High Performance Computing

High Performance Computing
Modern Systems and Practices

Thomas Sterling
Matthew Anderson
Maciej Brodowicz
School of Informatics, Computing, and Engineering
Indiana University, Bloomington

Foreword by C. Gordon Bell

Morgan Kaufmann is an imprint of Elsevier
50 Hampshire Street, 5th Floor, Cambridge, MA 02139, United States

Library of Congress Cataloging-in-Publication Data
A catalog record for this book is available from the Library of Congress

British Library Cataloguing-in-Publication Data
A catalogue record for this book is available from the British Library

ISBN: 978-0-12-420158-3

For information on all Morgan Kaufmann publications visit our website at https://www.elsevier.com/books-and-journals

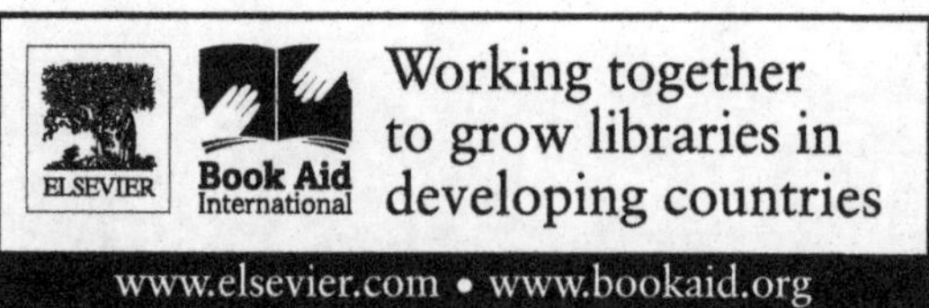

Publisher: Katey Birtcher
Acquisition Editor: Steve Merken
Developmental Editor: Nate McFadden
Production Project Manager: Punithavathy Govindaradjane
Designer: Mark Rogers

Typeset by TNQ Books and Journals

Dedicated to

Dr. Paul C. Messina

Leader, colleague, collaborator, mentor, friend

Contents

Foreword

High Performance Computing is a needed follow-on to Becker and Sterling's 1994 creation of the Beowulf clusters recipe to build scalable high performance computers (also known as a supercomputers) from commodity hardware. Beowulf enabled groups everywhere to build their own supercomputers. Now with hundreds of Beowulf clusters operating worldwide, this comprehensive text addresses the critical missing link of an academic course for training domain scientists and engineers—and especially computer scientists. Competence involves knowing exactly how to create and run (e.g., controlling, debugging, monitoring, visualizing, evolving) parallel programs on the congeries of computational elements (cores) that constitute today's supercomputers.

Mastery of these ever-increasing, scalable, parallel computing machines gives entry into a comparatively small but growing elite, and is the authors' goal for readers of the book. Lest the reader believes the name is unimportant: the first conference in 1988 was the ACM/IEEE Supercomputing Conference, also known as Supercomputing 88; in 2006 the name evolved to the International Conference on High Performance Computing, Networking, Storage, and Analysis, abbreviated SCXX. About 11,000 people attended SC16.

It is hard to describe a "supercomputer," but I know one when I see one. Personally, I never pass up a visit to a supercomputer having seen the first one in 1961—the UNIVAC LARC (Livermore Advanced Research Computer) at Lawrence Livermore National Laboratory, specified by Edward Teller to run hydrodynamic simulations for nuclear weapons design. LARC consisted of a few dozen cabinets of densely packed circuit board interconnected with a few thousand miles of wires and a few computational units operating at a 100 kHz rate. In 2016 the largest Sunway Light supercomputer in China operated a trillion times faster than LARC. It consists of over 10 million processing cores operating at a 1.5 GHz rate, and consumes 15 MW. The computer is housed in four rows of 40 cabinets, containing 256 processing nodes. A node has four interconnected 8 MB processors, controlling 64 processing elements or cores. Thus the 10.6 million processing elements deliver 125 peak petaflops, i.e., 160 cabinets $\times$ 256 physical nodes $\times$ 4 computers $\times$ (1 control + 8 $\times$ 8) processing elements or cores with a 1.31 PB memory (160 $\times$ 256 $\times$ 4 $\times$ 8 GB). Several of the Top 500 supercomputers have O(10,000) computing nodes that connect and control graphic processing units (GPUs) with O(100) cores. Today's challenge for computational program developers is designing the architecture and implementation of programs to utilize these megaprocessor computers.

From a user perspective, the "ideal high performance computer" has an *infinitely fast clock*, executes a *single instruction stream* program operating on data stored in an *infinitely large and fast single-memory*, and comes in any size to fit any budget or problem. In 1957 Backus established the von Neumann programming model with Fortran. The first or "Cray" era of supercomputing from the 1960s through the early 1990s saw the evolution of hardware to support this simple, easy-to-use ideal by increasing processor speed, pipelining an instruction stream, processing vectors with a single instruction, and finally adding processors for a program held in the single-memory computer. By the early 1990s evolution of a single computer toward the ideal had stopped: clock speeds reached a few GHz, and the number of processors accessing a single memory through interconnection was limited to a few dozen. Still, the limited-scale, multiple-processor shared memory is likely to be the most straightforward to program and use!

Fortunately, in the mid-1980s the "killer microprocessor" arrived, demonstrating cost effectiveness and unlimited scaling just by interconnecting increasingly powerful computers. Unfortunately, this multicomputer era has required abandoning both the single memory and the single sequential program ideal of Fortran. Thus "supercomputing" has evolved from a hardware engineering design challenge of the single (mono-memory) computer of the Seymour Cray era (1960–95) to a software engineering design challenge of creating a program to run effectively using multicomputers. Programs first operated on 64 processing elements (1983), then 1000 elements (1987), and now 10 million (2016) processing elements in thousands of fully distributed (mono-memory) computers in today's multicomputer era. So in effect, today's high performance computing (HPC) nodes are like the supercomputers of a decade ago, as processing elements have grown 36% per year from 1000 computers in 1987 to 10 million processing elements (contained in 100,000 computer nodes).

High Performance Computing is the essential guide and reference for mastering supercomputing, as the authors enumerate the complexity and subtleties of structuring for parallelism, creating, and running these large parallel and distributed programs. For example, the largest climate models simulate ocean, ice, atmosphere, and land concurrently created by a team of a dozen or more domain scientists, computational mathematicians, and computer scientists.

Program creation includes understanding the structure of the collection of processing resources and their interaction for different computers, from multiprocessors to multicomputers (Chapters 2 and 3), and the various overall strategies for parallelization (Chapter 9). Other topics include synchronization and message-passing communication among the parts of parallel programs (Chapters 7 and 8), additional libraries that form a program (Chapter 10), file systems (Chapter 18), long-term mass storage (Chapter 17), and components for the visualization of results (Chapter 12). Standard benchmarks for a system give an indication of how well your parallel program is likely to run (Chapter 4). Chapters 16 and 17 introduce and describe the techniques for controlling accelerators and special hardware cores, especially GPUs, attached to nodes to provide an extra two orders of magnitude more processing per node. These attachments are an alternative to the vector processing units of the Cray era, and typified by the Compute Unified Device Architecture, or CUDA, model and standard to encapsulate parallelism across different accelerators.

Unlike the creation, debugging, and execution of programs that run interactively on a personal computer, smartphone, or within a browser, supercomputer programs are submitted via batch processing control. Running a program requires specifying to the computer the resources and conditions for controlling your program with batch control languages and commands (Chapter 5), getting the program into a reliable and dependable state through debugging (Chapter 14), checkpointing, i.e., saving intermediate results on a timely basis as insurance for the computational investment (Chapter 20), and evolving and enhancing a program's efficacy through performance monitoring (Chapter 13).

Chapter 21 concludes with a forward look at the problems and alternatives for moving supercomputers and the ability to use them to petascale and beyond. In fact, the only part of HPC not described in this book is the incredible teamwork and evolution of team sizes for writing and managing HPC codes. However, the most critical aspect of teamwork resides with the competence of the individual members. This book is your guide.

Gordon Bell
October 2017

Preface

THE PURPOSE OF THIS TEXTBOOK

High performance computing (HPC) is a multidisciplinary field combining hardware technologies and architecture, operating systems, programming tools, software, and end-user problems and algorithms. Acquiring the necessary concepts, knowledge, and skills for capable engagement within HPC routinely involves an apprenticeship at one of a few rarefied sites with the essential experts, facilities, and mission objectives. Whether one's goals are associated with specific end-user domains such as science, engineering, medicine, or commercial applications, or focused on the enabling systems' technologies and methodologies that make supercomputing effective, the entry-level practitioner must embrace a wide range of distinct but interrelated and interdependent areas that require an understanding of their synergies to yield the necessary expertise. The study material could easily encompass a dozen or more books and manuals, but even together they would not deliver the necessary perspective that fully embodies the field as a whole and guides the student in pursuit of an effective path to achieve sufficient expertise.

This textbook is designed to bridge the gap between myriad sources of narrow focus and the need for a single source that spans and interconnects the range of disciplines comprising the HPC field. It is an entry-level text requiring a minimum of prerequisites, but provides a full understanding of the domains and their mutual effects that make supercomputing an interdisciplinary field. From a practical point of view, this textbook builds valuable and specific skill-sets for parallel programming, debugging, performance monitoring, system resource usage and tools, and result visualization among other useful techniques. These skills are provided in the reinforcing context of basic foundational concepts of prolonged relevance, and knowledge of detailed attributes of hardware and software system components more likely to evolve over time.

The textbook is chartered as support for a single-semester course for beginners to prepare themselves for a diversity of roles in supercomputing to pursue their chosen professional career goals. It is appropriate for future computational scientists who are dedicated to the use of supercomputers to solve science, engineering, or societal-domain applications, among others. It provides a base-level description of possible target capabilities for system designers and engineers in hardware and software. It also is a foundation for those who wish to proceed as researchers in supercomputing itself, as an introductory presentation of conventional systems and practices as well as a representation of the challenges facing this exciting domain of exploration. The book is equally appropriate for those engaged in supporting supercomputing environments, such as data centers and system administrators, operators, and management. In informing future professionals, the textbook can be used in multiple ways. It serves as a reference work of basic information for supercomputing. It provides a sequence of lecture content for classroom delivery. It supports a hands-on approach with substantial examples, all of which can be executed on parallel computers, and exercises to guide students as they learn by doing. It makes clear where skill-sets and training are presented, with an easy-to-learn tutorial style. Concepts are presented in a detailed but accessible form to establish the "why" of methods conveyed and assist future users in decision-making based on fundamental truths, factors, and sensitivities. Finally, this book unifies within the same context the many sets of facts associated with the multiplicity of subdisciplines that in combination make up the field of supercomputing.

ORGANIZATION OF THIS BOOK

This textbook serves as a bridge between the reader's initial curiosity, interests, and requirements in HPC and the ultimate knowledge, capabilities, and proficiency to be acquired through its study. It is a starting point for those in pursuit of a number of different possible professional paths that share a common foundation in the nature and use of these state-of-the-art systems. Whether the reader intends ultimately to be able to build hardware or software systems, use such systems as a critical tool in the pursuit of other fields in science, engineering, commerce, or security, conduct research to devise future means of pushing the state of the art in HPC, or administer, manage, and maintain HPC systems for other users, the textbook is structured to create a seamless flow of topics, each benefiting from those preceding while contributing to the foundations supporting those following. Thus the book presents its major subjects in an order that provides early basic skills of HPC use even as it conveys underlying concepts upon which a deeper understanding of these complex systems and their use is based. Where necessary, an introductory view of a topic is given with enough information to consider other topics that are dependent, only to return in greater depth in later chapters. The readers' understanding and capabilities are ratcheted up through incremental enhancement across the diversity of interrelated topical areas.

The textbook is about computing performance. For current and next-generation systems, this means the use and exploitation of workload parallelism to achieve scalability and the means of managing data to achieve efficiency of operation. The four principal overarching subject domains are listed below.

- System hardware architecture, and enabling technologies.
- Programming models, interfaces, and methods.
- System software environments, support, and tools.
- Parallel algorithms and distributed data structures.

This would suggest an obvious pedagogical organization of the textbook based on a logical flow. But there is another dimension to HPC: alternative strategies for organizing and coordinating parallelism and data management, and the roles of each of the component layers that contribute to them. This book presents four major strategies.

- Job stream parallelism, throughput, or capacity computing.
- Communicating sequential processes, or message passing.
- Multiple-threaded shared memory.
- SIMD or graphics processing unit (GPU) accelerated.

From a pedagogical perspective, the authors wish to convey three kinds of information to facilitate the learning process and hopefully also the enjoyment of the reader. At the foundational level are the concepts that establish understanding of the underlying principles that guide the form and function of HPC. There is a lot of basic information as well as some cultural (who, what, when) facts making up the necessary collection of knowledge that provides the framework (scaffolding) of the field. Finally, there are the skill-sets that teach how to do things. While admittedly not orthogonal to each other, the textbook approaches the presentation of all the material in each case as one of these three forms. For example, chapters with headings that begin "The Essential…" (such as "The Essential OpenMP") are crafted as skills modules with a tutorial presentation style for easiest learning. While the mixing of concepts and knowledge is unavoidable, separate sections emphasize one or the other. The importance of this distinction is that while much of the knowledge about this rapidly evolving field will change, and even become obsolete in some cases, the basic concepts offered are invariant with time and will serve the reader with strong long-term understanding even as the details of some specific machine or language may become largely irrelevant over time.

This textbook is organized first according to the four separate models of parallel computation, and then for each model according to the underlying concepts, the relevant knowledge with an emphasis on system architectures that support them, and the skills required to train the reader in how each class of system is programmed. In preparation for this approach, some initial material, including the introductory chapter, provides the basic premises and context upon which the textbook is established. Each of the four parallel computing models is described in terms of concepts, knowledge details, and programming skills. But while this covers a large part of the useful information needed to understand and program HPC systems, it misses some of the cross-cutting topics related to environments and tools that are an important, even pervasive, aspect of the full context of a system that makes it truly useful beyond the limits of an idealized beginner's viewpoint. After all, the intent of the textbook is to give the reader an effective working ability to take advantage of supercomputers in the professional workplace for diverse purposes. Thus a number of important and useful tools and methods of their use are given in an effective order. Finally, the reader is given a clear picture of the wide field of HPC, and where within this broader context the subject matter of this book fits. This can be used to guide planning for future pursuits and more advanced courses selected in part based on readers' ultimate professional goals. The overall structure and flow of this textbook are summarized below.

I. INTRODUCTORY AND BASIC IDEAS (CHAPTERS 1 AND 4)

These chapters provide a firm grounding on the basics, including an introduction to the domains of execution models, architecture concepts, performance and parallelism metrics, and the dominant class of parallel computing systems (commodity clusters). They give a first experience with running parallel programs through the use of a special kind of benchmarks that allow measurement and comparisons among different HPC systems. It is here that a sense of the history, the evolution of the contributing ideas, and the culture of the field is first given to the reader.

II. THROUGHPUT COMPUTING FOR JOB-STREAM PARALLELISM (CHAPTERS 5 AND 11)

Although among the simplest ways to take advantage of parallel computers, throughput computing (also referred to as capacity computing) as widely used is sufficient for many objectives and workflows. It can also prove to be among the most efficient, as it usually exhibits the most coarse-grained tasks and a minimum of control overheads. Widely used middleware that manages job-stream workloads such as SLURM and PBS are given in tutorial form for both independent jobs and related sets, such as parameter sweeps and Monte Carlo simulations.

III. SHARED-MEMORY MULTITHREADED COMPUTING (CHAPTERS 6 AND 7)

One of the dominant models of user parallel processing is task (or thread) parallelism in the context of shared memory. All the user data can be directly accessed by any of the user threads, and sequential consistency is assumed by hardware cache coherence. This part of the book describes this parallel execution model, the characteristics of shared-memory multiprocessors, and the OpenMP parallel programming language.

IV. MESSAGE-PASSING COMPUTING (CHAPTER 8)

For truly scalable parallel computing that may employ a million cores or more on a single application, the distributed-memory architecture and communicating sequential processing execution model is the dominant approach. This part of the book builds on topics associated with the nodes used for SMPs and the cluster approach previously described for throughput computing by adding the semantics of message passing, collective operations, and global synchronization. It is in this section that message-passing interface (MPI) is taught, the single most widely employed programming interface for scalable science and engineering applications.

V. ACCELERATING GPU COMPUTING (CHAPTERS 15 AND 16)

For certain widely used dataflow patterns, higher-level structures of specialized cores can provide exceptional performance and energy efficiency. Such subsystems, classified in the most general sense as "accelerators," can speed up applications by many times, sometimes by over an order of magnitude. Also referred to as GPGPUs, these often take the form of attached array processors, but in some cases are being integrated within single-socket packages or even the same die. This part of the textbook describes GPU structures, available products, and programming, with an emphasis on one programming interface, OpenACC.

VI. BUILDING SIGNIFICANT PROGRAMS (CHAPTERS 9, 10, AND 12–14)

By this point in the book the reader is well acquainted with the primary modes of HPC, knows the rules for the principal programming interfaces, and has hands-on experience with making basic parallel functions work within these frameworks. But for more complicated, more sophisticated, more useful, and frankly more professional supercomputing programs a number of additional methods and tools are required. This segment of the textbook takes the HPC novice from the beginner level to that of useful apprentice. Several key topics and skills are introduced here to give the student the necessary abilities to be useful in system design and application. First among these is a broad array of parallel algorithms for a diverse set of needs. Many of these are already made available in collections known as "libraries" that can save the application developer an enormous amount of time, if appropriately used. To get a program from its first draft to its final correct and efficient form requires a combined approach involving parallel debugging for correctness of answers and performance optimization through operation monitoring. Tools and methods for both are presented here, including the detailed skill-sets required. Finally, HPC runs tend to produce enormous amounts of data—as much as terabytes or petabytes of results in a single execution. Scientific visualization, the producing of images or even movies from such massive datasets, is the only practical way to achieve understanding of the results of a technical computing simulation. Examples of widely used tools for this purpose are presented, with essential techniques to make them useful.

VII. WORKING WITH THE REAL SYSTEM (CHAPTERS 11 AND 17–23)

The HPC system does not operate in a vacuum, and is of little value if it is not connected with the outside world. Throughout the book the reader is exposed to necessary bits of the system environment, but these chapters give a focused and comprehensive description of the operating system and its interface to the outside world. In particular, mass storage is described at both hardware and software levels for persistent storage of large blocks of data through the file system. As an example of the use of the file system, the map-reduce algorithm, which is very popular for big-data problems, is described in detail. The file system is also used to improve reliability through a method of checkpoint-restart. This technique periodically stores a snapshot of the intermediate data state of an application on mass storage in case a fault occurs in the system. Should this happen, the application program can be restarted not from the beginning but rather at the last known good checkpoint, thus saving a lot of time to get to a solution.

VIII. NEXT STEPS

At this point the reader will have come to the end of his or her introduction to HPC. But where does the reader go from here? There is much more to the field of such systems and their use than could be incorporated in any single textbook, although a good job of it has been done here. It is useful for the student to have a clear picture of what is out in front and, depending on one's interests or goals, which areas to pursue next. This chapter maps out the space of HPC beyond that contained in this text, and highlights the different areas as they relate to distinct professional objectives. But there is another dimension to the next steps: where is the field of HPC going itself, for it is changing very rapidly? The chapter concludes with a high-level description of the challenges facing HPC and the opportunities driving it forward.

WHO CAN BENEFIT FROM THIS TEXTBOOK?

This book is constructed so that the widest readership with diverse backgrounds can with a high probability of success take on the subject matter. For this reason it has been crafted with the minimal prerequisites of a working knowledge of programming in the C language and a familiarity of working within the context of a Unix-like operating system. But it is understood that even these requirements may be too stringent for some. For this reason, the appendix of the book includes two tutorials. One, "The Essential C," provides sufficient descriptive details in tutorial form to use the C programming language. It is not a primer of computer programming, as it is expected that the student has experience writing programs with some other programming language like Python, Java, Fortran, or MATLAB, but this tutorial is sufficient to support your needs through all the examples and exercises. Second, "The Essential Linux for Users," gives all the user interface descriptions and techniques that are required to fulfill all the tasks employed in this textbook.

This textbook may serve a broad community of possible readers including (but not limited to):

- Research scientists
- Computational scientists in end science, engineering, and societal domains
- HPC research faculty

- Future engineers and HPC system developers, and
- HPC system administrators and data center managers.

HOW TO USE THIS TEXTBOOK

The textbook is designed to serve multiple distinct approaches to learning and education, depending on the needs of the specific students.

- To achieve a full and in-depth understanding of HPC from an initial starting position, the book can be read from cover to cover. Its order of presentation of topical chapters is organized so that each builds on the material of the previous ones in the areas of concepts, knowledge, and skills. The examples embedded within the text are sufficient to represent the distinct points such that they are accessible to the reader.
- At the other extreme, the textbook can serve as a tutorial by reading the chapters and sections with titles/headings beginning with "The Essential…". These units are intended to develop the reader's skill-sets with minimal background and contextual information.
- Emphasis can be achieved by selecting the critical path chapters (or sections). Four models of parallel computing are represented: throughput, message passing, shared memory, and accelerated. But in some cases only one of these is required by the student or educator, thus a student may only need to be immersed in a subset of the chapters offered. For example, a course may use OpenMP or MPI but not both. For basic job-stream parallelism, both of these can be side-stepped and instead the student is focused on SLURM or PBS for throughput computing.

Acknowledgments

This textbook would not have been possible in either form or quality without the many contributions, both direct and indirect, of a large number of friends and colleagues. It is derivative of first-year graduate courses taught at both Louisiana State University (LSU) and Indiana University (IU). A number of people contributed to these courses, including Chirag Dekate, Daniel Kogler, and Timur Gilmanov. Amy Apon, a professor at the University of Arkansas, partnered with LSU and taught this course in real time over the internet and helped to develop pedagogical material, including many of the exercises used. Now at Clemson University, she continued this important contribution using her technical and pedagogical expertise. Andrew Lumsdaine, then a professor at IU, cotaught the first version of this course at IU. Amanda Upshaw was instrumental in the coordination of the process that resulted in the final draft of the book, and directly developed many of the illustrations, graphics, and tables. She was also responsible for the glossary of terms and acronyms. Her efforts are responsible in part for the quality of this textbook.

A number of friends and colleagues provided guidance as the authors crafted early drafts of the book. These contributions were of tremendous value, and helped improve the quality of content and form to be useful for readers and students. David Keyes of KAUST reviewed and advised on Chapter 9 on parallel algorithms. Jack Dongarra provided important feedback on Chapter 4 on benchmarking.

This textbook reflects decades of effort, research, development, and experience by uncounted number of contributors to the field of high performance computing. While not directly involved with the creation of this text, many colleagues have contributed to the concepts, components, tools, methods, and common practices associated with the broad context of high performance computing and its value. Among these are Bill Gropp, Bill Kramer, Don Becker, Richard and Sarah Murphy, Jack Dongarra and his many collaborators, Satoshi Matsuoka, Guang Gao, Bill Harrod, Lucy Nowell, Kathy Yelick, John Shalf, John Salmon, and of course Gordon Bell. Thomas Sterling would like to acknowledge his thesis advisor (at MIT) Bert Halstead for his mentorship to become the contributor that he has become. Thomas Sterling also acknowledges Jorge Ucan, Amanda Upshaw, co-authors who made this book possible, and especially Paul Messina who is his colleague, role model, mentor, and friend without whom this book would never occurred. Matthew Anderson would like to thank Dayana Marvez, Oliver Anderson, and Beltran Anderson. Maciej Brodowicz would like to thank his wife Yuko Prince Brodowicz. The authors would like to thank Nate McFadden of Morgan-Kaufmann who provided enormous effort, guidance, and patience that made this textbook possible.

DEDICATION TO PAUL MESSINA, WRITTEN BY THOMAS STERLING

The authors are pleased to dedicate this book to Dr Paul C. Messina, in acknowledgment of and gratitude for his exceptional contributions to and leadership in the field of high performance computing over a career of more than 4 decades. It is impossible to capture fully the importance of his impact, but many of the significant national programs have benefited from his guidance. Dr Messina has been a visionary, a strategist, and a leader of programs, projects, organizations, initiatives, and, perhaps most importantly, the careers of individual scientists who would come to deliver technical accomplishments and leadership of their own. Dr Messina was the founding director of the Mathematics and Computer Science Division at Argonne National Laboratory, a leading institution applying high performance computing to mission-critical problem domains of the US Department of Energy (DOE). He then founded and directed the Caltech Concurrent Supercomputing Facilities that staged the Intel Touchstone Delta massively parallel processor, the fastest computer in the world in 1991 and the prototype of a family of massively parallel processors that determined the future direction of high performance computing for the next 30 years. Caltech Concurrent Supercomputing Facilities evolved into the Caltech Center for Advanced Computing Research, at which two of the authors spent some of their most formative years. Paul was particularly instrumental and served as co-principal investigator for the pioneering NSF Teragrid and the National Virtual Observatory. He directed the DOE ASCI program for almost 3 years, building up the nation's high performance computing capabilities toward the leadership-scale computing it currently demonstrates. Most recently Paul Messina led the Exascale Computing Project, America's biggest undertaking in achieving exascale computing performance by the beginning of the 2020s. For some Paul has had a direct and meaningful effect on their individual careers. To author Thomas Sterling Paul has been a colleague, leader, mentor, and friend for many years.

CHAPTER

INTRODUCTION

1

CHAPTER OUTLINE

High Performance Computing. https://doi.org/10.1016/B978-0-12-420158-3.00001-0

Supercomputing, which means supercomputers and their application, is among the most important developments of the modern age, with unequaled impact across a vast diversity of fields of inquiry and practical effect. From the extremes of arcane sciences to the most immediate practical concerns, supercomputers play an essential role in the progress and advancement of human capabilities, environments, and understanding. No other single technology in the history of humanity has experienced a similar rate of growth, even in its relatively short existence. Within the span of a single human lifetime, supercomputers have expanded their ability to perform calculations by a factor of 10 trillion or 13 orders of magnitude, and this is a conservative estimate. From less than a 1000 basic operations per second in the late 1940s to today's performance in excess of a 100 quadrillion floating-point operations per second (over 100 petaflops), supercomputer speed has steadily improved by about a factor of 200 times every decade through a series of advances in technology, architecture, programming methods, algorithms, and system software (Fig. 1.1). High performance computing (HPC), synonymous with supercomputing, is a principal means of exploration complementing empirical methods used for more than 2 millennia and theory practiced in the age of enlightenment of the last 4 centuries. As the "third pillar" of investigation, supercomputing enables new paths of inquiry, new techniques of design, and new methods of operating process. Even discoveries correctly credited to other classes of tools and instrumentation, such as giant telescopes or particle accelerators, require the use of supercomputers as well to produce their final results through data analysis (sometimes referred to as "big data"). It can be asserted that supercomputing allows us to understand the past, to control the present, and in limited cases to predict the future.

The skills required to employ HPC are multiple and complex, while the means of acquiring such skills to a sufficient degree require potentially years of study and experience at least in normal practice.

FIGURE 1.1

The Titan petaflops machine fully deployed at Oak Ridge National Laboratory in 2013. It takes up more than 4000 sq ft and consumes approximately 8 MW of electrical power. It has a theoretical peak performance of over 27 petaflops and delivers 17.6 petaflops R_{max} sustained performance for the highly parallel Linpack (HPL) benchmark. This architecture includes Nvidia graphics processing unit accelerators.

Photo courtesy of Oak Ridge National Laboratory, US Dept. of Energy

This often means lengthy apprenticeships in research facilities in academia, industry, or national laboratories. There are many books written to teach particular programming languages; others describe in detail the structures and instruction sets of computer architectures; and still others discuss system software such as operating systems. But missing has been a single textbook that serves as an entry-level presentation of all these elements and their interrelationships in one place, combined with guided hands-on experience. This work, *High Performance Computing*, is developed as a carefully crafted synthesis of relevant elements of related disciplines, all of which contribute in critical ways to supercomputing and its use. This book presents the foundation concepts, in-depth relevant knowledge, and detailed skills that together will give you a meaningful understanding of HPC and an initial set of techniques to make you an effective, albeit incipient, practitioner in its use. Throughout this text the best practices employed by the community are presented with training, so you learn to do, the *how*, even as you are gaining understanding of the *what* and the *why*.

This textbook provides a comprehensive introduction to the field of HPC. It is presented in a form that will be both intellectually rewarding and practical in teaching useful basic skills. It combines perspectives about supercomputing concepts, knowledge about supercomputers, and techniques for using and programming supercomputers. But teaching a complex subject like HPC is challenging, in that just about everything is defined in terms of and relates to everything else. Yet by the nature of pedagogy, material must be presented in some sequential order. This first chapter is a brief introductory presentation of the essential elements of HPC to provide an overview of everything; a first pass that will allow successive in-depth chapters to be related to this broad context.

The chapter looks at the many facets which comprise HPC. The importance of the material is that it provides a complete, albeit simplified, perspective of HPC so that more detailed discussion of specifics can be understood within the full context. Because no piece makes sense without the others, almost all areas are briefly introduced in this chapter. To reinforce the interrelated broad-brush presentation of issues, this chapter concludes with a history of the field and its rapid evolution.

1.1 HIGH PERFORMANCE COMPUTING DISCIPLINES

As previously noted, HPC is really a collection of multiple interrelated disciplines, each providing an important aspect of the total field. To master HPC as a useful tool is to develop an understanding and associated skills in each of these corresponding areas. These broad areas are described here, including a formal definition of "high performance computing" that applies throughout the treatment of the field, end-user application problems that are the intended purpose of HPC across a wide range of science, engineering, societal, and security domains, the core concept of performance which is the distinguishing characteristic of HPC compared to other forms of computing, the hardware and software components that make up an HPC system, environments, tools, application programming, and the interfaces used. Each of these is presented in some detail in the following sections and together form a major portion of the concepts, knowledge content, and skills comprising this textbook.

1.1.1 DEFINITION

HPC is a field of endeavor that relates to all facets of technology, methodology, and application associated with achieving the greatest computing capability possible at any point in time and technology. It engages a class of electronic digital machines referred to as "supercomputers" to perform a wide array of computational problems or "applications" (alternatively "workloads") as fast as is possible. The action of performing an application on a supercomputer is widely termed "supercomputing" and is synonymous with HPC.

1.1.2 APPLICATION PROGRAMS

The purpose of HPC is to derive answers to questions that cannot be adequately addressed alone through means of empiricism, theory, or even widely available or accessible commercial computers (e.g., enterprise servers). Historically supercomputers have been applied to science and engineering, and the methodology has been described as the "third pillar of science" alongside and complementing both experimentation (empiricism) and mathematics (theory). But the range of problems that supercomputers can tackle extends far beyond classical scientific and engineering studies to include challenges in socioeconomics, big-data management and learning, process control, and national security. An application, then, is both the problem to be solved and the body of "code" or collection of ordered computing instructions that represent the means of solving the problem. The code is the means by which the user conveys to the supercomputer how it is to perform the necessary computations to achieve the objectives of the problem. The full set of code used is a "computer program" or just "program", and the person developing the application code is the "programmer".

1.1.3 PERFORMANCE AND METRICS

While the notion of performance may be intuitive, it is not simple. There is no single measure of performance that fully reflects all aspects of the quality of computer operation. A "metric" is a quantifiable observable operational parameter of a supercomputer. Multiple perspectives and related metrics are routinely applied to characterize the behavioral properties and capabilities of an HPC system. Two basic measures are employed individually or in combination and in differing contexts to formulate the values used to represent the quality of a supercomputer. These two fundamental measures are "time" and "number of operations" performed, both under prescribed conditions.

For HPC the most widely used metric is "floating-point operations per second" or "flops". A floating-point operation is an addition or multiplication of two real (or floating-point) numbers represented in some machine-readable and manipulatable form. Because supercomputers are so "powerful", to describe their capability would require phrases like "a trillion or quadrillion operations per second". The field adopts the same system of notation as science and engineering, using the Greek prefixes kilo, mega, giga, tera, and peta to represent 1000, 1 million, 1 billion, 1 trillion, and 1 quadrillion, respectively. The first supercomputers barely achieved 1 kiloflops (Kflops). Today's fastest supercomputer exhibits a peak performance in the order of 125 petaflops. The laptop computer upon which this textbook was written has a peak performance of a few gigaflops. A supercomputer is millions of times more powerful than a laptop by this metric.

The true capability of a supercomputer is its ability to perform real work, to achieve useful results toward an end goal such as simulating a particular physical phenomenon (e.g., colliding neutron stars to determine resulting electromagnetic burst signatures). A better measure than flops is how long a given problem takes to complete. But because there are literally thousands (millions?) of such problems, this measure is not particularly useful broadly. Thus the HPC community selects specific problems around which to standardize. Such standardized application programs are "benchmarks".

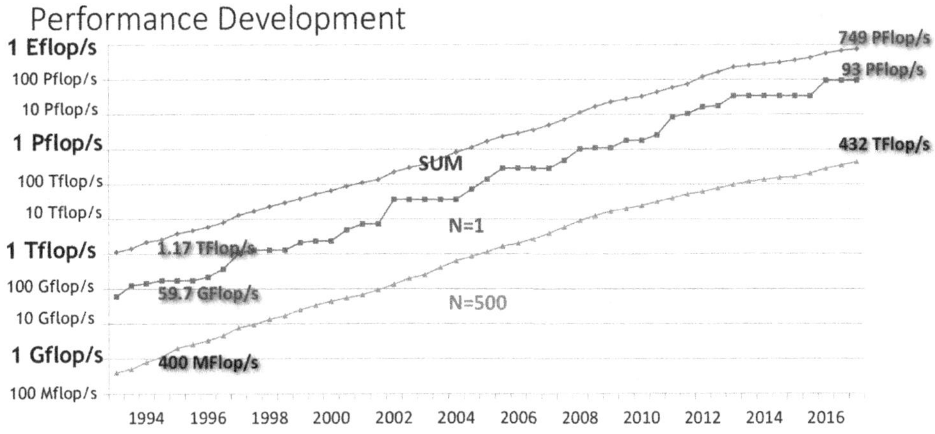

FIGURE 1.2

The evolution of the R_{max} from the HPL benchmark for supercomputing systems in the Top 500 list since the list began in 1993. The top line indicates the cumulative performance of all the computers in the list. The middle line shows the performance of the number one computer in the list. The bottom line shows the performance of the last computer in the list (number 500).

Image courtesy Erich Strohmaier

One particularly widely used supercomputer benchmark is "Linpack", or more precisely the "highly parallel Linpack" (HPL), which solves a set of linear equations in dense matrix form [1]. A benchmark gives a means of comparative evaluation between two independent systems by measuring their respective times to perform the same calculation. Thus a second way to measure performance is time to completion of a fixed problem. The HPC community has selected HPL as a means of ranking supercomputers, as represented by the "Top 500 list" begun in 1993 (Fig. 1.2). But other benchmarks are also employed to stress certain aspects of a supercomputer or represent a certain class of programs.

1.1.4 HIGH PERFORMANCE COMPUTING SYSTEMS

The most visible aspect of the field of HPC is the high performance computers, or simply supercomputers, themselves. Today these machines appear as rows upon rows of many racks taking up thousands of square feet and consuming potentially multiple megawatts of electrical power. To be in the presence of one (which often means to be literally inside it) offers a whole other experience in terms of noise, rapidly shifting temperature gradients, and many blinking lights. Even the most staid observer cannot help but be awestruck by the impressive massiveness of such systems, the engineering by which they are achieved, the commitment they represent to the edges of computing capability, and the problems only they can solve. And beyond what is visible even to the not-so-casual observer is the infrastructure that supports the operation of these systems, much of which is below floors, in adjacent rooms, and outside the building that houses the machine. The deployment of a state-of-the-art supercomputer is truly a major engineering undertaking involving time, expense, and expertise, as well as responsible management and maintenance throughout the lifetime of the system. And yet the visible, audible, and other sensory experiences barely reflect the true nature of the accomplishment embodied by these machines. At the heart of the HPC system is the structure and organization of its myriad components and the semantics or rules by which they operate and perform the user applications offered to them. Even more than the hardware, the HPC system is a vast array of software components that control the hierarchy of the physical components and manage the user workloads. If the physical hardware, racks and all, is what the visitor experiences, the system software, its interfaces, and functionality are what the user experiences (usually at a location far from the physical machine) when developing and running the applications and analyzing the results.

In one important sense, the high performance computer system has basic functionality and subsystems in common with the laptop personal computer upon which this textbook was written. These principal capabilities, shared by both extremes, include the following.

- The operational functions that transform input data values to output results.
- The internal memory that stores the data upon which the system operates.
- The communication channels through which intermediate data is transferred between different components and subsystems during application execution.
- The control hardware that coordinates the interoperability among the constituent components and subsystems.
- The mass storage that organizes and holds the persistent data, system software, and application programs.
- The input/output (I/O) channels and interfaces (like the keyboard I am typing on and the screen I am looking at) that connect users to the system.

Similarly, the software of an HPC system has much in common with the desk-side workstation or departmental enterprise server. Like these more pervasive albeit more modest computers, the supercomputer has a software structure that serves many of the same purposes of interface, control, and functionality, including but not limited to the following.

- The operating system that manages all aspects of the machine and its operation.
- The compilers that translate application programs written in human-readable syntactic languages (and other interfaces) to machine-readable binary code.
- File systems that present a logical abstraction of mass storage and organize the data on mass-storage devices (like hard-disk drives).
- The myriad software drivers of the I/O devices by which the computer communicates with the external world and users.
- The many tools that make up much of the expected user environments.

What distinguishes an HPC system from a conventional computer is the organization, interconnectivity, and scale of the component resources and the ability of the supporting software to manage the operation of the system at that scale (Fig. 1.3). By scale is meant the degree of physical and logical parallelism, i.e., the replication of key physical components such as processors and memory banks and the delineation of a number of tasks to be performed simultaneously. While even a single socket laptop incorporates some parallelism, an HPC system is structured in far more levels, each of which is usually much more substantial (but there are exceptions to this). It is this parallel organization, the methods by which the constituent subsystems are coordinated to solve a shared problem, and the additional functionality of the system software and programming models providing

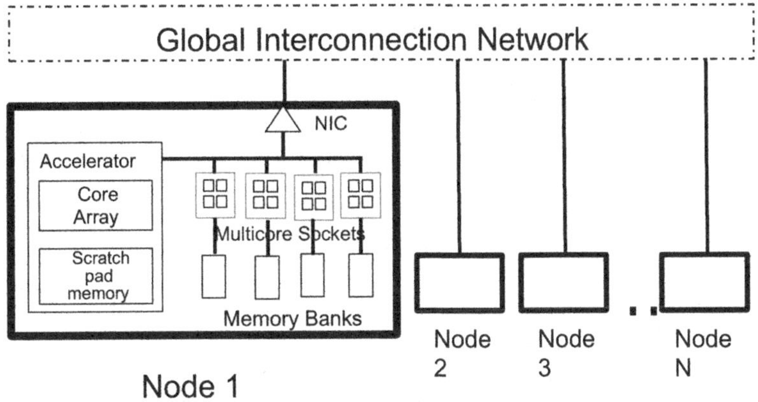

FIGURE 1.3

HPC systems are distinguished from a conventional computer by the organization, interconnectivity, and scale of the many component resources illustrated here. A "node" incorporates all the functional elements required for computation, and is highly replicated to achieve large scale.

such management that differentiate the supercomputer from its smaller counterparts. But from the viewpoint of the programmer, it is the need to think in parallel (many things happening at the same time) and distributed (things happening in different places separated by distance) that differentiates the supercomputer from the day-to-day computer [2]. This requires knowledge and skill in employing programming interfaces that expose and exploit application parallelism and algorithms that permit simultaneous operation of many parts of the computation contributing to the final answer.

1.1.5 SUPERCOMPUTING PROBLEMS

The field of supercomputing was born in the midst of revolutionary advances in experimental nuclear research, and has since grown to affect nearly all research fields driven by experiment. Because the genesis of supercomputing lies in simulating problems driven by nuclear physics, many supercomputing problems are framed in the context of tracking large systems of particles consisting of different species that may interact with one another and are not in equilibrium. Such nonequilibrium problems are generally difficult to compute analytically and can be very costly to explore experimentally. Consequently, these types of problems frequently appear on supercomputers, because of both the high-resolution probing ability of the simulation and the substantially reduced cost at which the computational experiment can be conducted [3].

Another class of supercomputing problem that overlaps with tracking large systems of particles with pair-wise interactions is the class that solves some set of partial-differential equations. For instance, a large fraction of supercomputing time is spent solving the Navier–Stokes equations for fluid flow because of their relevance to many engineering problems. As a second example, the direct detection of an astrophysical source of gravitational radiation in 2015 by the LIGO Scientific Collaboration was supported by millions of hours of supercomputing resources solving the Einstein field equations to simulate the merger of binary black holes.

Table 1.1 Supercomputing Problem Representatives and How They Are Used in Academia, Industry, and Government

Supercomputing Problem Representatives	Academia	Industry	Government
Solution of partial-differential equations	Navier–Stokes equations, Einstein equations, Maxwell equations	Black–Scholes equation, Navier–Stokes equations for compressible flow, oil reservoir modeling	Weather prediction, hurricane modeling, storm-surge modeling, sea-ice modeling
Large systems with pair-wise force interactions	Cosmology, molecular dynamics simulations	Medicine development, biomolecular dynamics	Plasma modeling
Linear algebra	Supporting solution of partial-differential equations, fundamental benchmarks of HPL and high performance conjugate gradients	Search engine PageRank, finite-element simulations	HPC machine evaluation, climate modeling
Graph problems	Systems research, machine learning	Fraud detection	Security services, data analytics
Stochastic systems	Radiation transport, particle physics	Risk analysis in finance, nuclear reactor design, process control	Public health, modeling spread of disease

Many classes of HPC problems are designed around the supercomputer's ability to solve problems in linear algebra. In science and engineering the result of discretizing partial-differential equations frequently results in a system of linear equations. This has led to the development of both direct and iterative solution techniques for supercomputers. The main benchmark currently used to measure a supercomputer's peak performance is a dense linear algebra problem.

While many HPC problems arise from mathematical models, some of the most important supercomputing problems today arise from graph problems. Graph problems often come from problems arising in knowledge management, machine intelligence, linguistics, networks, biology, dynamical systems, and collections of pair-wise systems.

HPC problem representatives and examples of their usage in academia, industry, and government are presented in Table 1.1.

The variety and novelty of supercomputing problems continue to expand far beyond its nuclear physics roots (see the example in Fig. 1.4). As supercomputing skill-sets and resources become increasingly commonplace, it is difficult to imagine an analytical field that will not be impacted by HPC in the future.

1.1.6 APPLICATION PROGRAMMING

The principal view the user has of a HPC system is through one or more programming interfaces, which take the form of programming languages, libraries, or other services. These are expanded by

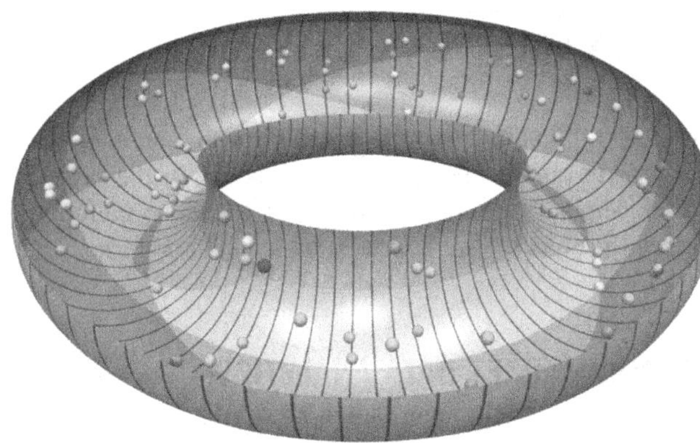

FIGURE 1.4

A particle-in-cell simulation from the Gyrokinetic Toroidal code (Princeton Plasma Physics laboratory) that simulates a plasma within a Tokomak fusion device. A sampling of some particles within the toroid is shown here colored according to their velocity, with different supercomputing processor boundaries delineated by the toroidal subdivisions.

additional sets of tools that assist in crafting, optimizing, and debugging application codes. Ironically, a major means of programming is the use of existing programs either directly or as templates to modify for specific purposes. There are hundreds of computer programming languages, from very low level including assemblers to very high reaching to the declarative regime. But for HPC the number of conventionally adopted programming interfaces is relatively few, in the order of dozens, although there are many more experimental or research models. At the risk of oversimplification, a programming language defines a set of named objects that can be manipulated, the basic operations that can be performed on these objects, the flow-control mechanisms for establishing the conditions and order of operation execution, the means of encapsulation for modularity, and I/O including mass storage.

Programming in the regime of supercomputing has additional requirements and characteristics. Performance is the driving requirement that differentiates HPC programming from other domains. It is second only to correctness and repeatability, which are of serious concern. Performance is most significantly represented by the need for representation and exploitation of computational parallelism: the ability to perform multiple tasks simultaneously. Parallel processing involves the definition of parallel tasks, establishing the criteria that determine when a task is performed, synchronization among tasks in part to coordinate sharing, and allocation to computing resources. A second aspect of programming for HPC is control of the relationship of allocations of data and tasks to the physical resources of the parallel and distributed systems. The nature of the parallelism may vary significantly depending on the form of computer system architecture targeted by the application program. Also of concern are issues of determinism, correctness, performance debugging, and performance portability.

Depending on the nature of the class of parallel system architecture, different programming models are employed. One dimension of differentiation is granularity of the parallel workflow. Very coarse-grained workloads with no interactivity, sometimes referred to as "embarrassingly parallel" or "job-stream" workflow, suggest one class of workflow managers. Fine-grained parallelism is emphasized in multiple-thread shared-memory system programming interfaces such as OpenMP and Cilk++. Medium- to coarse-grained parallelism, as reflected by highly scaled massively parallel processors (MPPs) and clusters, is primarily represented by communicating sequential processes such as the message-passing interface (MPI) and its many variants. Each of these forms of parallel programming is explored in this textbook, with extensive presentation and direct hands-on experience.

1.2 IMPACT OF SUPERCOMPUTING ON SCIENCE, SOCIETY, AND SECURITY

The broader HPC ecosystem today is a vibrant $23 billion market, projected to grow to more than $30 billion by 2020 and with a compound annual growth rate of 8%. HPC represents one of the fastest-growing markets, primarily driven by end-user demand in various application domains, including financial services, oil and gas, manufacturing, earth sciences, life sciences, national laboratories, and government intelligence.

1.2.1 CATALYZING FRAUD DETECTION AND MARKET DATA ANALYTICS

Rapidly growing global demand for financial services functions, including trading, banking, and financial transactions such as mortgage processing, is stressing financial information management systems to an unprecedented degree. Increasingly financial services companies such as proprietary trading firms, investment banks, and payment processing firms are deploying supercomputing to solve core business problems like backtesting, risk management, and fraud detection. Proprietary trading and investment management firms frequently deploy HPC systems (~100s of Tflops) to develop accurate trading strategies and predict market performance, enabling them to package highly profitable financial instruments. In many investment bank and mortgage/credit processing firms supercomputers (10–100s of Tflops) are used to process millions of records and accurately predict the risk of diverse portfolios. Payment processing firms are increasingly adopting supercomputing technologies for fraud prevention, using pattern detection and matching algorithms.

1.2.2 DISCOVERING, MANAGING, AND DISTRIBUTING OIL AND GAS

Oil and gas companies are some of the largest commercial users of supercomputing technologies, including all the publicly cited commercial petascale systems. Supercomputers drive all aspects of oil and gas workflows for exploration, production, and distribution. In exploration, supercomputers are deployed for the high-resolution seismic processing used to identify oil reservoirs through subsurface imaging (Fig. 1.5). In production workflows supercomputers are used in characterizing reservoirs and identifying the safest means of managing reserves. Increasingly oil and gas companies are using HPC capability to devise new predictive analytics for effective distribution of petroleum products. HPC is a crucial foundational capability for oil and gas companies today, and is widely deployed in exploration and production to minimize exploration risks and increase the safety of the overall processes involved.

1.2.3 ACCELERATING INNOVATION IN MANUFACTURING

Manufacturing encompasses a wide range of industries, including aerospace, automotive, consumer products, heavy industries, tire manufacturers, and electronics/semiconductor manufacturers. The common thread across these diverse industries is the use of computer-aided engineering applications for product design and manufacturing processes. In automotive industries supercomputers are used in simulating crashes, structural analysis of noise, vibration, hardness, and stress, and finally computational fluid-dynamics-driven product design. In aerospace supercomputers are primarily used

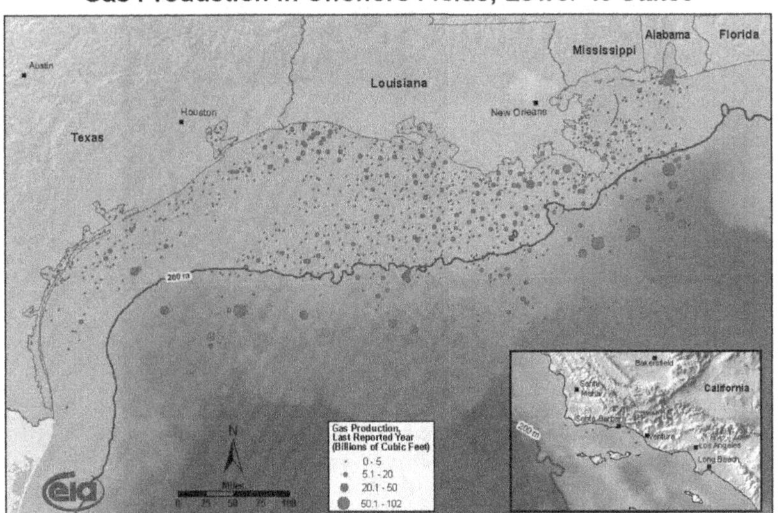

FIGURE 1.5

Researchers at BP use HPC to simulate subsurface geologies, using multidimensional analysis and characterization to identify oil reservoirs accurately.

Image by US Energy Information Administration via Wikimedia Commons

for computational fluid-dynamics-based aerodynamics simulations and virtual prototyping. By using simulation as opposed to physical testing in the design process, manufacturing firms are accelerating time to market through shortened design cycles while reducing development costs and delivering safer products to customers. HPC is perhaps one of the most important technologies in manufacturing today. Using simulation-driven engineering, organizations can improve the efficiency of jet engines, wind turbines, heavy machinery, and gas turbines (Fig. 1.6). Even a 2%–4% improvement in performance can result in billions of dollars in reduced operational and fuel costs.

1.2.4 PERSONALIZED MEDICINE AND DRUG DISCOVERY

Life sciences are another major vertical segment that relies on HPC technologies in various application areas. Supercomputing is used by researchers and enterprises for genome sequencing and drug discovery. Pharmaceutical companies often deploy supercomputers to accelerate the process of drug discovery using various molecular dynamic simulation methodologies. Using HPC and molecular dynamics simulations researchers are able to design new drugs and virtually test effectiveness, enabling significant optimization of the research process while resulting in safer and more effective drugs. HPC is also used to develop virtual models of human physiology (e.g., heart, brain, etc.), which enable scientists and researchers to understand ailments and potential treatments better (Fig. 1.7). Increasingly life sciences researchers and companies are engineering new methodologies combining genome sequencing and drug discovery to enable new and more effective forms of personalized medicine that could cure some of the most challenging diseases.

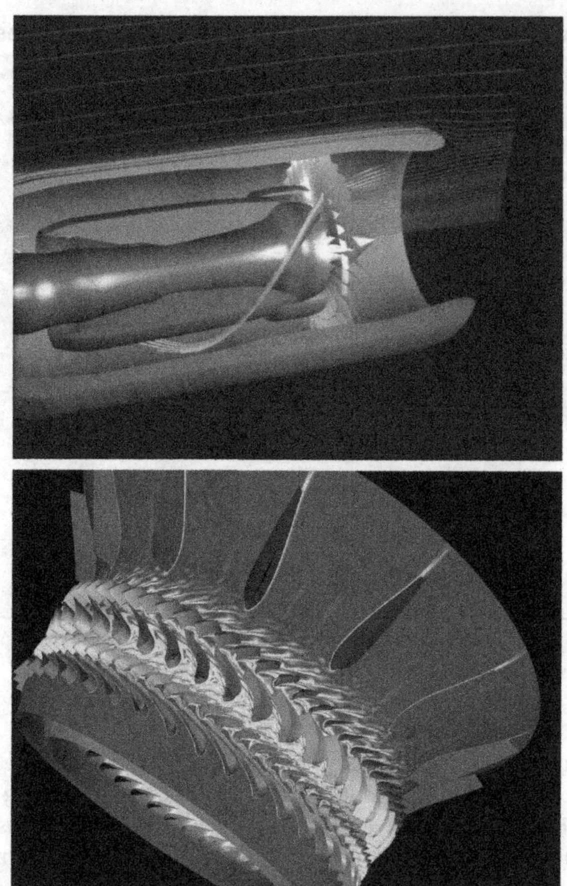

FIGURE 1.6

(Top) HPC is frequently used in high-fidelity virtual engine simulation and design. (Bottom) Researchers at NASA use HPC to simulate the design of next-generation turbines for both aviation and power production.

(Top) Simulation image via Wikimedia Commons; (Bottom) Simulation image by Dale Zante and Jay Horowitz via Wikimedia Commons

1.2.5 PREDICTING NATURAL DISASTERS AND UNDERSTANDING CLIMATE CHANGE

Another key field where HPC has delivered a transformational impact is Earth sciences. Supercomputing is frequently used to study climate change and its impact. Research organizations around the world rely on HPC to predict weather phenomena and enable highly accurate hyperlocalized forecasts. A crucial broader application area of these foundational domains is emergency preparedness, where HPC models are used to predict aspects of natural disasters such as intensity and impact of earthquakes, path and ferocity of hurricanes, direction and impact of tsunamis, and more (Fig. 1.8). The climate is ever changing, with increasing threats of intense hurricanes, heatwaves, and other

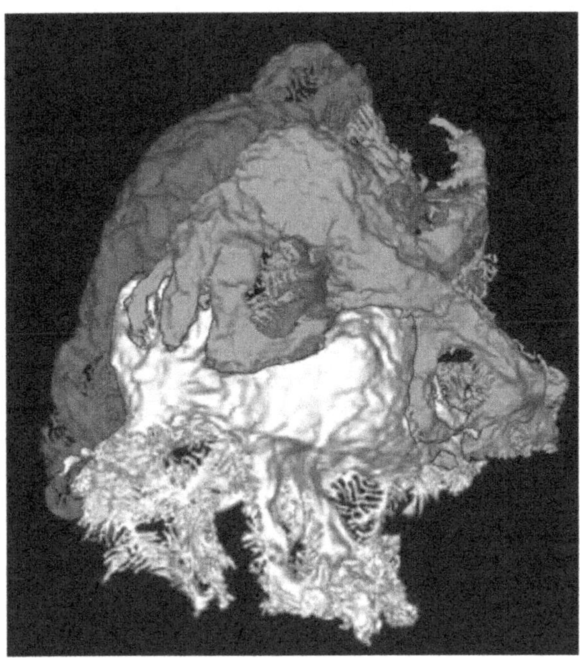

FIGURE 1.7

HPC is used to develop virtual models of kidney podocytes.

Image from C. Falkenberg et al. via Wikimedia Commons

extreme events necessitating the need for higher-fidelity computational models and more supercomputing capabilities.

In each of these application domains and beyond, supercomputers have a wide range of impact in accelerating innovation, optimizing business processes, saving lives, and delivering transformational socioeconomic impact. It is no surprise that HPC now forms a core strategic component in industrial innovation, research, and government policy development.

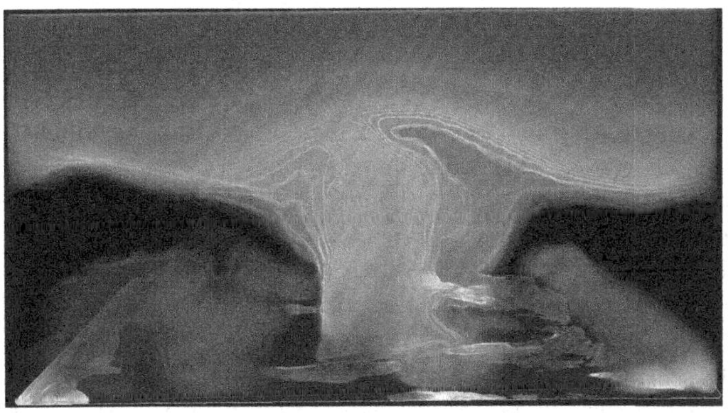

FIGURE 1.8

Researchers at Oak Ridge National Laboratory explore the advection of carbon dioxide in an atmospheric model.

Image courtesy of F. Hoffman and J. Daniel via Wikimedia Commons

Table 1.2 Broader Impacts of Supercomputing: How HPC Is Used by Different Application Domains to Accelerate Time to Innovation and Deliver Socioeconomic Impact

Vertical Segments	Common Workflows
Financial services	Fraud and anomaly detection, backtesting for algorithmic/proprietary trading, risk analytics
Oil and gas	Seismic processing, interpretation, reservoir modeling
Manufacturing	Materials simulation, structural simulations (noise/vibration/hardness and crash), aerodynamics simulations, design space exploration, thermal simulations and many more
Life sciences	Molecular dynamics, drug discovery, virtual modeling, genome sequencing and many more
Earth sciences	Atmospheric modeling, hydrodynamic modeling, ice modeling, coupled climate modeling

Table 1.2 highlights a subset of vertical segments that use HPC in their production environments to give faster time to innovation and deliver broad socioeconomic impact. Without supercomputing, these and other domains would be severely constrained in being able to deliver innovative, safer, and better products, with the pace of innovation far lower.

1.3 ANATOMY OF A SUPERCOMPUTER

To get a sense of what a modern supercomputer looks like, we give a brief description of Titan (Fig. 1.1), one of the fastest computers in the world. In November 2012 it was rated as the fastest; it has since been surpassed but is still among the top 10 supercomputers and the most powerful computer in the United States. Titan is true to its name in sheer size as well as in computational capability: it takes up more than 4000 sq ft and consumes approximately 8 MW of electrical power. Deployed at Oak Ridge National Laboratory in Tennessee, Titan was developed by Cray Inc. It incorporates the structure, function, and scale of elements found in most state-of-the-art high-end machines, with a theoretical peak performance of over 27 petaflops and delivering 17.6 petaflops R_{max} sustained performance for the HPL (Linpack) benchmark by which the Top 500 list is measured. Sponsored by the US Department of Energy and National Oceanic and Atmospheric Administration, the purpose of Titan is to do scientific research, at which it excels.

Titan is a Cray XK7 architecture: a heterogeneous architecture reflecting an important trend in HPC—the mixing of different kinds of processing units to provide the best possible operational support for distinctly different kinds of computation, even in the same application.

The block diagram of the system stack (Fig. 1.9) shows the layered hierarchy of the many physical and logical components contributing to a general-purpose supercomputer [4,5]. The bottom layer, the system hardware, represents the physical resources that are the most visible (and audible) aspect of a supercomputer like Titan. Even in this high-level view, the principal components of the system are perceived. The processors that perform the calculations and the memory which stores both the data and the program codes that operate on it are shown here, as well as the interconnection network that integrates potentially many thousands and eventually millions of such processor/memory "nodes" into a single supercomputer. Another family of hardware provides long-term storage of data and

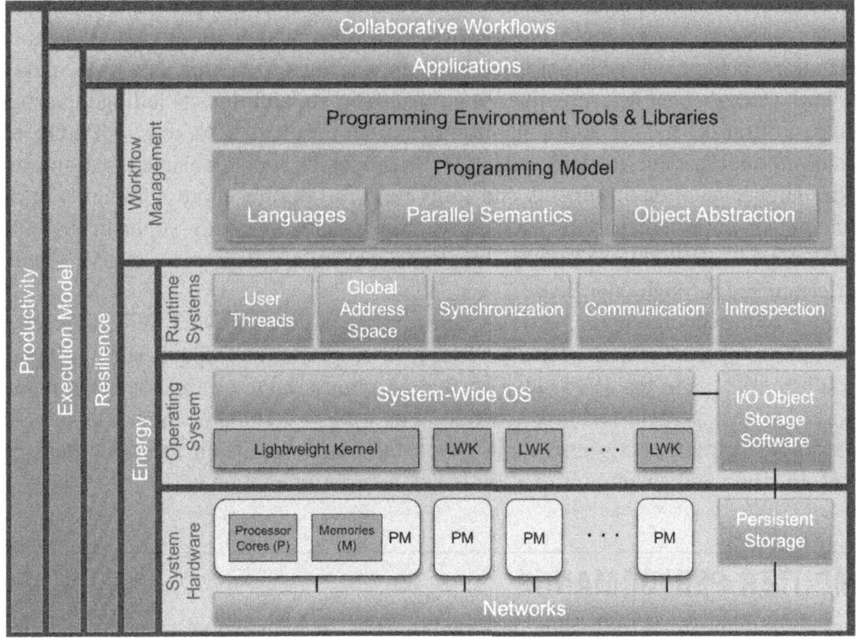

FIGURE 1.9

The system stack of a general supercomputer consists of a system hardware layer and several software layers. The first software layer is the operating system, encompassing both resource management and middleware to access input/output (I/O) channels. Higher software layers include runtime systems and workflow management.

programs. Hard-disk drives and archival tape storage can keep user data indefinitely and have much greater capacity than ephemeral main memory, but at a cost of significant access times.

The first levels of software that control the hardware and manage these resources are associated with the operating system, which is far more complex than the two layers shown would suggest. Each node has a local instance of an operating system controlling the physical memory and processor resources of the node as well as the interface to the external (to the node) system area network. An additional layer of the operating system, sometimes referred to as the middleware, logically integrates the many nodes and their local operating systems into a single system image to which users can submit their application programs and access standard I/O channels. In some supercomputers a separate front-end software environment running on a dedicated computer known as the host provides most of the user interfaces and services other than the scalable computing itself. The layered operating system reflects an abstract or virtual machine to the upper levels of the system, including the user-programming interface. It ensures a standardized set of user services upon which the application can depend, with common interface protocols independent of the specific system upon which it is performed. Among these services is the file system than manages much of the persistent storage and presents a structured organization of the diverse forms of user data.

Above the layers dedicated to resource management are those associated with the means of developing and executing user applications and workloads. Here "workloads" are defined as a collection of loosely coupled applications, each performing a different aspect of the total set of tasks that need to be computed. For example, one might have three applications, simulator, a data analyzer, and a visualization package, with each of these three applications streaming data to the next function. The overall work management layer involves several support capabilities, including the programming languages (e.g., Fortran, C, C++), additional libraries often for parallelism (e.g., MPI, OpenMP), and compilers that provide machine-readable code for the processor cores translated and optimized from the user code. Higher-level environments and tools help in building more complex workflows and managing them. An important part of such environments are the many sophisticated libraries of previously developed and highly optimized functions that many programs can use; these enhance programmer efficiency through code reuse.

One last layer of the supercomputer system is the runtime system software. While this level tends to be a rather thin layer in conventional HPC practices, in programming models such as Java it can be much more substantial, as in the JVM (Java Virtual Machine). HPC runtime systems manage some aspects of resource management and task scheduling as well as communication. It is possible that in future supercomputers runtime systems may play a far more significant role, but such claims are speculative at this time and await confirmation through experimentation.

1.4 COMPUTER PERFORMANCE

The principal defining property and value provided by HPC is delivered performance for an end-user application. Expressions of "speed" or "how fast" are common, describing, perhaps vaguely, the relationships among time, work as computation actions, system size, and other factors. But in spite of its central role in the domain of HPC, performance itself as a measure is ambiguous, has different and in some cases contradictory meanings, and can result in different conclusions depending on interpretation. Nonetheless, despite these vagaries, performance as both an achievement and a means to achievement is core to HPC as a discipline and means of accomplishment [6]. This section briefly introduces performance as a quality metric and describes its various aspects, even as attempts are made to measure and apply it to guide system and application development.

1.4.1 PERFORMANCE

Performance is an intuitive notion of a person or a machine going well. It is a natural part of how we think about athletes, vehicles on land, sea, and air, and more abstract accomplishments such as a grade in an exam. Performance for a computer could easily be thought of as how fast it runs or the speed of an application. While not wrong, this vague idea is inadequate to allow quantitative assessment or comparisons between separate machines running the same program, separate programs designed to get the same answer, or alternative support software (e.g., two different compilers or languages) facilitating both. It is necessary to define performance in one or more useful ways and establish the quantitative metrics used to measure it. As will be seen, there are multiple meaningful and useful definitions. They share the common parameters of time (seconds) and work (primitive operations). However, depending on the context in which the two are used, the meaning can be quite different and possibly lead to conflicting conclusions.

1.4.2 PEAK PERFORMANCE

Gordon Moore, the cofounder of Intel Corporation, noted that the number of transistors in an integrated circuit doubles roughly every 2 years. This observation is widely known as "Moore's law". *Photo by the Chemical Heritage Foundation via Wikimedia Commons*

Gordon Moore is the cofounder of Intel Corporation along with Robert Noyce and a pioneer in the semiconductor industry. Gordon Moore made an observation now known as "Moore's Law" which states that the number of transistors on an integrated chip doubles roughly every 2 years. Moore's law subsequently became a driving goal in the semiconductor industry that has resulted in enormous performance gains in computational science achieved simply by adopting the latest integrated chip, an era sometimes referred to as the "free ride." Gordon Moore is a recipient of the Presidential Medal of Freedom and the IEEE Medal of Honor.

Peak performance of a system is the maximum rate at which operations can be accomplished theoretically by the hardware resources of a supercomputer. Usually in HPC peak performance is measured in units of flops (megaflops, gigaflops, teraflops, petaflops), with peak performance by the end of this decade anticipated to hit exaflops. (Note that the "s" in flops is not the plural but rather stands for "seconds". This is a common error even among otherwise knowledgeable people.) But different kinds of operations may have different peak rates. Integer operations, floating-point operations, and memory access (load–store) operations will take different times (instruction issue to instruction retire) and there will be different numbers of such operations that can be performed concurrently. To complicate this, a given operation type may take different amounts of time depending on the circumstances of the action (e.g., load operation through a cache hierarchy).

Peak performance is determined by the combination of the clock rate provided by the device technology and the hardware parallelism determined by the computer architecture. Both are a function of device density, which has demonstrated a remarkable growth rate over the last 4 decades. This trend was captured by Gordon Moore, who predicted that device density would increase by a factor of two every 2 years. This has proven uncannily accurate. Reduced feature size (i.e., width of a wire on a die) reduces capacitance and natural time constants, permitting a higher clock rate. At the same time, more devices can be put on a single semiconductor die, which permits more sophisticated processor core architectures that can do more operations per cycle (at peak). The system architecture determines the number of processor cores that together comprise the total system and contributes to the total number of operations that can be performed at the same time. Thus peak performance in terms of operations per second is determined by clock rate and architecture.

1.4.3 SUSTAINED PERFORMANCE

Sustained performance is the actual or real performance achieved by a supercomputer system in running an application program. While sustained performance cannot exceed peak performance, it can be much less and often is. Throughout the period of computation the instantaneous performance can vary, sometimes quite dramatically depending on a number of variable circumstances determined by both the system itself and the immediate requirements of the application code. Sustained performance represents the total average performance of an application derived from the total number of operations performed during the entire program execution and the time required to complete the program, sometimes referred to as "wall clock time" or "time to solution". Like peak performance, it may be represented in terms of a particular unit (kind of operation) of interest, such as floating-point operations, or it can include all types of operations available by the computing system, such as integers (of different sizes), memory load and stores, and conditionals.

Sustained performance is considered a better indicator of the true value of a supercomputer than its specified peak performance. But because it is highly sensitive to variations in the workload, comparison of different systems only has meaning if they are measured running equivalent applications. *Benchmarks* are specific programs created for this purpose. Many different benchmarks reflect different classes of problems. The Linpack or HPL benchmark is one such application used to compare supercomputers: it is widely employed and referenced, and is the baseline for the Top 500 list that tracks the fastest computers in the world (at least those so measured) on a semiannual basis.

1.4.4 SCALING

"Scaling" or alternatively "scalability" is a relationship of performance to some measure of the size (or "scale") of the HPC system. It reflects the ability to achieve increased performance for an application by employing machines of ever-greater size. Although there are many ways to quantify a system's size, a simple and widely used measure is the number of processor cores employed, recognizing that there are multiple cores per processor socket and usually multiple processor sockets per system node. The added complexity of how these are distributed in their use for a given application (e.g., how many of the cores in a given socket are actually used) is largely ignored for this purpose, although it can in fact have a significant impact on the resulting performance.

As is explored at greater depth in later chapters, an important subtlety associated with performance scaling is the application program size employed as the system size is modified. For this purpose, the size of an application can be quantified as the amount of data used, such as the dimensions of a problem matrix (n by n). Over the last 2 to 3 decades, *weak scaling* has been an important way to take advantage of ever-larger systems where the size of the data (such as n) grows proportionally with the size of the system (again, number of cores). This keeps the amount of work that a given core does about the same even as the system scale increases. Granularity of a given task (process or thread) stays about the same and so does efficiency, at least for many regular problems. This has been an important enabler of the extraordinary apparent performance gain witnessed over the last 20 years. However, as systems grow in scale the amount of main memory incorporated does not grow proportionally due to costs. As a result, the amount of memory per core has been going down, limiting the opportunity for weak scaling. At one time it was presumed that there would be about 1 byte of main memory per 1 flops of performance. Now with the largest machines this factor has shrunk to below 10% (1% for TaihuLight) in some cases.

The alternative to weak scaling is the much more challenging but important approach of *strong scaling*, where the application dataset size remains constant in the presence of increased system size. The key measure for strong scaling is not flops but time to solution. If a system were to be doubled in scale (twice as many cores), the ideal case would exhibit an execution time of half. The total work performed would be the same, but with double the number of cores it should be possible to do this in half the time. As will be seen, there are many reasons why this often is not possible, and some experts dismiss strong scaling as no longer being a viable approach. While controversial, the position taken by this discussion is that both strong and weak scaling are important, although often for different purposes.

1.4.5 PERFORMANCE DEGRADATION

The causes that result in the degradation of performance from the (not to be exceeded) peak performance to the observed sustained performance are many and varied. But they all contribute to a failure to exploit all the resources all of the time. No single part of the system is responsible for this degradation, but rather it is the imperfect match of the user application code, the compiler translation of the high-level application specification to low-level binary representation, the potential intrusion and overheads of the operating system, and the many facets of the computer architecture at the system and microcore levels. Usually, it is no single element but rather the interplay of two or more such elements that together conspire against perfection of operation. Much of this book is about how such degradation occurs and what measures can be taken to mitigate it. However, at a more abstract level four principal factors determine the delivered (sustained or actual) performance for a given application running on a target platform, here briefly introduced. This formalization of performance degradation is referred to through the acronym *SLOW*, which identifies the sources as starvation, latency, overhead, and waiting for contention.

Starvation directly relates to a critical source of performance, parallelism. Peak performance is measured with the assumption that all functional units are operating simultaneously on separate operations. If sufficient application parallel work is not available at any instance in time to support issuing instructions to all functional units every cycle, then less work will be performed than is possible, at least ideally. The achieved performance will be less than the possible peak performance. Starvation is this absence of work. Either there is not enough parallelism exhibited by the user application to keep all the system resources busy, or while there is enough work it is not distributed evenly (load balanced). In this latter case, some resources have too much work to do while other have too little.

Latency is the time it takes for information to travel from one part of a system to another. If an operation requires some data from a remote resource to proceed, latency will contribute to the amount of time it takes for that data to be delivered and cause the associated execution unit to stall or cease functioning until the data is available and it can continue. If latency for all such requests is very short, the effect is small. But if an execution unit is blocked (cannot continue) until a request from across the system is delivered, the effect can be very significant. Latency occurs in many aspects of system operation, including (but not limited to) local memory accesses, data transfer between separate nodes, and length of execution pipeline (number of stages to completion of operation). To minimize its effects on performance, latency can be reduced through exploitation of locality where everything is retained relatively close to each other. Or latency can be "hidden" by making certain that blocking of functional unit operation does not occur, even in the presence of high-latency requests. This can be achieved if a unit can temporarily work on some other task. Cache hierarchies and multithreading hardware are examples of ways of mitigating the effects of latency. But locality management by the programmer and/or the system software dominates the means of limiting latency effects.

Overhead is the amount of additional work beyond that actually required to perform the computation (such as on a pure sequential processor). Overhead work is necessary to manage resources and task scheduling, control parallelism through synchronization, support communication, handle address translation, and perform many other support functions that do not actually contribute to the operations needed for the computation itself. Overhead degrades performance through a couple of mechanisms. It wastes operations, time, and resources that are not directly associated with the computation; this alone is cause for concern and corrective measures. But there is a subtle indirect effect as well. As will be seen when we explore scaling, overhead is associated directly with setting up individual tasks, and the duration of the overhead puts a lower bound on the granularity (length) of the task it is controlling to achieve effective operation. For a fixed amount of task work (for example for strong scaling), the amount of parallelism that can be exploited is dependent in part on the fineness of granularity that can be employed and therefore the total parallelism that may be available. Thus scalability (and starvation) is indirectly affected by overhead.

Waiting of threads of action for shared resources due to *contention* of access degrades performance. When two or more requests are made at the same time to be serviced by the same single resource, either hardware or software, only one can proceed. The other(s) must wait until the first request is retired and the required resource is freed. One effect is that the delayed actions are extended in time, taking longer to complete. This has a cascading effect as follow-on actions dependent on this first one will also be extended in their time of initiation. A second effect is that the hardware upon which the delayed action is being performed may be blocked and its potential capability wasted for the duration of the delay. Both time and energy are lost. Finally, such events occur unpredictably (in most cases) and create uncertainty in the execution, making optimization methods less effective. Typical examples include bank conflicts for main memory and insufficient bandwidth for communication networks.

1.4.6 PERFORMANCE IMPROVEMENT

With these factors in consideration, the HPC user can find a number of ways to improve delivered performance—referred to sometimes as "performance debugging". This textbook continuously describes techniques to improve one's performance, including hardware scaling, parallel algorithms, performance monitoring, work and data distribution, task granularity control, and other sometimes subtle means.

Something as simple as increasing the number of nodes employed in the execution of an application can be a major method of improving performance. But one will quickly experience limitations to scaling and efficiency due to contributing factors such as uniformity (or irregularity) of tasks on processor cores, distribution of data across memory affecting bank conflicts, cache and translation lookaside buffer (TLB) misses, and page faults. Minimization of data movement, especially between system nodes, will reduce latency effects. Granularity of tasks (e.g., processes, threads) and messages will amortize overhead and latency costs if it is made more heavyweight. Exploiting compiler optimizations correctly, increasing problem dataset sizes (weak scaling), algorithm improvements, and circumventing I/O bottlenecks are among additional methods that may result in performance gain. This list of strategies is very long, if not unending. Many of these basic techniques are demonstrated in the following chapters as they relate to the respective topics.

In general, the key to performance improvement is performance measurement and profiling. Entire classes of performance measurement toolkits and frameworks have been developed directly to fulfill this important role. Due to the intricacies of performance profiling on a supercomputer, an entire chapter is dedicated to this topic later in the text.

1.5 A BRIEF HISTORY OF SUPERCOMPUTING

The history of HPC is among the most dramatic examples of human achievement through innovations in scientific discovery and engineering. Without exaggeration, no other technology in the history of mankind has exhibited such extraordinary growth and in such a narrow time span. In the course of a single human lifetime, the capability of supercomputing as measured by floating-point operation throughput has achieved a growth factor of more than 10 trillion. It is not that somehow the field just got it wrong for a period of time and then suddenly got it right. Instead, through a series of half-a-dozen epochs, device technologies, system architectures, and programming approaches, the fastest computers at any point in time grew in performance by about a factor of 200 times each decade. This unique story is easily the subject of entire volumes. But the intent here is to grasp the lessons of this history as it defines current practices in HPC and guides future developments in to the era of exascale computing. Examples from the history of supercomputing illustrate and highlight critical ideas, and their importance in defining HPC and driving its progress. The overall pattern of the history of HPC provides a framework for future detailed discussions. But even in this initial presentation the fundamental concepts, touched on briefly above, are engaged as the fabric from which the more precise patterns of this story later evolve.

The age of modern computing has been powered by continuous and significant technology advances and achieved through innovations in computer architecture and programming models. But this accomplishment has only had true meaning and value due to the driving needs and empowerment of end-user goals: specifically domains of consideration that could only be addressed by computational means. The conceptual underpinnings of this constructive tension have been the continuous need to increase speed and concurrency while minimizing sources of inefficiencies. The changes in architecture were driven by a need to exploit the new opportunities enabled by new emergent technologies while addressing the challenges that each new advance imposed. Thus one perspective (there are many) of the history of supercomputing is to examine briefly seven epochs enabled through device technology and achieved through computer architecture supported with responsive programming models.

1.5.1 EPOCH I—AUTOMATED CALCULATORS THROUGH MECHANICAL TECHNOLOGIES

Vannevar Bush with US President Harry Truman. *Photo by Abbie Rowe via Wikimedia Commons*

Vannevar Bush's pioneering work on large-scale analog computers for solving differential equations paved the way for the tremendous expansion in computational science that continues to grow this day. The "differential analyzer", named and developed by Bush while at Massachusetts Institute of Technology (MIT), became the first general-purpose, large-scale analog computer for integration and served as a catalyst for the subsequent development of electronic digital computers. Apart from his influential impact on government support for big science and wartime management of scientific research, Bush is also considered an internet pioneer even though he had no direct involvement in the development of the internet. His influential 1945 essay describing a theoretical device that could store and access documents through associative linking was credited by information technology pioneer Theodor (Ted) Nelson with helping inspire the hypertext concept used in the internet today.

For multiple millennia mankind has sought aid in performing calculations through mechanical means, both to store intermediate values and to perform arithmetic operations on them. These methods increased speed and improved accuracy compared to pure mental or written methods. Although primitive, these techniques proved very effective and supported many important tasks associated with commerce, logistics, and even early science. Enumeration and summation were among the earliest computing tasks and these were facilitated by a family of simple recording media, such as the "tally sticks" used more than 10,000 years ago, culminating in the "abacus" in its many forms in Babylonia at about 2400 BCE. The abacus permitted integer numbers to be represented through physical arrangements of beads, and for addition and subtraction operations to be performed through mechanical actions. By 200 BCE the Chinese had developed the suanpan, an advanced form of abacus that has been employed up to the modern era in some parts of the world. This achieved two principles that are relevant to today's supercomputers: artificial representation and storage of numbers and the concept of process, a sequence of simple actions to achieve a more complex result. A third aspect of modern digital computation is manifest: the discrete data representation referred to now as "digital".

The 17th century and the age of enlightenment saw the first developments of the mechanical calculator. Blaise Pascal, a French mathematician, invented the "Pascaline" in 1642; this simplified the user interface such that anyone could use it and incorporated a carry mechanism for addition and subtraction. Gottfried Leibniz developed a "stepped reckoner" that performed the operation of digital multiplication in 1671. Throughout the 18th century many advances were made in mechanical calculators, culminating in 1820 with the "Arithmometer" developed by Charles de Colmar, which was mass produced from 1851 and performed division, addition, subtraction, and multiplication. This sequence of developments over a period of 2 centuries achieved practical artificial calculation delivered in a useful form to a wide market. It also provided a functional capability that would be embedded in all future modern computers, now referred to the "ALU" or "arithmetic logic unit".

At the beginning of the 19th century the second major advance toward fully automated computing was introduced by Joseph Jacquard for the special-purpose application of weaving. His contribution in 1801 was the concept of sequence of control through the storage of commands or instructions capable of eliciting specific automated action. The "punched card" was invented, which through a pattern of holes could define and activate a particular action of a possible set of many. The "Jacquard loom" was fed a sequence of such cards determining the color and pattern of weaving of threads to produce cloth. In 1890 the punched card storing data (rather than instructions) and the mechanical calculator were integrated to form the "tabulator", developed by Herman Hollerith and first applied to the US census. This provided the foundation for complex data processing by mechanical means that dominated commercial information management for almost a century and established what would become the world's largest computer company, IBM (originally the Tabulating Machine Company).

The basic concepts for general fully automated calculation by mechanical means were established by Charles Babbage, a British mathematician, starting in 1834 with his design of the "analytical engine" [7]. His earlier ideas of the "difference engine" which computed polynomial tables and was eventually built led to conceptual extensions for general-purpose computation. It embodied the principles of the mechanical ALU with that of punched-card sequence control. Babbage was not to see the realization of this dream, but he influenced the work of Konrad Zuse, who in 1938 completed the first programmable mechanical computer in Germany, and in 1944 Howard Aiken and IBM developed the "Harvard Mark 1". This final system was the culmination of 3 centuries of advances, starting with the Pascaline, that demonstrated the viability of automated computation, including the basic concepts of arithmetic function units, sequence control through stored instructions, intermediate data storage, and I/O. But despite all these innovations, the resulting calculating speed, i.e., the rate at which operations could be performed, was relatively slow: about 1 instruction per second (IPS). It would take a breakthrough in device technology, unanticipated in the time of Pascal and Leibniz, as well as further conceptual advances beyond that of Babbage to create the paradigm shift that led to the modern digital computer and supercomputer.

1.5.2 EPOCH II—VON NEUMANN ARCHITECTURE IN VACUUM TUBES

The second epoch of high-speed computing (what we would call "supercomputing") incorporated a paradigm shift that was enabled by a component technology revolution and driven by the crisis of war. Four fundamental concepts laid the groundwork for the modern computational age: Boolean logic, binary arithmetic, computability, and what would be called the von Neumann architecture. Logic was developed by the British mathematician George Boole in 1848 and provided the fundamental framework for the design of complex digital logic functions through the synthesis of basic Boolean operations (e.g., AND, OR, NOT), the basis of virtually all modern computers today. In 1937 Claude Shannon derived the basic unit of information, the "bit" (binary digit) that comprises the basis for binary arithmetic, the principal means of conducting calculations by artificial means (decimal or base 10 had also been used). A year earlier, in 1936, Alan Turing presented what would become the fundamental model of computation, the "Turing machine", which resolved a key issue of computability put forth by Hilbert and also addressed work by Church. Today we determine that a computing machine is general purpose if it is a "Turing equivalent". Finally, the mathematician John von Neumann, influenced by the work of Eckhart and Mauchly, described a class of general-purpose stored-program digital computing that has served as the basis of the architecture for almost all central processing unit (CPU) designs to this day. Central to this was the concept of the program counter and program representation as a sequence of encoded instructions stored in the main memory where the data also resides.

Alan M. Turing

June 23, 1912–June 7, 1954

Alan Turing laid the theoretic foundations of what would become the field of computer science, and in so doing defined what computability itself was. He applied his concepts and insights into the development of automated computing systems for breaking the German Enigma code during World War II, and developed one of the first stored-program digital electronic computers, the automatic computing engine (ACE). Due to his theoretical and applied research, Alan Turing is noted as one of the premier contributors to the establishment of modern computing.

Turing devised the concept of an abstract computing construct that would later come to be called the "universal Turing machine", and was employed to solve a central mathematical problem posed by the mathematician Hilbert, known as the halting problem. This established the principles of computability (also contributed to by Church with an alternate abstraction, the lambda calculus). Through this work a deep understanding of how all computers must work was devised, as well as the basic idea of computer algorithms. Any computer that can be fully general purpose is identified as a "Turing equivalent" to this day.

Turing brought his prodigious acumen and insights in mechanical computation to the requirements of crypto-analysis, and more specifically code breaking at Bletchley Park in England, where the challenge of decoding Enigma messages was a priority. His contributions to the development of advanced "bombes", electromechanical computers that tested many possible decoding combinations, are considered critical to bringing World War II to a successful and relatively fast conclusion and saving many lives. Among other effects, it was crucial to helping win the Battle of the Atlantic, enabling supplies and personnel to cross the ocean from the United States and Canada to Great Britain.

Alan Turing produced the first full design of a stored-program digital electronic computer, the ACE, which for various reasons was not built until after his premature death. However, a smaller version, the Pilot ACE, was implemented and the concepts incorporated in this early work had significant impact on future computer designs. Toward the end of his life, Turing considered the implications of mechanical computing and the idea of artificial intelligence. He conceived of a test that would mark the achievement of a thinking machine; this has come to be called the "Turing test" for machine intelligence.

–CONT'D

Photo via Wikimedia Commons

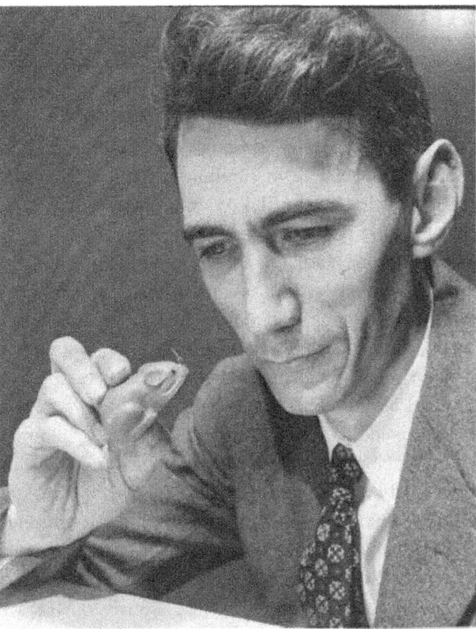

Photo from Wikimedia Commons

Claude Elwood Shannon is widely considered to be the father of modern information theory. He applied probability theory to the communication problem of finding the best way of encoding information for transmission. One of the fundamental

—CONT'D

concepts of this field, information entropy, describes the measure of information contents in a message. The unit of entropy has been named the "shannon" in his honor, and is equivalent to 1 bit.

Shannon created one of the first digital logic circuits based on the work of George Boole. At that time such circuits used arrangements of electromechanical relays, each of which could be in one of two states: "on" or "off". This corresponded to the 0 and 1 values used by binary Boolean algebras. Shannon expanded the concept by rigorously proving that digital circuits are capable of solving Boolean algebra problems, thus effectively establishing the theoretical foundations of digital logic design.

Shannon's research at Bell Laboratories focused on cryptography and weapons control systems during World War II. He proved that cryptographic one-time pads are unbreakable. He is credited with the invention of signal-flow graphs that may be used to describe signal propagation in a broad class of cyber-physical systems. He also introduced sampling theory that analyzes the relationships between the continuous-time (analog) signal and its uniformly sampled discrete-time representation. One outcome of this research is the famous Shannon—Nyquist theorem that quantifies the impact of signal aliasing. After leaving Bell Laboratories Shannon joined MIT, where he taught and worked at the Research Laboratory of Electronics until 1978.

During his prolific career Shannon maintained professional contacts with Alan Turing, Hermann Weyl, John von Neumann, Hendrik Bode, John Tukey, and many others. His achievements were recognized by numerous awards, including the Morris Liebmann Memorial Prize, Stuart Ballantine Medal of the Franklin Institute, AIEE Mervin J. Kelly Award, National Medal of Science, IEEE Medal of Honor, Royal Netherlands Academy of Arts and Sciences Joseph Jacquard Award, Audio Engineering Society Gold Medal, Kyoto Prize, and Eduard Rhein Foundation Basic Research Award, as well as multiple honorary doctorates bestowed by institutions of higher learning around the world. He was also inducted into the National Inventors' Hall of Fame in 2004.

MAURICE WILKES AND THE ELECTRONIC DELAYED STORAGE AUTOMATIC CALCULATOR

Maurice Wilkes was a pioneer in and major founder of the field of digital electronic computing. Arguably he is responsible for the first practical stored-program digital computer, the electronic delayed-storage automatic calculator (EDSAC), launched in May 1949. Wilkes spent his professional life primarily at the University of Cambridge as both a student and a professor, ultimately becoming director of the University of Cambridge Computer Laboratory. Throughout his career Professor Wilkes made a number of formative advances in computer principles and practices that led the field from its inchoate phase to commercial success; among these were EDSAC, microcontrollers, and microprogramming. His influence is felt even today after his death in 2010 at the age of 95.

EDSAC was derived from the concepts of von Neumann, Eckert, and Mauchly and from his in-depth experience with the electronics technology of the 1940s, primarily in radar during World War II. This included vacuum tube devices and circuits, mercury delay lines (tanks) for short-term data storage, and pulse transformers for data communication. Electromechanical devices used for tabulation and business data formation, search, and enumeration were employed for data entry and long-term storage on paper tape with teleprinters for output. The tanks held 1024 (initially 512) words, each of 18 bits. This was an accumulator machine with an additional buffer to aid in multiplication. It was a conservative machine, in that its clock rate was only about 660 Hz (1.5 ms), but this delivered the important reliability required for practical application computations. Double words of 35 bits could be used, and the accumulator was 71 bits long to hold two of these. The binary instruction set included a 5-bit op code, a 10-bit operand (often an address), a 1-bit length code, and a spare bit.

It was Maurice Wilkes who introduced the concept of microcontrollers to computer design. A microcontroller is a computer within a computer optimized to generate the control signals for the computer operations efficiently. By changing the microcode in the control store (usually a fast memory), the computer's instruction set could be added to or improved without changing the hardware. This solution was inspired by Wilkes's visit to MIT, where the Whirlwind computer was being developed using a similar hardwired controller with a sequence of rows of diodes determining the order of control signals. It was Wilkes's innovation to change the diodes to electronic switches. EDSAC-2 would later be the first computer to be microcoded, setting a trend that lasted at least 25 years.

MAURICE WILKES AND THE ELECTRONIC DELAYED STORAGE AUTOMATIC CALCULATOR—CONT'D

Maurice Wilkes and the EDSAC I under construction. *Copyright Computer Laboratory, University of Cambridge. Reproduced by permission*

John von Neuman. *Photo by Los Alamos National Laboratory via Wikimedia Commons*

John von Neumann's enormously wide-ranging scientific and mathematical work includes significant contributions to computer architecture, supercomputing algorithms, and cellular automata. His name is commonly associated with the

—CONT'D

stored-program architecture used by modern computers, even though the stored-program concept is also attributable to the developers of the electronic discrete variable automatic computer, J. Presper Eckert and John William Mauchly. John von Neumann's work on the electronic numerical integrator and computer (ENIAC) led to his realization that it could compute pseudorandom numbers, thereby paving the way for the first Monte Carlo simulations ever performed on an electronic computer in 1948. von Neumann was also involved in the first numerical weather predictions, also using the ENIAC. Both Monte Carlo simulations and numerical weather predictions are mainstays on supercomputers today.

The revolutionary enabling device technology that inaugurated modern computing was electronics, the amplification and control of electricity through the agent of active device components, the first of which was the vacuum tube. The vacuum tube was produced by the prolific inventor Thomas Edison by accident while working on the electric light in 1880. He witnessed the counterintuitive phenomenon of an electric current flowing in a vacuum between two disconnected elements (cathode and anode). Called the "Edison effect" (he patented it), it did little more than rectify an alternating current but served as the basic technology upon which electronics would be devised. The second breakthrough was the use of the vacuum tube as an amplifier by adding one or more screens between the cathode and the anode to which a much weaker signal could be applied. The Audion, the first amplifying vacuum tube, was produced by Lee De Forrest in 1906 and led to a series of advances, starting with the "Triode" that allowed a strong current to be controlled by the much weaker one. In 1937 John Atanosoff developed digital logic circuits for binary computing using vacuum tubes as electronic switches, replacing the mechanical counterparts employed by Zuse and Aiken and all of their forerunners.

During World War II Eckert and Mauchly in the United States and Turing in Great Britain developed special-purpose vacuum-tube-based digital electronic calculating systems for ballistics calculations (ENIAC) [8] and code breaking (Colossus), respectively. Immediately after the war, the von Neumann architecture concept was applied as the basis of the first generation of the modern digital computer for several projects in the US, England, and Germany. EDSAC was developed at Cambridge University by Maurice Wilkes in 1949 as the first full embodiment of the combination of principles and technologies described above [9]. In the United States a number of machines were implemented, including the MIT Whirlwind, the IBM 704, the IAS, and the UNIVAC I among others. Of these, Whirlwind was perhaps the supercomputer of the day. Performance of these systems ranged from below 1 KIPS to about 10 KIPS, and was principally limited by the speed of data-storage technology. After early flirtations with such primitive storage technologies as mercury delay lines and Williams' tubes, memory using small toroidal ferromagnetic cores to store magnetic fields was developed as part of the Whirlwind project and mass marketed by IBM to provide a stable, dense (relatively), three-dimensional (3D) matrix of memory bits that revolutionized digital computing and served as its main memory for more than 2 decades.

The first commercially produced computer was the LEO 1 developed by J. Lyons & Co. in the United Kingdom, based on EDSAC. It was capable of approximately 600 IPS. The first commercial digital electronic computer in the United States was the UNIVAC I, delivered in 1951 by Remington Rand. IBM produced its first scientific computer, the 701, and first mass-produced commercial machine, the 650, in the mid-1950s. The 701 was capable of 4 KIPS.

Performance for this first generation of digital electronic computers was a direct function of the clock rate of the CPU and the number of bits processed in parallel. Clock speed and parallelism would become the two principal dimensions driving the evolution of supercomputer performance. It was also dependent on the number of clock cycles required to perform each operation.

1.5.3 EPOCH III—INSTRUCTION-LEVEL PARALLELISM

The next technology breakthrough to revolutionize supercomputing was the development of the "transistor" in 1947 at Bell Laboratories. The transistor served as an alternative to the vacuum tube as an electronic switch. Unlike the tube, the transistor employed semiconductor materials to control the flow of electrons through a solid medium. It was much smaller and faster than the vacuum tube, required much less energy, and was more reliable. Eventually it became much more cost effective as well. Without exaggeration, the transistor made the digital computer practical and commercially viable to a large market, guaranteeing its positioning as a strategic technology. As a functional device, the transistor had three connections: emitter, collector, and base. These roughly compared to the older vacuum tubes' cathode, anode, and grid in their respective roles, with the weak current into the base being amplified as a much larger current between the emitter and collector. The transistor went through two phases of evolution: the first using germanium, and the second employing silicon. The latter demonstrated significant improvements over germanium, and once perfected largely replaced it. These bipolar transistors were themselves replaced with field-effect transistors that greatly increased input impedance, providing lower current drains between successive circuit stages and superior isolation between them for improved operational properties and easier circuit design [10].

The early transistor-based computers were first and foremost advances in circuit design, replacing the previous vacuum tube epoch with new logic circuits using transistors. Among the first experimental machines was the TX-0 developed by Lincoln Laboratories, demonstrating in principle the viability of transistor digital electronics for stored-program digital computing. As transistors improved in quality and reliability, design practices became standardized and printed circuit boards and modules were developed that reflected the higher abstraction of logical gates (Boolean functions) and latches (single-bit storage) with well-defined voltage levels representing binary 1 and 0 or Boolean true and false. From these, computer architectures were constructed. The IBM 1401 launched in 1959 (of which more than 10,000 were delivered in various configurations) and the DEC PDP-1 launched in 1960 (which began the minicomputer) and based on the TX-0 were two among many. They all executed one instruction at a time. The IBM 7090, also launched in 1959, was essentially a transistor version of the previous vacuum tube 709 but six times faster.

While every advance in delivered performance may be interpreted as improvement in HPC, it became clear even in the first generation of digital electronics that system design and programming for business purposes and scientific applications were different, with the former emphasizing long-term data storage and I/O devices while the latter required optimization for numeric computation with an emphasis on floating-point (real numbers) operations. As basic methods of circuit design, reliability, and cost were refined, these two distinct domains of computing began to be distinguished as two increasingly disparate system designs or architectures. Ultimately a machine architecture emerged which so dramatically reflected this demarcation of combined purpose-built design that it would be recognized as the first true supercomputer. That machine was the CDC 6600.

Developed under the leadership of Seymour Cray and designed by Jim Thornton, the CDC 6600 was delivered in 1964 by Control Data Corporation (CDC), and in its various forms was deployed at over 100 user sites. It was the first 1 megaflops (peak) supercomputer. While a *tour de force* in the use of the new silicon transistor technology that enabled it, providing an unprecedented 10 MHz clock rate, it was its use of innovative computer architecture to provide and exploit lightweight or instruction-level parallelism (ILP) that catalyzed a revolution in HPC, here categorized as the third epoch, arguably creating the supercomputer itself. It incorporated 10 separate logic units and was served by as many peripheral processors for accessing memory and I/O channels. Each was served in its turn by the CPU, overlapping the many operations and for the first time adding this new level of parallelism to achieve a dramatic performance increase.

1.5.4 EPOCH IV—VECTOR PROCESSING AND INTEGRATION

The SX-9. *Photo by GenGen via Wikimedia Commons*

Tadashi Watanabe is a computer architect and engineer, primarily responsible for the design of the highly successful SX series of vector supercomputers. The NEC SX-2, introduced in 1983, was the first machine to break the 1 GFlops barrier. It utilized four sets of pipelines feeding 16 vector arithmetic units implemented in high-density large-scale integration (LSI) logic and operating at a 6 ns machine cycle. It was also the first Japanese liquid-cooled supercomputer. Over the years the SX series significantly expanded in memory capacity and computational throughput while lowering the energy requirements, including, for example, the first single-image multinode installation in 1994 that performed at 1 TFlops peak utilizing 512 processors housed in 16 nodes, marketed as the SX-4. Later, the SX-6 served as the building block of the famous Earth Simulator that was used to perform the unprecedented whole-earth climate simulations at 10 km grid resolution. The best-performing member of the family, the SX-9, scales to 512 nodes that comprise a grand total of 8192 processors and 512 TB of memory, achieving in aggregate 839 TFlops. While at Riken R&D Center, Watanabe also influenced the design of another large-scale computer, K, that debuted at number one position in the Top 500 list in 2011, delivering over 8 PFlops in Linpack, and 6 months later was the first machine to cross the 10 PFlops threshold. For his achievements Tadashi Watanabe was honored with the IEEE-ACM Computer Society Eckert-Mauchly Award, the IEEE Computer Society Seymour Cray Award, the US National Academy of Engineering (Foreign Associate) Prize, and the Japan Academy Prize.

Seymour Cray and the Cray-1

September 28, 1925—October 5, 1996.

If any one person can be described as "the father of supercomputing", Seymour Cray is that person. Cray was largely responsible for the first true supercomputer while at CDC, the CDC-6600, delivered in 1965 with a performance well in excess of 1 megaflops on real-world applications. More than 100 of the 6600s were sold to national and academic laboratories. It was superseded in its status as "fastest computer in the world" in 1969 by the CDC-7600, also designed by Cray, and 10 times faster than the 6600 with a peak performance of about 36 Mflops. An attempt at a third-generation supercomputer, the CDC-8600, failed due to cost overruns.

Seymour Cray founded a new company, Cray Research Inc. (CRI), to chart the future direction in supercomputers, resulting in the Cray-1, the first true vector computer, launched in 1976 and beating just about anything on the market to a significant degree with a peak performance of 100 Mflops and more than 80 systems shipped. This was a really big success, and as much as any single machine defined supercomputing. The Cray-1 had both exceptional vector throughput and scalar speed.

Other teams at CRI extended the Cray-1 to the Cray-XMP and the Cray-YMP by employing multiple vector pipelines while improving clock rates and memory speeds. Seymour Cray developed the Cray-2, which was highly innovative but due to delays in delivery and poorer than expected memory speed technology failed to achieve a large market share. The design of the Cray-3 and Cray-4 by his new startup, Cray Computer Corporation (CCC), proved unsuccessful, with the ultimate bankruptcy of CCC due to heavy investments in gallium arsenide technology and the emergence of MPPs using very large-scale integration (VLSI) complementary metal-oxide semiconductor technologies which delivered superior performance to cost. Sadly, Cray died in a car accident in 1996 shortly after the founding of his last company, SRC.

Photo by Michael Hicks via Wikimedia Commons

As silicon transistor technology matured and feature size shrank it became possible to integrate more than one transistor along with diodes, resistors, and connecting wires on a single semiconductor die. The integrated circuit emerging in the late 1960s repeated the breakthrough of the original transistor, again pushing size, speed, power, and cost to new and unprecedented levels and driving the next revolution in supercomputing. This technology in its earliest phase was referred to as "SSI" for "small-scale integration" and incorporated one or more logical gates on a single die, exposing all their inputs and outputs via pins. SSI was formed in a number of basic technologies, such as resistor

FIGURE 1.10

The Cray-1 Supercomputer. First deployed in 1976 with a peak performance of 136 MFlops, this machine inaugurated the modern age of supercomputing.

Photo by Clemens Pfeiffer via Wikimedia Commons

transistor logic, diode transistor logic, transistor logic, and ECL (emitter coupled logic), among others. ECL was probably the fastest integrated logic at the time, but consumed more power.

As before, technology enabled significant advances in clock rate, but more importantly it inspired the next paradigm shift in supercomputer architecture: the exploitation of pipelining structures to process vectors of numbers. In 1976 Seymour Cray delivered the Cray-1 supercomputer to Los Alamos National Laboratory (Fig. 1.10) [11,12]. This architecture exploited the new technologies to achieve the then high clock rate of 80 MHz and vector pipelined processing for ultralightweight parallelism. But the pipelining did not just contribute to exposing and exploiting new levels of parallelism; it was also necessary to permit the 12.5 ns cycle time to be achievable by reducing the amount of logic that had to be processed at each physical point in the system. Further, the Cray-1 through this form of architecture addressed key factors of efficiency, specifically latency and overhead.

The key idea to pipelining is to divide a function into a balanced set of successive subfunctions, each of which takes much less time than performing the full function at one time. Each subfunction or pipeline stage operates simultaneously with the others but on different sets of operand data. Thus for a p-stage function pipeline, *p* different operations are being performed simultaneously, but at different stages of their completion. At the completion of a compute cycle, all the intermediate results of each stage are passed to their successive stage. A new set of operands is fed to the first stage of the pipeline, while the final result values are extracted from the final stage. The set of operand values forms a vector of length N, i.e., consisting of N values. If N is infinite, then the level of parallelism achieved is p. Because the vector length is finite, the average parallelism achieved is less, although when the pipeline is completely filled p parallelism is being exploited at that moment.

Latency is addressed in a vector processor by keeping communication distances very short and overlapping communication with actions of memory access and function operation. Multiple banks of memory are accessed in overlapping phases to get all the elements of a vector and place them in a vector register (a vector of single registers), permitting in effect multiple parallel memory accesses. Overhead is addressed in a vector computer by amortizing the control of an operation across the total set of vector elements rather than one at a time. The Cray-1 employed all these techniques based on the vector execution model to achieve the unprecedented peak performance of 136 megaflops.

There is an important limitation to the pure vector execution model and the architecture it implies. To increase vector parallelism, a pipeline needs to increase its number of stages, which means that the function to be performed needs to be divided into ever finer or shorter subfunctions. There is a limit to both this increasing division and its effectiveness, such that only so much useful parallelism can be extracted. Such factors include the time to communicate between successive stages, the imbalance in the processing time of each stage, and the limits of the logic gate depth of subfunction circuits. But for SSI and MSI (medium-scale integration) technologies, pipeline architecture and its underlying vector execution model proved an excellent blending of technology, architecture, and execution paradigm.

1.5.5 EPOCH V—SINGLE-INSTRUCTION MULTIPLE DATA ARRAY

Semiconductor fabrication and manufacturing processes continued to improve at an exponential rate, integrating an ever-increasing number of gates per silicon die. LSI augmented SSI and MSI to provide chips with higher functionality at lower size, cost, and power. Most notable of the advances in functionality is the advent of the microprocessor and dynamic random access memory (DRAM). The earliest microprocessors were extremely simple devices, but nonetheless capable of performing instruction sequences. At the time of the Cray-1, the first 8-bit microprocessors were available from Intel, Motorola, and Zilog among others, working on data stored in 1 Kbit DRAM memory chips. Clock rates of a few MHz were employed. While impressive, this class of component was not suitable for supercomputers that favored much faster logic parts, albeit less dense. But the same level of functional capability offered by LSI technology permitted alternative structures that would enable the next paradigm shift and levels of performance [13].

SIMD stands for single-instruction multiple data, and suggests the basic principle of a set of actors on separate data blocks all controlled by the same sequencer (Fig. 1.11). All the actors perform the same operation at the same time, but on their own dedicated block of data. Where the algorithm is suitable, SIMD-array architectures demonstrate great throughput and efficiency, and under these conditions performance to cost proved highly competitive. But other application algorithms were poorly served by this class of structure and suffered from significant inefficiencies.

FIGURE 1.11

The Thinking Machine CM-2. Single-instruction multiple data array machine with 64k simple functional cores and connected memory banks.

Photo by Don Armstrong via Wikimedia Commons

1.5.6 EPOCH VI—COMMUNICATING SEQUENTIAL PROCESSORS AND VERY LARGE SCALE INTEGRATION

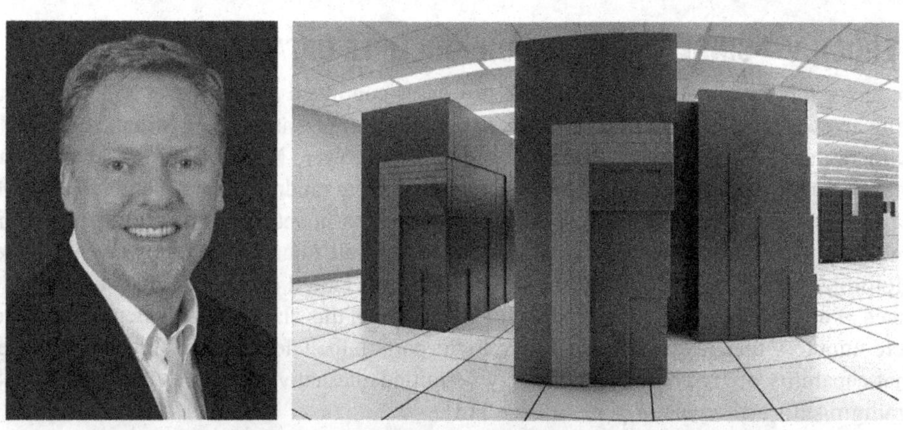

Left: Steve Scott. *Photo courtesy Cray Inc.*

Right: Cray T3E. *Photo courtesy NERSC/Lawrence Berkeley National Laboratory*

Steven Scott is a computer architect responsible for the design of several lines of Cray supercomputers. In 2005 he received the IEEE Seymour Cray Award "for advancing supercomputer architecture through the development of the Cray T3E, the Cray X1, and the Cray 'Black Widow'". The first of these machines, shown here, incorporated four-issue DEC Alpha processors clocked at between 300 and 675 MHz (EV5 and EV56 versions). T3E was a global address space distributed-memory computer that used a bidirectional 3D torus interconnect supporting up to 8 × 32 × 8 topology (2048 nodes), scalable in the Y dimension. Its custom router chips used five virtual channels to provide deadlock-free adaptive routing with

–CONT'D

a payload bandwidth of approximately 500 MB/s per link. This permitted efficient remote memory access with storage capacities ranging from 64 MB to 2 GB per node. One of the machine's unique features was self-hosting: no additional front-end system was required to manage its operation. A 1480-processor T3E system was the first to achieve a teraflops performance in a scientific application (simulation of metallic magnetism) in 1998. The Cray X1 combined the advanced network of the T3E with improved memory bandwidth and vector performance of up to 12.8 GFlops per processor to deliver over 50 TFlops aggregate in the largest configuration. The follow-on, the "Black Widow", introduced four-way symmetric multiprocessing nodes and a high-radix (64-port) yet another router chip that permitted growing the system to 32K processors in a fat-tree topology with the worst-case diameter of 7 hops.

While Scott's career was closely associated with CRI and Cray Inc., he also served as senior vice-president and chief technology officer of the Tesla business unit at Nvidia and principal engineer of the Platforms Group at Google. He holds 27 patents on interconnect, processor, and cache architecture, synchronization mechanisms, and parallel processing.

The previous epoch in HPC was triggered by the advent of VLSI technology, which has ultimately resulted in literally billions of transistors on a single semiconductor die. This technology demanded new strategies for making best use of the enormous capability now possible. It also opened up a new relationship between the special needs of supercomputing and the mass-market needs of general computing that was also enabled through VLSI. This was the era of the "killer micro".

VLSI permitted more concentration of functional ability on a single chip than ever before. This was most dramatically reflected by the microprocessor, a logical element with all the necessary functionality to perform complex computations and handle the workload of user application programs. Where once such a machine would cost a million dollars and fill a large machine room, by the beginning of this epoch a deskside or desktop box could do the same work and cost less than $40,000. Unlike the other epoch-spanning technologies, VLSI itself went through orders-of-magnitude transitions in device density throughout its 2-decade duration. Prior to this period, early microprocessors provided basic functionality with very limited performance. The first microprocessors actually entered the market in the 1970s, with 4-bit and 8-bit microprocessors being used in first-generation personal computers (PCs) and 16-bit microprocessors available at the start of the 1980s, causing a mitosis of the market between lower-cost PCs for personal use and higher-cost "workstations" for industrial-grade purposes. Early experiments were conducted in the late 1980s to explore the potential of integrating multiple microprocessors into ensemble systems, including the Caltech Cosmic Cube, MIT Concert, IBM RP2, Intel Touchstone Delta (Fig. 1.12), and others. In the meantime, farms of workstations on local area networks sharing I/O devices such as printers, early mass-storage systems, and access to the precursors to the internet were pursued as a means for cycle harvesting to perform large workloads on systems not in use (such as idle workstations at night).

By the beginning of the 1990s the first commercial MPPs with custom networks were being offered by vendors. Among these were the Intel Touchstone Paragon (1994), the Thinking Machines Corporation CM-5 (1992), and the IBM SP-2. With distributed-memory hardware a new model of programming was required, one in which each processor performed a separate process. Coordinated action was achieved through a combination of data exchange using message-passing methods and synchronization primitives, both across the interconnection network. CRI also introduced the T3D and later the T3E that integrated microprocessors, but in a configuration that permitted a degree of shared

FIGURE 1.12

Intel Touchstone Delta. With over 500 cores connected with a mesh topology, it delivered performance of 10–20 GFlops.

Photo courtesy of Dr. Paul Messina

memory across the entire system. Silicon Graphics, Inc and Convex extended the level of shared memory to include a nonuniform memory-access cache-coherent model through hardware.

A second strategy in the exploitation of VLSI microprocessor and high-density DRAM technologies emerged as a result of the success of the commercial market for workstations and the dramatically larger consumer market for PCs. The commodity cluster is a form of high performance computer assembled from commercially manufactured subsystems, each of which serves its own market niche as a standalone product. The cluster "node" is a computer that can be directly employed individually as a workstation, PC, desktop, or deskside machine, or as part of a set of independent computing facilities. Originally the network was derived from technology used as local area networks. In each case the markets for individual components greatly exceed the market for the components in cluster functions, enabling economy of scale to increase performance to cost dramatically with respect to custom-designed MPPs of the same scale (i.e., number of processor cores).

The concept of clustering of computing units predates this epoch, with perhaps the earliest example in the 1950s in the development and deployment of SAGE, a multiple computer system produced by IBM for North American Aerospace Defense Command to defend North America from the threat of air attack. The term "cluster" was first adopted by the DEC M31 Project (Andromeda), which assembled 32 VAX 11/750 minicomputers into a single ensemble system in the late 1980s. A number of early projects were initiated to investigate the feasibility and utility of harnessing the aggregate power of clustered systems, most notably the UC Berkeley Network of Workstations (NOWs) and the NASA Beowulf Project, both started in 1993. NOWs devised a series of increasingly sophisticated clusters of workstations, stressing the importance of the highest-quality and highest-performing components. In 1997 the first commodity cluster to be represented on the Top 500 list was the Berkeley NOW. The Beowulf Project pursued an alternative strategy, exploiting mass-market consumer-grade components to achieve the best possible performance to cost, even at the expense of efficiency and performance. Beowulf was also the first application of the inchoate Linux operating system for scientific parallel computing, to which the project contributed a large number of network drivers [14,15]. As this epoch comes to an end, the formula of commodity clusters now dominates the Top 500, with more than 82% of deployed systems in this category. The Beowulf integration of clusters of x86 processor architectures, the family of Ethernet networks, the Linux operating system, and message-passing programming modes all dominate in their respective categories the field of HPC due to the contributions of many researchers and developers in the field.

1.5.7 EPOCH VII—MULTICORE PETAFLOPS

It is controversial to assert that HPC is departing from the epoch of communicating sequential processes and being driven by technology toward something else in the petaflops era. But the now ubiquitous use of multicore sockets and graphics processing unit accelerators combined with exploration and experimentation of hybrid programming methods strongly suggests that the field is in a phase transition, with the ultimate outcome still undetermined [16]. Performance gains like never before are now determined by the growing number of cores employed, while programming models and methods are struggling to catch up. But some applications are failing to take full advantage of the hardware resources available, and are thus being dropped by the wayside as ever-fewer programs operate effectively across all systems.

A dominant trend is toward the synthesis of coarse-grained distributed-memory techniques using independent processes and medium-grained shared-memory techniques using interrelated multiple threads. Also being pursued is the addition of or replacement by lightweight processing cores for greater control state and higher memory-usage bandwidth. Nonetheless this is a rapidly evolving area, with large-scale system architectures evolving at least incrementally and programming methods changing to support them.

Even as this strategy is pursued, alternative pathfinding techniques are being explored to take advantage of dynamic adaptive computing methods supported by a new generation of runtime system software and programming interfaces. The future is far from known in this regard, but what will emerge when the smoke clears will be as interesting and exciting as any of the prior epochs.

1.5.8 NEODIGITAL AGE AND BEYOND MOORE'S LAW

The international HPC development community will extend many-core heterogeneous system technologies, architectures, system software, and programming methods from the petaflops generation to exascale in the early part of the next decade. But the semiconductor fabrication trends that have driven the exponential growth of device density and peak performance are coming to an end as feature size approaches nanoscale (approximately 5 nm). This is often referred to as the "end of Moore's law". This does not mean that system performance will also stop growing, but that the means of achieving it will rely on other innovations through alternative device technologies, architectures, and even paradigms. The exact forms these advances will take are unknown at this time, but exploratory research suggests several promising directions—some based on new ways of using refined semiconductor devices, and other complete paradigm shifts based on alternative methods. Other forms will be incremental changes to current practices benefiting from a legacy of experience and application.

While not commonly employed, the term "neodigital age" designates and describes new families of architectures that, while still building on semiconductor device technologies, go beyond the von Neumann derivative architectures that have dominated HPC throughout the last 6 decades and adopt alternative architectures to make better use of existing technologies. The von Neumann architecture emphasizes the importance of arithmetic floating-point units (FPUs) as precious resources which the remainder of the chip logic and storage is designed to support. It also enforces sequential instruction issue for execution control. Complexity of design offers many workarounds, but the fundamental principles prevail. Now FPUs are among the lowest-cost items and parallel control state is essential for scalability. New advances to current architecture and possible alternatives to von Neumann architectures may be among the innovations to extend the performance of semiconductor technologies beyond exascale.

More radical concepts are being pursued, at least for certain classes of computation. Special-purpose architectures where the logic design and dataflow communications match the algorithms can significantly accelerate computations for specific problems. Digital signal processing special-purpose chips have been employed since at least the 1970s. More recently architectures such as the Anton expand the domain of special-purpose devices to simulation of N-body problems, principally for molecular dynamics. Even more revolutionary approaches to computing are targets of research, including such techniques as quantum computing and neuromorphic architectures. Quantum computing exploits the physics of quantum mechanics to use the same circuits to perform many actions at the same time. Potentially some problems could be solved in seconds that would take conventional computers years to perform. Neuromorphic architecture is inspired by brain structures for such processes as pattern matching, searching, and machine learning. It is uncertain when such innovative concepts will achieve useful commercialization, but the future of computing systems and architecture is promising and exhibiting exciting potential.

1.6 THIS TEXTBOOK AS A GUIDE AND TOOL FOR THE STUDENT

This textbook is a graded introduction to the theory and practice of supercomputing. Each chapter brings in three or four key concepts, semantics, and technologies aimed at providing a *performance-oriented* and *systems-oriented* introduction to HPC. The topics are selected to provide both the theoretical background for understanding the abstract components of the field and a practical understanding of conventional practice needed to deploy applications, implement parallel algorithms, debug code, and monitor performance. While this textbook is intended for study under the guidance of an instructor in a college course, it is also suitable for individual study with the basic computing prerequisites covered in the appendices.

Chapters are organized to deliver three kinds of information: concepts, knowledge, and skills. Concept discussions aim to teach those ideas that have established theoretical foundations, enjoy longevity, and largely will not change. For instance, Amdahl's law, a performance model, is such a concept. Knowledge chapters aim to impart information about supercomputing to the reader that will evolve with time and will need to be added to in the future. For instance, the historical aspects of supercomputing fall into this category. Finally, skills needed for entry-level work in supercomputing are presented in tutorial style for ease of learning. These skills may change over time, but represent current conventional practice in the field. An example of this is the specifics on how to use the resource management tools on a supercomputer or how to program with a specific user application programming interface (e.g., OpenMP, MPI).

Exercises aimed at reinforcing understanding of the material are found at the end of each chapter. While much of the material will not require the use of a supercomputer to understand it fully, arranging access to a small cluster is recommended to attempt the practical coding exercises and examples given throughout the text.

Several of the chapters may serve as a reference guide to the specific technology they introduce. For example, the chapters on MPI, OpenMP, and essential resource management have also been written for self-contained reference usage.

The HPC field is replete both with freely available and proprietary software and toolkits designed to assist the practitioner and systems engineer in designing and deploying supercomputing applications. In general, this textbook provides a brief survey of such software and toolkits where relevant. However, for all examples and exercises only open-source and freely available software applications are utilized.

At the end of this course, the student can expect the following outcomes.

- A general overview of conventional practice in supercomputing in terms of both hardware architecture and software.
- A practical understanding of conventional practice in HPC software, including MPI, OpenMP, and OpenACC.
- A theoretical understanding of performance modeling and the key elements affecting parallel performance.
- A theoretical and practical understanding of file systems, resource management systems, debugging, and performance measurement.
- A theoretical and practical understanding of several key widely used parallel algorithms from a broad range of disciplines.
- A theoretical and practical understanding of the key operating systems in use by supercomputing systems.
- A broader view of the future directions of supercomputing in terms of both architecture and systems software.

1.7 SUMMARY AND OUTCOMES OF CHAPTER 1

- Definition of supercomputing and HPC. HPC incorporates all facets of three key disciplines: technology, methodology, and application. The principal defining property and value provided by HPC is delivered performance for an end-user application.
- Moore's law: the prediction by Intel cofounder Gordon Moore that device transistor density would increase by a factor of two every 2 years.
- Top 500 list. The Top 500 list ranks supercomputers in order of their performance running the HPL or "Linpack" benchmark for dense linear algebra. The list is updated twice a year.
- System stack of hardware and software comprising a supercomputer. The system stack of a supercomputer is a layered hierarchy of many physical and logical components, beginning with the system hardware and including processors, interconnection, and data storage. The system software that controls the hardware and manages the physical resources is associated with the

operating system, comprising both node-level instances controlling the node resources and the middleware which logically integrates many nodes and their local operating systems into a single system image. Software above the operating system abstraction includes resource management associated with executing user applications and workloads.

- Sustained and peak performance. Peak performance of a system is the maximum rate at which operations can be accomplished theoretically by the hardware resources of a supercomputer. Sustained performance is the actual or real performance achieved by a supercomputer system in the performance of an application program. While sustained performance cannot exceed peak performance, it can be much less.
- Benchmarks. The HPC community selects specific problems to compare and assess different HPC systems and capabilities. One of the most widely reported HPC benchmarks is HPL.
- Sources of performance degradation: starvation, latency, overhead, and contention. Starvation is when sufficient work is not available at any instance in time to support issuing instructions to all functional units every cycle. Latency is the time it takes for information to travel from one part of a system to another. Overhead is the amount of additional work beyond that which is actually required to perform the computation. Contention is when two or more requests are made at the same time and have to be serviced by the same single resource, either hardware or software, meaning that the requests can only proceed one at a time.
- Major epochs of supercomputing evolution based on technology drivers, execution models, and computer architecture. A perspective of seven epochs includes calculator mechanical technology, von Neumann architecture in vacuum tubes, ILP, vector processing, SIMD arrays, communicating sequential processes, and multicore petaflops.
- Possible future directions of HPC architecture. With the end of Moore's law, continued system performance growth will rely on other innovations through alternative device technologies, architectures, and even paradigms.

1.8 QUESTIONS AND PROBLEMS

1. Define or expand each of the following terms or acronyms.
    - HPC
    - Flops, gigaflops, teraflops, petaflops, exaflops
    - Benchmark
    - Parallel processing
    - OpenMP
    - MPI
    - Moore's law
    - Strong scaling
    - Starvation
    - Latency
    - Overhead
    - TLB, TLB miss
    - ALU
    - von Neumann architecture

- Turing machine
- SSI
- DRAM
- SIMD
- VLSI
- Distributed memory
- Commodity cluster
- NASA Beowulf Project
- Communicating sequential processors.

2. What is the primary requirement that differentiates HPC from other computers? What other requirements are also important?
3. Describe four reasons for performance degradation using the acronym SLOW. Give examples of each.
4. Give six techniques noted in the text for improving performance.
5. Name and give a brief description of the seven epochs in the history of supercomputing.
6. Describe the computer recognized as the first true supercomputer. Who developed it, and what company did he later form?
7. Suppose you have a computer that has a four-stage pipeline and a workload with an input set of operand values of size 100. Assuming that each stage takes one unit of time and passing results from one stage to the next is instantaneous, what is the average parallelism in your computer for this workload?
8. Describe Beowulf computers, with at least five characteristics. What makes them significant to supercomputing?
9. Describe what is meant by the "end of Moore's law".
10. What was the fastest computer in the year that you were born? What technologies were used in that fastest computer? How much faster is the world's fastest computer today?

REFERENCES

[1] J.J. Dongarra, P. Luszczek, A. Petitet, The LINPACK benchmark: past, present and future (PDF), John Wiley & Sons, Ltd. Concurrency and Computation: Practice and Experience (2003) 803–820.

[2] T. Rauber, G. Runger, Parallel Programming for Multicore and Cluster Systems, Springer, 2013, ISBN 978-3-642-37800-3.

[3] The Potential Impact of High-End Capability Computing on Four Illustrative Fields of Science and Engineering, Committee on the Potential Impact of High-End Computing on Illustrative Fields of Science and Engineering and National Research Council, October 28, 2008, ISBN 0-309-12485-9, p. 9.

[4] J.P. Singh, D. Culler, Parallel Computer Architecture, Nachdr. ed., Morgan Kaufmann Publ., San Francisco, 1997, ISBN 1-55860-343-3, p. 15.

[5] J.L. Hennessy, D.A. Patterson, J.R. Larus, Computer Organization and Design: The Hardware/software Interface, second ed., third print. ed., Kaufmann, San Francisco, 1999, ISBN 1-55860-428-6.

[6] A.O. Allen, Computer Performance Analysis with Mathematica, Academic Press, 1994.

[7] B. Collier, J. MacLachlan, Charles Babbage: And the Engines of Perfection, Oxford University Press, September 28, 2000, ISBN 978-0-19-514287-7, p. 11.

[8] ENIAC in Action: What It Was and How It Worked, ENIAC: Celebrating Penn Engineering History, University of Pennsylvania. Retrieved 2017.

[9] M.V. Wilkes, Memoirs of a Computer Pioneer, MIT Press, Cambridge, Mass, 1985, ISBN 0-262-23122-0.

[10] M.D. Hill, N.P. Jouppi, G.S. Sohi (Eds.), Readings in Computer Architecture, Morgan Kaufmann, September 23, 1999, ISBN 978-1558605398, p. 11.

[11] The Cray-1 Computer System (PDF), Cray Research, Inc, 1978.

[12] C.J. Murray, The Supermen: Story of Seymour Cray and the Technical Wizards behind the Supercomputer, 1997, ISBN 0-471-04885-2.

[13] K.E. Batcher, Design of a massively parallel processor, IEEE Transactions on Computers. C 29 (9) (September 1, 1980) 836–840, http://dx.doi.org/10.1109/TC.1980.1675684.

[14] D.J. Becker, T. Sterling, D. Savarese, J.E. Dorband, U.A. Ranawak, C.V. Packer, BEOWULF: a parallel workstation for scientific computation, Proceedings, International Conference on Parallel Processing 95 (1995).

[15] T.L. Sterling, Beowulf Cluster Computing with Linux, MIT Press, 2001, ISBN 0262692740.

[16] Blue Gene: A Vision for Protein Science Using a Petaflop Supercomputer (PDF), IBM Systems Journal, Special Issue on Deep Computing for the Life Sciences 40 (2) (2001).

CHAPTER

HPC ARCHITECTURE 1: SYSTEMS AND TECHNOLOGIES

2

CHAPTER OUTLINE

High Performance Computing. https://doi.org/10.1016/B978-0-12-420158-3.00002-2

2.1 INTRODUCTION

High performance computer architecture determines how very fast computers are formed and function. High performance computing (HPC) architecture is not specifically about the lowest-level technologies and circuit design, but is heavily influenced by them and how they can be most effectively employed in supercomputers. HPC architecture is the organization and functionality of its constituent components and the logical instruction set architecture (ISA) it presents to computer programs that run on supercomputers. HPC architecture exploits its enabling technologies to minimize time to solution, maximize throughput of operation, and serve the class of computations associated with large, usually numeric-intensive, applications. In recent years supercomputers have been applied to data-intensive problems as well, popularly referred to as "big data" or "graph analytics". For either class of high-end applications, HPC architecture is created to overcome the principal sources of performance degradation, including starvation, latency, overheads, and delays due to contention. It must facilitate reliability and minimize energy consumption within the scope of performance and data requirements. Cost is also a factor, affecting market size and ultimate value to domain scientists and other user communities. Finally, architecture shares in combination with the many other layers of the total HPC system the need to make application programming by end users as easy as possible.

A number of classes of HPC architecture have been employed for different technological niches over the decades, each addressing these key performance issues in the context of their respective enabling technologies. A unifying theme across HPC architectures is "parallelism", meaning the ability to perform multiple actions simultaneously and thus reduce the total time to accomplish the combined tasks and operations of a user workload. The different classes of architecture introduced in this chapter reflect some of the most widely employed forms of parallelism. While discussion of HPC is often focused on the largest systems, the field spans a wide range of performance operating points. More important than specific design points is the ability to bring orders of magnitude more capability to a valued problem than would be possible with a conventional uniprocessor or personal workstation. Thus the effect that defines a supercomputer and differentiates it from commercial (or even consumer) servers is that it delivers greatly enhanced performance to solve real-world problems. This can be realized with even a modest parallel computer, far smaller than the number one machine on the Top 500 list, but still much faster than the machine on which this textbook has been prepared.

2.2 KEY PROPERTIES OF HPC ARCHITECTURE

HPC architecture extracts performance from the underlying enabling technologies for the range of applications deemed important in the context of the user institution's mission. The organization of the architecture incorporates structures of the components that make best use of the devices and the dataflow patterns that move information between them. Three key properties of an architecture determine delivered performance: the speed of the components comprising the system, the parallelism or number of components that can operate concurrently doing many things simultaneously, and the efficiency of use of those components in the degree of utilization achieved. A simple relationship of these key factors shows their contributions to delivered performance in Eq. (2.1).

$$P = e \times S \times a(R) \times \mu(E) \tag{2.1}$$

where P is average performance, S is scaling (the number of units that can operate at the same time), a (which is a function of reliability, R) is availability, which is the total fraction of time the system is capable of performing a computation, and μ is the instruction retirement rate (usually the clock rate) of the processor core, which is a function of the power, E. Average performance is normally reported in terms of clock rate, while S and a are generally reported without units.

2.2.1 SPEED

HPC system performance is directly related to the speed of its components. A key parameter is the clock rate of its constituent processor cores, or basically the rate at which each retires instructions. But the technologies employed for different functionality have widely differing speeds or cycle times. Much architecture is devising structures and methods that match these disparate speeds. For example, a major concern is the speed of the processor, again the clock rate, with the cycle time of the main memory. Processor core clock rates may vary from slightly less than 1 GHz to approaching 3 GHz, with a few more extreme examples in both directions. Memory cycle times presented by dynamic random access memory (DRAM) devices to the processors are in the order of 100 times longer (substantial variation depends on details). But there are other forms of memory, specifically static random access memory (SRAM) technology, that depending on size and power consumption can operate at or near the speeds of the processor core logic. A modern architecture will include a memory hierarchy consisting of a mix of slower higher-density DRAMs for capacity with faster low-density SRAMs called "caches" to achieve speed. A third aspect of speed is the rate at which data can be transferred or communicated between any two points within the system. Two measures are applied for this communication speed. The bandwidth determines how much information can be moved between two points in unit time or the rate of data movement. The latency measures how long it takes to move data between the two points. These too can vary dramatically depending on the distances between the source and destination, as well as the type of technology employed and the amount used. Architecture is, among other things, the art of balancing these different time constants in structures and through methods that will yield the overall best delivered performance for a user workload (e.g., application) within normalizing cost factors like nonrecurring engineering (NRE), deployment, power, and user productivity.

2.2.2 PARALLELISM

No matter how fast the speed of the parts technology can be, it will never be fast enough alone to deliver the necessary performance required by major application problems. Fundamental limits such as the speed of light, atomic granularity, and the Boltzmann constant constrain how fast a single processor core can execute a stream of instructions. Thus HPC architecture is heavily dependent on structures that permit many actions to occur simultaneously: the ability to do many things at once. This is referred to as "parallelism", and the many different classes of parallel computer architecture are defined and distinguished by the diversity of structures that are employed to achieve parallelism in different ways. But HPC architecture is also determined by how such parallelism is controlled. Thus both the data path and the control path are factors in how parallelism is exploited by an HPC architecture.

2.2.3 EFFICIENCY

The third factor that determines delivered performance for a user workload is efficiency. Efficiency is primarily the utilization of the system, or the percentage of time that the critical components are employed. This is more complicated than it suggests. The question is: upon which components should efficiency be measured? For HPC, a common measure of efficiency is the ratio of the sustained floating-point performance to the theoretical peak floating-point performance, both measure in flops, floating-point operations per second (please note that the "s" is not the plural, but rather stands for "second").

$$e_{flops} = \frac{P_{sustained}}{P_{peak}} \tag{2.2}$$

where e_{flops} is floating-point efficiency such that $0 \le e_{flops} \le 1$, P_{peak} is the theoretical peak performance of the HPC architecture measured in flops, and $P_{sustained}$ is the achieved average floating-point performance.

However, this typical measure of efficiency reflects an earlier era when a floating-point operation was expensive, either taking a long time to perform or requiring expensive and complicated floating-point hardware. Today data movement and the costs of data access from memory are far more significant in die space, time, and energy than a register-to-register floating-point operation. Nonetheless, this is the metric that is most likely encountered.

2.2.4 POWER

Every computer, large or small, uses electrical power for its operation. The speed of processor cores is in part proportional to their clock rate, and this in turn relates to the power applied. As long as a computer like your laptop does not consume more power than is available via the typical electrical infrastructure, this is not an issue. For example, a laptop computer will require perhaps 80 W or less sustained power. A deskside workstation may demand 200–400 W depending on such features as number of screens and amount of disk capacity. These are well within the capacity of the electrical service infrastructure of a light industry building, even for many worker stations. Electricity is not only required to deliver power to drive the many integrated circuits, interconnection channels, and input/output (I/O) devices but also to remove the resulting heat from the system.

Thermal control is essential if the system is not to overheat and ultimately fail as a consequence. A high-end processor socket may consume anywhere from about 80 W to more than 200 W. Small to modest-size computers are air-cooled. Cold air is forced through the system modules and over the processor, memory, and control sockets to remove the heat generated as they operate. For higher-wattage parts, substantial metal radiator hardware is fitted directly on to the sockets for thermal conductivity, providing greater surface area and cooling capacity. This reduces the density of packaging and ultimate computing capability per unit module. Additional electrical power is required to chill the air and force it through the systems. This can easily be as much as 20% of the total power budget. Liquid cooling exploits the higher specific heat of fluids, most often water, to increase packing density and enable higher-power parts for higher clock rates or larger logic dies. There is a wide range of liquid cooling systems and mechanisms, and hybrids of combined air and liquid cooling.

Active thermal control is becoming increasingly important and common among the new generation of high performance computers. Measurement of temperatures throughout the system, including key chip temperatures, allows monitoring of thermal gradients and can support thermal control. Modern multicore processors permit variable clock rates, voltage adjustment, and variable numbers of active cores, all of which facilitate achieving a balance between power and performance. This requires some level of software management, either to establish settings at the beginning of an application program execution or to adjust these settings continually during runtime as application demands change.

2.2.5 RELIABILITY

No systems operations are perfect, and the reliability of HPC systems is additionally compounded by their scale. Errors can occur periodically due to hardware or software faults. "Hard" faults occur when some part of the hardware breaks permanently, causing an intrachip component to fail, a core of a processor socket to be inoperable, or the entire socket to become useless. Hard faults can affect cores, memory, communications, secondary storage, and control. A "soft" fault occurs when a part intermittently fails but otherwise operates correctly. Such transient failures are due to a number of possible causes, including occasional cosmic rays or "noise" resulting from low voltage margins among others. Software errors are due to flawed coding of either the user application program or the supporting system software, such as the operating system. Programmer errors are routine, and a process of program debugging is a part of the task of application development. An interruption due to a mistake by the operating system is more difficult to deal with, as it is usually the province of the system vendor.

Different application problems may require different responses to lead to a final and correct solution. For large computations of big problems on high-scale machines, a common methodology is "checkpoint/restart". Periodically the system will stop a computation being performed and store all the program state at that point ("checkpoint"), usually on secondary storage. If an error occurs after that time in the execution, the problem need not be restarted from the beginning but rather from the last checkpoint. If the error is caused by a hard fault, the system has to be reconfigured to eliminate the broken hardware from the part of the system being used prior to restarting the application. If it is a soft error, the program can be restarted from the last checkpoint without reconfiguration. In the case of a software bug, the code will have to be corrected by the user or application supplier before it can proceed. In all three cases, diagnosis is required to establish the cause and possible source of the error before execution proceeds.

2.2.6 PROGRAMMABILITY

How difficult it is to write or develop a complex application code reflects the programmability of the system. While other parameters such as performance or power can be readily defined and quantified, programmability largely defies specification although there have been many attempts; for example, standard lines of code (SLOC). Although less straightforward to define, it is nonetheless extremely important to the overall utility of HPC. While the cost of deploying a major HPC platform may reach hundreds of millions of dollars, the cost of the software that runs on it may reach billions of dollars in total. Many factors contribute to programmability (or the lack thereof), including the processor core and system architectures, the programming models and facility of the language, the effectiveness of the system software such as compilers, runtime systems, and operating system, and the skills of the programmers themselves. The level of effort required to write the application is strongly related to the performance ultimately achieved. Within a range of behaviors, the greater the performance required, the harder it is to optimize the user program. This interrelationship between performance achieved and programming effort is sometimes referred to as "productivity".

Improving the ease of use of HPC systems for domain applications benefits from a number of techniques making up a discipline of code development. Indeed, the best way to write an application code is "do not". Many libraries of common codes have been developed by experts and optimized for a diversity of HPC system types and scales. Code reuse is critical to managing application development complexity and difficulty. An application program can become as simple as building a high-level framework that calls a sequence of existing library routines and passing data between them successively. When programs get very complicated and are borrowed by many different users, management of the code base itself can become challenging. The discipline of "software engineering" provides principles and practices that guide overall control of workflow management, including testing. These and other methods contribute to programmability.

2.3 PARALLEL ARCHITECTURE FAMILIES—FLYNN'S TAXONOMY

There are many distinct classes of parallel architectures. Further, individual architectures may be hybrids incorporating characteristics and strengths of more than one type. This section introduces parallel architecture families in terms of structure of concurrent processing components and their parallel control. This overview is intended to convey a sense of the alternatives available, their relationship to the underlying enabling technologies, and to some degree how they address the key challenges to achieving sustained performance.

The 1970s saw a rapid increase in the practical application of parallel architecture for supercomputing, with a number of technology and organizational choices available. Michael Flynn proposed a taxonomy that simplified categorization of distinct classes of parallel architecture and control methods based on the relationships of data and instruction (control) with respect to parallelism of "streams". Although of limited value today, this nomenclature has stuck and is, if nothing else, part of our culture and vernacular. It also established the notion of data parallelism and task parallelism, to be encountered later in greater specificity.

Comprising four characters, it divides the world of computing structures into four mutually exclusive, collectively exhaustive classes that can be viewed in a two-dimensional space. One dimension concerns the data stream, "D", and whether there is one such stream, "S", or multiple data streams, "M". The other dimension relates to the control or instruction stream, "I", and similarly whether here too there is only a single stream of control or multiple instruction streams. From these Flynn proposed a set of four four-character acronyms as a codification of the parallel architecture choice space. It is still used today, more than 4 decades later.

SISD—single instruction stream, single data stream (pronounced "sisdee"): this represents the conventional sequential (serial) processor structure where a single thread of control, the instruction stream, guides the sequence of operations performed on a single set of data, one operand at a time. In truth, this is even more simplistic than today's conventional uniprocessors, which actually have several operations "in flight" at any one time.

SIMD—single instruction stream, multiple data stream (pronounced "simdee"): the first form of parallelism conveyed within this taxonomy is simultaneous operation on multiple datasets, controlled by the same set of instructions. Thus each operation at any one time is the same performed on different data arguments. Although simple in concept, SIMD has had long-term impact, first as the basis for entire systems and later as part of more complex control structures in today's heterogeneous microprocessors and supercomputers.

MIMD—multiple instruction stream, multiple data stream (pronounced "mimdee"): this category suggests that, like SIMD, there are many sets of data but in this case each dataset has its own instruction stream associated with it. At any one time there are many operations being performed, but they need not be the same and in fact are almost always different. As will be seen, this is the most widely used form of parallel architecture, but the category has many different subclasses.

MISD—multiple instruction stream, single data stream (pronounced "misdee"): surprisingly, the fourth of Flynn's categories is controversial, with some practitioners of the field considering it meaningless. It is not. One possible interpretation is a coarse-grained pipeline where each pipe stage accepts data from the previous stage, performs a set of operations on these data stream elements, and then passes on the results to the next stage. Another interpretation is a shared-memory multiprocessor (Section 2.8.1) where, as the name suggests, multiple processors each with its own instruction stream work on the same (therefore shared) data on which all the other processors operate.

One last related term, SPMD (pronounced "spimdee"), while not strictly part of Flynn's taxonomy, is related to and inspired by it. SPMD stands for "single program, multiple data stream" and reflects a practical variation of the SIMD model. Instead of issuing and broadcasting one instruction at a time to all the simple processing units of a SIMD-like machine, SPMD sends a function call of a coarse-grained procedure that is to be performed by all the processing units of the parallel machine. The invocation of heavyweight tasks rather than lightweight instructions amortizes the overheads and latency times involved in system control, and enables the operation of some forms of modern computing structures, including graphics processing unit (GPU) accelerators (Fig. 2.1) (Chapter 15).

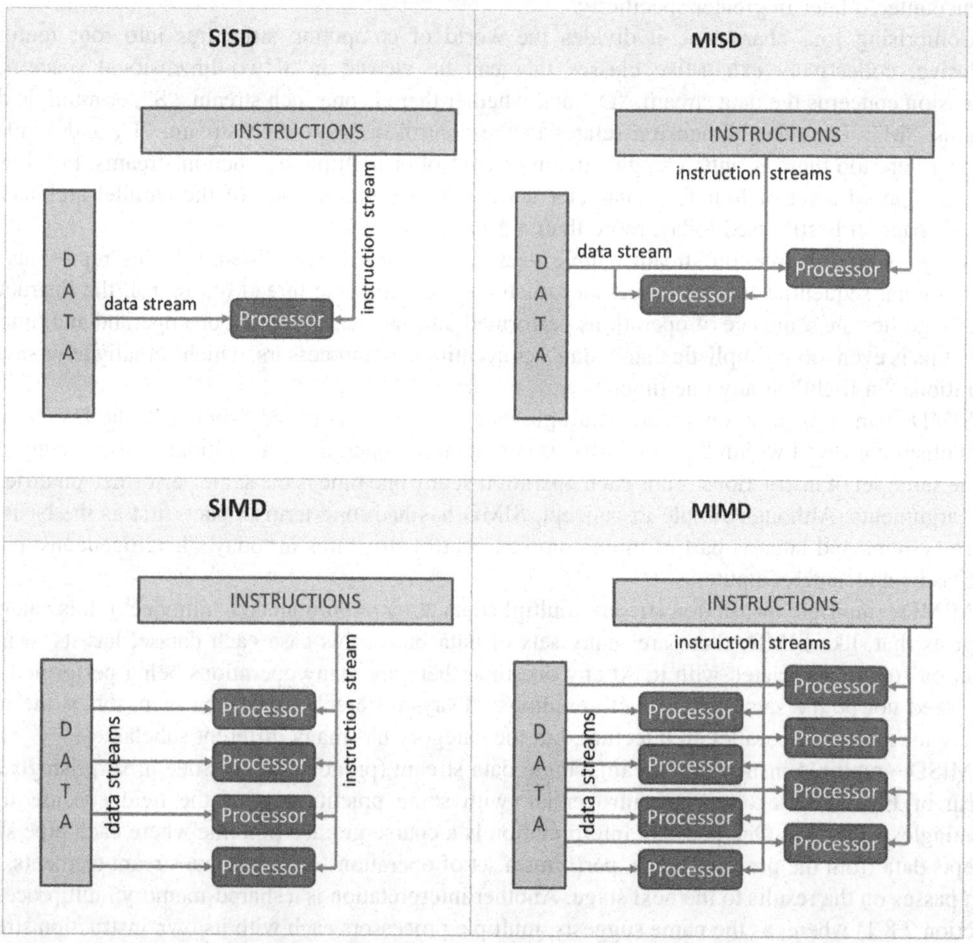

FIGURE 2.1

Flynn's taxonomy. *MIMD*, multiple instruction stream, multiple data stream; *MISD*, multiple instruction stream, single data stream; *SIMD*, single instruction stream, multiple data stream; *SISD*, single instruction stream, single data stream.

2.4 ENABLING TECHNOLOGY

HPC systems are products of opportunity enabled by device technologies. Such technologies may be derived through development unrelated but useful to HPC, created for the purpose of advancing computing, or result from incremental enhancements or extensions to existing HPC component types. Early digital electronics technologies were derived from radio and radar devices. Magnetic core memory was created to revolutionize data storage, which it did. Very large-scale integration (VLSI) circuits spanned more than 2 decades of continued improvement through increases in semiconductor device density and switching times. HPC architecture is strongly influenced by existing and emerging technologies to make best use of the opportunities that they may deliver and adjust to the challenges they impose.

2.4.1 TECHNOLOGY EPOCHS

Photo by Jitze Couperus via Wikimedia Commons

The Control Data Corporation (CDC) 6600 computer released in 1963 could perform over 3 million operations per second, operated at 10 MHz, was roughly 50 times faster than its immediate predecessor, the CDC-1604 released in 1960 (the fastest machine in the world at the time of its release), and was three times faster than the fastest IBM machine at the time, the IBM 7030 Stretch. The CDC-6600 was designed by Seymour Cray with a remarkably small staff of 34 people (with only one PhD among them) at his Chippewa Falls, Wisconsin, laboratory, and was innovative in using silicon-based transistors from Fairchild Semiconductor (cofounded by Robert Noyce, future cofounder of Intel Corporation) and Freon cooling rather than air cooling. Because of the unique cooling arrangement, the CDC-6600 was physically smaller than its CDC-1604 predecessor even though it was 50 times faster. The CDC-6600 was an enormous commercial success, selling over 100 units each costing US$8 million. Many of these machines were used at US national laboratories as part of the nuclear weapon simulations which helped contribute to the negotiations of the nuclear test ban treaty with the USSR in 1963.

US Army photo of the ENIAC via Wikimedia Commons

The electronic numerical integrator and computer (ENIAC) was the first large-scale electronic digital computer that could be reprogrammed for running different applications. It was developed at the University of Pennsylvania under contract by the US Army, and consisted of 18,000 vacuum tubes requiring 150 kW to operate. Its genesis was in World War II, when requests for improved tables for artillery and bombing overwhelmed the personnel developing such tables using mechanical calculators. Interestingly, at that time those people were called "computers". Unlike previous electromechanical devices, the ENIAC internals contained no mechanical moving parts, enabling it to produce an entirely electronic computation and significantly speed up work. It was reprogrammed by a lengthy process of manually changing switches and cables; even so, it was still used for over 9 years from 1946 to 1955. In April and May 1948, the first-ever electronic Monte Carlo simulations were successfully performed on the ENIAC, simulating the diffusion of neutrons. Monte Carlo methods remain today a mainstay of scientific computation.

Historically, epochs of device technology spanning the centuries of calculating machines may be delineated by key transitions of the components of which they are comprised. The following dates are approximate, with substantial overlapping between successive periods of technology adoption.

- 3000 BCE—primitive counting devices: enumeration or counting of amounts of important stock like domesticated animals, agricultural produce (units of grains, containers of olive oil), and products like lengths of textiles even at early stages of civilization in the Bronze Age and before required mechanical means of recording (storing) quantities and performing simple additions and subtractions to abstract actual real-world items. This inaugurated data storage, calculation, and abstraction through mechanical means. The abacus used in some areas up until the postwar era is a direct derivative.
- In 200–100 BCE one of the earliest known analog computers was developed, consisting of more than 80 pieces and 30 mechanical gears. Known as the Antikythera, this instrument was used for astronomical predictions (Fig. 2.2). The technology for this device was subsequently lost, and any widespread cultural impact of the Antikythera mechanism on the ancient world is generally considered controversial.

FIGURE 2.2

The Antikythera mechanism, one of the earliest known analog computers.

By Tilemahos Efthimiadis via Wikimedia Commons

- 1600—mechanical devices with gears and levers: the evolution of clockwork mechanisms, which were applied to relatively compact, reliable, and eventually sophisticated calculating devices that mastered sequencing of microoperations such as carries in decimal addition and multiplication. The Pascaline (see Fig. 2.3) developed by the mathematician Pascal is one of many such calculating devices, culminating in significant calculating engines like the difference engine invented by mathematician Charles Babbage in the early 19th century.
- 1850—electromechanical: motors, relays, punched cards. The inauguration of electricity offered new media for basic operation, sequencing, and data storage, both temporary and persistent. The tabulator (Fig. 2.4) devised by Hollerith for the 1890 US census led to the founding of IBM and 50 years of commercial data processing. The Mark I developed by Aiken at Harvard and

FIGURE 2.3

The Pascaline mechanical calculator.

By David Monniaux via Wikimedia Commons

FIGURE 2.4

The tabulator built for the 1890 US census.

Photo by Adam Schuster via Wikimedia Commons

manufactured by IBM was a culmination of the complex calculating systems enabled by these technologies, delivering approximately 1 operation per second (ops). Processor cores that separate instruction streams from data streams are still known as "Harvard architectures" today.

- 1940—vacuum tube: logic gate, flip-flop, magnetic core. With the emergence of electronics, initially by means of the amplifying vacuum tube, and their incorporation in digital logic by Atanasoff in the 1940s, calculators such as the US ENIAC and British Colossus increased computing rates 1000-fold and inspired the advanced architecture concept attributed to the mathematician John von Neumann, providing the foundation of the digital programmable computing paradigm. The three pivotal elements of the modern computer were firmly established and integrated into a form of which most future models would be derivatives. These elements were memory implemented as magnetic cores (old terminology; not processors), digital electronic logic using Boolean and binary encoding, and communication via digital signals through electrical wires.
- 1955—transistor: the replacement of vacuum-tube technology with semiconductor technology (germanium and silicon) dramatically reduced power consumption, cost, and size while greatly increasing speed and reliability.
- 1965—integrated circuits (small-scale integration/medium-scale integration): the placement and interconnection of multiple transistors with other components (e.g., resistors and capacitors) heralded another stage of cost and power reduction with speed and reliability increase by modularized logic gates on a single semiconductor die or "chip". The concept of the architecture family was introduced with the IBM 360 ("mainframe") and the Digital Equipment Corporation (DEC) PDP-8 ("minicomputer"), where multiple versions of computers with the same logical ISA could be sold with different performance-to-cost market points. Intermediate binary values were stored temporarily in semiconductor latches, with all intercommunication between functional modules encoded as digital signals. The CDC-6800 using multiple processing units and parallel ISA was among the first computers to deliver one megaflops.
- 1975—large-scale integration (LSI): large arrays of gates on a single chip permitted increasingly complex digital functional units to be implemented on single semiconductor dies, with core memory being replaced by semiconductor DRAM over this period. "Bit-slice" components allowed

full computers to be implemented with relatively few parts, yet permitted a wide diversity of ISAs through microcoding. High-speed technologies, although of lower density, drove new classes of supercomputers, like the Cray-1 vector processor delivering peak performance in excess of 100 megaflops. During this era, LSI also enabled the modern SIMD array computers such as the Maspar-1 and the CM-2. The first microprocessors were commercialized with 4-, 8-, and 16-bit architectures, and, while limited in performance, they dramatically reduced the costs of commercial and early consumer-grade computer electronics, including the first video games.

- 1990—VLSI with complementary metal-oxide semiconductor (CMOS): with increased device density through VLSI, significant single-chip microprocessors were possible, ultimately leading to 32-bit and eventually 64-bit data path architectures. These sparked a revolution, with the "killer micro" replacing more discrete component processor designs and ensembles of microprocessors replacing other forms of supercomputers. While a diversity of such multiprocessors were developed, three general classes emerged as dominant: the symmetric multiprocessor (SMP), the massively parallel processor (MPP), and the commodity cluster (e.g., Beowulf). Each has a different performance-to-cost design point.
- 2005—multicore heterogeneous with GPU: the modern era of technology and architectures emerged with the two combined trends of stagnant processor speed and multicore chips. Due to power constraints clock rates have remained relatively constant, although there is a significant spread of their values from below 1 GHz for embedded and mobile processors to over 3 GHz for the fastest. The continuing progress of Moore's law has made possible the incorporation of multiple processor cores on a single die to increase aggregate performance per chip. Special configurations of processing elements (PEs) can greatly accelerate important functions. The current era of supercomputers employ these two strategies to address these trends.

2.4.2 ROLES OF TECHNOLOGIES

Technologies play many different roles in enabling the implementation of computing systems and supporting their functionality. Three dominant classes of technologies largely define the design space for how HPC architectures evolve and the performance they are able to achieve. Throughout this text these fundamental aspects of HPC system implementation and operation will be examined. Here the dominant functional roles are introduced. The first technology class, digital logic, makes possible the actual basic operations that perform the calculations comprising the end-user work. It transforms one or more sets of input values, usually encoded as binary or Boolean information, into output values determined by the specified function (e.g., integer addition). The second technology class, memory, allows information to be stored temporarily (ephemeral) or permanently (persistent), to be accessed by logic elements, and to be modified (updated) as required. Memory technologies, even in a single architecture, are of a number of types that vary in speed and capacity. The third technology class, data communication, moves information from one part of the system architecture to another.

2.4.3 DIGITAL LOGIC

Digital logic technology is the workhorse of computer architecture. It occupies roles in every part of the computer system, from performing the actual operations of a calculation to controlling the memory subsystems and data communications. Digital logic is hierarchical (like architecture itself), in that the simplest devices are organized to create basic Boolean gates, which in turn are used to make more sophisticated functional units, and so on. The basic technology is an on/off switching device that permits or impedes the flow of electric current based on the state of an input signal. Alternatively, such switching devices determine the voltage exhibited at an output device, usually either a 0 V level or an alternative nonzero level to distinguish between two distinct associated Boolean or logical values, false or true, respectively, or "0" or "1" as they are often depicted. Over the last 7 decades these most basic switching devices have been successively vacuum tubes, discrete transistors, and integrated transistors (multiple transistors on a single semiconductor die).

Depending on the exact circuit design and basic physical technology, a number of switching devices are structured to work as logical gates or other simple functional units accepting one or a few input values (equivalent to Boolean 1 and 0) and producing one or more output values. The basic two-input logic gates represent every possible logical outcome, of which there are 16, including fixed values, invert, and, nand, or, nor, xor, and others, as shown in Fig. 2.5. Although circuits differ, typical gates are implemented with a dozen or so transistors. Key metrics of logic gate operation include switching rate and propagation delay. Switching rate is the highest frequency at which a logic gate output can change from a logical 1 to 0 (or 0 to 1) and back again. It is usually measured in gigaHertz (GHz) or billions of cycles per second. Propagation delay is the amount of time required for

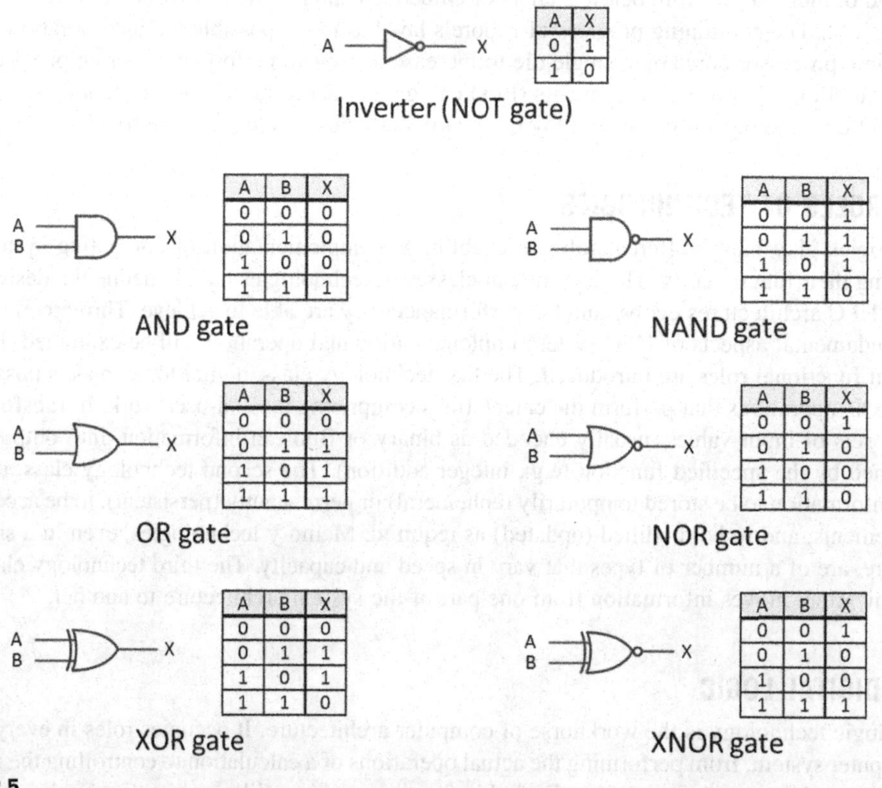

FIGURE 2.5

Basic two-input logic gates with corresponding logical functions.

a change in value of an input of a gate to be reflected by a corresponding change on the gate's output. This is usually measured in picoseconds or trillionths of a second. Fig. 2.6 illustrates these measures for an SN74AHC04 CMOS inverter manufactured by Texas Instruments, collected using a Tektronix MS5104 oscilloscope. A relevant excerpt from the datasheet for this integrated circuit is also shown in Fig. 2.6. Since propagation delay typically depends on the output load, such as the number of other gates driven by it, the workbench result differs somewhat from the specification.

Due to the limited number of states assumed by each connection in digital logic, representation of more complex concepts requires collections of multiple binary lines. To express integer numbers, an

(A)

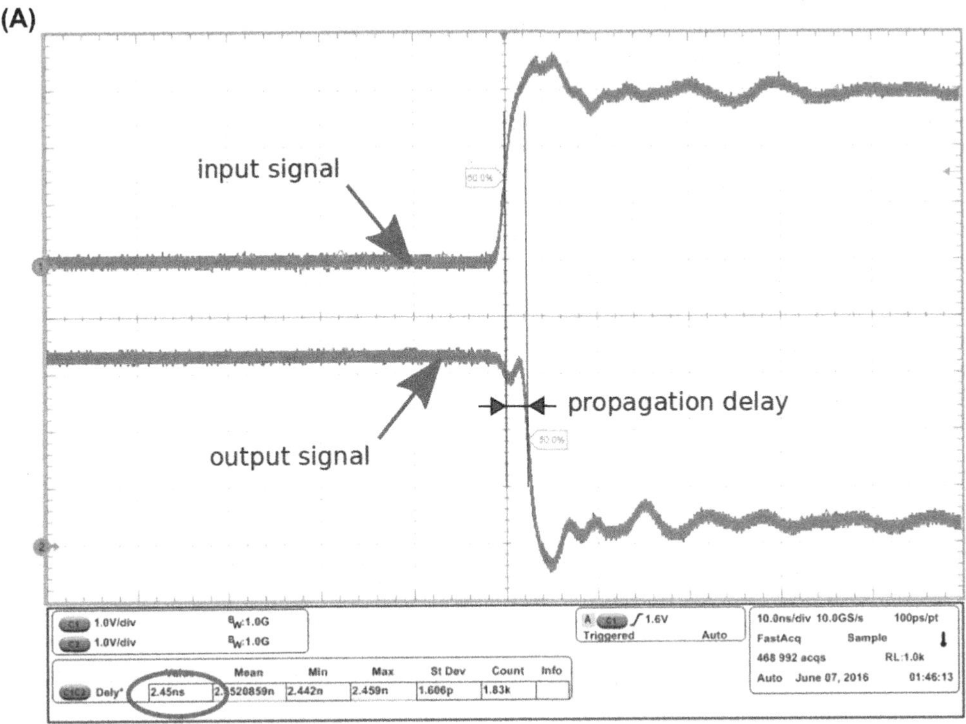

(B) **SWITCHING CHARACTERISTICS**

over recommended operating free-air temperature range, V_{CC} = 3.3 V ± 0.3 V (unless otherwise noted) (see Fig. 2.1)

PARAMETER	FROM (INPUT)	TO (OUTPUT)	LOAD CAPACITANCE	T_A = 25°C		T_A = −55°C TO 125°C SN54AHC04		T_A = −40°C TO 85°C SN74AHC04		T_A = −40°C TO 125°C Recommended SN74AHC04		UNIT
				TYP	MAX	MIN	MAX	MIN	MAX	MIN	MAX	
t_{PLH}	A	Y	C_L = 15 pF	5[(1)]	8.9[(1)]	1[(1)]	10.5[(1)]	1	10.5	1	10.5	ns
t_{PHL}				5[(1)]	8.9[(1)]	1[(1)]	10.5[(1)]	1	10.5	1	10.5	
t_{PLH}	A	Y	C_L = 50 pF	7.5	11.4	1	13	1	13	1	13	ns
t_{PHL}				7.5	11.4	1	13	1	13	1	13	

FIGURE 2.6

Timing in digital logic: (A) annotated oscilloscope trace showing propagation delay for a single inverter and (B) datasheet specification for the measured circuit.

Image (B): Courtesy Texas Instruments

ordering is imposed to signify the power of two each line's position is associated with, very much like the position of every digit in commonly used decimal numbers is associated with units, tens, hundreds, and so on (consecutive powers of 10). By convention, the least significant digit is written at the rightmost position in the number. For example, to express decimal number 6 as a binary number, it has to be converted to the sum of powers of two: $6 = 4 + 2 = 2^2 + 2^1 = 1 \cdot 2^2 + 1 \cdot 2^1 + 0 \cdot 2^0 = 110_2$ (subscript 2 denotes the radix, or the base of the number, to avoid confusion when numbers in different bases are used in the same place). The reverse conversion requires summation of powers of two corresponding to the positions of ones in a binary number: $1101_2 = 2^3 + 2^2 + 2^0 = 8 + 4 + 1 = 13$. Binary numbers consist typically of significantly more digits, or *bits*, than the equivalent decimal numbers. To keep verbosity in check, octal (radix 8) or hexadecimal (radix 16) notation is frequently used as an alternative to a binary base, while offering ease of conversion to and from the actual binary format. Each octal digit, spanning values from 0 to 7, represents an arbitrary group of three binary digits, while a hexadecimal digit replaces four bits. Since there are no decimal digits to express values from 10 to 15, letters A through F (upper or lower case) are customarily used to express them. This is illustrated in Fig. 2.7.

2.4.4 MEMORY TECHNOLOGIES

Memory technology in its alternative forms enables the storing, access, and changing of data. As in the case of digital logic, information is represented by collections of bits. Each bit is 0 or 1 (alternatively true or false), and they are usually grouped as 8-bit bytes or multiple byte words. Information is treated and encoded as distinct types, such as Boolean, character, strings, integers (of different lengths), and floating point (32 bit or 64 bit), among others.

(A)

Octal digit	Binary equivalent
0	000
1	001
2	010
3	011
4	100
5	101
6	110
7	111

(B)

Hexadecimal digit	Binary equivalent	Hexadecimal digit	Binary equivalent
0	0000	8	1000
1	0001	9	1001
2	0010	A	1010
3	0011	B	1011
4	0100	C	1100
5	0101	D	1101
6	0110	E	1110
7	0111	F	1111

FIGURE 2.7

Conversion between (A) octal and (B) hexadecimal and binary bases.

2.4.4.1 Early Memory Devices

WHIRLWIND—THE FIRST SUPERCOMPUTER

The Whirlwind vacuum-tube-based digital electronic computer was the first modern computer architecture and represented the state of the art in high-speed calculation. It may be considered the first general-purpose supercomputer. Developed at Massachusetts Institute of Technology (MIT) under successive projects sponsored by the US Navy and then the US Air Force, its intended applications stressed performance initially for flight simulation and ultimately for radar-based air defense. Whirlwind employed a bit parallel logic design with 16-bit words performed and simultaneously implemented with vacuum tubes. It stored and controlled access to 2048 words using electrostatic storage tubes with an original (never achieved) bit density of 1024 bits per unit. The control structure incorporated an innovative diode matrix for speed as well as simplicity and flexibility of design. Its initial design was completed in 1947 by Jay Forrester and Robert Everett; it became operational in 1951 and consisted of 5000 vacuum tubes. Whirlwind was upgraded in 1953 with a new kind of memory developed by Forrester that used arrays of magnetic cores in stacks, replacing the slow and less reliable vacuum-tube storage. The resulting performance of up to 40 K instructions per second made Whirlwind the fastest computer of its time, dramatically increased its reliability and reducing its cost of operation.

The Whirlwind computer and its many innovations had far-reaching impacts on the field of computing. The invention of core memory redefined computer architecture for the next 2 decades, and is one of the main reasons why digital computers became commercially practical. Bit-parallel logic units became the norm for data processing. The diode–matrix control unit inspired Maurice Wilkes to conceive of microcontrollers and microprogramming, upon which future computers would be based at least until the microprocessor era. Whirlwind was the prototype for the first major parallel computer system, SAGE, employed as the original US air defense system. A spinoff of the Whirlwind project was the founding of DEC, which invented the minicomputer and rose to become the world's second-largest computer company in the 1980s. A second spinoff, MITRE, a major defense research contractor, can also be attributed to Whirlwind. With the final operational deployment of the Whirlwind computer, the future direction of high performance computer architecture was established.

History's earliest forms of memory predate the use of the abstraction of the bit and took such primitive forms as grooves on wooden sticks, marks on clay and stone tablets, pebbles used for counting (sometimes in depressions of wooden boards or tables), and beads on rows of horizontal rods (of wood or metal). In the age of enlightenment starting in the 17th century and extending well into the 20th century the position of gears served as storage, often distinguishing among 10 items in support of the decimal system.

With the emergence of digital electronics enabled by the vacuum tube and derived from analog electronics components such as radio, amplifiers, and radar, a clear need was seen for a technology that could store information to complement the logic that was performing operations on that information.

The first generation (1940–1952) saw many memory technologies devised and applied as part of the earliest digital computers, which were the supercomputers of their day (compared to rooms full of women with mechanical calculators). Among the earliest were mercury delay lines, also called "tanks", developed for radar uses during World War II. A tank was, as the name implies, a container, filled with the liquid metal mercury. At one end of the tank was an acoustic speaker that would create sound impulses into the medium. At the other end a microphone was positioned to detect the same sound signals. A closed loop was created in which the detected sounds from the microphone (acoustic sensor) were amplified (electronically) and fed back to the speaker at the top of the tank. Thus any individual bit of information would continue in a perpetual loop. The number of bits that could be stored in the mercury tank was a function of the maximum pulse repetition frequency, the length of the tank, and the propagation delay of the medium. This is one form of a dynamic memory in which the information has to be continuously refreshed. It was also referred to as a "one-dimensional memory" because of the serial nature of the bit availability. Mercury delay lines were used in such first-generation computers as EDSAC [1] and the IBM 704 [2].

A two-dimensional memory was also developed in the mid-1940s: it stored electrostatic charges on a phosphorous screen on the inside of a vacuum tube, very much like the old-fashioned video tubes in televisions and oscilloscopes. Originally named the Williams tube after its British inventor, the small regions of charge were created on the rectangular surface and could be viewed from the outside as an array of glowing bits. This vacuum-tube memory was also dynamic, as the stored charge would slowly "leak" off of the phosphorous surface and have to be rewritten every few milliseconds. The capacity of the memory was dependent on the surface area of the screen and the granularity of the charge bit cells. The speed of the memory was a function of the electronic delays to send a signal to hit the bit cell with an electron beam and detect its scattered charge (if one was there). It was more than an order of magnitude faster than the mercury delay line memory. Vacuum-tube storage was used in such computers as EDVAC [3] and IAS [4].

The breakthrough storage technology of the first generation of digital electronic computers was "core memory". Developed as part of the MIT Whirlwind [5] project in the late 1940s and manufactured by IBM, core memories used doughnut-shaped ferromagnetic beads to represent bits and exploited the hysteresis of the magnetic properties to store statically the equivalents of 1s and 0s. If there was a magnetic flux in one direction around the core, it would be a 1; if there was no flux in the core, it represented a 0. Core memory was organized in stacks of planes of such cores, referred to as three-dimensional memories. Three wires went through the center of a core being accessed. Electric currents through two of the wires were applied at the same time to provide enough stimulus to cause a core bit to set its flux. When reading the memory, the third wire is used to sense the change in flux (or absence thereof). While static, in that it can retain state indefinitely without active recharge, it is an example of destructive reading. When a bit is read, the state is potentially erased in the process and has to be reset. Nonetheless, core memory enabled the modern digital electronic computer. It was faster than any other storage technology, higher density, lower cost per bit, and lower energy. Its impact was so extreme that it was employed for more than 2 decades and almost immediately replaced the earlier storage technologies described above.

Magnetism as a physical phenomenon has played a major role in data storage, far beyond its application to core memory. As the key element of a thin veneer, ferromagnetic oxides have been applied to strings, tapes, drums, hard disks, and floppy disks. In this general form, it represents among the longest-lasting technologies in computing, used from the 1940s to the present mass-storage systems. Its principal value has been the combination of density, cost, and persistence. Some machines, such as the IBM 1620 [6], used it as a main memory due to the relatively low cost. Today all mass-storage systems comprise giant arrays of hard drives, possibly in combination with tape-drive robots for even greater capacity.

Lest we forget, paper (yes, paper) has a long tradition in data storage and was among the longest and most effective technologies employed for the purpose. While usually overlooked, paper served directly as "scratch pads" for people to write partial results of calculations for many hundreds of years. More directly, throughout the history of modern computing printers employ paper as the primary medium of storing and presenting output results to end users. Mechanical printer devices dominated this last stage of computing over the first 40 years of its history, although the work is now primarily performed by laser printers (and some ink-jet printers). Punched cards and later paper tape used paper products with punched holes to represent data. Punched cards were first devised for Jacquard's loom to control the patterns for weaving cloth, introduced in 1801. Cards were connected in a sequence as a chain with the holes in the card controlling the threads that were woven cross-wise to make the fabric. Later Hollerith developed the tabulating machine for the 1890 US census. Each card represented a US citizen, and the holes encoded various characteristics. This was the supercomputer of the day and led to the establishment of IBM, with punched cards among its core technologies and employed well into the 1960s. Punched cards were used not just for data but to represent lines of code to describe computer programs, one line per card. The pattern of punched holes to represent characters was referred to as "Hollerith code". Punched cards were also used as a medium of output as well as data input and source code. Card punches were connected as output devices to early computers (e.g., the IBM 360) for the results of user programs to be returned. Paper tape in rolls or fan-folded provided a cheap way of storing program code and data for low-cost computers like the minicomputers of the 1960s and 1970s.

2.4.4.2 Modern Memory Technologies

Modern computer architecture incorporate three principal memory technologies dominant in supercomputing: DRAM, SRAM, and magnetic storage media, including hard-disk drives and tapes. A fourth, nonvolatile random access memory (NVRAM), is emerging as a technology sitting between DRAM and mass storage.

SRAM provides the highest-speed semiconductor memory. But it is also the largest, taking up the greatest die area, and it consumes by far the greatest power. SRAM cells use a number of transistors—between 6 and 12, depending on how they are employed within the total logic structure (Fig. 2.8A). The fastest SRAM devices are used for processor core registers and latches, and can operate at processor clock rates of less than 1 ns. These are relatively low density. As is discussed in future chapters, small memory blocks referred to as "caches" are used to take advantage of locality to give the effect of fast memory while holding only a small portion of the total program data. Caches may be divided into levels, with the L1 cache the fastest but the smallest, providing a throughout of one word per clock cycle. L2 caches can be much larger than L1 and hold much more data, but operate slower in the order of 4–20 cycles. A third level, the L3 cache, may also be included, but these are not usually SRAM.

The main memory is the primary component for storing data within a computer and is composed almost entirely of DRAM technology. DRAM is much denser than SRAM, holding far more bits per unit area. It consumes much less power as well, but it is much slower. It can take between 100 and 200 cycles for a processor to access data from DRAM. Each bit cell of a DRAM chip consists of a single transistor and a capacitor (Fig. 2.8B). A capacitor can store an electrostatic charge difference which represents a Boolean or binary state value of "1". No charge difference represents "0". The single

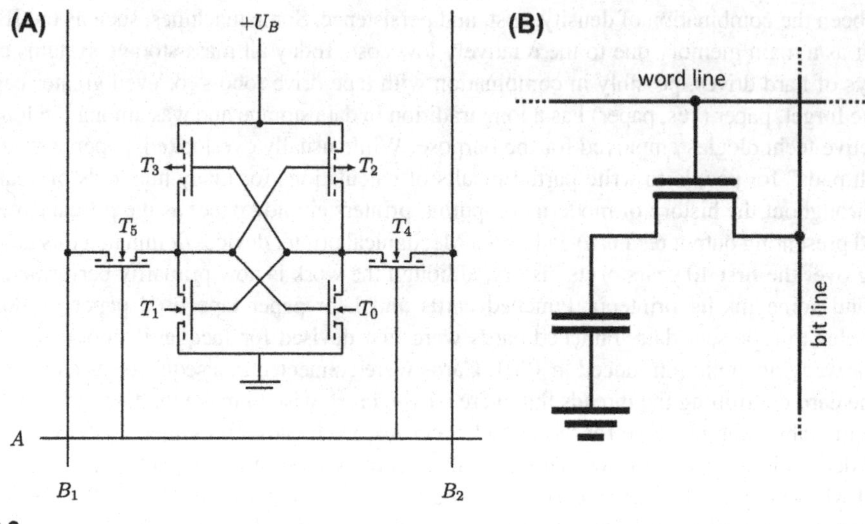

FIGURE 2.8

Single-bit storage cell structure in (A) static random access memory and (B) dynamic random access memory.

Image (A) by Martin Thoma via Wikimedia Commons

transistor isolates the capacitive charge from the sense lines to hold it and retain its state. Unfortunately, DRAMs are volatile. They require a destructive read where accessing a DRAM cell destroys its value and it has to be rewritten. Also, leakage from DRAM cells requires that they be refreshed in the order of tens of milliseconds.

2.5 VON NEUMANN SEQUENTIAL PROCESSORS

Although the word "supercomputer" may invoke mental images of specialized Cray vector machines or large concurrent-array systems, in fact the very first electronic digital stored-program computers were the supercomputers of their day. They delivered a level of performance 1000 times that of previous methods of calculation. The von Neumann architecture of sequential processing represents an important starting point in understanding how HPC is achieved. Initially a supercomputer in its own right, the original von Neumann architecture concepts and elements permeate in one form or another most of the modern and certainly the dominant form of supercomputer execution strategies.

Fig. 2.9 represents the principal elements of the von Neumann architecture conceived by Eckert, Mauchly, and the mathematician John von Neumann in the mid-1940s that has provided the recipe for most computing over the last 7 decades, admittedly with dramatic enhancements. This simplistic diagram offers an idealized picture of a sequential architecture. Nonetheless, most of the complicated elaborations have been devised to retain the image of this more perfect form and function. And while many of the key factors influencing performance are not shown by this template, speed is there, and provides a starting point to consider the extensions and elaborations embodied by the processing systems of today.

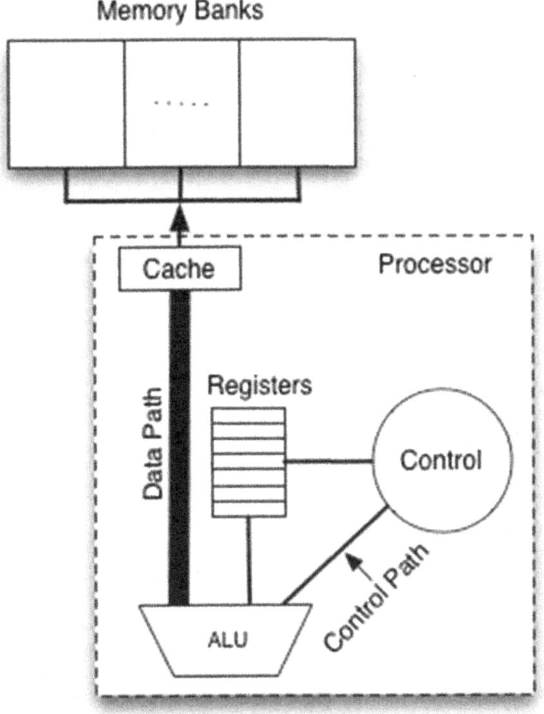

FIGURE 2.9

The principal elements of the von Neumann architecture. The caches and register banks were introduced at a later date.

Historically, the arithmetic logic unit (ALU) was considered the heart of the computer. It performed the actual numeric, character, and logical (Boolean) operations of the computation. It operates on argument values presented to it from some form of high-speed buffers, latches, or registers (shown here). Registers can be read and written to at the speed of the surrounding logic. In the earliest architectures, a single register, the accumulator, was used with an instruction set that referenced it implicitly. A bank of several registers has multiple ports so that simultaneous reads and writes can be performed. Unlike addresses for memory, registers have their own namespace, which usually cannot be operated on but only referenced.

The processor accesses the main memory of the computer system to store and use the values of the program variables making up the state of the calculation. While at first available main memory data was measured in thousands of bytes, today a typical processor core has direct access to billions of bytes (gigabytes) of memory. The largest HPC systems have an aggregate memory capacity in the order of a petabyte of main memory. A main memory is referred to as random access memory, as any of the storage locations may be designated by its hardware address to select one byte or word from the many. A load operation by the processor reads a word from the main memory and places its value into a designated register, to be used by the ALU at a later time. Because the cycle time of the memory is about two orders of magnitude slower than the clock rate of the processor, an intermediate level of storage referred to as "cache" is incorporated in the processor. Data that is accessed from memory is also copied to cache, with the expectation that it may be accessed again (a pattern referred to as temporal locality). When accessed in the future, the cached data can be acquired much faster from the cache than from the main memory itself. But the cache is much smaller than the main memory, so only some of the data can reside in the cache at any one time. Finding a sought-for value in cache is referred to as a "cache hit". The converse, not finding a required variable value in cache, is appropriately designated a "cache miss".

The operation of the processor is managed by the controller, which creates a sequence of signals to the hardware. Originally this was done as a series of phases: fetch instructions, execute operation, and write back to register (or memory). This would be repeated for each succeeding operation of the instruction stream. Far more complicated control sequences are required today, with multi-operation instructions performed with out-of-order completion, speculative execution for conditionals, reservation stations, and other advances to be considered in future chapters, all to achieve superior efficiency and ultimately performance.

2.6 VECTOR AND PIPELINING

EARTH SIMULATOR

Photo by Manatee_tw via Wikimedia Commons

The Earth Simulator (ES) was a hallmark supercomputer developed and deployed by the Japanese, with operations beginning in 2002 at the Earth Simulator Center in Yokohama, Japan. As measured by the highly parallel Linpack (HPL) benchmark, it was the fastest computer in the world then and for two more years, with a delivered performance of 35.9 teraflops. The ES is a milestone in supercomputing, as it marks the halfway point logarithmically between the first documented systems of the Top 500 list in 1993 and the current highest-rated system, which spans a range of approximately six orders of magnitude performance gain. The ES was a game changer, being about five times as fast as the previous top machine.

The ES was architecturally an elegant machine, built by NEC based on its SX-6 vector processor. It was an MPP with 640 nodes, each with eight vector processors that operated at a 3.2 GHz clock rate. Its total memory capacity was 20 TBs. The internode crossbar network had 10 TB/s bandwidth. The building in which the ES was housed was purpose built, and included lightening suppression and protection against earthquakes.

Pipelining is among the most widely employed and enduring forms of parallelism. It is so broad in applicability that it goes far beyond its use in computing and impacts many aspects of our daily lives. Mass production of automobiles is an example. Each frame moves from station to station to have one small assembly action (e.g., attaching a side mirror) performed on it. The vehicle then moves to the next station to have yet another assembly step performed, while at the previous station a new car frame rolls into place to get its mirror. Many different cars are being built at the same time on the assembly line, and it can take a long time for a car to be built—from hours to days. But the miracle is that a new car is finished every few minutes and driven out of the manufacturing plant.

Pipelining is used in many places within supercomputing system architecture, even today. At one time it was the principal form of parallelism exploited in a class of supercomputers referred to as vector computers, of which the Cray-1 [7] launched in 1975 is perhaps the archetype and recognized as the iconic supercomputer.

2.6.1 PIPELINE PARALLELISM

Pipeline parallelism is derived by dividing a complicated action into a sequence of simpler actions, each of which may be performed independently. For any one instance of the complex action, only one stage is performed at any one time and there is no concurrency. But when many instances of the same action have to be performed, they can be issued to the pipeline one at a time so that in each pipeline stage one of the concurrent operations is being performed. Thus a complex action is divided into a sequence of simpler steps and different parts of multiple operations are performed simultaneously. It is the combination of the number of separate instances of a given operation that need to be performed and the number of pipeline stages in which the operation may be divided that yields the parallelism. Further, exploitation of this kind of parallelism, as is the case for many other forms of parallelism, requires a combination of hardware architecture that can do many different things at the same time and software that exposes and controls the application parallel work to be performed. Thus except in special cases, both hardware and software have to work together to exploit this kind of parallelism.

A simple example will illustrate these basic ideas. We propose to increment (add one) to every integer of a block of numbers. To do this very fast we want to overlap the carries between successive bits (here four bits for ease of exposition). Thus the time to perform each stage is only that of a single bit full add rather than having to wait for the propagation of carries through the entire sequence of bits. This is illustrated in Fig. 2.10. Every stage of the addition pipeline consumes one bit of each input operand and generates a corresponding bit of output sum, starting with the least significant bit (bit 0). A dedicated chain of registers implements the intermediate storage for the carry bit. As the operation progresses, the input bits of operand A are successively replaced with the computed sum bits, finally resulting in the full sum and fours-bit addition carry bit produced at the end of stage 4.

The effective operation of a pipeline is a function of five parameters:

- t_s: operation time of each pipeline stage
- t_v: overhead to switch between successive stages
- p_s: number of stages
- n_d: number of input datasets
- t_m: execution time of a monolithic version of the same function.

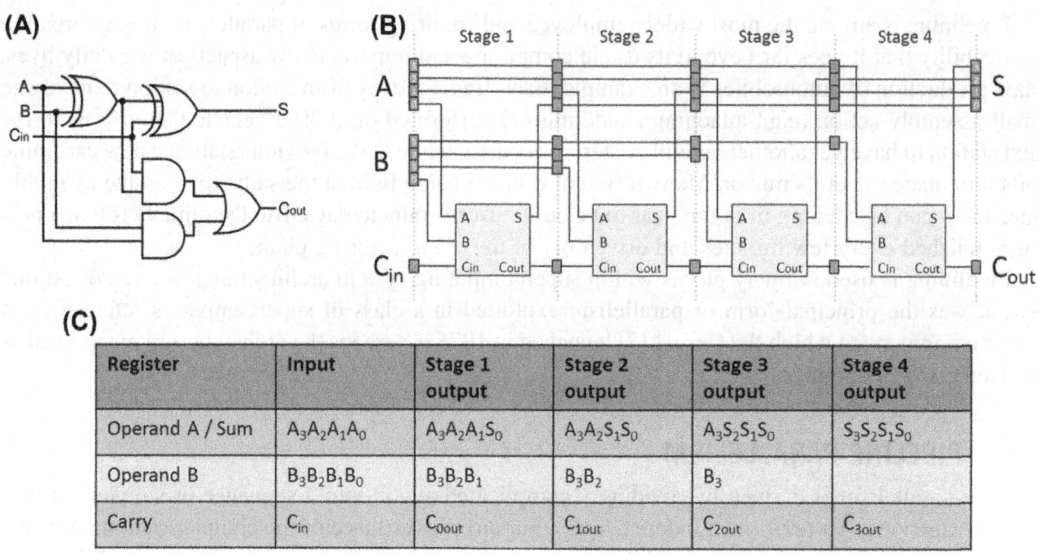

Register	Input	Stage 1 output	Stage 2 output	Stage 3 output	Stage 4 output
Operand A / Sum	$A_3A_2A_1A_0$	$A_3A_2A_1S_0$	$A_3A_2S_1S_0$	$A_3S_2S_1S_0$	$S_3S_2S_1S_0$
Operand B	$B_3B_2B_1B_0$	$B_3B_2B_1$	B_3B_2	B_3	
Carry	C_{in}	C_{0out}	C_{1out}	C_{2out}	C_{3out}

FIGURE 2.10

(A) Single-bit full adder. (B) Complete pipeline with input data, operation, and output. (C) Propagation of computations through individual pipeline stages.

The operation time of a pipeline stage is the propagation delay through the digital logic of the stage from when the input data is presented to it until it delivers the resulting data of that stage. The overhead is the small amount of time needed to control the movement of data from the output of a previous stage to the input of the next stage. Different kinds of functions can be divided into different number of parallel pipeline stages. Even for a given function there may be many alternative ways to divide the required workload into multiple successive stages. To determine the speedup of a pipeline structure, G, the total throughput rate is calculated and compared with the alternative monolithic structure.

$$G = \frac{T_m}{T_p} \tag{2.3}$$

$$T_m = t_m \times n_d \tag{2.4}$$

$$T_p = (t_v + t_s) \times (p_s + n_d), \; p_s > 1 \tag{2.5}$$

$$G = \frac{t_m \times n_d}{(t_v + t_s) \times (p_s + n_d)} \tag{2.6}$$

The total time to execute a set of data operands, T_m, employing a monolithic logical functional unit is simply the product of the time to perform the calculation of a single dataset and the number of such datasets to be processed. No parallelism is being used or exploited, except perhaps at the bit level within the logic design. The total time to execute all the sets of data operands, T_p, by a pipelined structure of logical stages is more complex. The finest-grain time is that of the propagation delay through a given stage, t_p, to which must be added a small amount of time to coordinate between successive stages and transfer partial results and operand values from each stage to its succeeding one, t_v, which is referred to as overhead time. The total number of steps to perform the complete computation for all the datasets is a function of both the number of such datasets, n_d, and the number of stages in the pipeline, p. It can be viewed as the number of steps to fill the pipeline with data plus the number of steps to empty the pipeline, which is the number of data elements.

The advantage achieved through pipelining or its performance gain, G, is given as the ratio of the monolithic logic execution time of all the data and the time required for the pipelined structured to complete the operation on the same argument dataset as presented in the equation above. A successful pipeline structure is one for which the following conditions hold:

$$\begin{aligned} t_p &\ll t_m \\ (p \times t_p) &> t_m \\ n_d &\gg p \\ t_p &\gg t_v \end{aligned} \tag{2.7}$$

Under these favorable conditions, the limit is:

$$\lim_{n_d \to \infty} G \cong \frac{t_m}{t_p} \tag{2.8}$$

This returns the optimal performance gain for a structure exploiting pipelined parallelism (Fig. 2.11). However, there are boundary conditions that limit the degree to which the performance gain can be increased through reduction of size to t_p. Major constraints are as follows.

1. The number of logic layers within a pipeline stage cannot be practically reduced below four- to six-gate depth, thus imposing a lower bound of a few gate delays.
2. The overhead, t_v, imposes a second bound on G when $t_v \geq t_p$.

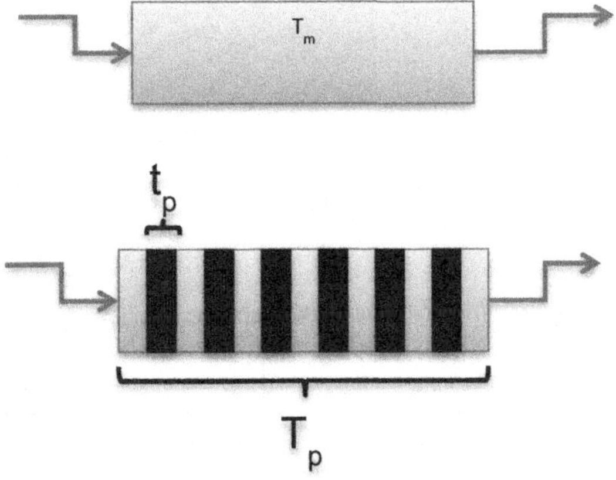

FIGURE 2.11

Pipeline parallelism.

3. The slowest pipeline stage (longest propagation delay) determines the clock rate of the entire pipeline.
4. When n_d becomes small with respect to p.

Performance gain is bounded by the overhead, t_v, limiting the degree of useful pipelining that can be achieved.

$$\lim_{p \to \infty} G = \frac{t_m}{t_v}, \quad \text{for } n_d \to \infty \tag{2.9}$$

While the propagation delay of a pipeline stage is much less than that of the monolithic logic version of the same function, the advantage of pipelining the logic is lost when n_d is very small or even length 1 (scalar). In this case, performance gain could be less than 1. The breakeven point for the special case of no overhead ($t_v = 0$) is:

$$n_d \geq \frac{p \times t_p}{t_m - t_p} \tag{2.10}$$

With $t_p \ll t_m$, this converges to: $n_d \geq p \times t_p / t_m$.

Pipeline structures are employed in many aspects of computer architecture. As is described later, a common application is in the execution pipeline, where many instructions can be executing at the same time, significantly increasing the rate of instruction throughput. However, the iconic use of pipelining for supercomputing was in the vector-processing architecture of the mid-1970s, described in the next subsection.

2.6.2 VECTOR PROCESSING

Vector-processing architecture exploits pipelining to achieve the advantages of fine-grain parallelism, latency hiding, and amortized control overheads (Fig. 2.12). Pipelining also permits a high clock rate for vector-based computer architecture by keeping the pipeline stages small in terms of the logic depth.

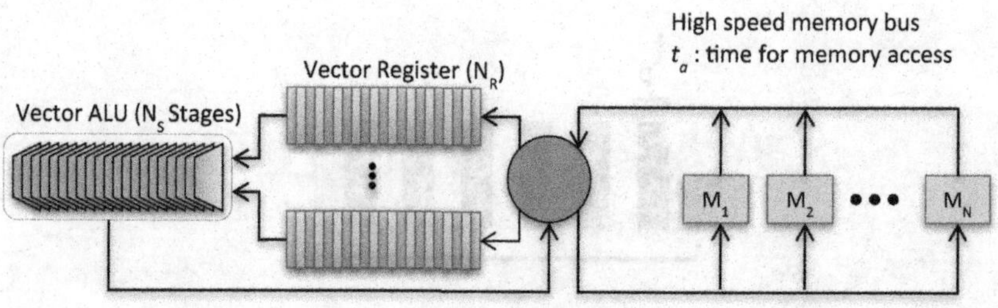

FIGURE 2.12

The vector-processing architecture.

2.7 SINGLE-INSTRUCTION, MULTIPLE DATA ARRAY

The SIMD array was a major class of parallel computer architecture in the 1980s and 1990s. It was particularly well suited to LSI technology, although such systems were implemented both before and after this era. This strategy for parallel processing is still found in subsystems of a wide range of computers today for specialized tasks and accelerators.

2.7.1 SINGLE-INSTRUCTION, MULTIPLE DATA ARCHITECTURE

The SIMD array class of parallel computer architecture consists of a very large number of relatively simple PEs, each operating on its own data memory (Fig. 2.13). The PEs are all controlled by a shared sequencer or sequence controller that broadcasts instructions in order to all the PEs. At any point in time all the PEs are doing the same operation but on their respective dedicated memory blocks. An interconnection network provides data paths for concurrent transfers of information between PEs, also managed by the sequence controller. I/O channels provide high bandwidth (in many cases) to the system as a whole or directly to the PEs for rapid postsensor processing. SIMD array architectures have been employed as standalone systems or integrated with other computer systems as accelerators.

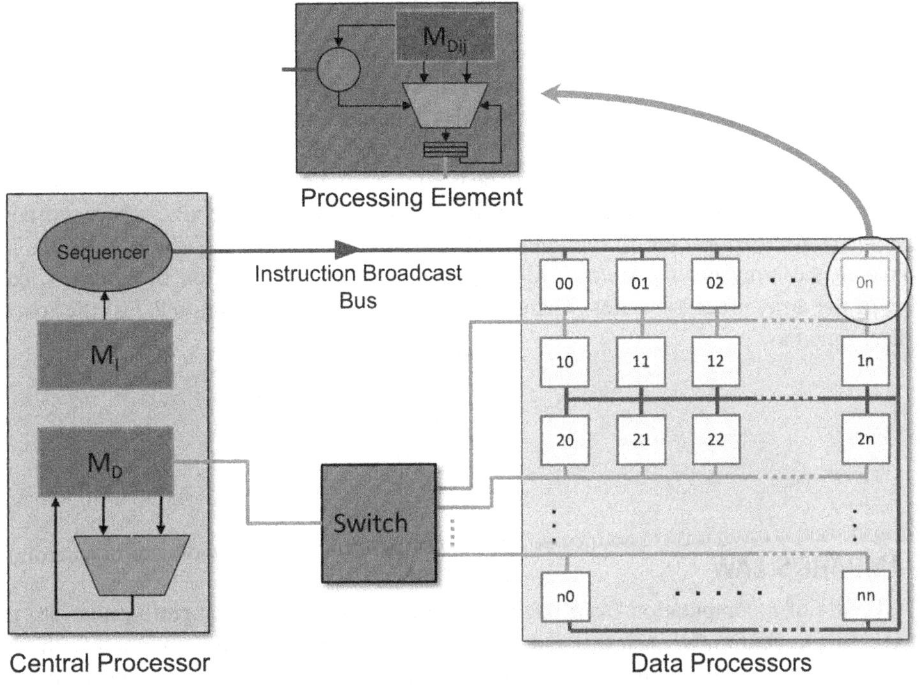

FIGURE 2.13

The SIMD array class of parallel computer architecture.

The PE of the SIMD array is highly replicated to deliver potentially dramatic performance gain through this level of parallelism. The canonical PE consists of key internal functional components, including the following.

- Memory block—provides part of the system total memory which is directly accessible to the individual PE. The resulting system-wide memory bandwidth is very high, with each memory read from and written to its own PE.
- ALU—performs operations on contents of data in local memory, possibly via local registers with additional immediate operand values within broadcast instructions from the sequence controller.
- Local registers—hold current working data values for operations performed by the PE. For load/store architectures, registers are direct interfaces to the local memory block. Local registers may serve as intermediate buffers for nonlocal data transfers from system-wide network and remote PEs as well as external I/O channels.
- Sequencer controller—accepts the stream of instructions from the system instruction sequencer, decodes each instruction, and generates the necessary local PE control signals, possibly as a sequence of microoperations.
- Instruction interface—a port to the broadcast network that distributes the instruction stream from the sequence controller.
- Data interface—a port to the system data network for exchanging data among PE memory blocks.
- External I/O interface—for those systems that associate individual PEs with system external I/O channels, the PE includes a direct interface to the dedicated port.

The SIMD array sequence controller determines the operations performed by the set of PEs. It also is responsible for some of the computational work itself. The sequence controller may take diverse forms and is itself a target for new designs even today. But in the most general sense, a set of features and subcomponents unify most variations.

As a first approximation, Amdahl's law may be used to estimate the performance gain of a classical SIMD array computer. Assume that in a given instruction cycle either all the array processor cores, p_n, perform their respective operations simultaneously or only the control sequencer performs a serial operation with the array processor cores idle; also assume that the fraction of cycles, f, can take advantage of the array processor cores. Then using Amdahl's law (see Section 2.7.2) the speedup, S, can be determined as:

$$S = \frac{1}{1 - f + \left(\frac{f}{p_n}\right)} \tag{2.11}$$

2.7.2 AMDAHL'S LAW

Ideally, all parts of a computation from beginning to end could be further partitioned into parallel pieces executing concurrently, such that many computing resources could be applied to the computation simultaneously to reduce time to solution uniformly (across the computation) and accelerate the rate of processing. While there are some extreme examples of this ideal case, more frequently application programs exhibit operational behavior such that some parts of the computation are indeed parallel, supporting acceleration through concurrent operation, while other parts show less or even no parallelism in the limit, operating purely sequentially and issuing only one instruction at a time. This computing profile combining both parallel and sequential fractions of the complete execution imposes an important bound on the maximum acceleration that can be achieved through parallelism. The most widely recognized formulation of this boundary condition is referred to as Amdahl's law after the famous computer architect who first codified it. While more broadly applicable to parallel computing in general, Amdahl's law is particularly well suited to modeling the performance of SIMD array computing (with some slight simplifying assumptions), and this motivates its introduction here. Later it is employed to understand other forms of parallel architectures.

Assume that a SIMD array has two modalities of execution, either sequential, where its central processor performs one instruction at a time, or parallel, where all the array processor cores perform their respective operations at the same time. For simplicity it is assumed that the clock rates of both the central processor and the array processors are the same, but this is of little importance to the implications of this performance model.

Figs. 2.14 and 2.15 show two timelines: the first a sequential execution of all the operations of a computation T_O, and the second with the fraction f of the operations, T_f, done in parallel, with a level of parallelism g. Ideally, the gain in performance would be g. But only T_F of the total T_O operations can be performed in parallel to at least some degree, with the remaining $T_O - T_F$ operations still done sequentially, where $f = T_F/T_O$. As shown below, the actual speedup, S, can be determined by the ratio of the times of the two solution times with and without g parallelism, such that $S = T_O/T_A$ where $T_A = T_F/g$. The resulting formulation for S is derived below as a function of g and f, independent of the exact times involved.

$$S = T_O/T_A \tag{2.12}$$

$$f = T_F/T_O \tag{2.13}$$

$$T_A = (1 - f) \times T_O + \left(\frac{f}{g}\right) \times T_O \tag{2.14}$$

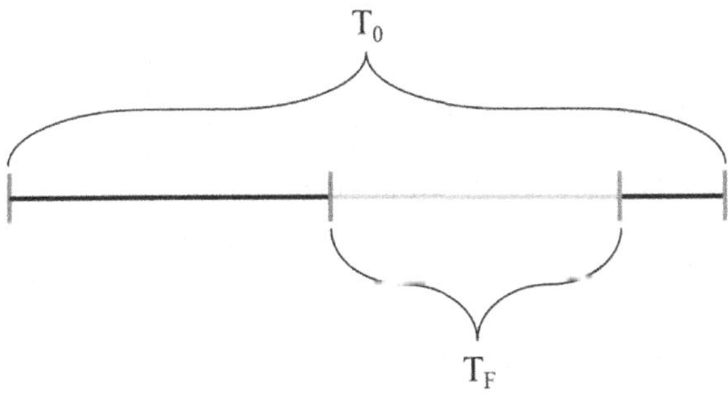

FIGURE 2.14

The timeline of a computation performed sequentially taking time T_O. The black segments of the line of execution represent the set of operations that have to be done in order. The green (light gray in print versions) segment of the line of execution represents the set of T_F operations that can be performed concurrently.

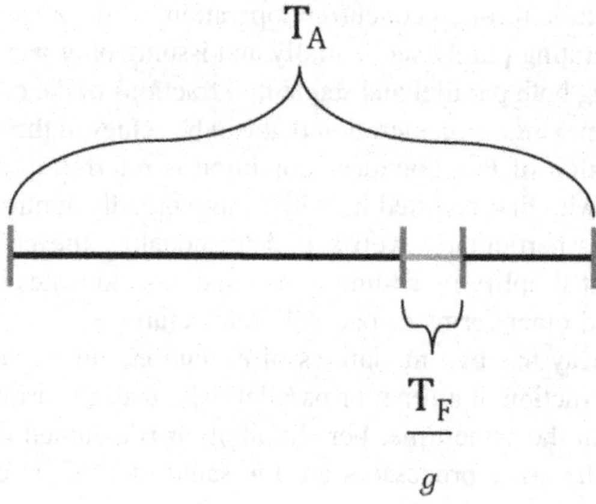

FIGURE 2.15

The timeline of a computation where those operations that can be done in parallel are performed concurrently with a parallelism of g, resulting in a shorter time to solution, T_A.

$$S = \frac{T_O}{(1-f) \times T_O + \left(\frac{f}{g}\right) \times T_O} \tag{2.15}$$

$$S = \frac{1}{1-f+\left(\frac{f}{g}\right)}, \tag{2.16}$$

where $T_O \equiv$ time for nonaccelerated computation; $T_A \equiv$ time for accelerated computation; $T_F \equiv$ time of portion of computation that can be accelerated; $g \equiv$ peak performance gain for accelerated portion of computation; $f \equiv$ fraction of nonaccelerated computation to be accelerated; $S \equiv$ speedup of computation with acceleration applied.

This formulation of Amdahl's law can be understood by considering various possible operating points. In the limits, if the entire code can be executed (equally) in parallel by a concurrency of g, then the fraction $f = 1$ and the total speedup is the ideal case of g. But if none of the code can be performed in parallel despite having g-level hardware parallelism, $f = 0$ and $S = 1$, so there is no gain as one would expect. What is more sobering, and why Amdahl's law is so important, is seen with yet another operating point. Suppose the parallel hardware exhibits an ideal gain of 1 million, that is $g = 1{,}000{,}000$, and half the code can be done concurrently, $f = 0.5$. Simple substitution shows that in spite of this enormous potential gain, the actual delivered speedup is less than 2; $S < 2$. In fact, even if g were infinity, with a fraction of 0.5, you would still not get a speedup greater than 2. A range of speedups is shown in Fig. 2.16 with respect to the fraction of total time to be accelerated with different ideal accelerator gains.

Example. Consider a SIMD array computer with an 8×8 array of core processors and one sequential control processor. In a given computing cycle, either the control processor performs an operation or all the array cores perform the same operation on their respective data. What fraction of the total workload needs to be performed by the core array to deliver an overall speedup of eight times?

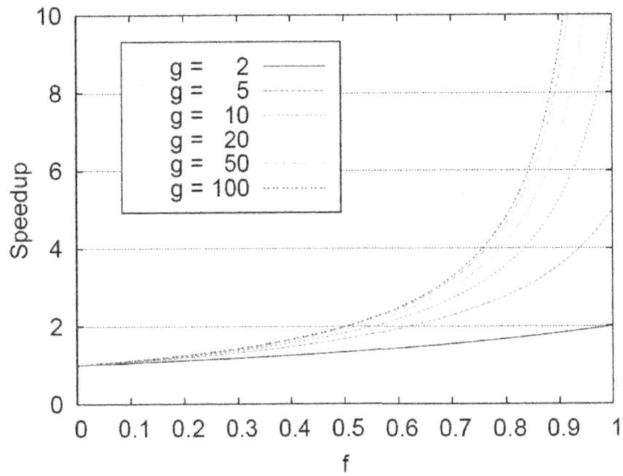

FIGURE 2.16

Examples of delivered speedup with respect to the fraction of code that can be parallelized and the gain of the accelerator hardware.

The total speedup, $S = 8$, is required with an acceleration gain, $g = 64$. Substituting appropriately:

$$S = \frac{1}{1 - f + \dfrac{f}{g}}$$

$$8 = \frac{1}{1 - f + \dfrac{f}{64}}$$

$$8 - 8f + \frac{f}{8} = 1$$

$$64 - 63f = 8$$

$$56 = 63f$$

$$f = \frac{56}{63} = 0.889$$

here it is seen that to achieve only 12.5% of the peak gain of 64 requires almost 90% of the workload to be able to be parallelized. Experience throughout this course will demonstrate that this is a tall order and difficult to achieve.

2.8 MULTIPROCESSORS

The multiprocessor class of parallel computer is the dominant form of supercomputer today. Most broadly, it is any system comprising a set of individual self-controlled computers integrated by a communications network and coordinated to perform a single workload. By the Flynn taxonomy the multiprocessor is a MIMD-class machine. Each processor making up the system has its own data-processing units controlled by its own local instruction stream controller. Multiprocessors have a long history reaching back to the 1950s and SAGE, consisting of MIT Whirlwind-class computers deployed by IBM for the US Air Force at North American Aerospace Defense Command. A number of commercial multiprocessors consisting of two processors were deployed, with one processor dedicated to the computing (heavy lifting) while the other managed I/O tasks.

Multiprocessors grew in importance for supercomputing with the advent of VLSI technology and the development of microprocessor architecture. This represented an important change in the trend and direction of supercomputer architecture. Cost benefits through the exploitation of economy of scale derived from the mass market of general-purpose microprocessors defined the next generation of high performance computers. The integration of microprocessors derived for the broader markets of workstations, personal computers, and enterprise servers as the principal compute engines of supercomputers had a dramatic impact on large-scale system architecture, largely displacing the previous specialized designs. One visible impact was the sheer physical size of supercomputers, which greatly escalated to multiple rows of racks, each incorporating many VLSI microprocessors. Today the multiprocessor has made yet another leap in technology, with a decade of multicore technology where each socket now incorporates multiple processors, referred to as "cores".

There are three mainstream configurations in use: SMPs, MPPs, and commodity clusters. A single processor system reflects a unified memory in which all of your data sits in the same memory subsystem. When multiple processors are used, a choice has to be made about how the processors and memory are interrelated. Do all the processors within the system share the same memory subsystem, or does each processor have its own separate memory? A third choice is somewhere in between: groups of processors share a memory block while the different groups, often referred to as "nodes", have distinct memory blocks. With multicore sockets this last is often the structure employed. These different classes of multiprocessor system architectures are described in detail in the following subsections.

2.8.1 SHARED-MEMORY MULTIPROCESSORS

A shared-memory multiprocessor is an architecture consisting of a modest number of processors, all of which have direct (hardware) access to all the main memory in the system (Fig. 2.17). This permits

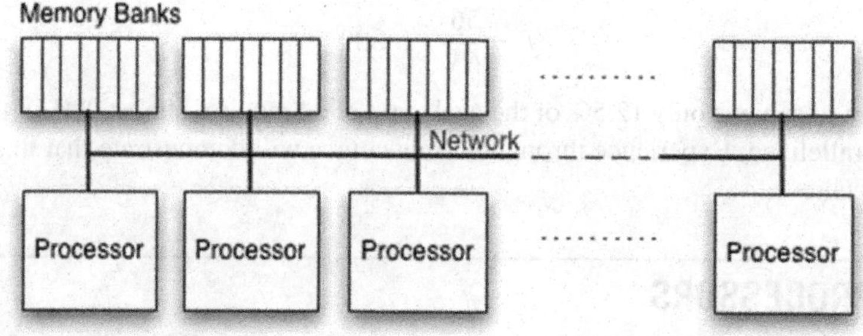

FIGURE 2.17

The shared-memory multiprocessor architecture.

any of the system processors to access data that any of the other processors has created or will use. The key to this form of multiprocessor architecture is the interconnection network that directly connects all the processors to the memories. This is complicated by the need to retain cache coherence across all caches of all processors in the system.

Cache coherence ensures that any change in the data of one cache is reflected by some change to all other caches that may have a copy of the same global data location. It guarantees that any data load or store to a processor register, if acquired from the local cache, will be correct, even if another processor is using the same data. The interconnection network that provides cache coherence may employ any one of several techniques. One of the earliest is the modified exclusive shared invalid (MESI) protocol, sometimes referred to as a "snooping cache", in which a shared bus is used to connect all processors and memories together. This method permits any write of one processor to memory to be detected by all other processors and checked to see if the same memory location is cached locally. If so, some indication is recorded and the cache is either updated or at least invalidated, such that no error occurs.

Shared-memory multiprocessors are differentiated by the relative time to access the common memory blocks by their processors. A SMP is a system architecture in which all the processors can access each memory block in the same amount of time. This capability is often referred to as "UMA" or uniform memory access. SMPs are controlled by a single operating system across all the processor cores and a network such as a bus or cross-bar that gives direct access to the multiple memory banks. Access times can still vary, as contention between two or more processors for any single memory bank will delay access times of one or more processors. But all processors still have the same chance and equal access. Early SMPs emerged in the 1980s with such systems as the Sequent Balance 8000. Today SMPs serve as enterprise servers, deskside machines, and even laptops using multicore chips, and thus play a major role in the medium-scale computing which is a major part of the commercial market. SMPs also serve as nodes within much larger MPPs.

Nonuniform memory access (NUMA) architectures retain access by all processors to all the main memory blocks within the system (Fig. 2.18). But this does not ensure equal access times to all

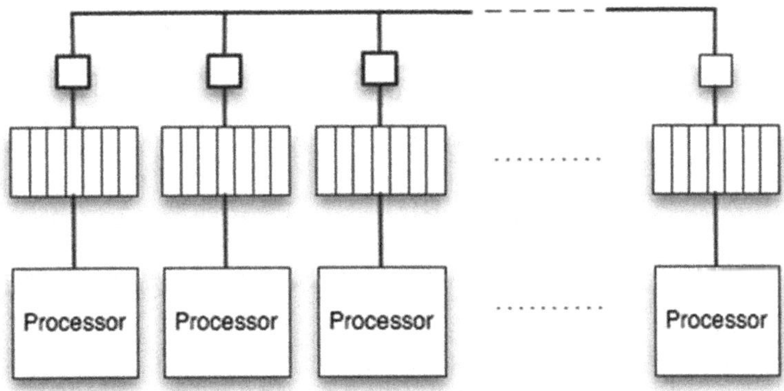

FIGURE 2.18

Nonuniform memory access architectures retain access by all processors to all the main memory blocks within a system, but does not ensure equal access times to all memory blocks by all the processors.

memory blocks by all processors. This is motivated by the architecture opportunity provided by modern microprocessor designs to exploit high-speed local memory communication channels while providing access to all the memory through external, albeit slower, global interconnection networks. NUMA architectures benefit from scaling, permitting more processor cores to be incorporated into a single shared-memory system than SMPs. However, because of the difference in memory access times, the programmer has to be conscious of the locality of data placement and use it to take best advantage of computing resources. NUMA multiprocessor architectures first emerged with such systems as the BBN Butterfly multiprocessors, including the GP-1000 and the TC-2000.

2.8.2 MASSIVELY PARALLEL PROCESSORS

MPP architecture is the structure that most easily scales to the extremes of computing system size and performance (Fig. 2.19). The largest supercomputers today, comprising millions of processor cores, are of this class of multiprocessor. MPPs are (in most cases) not shared-memory architectures, but are distributed memory. In an MPP separate groups of processor cores are directly connected to their own local memory. Such groups are colloquially referred to as "nodes", and there is no sharing of memory between them; this simplifies design and eliminates inefficiencies that impede scalability. But in the absence of shared memories, a processor core in one group must employ a different method to exchange data and coordinate with cores of other processor groups. The logical capability for message passing is enabled by the physical system area network (SAN) that integrates all the nodes to form a single system. As discussed in greater detail in Chapter 8, a message is transferred between two processor cores of the system, with each core running a separate process. By this means a receiving process and its host processor can acquire data from a sending processor's process. The same network can be used to synchronize processes running on separate processors. By 1997 the first system capable of teraflops (HPL benchmark) was the Intel ASCI Red MPP deployed at Sandia National Laboratories.

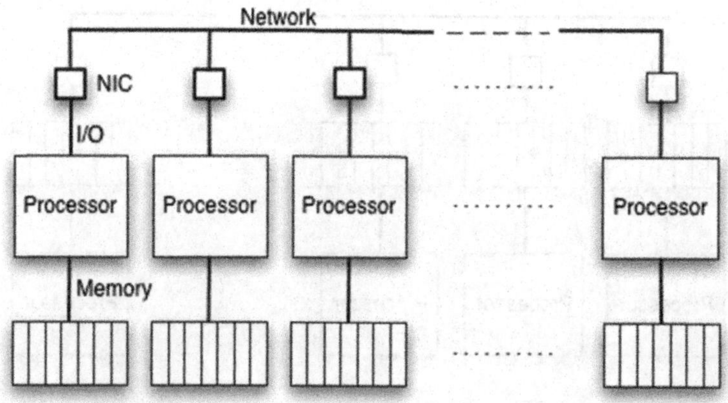

FIGURE 2.19

The massively parallel processor class of parallel computer architecture.

2.8.3 COMMODITY CLUSTERS

While all current generations of supercomputers exploit the economic advantages of incorporating VLSI microprocessors and DRAM main memory that are mass produced for commercial and consumer markets, the systems discussed thus far are still based on special-purpose designs to provide tight coupling among processor cores for superior performance. However, the dominant class of deployed supercomputers, the commodity clusters, take exploitation of mass-market economics one step further to introduce even an greater cost advantage. As the name suggests, such systems consist exclusively of commodity subsystems, sometimes referred to as COTS (commodity off-the-shelf) components. Dongarra et al. [8] defines a "commodity cluster" as "a cluster in which both the network and the compute nodes are commercial products available for procurement and independent application by organizations (end users or separate vendors) other than the original equipment manufacturer". The key idea is that a supercomputer can be made up of component subsystems, all of which can be procured by and are produced for a much larger user market than the deployed base of supercomputers, thus leveraging economy of scale for dramatic improvements of performance to cost.

Emerging in the mid-1990s, such improvements often exceeded an order of magnitude when using consumer-grade system components. In 1997 the network of workstations (NOW) cluster [9] of commercial-grade workstations from the University of California at Berkeley was the first commodity cluster to be placed in the Top 500 list, and the Beowulf cluster [10] (of consumer-grade personal computers) from NASA Jet Propulsion Laboratory and the California Institute of Technology was the first to be awarded the Gordon Bell Prize (Fig. 2.20). As this early history suggests, there were two levels of commodity clusters due to two corresponding levels of microprocessors. Commercial-grade microprocessors were used for industrial-grade workstations where performance mattered, while consumer-grade microprocessors were used for personal computers where cost was of the greatest importance. Eventually this differentiated market merged, as 32-bit and eventually 64-bit architectures became common.

FIGURE 2.20

An example of the Beowulf class of parallel computer architecture.

Typically commodity clusters exhibit lower efficiencies with respect to number of cores than MPPs. While contemporary MPPs may demonstrate efficiency approaching 90% on some workloads, commodity clusters are more likely to yield efficiency between 60% and 70% (HPL benchmark). However, workloads vary significantly in terms of degree of coupling, and clusters are excellent for throughput computing such as parameter sweeps that rely less on intercommunication and more on local processing capabilities.

Today the fastest supercomputers are a mix of MPPs and commodity clusters. Clusters currently exceed 80% (four out of five) of all the systems rated by the Top 500 list. Not surprisingly, due to the superior properties of the MPPs purpose built for supercomputing with their optimized SANs, the majority of the fastest machines are of this class. Historically commodity clusters have employed a number of COTS networks, including such early offerings as asynchronous transfer mode (ATM), Myrinet, and Ethernet 100BaseT. Current-generation clusters principally employ Gigabit Ethernet or Infiniband Networks.

2.9 HETEROGENEOUS COMPUTER STRUCTURES

The homogeneous computing systems described so far employ a single type of processing component to perform all computation, such as a typical multicore processor socket component. The majority of supercomputers are of this type. However, for certain patterns of computing, other core designs and structures made of them can deliver sometimes dramatic performance improvements, at least for some kinds of computing algorithms. Systems comprising two or more types of computer cores, sockets, and nodes are distinguished from homogeneous computing systems that have only one type, and are designated as heterogeneous systems. Accelerators, sometimes known as GPUs, are attached to a system node via the I/O bus, principally the peripheral component interconnect bus, and can be accessed by any of the conventional processor cores of the system within the same node. Accelerators are designed to perform certain classes of computation extremely well, like linear algebra and signal processing problems. Heterogeneity is also finding its way directly into chip design, thus circumventing the intermediary I/O bus.

While each of these classes of architecture, both sequential and multiple forms of parallel, has been presented as separate and distinct, modern computer architecture such as MPPs in the broadest sense often incorporate the best aspects of all of them. A modern microprocessor socket incorporates structures derived from each of these main types, including sequential, pipelining, SIMD, and multiprocessor organizations.

2.10 SUMMARY AND OUTCOMES OF CHAPTER 2

- Computer architecture is the structure and semantics of a computer. HPC architecture is optimized to achieve high speed through aggressive exploitation of fast technologies and parallel organization of its component modules.

- Key properties of HPC architecture include speed of operation, parallelism for doing multiple operations at the same time, efficient use of critical components, the electrical power that it consumes, reliability, and how easy it is to program.
- Flynn's taxonomy of parallel architectures, while a bit stale, is still widely cited. It includes SISD, SIMD, and MIMD, which can be applied to system types today.
- HPC has advanced over many generations, with progress determined in part by evolving device technologies, including simple devices (e.g., abacus), mechanical gears, electromechanical, such as the Hollerith, and electronics, including vacuum tubes, transistors, and integrated circuits.
- Technologies serve multiple purposes. These include storing information in binary (base 2) form in memory (e.g., magnetic cores and DRAM), performing operations using Boolean logic, and moving data on buses and network interconnect channels.
- The von Neumann architecture is the foundational concept for sequential stored-program computers, which are the basis for essentially all modern supercomputers today.
- HPC systems are derivatives of the von Neumann architecture through many innovations, which include diverse forms of parallelism, memory hierarchies, and advanced networks to integrate the many subsystems together.
- Pipelining connects successive component stages together so data can pass from one stage to the next for rapid throughput.
- Vector architectures (e.g., the Cray-1) exploit pipelining for high-speed arithmetic units, register loads and stores, and overlapping memory accesses.
- SIMD array processing uses many lightweight cores dedicated to separate partitioned memory banks. All cores perform the same kind of operation at the same time but on their local data, to achieve a high degree of parallelism managed by a control processor.
- MPPs are single systems comprising many integrated computer processors. There are diverse forms of multiprocessor, differentiated by the way they are interconnected and the relationship between processors and memory banks.
- Shared-memory multiprocessors combine individual processors with multiple memory banks, such that all processors are able to access all the shared memory banks. SMPs have equal access to all memory in terms of time and bandwidth. Distributed shared-memory (DSM) architectures also share the same memories but have preferential access to some memory banks in lieu of others. SMPs are referred to as UMA, while DSMs exhibit NUMA behavior.
- Commodity clusters are another form of multiprocessor, made entirely from subsystems that are COTS to exploit economy of scale for superior performance to cost.
- Amdahl's law relates achievable delivered speedup to the gain of a parallel accelerator and the fraction of the total workload that can be performed in parallel.

2.11 QUESTIONS AND PROBLEMS

1. Define or expand each of the following terms or acronyms.

- Computer architecture
- ISA
- Parallelism
- GHz
- DRAM
- SRAM
- NVRAM
- Cache
- Bandwidth
- Latency
- NRE
- Botzmann constant
- Data path
- Control path
- Efficiency, floating-point efficiency
- Hardware fault
- Software fault
- Hard fault, soft fault
- Cosmic ray
- Checkpoint/restart
- Programmability
- SLOC
- Programming model
- Productivity
- Software engineering
- Workflow management
- Flynn's taxonomy, Michael Flynn
- SISD
- SIMD
- MIMD
- MISD
- SPMD
- GPU accelerator
- Abacus
- Harvard architecture
- Chip
- Mainframe
- Minicomputer
- Vector processor
- SIMD array
- CMOS
- SMP
- MPP
- Vacuum tube
- Discrete transistor
- Integrated transistor
- Logic gate
- Circuit
- Switching rate
- Propagation delay
- Mercury tank
- One-dimensional memory
- Two-dimensional memory
- Core memory
- Punched cards
- Paper tape
- Cycle time
- Volatile
- Destructive read
- Register
- Accumulator
- PE
- Interconnection network
- Data path
- I/O channel
- Amdahl's law
- Shared-memory multiprocessor
- Cache coherence
- MESI protocol
- Snooping cache
- SMP
- UMA
- NUMA
- SAN
- COTS
- ATM
- Myrinet
- Gigabit Ethernet
- Infiniband
- Heterogeneous system architecture
- Microprocessor socket

2. State whether each of the following statements is true or false.

- HPC architecture is concerned with only the lowest-level technologies and circuit design.
- An HPC system will never be fast enough to deliver the necessary performance required by major application problems.

- The time to do a floating-point operation is the most important aspect of the efficiency of an HPC system.
- The cost of the software on an HPC system is much less than the cost of the hardware platform.
- The greater the performance that is required, the harder it is to optimize the user program.
- Code reuse is critical to managing application development complexity and difficulty.
- Magnetism is the longest-lasting technology in computing, having been used from the 1940s to the present (2010s).

3. HPC architecture exploits enabling technologies to minimize ____, maximize ____, and serve ______. In recent years HPC has been applied to ______.
4. Name and describe the four principal sources of performance degradation. In addition to performance, name and describe four factors that are of concern for HPC.
5. Explain what distinguishes a supercomputer from a commercial or consumer-grade server.
6. Name and describe three key properties that determine the performance of an HPC architecture. Give a formula that shows the relationship of these properties. Name and describe two additional factors that influence HPC systems operation.
7. Which has better performance, a supercomputer with 10,000 CPUs that can operate in parallel at a clock rate of 2.9 GHz and is available 80% of the time, or a supercomputer with 10,000 CPUs that can operate in parallel at a clock rate of 2.7 GHz and is available 95% of the time?
8. Name and describe three aspects of speed of an HPC system. What are the two measures for communication speed?
9. Describe how air cooling works. Explain why liquid cooling is sometimes used.
10. Describe three types of faults in an HPC system. Describe how recovery from a fault can work.
11. Describe two modern architecture strategies that address the two trends of stagnant processor speed and multicore chips.
12. Name and briefly describe the three dominant classes of technologies that define the design space for HPC architecture.
13. Describe the purpose of cache memory. Describe the purpose of L1, L2, and L3 cache.
14. Discuss at least three different features of SRAM, DRAM, and NVRAM, including their relative access speeds.
15. Draw a figure that illustrates the principal elements of the von Neumann architecture.
16. Suppose that you want to optimize an automotive assembly plant. In your plant the automotive frame and whole components arrive at the plant and the task is to assemble the complete automobile. For simplicity, let us assume there are five steps to assembling an automobile: add and configure engine in frame; add seats; assemble wheel subsystem; assemble steering; and assemble and configure braking system. Also for simplicity, assume that these can be done in any order and can be done at the same time, except that the assembly of the seats cannot happen at the same time as the assembly of the steering system, and assembly of the brakes has to come after the assembly of the wheels. Also assume that the time for all steps is the same, except that the time to assemble the braking system is two times the time required for each of the other steps.
    - Discuss at least three alternatives that are possible for an automotive assembly strategy. Include SISD, SIMD, MISD, and MIMD alternatives in your discussion.

- Design an effective automotive assembly strategy that includes a pipeline. Analyze your design, including a calculation of the throughput of your system and the performance gain of your system over a simple monolithic assembly system. State your assumptions explicitly in your analysis.

17. Name and describe the key internal functional components of an SIMD array.
18. Suppose that 5% of my program is sequential and cannot be parallelized. If I can execute my program in 10 min on one processor, how fast can I expect it to run on 10 processors according to Amdahl's law? What is the maximum speedup that I can obtain, no matter how many processors I use, according to Amdahl's law.
19. Discuss the efficiency that is likely obtainable with commodity clusters versus MPPs. How can workload affect efficiency?

REFERENCES

[1] M.W. Wilkes, W. Renwick, The EDSAC (electronic delay storage automatic calculator), Mathematics of Computation 4 (1950) 61–65.

[2] IBM Corp, 704 Data Processing System, August 30, 2013 [Online]. Available: http://www-03.ibm.com/ibm/history/exhibits/mainframe/mainframe_PP704.html.

[3] J. von Neumann, First Draft of a Report on the EDVAC, University of Pennsylvania, 1945.

[4] Institute for Advanced Study, IAS Electronic Computer Project, 2017 [Online]. Available: https://www.ias.edu/electronic-computer-project.

[5] Massachussets Institute of Technology, Project Whirlwind, MIT Institute Archives & Special Collections, 2008 [Online]. Available: https://libraries.mit.edu/archives/exhibits/project-whirlwind/.

[6] I.B.M. Corp., 1620 Data Processing System, August 30, 2013 [Online]. Available: https://www-03.ibm.com/ibm/history/exhibits/mainframe/mainframe_PP1620.html.

[7] Cray Research, Inc., Cray-1 Computer System Hardware Reference Manual, 1977 [Online]. Available: http://history-computer.com/Library/Cray-1_Reference%20Manual.pdf.

[8] J. Dongarra, T. Sterling, H. Simon, E. Strohmaier, High-performance computing: clusters, constellations, MPPs, and future directions, Computing in Science & Engineering 7 (2) (2005) 51–59.

[9] T.E. Anderson, D.E. Culler, D.A. Patterson, A case for NOW (networks of workstations), IEEE Micro 15 (1) (1995) 54–64.

[10] D.J. Becker, T. Sterling, D. Savarese, J.E. Dorband, U.A. Ranawak, C.V. Packer, BEOWULF: a parallel workstation for scientific computation, in: In Proceedings of the 24th International Conference on Parallel Processing, 1995.

CHAPTER

COMMODITY CLUSTERS

3

CHAPTER OUTLINE

High Performance Computing. https://doi.org/10.1016/B978-0-12-420158-3.00003-4

3.1 INTRODUCTION

The commodity cluster [1] represents possibly the single most successful form of supercomputing in the history of high performance systems. It exploits technology advancements in the areas of very large-scale integration microprocessors, dynamic random access memory (DRAM), and networking, as well as improving performance relative to cost through the economy of scale of mass production. The secret of the success of commodity clusters is that they comprise major components that are standalone computers in their own right, marketed to a much larger market segment than the narrower high performance computing (HPC) community, and delivering an economy of scale benefit from the larger consumer base. But the commodity cluster is also successful because it provides great flexibility of system configuration and tremendous accessibility for a broad range of users, from the most arcane national laboratory scientists to high-school students. Indeed, commodity clusters may constitute the third revolution in supercomputing since its inception in the late 1940s. For our purposes, the commodity cluster will serve as the archetype of the conventional scalable HPC system, and its description will delineate the many system component layers that comprise a full supercomputer in terms of both hardware and software.

3.1.1 DEFINITION OF "COMMODITY CLUSTER"

The commodity cluster is a group of integrated computer systems. The component computers are standalone, capable of independent operation, and marketed to a much broader consumer base than the scaled clusters which they comprise. The integration network employed is separately developed and marketed for use by a systems integrator. Mass storage devices are off the shelf and either physically installed within the system nodes or connected externally. All interfaces adhere to industry standards for both attached devices (e.g., USB [2], peripheral component interconnect express [PCIe] [3]) and system networking. Although not required, system software is usually open-source, nonproprietary, and Linux based. Programming interface libraries are bound to C, C++, or Fortran and employ a message-passing interface (MPI), OpenMP, or both.

3.1.2 MOTIVATION AND JUSTIFICATION FOR CLUSTERS

While the motivation for adopting commodity clusters may differ among individuals and institutions, there are clear attributes that have justified their adoption for the last 2 decades. Some of the most prevalent among these are briefly discussed below.

Accessibility—more likely than not, access to a medium-scaled supercomputer will link to a commodity cluster of moderate scale. This is in part because they are by far the most prevalent form of supercomputer available. But it is also true that due to their cost, commodity clusters make up a disproportionate number of systems deployed at institutions where entry-level experience is likely to be acquired.

Performance relative to cost—the relatively low cost of acquisition and within some environments the low cost of ownership are often the dominant reason for the procurement choice of commodity clusters. Simply put, one gets more peak performance for a given price than using more tightly coupled, admittedly more efficient alternatives.

Scalability—unlike symmetric memory processor (SMP) systems, commodity clusters are scalable in that the number of nodes can vary widely dependent on need, space, power, and cost. As above, for a given scale the cost is probably less than for alternative custom systems. However, this claim may be primarily in the domain of throughput computing rather than capability computing, for which the overheads, latencies, and bandwidths may be less substantial than using custom systems.

Configurability—the flexibility of configuration for commodity clusters has been historically greater than vendor-configured custom systems. Not only is variability of scale more flexible, but topology of node interconnects, node memory, and processor sockets, external input/output (I/O) components, and other properties can be easily specified by the end-user institution. Because of exploitation of industry standards and multiple sources of system elements, a diversity of choices gives even greater flexibility and more alternatives. Also, systems can be modified over time rather than remaining stagnant throughout their lifetime.

Latest technology—clusters are made of subsystems that have large markets, hence the economy of scale through mass production. As a consequence, such subsystems are targets by vendors for incorporation of the latest technologies to remain competitive in large markets such as enterprise servers or SMP platforms. The integration of these leading-edge subsystems guarantees that commodity clusters, even those provided by system integrators, will incorporate the state of the art in component technologies.

Programming compatibility—while very different in appearance and cost, commodity clusters are compliant in for if not function to massively parallel processors (MPPs). The approach to programming both is quite similar although optimizations may differ. Both clusters and MPPs consist of microprocessor cores, tightly coupled nodes of processors and memories, and integration networks of various topologies. This permits an MPI to be employed in programming both classes of supercomputer, and the use of OpenMP for programming the individual system nodes. This compatibility permits application codes and libraries to be shared between clusters and MPPs, and similar skill sets to be used for both as well.

Empowerment—a sociological aspect of commodity clusters, unanticipated by their original developers, was that users in labs and academia principally found that they had control of their system and were not bound or constrained by commercial fixed product specifications or proprietary software. There was an excitement about supercomputers, an ease of engagement in doing it with off-the-shelf components, and it was fun. Due to this a whole new generation was attracted to this form of supercomputing, and it continues to draw young people into the field to this day.

3.1.3 CLUSTER ELEMENTS

There are widely varying alternative structures for commodity clusters, this being one of their features for scalability and configurability. But in one form or another, almost all clusters comprise the same four classes of component types.

- Node—the principal element that contains the major processing and main memory components to perform user computations. The node is a standalone computer capable of handling independent user workloads. Even as part of a larger cluster, a node may be used to perform a single computation with other nodes doing separate work in the mode of throughput computing. Additional components of nodes usually include communication channels for processor to memory access and processor to I/O controllers, and the node "chip-set" that manages the node transparently to the user while providing basic primitives for the OS and bootstrapping the node from the powered-down state. The node may include a diversity of I/O controllers for various purposes, including but not limited to the system area network(s) (SANs).

- The system area network, or SAN—the off-the-shelf communication channel that interconnects all the nodes together into a single distributed computing system. The network supports data message passing between nodes, interprocess synchronization such as global barriers, and other collective actions such as reduction operations. It also may support communication with external system I/O devices and the internet. The network consists of the physical data paths of either copper wires or fiber optics, network interface controllers (NICs) to move node data to the data paths, and routers for switching data between data paths to arrive at the destination node.
- Host—a special node to support user services, including login accounts, administration, resource allocation and scheduling, and user directories. The host node may serve multiple users simultaneously even as it spatially partitions the compute nodes among user jobs. The host node may have its own secondary storage, use the clusterwide mass storage, or access an external file system. Users usually log in to the host node through an institution's local area network (LAN).
- Secondary storage—associated with the commodity cluster provides persistent storage for user files and directories, user programs, input data, and result data associated with the jobs that run on the cluster. Logically, the storage is exported to the user through the operating system file system. Physically the storage is a set of disk drives (and possibly tape drives) combined with controller hardware and connections between the controllers and the hard drives. Each node may have its own disk(s) built into the node or have access to a set of disk drives comprising the systemwide file system, sometimes referred to as the "storage area network". Alternatively, the file system may be external to a cluster in the form of a network file system.

The canonical commodity cluster block diagram shown in Fig. 3.1 contains these principal components.

3.1.4 IMPACT ON TOP 500 LIST

As previously discussed, the field of HPC tracks its progress by measuring the performance of systems executing a derivative of the Linpack benchmark, high performance Linpack, and listing the fastest 500

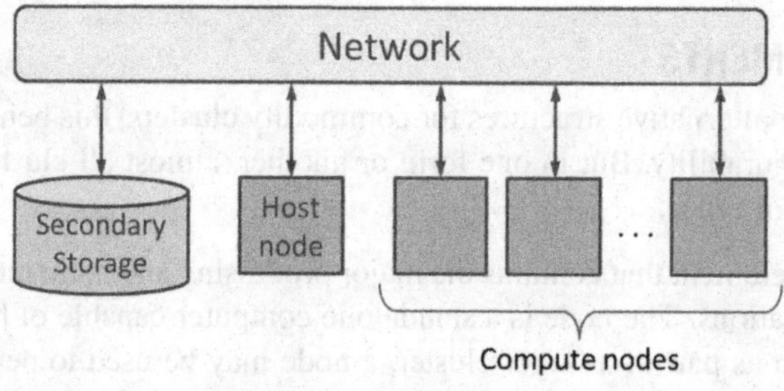

FIGURE 3.1

Commodity cluster components.

machines every 6 months. Over this period, observed performance has experienced a gain factor of more than a billion (>10^9 times). Fig. 3.2 represents this history in terms of the class of HPC systems contributing to the list at any period of review. Commodity clusters did not even show up on the list until 1997, with the entry of the network of workstations (NOW) system. In 2005 commodity clusters constituted half of all systems in the Top 500 list; today that proportion has grown to about 85%, and has been above 80% for the last 8 years.

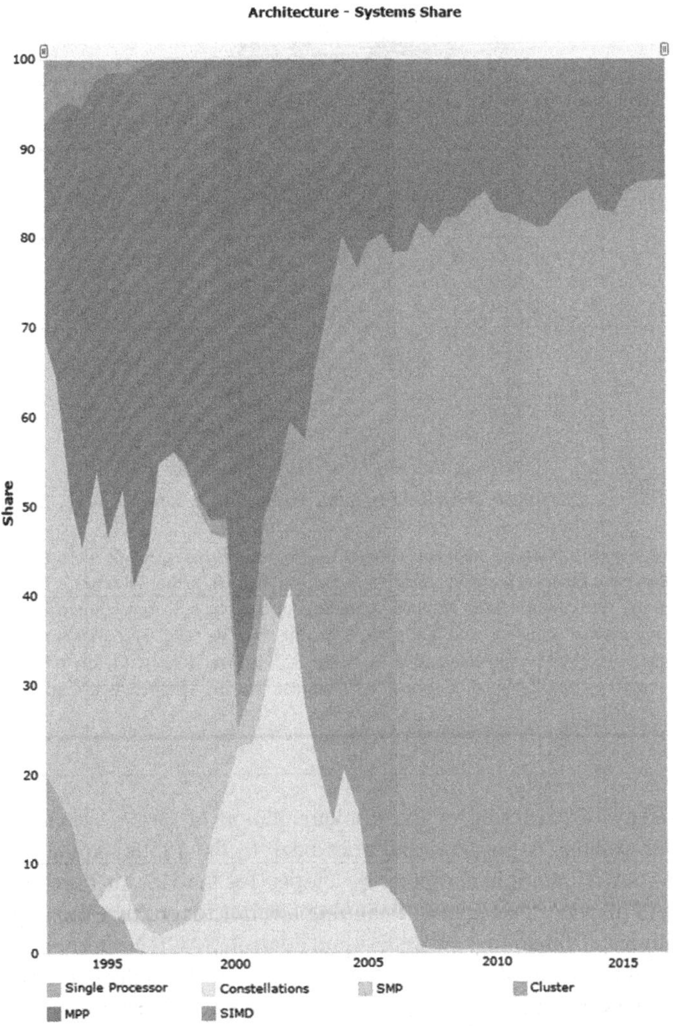

FIGURE 3.2

The dominant system architecture classes comprising the fastest 500 computers over the last 24 years.

Courtesy Top500.org

3.1.5 BRIEF HISTORY

Robert Metcalf. *Photo from wikimedia commons*

Robert Metcalfe is an American electrical engineer who helped to invent Ethernet while working at the Xerox Palo Alto Research Center. He also gave Ethernet its name, borrowing the term from the ether incorrectly thought to be the medium for light propagation in the 19th century. After leaving Xerox he founded 3Com Corporation in his Palo Alto apartment in 1979, initially producing network adapters and going on to produce a wide range of computer network products. 3Com was ultimately acquired by Hewlett-Packard in 2010 for $2.7 billion. Robert Metcalfe is the recipient of the National Medal of Technology, IEEE Medal of Honor, ACM Grace Murray Hopper Award, and IEEE Alexander Graham Bell Medal.

The general strategy of clustering or the implementation of larger systems from smaller fully operational computer systems is not new, and goes back to the 1950s. Among the most prominent system was the IBM SAGE multiple computer developed for the US Air Force NORAD air defense system to acquire and display radar data of incoming aircraft (over the polar regions) to provide an early instance of automated situational awareness and control. SAGE comprised a number of systems that were derivatives of the Whirlwind computer developed by MIT in the late 1940s, a 16-bit vacuum tube architecture that was the supercomputer of its day. The SAGE cluster was motivated by the need for high throughput of large (for that day) datastreams and many-user simultaneous access. It was a pioneer in the use of real-time visual display and screen–input interface. SAGE was also designed to provide enhanced reliability through the multiplicity of identical component systems. When one failed, the others could assume the added workload for nonstop operation.

Although not as exotic, two-way clusters were adopted commercially in the late 1950s, where one system was employed to perform the computing workload while the other was assigned the task of controlling I/O devices such as tapes, disk drives, punched-card handlers, and printers. The IBM 7090/7040 was a very successful example of these dual-node commercial clusters.

The term "cluster" itself was first employed in the late 1980s by Digital Equipment Corporation for its Andromeda project. This early cluster combined 32 VAX 11/750 minicomputers and served as a testbed for experimental studies of hardware system interconnection and software support. This cluster system was never commercialized.

During the 1970s and 1980s network technologies were devised to serve as LANs to allow multiple standalone computer systems in the same environment to share resources such as file systems, laser printers, and ports to external wide area networks such as the emerging internet. The IBM token ring, ATM, and Ethernet were among the most prominent of these. Ultimately, Ethernet emerged as dominant and eventually superseded the others. Ethernet, developed by Metcalf and Boggs [4], was first successfully deployed commercially as a multidrop carrier-sensed arbitration protocol in 1980, permitting multiple systems to share a single interconnection framework to move data between them. These first Ethernet LANs operated at a peak bandwidth of 2.94 Megabit/second in 1973, but were soon replaced with a more pervasive 10 Megabit/s commercial standard in the mid-1980s. It was the establishment of dependable and relatively low-cost LAN interconnection capabilities that set the stage for the next steps to commodity clusters.

The microprocessor was invented by Intel in 1971 [5] and by 1980 was employed in a number of personal computers (PCs), such as the TRS 80, Apple 2, and IBM PC. These were quickly followed by higher grades of single-person direct-access computers employing 16-bit microprocessors referred to as workstations, including the IBM RS-6000, the Sun-1, and others. PCs offered a consumer-grade computer that was relatively slow, with limited main memory and storage, and limited resolution and screens. Their saving virtue was their price, due to large and growing mass market resulting in economy of scale. Workstations provided far more performance, memory, storage, and visual presentation resolution for industrial-grade applications. The difference in cost between a workstation and a PC could be as much as an order of magnitude.

In the late 1980s and early 1990s the combination of LANs integrating workstations offered an opportunity that emerged as workstation farms for sharing batch workloads made up of many user jobs. It was recognized that workstations were often high-availability, low-utilization devices supporting real-time user access but not always fully busy with executing intensive computing tasks. Software was developed, such as the widely used Condor system by Miron Livny, to distribute pending jobs from workstations within the farm to idle workstations. At the job grain boundary, such farms supported parallel job throughput or capacity computing. This would portend the later evolution of workstation clusters.

In 1993 Chuck Sites, former professor at California Institute of Technology, invented the SAN, optimized to connect workstations so they could work together on a common workload. The Myrinet, manufactured and marketed by Myricom, had significantly lower communication latency and higher bandwidth than prior LANs.

Also in 1993 two cluster projects were started: the UC Berkeley Network of Workstations (NOW) Project and the NASA Beowulf Project. The NOW Project pursued the premise that many powerful small-scale computers, in this case workstations, could together outperform a single very large computer such as a mainframe or supercomputer of the day. The NOW Project implemented a series of clusters constructed from high-end workstations, specifically SUN workstations, and the Myrinet network. By 1997 the NOW Project was represented as the first cluster on the Top 500 list; the same year as the first Teraflops computer, the Intel ASCI Red.

As discussed in the next section, the NASA Beowulf Project used a distinctly different approach, incorporating low-end consumer-grade PCs and integrating them with the widely used Ethernet LAN. It also introduced Linux to the supercomputing community. For much of the succeeding 2 decades, this formula dominated commodity clusters and ultimately supercomputing as a whole.

Throughout the late 1980s and the early 1990s a series of message-passing programming interfaces were developed by industry, national laboratories, and academia. These represented in one form or the other the communicating sequential processes execution model derived by Anthony Hoare in the late 1970s [6]. Ultimately this body of work culminated in the communitywide application programming interface being developed and agreed upon, MPI. Shortly thereafter, MPI over CHameleon (MPICH) [7] was developed as a first reduction to practice by Argonne National Laboratory, making MPI widely accessible to a broad user community and establishing it as the premier programming library for both MPPs and commodity clusters.

By the late 1990s commodity clusters emerged as one of several forms of supercomputing systems contending for supremacy. By 2005 and throughout the succeeding decade commodity clusters achieved primary status in terms of number of deployed systems on the Top 500 list.

3.1.6 CHAPTER GUIDE

This chapter describes commodity clusters in breadth, providing an overview of this class of supercomputer and a good picture of supercomputing overall. The next section delivers a technical history of a major milestone in the development of commodity clusters, the Beowulf Project in the mid-1990s, and in so doing introduces many of the components, hardware and software, making up the modern commodity cluster. Section 3.3 gives a detailed description of the hardware components making up the commodity cluster, including the processing nodes, the SAN for integration, communication, and synchronization, and the mass storage for nonvolatile data archiving. Section 3.4 presents the principal ways in which commodity clusters are programmed, involving sequential programming languages combined with parallel programming interfaces and libraries. Section 3.5 provides a software counterpart to the previous hardware discussion, describing the principal system software components, environments, and tools such as the operating system and resource management middleware. Section 3.6 begins the process of hands-on skill-set development. It walks the student through the simplest of actions for logging in to clusters and moving through the user directory hierarchy, running parallel programs, compiling application source codes, and visualizing result data, among other tasks. Section 3.7 closes with a set of conclusions and outcomes of the chapter content.

3.2 BEOWULF CLUSTER PROJECT

Thomas Sterling in front of a commodity cluster built as part of the Beowulf Project. Such commodity clusters are now frequently referred to as belonging to the Beowulf class of supercomputer.

Thomas Sterling is widely known as the father of the Beowulf class of supercomputers. His pioneering work in 1994 along with Don Becker in creating a cluster comprised of commodity-grade computers, collectively referred to as a "Beowulf cluster", significantly reduced the cost of supercomputing and later resulted in the widespread adoption of commodity clusters for scientific computing. This effort resulted in Beowulf being awarded the 1997 Gordon Bell prize in the price–performance category. The Beowulf Project's adoption and software support of the Linux operating system also contributed to the widespread adoption of this operating system in supercomputing systems worldwide. Apart from being the "father of Beowulf", Thomas Sterling's contributions to the hybrid technology multithreaded architecture based on superconducting logic continue to have impacts on high-end computer system architecture design. Thomas Sterling is the recipient of the American Association for the Advancement of Science and HPC Vanguard Awards.

As the history of cluster computing in the previous section indicates, many projects from industry, academia, and government across the international community contributed to the culmination of commodity clusters as the dominant form of supercomputing applicable to a wide range of problem domains and system scales. Nonetheless, one project stands out as the preeminent milestone in the emergence of commodity clusters into the mainstream: the Beowulf Project, begun in the fall of 1993 at the NASA Goddard Space Flight Center by Thomas Sterling and James Fischer, and soon joined by Donald Becker at the start of 1994.

The Beowulf Project explored the potential of deploying systems of a peak performance of 1 Gigaflops and sufficient memory and disk storage to hold scientific data for problems of interest, notably in the earth and space sciences, at a cost that justified systems dedicated to individual computational scientists. At this time, the cost of a high-end workstations was about $50,000 and a

FIGURE 3.3

The 1996 1 Gigaflops Beowulf cluster.

system capable of the abovementioned peak performance was around a million dollars. In the summer of 1994 the first system, "Wiglaf", was deployed, constructed of 16 PC nodes each with one Intel 80486 at 100 MHz, 16 Mbytes of memory, and dual 10BASE-T Ethernet, at a cost of approximately $40,000. By 1996 the third-generation Beowulf Project proof-of-concept system, "Hyglac", achieved sustained performance on a real code in excess of 1 Gigaflops, again with 16 nodes (Fig. 3.3). This time the processors were Intel Pentium Pros at 200 MHz, with a total of 2 Gigabytes of main memory and employing a much-improved 100BASE-TX Fast Ethernet with a nonblocking switch. While the details have changed, this represented the trajectory for future mainstream commodity clusters.

The Beowulf Project also broke ground in its use of the open-source Linux operating system. It made major contributions by providing almost all network driver software employed by Linux at that time and for years to come (for which Donald Becker would rightfully be credited worldwide). This began a process by which Linux ultimately became the number one operating system used in the field of supercomputing up to this day. The Beowulf Project adopted the use of the initial MPICH libraries developed by Bill Gropp and his team at Argonne National Laboratory, which too through evolution would become the standard for programming distributed clusters.

By 1997 a new phase of the Beowulf Project engaged multiple research sites. That year a joint team including Salmon, Warren, Becker, and Sterling won the Gordon Bell Prize for performance to cost. This team also presented a series of tutorials at various conferences that ultimately led to the publication of the popular "How to Build a Beowulf" by Sterling, Salmon, Becker, and Savarese by MIT Press [8]. Later, a second, more comprehensive and up-to-date book, also published by MIT Press and entitled "Beowulf Computing with Linux", was authored by Bill Gropp, Rusty Lusk, and Sterling, and eventually went into a second edition [9].

Beowulf is not the creation of a single individual or even a group; rather it is a synthesis of a set of diverse accomplishments in hardware technology, software libraries, and application programming developed concurrently by many different individual contributors, teams of experts, and product vendors. One example is the community driven development of the MPI programming interface and the MPICH reduction to practice. But while considered an obvious outcome, it was not obvious to mainstream practitioners at the time—in fact for at least 3 years there was strong resistance, even intransigence, at all levels of the supercomputing community to the introduction of commodity clusters as a medium of HPC. It was the vision, tenacity, and trial and error or experimentalism of the early explorers that brought this strategy in hardware and software to the realm of scientific and engineering problem solving. Eventually, the vendors themselves recognized the market opportunity and enhanced aspects of node systems and packaging as well as networking to facilitate commodity clusters and their effective usage. Many hardware vendors and independent software vendors would provide an ever-growing customer base with higher-density, full-featured, highly scalable, and more efficient commodity cluster systems.

Today both within the United States and worldwide, commodity clusters have become a vehicle to excite and educate college students in parallel processing and supercomputing. Major contests are held every year at both the Supercomputing Conference in the United States and the International Supercomputing Conference in Germany. Even high-school students have been attracted to the hands-on aspects of Beowulf computing. In closing, the term "Beowulf computing" was not coined by the original team of developers; they were only responsible for naming a project Beowulf and so injecting the word into the lexicon. Someone else in the public media, and it may never be known whom, used the phrase in print and it caught on. More than 20 years after its first humble and uncertain beginnings, Beowulf computing in the form of commodity clusters now dominates the field of supercomputing.

3.3 HARDWARE ARCHITECTURE

Commodity cluster hardware is, by definition, all commodity off the shelf (COTS) to maximize the benefit of economy of scale and achieve the best performance to cost. The hardware architecture of the commodity cluster is therefore driven and constrained by this requirement. As briefly discussed in Section 3.1, the principal system components in a commodity cluster are the computer nodes, SAN, host node, and mass storage. The architecture of a cluster exploits these resource classes, but is also limited by them and additional support components (e.g., graphics processing units) that conform to industry interface standards. The hardware architecture of a cluster reflects the choices of the specific component types, their number, and the structure in which they are organized and integrated via associated networks. These components and their effect on system architecture are described below, with further expansion and details on specific component types presented in later chapters.

3.3.1 THE NODE

The principal system component of the commodity cluster is most commonly referred to as the "node", and includes most of the active components that make up the aggregate cluster computer. The replicated nodes, also referred to as "the compute nodes", in combination with the integrating interconnection network and the mass (secondary) storage comprise the complete scalable commodity cluster with associated mass storage. But the node itself is a full and self-contained computer that alone and individually serves a much larger user market and therefore benefits from economy of scale to deliver exceptional performance relative to cost, at least for some important institutional workloads. The peak performance and capacity of a cluster are essentially the aggregate capability of all of the compute nodes in combination.

The responsibility of the node is to perform useful computing work for the end user. This is achieved through the collection of processor cores. A modern cluster node is made up of one or more multicore chips, also referred to as "processors", "sockets", "processor sockets", and so on. Depending on the type and number of cores on the chip, the term "many core" may be used. A core is the workhorse of any modern computer. It issues a sequence of user instructions, each potentially designating multiple operations to be performed. A multistage execution pipeline carries out the microoperations required in succession to complete a given instruction and retire it when results are written back into the associated register, to the memory system, or to an I/O channel (other effects are possible as well). A processor socket contains multiple cores, one or more layers of memory cache for high memory bandwidth and low latency access, and chip networks that integrate the cores, caches, and external I/O ports together. In many cases a cluster node incorporates multiple multicore processor sockets. As is discussed in more detail in the following chapters, the microarchitecture of the node cores varies depending on manufacturer and system integrator. Popular processors have variants of two separate architectures by Intel, the IBM Power architecture family, x86 variants by AMD, and the ARM architecture, which is becoming increasingly interesting although it has not as yet had significant impact on the cluster market.

The node is also the container for the main system memory, which primarily uses DRAM technology. Although there are many variants of technology and design, a typical DRAM bit cell consists of a switching transistor and associated capacitor for high-density, low-cost, and moderate-speed data access, both read and write. Although core and main memory are both made from semiconductor devices, they are usually on separate chips because the respective manufacturing processes are very different for optimal behavior of each. Multiple DRAM chips are mounted on single cards, and a number of cards are plugged into industry standard interfaces. The sum of these cards determines the total main memory capacity of the node, with the number of nodes then determining the total main memory of the commodity cluster.

The onboard network channels of the node support intranode communication to move data between the processor sockets, the main memory boards, and the external I/O ports of the node. These networks are transparent to the user and controlled either by the low-level "chip-set" also on the node motherboard or by the node operating system. One of these communications channels is open to the user institution at the time of deployment or when reconfiguration is being conducted. The PCI "bus" is a standardized multiport I/O device that permits additional subsystems to be added in a "plug-and-play" manner to the node without additional hardware changes. Several generations of PCI interconnects have been employed in succession, the latest being PCIe. Even for this single specification, there are many distinct scales for each generation. Other interface ports, some of which go through the PCI bus on the node, are available, such as the ubiquitous USB ports and more obscure accesses for maintenance and administration. Of particular importance is possible direct access to hard disk drives for secondary storage, network controllers for the LAN, and an additional NIC for the SAN discussed below.

3.3.2 SYSTEM AREA NETWORKS

The SAN is the central and differentiating attribute of a commodity cluster that varies in industry standards for communications. It is the principal distinction between a commodity cluster and a more generalized clustering of components where the network is custom designed, such as the Intel Omnipath. Many different networks have served this purpose. In 1994–1995 two approaches were explored. The first was the invention of the SAN by Chuck Seitz, a former professor at Caltech, who created and manufactured the "Myrinet" that was very high performance and low latency for its day. It was also expensive. It was employed by the UC Berkeley NOW project that used Sun Microsystems workstations (hence network of workstations), which were also relatively expensive.

The second was the adoption of the Ethernet LAN to this purpose by the NASA Beowulf Project using low-cost, but low-performance, PCs based on the x86 Intel microprocessor architecture. Both approaches were heavily used throughout the following decade in commodity clusters. Myricom, the vendor and distributor for Myrinet, is no more, but Ethernet continues to this day, only recently being surpassed by the Infiniband network architecture, "IBA". Ethernet has dominated the low-cost SAN market and those clusters employed primarily for throughput computing, while IBA is widely used for more tightly coupled commodity clusters with higher bandwidth and significantly lower latency. Both branches of the SAN technology continue to evolve. Some commodity clusters will incorporate both types of network, with the actual computing being conducted over the IBA network and the "out-of-band" activities for administration and system maintenance being performed over the Ethernet network.

SANs comprise physical channels for data transfer over distances of a few centimeters to hundreds of meters. These may be either conductors, usually copper, or optical fiber depending on issues of cost, energy, and bandwidth requirements. They are connected to nodes by NICs. These may be hardwired into the node motherboard, as is found with GigE (1 Gigabit per second Ethernet) in many cases, or with separate NIC cards often plugged into the nodes' PCIe connectors. The NIC converts data provided by the processors or directly from main memory into message packets of varying length to be sent to destination nodes. The third component is the router or switch used to create topologies of multilayer network structures for higher degree of nodes. Switches are characterized by their degree (number of ports) and their time to transfer a packet from input port to output port, including the time to set up the internal switching configuration. For very large systems, switches can make up a large investment and a major part of the system total cost as well as energy usage.

3.3.3 SECONDARY STORAGE

Persistent storage in one or more forms is essential for computing to retain indefinitely user programs, libraries, and input and result data. Commodity clusters may directly employ hard disk drives or solid-state devices (SSDs) built in to each node. Alternatively, a storage subsystem with its own controllers and possibly its own network may be included as a separate unit within the cluster. Finally, the commodity cluster may access an external mass storage system via the LAN and share it with other user systems. A mix of these is possible and often used. One advantage of not having hard disks integrated within the node is a significant reduction in node power consumption and improved reliability. Disk drives are mechanical and therefore have a higher failure rate (like fans), so avoiding them in the node improves the node's downtime. These would be referred to appropriately as "diskless nodes". However, the recent rapid growth of use of nonvolatile random access memories fabricated from semiconductors eliminates the use of mechanicals and can largely resolve this problem. Separate file systems are usually built from faster hard disks and incorporate redundancy (e.g., RAID) to circumvent downtime due to single disk failures. This is often a cost-effective and operationally better approach to providing persistent storage for users.

3.3.4 COMMERCIAL SYSTEMS SUMMARY

Table 3.1 gives an overview of several commercially available commodity clusters.

Table 3.1 Overview of Components of Several Commercially Available Commodity Clusters

Machine	Network	Processor	Cores per Node	Memory Capacity	Blades	Vendor	Secondary Storage	Nodes per Rack
SuperMUC	Infiniband-FDR (41.25 Gb/s) Mellanox	Sandy Bridge–EP Intel Xeon E5-2680 8C, 2.7 GHz (Turbo 3.5 GHz)	16	32 GB/node	Yes	IBM/ Lenovo	15 PB (scratch) 3.5 PB (home)	512
Mistral	Infiniband-FDR	Xeon E5-2680v3 12C 2.5 GHz/ E5-2695v4 18c 2.1 GHz	24	64 GB/node	No	Bull, Atos		18
Cray CS-Storm	Infiniband-FDR	Xeon E5-2660v2 10C 2.2 GHz	20	Up to 1024 GB/node	No	Cray		23
Stampede	Infiniband-FDR (56 Gbps)	Xeon E5-2680 8C 2.7 GHz	16	32 GB/node	No	Dell	14 PB (shared) 1.6 PB (local aggregate)	40
HPC4 HP POD	Infiniband-FDR	Xeon E5-2697v2 12C 2.7 GHz	24		Yes	Hewlett–Packard	1.8 PB (shared) 0.75 PB (midterm shared) 1.5 PB (local aggregate)	160

3.4 PROGRAMMING INTERFACES

The principal programming modes for parallel programming involve using parallel library application programming interfaces that have bindings to sequential languages. This is the main modality that will be presented here.

3.4.1 HIGH PERFORMANCE COMPUTING PROGRAMMING LANGUAGES

Among programming languages frequently used in HPC, the most popular continue to be Fortran, C, and C++. Some other languages are growing in popularity for HPC applications, including the Python scripting language.

Fortran was developed by John Backus at IBM and first released in 1957. The name derives from the original description of the language as a formula translating system, and it is designed to be well suited for high-level programming of numerical calculations. In fact, many have described Fortran as a domain-specific language for mathematics. Subsequent standardizations followed, including Fortran 66, Fortran 77, Fortran 90, Fortran 95, Fortran 2003, and Fortran 2008.

The C language emerged in the late 1960s and early 1970s from Bell Laboratories using work by Dennis Ritchie. It was first standardized in 1989 and has gone through multiple updates, including C95, C99, and C11. In 1978 Brian Kernighan and Dennis Ritchie published one of the most influential books and tutorials on C programming, "The C Programming Language" [10], which continues to influence C programmers today.

The C++ language emerged in the early 1980s, developed by Bjarne Stroustrup. The name arises from the "++" increment operator and indicates the "evolutionary nature of the changes from C" [11]. Just as in the case for the C language, the C++ creator also wrote a highly influential book entitled "The C++ Programming Language", which has gone through multiple editions and continues to influence C++ programmers strongly. The C++ standard continues to evolve, from C++98 to C++03, C++11, and C++14.

3.4.2 PARALLEL PROGRAMMING MODALITIES

There are three main parallel programming modalities present in most clusters today: throughput computing, message passing, and shared-memory multiple-thread applications.

Throughput computing involves efficiently running a large number of jobs that may be either entirely independent of one another or require minimal communication or coordination between them. An example is conducting an application parameter survey where a single application is run with thousands of different input parameters concurrently to explore its parameter space. Throughput computing is covered in greater detail in Chapter 19.

In contrast to throughput computing, a single message-passing application requires a significant amount of communication and coordination within the application to speed up the time to solution. The principal programming model for achieving this speed up is the communicating sequential processes model, as exemplified by the MPI (Chapter 8).

Like message passing, shared-memory multiple-thread applications also focus on speeding up the time to solution for a single application rather than efficiently executing a large number of mostly independent applications, as in throughput computing. However, as the name implies, shared-memory multiple-thread applications are restricted to shared memory as opposed to distributed memory, as in the case of message passing. The shared-memory multiple-thread parallel programming modality is exemplified by the OpenMP programming model (Chapter 7).

3.5 SOFTWARE ENVIRONMENT

The software environment is a critical element of every computer's operational infrastructure. It exposes and manages functionality supported by hardware, provides different access and usage modalities for different users, manages global and local resources, and offers tools to expand the installed software base further. The latter is accomplished through utilities focusing on development, testing, optimization, configuration, performance monitoring and tuning, and trackable incorporation of new software modules into the existing code base. Below is a necessarily brief discussion of common software components composing a cluster's operational environment. A number of usage examples are also provided to help readers who have not been exposed to this class of systems before.

3.5.1 OPERATING SYSTEMS

The operating system (OS) provides the software environment and services necessary to use the computer and execute custom applications. It consists of a *kernel* that manages hardware resources and arbitrates access to them from other software layers, *system libraries* that expose a common set of programming interfaces permitting application writers to communicate with the kernel and underlying physical devices, additional system *services* performed by the background processes, and various administrator and user *utilities* that comprise programs invoked by users of the computer to accomplish specific minor tasks. The reader is likely familiar with OSs commonly found on desktop and laptop computers such as Microsoft Windows or Apple OS X. Traditionally, however, this space on "big-iron" systems was reserved to several variants of the UNIX OS—a proprietary OS developed by Bell Laboratories in 1970. Thus one could find AIX on IBM machines, HP-UX on Hewlett–Packard computers, UNICOS on Cray, IRIX on SGI, and Solaris on Oracle products, in addition to academic equivalents such as Minix and Berkeley Software Distribution (BSD and its subsequent forks, OpenBSD, NetBSD, and FreeBSD). Note that the series of Apple Mac OSs mentioned above are also a derivative of FreeBSD. Another important UNIX-like OS that has been steadily gaining in prominence over that last 2 decades is Linux. Linux is frequently employed as the OS of choice on servers and clusters, although it is also used in a broad range of mobile computing devices, for example providing the core implementation for Android OS. While successful in mobile and enterprise markets, Linux desktop penetration oscillates at around only 1%–2% depending on the statistics.

The development of the Linux kernel was started by Linus Torvalds in 1991. Since then many individual developers and companies have contributed to its source, making it a truly multiplatform product, effectively supporting an impressive number of hardware devices through the available driver pool and execution environments, ranging from small embedded devices to large multiprocessor systems. The Linux kernel is an open-source product licensed under GPLv2.

On most systems the Linux kernel is accompanied by an open-source suite of libraries and utilities primarily contributed by the GNU Project. These tools were developed and refined over the course of several decades in a massive online collaboration that originated in 1983, and include the following among many other entries.

- C library (*glibc*)
- C, C++, Fortran, and a compiler for several other languages (*gcc*)
- Debugger (*gdb*)
- Binary utilities comprising linker, assembler, symbol table tools, simple archive manager, and others (*binutils*)
- Application build system support (*make*, *autoconf*, *automake*, *libtool*)
- Command-line shell (*bash*)
- Core utilities that support low-level operations on file systems and contents of stored files (*coreutils*, *less*, *findutils*, *gawk*, *sed*, *diffutils*)
- Text editors (*emacs*, *vi*, *nano*)
- Email utilities (*mailutils*)
- Terminal emulator (*screen*)
- Archiving and compression tools (*tar*, *gzip*).

While these utilities provide a near-complete basic UNIX-like operating environment, most Linux distributions include additional open-source software packages, many of them released under a GPL license. They enable more flexible process management, bootstrap service configuration, network tools, improved email client and server programs, graphical environments (X Window System, Wayland), and desktop environments (Gnome, KDE) in addition to a plethora of other special-purpose programs. To ensure broad compatibility, most of the software conforms to the IEEE POSIX standards, effectively enabling drop-in replacement for proprietary implementations.

3.5.2 RESOURCE MANAGEMENT

Large computers employ resource management systems to coordinate accesses to multiple execution units, memory allocation, network selection, and persistent storage allocation. The number of users of even a single machine can easily reach several thousands, and each of them may potentially execute multiple applications with different properties, requirements, and run time. Manual management of every aspect of machine resource allocation by the operators is therefore prohibitive. Fortunately, several sophisticated resource management packages have been developed and are in extensive use today to automate the tasks related to distribution of user workloads across the compute nodes and monitoring the progress of their execution. One of the most widespread resource management systems is Slurm. The example commands described below may be directly used on any correctly configured system equipped with Slurm.

The resource management programs encapsulate user workloads in self-contained units, or *jobs*, that specify at the very least the program to be run, its input and output datasets, the number of nodes (or cores) to be used for its execution, and the maximum time the program is expected or required to work. These parameters are encoded in *job scripts*, which are discussed in greater detail in Chapter 5.

The user informs the system of the intended workload and its resource requirements by submitting a job script to the execution queue. This is done using the *sbatch* command:

```
sbatch job_script
```

If the script `job_script` is an existing file, this command will create a new job, append it to the default job queue, and print a confirmation similar to the following:

```
Submitted batch job 12345
```

In this output, "12345" is a unique job number assigned by the system to the job that has just been queued. The user may subsequently refer to this number to examine the job status using the *squeue* command:

```
squeue -j 12345
```

The resulting output contains among other information the name of the queue the job was stored in (PARTITION field), the name of the job (NAME), the submitting user's ID (USER), and the execution status (ST). The example output may look as follows:

```
JOBID PARTITION   NAME    USER ST    TIME NODES NODELIST(REASON)
12345    batch job_scri  user03 R    0:13     1 node01
```

In this particular case, the job was submitted to the "batch" queue by user "user03" and is already running (status "R") on one node of the cluster. Other noteworthy status flags include "CA" for canceled jobs, "CD" for completed, "F" for failed, "TO" for timed out, and "PD" for pending. The latter marks jobs that await allocation of resources to avoid conflicts with other jobs that are already executing.

A pending or running job may be at any time canceled using the command:

```
scancel 12345
```

If successful, the command does not print any confirmation after removing the job from the queue or killing the related executing application and releasing the affected nodes. Errors (for example an invalid job number given as the argument) will cause an explicit error message to be printed on the console.

3.5.3 DEBUGGER

A debugger enables the programmer to step through code in execution, place breakpoints in the code, view memory, change variables, and track variables, among other capabilities. One of the most common serial debuggers available is the gnu debugger (gdb). The gdb debugger is a command-line debugger where the user can give a series of commands to set a break point, continue execution, examine a variable, set a watch point, etc. Table 3.2 gives a few of the basic gdb commands.

To debug a code, that code must be compiled with debugging information included. For most compilers this is accomplished by adding the "-g" flag to the list of compiler flags when compiling. An example of this using the gnu debugger to alter the execution flow of a serial dot-product computation is provided in Fig. 3.4.

Debugging a parallel application on a commodity cluster introduces several complications. These are addressed in further detail in Chapter 14. A simple and straightforward way to debug a parallel application on a commodity cluster is to launch a serial (nonparallel) debugger for each process. An example is provided in Fig. 3.5.

3.5.4 PERFORMANCE PROFILING

Profiling the performance of an application on a commodity cluster can be carried out in a very similar way to debugging, by launching serial performance profilers on one or several processes. The Linux *perf* utility provides a simple interface for profiling a serial application and can be launched on a single process of a parallel application. An example of launching the serial performance profiler *perf* in conjunction with an MPI supercomputing code is given in Figs. 3.6 and 3.7. Further discussion and details of performance profiling on supercomputers are given in Chapter 13.

3.5.5 VISUALIZATION

There are many open-source and proprietary solutions for visualization of data generated in a commodity cluster. One ubiquitous command-line and script-driven solution is *gnuplot*. An example

Table 3.2 A Few Basic gnu Debugger Commands

gdb Command	Function
gdb <executable name>	Starts the gnu debugger on the specified executable
r	Starts executing the code
l	Lists the current source code where execution is paused
bt	Provides a back trace from the stack
p <variable name>	Prints the variable value
set var <var> = <value>	Sets the value of the specified variable
watch <var>	Sets watch point on specified variables
b <filename>:<line number>	Set break point at specified source code line number
c	Continue execution after pausing after a break point or some other pause
quit	Quit

```
1 #include <stdlib.h>
2 #include <stdio.h>
3
4 int main(int argc,char **argv) {
5   int i;
6   // Make the local vector size constant
7   int local_vector_size = 100;
8
9   // initialize the vectors
10  double *a, *b;
11  a = (double *) malloc(
12       local_vector_size*sizeof(double));
13  b = (double *) malloc(
14       local_vector_size*sizeof(double));
15  for (i=0;i<local_vector_size;i++) {
16    a[i] = 3.14;
17    b[i] = 6.67;
18  }
19  // compute dot product
20  double sum = 0.0;
21  for (i=0;i<local_vector_size;i++) {
22    sum += a[i]*b[i];
23  }
24  printf("The dot product is %g\n",sum);
25
26  free(a);
27  free(b);
28  return 0;
29 }
```

Launch gdb on the executable (*a.out* here):

```
andersmw@cutter:~/learn$ gdb ./a.out
```

Command line interaction with gdb:

```
Reading symbols from ./a.out...done.
(gdb) b dotprod_serial.c:17
Breakpoint 1 at 0x4005ef: file dotprod_serial.c, line 17.
(gdb) r
Starting program: /home/andersmw/learn/a.out

Breakpoint 1, main (argc=1, argv=0x7fffffffdfe8) at dotprod_serial.c:17
17            b[i] = 6.67;
(gdb) p i
$1 = 0
(gdb) l
12                local_vector_size*sizeof(double));
13          b = (double *) malloc(
14                local_vector_size*sizeof(double));
15          for (i=0;i<local_vector_size;i++) {
16            a[i] = 3.14;
17            b[i] = 6.67;
18          }
19          // compute dot product
20          double sum = 0.0;
21          for (i=0;i<local_vector_size;i++) {
(gdb) set var i=100
(gdb) c
Continuing.
The dot product is 0
[Inferior 1 (process 24118) exited normally]
(gdb)
```

FIGURE 3.4

Example usage of the gnu debugger. The left panel illustrates a simple serial dot-product computation. The right panel illustrates command-line interaction with the gnu debugger, including the setting of break points, printing variables, setting variables, and continuing execution. In the gnu debugger interaction, the loop variable in source code line 15 is reset to be 100, forcing the exit of the loop and the null dot-product result.

```
andersmw@cutter:~/learn$ mpirun -np 2 xterm -e gdb ./a.out
```

```
gdb
GNU gdb (Ubuntu 7.7.1-0ubuntu5~14.04.2) 7.7.1
Copyright (C) 2014 Free Software Foundation, Inc.
License GPLv3+: GNU GPL version 3 or later <http://gnu.org/licenses/gpl.html>
This is free software: you are free to change and redistribute it.
There is NO WARRANTY, to the extent permitted by law.  Type "show copying"
and "show warranty" for details.
This GDB was configured as "x86_64-linux-gnu".
Type "show configuration" for configuration details.
For bug reporting instructions, please see:
<http://www.gnu.org/software/gdb/bugs/>.
Find the GDB manual and other documentation resources online at:
<http://www.gnu.org/software/gdb/documentation/>.
For help, type "help".
Type "apropos word" to search for commands related to "word"...
Reading symbols from ./a.out...(no debugging symbols found)...done.
(gdb)
```

```
gdb
GNU gdb (Ubuntu 7.7.1-0ubuntu5~14.04.2) 7.7.1
Copyright (C) 2014 Free Software Foundation, Inc.
License GPLv3+: GNU GPL version 3 or later <http://gnu.org/licenses/gpl.html>
This is free software: you are free to change and redistribute it.
There is NO WARRANTY, to the extent permitted by law.  Type "show copying"
and "show warranty" for details.
This GDB was configured as "x86_64-linux-gnu".
Type "show configuration" for configuration details.
For bug reporting instructions, please see:
<http://www.gnu.org/software/gdb/bugs/>.
Find the GDB manual and other documentation resources online at:
<http://www.gnu.org/software/gdb/documentation/>.
For help, type "help".
Type "apropos word" to search for commands related to "word"...
Reading symbols from ./a.out...(no debugging symbols found)...done.
(gdb)
```

FIGURE 3.5

Using the "mpirun" command, the gnu debugger is launched for each process to enable parallel debugging. Two processes are launched here. More details on parallel debugging are given in Chapter 14.

```
andersmw@cutter:~/learn$ mpirun -np 7 ./a.out : -np 1 perf record ./a.out
The sum of the ranks is 28
[ perf record: Woken up 1 times to write data ]
[ perf record: Captured and wrote 0.034 MB perf.data (~1474 samples) ]
```

FIGURE 3.6

In this example, a parallel application is run on eight cores where the serial Linux performance counter tool, perf, is run on the application (called a.out here) in just one of those cores. The perf utility is given the instruction to "record" the events in this example for postprocessing. Postprocessing is shown in Fig. 3.7.

```
Samples: 125  of event 'cycles', Event count (approx.): 68985441
Overhead  Command  Shared Object           Symbol
   5.76%  a.out    ld-2.19.so              [.] do_lookup_x
   5.13%  a.out    ld-2.19.so              [.] _dl_lookup_symbol_x
   4.16%  a.out    libc-2.19.so            [.] memset
   4.07%  a.out    [kernel.kallsyms]       [k] perf_event_aux_ctx
   3.20%  a.out    libc-2.19.so            [.] __strncmp_sse2
   2.87%  a.out    [kernel.kallsyms]       [k] __d_lookup_rcu
   2.87%  a.out    [kernel.kallsyms]       [k] clear_page_c
   2.79%  a.out    [kernel.kallsyms]       [k] native_write_msr_safe
   2.63%  a.out    [kernel.kallsyms]       [k] format_decode
   2.58%  a.out    [kernel.kallsyms]       [k] shmem_getpage_gfp
   2.52%  a.out    [kernel.kallsyms]       [k] __rmqueue
   2.42%  a.out    libopen-pal.so.13       [.] opal_memory_ptmalloc2_malloc
   2.35%  a.out    libc-2.19.so            [.] vfprintf
   2.31%  a.out    libc-2.19.so            [.] malloc
```

FIGURE 3.7

The postprocessing of the results from the serial performance record in Fig. 3.3 originating from a parallel execution is reported using the "perf report" command.

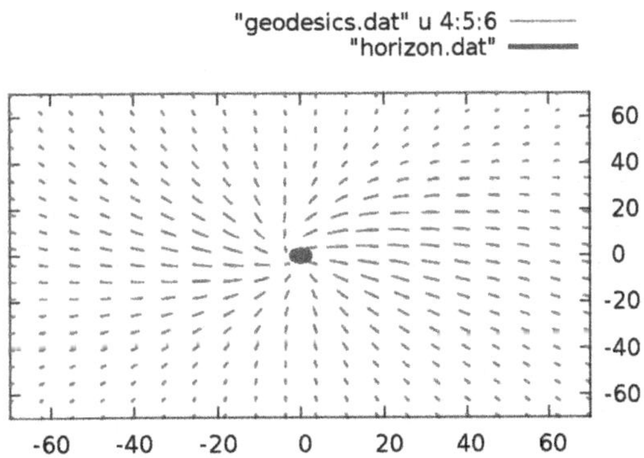

FIGURE 3.8

Visualization of the bending of light around a spinning black hole using gnuplot.

```
# To run this file, type: gnuplot -persist plot.gnu
sp[-70:70][-70:70][-50:50] "geodesics.dat" u 4:5:6 w lines
unset ztics
set style line 1 lt 1 lw 3 pt 3 linecolor rgb "blue"
replot "horizon.dat" with lines ls 1
# bottom
set view 0,0
replot
```

FIGURE 3.9

Script to generate Fig. 3.8. The fourth, fifth, and sixth columns of the file "geodesics.dat" are used to plot the light rays; the spinning black hole horizon is added to the figure from the "horizon.dat" file. These data files are available for download at the textbook website.

of *gnuplot* visualization is provided in Figs. 3.8 and 3.9. Visualization is covered in greater detail in Chapter 12.

3.6 BASIC METHODS OF USE

3.6.1 LOGGING ON

Some readers may already be familiar with the login procedure on common desktop machines. It typically requires providing the user identifier (or clicking on a corresponding icon) and typing a correct password to verify that the person attempting to log on is the same as the one who set up the password. Unfortunately, this method requires direct proximity to the target computer, which is not practical with systems hosting thousands of users or located far away. Hence the login has to be performed over the network utilizing a computer local to the user to act as a connection client. Most supercomputers provide the Secure Shell (SSH) managed logins, which require that an SSH client is installed on the user's machine. Secure connections are preferred, as they thwart most eavesdropping attempts by using strong encryption of all communications, including login information and passwords. Most UNIX-like computers are typically configured to include the SSH program used for this purpose, and on Windows one can install the popular PuTTY package to achieve the same goal. While PuTTY provides a dialog window that manages the login procedure, a login sequence using a command prompt in a terminal window or console is described below. For those unfamiliar with UNIX systems, launching the program called *xterm* is recommended to get the command prompt. Depending on the system, there may be other graphical terminal emulators available, such as *gnome-terminal*, *konsole*, or *urxvt*. If using a console directly (and after a successful login to the local computer), secure communication with a target computer is achieved after typing at the command prompt:

```
ssh -l user03 cluster.hostname.edu
```

In this example the SSH client connects to the account of `user03` on the login node `cluster.hostname.edu`. Note that the user ID refers to the user's login name on the *target* machine, here identified as `cluster.hostname.edu`, and not the one on which SSH was invoked. After the connection is established, the SSH client prints a password prompt on the client machine and the user should supply the account password, again for the target machine. Alternatively, the above command may be invoked as:

```
ssh user03@cluster.hostname.edu
```

If the password is accepted, SSH will respond with the remote machine command prompt in the local terminal. Arbitrary commands may be entered at this prompt and executed in the same way as if they were invoked directly on the remote machine. To finish the interactive session on the remote computer and return to the local shell prompt, it is necessary to type `exit` or simultaneously press Control and D keys.

Another utility, *scp*, is a close companion to SSH and often installed with it. It enables secure transfer of files between the local and remote computers. For example:

```
scp ./myfile user03@cluster.hostname.edu:
```

This copies the local file `myfile` from the current working directory on the local machine to the home directory on the `cluster.hostname.edu` host. Note that the colon following the remote host name is required to inform the *scp* that the second argument is a host and not a file name. Transfer of directories is accomplished by specifying the `-r` option:

```
scp -r user03@cluster.hostname.edu:/tmp/user03/dir
```

This command copies the directory `/tmp/user03/dir` with all its contents to the current working directory on the local machine. An absolute path was specified for the source directory, but only its last component, `dir`, will be created and populated on the local machine.

3.6.2 USER SPACE AND DIRECTORY SYSTEM

Persistent information in a computer has to be stored in a secondary storage system (such as a disk or SSD), since the contents of RAM are volatile. *File systems* organize this information into hierarchical name spaces, where each chunk of data can be properly named and attributed for access. The individual datasets and program executables are stored in *files*. Which parts of the data belong in each file and how to subdivide the computational datasets into files is at the discretion of the user. Each file in a file system has a unique name by which it can be accessed by executing programs. Files are stored in logical containers called *directories*; a directory may also include other directories, permitting building of tree-like structures with arbitrary depth. Like files, directories also have unique names. UNIX-like systems use single-rooted name spaces for all file systems in current use.

A *path* describes a file or directory identifier that is sufficient to locate it in the file system hierarchy. Path components, from left to right, name the subsequent containing directories in descending order (from the root downwards). The last component of a path identifies the target file or directory in its immediate containing unit. In UNIX (and therefore Linux), path components are separated by forward slashes ("/"), hence the individual directory or file names should not contain forward slashes to avoid confusion. By convention, "/" denotes the topmost directory in a file system, referred to as the "root". "/tmp/myfile" identifies a file called "myfile" stored in a directory called "tmp", one level below the root. The typical location of files owned by a specific user on most machines is in the directory "/home/*user*", where "*user*" is substituted with the login ID of that user. The users are free to create their own subtrees of directories and files in these locations. While the exact details of name space taxonomy may vary from system to system, in Linux they are regulated by an informal specification, Filesystem Hierarchy Standard (FHS) [12], maintained by the Linux Foundation. It defines the typical layout as containing the following directories.

- "/bin" contains critical executables that may be used during system boot
- "/sbin" contains critical system executables that may be used during system boot
- "/lib" includes libraries for the essential executables in "/bin" and "/sbin"
- "/usr" is a root of secondary hierarchy containing mostly read-only data. Notable subdirectories of "/usr" include the following.
  - "/usr/bin" contains nonessential executables, typically system-wide application binaries.
  - "/usr/sbin" contains nonessential system executables such as auxiliary services and daemons.
  - "/usr/lib" holds libraries used by executables in "/usr/bin" and "/usr/sbin".
  - "/usr/include" contains "include" files (headers) used by compilers.
  - "/usr/share" includes shared, architecture-independent data frequently associated with the installed systemwide applications.
  - "/usr/local" stores local, host-dependent data. It has additional subdirectories similar to those of "/usr", such as "bin", "include", "lib", and others.
- "/home" hosts individual user subdirectories with their own settings, configuration files, and custom user datasets.
- "/tmp" is a systemwide store for temporary data that is cleaned after every reboot. While on desktop machines its capacity may be limited, on cluster computing nodes with dedicated storage it is often configured to provide a sizable scratch space with its own data retention policy.
- "/dev" keeps entries representing physical and logical devices under the control of the OS. These entries are not regular files, and special care should be exercised when accessing them.
- "/etc" stores host-specific configuration files.
- "/var" contains logs, spools, email, temporary files, and other variable datasets.
- "/root" provides a dedicated home directory for the superuser (administrator).
- "/opt" is used to store optional packages, frequently third-party proprietary or licensed software.
- "/mnt" contains temporarily mounted file systems.
- "/media" includes mount points for external removable storage media such as USB drives (including flash), e-SATA drives, and CD- or DVD-ROMS.
- "/proc" and "/sys" are pseudo-file systems (not backed up by physical storage devices) providing runtime process data, memory allocation, I/O statistics, performance information, and device configuration and status. These file systems are frequently used by monitoring programs and scripts to obtain access from user space to certain types of information maintained by the OS kernel.

Unlike some other OSs, UNIX-compatible systems do not introduce distinct directory hierarchies for each storage device. Instead, the contents of a file system associated with a specific device are *mounted* under some predefined directory (called a *mount point*). The location of that directory in the hierarchy may be arbitrary, and is typically preselected by the system administrator or a suitable device access daemon. This offers the benefit of being potentially able to reach any of the files and directories available in the entire node by performing a recursive traversal of the hierarchy starting from its root. To examine the currently mounted file systems, the user may issue the "disk free" command:

```
df -h
```

The example output may look as follows:

```
Filesystem               Size  Used Avail Use% Mounted on
udev                      16G   12K   16G   1% /dev
tmpfs                    3.2G  1.7M  3.2G   1% /run
/dev/sda2                235G  146G   78G  66% /
none                     4.0K     0  4.0K   0% /sys/fs/cgroup
none                     5.0M     0  5.0M   0% /run/lock
none                      16G  3.3G   13G  21% /run/shm
none                     100M     0  100M   0% /run/user
/dev/sda1                290M  175M   96M  65% /boot
/dev/mapper/vg0-home     6.8T  4.6T  1.9T  72% /home
```

The devices representing individual component file systems are listed in the leftmost column and the corresponding mount points in the rightmost column. The command also presents the actual size of storage devices suffixed with a proper unit ("K" for kilobytes, "M" for megabytes, "G" for gigabytes, and "T" for terabytes). For users generating a lot of data, "Avail" and "Use%" columns are of particular interest, as they show how much free space is remaining on each device.

To list the contents of any directory an *ls* command is used. If invoked without any options, it will simply print the names of all files in the *current working directory* in several columns. It is far more useful to see various attributes of files, such as their sizes, access permissions, modification time-stamps, and so on. For example:

```
ls -halF /some/path
```

This command is going to output information about all files and directories contained in "/some/path" directory, or, if "/some/path" is a file, only about that file. The output data produced with the "long" ("-l") option shows the file ownership (user and group), its size, the last modification date and time, and file name. Other options add useful features: "-a" will list "hidden" entries (all items whose names start with a period "."); "-h" converts numbers to "human-readable" format with suffixes instead of printing size data in bytes; and "-F" appends a symbol after each name indicating the type of entry. Thus directory entries will end in "/" and executable files in "*". The *ls* command offers many more useful options; to see what they do one can access the relevant manual page by typing

```
man ls
```

Of course, the *man* command can also display information about other commands available in the system. Exploration is strongly encouraged!

To navigate the directory hierarchy, one of the most useful commands is "change directory". For example, typing:

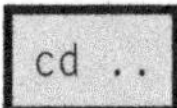

at the prompt will move the shell context to the closest encompassing directory. The double dot notation is a special shortcut to denote the parent directory; similarly, single dot (".") has a special meaning indicating the current directory. This notation introduces another important concept, namely that of *relative* paths. So far, all examples have used paths that begin at the root (the first character is "/"). To reach the final component of such a path, called the *absolute* path, the system needs to start at the root and traverse all component subdirectories. However, it is frequently more convenient (and on occasion faster) to indicate the target location relative to the current working directory. Thus specifying "../tmp/some_file" while located in "/usr" directory would effectively refer to a file described by an equivalent absolute path "/tmp/some_file". To verify that the directory change performed by the last command actually happened, a "print working directory" command may be called:

If the previous command was invoked in the user's home directory, the result of the last command will likely be "/home". Another useful path shortcut is a tilde ("~"), which expands to the user's home directory. Hence executing the following will change the working directory to the parent directory of the user's home independent of where it is invoked:

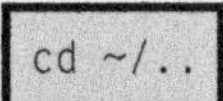

Both files and directories can be added to and removed from the hierarchy at will. To create a new directory, a "make directory" command is issued:

```
mkdir /tmp/user13
```

This will create an empty "user13" subdirectory in the systemwide temporary data directory. Since it is owned by the creating user, it may subsequently be used to store arbitrary data attributed to that user. Very few system directories delineated by FHS have this property; typically creation of new entries in system directories by regular users will be denied (for good reasons!) due to insufficient access rights. Note that creating directories with paths containing multiple components that do not exist yet requires a "-p" option (for "parents"). Removal of files and directories is achieved with "remove" or the *rm* command. Thus:

```
rm -r ~/my_jobs
```

deletes the "my_jobs" subdirectory from the user's home. While removing files does not require any special options, for directories one needs to specify "-r" (meaning "recursive") to scan for and eliminate all the contents within the directory. Since the *rm* command is frequently configured with a fail-safe interactive mode that requires the user to confirm deletion of every entry, this is often impractical for subdirectories containing thousands of files. For that reason a "-f" or "force" option may be specified to suppress any confirmation prompts.

Note that *rm –fr* is one the most dangerous commands on UNIX systems. Since there is no undelete functionality integrated with most file systems, all deleted files and directories are usually irretrievably lost.

Another useful set of commands performs moving, renaming, and copying of file system entries. To relocate a file or directory to another location, a "move" command is used, with the first argument being the source path and the second being the destination path:

```
mv /tmp/user13/src ~/dst
```

Interestingly, the outcome of this command depends on whether "dst" exists and is a file or directory. If it is a directory, "src" will be removed from the "/tmp/user13" directory and stored in the "dst" directory (this works independently of the original "src" being a file or directory). If both "src" and "dest" are files, "src" will be removed from "/tmp/user13" and stored in the user's home under a new name, "dst". Since this operation also destroys the original contents of the file "dst", *mv* typically will ask the user to confirm the operation. If "src" is a directory but "dst" is a file, the command unconditionally fails (one cannot move a directory into a file). Finally, if there is no object named "dst" in the home directory, the operation removes the original entry from "/tmp/user13" and stores it in the user's home renamed as "dst". Since no preexisting files are overwritten, *mv* does not issue confirmation prompts in this case. As can be seen, the *mv* command is quite multifaceted in that it combines the semantics of relocating the objects in the file system hierarchy, object deletion, and object name modification.

Most of the remarks described for move can be applied for the copy command, or *cp*. There are two crucial differences: *cp* does not remove the original entry referenced by the source path, and the explicit "-r" option has to be specified for all operations in which the source path is a directory. Thus

```
cp -r ~/data/set5 .
```

replicates "set5" directory in the current working directory, leaving the source directory intact.

While this guide introduces some of the most essential file system operations, the world of POSIX commands has much more to offer. Listed below are other commonly available commands suggested for further exploration that can be carried out by consulting the related manual pages (using the *man* command) in a working system:

- *cat* concatenates the contents of multiple files, but is also useful for printing their contents
- *less* permits browsing the contents of text files, scrolling line by line or page by page, or advancing directly to points requested by the user
- *chmod* changes the access permission flags for a file or directory
- *chown* changes the file ownership (user and group)
- *ln* creates a link (named reference) to a file system object
- *du* computes the total storage usage by a specific file or directory
- *touch* updates the file timestamp or creates an empty file
- *head* prints out the starting lines of a file
- *tail* prints out the final lines in a file
- *wc* computes the count of characters, words, and lines
- *file* guesses the file format based on its contents (not extension)
- *find* searches for specific files and directories
- *grep* searches for patterns and phrases in files
- *uname* prints out brief information about the system in use
- *ps* lists processes in the system
- *top* ranks the processes in order of resource usage
- *kill* sends signals to processes, in particular allowing their termination
- *bash* is the primary shell on most systems.

The suggested topics to master include I/O redirection, pipelines, globing, command aliasing, user environment initialization, variable expansion, job control, and basics of scripting.

3.6.3 PACKAGE CONFIGURATION AND BUILDING

The source code of most software packages is distributed in the form of so-called *tar archives*. *tar* is a utility to create, examine, and unpack the contents of these archives. They retain the original directory layout and file contents of the package-build directory and include the configuration data required to build the binaries on another platform. In addition, the archives may be compressed to save storage space. The following command lists the contents of the archive "package.tgz":

```
tar tvf package.tgz
```

The archives may use different extensions depending on the used compression algorithm. Thus ".tar" indicates an uncompressed archive, files ending in ".tgz" and ".tar.gz" were prepared using *gzip* compression, while ".tbz2" and ".tar.bz2" are the result of applying the *bzip2* tool. Other compression formats are also possible. Recent versions of *tar* are capable of recognizing the compression algorithm automatically and do not require specific command-line options for that purpose. The archive is unpacked by invoking:

```
tar xf package.tgz
```

Typically the command will create a subdirectory tree in the current working directory containing the package source files and configuration scripts. There may also be README and INSTALL files providing additional configuration and installation instructions. Before initiating the build process, it is worth examining various configuration options to customize the features of created executables and libraries properly. After changing the working directory to the top directory of the unpacked archive contents, it may be done with:

```
./configure --help
```

Most commonly, options like "–prefix" that determines the final installation directory, "–with-mpi" that includes MPI support, and "–with-omp" that enables OpenMP-based multithreading are of interest. The final configuration may be then generated as:

```
./configure --prefix=/home/user13/some_package
```

The last command creates the necessary *makefiles*, which are files that contain various definitions, rules, and commands required to execute the build process successfully. Makefiles are utilized by the *make* utility, which optimizes the build process by only executing commands for which the dependencies are newer than the build target. Default makefile names include "makefile", "Makefile", and "GNUmakefile", although the last should be used only for build scripts that contain GNU-specific extensions. To start the build process, one needs to issue:

```
make -j9
```

While the *make* command alone would suffice, the "-j" option initiates a much faster parallel build using multiple processors in the system. The commonly applied rule of thumb suggests passing it an argument that equals the number of available cores plus one, thus the above command should work well on eight-core platforms. The final step when preparing new packages for use is installation of the generated programs, libraries, and data to the target directory. This is accomplished through:

```
make install
```

3.6.4 COMPILERS AND COMPILING

Cluster supercomputers provide several suites of compilers and debugging tools to support the diverse user community using the cluster. The individual user environments are most frequently customized using a module system. Using modules, the compilers and relevant environment paths can be changed in a dynamic way transparent to the user. A list of the most common module commands is given in Table 3.3. An example of module usage on a Cray XE6 is provided in Fig. 3.10.

With the specific compiler flavor and version controlled by loading modules, compiling a source code usually translates into invoking a compiler wrapper and supplying compiler flags along with the

Table 3.3 A List of Commonly Uses Module Commands for Dynamically Controlling the User's Software Environment

Module Command	Description
module load [module name]	Loads the specified module
module unload [module name]	Unloads the specified module
module list	Lists the modules already loaded in the user environment
module avail <string>	Lists the available modules that can be loaded; if a string is provided, only those modules starting with that string are listed
module swap [module 1] [module 2]	Swaps out module 1 for module 2

An example of some usage of these commands is shown in Fig. 3.10. Brackets indicate required arguments, while angle brackets indicate optional arguments.

```
hpstrn01@login1:/N/dc2/scratch/hpstrn01> module list
Currently Loaded Modulefiles:
  1) modules/3.2.10.3                          13) gni-headers/4.0-1.0502.10859.7.8.gem
  2) eswrap/1.1.0-1.020200.1231.0              14) xpmem/0.1-2.0502.64982.5.3.gem
  3) craype-network-gemini                     15) dvs/2.5_0.9.0-1.0502.2188.1.113.gem
  4) cce/8.4.6                                 16) alps/5.2.4-2.0502.9774.31.12.gem
  5) craype/2.4.2                              17) rca/1.0.0-2.0502.60530.1.63.gem
  6) totalview-support/1.2.0.2                 18) atp/1.8.3
  7) totalview/8.14.0                          19) PrgEnv-cray/5.2.82
  8) cray-libsci/13.2.0                        20) craype-interlagos
  9) udreg/2.3.2-1.0502.10518.2.17.gem         21) cray-mpich/7.2.6
 10) ugni/6.0-1.0502.10863.8.28.gem            22) moab/8.0.1
 11) pmi/5.0.10-1.0000.11050.179.3.gem         23) torque/5.0.1
 12) dmapp/7.0.1-1.0502.11080.8.74.gem
hpstrn01@login1:/N/dc2/scratch/hpstrn01> module avail PrgEnv

----------------------------------- /opt/cray/modulefiles ------------------------
PrgEnv-cray/5.2.82(default)  PrgEnv-intel/5.2.82(default)
PrgEnv-gnu/5.2.82(default)   PrgEnv-pgi/5.2.82(default)
hpstrn01@login1:/N/dc2/scratch/hpstrn01> module swap PrgEnv-cray PrgEnv-gnu
hpstrn01@login1:/N/dc2/scratch/hpstrn01> █
```

FIGURE 3.10

An example of using modules to control a user's software environment dynamically. The first command, module list, lists the modules already loaded. The second command lists the modules available for loading, which begin with the string "PrgEnv". The last command swaps out the Cray programming environment for the GNU programming environment.

source code in the same way as is done when compiling a serial (nonparallel) application. In cluster environments, the C compiler wrapper for applications using the MPI (see Chapter 8) is most frequently called *mpicc*.

3.6.5 RUNNING APPLICATIONS

After accessing compute nodes from the resource management system, as summarized in Section 3.5.2 and detailed in Chapter 5, the user can launch a parallel application on the compute nodes using a shell script to start the computation if using an application in a distributed memory context. In the case of using the MPI, this shell script is most often called *mpirun*. The most important argument it takes is the flag specifying the number of processes to launch, usually given by *−n* <# of processes>. Other options and flags associated with the *mpirun* script can be found by passing to the script the help flag, *-h*. In the case of launching a shared memory application with OpenMP (see Chapter 7), no shell script is needed to start the application.

3.7 SUMMARY AND OUTCOMES OF CHAPTER 3

- A commodity cluster is a group of integrated computer systems. The component computers are standalone, capable of independent operation, and marketed to a much broader consumer base than the scaled clusters which they comprise. The integration network employed is separately developed and marketed to be used by a systems integrator.
- A commodity cluster is constructed from a set of processing nodes, one or more interconnection networks that integrate the nodes, and secondary storage.
- A node of a cluster contains all the components required to serve as a standalone computer.
- Commodity clusters benefit from high performance relative to cost due to the economy of scale achieved by mass production.
- A node incorporates one or more processor cores and sockets, main memory banks, a motherboard controller, an onboard network connecting all the components, external I/O interfaces including an NIC to the SAN, possibly one or more disk drives for nonvolatile storage of data, user program code, and system libraries.
- The principal programming modes for parallel programming involve using parallel library application programming interfaces that have bindings to sequential languages.
- The OS provides the software environment and services necessary to use the computer and execute custom applications. It consists of a *kernel* that manages hardware resources and arbitrates access to them from other software layers, *system libraries* that expose a common set of programming interfaces permitting the application writers to communicate with the kernel and underlying physical devices, additional system *services* performed by the background processes, and various administrator and user *utilities* that comprise programs invoked by users of the computer to accomplish specific minor tasks.
- Large computers employ resource management systems to coordinate accesses to multiple execution units, memory allocation, network selection, and persistent storage allocation.
- A debugger enables the programmer to step through code in execution, place break points in the code, view memory, change variables, and track variables.

- A simple and straightforward way to debug a parallel application on a commodity cluster is to launch a serial (nonparallel) debugger for each process.
- Persistent information in a computer has to be stored in a secondary storage system (such as a disk or SSD), since the contents of RAM are volatile. *File systems* organize this information into hierarchical name spaces, where each chunk of data can be properly named and attributed for access.
- Cluster supercomputers provide several suites of compilers and debugging tools to support the diverse community using the cluster. The individual user environments are most frequently customized using the module system.

3.8 QUESTIONS AND EXERCISES

1. What are the four principal components of a commodity cluster? Describe their functions.
2. Name the required and optional hardware components of a cluster node and describe their properties. Which of them would be more suitable for installation in a compute node and which in a host node? What would be their preferred traits and parameters in each of these environments?
3. Expand and explain the COTS acronym. What is the role of COTS components in a commodity cluster?
4. Contrast a commodity cluster and NOW. What are the drawbacks and benefits of each?
5. List elements of the software environment critical to cluster operation. Which of these components directly involve interaction with the user?
6. What are the steps required to develop and execute a custom application on a cluster?
7. Describe two primary named entities supported by file systems. Why is maintaining consistent organization of file system hierarchy such as the one suggested by FHS important to daily operation of a computing center?

REFERENCES

[1] M. Baker, R. Buyya, Cluster computing: the commodity supercomputer, Software – Practice and Experience 29 (6) (1999) 551–576.

[2] USB-IF, Universal Serial Bus Revision 3.1 Specification, Revision 1.0, July 26, 2013 [Online]. Available: http://www.usb.org/developers/docs/usb_31_061917.zip.

[3] PCI Special Interest Group, PCI-Express Base Specification Revision 3.1a, December 7, 2015 [Online]. Available: http://pcisig.com/specifications/pciexpress/.

[4] R.M. Metcalfe, D.R. Boggs, Ethernet: distributed packet switching for local computer networks, Communications of the ACM 19 (7) (1976) 395–404.

[5] F. Faggin, M.E. Hoff, S. Mazor, M. Shima, The history of the 4004, IEEE Micro 16 (6) (1996) 10–20.

[6] C.A.R. Hoare, Communicating sequential processes, Communications of the ACM 21 (8) (1978) 666–677.

[7] MPICH: High-Performance Portable MPI, [Online], 2017. Available: https://www.mpich.org.

[8] T.L. Sterling, J. Salmon, D.J. Becker, D.F. Savarese, How to Build a Beowulf, MIT Press, 1999.

[9] W. Gropp, E. Lusk, T. Sterling, Beowulf Cluster Computing with Linux, second ed., MIT Press, 2003.

[10] B.W. Kernighan, D.M. Ritchie, The C Programming Language, Prentice Hall, 1978.

[11] B. Stroustrup, The C++ Programming Language, fourth ed., Addison-Wesley, 2013.

[12] The Linux Foundation, Filesystem Hierarchy Standard (FHS), July 19, 2016 [Online]. Available: https://wiki.linuxfoundation.org/lsb/fhs.

CHAPTER

BENCHMARKING

4

CHAPTER OUTLINE

4.1 INTRODUCTION

Benchmarking efforts for evaluating the performance of a computer have been ongoing since the beginning of the age of general-purpose computers. The nature of those benchmarks has generally reflected the intended purpose for which the computer was built, while also providing an empirical performance measure that can be compared against the manufacturer's theoretical performance estimate. In the case of the first general-purpose electronic computer, the electronic numerical integrator and computer (ENIAC) (1946) [1], the *de facto* performance benchmark was computing an artillery trajectory and comparing the time to solution against a human computing the same trajectory. Modern supercomputers employ a wide variety of benchmarks, ranging from linear algebra to graph applications, reflecting the diversity of users on modern systems. Just as in the case of the artillery trajectory calculation on the ENIAC, however, user applications are also used on modern supercomputers as *de facto* benchmarks even though they are generally not standardized nor qualified for generic use as a benchmark.

One of the earliest general-purpose benchmarks for evaluating computer performance was the Whetstone [2], named after Whetstone village in Leicestershire, England, where the Whetstone compiler was developed. This benchmark, first released in 1972, consisted of multiple programs that

High Performance Computing. https://doi.org/10.1016/B978-0-12-420158-3.00004-6

JACK DONGARRA AND THE LINPACK BENCHMARK

Photo by the University of Tennessee, Knoxville via Wikimedia Commons

Jack Dongarra is one of the most prolific academic researchers, contributing practical advances to high performance computing (HPC) applications, algorithms, and tools over a period of 4 decades. With a principal focus on the central problem of linear algebra critical to many important applications, Dongarra has advanced methods and libraries for effective, efficient, and scalable use of HPC. In so doing he has contributed significantly and provided leadership for such open-source libraries as basic linear algebra subprograms (BLAS), Linpack, Lapack, and ScaLapack among others. From this work came the most widely recognized computing benchmark, highly parallel Linpack (HPL), as a derivative of the earlier Linpack. HPL is the metric by which the Top 500 list of the last 25 years has been measured, essentially defining progress in the field of HPC. Dongarra's more recent work on the high performance conjugate gradients (HPCG) benchmark (conjugate gradient) provided another powerful means to explore the capabilities of emerging HPC systems, stressing more aspects of their architectural properties. Jack is the founding director of the Innovative Computing Laboratory at the University of Tennessee at Knoxville, a Distinguished Research Staff at the Department of Energy Oak Ridge National Laboratory, and a member of the National Academy of Engineering.

created synthetic workloads for evaluating kilo Whetstone instructions per second. In 1980 it was updated to report floating-point operations per second (flops). While this was a serial benchmark not specifically designed for supercomputing systems, it became an industry standard and was used to evaluate the performance of the microprocessors being used in some supercomputers.

In 1984 a benchmark with a standardized synthetic computing workload, named Dhrystone, was released. This benchmark became an industry standard for measuring integer performance. Its name reflects its function as the counterpart to the Whetstone benchmark, but intended for integer performance rather than floating-point performance. Like Whetstone, Dhrystone was not created as a supercomputing benchmark but has been used for evaluating microprocessor components of supercomputers. Dhrystone has since been superseded by the SPECint suite [3].

The genesis of one of the most widely used benchmarks in supercomputing is the Linpack benchmark introduced by Jack Dongarra in 1979 and based on the Linpack linear algebra package developed by Dongarra, Jim Bunch, Cleve Moler, and Gilbert Stewart [4]. While the Linpack linear algebra package has since been superseded by the Lapack library [5] and other competitors, the Linpack benchmark continues to exert a strong influence in the field. It provides an estimate of the system's effective floating-point performance. Beginning in 1979, results from the Linpack benchmark on various systems have been collected by Dongarra. This list started with just 23 computer systems and ultimately grew to include hundreds.

The Linpack benchmark employs a workload that solves a dense system of linear equations. That is, it solves for x in

$$Ax = b \tag{4.1}$$

where b and x are vectors of length n and A is an $n \times n$ matrix with very few or no zero elements. The original Linpack benchmark solved matrices with $n = 100$ and was written for serial computation. No changes to the source code were allowed; only optimizations achieved through compiler flags were permitted. A second iteration of the benchmark used matrices with $n = 1000$ and allowed user modifications to the factorization and solver portions of the code. An accuracy bound on the final solution was also introduced. The third iteration of the benchmark, HPL, allows variations in both problem size and software and can run on a distributed-memory supercomputer. This version of the benchmark is used to generate the Top 500 list that is frequently used to rank supercomputers around the world. Section 4.3.1 discusses HPL in greater detail.

Today there are a wide variety of general-purpose benchmarks used for evaluating the performance of supercomputers and supercomputing elements. These benchmarks often originate from a specific application domain with a workload motivated by that application class rather than from a synthetic workload to achieve better relevance with respect to actual user applications. Table 4.1 provides a brief summary of some of the benchmarks available for HPC users, along with their motivating application domain and characteristics. Some of the most highly used benchmarks come in suites containing multiple individual benchmarks. Two widely used versions are the HPC Challenge suite [6] consisting of seven individual benchmarks (including HPL), and the NAS parallel benchmarks [7] (NPB) consisting of 19 benchmark specifications and reference implementations. These suites are discussed further in Sections 4.5 and 4.7 respectively.

4.2 KEY PROPERTIES OF AN HPC BENCHMARK

HPC benchmarks fulfill several important roles in the HPC community. Benchmarks are frequently used to help decide the size and type of a supercomputer that an institution procures. In this role, many different benchmarks may be used to assess if a candidate supercomputer will adequately address the needs of its users. In a similar role, benchmarks are often called upon to estimate the performance of certain user applications at processor scales and dataset sizes much larger than those available to the user. Benchmarks also help identify and quantify performance upper bounds and limitations for specific application algorithms. For emerging technologies, benchmarks play a key role in comparing performance between conventional practice and a new technology using the same workloads. On many supercomputing systems, benchmarks provide performance milestones against which users can compare their specific application performance and make assessments about the efficiency of their application. Benchmark results form an important historical record for exploring trends in HPC. Finally, benchmarks play an important role in quantifying what percentage of the theoretical peak performance a supercomputer can achieve.

Good benchmarks share several key properties. First, they are relevant and meaningful to the target application domain. Second, they are applicable to a broad spectrum of hardware architectures. Third, they are adopted both by users and vendors and enable comparative evaluation.

Table 4.1 Brief Summary of Some Benchmarks Used in the HPC Community

Benchmark	Application Domain Workload	Aim	Parallelism	Characteristics
HPL	Dense linear algebra	Estimate system's effective flops	MPI (message passing interface)	Part of HPC Challenge suite; used for Top 500 list
STREAM	Synthetic	Estimate sustainable memory bandwidth (GB/s)	None	Part of HPC Challenge suite
RandomAccess	Synthetic	Estimate system's effective rate of integer random updates of memory, reported as giga updates per second (GUPS)	MPI, OpenMP	Part of HPC Challenge suite
HPCG	Sparse linear algebra	Estimate system's effective flops for those applications poorly represented by HPL	MPI + OpenMP	Used for HPCG list ranking
SPEC CPU 2006	Various	Estimate system's effective processor, memory, and compiler performance	None	Commercial
High performance geometric multigrid (HPGMG)	Geometric multigrid	Estimate system's effective evaluation of number of degrees of freedom per second (DOFS)	MPI + OpenMP + CUDA	Used for HPGMG list ranking Comes in two flavors: finite element and finite volume
IS	Computational fluid dynamics	Estimate system's effective integer sort and random access performance	MPI, OpenMP	Part of NPBs
Graph500	Data-intensive applications	Estimate system's effective traversed edges per second (TEPS) for a graph traversal	MPI, OpenMP	Used for Graph500 list ranking

Some other *de facto* properties of successful HPC benchmarks are worth noting. One is that most HPC benchmarks are short. Table 4.2 gives the line count for each of the nonproprietary benchmarks summarized in Table 4.1. While many HPC user applications regularly exceed 100,000 lines of source code, the benchmarks used for evaluating supercomputing resources are generally much smaller.

Table 4.2 Approximate Line Count, Parallelism Application Programming Interface (API), and Language for the Nonproprietary Benchmarks in Table 4.1

	Approximate	Parallelism		Language	
Benchmark	**Line Count**	**MPI**	**OpenMP**	**C**	**C++**
HPL	26,700	X		X	
STREAM	1500			X	
RandomAccess	5800	X	X	X	
HPCG	5700	X	X		X
IS	1150	X	X	X	
Graph500	1900	X	X	X	
HPGMG	5000	X	X	X	

HPC benchmarks in general specify guidelines about how the benchmark may be run and optimized. Similarly, the results from the benchmark can be archived and shared. Among the benchmarks in Table 4.2, there are four maintained supercomputer ranking lists associated with four benchmarks: HPL [8], HPCG [9], HPGMG [10], and Graph500 [11]. The top supercomputer on each of the lists in June 2017 is provided in Table 4.3.

In addition to providing guidelines for execution, optimization, and result reporting, HPC benchmarks generally use standard parallel programming APIs such as OpenMP and message passing

Table 4.3 The Top-Performing Supercomputer in June 2017 for Each of the Four Benchmarks

Benchmark	Supercomputer	Location	Performance Result	Cores
HPL	Sunway TaihuLight	Jiangsu, China	93.0 petaflops	10,649,600
HPGC	K computer	Kobe, Japan	0.6027 petaflops	705,024
Graph500	K computer	Kobe, Japan	38621.4 GTEPS	705,024
HPGMG	Cori	Berkeley, CA, USA	859 gigaDOFS	632,400

The rank of each supercomputer cross-listed on each list is shown in Table 4.4.

Table 4.4 Ranking of the Top-Performing Supercomputers in June 2017 for Each of the Maintained Ranking Lists

Supercomputer	Top 500 List Ranking	Graph500 List Ranking	HPCG Ranking	HPGMG Ranking
Sunway Taihu Light	1	2	3	2
Tianhe-2	2	8	2	
K computer	8	1	1	
Cori	6		6	1

interface (MPI) (discussed in Chapters 7 and 8, respectively). They also enable the use of different dataset sizes as part of the optimization. For example, the fastest-performing supercomputer for the Graph500 benchmark in June 2016, the K computer in Kobe, Japan, used a graph problem size that was smaller than the third-fastest machine in the list even while they benchmarked against the same type of workload. For HPC benchmarks in general, while the type of workload may be the same within a list of benchmark results, the size of that workload may differ considerably.

One of the most important properties of an HPC benchmark is that its workload should represent some appropriate set of real supercomputer application workloads. This is often one of the most difficult properties for a benchmark, and the performance impact of the type of workload can be significant. The HPCG benchmark mentioned in Tables 4.1–4.4 is intended to complement the HPL benchmark by exploring workloads with data access patterns not exhibited by HPL. The difference between the peak performance of these two types of workloads can be seen in Table 4.3. The fastest HPCG performance is typically less than 1% of the fastest HPL performance, illustrating a huge performance disparity between these two different types of workloads. In June 2017 the notable exception to this was the K computer, which achieves a remarkable 5.3% of the theoretical HPL peak performance. HPC benchmarks with workloads that represent real applications enable better performance estimation and evaluation.

4.3 STANDARD HPC COMMUNITY BENCHMARKS

Sections 4.4–4.8 explore several of the most widely used benchmarks in the HPC community. The most important of these benchmarks, HPL, is part of the HPC Challenge benchmark suite but is singled out in Section 4.4 because of its impact on the HPC industry. The HPC Challenge suite contains seven different benchmarks examining a wide array of memory access patterns and workload types. Complementing the HPC Challenge suite but not part of it is the HPCG benchmark, which covers a large number of applications with workloads not represented by the dense linear solver in HPL and better represents applications with sparse systems of equations. Another important suite of benchmarks is the NPB, which consisted originally of written algorithm specifications for benchmarks with later reference implementations that ultimately ended up becoming the benchmarks themselves in subsequent iterations. This benchmark suite is intended to represent workloads commonly seen in computational fluid dynamics applications. Lastly, the Graph500 benchmark and its associated graph traversal workload are described.

4.4 HIGHLY PARALLEL COMPUTING LINPACK

HPL is one of the most influential HPC benchmarks in the HPC community. It solves a dense system of linear equations and is well suited for floating-point-intensive computations. As noted in Section 4.1, its genesis is the Linpack benchmark introduced by Jack Dongarra in 1979. HPL also serves as the benchmark for determining the supercomputer ranking on the Top 500 list. HPL is written in C and targets distributed-memory computers.

The key workload algorithm in HPL is lower/upper (LU) factorization. Given a problem size n, HPL will perform $O(n^3)$ floating-point operations while only performing $O(n^2)$ memory accesses. Consequently, HPL is not strongly influenced by memory bandwidth and is well suited for empirically exploring the peak floating-point computation capability of a supercomputer.

HPL contains many possible variations in the way it is executed so the best-performing approach for a particular supercomputer can be found empirically. The user is also allowed to replace the LU factorization and solver step reference implementation entirely with an alternative implementation if so desired. Unlike the earlier versions of Linpack, there are no restrictions on problem size in HPL.

HPL is available through netlib.org at www.netlib.org/benchmark/hpl, with the most recent version developed by Antoine Petitet, Clint Whaley, Jack Dongarra, Andy Clear, and Piotr Luszczek. There are two external dependencies for HPL: MPI and the BLAS routines. The compressed tarball is uncompressed as follows:

```
tar -zxf hpl-2.2.tar.gz
```

The directory hpl-2.2 will then appear. In the setup directory there are several examples of compile settings for various architectures. For this example, the make_generic script is executed to produce a template for creating compile settings.

```
cd hpl-2.2/setup
sh make_generic
cp Make.UNKNOWN ../Make.linux; cd ..
```

The Make.linux file now needs to be modified to reflect the location of the hpl-2.2 directory and the BLAS libraries, and the name of the C compiler. In Make.linux the location of the BLAS libraries can be specified in line 97 immediately before the -lblas:

```
95 LAdir    =
96 LAinc    =
97 LAlib    = -lblas
```

A library location is given to the compiler using the −L flag. For example, if the BLAS libraries were located in /usr/local/lib, line 97 would be changed to read:

```
95 LAdir    =
96 LAinc    =
97 LAlib    = -L/usr/local/lib -lblas
```

The location of the hpl-2.2 directory can be specified at line 70. The architecture name can be changed from UNKNOWN to linux in line 64:

```
64 ARCH     = linux
65 #
66 # ----------------------------------------------------------------------
67 # - HPL Directory Structure / HPL library ------------------------------
68 # ----------------------------------------------------------------------
69 #
70 TOPdir   = /your/path/to/hpl-2.2
```

```
0001 HPLinpack benchmark input file
0002 Innovative Computing Laboratory, University of Tennessee
0003 HPL.out         output file name (if any)
0004 6               device out (6=stdout,7=stderr,file)
0005 4               # of problems sizes (N)
0006 29 30 34 35     Ns
0007 4               # of NBs
0008 1 2 3 4         NBs
0009 0               PMAP process mapping (0=Row-,1=Column-major)
0010 3               # of process grids (P x Q)
0011 2 1 4           Ps
0012 2 4 1           Qs
0013 16.0            threshold
0014 3               # of panel fact
0015 0 1 2           PFACTs (0=left, 1=Crout, 2=Right)
0016 2               # of recursive stopping criterium
0017 2 4             NBMINs (>= 1)
0018 1               # of panels in recursion
0019 2               NDIVs
0020 3               # of recursive panel fact.
0021 0 1 2           RFACTs (0=left, 1=Crout, 2=Right)
0022 1               # of broadcast
0023 0               BCASTs (0=1rg,1=1rM,2=2rg,3=2rM,4=Lng,5=LnM)
0024 1               # of lookahead depth
0025 0               DEPTHs (>=0)
0026 2               SWAP (0=bin-exch,1=long,2=mix)
0027 64              swapping threshold
0028 0               L1 in (0=transposed,1=no-transposed) form
0029 0               U  in (0=transposed,1=no-transposed) form
0030 1               Equilibration (0=no,1=yes)
0031 8               memory alignment in double (> 0)
```

FIGURE 4.1

An example parameter file, HPL.dat for HPL. Parameter inputs separated by spaces on each line are each explored and reported independently by HPL to ease the tuning of HPL.

Once the Make.linux file is prepared, HPL can be compiled by issuing the following command:

```
make arch=linux
```

This will create the HPL executable, xhpl, in the bin/linux directory.

Accompanying the *xhpl* executable is a parameter file to tune HPL for the supercomputer. An example is provided in Fig. 4.1.

The parameter space for tuning HPL is very large, so parameter inputs separated by a space on each line are run independently. For example, the default parameter file in Fig. 4.1 will run HPL through 864 ($= 4 \times 4 \times 3 \times 3 \times 2 \times 3$) distinct parameter combinations with a separate report of Gflops for each unique combination.

A brief explanation of the HPL tuning parameters is as follows.

- Lines 1–2 are ignored.
- Line 3 specifies the name of the file where any output should be redirected if requested in line 4.
- Line 4 specifies whether to print the output to screen or to a file.
- Line 5 indicates the number of different problem sizes explored in this parameter file. It cannot be greater than 20.

- Line 6 gives a space-separated list of the matrix problem sizes. If the number of problem sizes given exceeds the number specified in line 5, those excess problem sizes will be ignored.
- Line 7 gives the number of block sizes explored in this parameter file.
- Line 8 gives a space-separated list of those block sizes.
- Line 9 indicates how MPI processes are mapped on to the nodes, and whether row major or column major.
- Line 10 indicates the number of process grid configurations specified in this parameter file.
- Lines 11–12 specify those process grid configurations.
- Line 13 specifies a threshold used for flagging residuals as failed. In general, residuals will be order 1. Specifying a negative threshold turns off checking and allows faster parameter space sweeps.
- Lines 14–31 specify algorithmic variations in HPL. HPL has a number of different algorithm options, including six different virtual panel broadcast topologies (line 23), a bandwidth-reducing swap-broadcast algorithm (line 26), back substitution with a look-ahead depth of one (line 24), and three different LU factorization algorithms (lines 21) among other options. Tuning for these parameters on a specific supercomputer is a routine task with HPL.

Output for each parameter combination choice is reported in Gflops.

```
================================================================================
T/V                N    NB     P     Q               Time                 Gflops
--------------------------------------------------------------------------------
WR11C2R4        1000    80     2     2               0.09              7.694e+00
--------------------------------------------------------------------------------
||Ax-b||_oo/(eps*(||A||_oo*||x||_oo+||b||_oo)*N)=        0.0072510 ...... PASSED
================================================================================
```

For a certain problem size N_{max}, the cumulative performance in Gflops reaches its maximum value, R_{max}. The R_{max} value is what is reported for the Top 500 list ranking supercomputers. Another interesting metric from the HPL benchmark is $N_{1/2}$, which is the problem size where the maximum performance achieved is $R_{max}/2$.

4.5 HPC CHALLENGE BENCHMARK SUITE

The HPC Challenge benchmark suite consists of seven different tests that cover a range of application types and memory access patterns. The first, HPL, was discussed in Section 4.4 because of its large impact on the HPC community. The other six tests are:

- DGEMM—double-precision matrix–matrix multiplication
- STREAM—synthetic workload to measure sustainable memory bandwidth
- PTRANS— parallel matrix transpose
- RandomAccess—reports the rate of integer random updates of memory in giga updates per second (GUPS)
- FFT—double-precision complex one-dimensional discrete Fourier transform
- B_eff—reports latency and bandwidth for several different communication patterns.

The HPC Challenge benchmark suite can be accessed from the HPC Challenge website [6]. The code is uncompressed and accessed as follows:

```
tar -zxf hpcc-1.5.0.tar.gz
```

The directory hpcc-1.5.0 will then appear. The build methodology for the HPC Challenge benchmark is the same as for HPL: a Make.architecture file is created specifying the compiler and any dependency and optimization information for the supercomputer. Example Make.architecture files are found in the hpcc-1.5.0/hpl/setup directory:

```
cd hpcc-1.5.0/hpl/setup
sh make_generic
cp Make.UNKNOWN ../Make.linux
```

The same changes are made to Make.linux as were done in Section 4.3.1. The benchmark suite is then compiled as follows:

```
make arch=linux
```

This will produce an executable called *hpcc* in the hpcc-1.5.0 directory. The parameter file is called hpccinf.txt and an example version is provided. This parameter file has nearly the same format as the HPL.dat parameter file of Section 4.3.1 but has been augmented slightly to incorporate parameters specific to the matrix transpose benchmark, PTRANS. This change is noted in the parameter file itself:

```
32 ##### This line (no. 32) is ignored (it serves as a separator). ######
33 0                              Number of additional problem sizes for PTRANS
34 1200 10000 30000               values of N
35 0                              number of additional blocking sizes for PTRANS
36 40 9 8 13 13 20 16 32 64       values of NB
```

where lines 1−32 have the same meaning as those in Fig. 4.1. Additionally, the process grid configurations specified in lines 11−12 and the residual threshold in line 13 are used for PTRANS. An example of running the HPC Challenge benchmark is as follows:

```
mpirun -np 16 ./hpcc
```

This produces output from each of the seven benchmarks, summarized in Figs. 4.2−4.8.

```
DGEMM_N=288
StarDGEMM_Gflops=2.44343
SingleDGEMM_Gflops=2.45875
```

FIGURE 4.2

Example DGEMM summary section output.

```
PTRANS_GBs=2.17378
PTRANS_time=0.000628948
PTRANS_residual=0
PTRANS_n=500
PTRANS_nb=80
PTRANS_nprow=2
PTRANS_npcol=2
```

FIGURE 4.3

Example PTRANS summary section output.

```
MPIRandomAccess_GUPs=0.144392
StarRandomAccess_LCG_GUPs=0.11601
SingleRandomAccess_LCG_GUPs=0.118885
StarRandomAccess_GUPs=0.0829133
SingleRandomAccess_GUPs=0.083817
```

FIGURE 4.4

Example RandomAccess summary section output.

```
STREAM_VectorSize=83333
STREAM_Threads=1
StarSTREAM_Copy=5.14952
StarSTREAM_Scale=5.27086
StarSTREAM_Add=7.09093
StarSTREAM_Triad=5.0111
SingleSTREAM_Copy=5.33624
SingleSTREAM_Scale=5.53154
SingleSTREAM_Add=7.25028
SingleSTREAM_Triad=6.75953
```

FIGURE 4.5

Example STREAM summary section output.

```
MaxPingPongLatency_usec=0.55631
RandomlyOrderedRingLatency_usec=0.768096
MinPingPongBandwidth_GBytes=4.28756
NaturallyOrderedRingBandwidth_GBytes=0.533907
RandomlyOrderedRingBandwidth_GBytes=0.576042
MinPingPongLatency_usec=0.238419
AvgPingPongLatency_usec=0.390631
MaxPingPongBandwidth_GBytes=9.36751
AvgPingPongBandwidth_GBytes=6.48206
NaturallyOrderedRingLatency_usec=0.751019
```

FIGURE 4.6

Example b_eff summary section output.

```
================================================================================
T/V                N    NB     P     Q               Time                 Gflops
--------------------------------------------------------------------------------
WR11C2R4        1000    80     2     2               0.09              7.694e+00
--------------------------------------------------------------------------------
||Ax-b||_oo/(eps*(||A||_oo*||x||_oo+||b||_oo)*N)=        0.0072510 ...... PASSED
================================================================================
```

FIGURE 4.7

Example HPL summary section output.

```
FFT_N=32768
StarFFT_Gflops=0.594992
SingleFFT_Gflops=0.613019
MPIFFT_N=262144
MPIFFT_Gflops=6.17472
MPIFFT_maxErr=1.28804e-15
MPIFFT_Procs=16
```

FIGURE 4.8

Example FFT summary section output.

4.6 HIGH PERFORMANCE CONJUGATE GRADIENTS

The HPCG benchmark was created by Jack Dongarra (HPL creator), Michael Heroux, and Piotr Luszczek (HPL developer), with the first release in 2000 and the most recent version released in 2015. It aims to complement the HPL benchmark in exploring memory and data-access patterns in application workloads that are not well represented by HPL. The workload in HPCG centers on a sparse system of linear equations arising from the discretization of a three-dimensional (3D) Laplacian partial differential equation with a 27-point stencil. Like HPL, the workload in HPCG is geared for solving Eq. (4.1), but the *A* matrix is dominated by zeros in the HPCG workload. Unlike HPL, the solution method in HPCG is driven by a Krylov subspace solver known as conjugate gradient. Krylov subspace solvers are iterative solvers requiring multiple iterations to produce an approximate solution to Eq. (4.1) to within a certain tolerance, and are among the most common methods used for solving sparse linear systems of equations. Because the matrix in HPCG is dominated by zeros, the nonzero elements of the matrix are stored in contiguous memory locations for each row.

The sparse nature of the workload in this benchmark requires many more memory accesses than in HPL. For a problem size n, HPCG will perform $O(n)$ floating-point operations while also requiring $O(n)$ memory accesses. Given this, it is no great surprise that in Table 4.3 the peak flops measured for HPL and HPCG differ by over a factor of 150.

The HPCG benchmark incorporates five major kernels: sparse matrix vector multiplication, symmetric Gauss–Seidel smoothing, global dot product evaluation, vector update, and multigrid preconditioning. In addition, the benchmark provides seven different reference routines, which can be replaced in their entirety by user code optimized for the intended supercomputer in accordance with some specific guidelines.

For Krylov subspace solvers, a significant portion of the solve time is spent in sparse matrix vector multiplication, thereby making the HPCG sparse matrix vector multiplication kernel performance very relevant to performance in many user applications. For a matrix of size $N \times N$ and a vector of size N, matrix vector multiplication is given by Eq. (4.2)

$$x_i = \sum_{j=0}^{N-1} A_{ij} b_j \tag{4.2}$$

where A_{ij} is the (i,j)th element of the matrix and b_j is the jth element of the vector. Because nonzero elements of sparse matrix are stored in contiguous memory locations for each row, Eq. (4.2) can be modified to reflect that zero matrix entries in HPCG are neither stored nor manipulated:

$$x_i = \sum_{j=0}^{n_i} A_{ij} b_j \tag{4.3}$$

where n_i indicates the number of nonzeros in sparse matrix A for the ith row. The sparse matrix vector multiplication kernel in HPCG evaluates Eq. (4.3) in distributed memory requiring some exchange of needed b_j values between memory localities. This is an example of *halo exchange* and is explored in detail in Chapter 9. Both the halo exchange routine and the entire sparse matrix vector multiplication kernel code in HPCG can be replaced or altered with certain restrictions by the user.

Gauss−Seidel smoothing is an iterative solution method for linear systems of equations. The Gauss−Seidel kernel in HPCG tests recursive execution and has memory access characteristics similar to that of the sparse matrix vector multiplication kernel. Like the sparse matrix vector kernel, the entire reference implementation of Gauss−Seidel smoothing can be modified or replaced in the benchmark by the user under specified guidelines.

One of the most important collective communication-type operations in HPCG is computing a global dot product of two vectors in distributed memory to produce a single scalar value available to all processing elements. This type of operation is common in most user applications. HPCG reporting includes the minimum, maximum, and average MPI allreduce time when using MPI for the benchmark. A user-provided dot product routine can be substituted for the reference implementation. The same is true for the vector update and multigrid preconditioner, where all the key kernels of HPCG are tested using four different grid sizes.

Compiling the HPCG benchmark on a supercomputer is straightforward. The MPI-OpenMP reference implementation of the benchmark can be downloaded from the HPCG website, www.hpcg-benchmark.org. The benchmark tarball is unpacked with the following command:

```
tar -zxf hpcg-3.0.tar.gz
```

A resulting directory, hpcg-3.0, containis the source code for the benchmark. HPCG supports out-of-source builds to avoid cluttering the source code directories with build-related files. To compile, a build directory is created; for simplicity this is placed in the hpcg-3.0 directory:

```
cd hpcg-3.0
mkdir build; cd build
```

In the build directory, execute the configure script and pass it the name of the architecture for which the build is desired. The compiler flags and commands for several standard options are already in the setup directory. In the example below, the Linux_MPI configuration option is used.

```
../configure Linux_MPI
make
```

The hpcg executable, called *xhpcg*, will appear in the build/bin directory along with a parameter file named *hpcg.dat*.

Unlike the HPL parameter file, the HPCG parameter file is very simple and only contains four lines:

```
1 HPCG benchmark input file
2 Sandia National Laboratories; University of Tennessee, Knoxville
3 104 104 104
4 60
```

The first two lines are unused and can be replaced with user-motivated descriptions. The third line specifies the dimensions of the problem that are local to each MPI process. Consequently, the global problem size changes for HPCG depending on the number of processes launched, while the local problem size stays the same. In this sense, HPCG is already set up for weak scaling tests. The third line contains three space-separated numbers which correspond to the number of collocation points in a cubic grid used for discretizing the 3D Laplacian partial differential equation that is at the heart of the HPCG workload. The fourth line specifies how long in seconds the benchmark should run (60 s in this example parameter file). To submit official HPCG results, the benchmark should run for at least 1800 s. The parameter file should reside in the same directory as the executable when running.

To run the benchmark using MPI, the mpirun script will launch the executable on the desired number of processes, 16 in this example:

```
mpirun -np 16 ./xhpcg
```

Two files result from this operation, named HPCG-Benchmark-3.0_<today's date and time>.yaml and hpcg_log_<today's date and time>.txt. The hpcg_log file contains the log of output from the HPCG execution; the benchmark results are in the yaml file. Extracts from an example yaml file output from HPCG are shown in Fig. 4.9.

Current HPCG implementations generally achieve only a small fraction of peak flops (most around 1%–2%) on the fastest 10 supercomputers in the Top 500 list while they achieve as much as 90% of the theoretical peak performance for HPL. This highlights the different nature of the HPCG benchmark versus HPL, even though they both report flops as the final overall rating. Fig. 4.10 shows the HPCG and HPL performance for the top 10 supercomputers. One outlier is the K computer, which achieves a staggering 5.3% fraction of peak HPL performance with HPCG. In general, the low efficiency in terms of flops exhibited by HPCG is because even small problems for HPCG do not fit in the (L3) cache, halo exchange and allreduce become network bottlenecks as the number of nodes becomes large, and sparse matrix vector multiplication is limited by memory bandwidth.

```
HPCG-Benchmark version: 3.0
Release date: November 11, 2015
Machine Summary:
  Distributed Processes: 16
  Threads per processes: 1
Global Problem Dimensions:
  Global nx: 416
  Global ny: 208
  Global nz: 208
Processor Dimensions:
  npx: 4
  npy: 2
  npz: 2
Local Domain Dimensions:
  nx: 104
  ny: 104
  nz: 104
```

```
########## V&V Testing Summary  ##########:
Spectral Convergence Tests:
  Result: PASSED
  Unpreconditioned:
    Maximum iteration count: 11
    Expected iteration count: 12
  Preconditioned:
    Maximum iteration count: 2
    Expected iteration count: 2
Departure from Symmetry |x'Ay-y'Ax|/(2*||x||*||A||*||y||)/ep
  Result: PASSED
  Departure for SpMV: 3.15835e-08
  Departure for MG: 4.00058e-09

GFLOP/s Summary:
  Raw DDOT: 4.48213
  Raw WAXPBY: 7.70723
  Raw SpMV: 7.3242
  Raw MG: 7.07338
  Raw Total: 7.05082
  Total with convergence overhead: 7.05082
```

```
__________ Final Summary __________:
  HPCG result is VALID with a GFLOP/s rating of: 6.88674
```

FIGURE 4.9

Some extracts from the HPCG benchmark yaml output file. The raw Gflops summary of several of the key HPCG kernels is itemized independently in addition to providing an overall Gflops rating. Verification and validation testing is also reported. The local problem size, 104 × 104 × 104, was specified in the hpcg.dat parameter file, while the HPCG output also reports the global problem size as determined by the number of MPI processes launched.

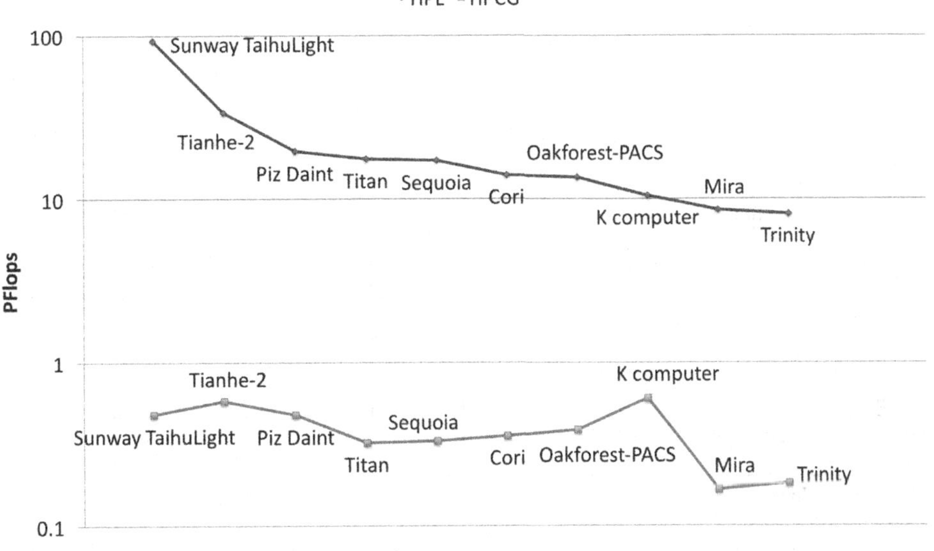

FIGURE 4.10

Comparison of HPL and HPCG performance for the top 10 supercomputers in the Top 500 list in June 2017.

4.7 NAS PARALLEL BENCHMARKS

NPB is a series of small self-contained programs that encapsulate the performance attributes of a large computational fluid dynamics application. It originated from the NASA Ames research center in 1991, and the first version of the benchmark consisted of eight problems that were specified entirely in a "pencil-and-paper" fashion: there was no reference implementation, as in other benchmarks, and the benchmark programs were specified algorithmically. In 1995 the second version of NPB was announced, where reference versions based on MPI and Fortran77 were distributed. Subsequently a third version of NPB was released, which included a number of additions to the original eight problems as additional parallel programming APIs beyond MPI, such as OpenMP, high performance Fortran, and Java.

The original eight problems in NPB are a large integer sort for testing both integer computation speed and network performance, embarrassingly parallel random number generation for integral evaluation, a conjugate gradient approximation to compute the smallest eigenvalue of a sparse symmetric matrix, a multigrid solver for computing a 3D potential, a time integrator of a 3D partial differential equation using fast Fourier transform, a block tridiagonal solver with a 5×5 block size, a pentadiagonal solver, and an LU solver for coupled parabolic/elliptic partial differential equations. These problems are referred to by the two-letter abbreviations IS, EP, CG, MG, FT, BT, SP, and LU respectively. A brief summary of these benchmarks is given in Table 4.5.

The latest version, NPB3, can be downloaded from the NPB page [7] and uncompressed as follows:

```
tar -zxf NPB3.3.1.tar.gz
```

Table 4.5 Some Characteristics of the NAS Parallel Benchmarks (NPB)

NPB	Approximate Line Count	Parallelism		Language	
		MPI	OpenMP	Fortran	C
IS—Integer Sort	1150	X	X		X
EP—Embarrassingly Parallel	400	X	X	X	
CG—Conjugate Gradient	1900	X	X	X	
MG—Multigrid	2600	X	X	X	
FT—Discrete 3D Fast Fourier Transform	2200	X	X	X	
BT—Block Tridiagonal Solver	9200	X	X	X	
SP—Scalar Pentadiagonal Solver	5000	X	X	X	
LU—Lower Upper Gauss–Seidel Solver	6000	X	X	X	

This will create a directory called NPB3.3.1, wherein can be found the MPI versions of the benchmark that are demonstrated here. To compile, enter the NPB MPI version directory:

```
cd NPB3.3.1/NPB3.3-MPI
```

Compiling the benchmark problems requires specifying a compiler choice for C and Fortran in the make.def file located in the config directory:

```
cd config
cp make.def.template make.def
```

Now modify the make.def file in the config directory by specifying the Fortran and C compilers on lines 32 and 78, respectively:

```
29 # ---------------------------------------------------------------------------
30 # This is the fortran compiler used for MPI programs
31 # ---------------------------------------------------------------------------
32 MPIF77 = mpif90

75 # ---------------------------------------------------------------------------
76 # This is the C compiler used for MPI programs
77 # ---------------------------------------------------------------------------
78 MPICC = mpicc
```

Return to the NPB3.3-MPI directory to compile the specific benchmark problem. To compile, three pieces of information must be given to the Makefile: the two-letter (lower-case) reference to the benchmark problem, the number of processes on which to run, and the class of problem where the class is one of S, W, A, B, C, D, or E. S indicates a small problem size; W indicates a problem for a 1990s-era workstation; A, B, and C indicate standard problem sizes increasing by a factor of 4 with each letter; and D and E indicate large test problems increasing by a factor of 16 by each letter.

An example compiling the IS benchmark problem for the smallest problem size on four cores is as follows:

```
cd ..
make is NPROCS=4 CLASS=S
```

The executable will be placed in the bin directory with a name indicating the number of processes and the class for which it was compiled, is.S.4 in this case:

```
cd bin
mpirun -n 4 ./is.S.4
```

Output is shown in Fig. 4.11.

```
NAS Parallel Benchmarks 3.3 -- IS Benchmark

Size:  65536  (class S)
Iterations:   10
Number of processes:     4


IS Benchmark Completed
Class           =                        S
Size            =                    65536
Iterations      =                       10
Time in seconds =                     0.00
Total processes =                        4
Compiled procs  =                        4
Mop/s total     =                   274.91
Mop/s/process   =                    68.73
Operation type  =              keys ranked
Verification    =               SUCCESSFUL
Version         =                    3.3.1
Compile date    =              16 Aug 2016

Compile options:
   MPICC        = mpicc
   CLINK        = $(MPICC)
   CMPI_LIB     = -L/usr/local/lib -lmpi
   CMPI_INC     = -I/usr/local/include
   CFLAGS       = -O
   CLINKFLAGS   = -O


Please send feedbacks and/or the results of this run to:

NPB Development Team
npb@nas.nasa.gov
```

FIGURE 4.11

Output from the parallel IS benchmark for a small class problem size run on four processes.

4.8 GRAPH500

The Graph500 benchmark was announced in 2010, and is intended to represent data-intensive workloads rather than floating-point-intensive computations as in HPL. With support from an international steering committee of over 50 members and led by Richard Murphy, the Graph500 benchmark targets three key problems in the context of data-intensive applications: concurrent search, the single-source shortest path, and the maximal independent set. At present only the concurrent search problem has been specified as Graph500 benchmark 1, and is sometimes known as the Graph500 benchmark. In this subsection the Graph500 benchmark 1 is referred to as the Graph500 search benchmark to avoid confusion.

The Graph500 search benchmark implements the breadth-first search algorithm on a large graph. An illustration of this algorithm is given in Fig. 4.12.

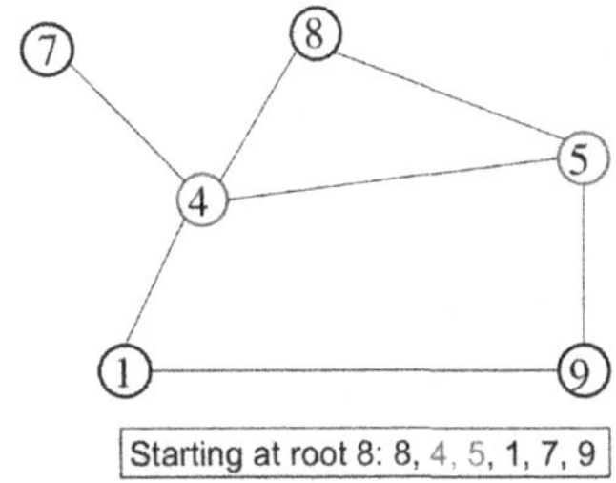

FIGURE 4.12

Example of breadth-first search traversal of this graph data structure starting at vertex 8. The starting vertex is also called the root. The adjacent vertices to the root are 4 and 5, colored red (light gray in print versions). The adjacent vertices to those are 1, 7, and 9, colored blue (dark gray in print versions). Lines connecting the vertices are called edges.

The reference implementation comes with parallelism in several forms, including MPI and OpenMP for distributed and shared-memory settings, and was developed by David Bader, Jonathan Berry, Simon Kahan, Richard Murphy, Jason Riedy, and Jeremiah Willcock. It includes both a graph generator and a breadth-first search implementation. The benchmark starts with a root and finds all reachable vertices from that root; 64 unique roots are checked. There is only one kind of edge and there are no weights between vertices. The output performance metric is traversed edges per second (TEPS). The resulting search tree is validated to ensure it is the correct tree given the root. The graph construction and graph search are both timed in the Graph500 search benchmark.

The reference implementation may be downloaded from www.graph500.org. The tarball is uncompressed and untarred as follows:

```
bzip2 -d graph500-2.1.4.tar.bz2
tar -xf graph500-2.1.4.tar
```

This will create a directory called graph500-2.1.4. In this directory there are several implementations, including MPI. To build the MPI version:

```
cd mpi
make
```

The *Makefile* for the reference implementation automatically assumes the use of the gnu compilers and that the MPI compiler wrapper *mpicc* is available in the user's path. The *Makefile* can be directly modified for alterations to these assumptions. No external libraries or dependencies are needed.

Five different executables result from the compile process, reflecting different ways of implementing the breadth-first search algorithm with graph500_mpi_simple being the standard level-

```
Usage: ./graph500_mpi_simple SCALE edgefactor
  SCALE = log_2(# vertices) [integer, required]
  edgefactor = (# edges) / (# vertices) = .5 * (average vertex degree) [integer, defaults to 16]
(Random number seed and Kronecker initiator are in main.c)
```

FIGURE 4.13

Usage reminder for the Graph500 search benchmark.

synchronized breadth-first search algorithm with a bitmap and two queues. This algorithm is explored in detail in Chapter 9. It requires at least one input to run and can take a second input. The usage for the benchmark shown in Fig. 4.13 appears in the event the user attempts to run the benchmark without arguments.

The first input supplies the code with the number of vertices:

$$N_{vertices} = 2^{scale} \tag{4.4}$$

The number of edges is given by product of the number of vertices and the edgefactor:

$$N_{edges} = edgefactor \times N_{vertices} \tag{4.5}$$

The default edgefactor is 16. Problem sizes in the Graph500 search benchmark are classified into six categories: toy, mini, small, medium, large, and huge. These are also referred to as levels 10–15, with level 10 being toy and level 15 huge. The scale factor for each of these and the associated memory requirements for the graph are given in Table 4.6.

An example execution of the Graph500_simple executable is as follows:

```
mpirun -np 16 ./graph500_mpi_simple 9
```

At this point the graph is constructed and the timing output for that graph is printed to screen, as shown in Fig. 4.14.

The timing for the breadth-first search kernel then prints to screen for each of the 64 roots, followed by a validation phase, as partially shown in Fig. 4.15.

Table 4.6 Problem Size Classes, Number of Vertices, and Memory Requirements for Graph500 Search Benchmark

Level	Scale	Size	Vertices (Billions)	Terabytes
10	26	Toy	0.1	0.02
11	29	Mini	0.5	0.14
12	32	Small	4.3	1.1
13	36	Medium	68.7	17.6
14	39	Large	549.8	141
15	42	Huge	4398.0	1126

```
graph_generation:          0.115093 s
construction_time:         0.224907 s
```

FIGURE 4.14

Graph generation statistics output from Graph500 search benchmark.

```
Running BFS 0
Time for BFS 0 is 0.007095
Validating BFS 0
Validate time for BFS 0 is 1.805835
TEPS for BFS 0 is 1.15464e+06
Running BFS 1
Time for BFS 1 is 0.000358
Validating BFS 1
Validate time for BFS 1 is 2.007691
TEPS for BFS 1 is 2.28912e+07
Running BFS 2
Time for BFS 2 is 0.000500
Validating BFS 2
Validate time for BFS 2 is 1.967331
TEPS for BFS 2 is 1.63852e+07
```

FIGURE 4.15

Partial output of the breadth-first search output for each of the 64 roots.

At the end of the graph traversal for each of the 64 roots, the final statistics for the graph500 search benchmark will print to screen, as shown in Fig. 4.16.

The Graph500 search benchmark does not output flops, but rather TEPS. This makes a comparison like that between HPL and HPCG difficult for the Graph500 search benchmark. However, two important trends for this benchmark are noticeable. First, while the HPL benchmark continues to show exponential improvement on newer supercomputers, the Graph500 search benchmark performance has gone flat. This is illustrated in Fig. 4.17, where the best performance of the Graph500 search benchmark is plotted as a function of time. This can be compared to Fig. 1.2, where the HPL performance for the Top 500 list continues to grow exponentially while the Graph500 performance has flat-lined.

The second noticeable trend is that the effective giga-traversed edges per second (GTEPS) per core is much lower for distributed-memory architectures than for shared memory. This is illustrated in Fig. 4.18, where the effective GTEPS/core in the best distributed and shared-memory results for each of problem scales 31–34 are plotted and the problem scale = $\log_2(N_{vertices})$.

4.9 MINIAPPLICATIONS AS BENCHMARKS

While benchmarks continue to serve an important role in the HPC community, there are many criticisms about their validity in fully capturing real application behavior. One of the principal concerns is that HPC benchmarks are too simple to assess a supercomputer's performance properly with respect to a dynamic application. HPC benchmarks generally aim to be specific to a small subset of independent HPC system performance attributes by design. To complement HPC benchmarking efforts and better capture real application behavior, many in the HPC community have turned to using miniapplications.

```
SCALE:                          9
edgefactor:                     16
NBFS:                           64
graph_generation:               0.115093
num_mpi_processes:              16
construction_time:              0.224907
min_time:                       0.000169039
firstquartile_time:             0.000205517
median_time:                    0.000227094
thirdquartile_time:             0.000342607
max_time:                       0.0959749
mean_time:                      0.00589841
stddev_time:                    0.019746
min_nedge:                      8192
firstquartile_nedge:            8192
median_nedge:                   8192
thirdquartile_nedge:            8192
max_nedge:                      8192
mean_nedge:                     8192
stddev_nedge:                   0
min_TEPS:                       85355.6
firstquartile_TEPS:             2.39107e+07
median_TEPS:                    3.60732e+07
thirdquartile_TEPS:             3.98605e+07
max_TEPS:                       4.84623e+07
harmonic_mean_TEPS:             1.38885e+06
harmonic_stddev_TEPS:           585773
min_validate:                   1.72823
firstquartile_validate:         1.86437
median_validate:                1.91839
thirdquartile_validate:         2.00359
max_validate:                   2.11599
mean_validate:                  1.92975
stddev_validate:                0.0889681
```

FIGURE 4.16

Final statistical output from the Graph500 search benchmark.

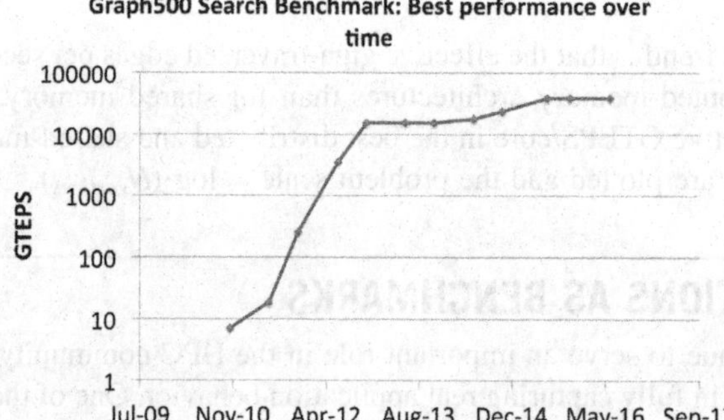

FIGURE 4.17

The Graph500 best performance as a function of time. Performance has gone flat, while the HPL performance continues to grow exponentially.

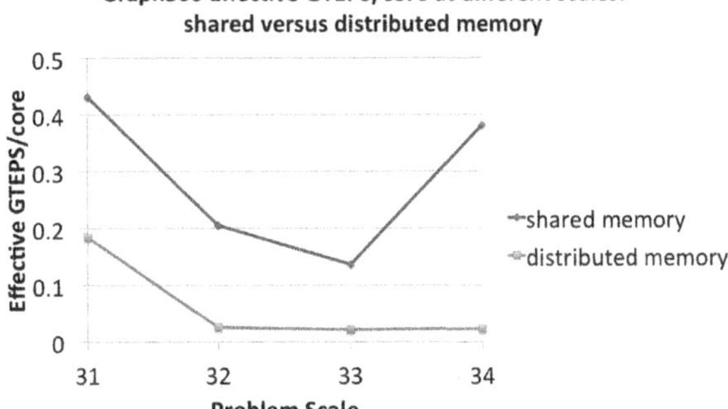

FIGURE 4.18

Results from the June 2016 Graph500 list comparing the effective GTEPS/core for the best results in shared memory and distributed memory at problem scales 31–34.

As the name implies, miniapplications are smaller versions of real applications. They originate from a large number of scientific disciplines and are generally much longer than HPC benchmarks. They do not generally output any standardized metric like flops, GUPS, TEPS, or degrees of freedom per second (DOFS), but do provide time to solution for various kernels as well as strong and weak scaling information. Table 4.7 provides an overview of some common miniapplications from the Mantevo suite [12] organized by Michael Heroux (HPCG benchmark cocreator) and Richard Barrett.

Miniapplications fulfill several roles that are difficult for standard HPC benchmarks. They enable large application developers to interact with a broader software engineering community by producing simplified, smaller, open-source versions of their application for outside scrutiny and optimization. Miniapplications also serve an important role in testing emerging programming models outside the scope of conventional parallel programming APIs like MPI and OpenMP. Miniapplications are well suited for performing scaling studies, especially in the context of dynamic simulations and on emerging hardware architectures. Finally, miniapplications are sufficiently complex yet small enough to explore the parameter and interaction space of memory, network, accelerators, and processor elements.

Table 4.7 Some Characteristics of Miniapplications from the Mantevo Suite

Mini-Application	Approximate Line Count	Parallelism			Language		
		MPI	OpenMP	Other	Fortran	C	C++
MiniAMR	9,400	X				X	
MiniFE	14,200	X	X	CUDA, Cilk			X
MiniGhost	12,770	X	X	OpenACC	X		
MiniMD	6,500	X	X	OpenCL, OpenACC			X
CloverLeaf	9,300	X	X	OpenACC, CUDA	X	X	
TeaLeaf	6,500	X	X	OpenCL	X		

The Mantevo suite contains a large number of open-source miniapplications from a wide array of application domains, including those listed below.

- MiniAMR—a miniapplication for exploring adaptive mesh refinement and dynamic execution with refinement and coarsening of meshes driven by objects passing through the mesh.
- MiniFE—a miniapplication for finite element codes.
- MiniGhost—a miniapplication for exploring halo exchange in the context of a finite differencing application on uniform 3D mesh.
- MiniMD—a miniapplication based on a molecular dynamics workload.
- Cloverleaf—a miniapplication for solving compressible Euler equations.
- TeaLeaf—a miniapplication based on a workload for solving linear heat conduction equation.

Some of these miniapplications are revisited in the context of the software libraries discussion in Chapter 10.

In addition to the Mantevo suite, a large number of miniapplications are maintained at the many supercomputing centers around the world. These miniapplications often complement standard HPC benchmarks by playing a significant role in procurement decisions. Consequently, they have significant supercomputing vendor involvement as well. As an example, in the collaboration of Oak Ridge, Argonne, and Livermore US National Laboratories (CORAL) to procure two 150 petaflops machines, results from over 25 miniapplications were requested from hardware vendors [13] in addition to several of the benchmarks mentioned in this chapter.

4.10 SUMMARY AND OUTCOMES OF CHAPTER 4

- Benchmarking is a way to measure the performance of a supercomputer empirically. A benchmark provides some standardized type of workload that may vary in size or input dataset.
- Computational benchmark workloads come in two types: synthetic, where workloads are designed and created to impose a load on a specific component in the system; and application, where the workload is derived from a real-world application.
- Good benchmarks are relevant and meaningful to the target application domain, applicable to a broad spectrum of hardware architectures, adopted by both users and vendors, and enable comparative evaluation.
- Early benchmarks include the floating-point-intensive Whetstone benchmark and the integer-oriented Dhrystone benchmark.
- The Linpack benchmark solves a dense, regular system of linear equations and provides an estimate of a system's effective floating-point performance.
- The HPL benchmark is used for ranking supercomputers in the Top 500 list.
- HPL is part of the HPC Challenge benchmark suite that contains seven widely used HPC benchmarks.
- The HPCG benchmark is meant to complement the HPL benchmark in exploring memory and data-access patterns in application workloads that are not well represented by HPL. The workload in HPCG centers on a sparse system of linear equations arising from the discretization of a 3D Laplacian partial differential equation with a 27-point stencil.

- HPCG performance continues to be, at best, a very small fraction of HPL performance on even the fastest supercomputers in the Top 500 list.
- NPB is a series of small self-contained programs that encapsulate the performance attributes of a large computational fluid dynamics application.
- NPB started as a pencil-and-paper benchmark, but later reference implementations became the benchmark itself in NPB iterations.
- The Graph500 benchmark is intended to represent data-intensive workloads.
- The Graph500 search benchmark implements the breadth-first search algorithm and reports TEPS as a key metric.
- Graph500 benchmark performance has gone flat even while HPL benchmark performance continues to grow exponentially.
- To complement HPC benchmarking efforts and better capture real application behavior, many in the HPC community have turned to using miniapplications.
- Miniapplications fulfill several roles that are difficult for standard HPC benchmarks, including exploring the parameter and interaction space of memory, network, accelerators, and processor elements, especially in terms of emerging hardware and programming models.

4.11 EXERCISES

1. Run the HPL benchmark on an accessible supercomputer and an available laptop. Tune the input parameters independently for each system to get the best possible performance. For what matrix size does the supercomputer give the best HPL performance? At what matrix size does the laptop give the best HPL performance? Explain your results in terms of the system architecture and memory characteristics of HPL.
2. Run the HPCG benchmark on an accessible supercomputer. Compare the peak HPCG performance versus the peak HPL performance. Which performs best and why?
3. Compile and run the HPC Challenge benchmark suite on an accessible supercomputer and an available laptop. Provide a table with the final results (number and units) of each of the seven problems. Your table should have two columns: test name, and a numeric value of a certain metric with its units. Pick only one metric for each problem. Compare the performance between the supercomputer and the laptop.
4. Run the Graph500 benchmark on an accessible supercomputer. Plot the performance of the Graph500 in GTEPS as a function of graph size. What is the biggest graph problem that you can run on the supercomputer?
5. Explore the performance of the discrete 3D Fourier transform on an accessible supercomputer using the FT NPB. Plot the performance in gigaflops as a function of problem size. What is the peak gigaflops achieved for FT compared with the peak gigaflops achieved for the HPL benchmark on the same supercomputer?

REFERENCES

[1] Wikipedia, ENIAC, [Online]. https://en.wikipedia.org/wiki/ENIAC.
[2] R. Longbottom, History of Whetstone, [Online]. http://www.roylongbottom.org.uk/whetstone.htm.

[3] Standard Performance Evaluation Corporation, SPEC CPU, 2006 [Online], https://www.spec.org/cpu2006/.
[4] Netlib, Linpack FAQ, [Online]. http://www.netlib.org/utk/people/JackDongarra/faq-linpack.htm.
[5] LAPACK, [Online]. http://www.netlib.org/lapack/.
[6] Innovative Computing Laboratory, The University of Tennessee, HPC Challenge Benchmark Suite, [Online]. http://icl.cs.utk.edu/hpcc/.
[7] NASA, NAS Parallel Benchmarks, [Online]. http://www.nas.nasa.gov/publications/npb.html.
[8] Top500, Top500 List, [Online]. https://www.top500.org/lists/.
[9] HPCG, HPCG Benchmark, [Online]. http://www.hpcg-benchmark.org/.
[10] Computational Research, Berkeley Laboratory, HPGMG Performane Results, [Online]. https://crd.lbl.gov/departments/computer-science/PAR/research/hpgmg/results/.
[11] Graph500, Graph500, [Online]. http://graph500.org/.
[12] M. Heroux, Mantevo Suite of Mini Apps, [Online]. https://mantevo.org.
[13] Lawrence Livermore National Laboratory, Coral Benchmarks, [Online]. https://asc.llnl.gov/CORAL-benchmarks.

CHAPTER

THE ESSENTIAL RESOURCE MANAGEMENT

5

CHAPTER OUTLINE

High Performance Computing. https://doi.org/10.1016/B978-0-12-420158-3.00005-8

5.1 MANAGING RESOURCES

Supercomputer installation frequently represents a significant financial investment by the hosting institution. However, the expenses do not stop after the hardware acquisition and deployment is complete. The hosting data center needs to employ dedicated system administrators, pay for support contracts and/or a maintenance crew, and cover the cost of electricity used to power and cool the machine. Together these are referred to as "cost of ownership". The electricity cost is frequently overwhelming for large installations. A commonly quoted average is over US$1 million for each megawatt of power consumed per year in the United States; in many other countries this figure is much higher. It is not surprising that institutions pay close attention to how supercomputing resources are used and how to maximize their utilization.

Addressing these concerns, resource management software plays a critical role in how supercomputing system resources are allocated to user applications. It not only helps to accommodate different workload sizes and durations, but also provides uniform interfaces across different machine types and their configurations, simplifying access to them and easing (at least some) portability concerns. Resource management middleware provides mechanisms by which computing systems may be made available to various categories of users (including those external to the hosting institution, for example via collaborative environments such as the National Science Foundation XSEDE [1]) with accurate accounting and charging for the resource use. Resource management tools are an inherent part of the high performance computing (HPC) software stack. They perform three principal functions: resource allocation, workload scheduling, and support for distributed workload execution and monitoring. Resource allocation takes care of assigning physical hardware, which may span from a fraction of the machine to the entire system, to specific user tasks based on their requirements. Resource managers typically recognize the following resource types.

- *Compute nodes*. Increasing the number of nodes assigned to a parallel application is the simplest way to scale the size of the dataset (such as the number of grid points in a simulation domain) on which the work is to be performed, or reduce the execution time for a fixed workload size. Node count is therefore one of the most important parameters requested when scheduling an application launched on a parallel machine. Even single physical computers may include various node types; for example differing in memory capacity, central processing unit (CPU) types and clock frequency, local storage characteristics, available interconnects, etc. Properly configured resource managers permit selection of the right kind of node for the job, precluding assigning resources that will likely go unused.

- *Processing cores (processing units, processing elements).* Most modern supercomputer nodes feature one or more multicore processor sockets, providing local parallelism to applications that support it through multithreading or by accommodating several concurrent single-threaded processes. For that reason, resource managers provide the option of specifying *shared* or *exclusive* allocation of nodes to workloads. Shared nodes are useful in situations where already assigned workloads would leave some of the cores unoccupied. By coscheduling different processes on the remaining cores, better utilization may be achieved. However, this comes at a cost: all programs executing on the shared node will also share access to other physical components, such as memory, network interfaces, and input/output (I/O) buses. Users who perform careful benchmarking of their applications are frequently better off allocating the nodes in exclusive mode to minimize the intrusions and resulting degradation due to contention caused by unrelated programs. Exclusive allocation can also be used for programs that rely on the affinity of the executing code to specific cores to achieve good performance. For example, programs that rely on lowest communication latency may want to place the message sending and receiving threads on cores close to the PCI express bus connected to the related network card. This may not be possible when multiple applications enforce their own, possibly conflicting, affinity settings at the same time.
- *Interconnect.* While many systems are built with only one network type, some installations explicitly include multiple networks or have been expanded or modernized to take advantage of different interconnect technologies, such as GigE and InfiniBand architecture in combination. Selection of the right configuration depends on the application characteristics and needs. For example, is the program execution more sensitive to communication latency, or does it need as much communication bandwidth as possible? Can it take advantage of channel bonding using different network interfaces? Often the answer may be imposed by the available version of the communication library with which the application has been linked. For example, it is common to see message-passing interface (MPI) installations with separate libraries supporting InfiniBand and Ethernet if both such network types are available. Selecting a wrong network type will likely result in less efficient execution.
- *Permanent storage and I/O options.* Many clusters rely on shared file systems that are exported to every node in the system. This is convenient, since storing a program compiled on the head node in such a file system will make it available to the compute nodes as well. Computations may also easily share a common dataset, with modifications visible to the relevant applications already during their runtime. However, not all installations provide efficient high-bandwidth file systems that are scalable to all machine resources and can accommodate concurrent access by multiple users. For programs performing a substantial amount of file I/O, localized storage such as local disks of individual nodes or burst buffers (fast solid-state device pools servicing I/O requests for predefined node groups) may be a better solution. Such local storage pools are typically mounted under a predefined directory path. The drawback is that the datasets generated this way will have to be explicitly moved to the front-end storage after job completion to permit general access (analysis, visualization, etc.). Since there is no single solution available, users should consult

local machine guides to determine the best option for their application and how it can be conveyed to the resource management software.

- *Accelerators*. Heterogeneous architectures that employ accelerators (graphics processing units (GPUs), many integrated cores (MICs), field programmable gate array modules, etc.) in addition to main CPUs are a common way to increase the aggregate computational performance while minimizing power consumption. However, this complicates resource management, since the same machine may consist of some nodes that are populated with accelerators of one type, some nodes that are populated with accelerators of a different type, and some nodes that do not contain any accelerating hardware at all. Modern resource managers permit users to specify parameters of their jobs so that the appropriate node types are selected for the application. At the same time, codes that do not need accelerators may be confined to regular nodes as much as possible for best resource utilization over multiple jobs.

Resource managers allocate the available computing resources to *jobs* specified by users. A job is a self-contained work unit with associated input data that during its execution produces some output result data. The output may be as little as a line of text displayed on the console, or a multiterabyte dataset stored in multiple files, or a stream of information transmitted over the local or wide area network to another machine. Jobs may be executed *interactively*, involving user presence at the console to provide additional input at runtime as required, or use *batch processing* where all necessary parameters and inputs for job execution are specified before it is launched. Batch processing provides much greater flexibility to the resource manager, since it can decide to launch the job when it is optimal from the standpoint of HPC system utilization and is not hindered by the availability of a human operator, for example at night. For this reason, interactive jobs on many machines may be permitted to use only a limited set of resources.

Jobs may be monolithic or subdivided into a number of smaller *steps* or *tasks*. Typically each task is associated with the launch of a specific application program. In general, individual steps do not have to be identical in terms of used resources or duration of execution. Jobs may also mix parallel application invocations with instantiations of single-threaded processes, dramatically changing the required resource footprint. An example is a job that first preprocesses input data, copying them to storage local to its execution nodes, then launches the application that gives high-bandwidth access to the data, and finally copies the output files to shared storage using shell commands.

Pending computing jobs are stored in job *queues*. The job queue defines the order in which jobs are selected by the resource manager for execution. As the computer science definition of the word suggests, in most cases it is "first in, first out" or "FIFO", although good job schedulers will relax this scheme to boost machine utilization, improve response time, or otherwise optimize some aspect of the system as indicated by the operator (user or system administrator). Most systems typically use multiple job queues, each with a specific purpose and set of scheduling constraints. Thus one may find an interactive queue solely for interactive jobs. Similarly, a debug queue may be employed that permits jobs to run in a restricted parallel environment that is big enough to expose problems when running on multiple nodes using the same configuration as the production queue, yet small enough that the pool of nodes for production jobs may remain substantially larger. Frequently there are multiple production queues available, each with a different maximum execution time imposed on jobs or total job size (short versus long, large versus small, etc.). With hundreds to thousands of jobs with different properties pending in all queues of a typical large system, it is easy to see why scheduling algorithms are critical to achieving high job throughput. Common parameters that affect job scheduling include the following.

- *Availability of execution and auxiliary resources* is the primary factor that determines when a job can be launched.
- *Priority* permits more privileged jobs to execute sooner or even preempt currently running jobs of lower priority.
- *Resources allocated to the user* determines the long-term resource pool a specific user may consume while his or her account on the machine remains active.
- *Maximum number of jobs* that a user is permitted to execute simultaneously.
- *Requested execution time* estimated by the user for the job.
- *Elapsed execution time* may cause forced job termination or impact staging of pending jobs for upcoming execution.
- *Job dependencies* determine the launching order of multiple related jobs, especially in producer—consumer scenarios.
- *Event occurrence*, when the job start is postponed until a specific predefined event occurs.
- *Operator availability* impacts the launch of interactive applications.
- *Software license availability* if a job is requesting the launch of proprietary code.

Resource managers are equipped with optimized mechanisms that enable efficient launching of thousands or more processes across a comparable number of nodes. Naïve approaches, such as repeated invocation of a remote shell, will not yield acceptable results at scale due to high contention when transferring multiple programs' executables to the target nodes. Job launchers employ hierarchical mechanisms to alleviate the bandwidth requirements and exploit network topology to minimize the amount of data transferred and overall launch time. Resource managers must be able to terminate any job that exceeds its execution time or other resource limits, irrespective of its current processing status. Again, distributed termination should be efficient to release the allocated nodes to the pool of available nodes as quickly as possible. Finally, resource managers are responsible for monitoring application execution and keeping track of related resource usage. The actual resource utilization data is recorded to enable accounting and accurate charging of users for their cumulative system resource usage.

A number of resource management suites have been created that differ in their features, capabilities, and adoption level. The software commonly used today includes the following.

- *Simple Linux Utility for Resource Management (SLURM)* [2] is a widely used free open-source package.
- *Portable Batch System (PBS)* [3] was originally available as proprietary code as well as several open implementations with compatible application programming interface and commands.
- *OpenLava* [4] is an open source scheduler based on the Platform Load Sharing Facility and originally developed at the University of Toronto.
- *Moab Cluster Suite* [5], based on the open-source Maui Cluster Scheduler, is a highly scalable proprietary resource manager developed by Adaptive Computing Inc.
- *LoadLeveler* [6], currently known as the Tivoli Workload Scheduler LoadLeveler, is a proprietary IBM product originally targeting systems running the AIX operating system (OS) but later ported to POWER and x86-based Linux platforms.

- *Univa Grid Engine* [7] uses technology originally developed by Sun Microsystems and Oracle that supports multiple platforms and OSs.
- *HTCondor* [8], formerly known just as Condor, is an open-source framework for coarse-grain high-throughput computing.
- *OAR* [9] provides database-centered resource and task management for HPC clusters and some classes of distributed systems.
- *Hadoop Yet Another Resource Negotiator (YARN)* [10] is a broadly deployed scheduler specifically tailored to MapReduce applications, discussed in detail in Chapter 19.

Unfortunately there is no common standard specifying the command format, language, and configuration of resource management. Every system mentioned above uses its own interface and supports different sets of capabilities, although the basic functionality is essentially similar. Thus two widely used examples of resource managers are described here in detail, SLURM and PBS. Both have particularly broad adoption in the HPC community. These sections are presented in tutorial form to build the reader's skill-set.

5.2 THE ESSENTIAL SLURM

SLURM is an open-source, modular, extensible, scalable resource manager and workload scheduling software for clusters and supercomputers running Linux or other Unix-compatible OS. Its origins date back to 2001, when a small team of developers started by Morris Jette at Lawrence Livermore National Laboratory originated work on advanced scheduling systems for HPC. Since that time SLURM development has grown significantly, extending to nearly 200 contributors as well as multiple institutions, including SchedMD LLC (currently the core company responsible for its development, support, training, and consulting services), Linux NetworX, Hewlett–Packard, Groupe Bull, Cray, Barcelona Supercomputing Center, Oak Ridge National Laboratory, Los Alamos National Laboratory, Intel, Nvidia, and many others. In June 2014 SLURM was among the most dominant resource management systems, being utilized in approximately 60% of machines in the Top 500 list [11].

The popularity of SLURM is in no small part due to its impressive list of operational features. As an open-source solution it is available and affordable to even the smallest computing centers and schools. Its core functionality may be extended using plugins written in C or Lua, thus providing complex configuration options and support for various interconnect types, scheduling algorithms, MPI implementations, accounting, and more. SLURM scales to the largest systems in use today, including the fastest supercomputer of 2016, Sunway TaihuLight, with its 40,000 CPUs (over 10 million cores). Five of the top 10 machines are managed by SLURM. It can handle up to a 1000 job submissions and 500 job executions per second. A number of strategies are available to optimize power consumption, ranging from the ability to specify clock frequency for CPUs to powering down unused nodes completely—an important feature when power draw for the largest platforms may exceed 10 MW. Adjusted power levels can be entered in job records to account more accurately for resource usage. Single points of failure are eliminated through the use of multiple backup daemons, permitting the affected applications to continue running and request resources to replace those that fail. Network topology factors into resource allocation to minimize communication latency when it is critical to application execution. SLURM maintains detailed architectural information about each component node, including distribution of cores across nonuniform memory access domains and hyperthread affinities. The user may utilize these parameters to optimize binding of tasks to resources. Job sizes are not necessarily fixed over their execution time; they may grow or shrink in accordance with the specified size and time limits. Sophisticated scheduling algorithms are available, including gang scheduling and preemption. Control over scheduling policies is enabled through constraints specified by the user, a bank account, or quality of service metrics. Finally, SLURM integrates support for execution on heterogeneous components, such as GPUs, MIC processors, and other accelerators. An optional database may be used to store each job's execution profile, detailing CPU, memory, network, and I/O usage, providing the means for postmortem analysis and optimization of system allocation in the future.

5.2.1 ARCHITECTURE OVERVIEW

To support its extensive functionality, SLURM employs a collection of daemons (programs continuously running in the background) to interpret user commands and distribute work to individual nodes in the system. Similar arrangements are commonly used by other cluster resource management systems. Users, including programmers and system administrators, issue commands on one of the head nodes. These commands typically communicate with local control daemons *slurmctld*, which relay specific management tasks to the *slurmd* daemons running on the compute nodes. Some commands may directly interact with *slurmd* backends. Each *slurmd* daemon listens to a network connection to accept an incoming work item, execute it, return completion status, and wait for another work unit. These daemons are organized hierarchically to optimize communication and provide fault tolerance, as illustrated in Fig. 5.1. SLURM may optionally support a performance collection database, shown in the figure as an external storage component marked *db* and managed by a dedicated daemon, *slurmdbd*. *Slurmdbd* may also connect to other machines to provide a central recording of accounting information for multiple clusters that run the SLURM software suite.

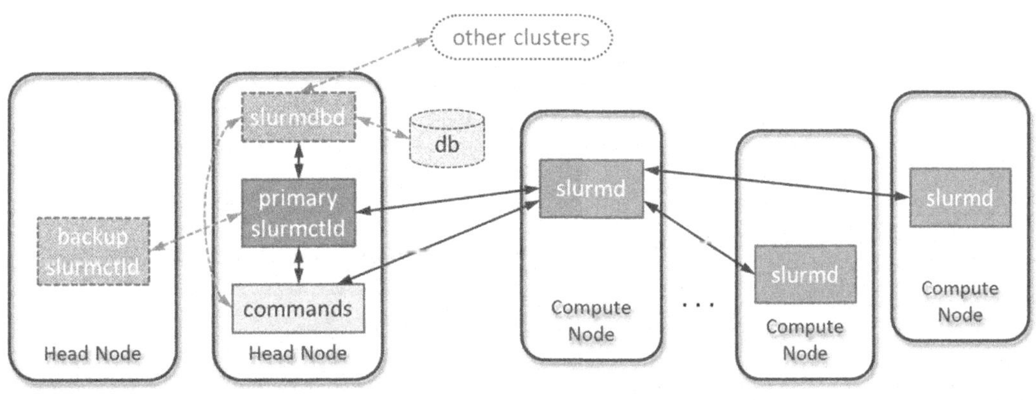

FIGURE 5.1

Simplified architecture of SLURM. Components framed by *dashed lines* are optional.

5.2.2 WORKLOAD ORGANIZATION

One of the primary resource types managed by SLURM is the compute node. Nodes are divided into logical sets called *partitions*. Partitions in SLURM represent individual job queues and thus impose specific constraints on user jobs. Depending on the prevalent characteristics of computational workloads and user needs, the cluster administrator may decide to create completely disjoint or overlapping partitions. The latter may be useful to permit the allocation of all available execution resources to certain, usually severely constrained, job types.

The scheduler assigns the available nodes in the partition to the highest-priority eligible jobs until the pool of available nodes is exhausted. The individual tasks composing a job, called *job steps*, may utilize the entire set of nodes allocated to the parent job or only a fraction. The example in Fig. 5.2 shows a 20-node cluster that has been partitioned into two disjoint node sets, `Partition 1` and `Partition 2`. As illustrated in the figure, `Job 1` has been assigned all nodes in `Partition 1` and all are currently utilized by `Job Step 1`. In `Partition 2` the scheduler designated only 9 out of 12 available nodes for `Job 2` and 8 of them are in use by two concurrent job steps, `Job Steps 5` and `6` (they could be a physics simulation application and connected visualization engine executing in parallel). The remaining three nodes in `Partition 2` could be allocated to another job concurrent with `Job 2` as long as its resource constraints can be satisfied. A typical system would use more meaningful partition names indicative of their function in the system, such as `debug` or `main`. Similarly, good practice calls on users to label their jobs in a way that permits easy identification of their purpose and configuration variant.

SLURM uses the concept of *job arrays* to provide a highly efficient means for submission and management of collections of similar jobs. While their initial parameters, such as time limit or size, have to be identical, they may be changed later on a per-array or per-job basis. Job arrays may only be batch processed.

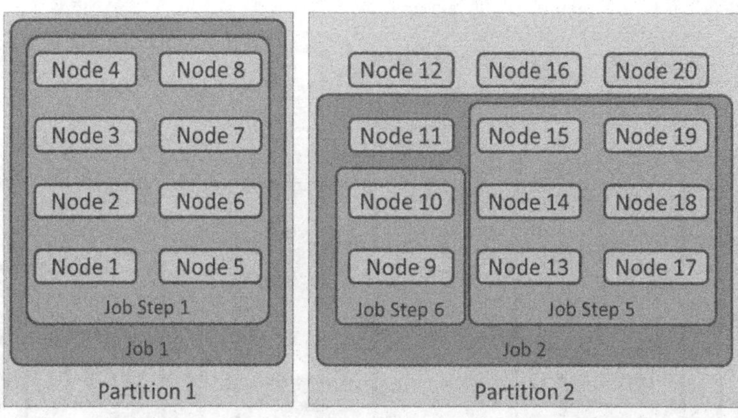

FIGURE 5.2

Relationships between partitions, jobs, and job steps in SLURM.

5.2.3 SLURM SCHEDULING

SLURM employs relatively simple default scheduling algorithms to comply with its design goals of efficiency and simplicity. Whenever a job is submitted or completed, or system configuration changes, only a limited and predefined number of jobs at the front of the queue will be considered for scheduling. This is called event-triggered scheduling. This algorithm is complemented by another that attempts to take into consideration all queued jobs before making scheduling decisions. Due to significantly increased overheads, the latter runs at much less frequent intervals. The scheduling algorithm marks the subset of highest-priority eligible jobs that in aggregate satisfy the available resource footprint as pending for execution. As long as there are any pending jobs in a partition, scheduling for that partition is disabled.

SLURM also provides a *backfill* scheduler plugin that can considerably improve the overall arrangement of job execution compared to the priority-based FIFO scheduling. For example, low-priority jobs requesting a significant amount of resources could be delayed indefinitely in the queue if the influx of small, higher-priority jobs is large. Due to a larger number of jobs considered for execution, the system utilization may also improve. The backfill scheduler will attempt to start lower-priority jobs if this will not delay the expected start time of any of the higher-priority jobs. Making accurate scheduling decisions relies heavily on job completion estimates, defined as the queue configuration parameters and submitted as wallclock limit estimates with individual jobs. Thus the administrators of many systems recommend that their users specify these constraints as accurately as possible.

Job scheduling in SLURM is a complex topic, with many additional improvements and scheduler variants available through plugins. The following is a brief discussion of some of the more prominent concepts.

5.2.3.1 Gang Scheduling

Gang scheduling supports a scheduling approach in which two or more jobs with similar characteristics are allocated the same set of resources. These jobs are then executed in an alternating fashion so that only one of them obtains the exclusive access to the resources at a time. The time for which a single job retains access to the resources, or a *timeslice*, is a configurable parameter. This scheduling mode permits shorter jobs to be started ahead of longer jobs as long as there are available resources, instead of being forced to wait in the queue behind the longer job. As a result they may be started (and finished) earlier, increasing the overall throughput of the system.

SLURM spawns a dedicated timeslicer thread that prevents starvation of gang-scheduled jobs. The timeslicer wakes up periodically (at the start of each timeslice period) and checks for suspended jobs. If there are any, the currently running jobs are moved to the end of queue. The timeslicer then calculates a new allocation for the partition by scanning the queue for suspended jobs which have been waiting longest to run. If there are other active jobs that can be run concurrently with the newly computed allocation, they are added to it. All other currently running jobs that do not fit into the new allocation are suspended.

5.2.3.2 Preemption

Closely related to gang scheduling is preemption, or stopping lower priority jobs to permit the execution of higher-priority jobs. Preemption is implemented using a variant of gang scheduling.

Whenever a high-priority job receives a resource allocation that overlaps the allocation already assigned to one or more low-priority jobs, the affected low-priority jobs are preempted. They may resume once the high-priority job completes or, in newer versions of SLURM, be requeued and started using a different set of resources.

5.2.3.3 Generic Resources

Generic resources (GRES) in SLURM terminology refer to other hardware devices associated with nodes, most commonly accelerators. SLURM currently supports Nvidia GPUs and Intel MICs through a plugin mechanism. As there is no default configuration available, the system administrator has to specify the resource name, count, CPUs that may access the resource, device type, and file system pathname that can be used to access or exclusively allocate the device. Only the permitted CPUs may access the device, even though there may be no physical counterindications to disable access for the remaining CPUs in the node. Unlike other execution resources, GRES allocated to a job will not become available to other jobs when that job gets suspended. The job steps may request fewer GRES than the amount allocated to the parent job (by default they are allocated all the GRES that the job holds). This permits easy partitioning of GRES among concurrent jobs steps.

5.2.3.4 Trackable Resources

SLURM provides additional options to track the use of or enforce custom constraints on various kinds of resources. Such trackable resources (TRES) are identified by their types and names; examples include burst buffers, CPUs, energy, GRES, licenses, memory, and nodes. This feature helps establish more accurate formulas to bill for computer usage in which predefined weights may be assigned to each TRES type.

5.2.3.5 Elastic Computing

Elastic computing refers to a scenario in which the overall resource footprint available in a system or consumed by a specific job can grow or shrink on demand. This usually relies on external cloud computing services, where the local cluster provides only part of the resource pool available to all jobs. However, elastic computing may also be implemented on standalone clusters.

Elastic computing may improve power efficiency by explicitly turning off nodes that are not in use. These nodes will be restored to normal operation as soon as there are any jobs assigned to them. To prevent power surges, which are inevitable when powering up or down large groups of nodes, SLURM gradually changes power consumption at a configurable rate. This typically requires CPU throttling support built into the OS kernel on the affected nodes. The power-saving algorithms drive the node provisioning logic in coordinating reservation and relinquishing the external nodes to the cloud as needed.

5.2.3.6 High-Throughput Computing

SLURM provides rudimentary support for high-throughput computing, in which large numbers of relatively small, loosely coupled jobs are launched over an extended period of time. A correctly tuned SLURM system may execute as many as 500 simple batch jobs per second (sustained), with bursts significantly exceeding this number. SLURM high-throughput job selection logic has been significantly optimized, retaining roughly half of the original scheduling code.

5.2.4 SUMMARY OF COMMANDS

The purpose of this subsection is to familiarize the reader interested in using a system equipped with the SLURM resource manager with the basic commands to perform job submission, job status retrieval, system status query, and basic management of jobs. Commands primarily targeting system administration are beyond the scope of this presentation. Along with each command description listed are the most frequently used options (both short and long forms are provided if available) and usage examples. The option syntax used below shows literal parameter names and operators except for the following cases:

- angle brackets, "<" and ">", signify a parameter name, which may expand to a number or a string depending on the context
- square brackets, "[" and "]", denote an optional entry
- braces, "{" and "}", encompass a list to describe selection of one of the items in that list.

SLURM commands start with lower-case "s" and include the following.

5.2.4.1 srun

srun [<options>] <executable> [<arguments>]

The srun command is used to start parallel jobs or job steps on a cluster. If the resources to run the job have not been allocated yet (for example, the command is executed on the head node's terminal), the resource allocation will be performed first. If invoked from an already started job, such as the job's batch script, srun starts a new job step. If the resources to start the job are available, the job is started immediately, otherwise the command blocks until the resources become available.

The list of options presented below is comprehensive, but in no way exhaustive. Many of these options also apply to resource allocation used by other SLURM commands.

-N or **--nodes=<min_nodes>[-<max_nodes>]**

This allocates nodes for a job to be executed. The number of nodes has to be at least **min_nodes** but not exceed **max_nodes**. The numbers may be followed by the suffix "k" or "m" to signify a multiplier of 1024 (2^{10}) or 1,048,576 (2^{20}). SLURM will allocate as many nodes in the range specified as possible without causing additional delays.

Example

```
srun -N1 /bin/bash
```

This starts an interactive shell on one of the compute nodes for the default period of time.

-n or **--ntasks=<number_of_tasks>**

-c or **--cpus-per-task=<number_of_cpus>**

The **ntasks** option specifies the number of tasks (processes) to run and requests allocation of a sufficient number of nodes for them. By default one task per node is started, unless overridden by the

cpus-per-task option, which defines the maximum number of cores assigned to each process. The latter may be used to launch multithreaded processes.

Example

```
srun -n4 -c8 my_app
```

This launches four processes using executable my_app, each limited to eight threads of execution. If the cluster has 16-core nodes, 2 nodes will be allocated for the job, unless the **exclusive** option is used (see below).

--mincpus=<number_of_cpus>

This allocates nodes for job that have at least number_of_cpus cores per node available.

Example

```
srun -n4 -c8 --mincpus=32 my_app
```

This will place all four instances of my_app on a single node.

-B or **--extra-node-info=<sockets_per_node>[:<cores_per_socket>[:<threads_per_core>]]**

--cores-per-socket=<number_of_cores>

--sockets-per-node=<number_of_sockets>

--threads-per-core=<number_of_threads>

The first form allocates nodes with a specific number of sockets (physical processors), and optionally given a count of cores per socket and threads per core. The last parameter applies to architectures that permit concurrent threads effectively to share execution units, such as Intel processors with hyperthreading. The remaining three options enable independent specification of each parameter.

Example

```
srun -N1 -B2:4 my_app
srun -N1 --cores-per-socket=4 --sockets-per-node=2 my_app
```

Both examples are equivalent, and will allocate one node for application my_app with at least two physical CPUs each containing at least four cores.

-m or **--distribution=<node_distr>[:<socket_distr>[:<core_distr>]][,{Pack,NoPack}]**

This specifies different distribution modes of the job's tasks across system resources. It may have dramatic implications for application performance, e.g., due to grouping related threads on topologically close resources and separating unrelated tasks. The option argument contains up to three entries separated by colons, “:”, that determine process assignment to nodes, sockets, and cores, respectively. Only the first entry (node distribution) is required. The argument may optionally contain the **Pack** or **NoPack** directive, which either directs the allocator to pack the tasks on the nodes as tightly as possible or forces as even a task distribution as possible. The node distribution parameters are as follows:

- * to accept the default distribution, typically **block**
- **block** will try to assign consecutive tasks to the same node before moving to the next node
- **cyclic** distributes consecutive tasks over consecutive nodes in a round-robin fashion
- **plane=<size>** distributes the processes in blocks of specified **size**; after placing block of **size** processes on one node, it moves to the next node to assign the next block, and so on
- **arbitrary** mode distributes the tasks in the order specified in the environment variable SLURM_HOSTFILE, defaulting to **block** if the variable is unspecified.

The supported socket and core distribution parameters are identical, and include:

- * default mode, which is **cyclic** for sockets and derived from the socket distribution for cores
- **block** assigns consecutive tasks to the same socket/core before moving to the next socket or core
- **cyclic** will assign CPUs consecutively from the same socket/core to the same task and from the next socket/core for the next task in a round-robin fashion.
- **fcyclic** or “full cyclic” assigns CPUs to tasks across consecutive sockets/cores in a round-robin fashion without trying to group them based on task boundary.

Example

```
srun -n6 -c2 -m'block:cyclic' my_app
srun -n6 -c2 -mplane=2:fcyclic,NoPack my_app
```

If the first example is submitted on a machine equipped with dual quad-core processors (each core supporting single thread of execution), two nodes will be allocated for the job. Assuming the first socket of node 0 includes cores numbered 0–3 and the second cores 4–7, task 0 will run on cores 0 and 1, task 1 on cores 4 and 5, task 2 on cores 2 and 3, and task 3 on cores 6 and 7. The remaining tasks will be instantiated on node 1, with task 4 using cores 0 and 1 and task 5 cores 4 and 5.

Launching the second example on the same platform results in allocation of three nodes. Tasks 0 and 1 are assigned node 0, tasks 2 and 3 node 1, and tasks 4 and 5 node 3. Individual tasks within the node use cores 0 and 4 (first task) and 1 and 5 (second task).

-w or **--nodelist=<list_of_nodes>**

This requests specific nodes for job execution. The list may contain individual node names separated by commas, or node ranges. If **list_of_nodes** contains a “/” (forward slash character), it will be assumed to represent a path to file containing the node list. Note that if the specified node list is not sufficient to support the job, the system will attempt to allocate additional nodes as required.

Example

```
srun -wnode0[4-6],node08 -N6 my_app
```

This will allocate nodes 4, 5, 6, and 8 plus two more not explicitly specified nodes for the total of six required tasks.

--mem=<megabytes>

--mem-per-cpu=<megabytes>

This controls the allocation of physical memory. The first form specifies the total memory per node required for job execution. The value of zero specified in the job step invocation restricts that job step to memory allocated to the parent job. The second option is used to limit the amount of memory allocated to individual processors.

Only one of these options may be specified at a time.

Example

```
srun -N2 -c8 --mem-per-cpu=4096 my_app
```

Here "my_app" will be allocated 32 GB of memory (or 4 GB per core) on each of the two assigned nodes.

--hint=<type>

This allocates resources based on a literal hint describing the job's properties:

- **compute_bound** causes allocation of all cores in each socket with one thread per core
- **memory_bound** uses one core in each socket and one thread per core
- **[no]multithread** instructs the system (not) to use multiple threads per core, which could improve the performance of communication-intensive applications.

Example

```
srun -N48 --hint=compute_bound bh_mol
```

This will start the compute-bound application "bh_mol" on all cores of 48 assigned nodes.

--ntasks-per-core=<number>
--ntasks-per-socket=<number>
--ntasks-per-node=<number>

These set the upper bound for the number of tasks per core, socket, and node, respectively. The last option is useful for starting mixed MPI/OpenMP jobs which require that only one MPI process is created per node that utilizes multiple threads for increased local parallelism.

Example

```
srun -N16 --ntasks-per-node=16 mpirun my_sim
```

This will launch an MPI application on 16 nodes utilizing a total of 256 threads.

--multi-prog

This runs a job consisting of different programs with different arguments. A configuration file listing the applications with related arguments for each task is required. A path to that file replaces the usual executable name at the end of the **srun** command line. The syntax of this file is explained in the Section 5.2.5 discussing job scripting in detail.

--exclusive[=user]

-s or **--oversubscribe**

These affect resource undersubscription and oversubscription. The first option suppresses node sharing with other jobs. If the optional parameter **user** is specified, the node will not be shared with jobs submitted by other users, but may be available to jobs owned by the same user. When used for job step launch, each of the concurrently executing job steps is assigned a separate processor. If such assignment is not possible at the time of invocation, launch of the job step may be deferred.

The **oversubscribe** option permits the resource oversubscription with other jobs that may apply to nodes, sockets, cores, and hyperthreads depending on system configuration. Jobs enabling oversubscription may obtain their resource allocation sooner and thus be started earlier than in exclusive mode.

Example

```
srun -n4 -c2 --exclusive my_app
```

This launches each of the four my_app instances on a separate node, even if the nodes have four or more cores.

--gres=<resource_list>

The first option is used to specify GRES. Each entry in the list has a format of **<name>[[:<type>]:count]**, where name is the name of the resource, count indicates the number of allocated units (one being the default), and type further restricts the resource to a specific class. When used with job steps, using **--gres=none** prevents a specific job step from using any of the resources allocated to the job (by default job steps are permitted to use all GRES allocated to the job). Simultaneous job steps may also partition the job resources by defining their own GRES allocations.

Example

```
srun -N16 --gres=gpu:kepler:2 my_app
srun --gres=help
```

The first example allocates 16 nodes each equipped with two Kepler GPUs for the my_app job. The second invocation may be used to obtain the description of all GRES defined in the specific system.

-C or **--constraint=<features>**

This specifies additional resource constraints that will apply. The option parameter may be a feature name, feature name with associated node count, or an expression formed by concatenating its clauses using the following operators.

- AND ("&"): only the nodes containing all specified features are selected.
- OR ("|"): only the nodes containing at least one of the listed features are chosen.
- Matching OR ("[<feature1>|<feature2>|...]": variant of OR where precisely one of the alternatives is matched.

Currently, jobs steps may only use a single feature name as a constraint (no operators are supported). Features are defined by administrators, and therefore meaningful only on a specific system.

Example

```
srun -n4 -C 'big_mem*2|small_mem*4' my_app
srun -N8 -C '[rack1|rack3|rack5]' my_app
```

The first example reserves two large memory nodes or four nodes with small memory capacity, and starts four user processes on the selection. The second command allocates eight nodes within a single rack selected from three possibilities.

-t or **--time=<time>**

This is one of the most frequently used options, and limits the total runtime of the job allocation. When the execution time limit is reached, all running tasks are sent a TERM signal followed soon thereafter by a KILL signal. Intercepting the first signal may be used to arrange for graceful termination of affected processes. Time resolution is 1 min (seconds are rounded up to the next minute) with allowed specification formats of [<hours>:]<minutes>:<seconds>, <minutes>[:<seconds>], <days>-<hours>[:<minutes>[:<seconds>]]. SLURM is frequently configured to permit a reasonable grace period following the expiration of the job allocation. A time value of zero imposes no temporal limit on the execution.

Example

```
srun -N1 -t15 my_app
srun -N8 -t1-3:30 my_app
```

The first command executes the job for 15 min on one node. The second will allocate eight nodes for 1 day, 3 h, and 30 min.

-i or **--immediate[=<seconds>]**

--begin=<time>

--deadline=<time>

These options additionally affect the temporal aspect of job scheduling. The first attempts to start the job within a specified period given in seconds (resources must be available right away if no argument is present). The job is not started if the resources cannot be allocated within the time indicated. The last two options may be used either to postpone the start of the job until a specific time (**begin**) or to make sure that it finishes before a certain time (**deadline**). The latter removes the job if completion by the deadline is not possible. The time specification format for both is YYYY-MM-DD [THH:MM[:SS]] for each letter standing for year, month, day, hour (24 h clock), minute, and second. Letter "T" separates the date from the time. If launching on the same day, just the time specification may be used without the letter "T" and with optionally appended "AM" or "PM". Both options offer additional time formats for convenience (see the examples).

Example

```
srun -N4 --deadline=5/27-16:30 -t1-0 my_app
srun -N8 --begin="now+300" my_app
srun -N1 --begin=noon my_app
```

The first example sets the completion deadline for an application estimated to run for a single day to May 27th at 4:30 p.m. in the current year. The second command will attempt to schedule the application within the next 5 min after submission (default units are seconds, but "minutes" and "hours" may be specified following the number). Finally, the third example will limit the job start to no later than noon (note that this may be the current or the following day, depending on the time of submission). Other predefined times of day include **midnight**, **teatime** (4 p.m.), and **fika** (3 p.m.).

-d or **--dependency=<list_of_dependencies>**

This defers job execution until the listed dependencies are satisfied. This option applies only to full jobs and not job steps. list_of_dependencies may assume one of two forms, one using commas, ",", to separate the entries, while the other uses question marks, "?". With the first format all specified dependencies must be satisfied for the job to be launched. The other form means that satisfying any of the dependencies is sufficient for the dependent job to be started. Each entry assumes one of the following expressions:

- **after:<id>[:<id>...]** delays the dependent job start until all listed jobs start the execution
- **afterany:<id>[:<id>...]** defers the dependent job until the listed jobs terminate
- **aftercorr:<id>[:<id>...]** is used to start tasks in the current job array after successful completion of the corresponding tasks in the listed job array
- **afternotok:<id>[:<id>...]** specifies dependency on failed jobs (timed out, nonzero exit code, node failure, and others)

- **afterok:<id>[:<id>…]** starts the job after successful completion of listed jobs (completed with zero exit code)
- **expand:<id>** indicates that resources allocated to this job are used to expand the job <id>, which must execute in the same partition
- **singleton** defers the execution of this job until all previously started jobs with the same name and by the same user terminate.

Example

```
srun -N4 --dependency=afterok:1234 my_app
```

This will not start the job involving "my_app" until job 1234 completes successfully.

-J or **--job-name=<name>**

This permits the user to specify the job name. The default is to use the submitted executable name. The job name is displayed alongside the job ID when listing the queue contents.

Example

```
srun -N4 --job-name=gamma_ray_4n my_sim
```

This will change the default job name `my_sim` to `gamma_ray_4n`.

--jobid=<id>

This initiates a job step under an already allocated job with the specified ID. For regular users, this command is limited to job step control only and should not be used for full job allocations.

--checkpoint=<time>

--checkpoint-dir=<path>

--restart-dir=<path>

These handle automatic checkpointing and restart. The first option will create checkpoints at regular intervals specified by the time argument. The time format is identical to that used by the **time** option. The default is not to generate checkpoints. The directory to store the checkpoint data is defined by the second option, defaulting to the current working directory. The third option specifies the directory from which the checkpoint data will be read when restarting a job or job step.

Example

```
srun -N4 -t40:00:00 --checkpoint=120 --checkpoint-dir=/tmp/user036/chckpts my_app
```

This will run the job for 40 h, checkpointing its state every 2 h. The checkpoint files are stored in a user's subdirectory on a temporary file system.

-D or **--chdir=<path>**

This changes the current working directory to the path specified before initiating job execution. The default is the working directory used for job submission. The path may be absolute or relative to the current working directory.

Example

```
srun -N64 -t10:00 -D /scratch/datasets/0015 dataminer.sh
```

This will switch the working directory to scratch storage before starting the application.

-p or **--partition=<partition_name>**

This specifies a partition (queue) to be used. A comma-delimited list of partitions may be specified to accelerate the job allocation.

Example

```
srun -N4 -t30 -p small,medium,large my_app
```

This will start the application in the small, medium, or large job queue, whichever becomes available first.

--mpi=<mpi_type>

This identifies the MPI implementation to use. Supported types (which may not be supported on all systems) include:

- **openmpi** enables the use of OpenMPI library and implementation
- **mvapich** supports MPI implementation on InfiniBand
- **lam** with one *lamd* process per node and appropriate environment variables
- **mpich1_shmem** launches one process per node and environment initialized for shared memory support in either MPICH1 or MVAPICH shared memory build
- **mpichgm** to be used with Myrinet networks
- **pmi2** if the underlying MPI implementation supports the process management interface (PMI2)
- **pmix** includes support for PMI1, PMI2, and PMIx, and requires that SLURM is configured accordingly
- **none** used for other MPI environments.

Example

```
srun -N64 -t300 --mpi=mvapich mpirun my_sim
```

This will run the MPI application `my_sim` on 64 nodes using InfiniBand interconnect.

-l or **--label**

This prepends a task number to every output line (for both stdout and stderr) generated while running the job. Since the output of all processes may be interleaved on the console, this option helps identify and sort the output lines printed by individual tasks. This has uses in debugging and post-mortem analysis of applications.

Example

```
srun -N4 -l hostname
```

A possible output is shown below:

```
1: node06
0: node05
3: node08
2: node07
```

-K or **--kill-on-bad-exit[={0,1}]**

This determines whether to terminate the job if one of its tasks fails (exits with nonzero status). The job will not be terminated if the argument "1" is specified; in all other cases ("0" or no argument) task failure will imply the job's failure.

-W or **--wait=<seconds>**

This specifies the waiting period in seconds for other task termination after completion of the first task. "0" signifies unlimited waiting time, with a warning issued after the first 60 s. The **kill-on-bad-exit** option takes precedence over **wait**, causing the immediate termination of other tasks after the first one exits with nonzero status.

5.2.4.2 salloc

salloc [<options>] [<command> [<command_arguments>]]

The **salloc** command obtains resource allocation and runs the command specified by the user. The allocation is relinquished after the user's command completes. The **salloc** command manipulates terminal settings and therefore should be executed in the foreground. The command may be an arbitrary program or possibly shell script containing **srun** commands. The job output is shown directly on the terminal from which the command was invoked. The resource allocation options are identical to those listed for **srun** above, with the addition of the following:

-F or **--nodefile=<path>**

Similarly to the nodelist option described above, this explicitly specifies names of the nodes to be used for allocation. The names are stored in a file identified by **path** argument. The node names may be listed in multiple lines. Duplicates and ordering do not matter, as the list will be sorted by SLURM.

5.2.4.3 sbatch

sbatch [<options>] [script [<arguments>]]

The **sbatch** command is used to submit batch scripts for execution to the SLURM system. This is the preferred way of running large or long jobs, as it allows the scheduler to pick the right moment for their launch to maintain high system utilization and job throughput. The job parameters are fully described by **sbatch** command line options and script contents, including I/O stream redirection. This frees the user from being continuously present at the terminal. The script may be a file or, if omitted on the command line, entered directly on the terminal. Batch script contents are described in more detail in the next subsection.

Normally, **sbatch** exits as soon as the script is successfully submitted to the SLURM controller daemon. This does not mean that the job has executed, or even that it has been allocated resources, only that it has been queued. When the resources for execution are granted, SLURM starts a copy of the submitted script on the first of the assigned nodes. If commands executed by the script generate any output, it is stored in files with the name "slurm-%j.out", where "%j" is the job number. For job arrays the output is captured in files named "slurm-%A_%a.out", with "%A" denoting job identifier and "% a" job index.

Like **sallocate**, **sbatch** recognizes many of the same resource allocation options, but also supports a few of its own.

-a or **--array=<index_list>**

This submits a job array containing multiple jobs with the same parameters. The **index_list** specifies numerical IDs of individual jobs and may use comma-delimited numbers, ranges (two numbers separated by a dash), and step functions (range followed by a colon and a number). Additionally, the user may put a restriction on a number of simultaneously executing tasks from the job array by suffixing the index_list with a "%" (percent sign) and a number.

Example

```
sbatch -N6 -a5-8,10,15%3 script.sh
sbatch -N2 -a0-11:5 script.sh
```

This will create a six-job array with job indexes 5, 6, 7, 8, 10, and 15 while limiting the number of concurrent tasks to three. The second command creates a job array with three jobs indexed 0, 5, and 10.

-o or **--output=<pattern>**

This redefines the default file name to store the job script's output stream with a **pattern**. The pattern may be an arbitrary literal that could be used as a file name by the underlying file system with special character sequences that are expanded by SLURM using current job parameters. They include:

- \\ to suppress the processing of expansion sequences
- **%%** to insert the single "%" character
- **%A** expands into the job array's master job allocation number
- **%a** produces a job index within a job array
- **%j** yields a job allocation number
- **%N** is the node name of the first node used by the allocation
- **%u** converts to the user's name.

Example

```
sbatch -N10 -o"ljs-%u-%j.out" ljs.sh
```

This will capture the job's output in file "ljs-joe013-1337.out" if submitted by user joe013 and the allocated job number was 1337.

-W or **--wait**

This postpones the **sbatch** exit until the submitted job terminates. The exit code of **sbatch** will be the same as the exit code of the job, and for job arrays it will be the highest recorded exit code of all jobs in the array.

5.2.4.4 *squeue*

squeue [<options>]

The **squeue** command displays information about jobs and job steps in SLURM queues. It may be used to examine the status of queued, running, and suspended jobs, and show their resource allocations, time limits, associated partitions, and job owners. The frequently used options are as follows.

--all

-l or **--long**

These force additional information to be shown. The **all** option displays the status of jobs in all partitions, including hidden partitions and partitions that are unavailable to the user invoking the command. The **long** option is specified to list the contents of additional fields, e.g., time limit for each job.

-M or **--clusters=<cluster_list>**

-p or **--partition=<partition_list>**

-u or **--user=<user_list>**

-t or **--states=<state_list>**

These restrict the reported information to specific clusters, partitions, users, or states. Each option accepts a single name or comma-separated list of applicable names (for the first three options they are system dependent). The **states** option accepts the following state IDs, listed here in full and shortened format: PENDING (PD), RUNNING (R), SUSPENDED (S), STOPPED (ST), COMPLETING (CG), COMPLETED (CD), CONFIGURING (CF), CANCELLED (CA), FAILED (F), TIMEOUT (TO), PREEMPTED (PR), BOO_TFAIL (BF), NODE_FAIL (NF), and SPECIAL_EXIT (SE). The state IDs are case insensitive.

Example

```
squeue -presearch -tPD,S -i60
```

This lists all pending and suspended jobs for the research partition of the currently used cluster, and updates it every minute.

-i or **--iterate=<seconds>**

This repeatedly updates the displayed information every given number of seconds. The time stamp of the last update is included in the header.

--start

This shows the expected start time and resource allocation for pending jobs if the SLURM scheduler is configured with the backfill plugin. The output is ordered by increasing start time.

-r or **--array**

This prints each job element per line when showing job arrays. If not specified, the output contains condensed information about job arrays combining all information about each job array into a single line.

5.2.4.5 scancel

scancel [<options>] [<job_id>[_<array_id>][.<step_id>]]...

The **scancel** command cancels or delivers signals to jobs, job arrays, and job steps. Besides the options, **scancel** accepts any number of arguments denoting the identifiers of specific jobs or job steps. An underscore ("_") is used to specify the individual elements of a job array. Both regular jobs and job array elements may append a step identifier after a period (".") to limit the scope of signal delivery to the specific job steps. The target job subset may also be identified by application of filters, in which case no explicit job identifiers need be given.

The essential command options include the following.

-s or **--signal=<signal>**

This determines the type of Unix signal to be delivered. The **signal** argument may be either the signal's name or its number, and is typically one of HUP, INT, QUIT, ABRT, KILL, ALRM, TERM, USR1, USR2, CONT, STOP, TSTP, TTIN, and TTOU. Absence of this option causes job termination.

Example

```
scancel -sSTOP 12345
```

This will send the STOP signal to job number 12345.

-n or **--name=<job_name>**

-p or **--partition=<partition_name>**

-t or **--state=<job_state>**

-u or **--user=<user_name>**

These options restrict the set of jobs affected by **scancel**. The job filtering may be done by job name, partition name, state, or user ID of the job's owner, respectively. The job state must be PENDING, RUNNING, or SUSPENDED.

Example

```
scancel -tPENDING -ujoe013
```

This terminates all pending jobs owned by user "joe013".

-i or **--interactive**

This enables an interactive mode in which the user has to confirm the cancellation of each affected job.

5.2.4.6 sacct

sacct [<options>]

This retrieves job accounting data from SLURM logs or databases. Information is collected on jobs, job steps, their status, and exit codes. This command may also be used to access the status of no longer existing jobs to determine if they completed successfully. The options available to the regular user include the following:

-a or **--allusers**

-L or **--allclusters**

-l or **--long**

-D or **--duplicates**

The options listed above increase the amount of information reported by **sacct**. The first outputs data related to jobs owned by all users of the cluster (note that this may be restricted in some environments). Similarly, **allclusters** includes data collected for all clusters under SLURM control; otherwise the output is limited to the machine from which the command is invoked. The **long** option provides practically all information that has been retained in logs pertaining to the finished job. Finally, the last option provides information for all jobs that used the same ID. Normally, only the records with the most recent timestamp are reported for each job ID.

-b or **--brief**

-j or **--job=<job>[.<step>]**

--name=<jobname_list>

-s or **--state_list=<state_list>**

-i or **--nnodes=<min_nodes>[-<max_nodes>]**

-k or **--timelimit-min=<time>**

-K or **--timelimit-max=<time>**

-S or **--starttime=<time>**

-E or **--endtime=<time>**

Options in this group filter or otherwise restrict the output of the **sacct** command. The **brief** option shortens the listing to just job ID, status, and exit code. The **job** and **name** take arguments that identify the specific job (or job steps) and job names of interest. The **state_list** will list jobs that are pending, executing, or terminated in a specific state. The state mnemonics include (short form in parentheses) CANCELED (CA), COMPLETED (CD), COMPLETING (CG), CONFIGURING (CF), PENDING (PD), PREEMPTED (PR), RUNNING (R), SUSPENDED (S), RESIZING (RS), TIMEOUT (TO), DEADLINE (DL), FAILED (F), NODE_FAIL (NF), and BOOT_FAIL (BF). The **nnodes** option shows only entries that allocated a specific number of nodes (a range may be specified). The remaining options are used to limit the retrieved records by the range of execution time limits (**timelimit-max** may only be specified if **timelimit-min** is set), and actual start and end times. The time format is the same as for the **srun time** option.

Example

```
sacct -sF,NF,BF -a -D
```

This will list all failed jobs (including errors due to node failures) on the current machine.

5.2.4.7 sinfo

sinfo [<options>]

This shows information about system partitions and nodes managed by SLURM. The options **all**, **long**, **clusters**, **partition**, and **iterate** are available, and have the same semantics as described above for **squeue**. In addition to these, **sinfo** interprets the following options.

-n or **--nodes=<node_list>**

This displays information only about the specified nodes. Node names may be individually listed in a comma-separated list or use range syntax, as described for the **nodelist** option of **srun**.

-r or **--responding**

-d or **--dead**

These limit the report to either alive (responding) or dead (nonresponding) nodes.

-e or **--exact**

-N or **--Node**

These change the way system information is presented. The first prevents grouping the data related to multiple nodes, unless they have identical configurations. If not specified, the memory size, CPU count, and disk space are listed as a minimal value followed by a plus sign for all nodes in the same state and the same partition. The **Node** option forces output of one line per node instead of using a partition-oriented format.

Example

```
sinfo -N -pbatch
```

This produces the following output showing the status of all nodes configured in the "batch" partition:

```
NODELIST                     NODES PARTITION STATE
node[01,04]                      2    batch* alloc
node[02-03,05-08,10-16]         13    batch* idle
node09                           1    batch* down*
```

5.2.5 SLURM JOB SCRIPTING

The majority of cluster execution resources are utilized by batch processing. Individual workloads (jobs) submitted to the batch queue must be correctly described through job submission scripts. While SLURM attempts to detect errors as early as possible (which results in immediate job rejection), some errors are only manifest when the job is run. This section gives a brief introduction to the basics of batch script writing.

5.2.5.1 Script Components

Job submission script is a shell script, most commonly *sh* or *bash*. To indicate the type of shell to be used to execute the script contents, the very first line must be in the form

```
#!/bin/bash
```

Formally, the first character ("#") denotes a comment that spans to the end of line; therefore the shell ignores its contents. By convention, if the comment marker is followed by the exclamation point ("!"), the remainder of the line is assumed to be the path to the executable that will interpret the script contents. It is good practice to use an absolute path to eliminate reliance on PATH environment variables which may not always be set on compute nodes and ensure that the specific shell executable is started.

Additional job parameters and resource descriptions may be defined in the lines that follow. This part of the script is optional. Note that command-line options for **sbatch** may override the settings specified in the script. Each line starts with a comment marker followed by "SBATCH" and the relevant **sbatch** command option accompanied by an argument. For example:

```
#SBATCH --nodes=16
#SBATCH --time=100
#SBATCH --job-name=experiment4
```

The final portion of the batch script contains commands along with their options and arguments. The commands are executed in the order they are listed within the script. They may be regular Unix utilities or parallel programs, but to invoke them in parallel (create multiple processes), the **srun** command should be used. As mentioned, when called from a batch script the **srun** command initiates a new job step. This gives the script writer the means to modify the resource footprint assigned to individual applications through **srun** command-line options.

5.2.5.2 MPI Scripts

The simplest batch script to launch an MPI job looks as follows:

```
#!/bin/bash
mpirun hello_world
```

Since there are no job parameters set in the script, one should specify at least the required number of nodes or tasks and the estimated runtime on the **sbatch** command line. The execution may fail on some platforms due to the `mpirun` command not being found. As many platforms provide multiple MPI implementations, adding "`module load openmpi`" (or its equivalent on local machine) before the last line will correctly initialize the MPI environment (library and executable search directories and possibly other critical environment variables). Finally, the command mpirun need not be preceded by `srun` since it has already been properly configured to interact with SLURM's parallel job launch facilities. The node count option to mpirun is no longer required, since it is derived from the environment set up by SLURM.

5.2.5.3 OpenMP Scripts

Since OpenMP applications do not cross the node boundary, they do not require any special treatment. The only requirement is to make the number of threads requested by the user known to the OpenMP environment. This is demonstrated by the script below:

```
#!/bin/bash
export OMP_NUM_THREADS=$SLURM_CPUS_PER_TASK
./omp_hello_world
```

5.2.5.4 Concurrent Applications

It is possible to use the batch system to launch different applications at the same time within the confines of the same job. The first way to do this involves the **multi-prog** option of **srun**. This option requires a configuration file that specifies in each line the task numbers or their ranges, followed by the command line (executable with options and arguments) for each application used. The program arguments in the configuration file may contain percent sign ("%") expressions that will be replaced by relevant job parameters when actually run:

- **%t** is replaced by the task number under which the application executes
- **%o** expands to task offset within a range specified at the start of the line for the application.

For example, we can create the file "multi.cf" with the following contents:

```
2,7     hostname
0-1,6   echo sample task A: task=%t offset=%o
3-5     echo sample task B: task=%t offset=%o
```

We use the script shown below to execute the job:

```
#!/bin/bash
#SBATCH --ntasks=8
#SBATCH --ntasks-per-node=4
srun -l --multi-prog multi.cf
```

Option **ntasks-per-node** forces the distribution of tasks across two nodes, while the **–l** option passed to **srun** causes it to prefix every output line with the number of the task that prints it out. Script execution produces the following output:

```
0: sample task A: task=0 offset=0
1: sample task A: task=1 offset=1
3: sample task B: task=3 offset=0
2: node02
5: sample task B: task=5 offset=2
6: sample task A: task=6 offset=2
7: node03
4: sample task B: task=4 offset=1
```

The second method to achieve concurrent execution of different applications is by spawning simultaneous job steps. The following script illustrates the concept:

```
#!/bin/bash
#SBATCH --ntasks=1536
#SBATCH --time=1:00:00
srun -n1 ./single_process &
srun -n16 mpirun ./small_mpi_app &
srun -n1024 mpirun ./big_mpi_app &
wait
```

The concurrent job steps are created by placing an ampersand ("&") at the end of the relevant lines, which cause the **srun** command to execute in the background. Note that unlike **multi-prog**, this method enables concurrent execution of parallel applications. The `wait` statement is required to prevent script exit before all the background job steps complete. On systems with installed PMI, the `mpirun` commands may be dropped, since the MPI applications already include support for parallel launch. Also, the resource requests in the script header need not exactly match the aggregate resource allocations of all simultaneous job steps. However, if they are significantly overestimated the unnecessarily increased amount of requested resources may delay job execution. As a general rule, creating multiple job steps is preferable to submitting multiple jobs, as the mechanisms used to launch the job steps introduce much lower overheads than full-scale job resource allocation and scheduling.

5.2.5.5 Environment Variables

The execution of scripts may be further modified by using environment variables that are provided by SLURM to reflect the details of resource assignment to a particular job and expose information that is not known prior to its execution. These environment variables (only a subset is shown) may be categorized in the following groups.

- Propagated option values

  SLURM_NTASKS or **SLURM_NPROCS**

  SLURM_NTASKS_PER_CORE

  SLURM_NTASKS_PER_NODE

  SLURM_NTASKS_PER_SOCKET

  SLURM_CPUS_PER_TASK

  SLURM_DISTRIBUTION

  SLURM_JOB_DEPENDENCY

  SLURM_CHECKPOINT_IMAGE_DIR
  These variables reflect the values of **sbatch** options specified either on the **sbatch** command line or in the job script header. They correspond respectively to the **ntasks**, **ntasks-per-core**, **ntasks-per-node**, **ntasks-per-socket**, **cpus-per-task**, **distribution**, **dependency**, and **checkpoint-dir** options.

- Counts of resources allocated to the job:

  SLURM_JOB_NUM_NODES or **SLURM_NNODES** holds the total number of nodes allocated to the job

  SLURM_JOB_CPUS_PER_NODE, depending on the scheduler, indicates the total number of CPUs (cores) available on the local node or the actual number of CPUs allocated to the job

  SLURM_CPUS_ON_NODE indicates the number of CPUs on the current node.

- Runtime assigned IDs and enumerations:

  SLURM_SUBMIT_HOST specifies the name of the host on which the job was submitted

  SLURM_CLUSTER_NAME contains the name of the cluster on which the job is running

  SLURM_JOB_PARTITION names the partition in which the job is running

  SLURM_JOB_ID or **SLURM_JOBID** indicates the ID of the current job

SLURM_LOCALID indicates the ID of the node-local task corresponding to the current process

SLURM_NODEID is the ID of the allocated node

SLURM_PROCID specifies the global relative ID of the current process (MPI rank if the process is a part of MPI process group)

SLURM_JOB_NODELIST or **SLURM_NODELIST** contains a list of node names that were allocated to the job; it may contain node ranges or individual entries

SLURM_TASKS_PER_NODE shows the number of tasks executing on each node; entries in the list correspond to host names in the **SLURM_JOB_NODELIST** variable, with some space-saving notation applied to identical consecutive entries (e.g., 4(x2) indicates two consecutive nodes with a task count of 4)

SLURM_ARRAY_TASK_ID stores the index of job array elements

SLURM_ARRAY_TASK_MIN and **SLURM_ARRAY_TASK_MAX** provide the minimum and maximum indices used by the job array

SLURM_ARRAY_TASK_STEP indicates the step by which the index is increased in the job array

SLURM_ARRAY_JOB_ID specifies the ID of the master job in the job array.

- Other

  SLURM_SUBMIT_DIR contains the directory name from which the job was submitted

  SLURM_RESTART_COUNT stores the current count if the job has been restarted due to failure or requeueing.

Importing the actual configuration parameters into the script and application space through environment variables permits nearly arbitrary customization of job execution. It also enables creation of more flexible job scripts. For example, the following script calculates the total number of cores allocated to the job and selects the appropriate input configuration based on the outcome. It also provides a unique log file name to be generated by the master task, reflecting the job number and used resource geometry.

```
#!/bin/bash

job=$SLURM_JOB_ID
nodes=$SLURM_JOB_NUM_NODES
cores=$SLURM_JOB_CPUS_PER_NODE
total=$((nodes * cores))

config=small.conf
[ $total -ge 4096 ] && config=medium.conf
[ $total -ge 16384 ] && config=large.conf

mpirun ./my_sim -i $config -o sim_${job}_${nodes}x${cores}.log
```

SLURM environment variables may be helpful in staging files to a higher performance file system than shared Network File System storage (frequently used to provide global access to home directories). The script listed below creates a unique temporary directory for each task in local temporary storage, copies the dataset `data.in` prepared in the submission directory, spawns tasks that modify it, and copies the results back. It assumes that the cluster supports a passwordless secure shell on login and compute nodes.

```
#!/bin/bash

host=$SLURM_SUBMIT_HOST
hostdir=$SLURM_SUBMIT_DIR
tmpdir=/tmp/${USER}/${SLURM_JOB_ID}

srun mkdir -p $tmpdir/$SLURM_PROCID
srun scp ${host}:${hostdir}/data.in \
  $tmpdir/$SLURM_PROCID/data

srun ./update_file $tmpdir/$SLURM_PROCID/data

srun scp $tmpdir/$SLURM_PROCID/data \
  ${host}:$hostdir/data.out.${SLURM_PROCID}
```

5.2.6 SLURM CHEAT SHEET

This subsection contains a collection of commands that accomplish frequently performed tasks but may sometimes be difficult to locate in the manual. They are presented in the way they would be typed by a user at the login shell prompt, although many of them can be converted to the equivalent job scripts. The examples below serve primarily as a template, since in many cases the option arguments are strongly platform dependent. For commands that require resource allocation, both the time limit and the number of nodes or tasks are specified to enforce good practices.

Invoke the interactive shell on the allocation:

```
srun -N4 -t30 --pty /bin/bash
```

Enable X windows forwarding for graphical applications (requires an X11 plugin installed):

```
srun -N1 -t30 --x11 xterm
```

(Here xterm is used as an example application).

Submit job to the specific queue ("debug" in this case):

```
sbatch -N4 -t30 -pdebug job.sh
```

Submit a multithreaded MPI job (MPI with OpenMP). The command below spawns 16 MPI processes with 8 OpenMP threads each, placing 2 processes per node:

```
env OMP_NUM_THREADS=8 sbatch -n16 -c8 -t30 \
--ntasks-per-node=2 job.sh
```

Specify memory requirements for the job (4 GB = 4096 MB per node shown):

```
sbatch --mem=4096 -n2 -t30 job.sh
```

Find out the estimated start of execution time (1234 is the queued job identifier):

```
squeue --start -j 1234
```

Ask to be notified by email when the job terminates or fails:

```
sbatch --mail-type=END,FAIL -N4 -t30 job.sh
```

Kill a submitted or currently running job (1234 is the identifier of the queued job):

```
scancel 1234
```

5.3 THE ESSENTIAL PORTABLE BATCH SYSTEM

5.3.1 PORTABLE BATCH SYSTEM OVERVIEW

PBS is one of the oldest resource management suites. It originated in 1991 as a contract project for NASA, with the bulk of the proprietary code developed by MRJ Technology Solutions. The PBS interface was based on the POSIX 1003.2d standard defining batch environments, which was ultimately released in 1994. The underpinnings of the initial PBS design were the result of collaboration between NASA Ames, Lawrence Livermore National Laboratory, and the National Energy Research Scientific Computing Center. Further developments brought integration with operating environments on Cray (UNICOS), Intel Paragon, and iPSC/860, as well as checkpoint/restart, interactive job support, and initiated experiments resulting in execution of workloads on supercomputers located at opposite ends of the United States (NASA Metacenter). In 1998 the PBS team led by Bill Nitzberg released version 2.0 of the resource manager code, which included the ability to add and remove execution nodes dynamically. Two years later Veridian Corp. announced the first commercial release of PBS,

PBS Pro 5.0. At this point PBS supported an advanced reservation mechanism and peer scheduling, and was capable of managing grid workloads using Globus. The intellectual property behind the proprietary version of PBS has been acquired by Altair Engineering, which remains its home to this day. The improvements that followed include topology-aware scheduling, on-demand computing, scheduling on GPUs, and support for performance data analysis and visualization. In May 2016 Altair opened the code base of PBS Professional to stimulate innovation across all markets important to the HPC community.

Several open-source PBS implementations compatible in essential functionality but not in all of the features have been developed over the years. The most notable are the following.

- **OpenPBS**, deriving from the revision open sourced by the MRJ in the late 1990s. This version is no longer in development.
- **TORQUE**, or Terascale Open-Source Resource and Queue Manager. TORQUE was developed and is supported by Adaptive Computing with significant community contributions. It includes such features as job arrays, GPU scheduling, high-throughput support, advanced diagnostics, log and statistics collection, node health monitoring, and high availability.

Both open and proprietary versions of PBS were extensively used by among others the NASA Goddard Space Flight Center, Chevron, Conoco, Wolfram Research, Nvidia, the US Department of Defense, Department of Energy national laboratories, National Center for Supercomputing Applications, and Australian National Computational Infrastructure. Altair Engineering and Adaptive Computing formed partnerships with Hewlett-Packard, Cray, Silicon Graphics International, Fujitsu, Groupe Bull, and others as resellers of resource management products. Software from both companies was also awarded the Intel "cluster ready" certification. PBS maintains a very strong presence in the HPC community and is one of the most popular and broadly used resource management systems.

5.3.2 PORTABLE BATCH SYSTEM ARCHITECTURE

Similar to SLURM, PBS consists of a number of daemons accepting user commands and sharing job execution duties. User-command processing, job creation, monitoring, and dispatch, and protecting

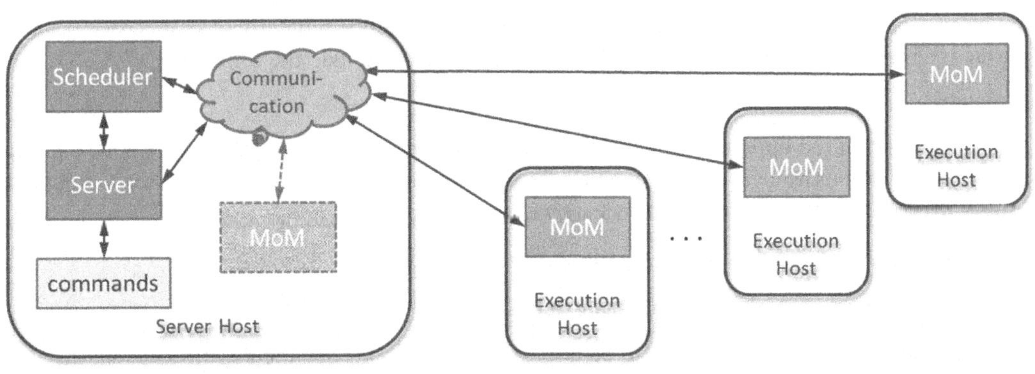

FIGURE 5.3

Simplified PBS architecture.

From Altair/PBS

against system failures are the responsibility of the server daemon (Fig. 5.3). The server runs on the cluster's head node, or server host in PBS terminology, and interacts with other entities in the system via the communication daemon. The communication daemon is based on the internet protocol. There is one server for each set of resources.

The compute nodes (execution hosts in PBS) typically run only the machine-oriented miniserver (MoM) daemons, one instance per node. MoMs play the role of job executors, and are more commonly described as "the mother of all executing jobs". MoMs communicate with the server to receive the jobs to be run on local execution resources. They are also responsible for faithfully instantiating shell-like user sessions, including the correct initialization of the related environment (in particular execution of the appropriate shell initialization scripts and set up of environment variables) as well as proper redirection of I/O and error streams.

The scheduler is responsible for monitoring the state of system resources and deciding when and on which subset of resources each job is to run. It does so by polling the MoM daemons to obtain the most current utilization data. The scheduler also communicates with the server to sample the status of job queues and thus determine the next most eligible jobs to execute.

The configuration described above is most typical for small and medium-scale platforms. Optionally, a PBS installation may include additional server hosts to reduce the amount of resources that need to be managed per server instance. In some cases MoM daemons may be permitted to execute on server hosts to extend the pool of available resources. Finally, PBS allows the inclusion of nodes whose only function is command submission.

5.3.3 SUMMARY OF PBS COMMANDS

5.3.3.1 qsub

qsub [<options>] [<script_name>]

The **qsub** command is likely the most frequently used command in PBS. It allows users to submit jobs to the batch system, along with their resource requirements and additional attributes. If the name of the script file is omitted, **qsub** reads the equivalent statements from the terminal input or starts the application specified on the command line. After the submission is successfully accepted, **qsub** prints the job identifier in the form `<sequence_number>.<server_name>` or, for job array, `<sequence_number>[].<server_name>`. Job parameters can be defined directly in scripts (discussed in Section 5.3.5) or passed through command-line options. These include the following.

-l <resource_list>

This frequently used option requests resources, specifies distribution of job components, and imposes limits on various aspects of job execution. To allocate job-wide resources, the option's argument assumes the format:

<resource_name>=<value>[,<resource_name>=<value>...]

The following are some of the supported resource names.

- **Nodes**—number and type of nodes to be allocated for the job. They are described using the following format:

<node_spec>[+<node_spec>...]

where each **<node_spec>** starts with the number of nodes followed by one or more named properties separated by colons, ":". If no number is provided, "1" is assumed. The properties may be:

  - name of the node (hostname)
  - **ppn=<processors_per_node>** (defaults to 1)
  - another string assigned by the system administrator which may identify additional parameters of interest, such as memory size, CPU type, or accelerator availability.

- **Walltime**—the maximum amount of time a job is permitted to run.
- The names **cput** and **pcput** refer respectively to the aggregate CPU time used by all processes and the maximum time used by any of the job's processes (unit: time).
- The names **pmem**, **pvmem**, and **vmem** are respectively the maximum physical memory used by any of the processes, maximum virtual memory used by any of the processes, and maximum virtual memory used by all processes in aggregate (unit: size).
- **File**—the maximum size of any of the files created by the job (unit: size).

The **qsub** command also offers new style resource selections and job placement statements. The new syntax uses the abstraction of *vnodes* (virtual nodes) to make the resource allocation and partitioning more flexible. Vnodes represent a set of resources that are a usable part of a machine. A vnode can be an entire host or a part of it, such as a single processing blade. A host may comprise multiple vnodes.

The new style resource allocation formats are incompatible with the syntax described above, thus mixing these two approaches in a single job will result in an error. The resource selection is specified using the following format:

select=[<number>:]<chunk>[+[<number>:]<chunk>...]

where **<number>** determines how many instances of **<chunk>** are needed. Each chunk is a list of **<resource_name>=<value>** assignments separated by colons (":"). Some of the commonly used built-in resources include:

- **arch**—type of the architecture (site dependent)
- **ncpus**—number of processing cores
- **mem**—amount of physical memory allocated to the chunk
- **mpiprocs**—number of MPI processes per chunk
- **accelerator**—indicates whether the chunk contains an accelerator
- **naccelerators**—number of accelerators on the host (host-level resource)
- **accelerator_memory**—amount of memory with which accelerators on this vnode are equipped
- **accelerator_model**—type of accelerator associated with a vnode
- **ompthreads**—number of OpenMP threads

- **host**—name of host to execute the job on
- **vnode**—name of virtual node to be used for execution.

The placement format supported by the **-l** option must conform to the following:

place=[<arrangement>][:<sharing>][:<grouping>]

The following rules apply.

- *arrangement* may be one of **free**, **pack**, **scatter**, or **vscatter. free** will place the job on any of the vnodes, **pack** will put all chunks on a single host, **scatter** will assign only one MPI chunk to a host (although nonMPI chunks may be assigned to the same node), and **vscatter** takes one chunk from one vnode.
- *sharing* keywords include **excl**, **shared**, and **exclhost**. They determine the exclusivity of vnode allocation for the job. The first permits only this job to use the allocated vnodes, the second allows vnode sharing, and **exclhost** allocates the entire host to the job.
- *grouping* determines how chunks are grouped according to a resource. It takes the form of **<group>=<resource>** with **<resource>** being either a built-in resource host or a node-level resource that is site specific.

Some of the option variants expect arguments that express time. The time value must conform to the string in the format **[[<hours>:]<minutes>:]<seconds>[.<milliseconds>]**. Other arguments denote size, which is expressed by a number followed by either **b** or **w** for bytes or words, respectively. The actual word size in bytes is system dependent and equal to the native word size on the execution host. The specification permits **k**, **m**, and **g** (kilo, mega, and giga) prefixes that scale the basic unit 2^{10}, 2^{20}, and 2^{30} times, respectively.

Example

```
qsub -l nodes=16 -l walltime=15:00 my_job.sh
```

This will submit a job described by the script `my_job.sh` to be executed on 16 nodes for at most 15 min.

```
qsub -l nodes=node01+node20+node21,walltime=1:00:00 my_job.sh
```

This will execute the job on three specific hosts, named "node01", "node20", and "node21", for up to 1 h.

```
qsub -l select=2:ncpus=4:mem=2gb my_job.sh
```

This will submit the job, requesting allocation of two resource chunks with four cores and 2 GB memory each.

-q <destination>

Depending on the argument, this sends the job to a specific queue, server, or queue at a server. The argument format corresponding to these cases is **<queue>**, **@<server>**, and **<queue>@<server>**.

Example

```
qsub -l nodes=2 -q debug test.sh
```

This will submit a two-node job to the debug queue.

-N <name>

The first option permits the user to associate a name with the job. If omitted, it defaults to the name of the script or `STDIN` if submitted from the standard input on the console.

Example

```
qsub -l nodes=12,walltime=10:00:00 -N hurricane job.sh
```

This will submit a job named "hurricane" to the pending job queue.

-J <range>

This declares a job array. The range argument assumes the form **<x>-<y>[:<z>]**, with *x* being the starting index of the array, *y* being the upper bound on the index value, and *z* the step (index increment) value. By default, the step value is one.

Example

```
qsub -J 5-22:5 -l walltime=25:00 job.sh
```

This will create a job array with element job indices of 5, 10, 15, and 20.

-a <date_time>

This postpones job execution at least until the specified time. The argument format is **[[[[CC]YY]MM]DD]hhmm[.SS]**, where **CC** is the century, **YY** is the year, **MM** is the month, **hh** is the hour in 24 h format, **mm** is the minute, and **SS** is the second. The omitted components of **<date_time>** are extracted from the current date and time as long as they specify a time point in the future. If not, the nearest time in the future matching the specified **<date_time>** string is assumed.

Example

```
qsub -l nodes=1600 -a 151630 big_one.sh
```

If submitted on June 17, this will schedule the job execution for on or after July 15, 4:30 p.m., in the same year.

-W <attribute_name>=<value>[,<attribute_name>=<value>...]

This specifies additional job attributes. Due to limited space, only a subset is presented here.

- **depend=<dependency>[,<dependency>...]**

  where the individual dependencies may be
  - **after:<job_id>[,<job_id>...]** delays the execution of this job until all jobs in the list have started execution
  - **afterok:<job_id>[,<job_id>...]** does not start the job until all jobs in the list have terminated successfully
  - **afternotok:<job_id>[,<job_id>...]** waits until all jobs in the list terminate with errors
  - **afterany:<job_id>[,<job_id>...]** postpones the job start until all jobs in the list terminate with any exit status
  - **before:<job_id>[,<job_id>...]** jobs specified in the list may begin execution only after this jobs starts execution
  - **beforeok:<job_id>[,<job_id>...]** jobs in the list may start execution only after this job's successful termination
  - **beforenotok:<job_id>[,<job_id>...]** jobs in the list may execute after the current job terminates with an error
  - **beforeany:<job_id>[,<job_id>...]** argument jobs may begin execution only after this job terminates
  - **on:<number>** this job may start execution only after <number> of dependencies on other jobs has been satisfied.
- **block=true** causes **qsub** to block until the submitted job terminates. The command returns the job's exit status.
- **run_count=<number>** sets the number of times the job should be run.

Example

```
qsub -l nodes=1 -W depend=afterok:simulate.cluster.edu \
 postprocess
```

This makes the `postprocess` job dependent on the successful termination of the job `simulate`.

-V

-v <variable_list>

These options control the export of environment variables to the job's environment. The first one forces copying of all environment variables and shell functions from the user login environment in which **qsub** is run. The second uses an explicit list of variables to be exported. The entries on the list are separated by commas and take the form **<variable>** or **<variable>=<value>**. The first form simply names the variable to be exported (such a variable must exist in the login environment in which **qsub** is invoked), while the second defines both the name and the value of the exported variable.

-I

-X

These start an interactive job, causing the stdin, stdout, and stderr streams of the job to be connected to the terminal session in which qsub is running. If a job script is provided, only its PBS directives are processed. Jobs belonging to a job array cannot be interactive.

The second option enables an *interactive* job to open X windows on the user's display.

-e <path>

-o <path>

-j {oe,eo,n}

These affect handling of the output and error streams of the job. The first two options save the contents of respectively error and standard output streams to specified files. If omitted, stderr is captured in the file **<job_name>.e<number>**, while stdout stream is redirected to **<job_name>.o<number>**, where **<number>** is the job's ID. The **<path>** may be expressed as **[<host>:]<path>**. Both relative and absolute paths are permitted; in the first case they are relative to the current working directory during **qsub** invocation.

The third option describes how standard error and output streams are merged. The parameters listed above correspond to both merged into stdout, both merged into stderr, and not merged.

-S <path>[@<host>][,<path>[@<host>]...]

-C <prefix>

These options may be used to modify how job scripts are processed by PBS. The first specifies the path to the shell executable acting as an interpreter for the job script. By default the user's login shell is used. If the host name is not entered, only one shell path may be listed that applies to all execution hosts. The second option specifies the literal to be used as a prefix for PBS directives inside the script, nominally "#PBS".

Example

```
qsub -l nodes=1 -S $PBS_EXEC/bin/pbs_python test.py
```

This will execute a python script on the target host.

5.3.3.2 qdel

qdel [<options>] <job_id> [<job_id>...]

This deletes specified job(s). If used without any options, **qdel** removes any queued, running, or suspended jobs. In such a case, the job history is retained. Job deletion begins by sending the affected processes the SIGTERM signal. Afterwards, if there are still any remaining processes belonging to the job, they are sent SIGKILL. Supported options include the following.

-W force

This deletes the job even if the execution host cannot be reached.

-x

This applies to all jobs in the system, including finished and moved jobs. The related job history is also removed.

Example

```
qdel -x mpi_sparse8.some.host.com
```

This will delete job `mpi_sparse8` from the server `some.host.com` irrespective of its status. The job's history will also be erased.

5.3.3.3 qstat

The **qstat** command displays on the standard output status of jobs, queues, or servers. Each of these functions requires a different set of options and command-line arguments, which are briefly discussed below.

5.3.3.3.1 Job Status Query

qstat [<options>] [{<job_id>,<destination>}...]

These are default job status options, as follows.

-J

This shows the status of job arrays only.

-t

This displays the status of jobs, job arrays, and subjobs. When combined with **-J**, it only shows the subjob status.

-p

This replaces values in the time-use column with completion percentages. For job arrays, it lists the percentage of subjobs completed.

-x

In addition to queued and running jobs, this displays the status of finished and moved jobs.

For alternative job status options, the command argument in this mode may be a job ID, which causes the printed information to be limited to that specific job, or a server name, in which case the information is restricted to jobs managed by that server.

-a

The status of running and queued jobs is reported.

-H

This displays the status of finished and moved jobs.

-i

This shows information about waiting, held, and queued jobs.

-r

This lists running and suspended jobs.

-T

This replaces the `Elap Time` field with the estimated time for queued jobs.

-u <user.[,<user>…]

This shows information about jobs owned by a specific user(s).

Long job status options are available from:

-f

The *full* option lists the job information in long format, including job ID, job attributes (one per line), job submission arguments, the job's executable, and the argument list.

5.3.3.3.2 Queue Status Query

qstat -Q [-f] [<destination>[,<destination>…]]

qstat -q {-G,-M} [<destination>[,<destination>…]]

Queue status may be examined using one of two forms. The first displays the status of specified queues, one queue per line. If the **-f** option is given, the full status of each queue is listed, one attribute per line. The destination argument may be **<queue_name>**, **<quque_name>@<server>**, or **@<server>** (the last reports on all queues managed by the specified server).

The second form shows queue status in alternate format, one queue per line. The additional options are as follows.

-G

This shows size in gigabytes.

-M

This shows size in megawords (8 bytes per word).

5.3.3.3.3 Server Status Query

qstat -B [-f] [-G] [-M] [<server>[,<server>...]

The arguments of this command must be server names. The meaning of options is analogous to that described above for queue status query.

5.3.3.4 tracejob

tracejob [<options>] <job_id>

This extracts and outputs log information about a specific job. Log data includes server (time when the job was queued or modified), scheduler (circumstances that prevent the job from running), accounting (track of the job entering the queue, starting execution, termination, and deletion), and MoM (what happened to job while it was running) information. Supported options are:

-a

-l

-m

-s

Each of these options suppresses the presentation of the respective class of data, in order: accounting, scheduler, MoM, and server. Note that to retrieve MoM's log, **tracejob** has to be invoked on the node where the examined MoM daemon runs.

-c <number>

-n <day_count>

-f <filter>

These options provide additional filtering of displayed data. The first limits the count of specific messages to the **number** of most recent occurrences. The second accesses only the logs that go back no more than **day_count** days. Finally, the filter option excludes specific events from the printout. The filter argument is any of the keywords listed below, or a number formed by using OR on the flags given in parentheses:

- **error** (0x0001) filters internal errors
- **system** (0x0002) filters system errors
- **admin** (0x0004) filters administrative events
- **job** (0x0008) filters job-related events
- **job_usage** (0x0010) filters job accounting information
- **security** (0x0020) filters security violations
- **sched** (0x0040) filters scheduling events
- **debug** (0x0080) filters common debug messages

- **debug2** (0x0100) filters less common debug messages
- **resv** (0x0200) filters reservation debug messages
- **debug3** (0x0400) filters debug messages less common than **debug2**
- **debug4** (0x0800) filters debug messages less common than **debug3.**

-v

This increases the verbosity of presented information. Using this option will include additional error messages in the output.

Example

```
tracejob -a -n 7 -f 0x84 1234
```

This will display log information related to jobs with IDs of 1234 and collected in the past week. Accounting, administrative, and debugging information will not be included.

5.3.3.5 pbsnodes

pbsnodes [<options>] [<host>[<host>...]]

The **pbsnodes** command is used to examine the status of system hosts. This information is obtained through interaction with the PBS server. The command supports a number of different invocation formats that use different option subsets. Necessarily, only some of them are described below.

-a

This lists all hosts and their attributes. The attributes may include jobs that are currently running on the specific hosts and resources that are used by running jobs. Summary information about all consumable resources across all vnodes is reported for each host.

-H <host>[,<host>...]

This outputs all attributes with nondefault values on all hosts listed and their vnodes.

-j

-S

These change the format of information displayed for each vnode. The first includes job-related fields such as vnode name, vnode state, number of jobs per vnode, running and suspended jobs, and total and free memory, CPUs, MICs, and GPUs per vnode. The second option presents system-oriented information that besides vnode name and state contains the values of OS custom and hardware resources, host name, queue attribute, amount of vnode memory, and the count of CPUs, MICs, and GPUs.

-L

This causes pbsnodes to produce output in long format with no restrictions on column width.

5.3.4 PBS JOB SCRIPTING

PBS job scripts share many similarities with SLURM scripts. In both cases the scripts are executed by an interpreter, which is typically a shell such as bash or csh. They also use prefixed comments in the script header to define job parameters. Each line of the PBS script header needs to begin with a "#PBS" prefix, which is followed by the qsub command option. For example:

```
#!/bin/bash
#PBS -J 0-3
#PBS -l nodes=4
#PBS -l walltime=30:00
/home/user13/my_app
```

This will start four instances of the my_app program (one per host) as a job array with an execution time limit of half an hour. While SLURM relies on the built-in shell mechanisms to start the appropriate interpreter (following "#!" in the first line of the script), in PBS this can be changed explicitly using the **-S** option. In addition, the PBS **-C** option may redefine the directive prefix to something other than "#PBS". This helps to accommodate scripts and shells in which comments do not start with the "#" character.

Despite many similarities between PBS and SLURM, there are some noteworthy differences in the default setup of the execution environment. While SLURM exports all environment variables set in a user's login shell to a job's environment, by default PBS does not export anything. The user must therefore use **-v** or **-V** options to control explicitly what is copied to the target job's environment. While SLURM attempts to emulate running in the current directory as much as possible (one may use file paths relative to the submission directory and the captured standard outputs are also placed there), PBS runs in a spool directory. Finally, PBS does not merge the standard output and error streams by default.

5.3.4.1 OpenMP Jobs

In contrast to uniprocessor jobs, OpenMP scripts must explicitly request the number of cores required to support the multithreaded application. This is illustrated below:

```
#!/bin/bash
#PBS -l nodes=1:ppn=16
#PBS -l walltime=45:00
export OMP_NUM_THREADS=16
./my_omp_prog
```

The above script allocates one node with 16 cores for the job. Note that the OMP_NUM_THREADS is in this case set explicitly in the script, but it may also be defined using the **-v** option on the command line. The equivalent script using the new style of "chunked" resource requests is presented below:

```
#!/bin/bash
#PBS -l select=1:ncpus=16:ompthreads=16
#PBS -l walltime=45:00
./my_omp_prog
```

Note that since the **ompthreads** directive automatically sets the OMP_NUM_THREADS environment variable, it is no longer necessary to export it explicitly.

5.3.4.2 MPI Jobs

The basic MPI job script is shown below:

```
#!/bin/bash
#PBS -l nodes=16:ppn=8
#PBS -l walltime=1:00:00
module load openmpi
mpirun mpi_app mpi_app_arg
```

It will allocate 16 execution hosts for the job, scheduling eight single-threaded MPI processes on each of them for a total of 128 parallel processes. Expressing the same using the new syntax yields:

```
#!/bin/bash
#PBS -l select=16:ncpus=8
#PBS -l walltime=1:00:00
module load openmpi
mpirun mpi_app mpi_app_arg
```

As PBS does not automatically export the user's environment to the job, the note in the SLURM section about properly setting up the MPI environment is particularly important here. While SLURM users who forget to do this may be "saved" in some cases by SLURM's automatic propagation of the environment, in PBS the task has to be performed explicitly. In the scripts above, this is ensured by the `module` statements. In general, however, the specific command for the task is platform dependent and should be checked with the system administrator or online manuals.

5.3.4.3 Environment Variables of Interest

- **PBS_ENVIRONMENT**—either PBS_BATCH or PBS_INTERACTIVE.
- **PBS_NODEFILE**—name of the file containing the assigned execution vnodes.

- **NCPUS**—number of usable threads per vnode.
- **PBS_TASKNUM**—the process number on this vnode.
- **PBS_ARRAY_INDEX**—index of subjobs in the job array.
- **PBS_ARRAY_ID**—identifier of the job array.
- **PBS_JOB_ID**—job or subjob identifier; if the latter, the <job_id>[<index>].<server> format is used
- **PBS_JOBNAME**—user-defined job name
- **PBS_QUEUE**—queue from which the job is executed
- **PBS_SERVER**—default submission server.
- **PBS_JOBDIR**—the staging and execution directory for the job.
- **PBS_TMPDIR**—a job-specific temporary directory.
- **PBS_O_WORKDIR**—the absolute path to the job submission directory.
- **PBS_O_HOME**—the value of the HOME variable from the submission environment.
- **PBS_O_HOST**—host name of the machine on which **qsub** was invoked.
- **PBS_O_SHELL**—value of the SHELL variable from the submission environment.
- **PBS_O_PATH**—value of the PATH variable from the submission environment.

5.3.5 PBS CHEAT SHEET

Invoke the interactive shell on the allocation:

```
qsub -I -l nodes=4,walltime=30:00
```

Enable X windows forwarding for graphical applications:

```
qsub -X -I -l nodes=4,walltime=30:00 xterm
```

(Here xterm is used as an example application.)
Submit the job to the specific queue ("debug" in this case):

```
qsub -q debug -l nodes=4,walltime=30:00 job.sh
```

Submit the multithreaded MPI job (MPI with OpenMP). The command below spawns 16 MPI processes with eight threads each:

```
qsub -l select=16:ncpus=8:mpiprocs=1:ompthreads=8 \
  --walltime=30:00 job.sh
```

Specify the memory requirements for the job (4 GB per vnode shown):

```
qsub -l select=2:mem=4gb,walltime=30:00 job.sh
```

Find out the estimated start of execution time (1234.host.org is the queued job identifier):

```
qstat -T 1234.host.org
```

Ask to be notified by email when the job gets aborted or terminates:

```
qsub -m ae -l nodes=4,walltime=30:00 job.sh
```

Kill a submitted or currently running job (1234.host.org):

```
qdel 1234.host.org
```

5.4 SUMMARY AND OUTCOMES OF CHAPTER 5

- Resource management tools are an inherent part of the HPC software stack and perform three principal functions: resource allocation, workload scheduling, and support for distributed workload execution and monitoring.
- Resource allocation takes care of assigning physical hardware, which may range from a fraction of the machine to the entire system, to specific user tasks based on their requirements.
- Resource managers typically recognize the resource types of compute nodes, processor cores, interconnects, permanent storage and I/O devices, and accelerators.
- Resource managers allocate the available computing resources to jobs specified by users.
- Jobs may be executed interactively or batch processed. Batch processing requires all necessary parameters and inputs for job execution to be specified before it is launched.

- Jobs may be monolithic or subdivided into a number of smaller steps or tasks. Each such task is associated with the launch of a specific application program.
- Pending computing jobs are stored in job queues, which define the order in which jobs are selected by the resource manager for execution.
- Most systems use multiple job queues, each with a specific purpose and set of scheduling constraints.
- Common parameters that affect job scheduling include availability of execution and auxiliary resources, priority, resources allocated to the user, maximum number of jobs, requested execution time, elapsed execution time, job dependencies, event occurrence, operator availability, and software license availability.
- Job launchers employ hierarchical mechanisms to alleviate bandwidth requirements and exploit network topology to minimize the amount of data transferred and overall launch time.
- Resource managers must be able to terminate any job that exceeds its execution time or other resource limits, irrespective of its current processing status.
- The software commonly used today includes SLURM, PBS, OpenLava, Moab Cluster Suite, LoadLeveler, Univa Grid Engine, HTCondor, OAR, and YARN.
- There is no common standard specifying the command format, language, and configuration of resource management.
- SLURM is an open-source, modular, extensible, scalable resource manager and workload scheduling software for clusters and supercomputers running Linux or other Unix-compatible OSs.
- SLURM scales to the largest systems in use today, including the fastest supercomputer of 2016, the Sunway TaihuLight, with its 40,000 CPUs (over 10 million cores). It is also used on 5 of the top 10 machines. It can handle up to 1000 job submissions and 500 job executions per second.
- Single points of failure are eliminated through the use of multiple backup daemons, permitting the affected applications to continue running and requesting resources to replace those that fail.
- Job sizes are not necessarily fixed over their execution time; they may grow or shrink, but should not exceed the maximum specified size and time limits. Sophisticated scheduling algorithms are available, including elastic scheduling, gang scheduling, and preemption.
- SLURM integrates support for execution on heterogeneous components, such as GPUs, MIC processors, and other accelerators.
- Gang scheduling supports a scheduling approach in which two or more jobs with similar characteristics are allocated the same set of resources. These jobs are then executed in an alternating fashion, so that only one of them obtains exclusive access to the resources at a time.
- PBS is a resource management suite that is among the most widely employed within HPC, including open-source versions such as OpenPBS and TORQUE.
- PBS consists of a number of daemons accepting user commands and sharing the job execution duties. User-command processing and job creation, monitoring dispatch, and protecting against system failures are the responsibility of the server daemon.
- The PBS server runs on the cluster's head node, or server host in PBS terminology, and interacts with other entities in the system via the communication daemon. Communication is based on the internet protocol, with one server for each set of resources.
- The compute nodes run typically only MoM daemons, with one instance per node.
- The PBS MoMs play the role of job executors.

- MoMs communicate with the server to receive the jobs to be run on local execution resources.
- The scheduler is responsible for monitoring the state of the system resources and deciding when and on which subset of resources each job is to run.

5.5 QUESTIONS AND PROBLEMS

1. Describe the role of resource management systems. Can they be implemented as a part of a conventional OS? Elaborate.
2. Based on Figs. 5.1 and 5.3, what are the primary software components of a resource management system in a cluster? Which physical system components do they rely on?
3. What are the two primary types of jobs? Why are they needed?
4. What are the differences between a job array and job step in SLURM?
5. Imagine you are a system administrator for a newly installed computer composed of 260 nodes in total. Of those, 64 come equipped with GPUs and 36 have substantially larger memory capacity. Your users execute both regular and (infrequently) high-priority jobs. The latter require exclusive access to nonaccelerated hardware resources, but never occupy more than 128 nodes.
   a. Propose a partitioning scheme (enumerate the types and sizes of SLURM partitions) that provides good utilization of the entire machine. Identify any partition overlaps.
   b. What kind of provisions would you implement to facilitate parallel job debugging?
   c. Which SLURM features would you take advantage of to minimize the impact of conflicts between jobs of different priorities?
6. What is backfill? How does it affect computer utilization?
7. Provide a couple of realistic cases that would utilize job dependencies in batch processing. Why would emulating this functionality with blocking statements inside job scripts be ill advised?
8. Write a SLURM command line to schedule an MPI application "mpi_compute" that takes input file argument "my_file.dat" stored in the user's home directory. The application must run on 10,240 cores on a machine equipped with 16-core compute nodes that are available in the "production" partition. The anticipated execution time is 1.5 hours. Also provide an equivalent job script with a correctly formed header.
9. Provide the PBS equivalent of the command described in Question 8.
10. List notable user interface differences between SLURM and PBS. How would you instruct a novice SLURM user with experience in PBS to make her/his initial interactions with the job manager more productive?
11. The following PBS job script was submitted on a machine equipped with dual eight-core CPUs per node:

```
#!/bin/bash
#PBS -N sim3-grid25x4
#PBS -l select=4:ncpus=4:ompthreads=4
#PBS -l place=pack
#PBS -l walltime=2:30:00
#PBS -o ${PBS_O_WORKDIR}/${PBS_JOB_ID}.out
#PBS -j oe
mpirun sim3 -x 25 -y 4
```

What information can be inferred about the scheduled job? How are the application's processes and threads distributed across the physical execution resources? How is the distribution going to change if the fourth line is replaced with:

```
#PBS -l place=scatter
```

REFERENCES

[1] XSEDE: Extreme Science and Discovery Environment, 2011 [Online]. Available: https://www.xsede.org.

[2] SchedMD, Slurm Workload Manager Version 17.02, November 2, 2016 [Online]. Available: https://slurm.schedmd.com.

[3] Altair Engineering, Inc., PBS Professional Open Source Project, 2016 [Online]. Available: http://www.pbspro.org.

[4] OpenLava: Open Source Workload Management, 2011–2015 [Online]. Available: http://www.openlava.org.

[5] Adaptive Computing, Inc., MOAB HPC Suite, 2017 [Online]. Available: http://www.adaptivecomputing.com/products/hpc-products/moab-hpc-basic-edition/.

[6] IBM, IBM DeveloperWorks: Tivoli Workload Scheduler, [Online]. Available: https://www.ibm.com/developerworks/community/wikis/home?lang=en#!/wiki/Tivoli%20Documentation%20Central/page/Tivoli%20Workload%20Scheduler.

[7] Univa, Grid Engine, 2017 [Online]. Available: http://www.univa.com/products/.

[8] University of Wisconsin-Madison, HTCondor High Throughput Computing, April 23, 2017 [Online]. Available: https://research.cs.wisc.edu/htcondor/.

[9] OAR Home Page, February 25, 2016 [Online]. Available: http://oar.imag.fr.

[10] A. Murthy, Apache Hadoop YARN – Concepts and Applications, August 15, 2012 [Online]. Available: https://hortonworks.com/blog/apache-hadoop-yarn-concepts-and-applications/.

[11] Top 500. The List, 1993–2016 [Online]. Available: https://www.top500.org.

CHAPTER

SYMMETRIC MULTIPROCESSOR ARCHITECTURE 6

CHAPTER OUTLINE

6.1 INTRODUCTION

The most widely used form of high performance computer is the symmetric multiprocessor (SMP). It represents a class of parallel architectures that exploits multiple processor cores to increase performance through parallelism while maintaining a single image of common memory across the entire

High Performance Computing. https://doi.org/10.1016/B978-0-12-420158-3.00006-X

Table 6.1 Some Examples of SMPs and Their Characteristics

Vendor and Name	Processor	Number of Cores	Cores per Central Processing Unit	Memory Capacity	PCIe Slots	Storage Slots
IBM S822LC	IBM POWER8 2.92 GHz	20	10	256 GB	2 × 16-lane Gen.3 3 × 8-lane Gen.3	12 LFF
HPE rx2800 i6	Intel Itanium 9760 2.66 GHz	16	8	384 GB	3 × 16-lane Gen.2 2 × 8-lane Gen.2	8 SFF
Dell PowerEdge R930	Intel E7-8870v4 2.1 GHz	80	20	12 TB	10 Gen.3	24 SFF 8 NVMe
Oracle SPARC T7-4	SPARC M7 4.13 GHz	128	32	4 TB	8 × 16-lane Gen.3 8 × 8-lane Gen.3	8 SFF
HPE ProLiant DL385p Gen8	AMD Opteron 6373 2.3 GHz	32	16	384 GB	3 × 16-lane Gen.2 3 × 8-lane Gen.2	8 SFF

parallel computer. This global virtual address space shared by all of the incorporated processors minimizes the changes from a single processor machine thus simplifying the transformation from sequential applications to parallel programs. SMPs are also referred to as *shared-memory* machines or *cache-coherent* computers. The "S" in SMP stands for symmetric, which refers to the property of equal access times by any processor core to any of the main memory banks. As will be seen, this is at best an approximation as secondary effects cause some variability in load/store operations. But overall SMPs provide balanced operations where data placement need not be a major consideration. This differs from the distributed-memory systems discussed in detail elsewhere in the text.

The principal strength of the SMP architecture family is that it is tightly coupled, i.e., all the components are close together in terms of time–distance of operations, data manipulation, and communication. Some examples of SMPs and their characteristics are provided in Table 6.1.

6.2 ARCHITECTURE OVERVIEW

An SMP is a full-standing self-sufficient computer system with all subsystems and components needed to serve the requirements and support actions necessary to conduct the computation of an application. It can be employed independently for user applications cast as shared-memory multiple-threaded programs or as one of many equivalent subsystems integrated to form a scalable distributed-memory massively parallel processor (MPP) or commodity cluster. It can also operate as a throughput computer supporting multiprogramming of concurrent independent jobs or as a platform for multiprocess message passing jobs, even though the interprocess data exchange is achieved through shared memory transparent to the parallel programming interface. The following sections describe the key subsystems in some detail to convey how they contribute to achieving performance, principally through parallelism and diverse functionality with distinct technologies. This section begins with a brief overview of the full organization of an SMP architecture and the basic purposes of its major components, to provide a context for the later detailed discussions.

Like any general-purpose computer, an SMP serves a key set of functions on behalf of the user application, either directly in hardware or indirectly through the supporting operating system. These are typically:

- instruction issue and operation functions through the processor core
- program instruction storage and application data storage upon which the processor cores operate
- mass and persistent storage to hold all information required over long periods of time
- internal data movement communication paths and control to transfer intermediate values between subsystems and components within the SMP
- input/output (I/O) interfaces to external devices outside the SMP, including other mass storage, computing systems, interconnection networks, and user interfaces, and
- control logic and subsystems to manage SMP operation and coordination among processing, memory, internal data paths, and external communication channels.

The SMP processor cores perform the primary execution functions for the application programs. While these devices incorporate substantial complexity of design (described later), their principal operation is to identify the next instruction in memory to execute, read that instruction into a special instruction register, and decode the binary instruction coding to determine the purpose of the operation and the sequence of hardware signals to be generated to control the execution. The instruction is issued to the pipelined execution unit, and with its related data it proceeds through a sequence of micro-operations to determine a final result. Usually the initial and resulting data is acquired from and deposited to special storage elements called registers: very high-speed (high bandwidth, low latency) latches that hold temporary values. Somewhat simplistically, there are five classes of operations that make up the overall functionality of the processor core.

1. The basic register-to-register integer, logic, and character operations.
2. Floating-point operations on real values.
3. Conditional branch operations to control the sequence of operations performed dependent on intermediate data values (usually Boolean).
4. Memory access operations to move data to and from registers and the main memory system.
5. Actions that initiate control of data through external I/O channels, including transfer to mass storage.

Until 2005 essentially all processors in the age of very large-scale integration (VLSI) technology were single-microprocessor integrated circuits. But with the progress of semiconductor technology reflecting Moore's law and the limitations of instruction-level parallelism (ILP) and clock rates due to power constraints, multicore processors (or sockets) starting with dual-core sockets have dominated the processor market over the last decade. Today processors may comprise a few cores, 6–16, with new classes of lightweight architectures permitting sockets of greater than 60 cores on a chip. An SMP may incorporate one or more such sockets to provide its processing capability (Fig. 6.1). Peak performance of an SMP is approximated by the product of the number of sockets, the number of cores per socket, the number of operations per instruction, and the clock rate that usually determines the instruction issue rate. This is summarized in Eq. (6.1).

$$P_{peak} \sim N_{sockets} * N_{cores\ per\ socket} * R_{clock} * N_{operations\ per\ instruction} \tag{6.1}$$

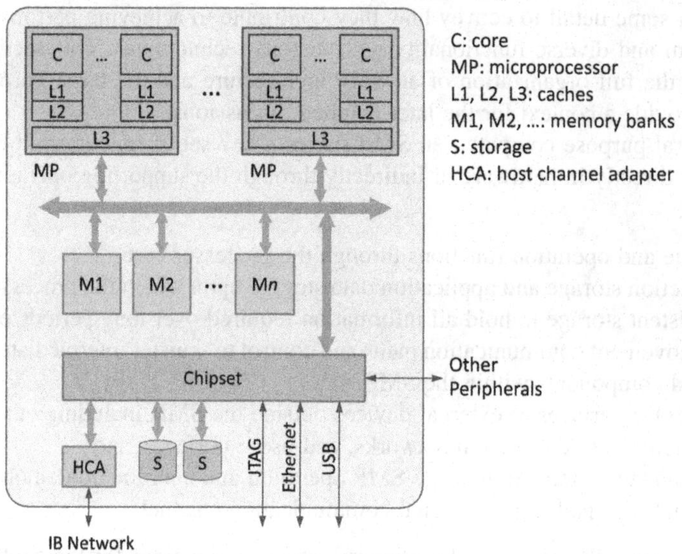

FIGURE 6.1

Internal to the SMP are the intranode data paths, standard interfaces, and motherboard control elements.

The SMP memory consists of multiple layers of semiconductor storage with complex control logic to manage the access of data from the memory by the processor cores, transparent vertical migration through the cache hierarchy, and cache consistency across the many cache stacks supporting the processor core and processor stack caches. The SMP memory in terms of the location of data that is being operated on is, in fact, three separate kinds of hardware. Already mentioned are the processor core registers; very fast latches that have their own namespace and provide the fastest access time (less than one cycle) and lowest latency. Each core has its own sets of registers that are unique to it and separated from all others. The main memory of the SMP is a large set of memory modules divided into memory banks that are accessible by all the processors and their cores. Main memory is implemented on separate dynamic random access memory (DRAM) chips and plugged into the SMP motherboard's industry-standard memory interfaces (physical, logical, and electrical). Data in the main memory is accessed through a virtual address that the processor translates to a physical address location in the main memory. Typically an SMP will have from 1–4 gigabytes of main memory capacity per processor core.

Between the processor core register sets and the SMP main memory banks are the caches. Caches bridge the gap of speeds between the rate at which the processor core accesses data and the rate at which the DRAM can provide it. The difference between these two is easily two orders of magnitude, with a core fetch rate in the order of two accesses per nanosecond and the memory cycle time in the order of 100 ns. To achieve this, the cache layers exploit temporal and spatial locality. In simple terms, this means that the cache system relies on data reuse. Ideally, data access requests will be satisfied with data present in the level 1 (L1) cache that operates at a throughput equivalent to the demand rate of a processor core and a latency of one to four cycles. This assumes that the sought-after data has already been acquired before (temporal locality) or that it is very near data already accessed (spatial locality). Under these conditions, a processor core could operate very near its peak performance capability. But due to size and power requirements, L1 caches (both data and instruction) are relatively small and susceptible to overflow; there is a need for more data than can be held in the L1 cache alone. To address this, a level 2 (L2) cache is almost always incorporated, again on the processor socket for each core or sometimes shared among cores. The L2 cache holds both data and instructions and is much larger than the L1 caches, although much slower. L1 and L2 caches are implemented with static random access memory (SRAM) circuit design. As the separation between core clock rates and main memory cycle times grew, a third level of cache, L3, was included, although these were usually implemented as a DRAM chip integrated within the same multi-chip module packaging of the processor socket. The L3 cache will often be shared among two or more cores on the processor package.

This contributes to achieving the second critical property of the SMP memory hierarchy: cache coherency. The symmetric multiprocessing attribute requires copies of main memory data values that are held in caches for fast access to be consistent. When two or more copies of a value with a virtual address are in distinct physical caches, a change to the value of one of those copies must be reflected in the values of all others. Sometimes the actual value may be changed to the updated value, although more frequently the other copies are merely invalidated so an obsolete value is not read and used. There are many hardware protocols that ensure the correctness of data copies, started as early as the 1980s with the modified exclusive shared invalid [1] family of protocols. The necessity to maintain such data coherence across caches within an SMP adds design complexity, time to access data, and increased energy.

Many SMP systems incorporate their own secondary storage to hold large quantities of information, both program codes and user data, and do so in a persistent manner so as to not lose stored information after the associated applications finish, other users employ the system, or the system is powered down. Mass storage has usually been achieved through hard magnetic disk technology with one or more spinning disk drives. More recently, although with somewhat lower density, solid-state drives (SSDs) have served this purpose. While more expensive, SSDs exhibit superior access and cycle times and better reliability as they have no moving parts. Mass storage presents two logic interfaces to the user. Explicitly, it supports the file system consisting of a graph structure of directories, each holding other directories and end-user files of data and programs. A complete set of specific file and directory access service calls is made available to users as part of the operating system to use the secondary storage. A second abstraction presented by mass storage is as part of the virtual memory system, where "pages" of block data with virtual addresses may be kept on disk and swapped in and out of main memory as needed. When a page request is made for data that is not found in memory, a page fault is indicated and the operating system performs the necessary tasks to make room for the requested page in main memory by moving a less-used page on to disk and then bringing the desired page into memory while updating various tables. This is performed transparently to the user, but can take more than a million times longer than a similar data access request to cache. Some SMP nodes, especially those used as subsystems of commodity clusters or MPPs, may not include their own secondary storage. Referred to as "diskless nodes", these will instead share secondary storage which is itself a subsystem of the supercomputer or even external file systems shared by multiple computers and workstations. Diskless nodes are smaller, cheaper, lower energy, and more reliable.

Every SMP has multiple I/O channels that communicate with external devices (outside the SMP), user interfaces, data storage, system area networks, local area networks, and wide area networks, among others. Every user is familiar with many of these, as they are also found on deskside and laptop systems. For local area and system area networks, interfaces are most frequently provided to Ethernet and InfiniBand (IB) to connect to other SMPs of a larger cluster or institutional environments such as shared mass storage, printers, and the internet. The universal serial bus (USB) has become so widely employed for diverse purposes, including portable flash drives, that it is ubiquitous and available on essentially everything larger than a screen pad or laptop, and certainly on any deskside or rack-mounted SMP. JTAG is widely employed for system administration and maintenance. The Serial Advanced Technology Attachment (SATA) is widely used for external disk drives. Video graphics array and high-definition multimedia interface provide direct connection to high-resolution video screens. There is usually a connection specifically provided for a directly connected user keyboard. Depending on the system, there may be a number of other I/O interfaces.

6.3 AMDAHL'S LAW PLUS

Consider a situation analogous to one that dominates computing: whether to fly or drive to get from one city to another nearby city. The airplane travels about 10 times faster than a car. At first thought, it would be obvious that flying is better than driving with a peak performance gain of an order of magnitude. But door to door may not be an advantage: it takes about the same amount of time either way. The overheads of getting to and from the airport, the waiting time at the airport, waiting at baggage claim, the delay in getting a rental car or taxi, and even the time to check in at the hotel all degrade the positive effect of having a significant accelerator (the jet airplane versus the automobile) over the majority of the distance. A very similar situation dominates computing: it is codified in an observation made by Gene Amdahl, and is appropriately referred to as "Amdahl's law".

As previously presented, the SLOW performance model identifies key factors that determine delivered (or sustained) performance, including parallelism (starvation), latency, overheads, and contention (waiting for arbitration for shared resources). The effective operation of SMP-class architecture can be measured as the ratio of the delivered performance to the theoretical peak performance of the system. Amdahl's law is an important relation that captures a critical aspect of the SLOW performance model, specifically the effect of the program parallelism that provides the performance gain. If, with some simplification, a computation is divided between the part or fraction (f, where $0 < f < 1$) that can benefit from acceleration, such as the number of processor cores available for parallel execution and the remaining part of the computation ($1 - f$) that is forced to perform at the rate of a single-thread execution, a total performance gain, S, with respect to the full computation being performed at sequential speed can be determined. This is illustrated in Fig. 6.2.

In Fig. 6.2 the upper line represents the computation being performed in a purely sequential manner from start to end over a period of T_O. The part of the total execution that is available for acceleration, shown as the lighter shaded line, is T_F where $T_F < T_O$. The fraction of the computation that can benefit from performance gain is $f = T_F/T_O$. With acceleration applied to the fraction designated, the total speedup is $S = T_O/T_A$, where T_A is the time to solution of the accelerated code. The derivation for S is shown in Eqs. (6.2)–(6.6), where g is the gain of the accelerator over the conventional execution rate. This is known as Amdahl's law:

$$S = T_O/T_A \tag{6.2}$$

$$f = T_F/T_O \tag{6.3}$$

$$T_A = (1-f) * T_O + \frac{f}{g} * T_O \tag{6.4}$$

$$S = \frac{T_O}{(1-f) * T_O + \frac{f}{g} * T_O} \tag{6.5}$$

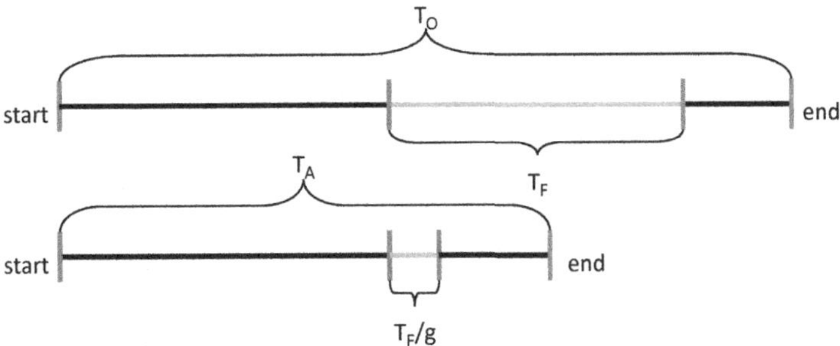

FIGURE 6.2

The time required to complete the serial execution (T_0) and accelerated (parallel) execution (T_A) of an application. A fraction of the application can be accelerated, indicated in green (light gray in print versions), requiring a non-accelerated time of T_F and an accelerated time of T_F/g. The total performance gain of the acceleration, S, is T_0/T_F.

$$S = \frac{1}{1 - f + \frac{f}{g}} \tag{6.6}$$

where T_0 is time for the nonaccelerated computation; T_A is time for the accelerated computation; T_F is time of the portion of computation that can be accelerated; g is peak performance gain for the accelerated portion of computation; f is fraction of the nonaccelerated computation to be accelerated; and S is speedup of the computation with acceleration applied.

The fundamental consequence of Amdahl's law is that independent of the size of the accelerator's peak performance gain, g, the sustained performance is bounded by the fraction, f, of the original code that can be accelerated. As a trivial limit, imagine that you have an accelerator capable of instantaneous execution no matter what the code, and that half the problem can be executed this way; that is, consider the case of infinite gain. The speedup for infinite gain and $f = 0.5$ is only $S = 2.0$. Fig. 6.3 shows the speedup with respect to the fraction of code accelerated for several values of g.

It is clear from the set of curves in Fig. 6.3 that sustained speedup is highly sensitive to the fraction of the computation that can benefit from acceleration. Where the fraction, f, to which g can be applied is less than 0.5 or so, S remains relatively low even if g is greater than an order of magnitude. It is only when f approaches 1.0 that dramatic reductions of time to solution result. For an SMP comprising p processor cores, g can be approximated by p_A, which is the number of cores applied to the parallel segments of the code ($p_A \leq p$).

Example

What is the minimum number of processor cores one must employ in an SMP to achieve a speedup of 3× where 75% of the user application can be fully parallelized?

Here $S = 3$, and $f = 0.75$ where we are seeking p_A as the minimum value of g required. Using the formulation for Amdahl's law derived above, the calculation follows:

$3 = 1/(1 - 0.75 + (0.75/g))$ or $g = 9$.

At least nine cores of the SMP must be used to get a speed up of 3× with this code.

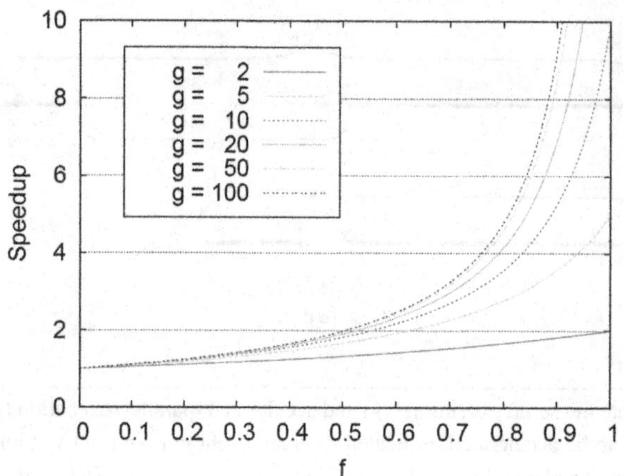

FIGURE 6.3

The speedup with respect to the fraction of code accelerated for several values of g.

But that is the good news. There are other sources of performance degradation that also come into play; in particular the overhead, v, of managing the parallel tasks, which does not contribute to the real work but does add to the critical time to solution. The timelines in Fig. 6.2 suggest that all the work that can be accelerated occurs in one large chunk, when in reality it is usually partitioned in a sequence of chunks, each controlled by some amount of overhead work, as shown in Fig. 6.4.

As seen in the top sequential (nonaccelerated) timeline of Fig. 6.4, the fraction of the computation that can be accelerated is broken into $n = 4$ partitions, which together make up the fraction f of the total work that can be accelerated. If this were the only difference, with a bit of manipulation the formulation of speedup would remain the same as that originally derived. However, for each partition of code to be accelerated, there is hopefully only a small amount of overhead work added to the critical path of execution time. Unfortunately, the size of the overhead is usually relatively constant independent of the granularity of the parallelized useful work parts. Further, the more partitions, n, into which the work is

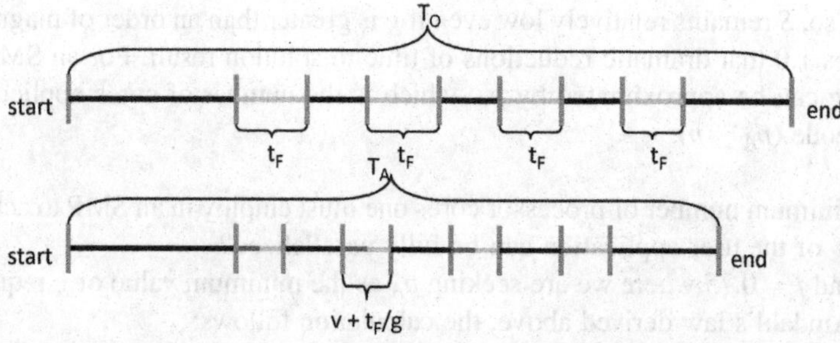

FIGURE 6.4

Timelines for nonaccelerated (T_O) and accelerated (T_A) executions, similar to Fig. 6.2 but including overhead, v.

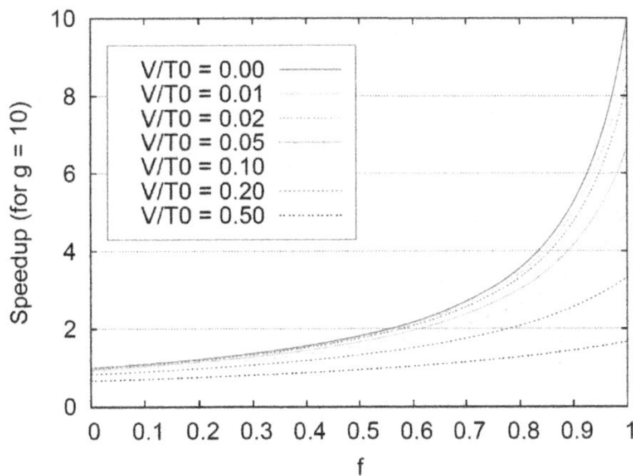

FIGURE 6.5

The speedup for various overhead ratios as a function of the fraction of code that can be accelerated for a fixed gain ($g = 10$).

divided, the more the additional overhead. By considering this overhead, a new extended version of Amdahl's law is derived in Eqs. (6.7)–(6.9).

$$T_A = (1 - f) * T_0 + \frac{f}{g} * T_0 + n * v \tag{6.7}$$

$$S = \frac{T_0}{T_A} = \frac{T_0}{(1 - f) * T_0 + \frac{f}{g} * T_0 + n * v} \tag{6.8}$$

$$S = \frac{1}{(1 - f) + \frac{f}{g} + \frac{n * v}{T_0}} \tag{6.9}$$

where v is the overhead of an accelerated work segment and V is total overhead for the total accelerated work, $\sum_i^n v_i$.

Using the new equation for speedup given in Eq. (6.9), there is a new ratio added to the denominator that is proportional to the overhead v and the number of partitions, n. If there is no overhead ($v = 0$), the results are the same as the original formulation of Amdahl's law. If there is only a single large fraction of the code to be accelerated ($n = 1$), the result is almost the same. But as the parallelism is increased in the number of separate components, the overhead has an increasingly degrading effect. This is shown in Fig. 6.5.

As in Fig. 6.3, the abscissa axis in Fig. 6.5 is the fraction of code that can be accelerated, f, but g here is constant for all curves. A new independent variable, overhead v, is added to the plot, while T_0 is constant. As the overhead increases, performance gain, S, is reduced.

6.4 PROCESSOR CORE ARCHITECTURE

The modern multicore processor, sometimes called a "socket", consists of a number of cores, a potentially complex cache hierarchy, one or more interfaces to external main memory and I/O buses, and ancillary logic. While differing in details, most common processors can be characterized by a

Table 6.2 Characterization of Several SMP Processors

Processor	Clock Rate	Caches (per Core)	ILP (Each Core)	Cores Per Chip	Process and Die Size	Power (W)
AMD Opteron 6380	2.5 GHz (3.4 GHz turbo)	L1I: 32 KB L1D: 16 KB L2: 1 MB L3: 16 MB total	4 FPops/cycle 4 intops/cycle	16	32 nm, 316 mm^2	115
IBM Power8	3.126 GHz (3.625 GHz turbo)	L1I: 64 KB L1D: 32 KB L2: 512 KB L3: 8 MB L4: 64 MB total	16 FPops/cycle	12	22 nm, 650 mm^2	190/247
Intel Xeon E7-8894V4	2.4 GHz (3.4 GHz turbo)	L1I: 32 KB L1D: 32 KB L2: 256 KB L3: 60 MB total	16 FPops/cycle	24	14 nm	165

shared set of parameters, shown in Table 6.2. Among these are the number of cores per socket, the size and interconnectivity of the cache levels (usually two or three levels), the clock rate of the core, the number and type of arithmetic logic units per core (ILP), the die size (between one and four square centimeters), the feature size, and the delivered performance for one or more standardized benchmarks. For the application programmer many of the details may not matter, but the rate at which instructions are issued, the number of operations performed per instruction issue, the average time per memory access, and the delays due to I/O requests are principal in determining the delivered performance. In this section the major structures of the processor core are described and how they contribute to achieved performance. Section 6.5 examines the memory and cache hierarchy in depth to understand the role of locality in reducing average memory access time.

6.4.1 EXECUTION PIPELINE

The earliest generation of sequential computers issued and completed one instruction at a time using the oft-quoted "fetch–execute–writeback" cycle. With the low clock rates possible in early vacuum-tube and transistor technologies, this was satisfactory. But as clock rates improved with advanced technologies (e.g., small- and medium-scale integration), this straightforward approach became untenable. The complexity of the full issue to completion of instructions required too many layers of logic, with the resulting latency bounding the feasible clock rate.

A pipelined structure was adopted to partition the full compute operation into a sequence of microoperations which together achieved the same functionality. The time from instruction issue to completion would actually be longer than for a single logical function of the same purpose, but each stage of the pipeline would take much less time. As the clock rate was limited by the instruction issue cycle time, which was itself determined by the propagation delay through the longest stage of the pipeline, an execution pipeline with as many stages as possible each of the same delay allowed the clock rate to be increased appreciably. Early execution pipelines with four or five stages were eventually superseded by much longer pipelines.

As discussed in Chapter 2, pipeline logic structure is a general way of exploiting a form of very fine-grain parallelism, as each pipeline stage operates simultaneously. Ideally, the parallelism of a functional pipeline is equal to the number of stages of which the total pipeline is formed. Execution pipelines benefited from both the reduction in clock cycle times and the parallelism of their constituent stages. But a number of other factors imposed limits on the degree of pipelining that could be effectively employed. Among these are:

1. The size of the total function limited the number of logic layers that were required and thus the maximum number of stages into which the pipeline could be divided.
2. Imbalance in the number of logic layers in each stage made some stages slightly longer than others and therefore slowed down the rate at which signals could propagate through the execution pipeline.
3. The overhead of the interface between successive stages of the pipeline added additional propagation delay to each stage, bounding how fast the signals could proceed through the execution pipeline.
4. Not all execution functions were the same, and they did not necessarily require the same number of function stages. Those requiring more stages would waste some of the hardware when other execution cycles required fewer stages.
5. Intermediate values of one operation might be required for a following operation, but would be unavailable in time for the succeeding operation to be issued at its earliest opportunity. Alternatively, it would stall waiting for the results of the earlier operation to complete.
6. Conditional operations complicate the efficient use of an execution pipeline. Their function is to perform a branch to a noncontiguous instruction location, but to do so only if a predicate value is true, which must also be determined. This extends the number of microaction sequences, disrupting the flow within the execution pipeline and causing delays or "bubbles" to be inserted, thus slowing down execution.

To speed up execution despite these inhibiting factors, the core architecture has evolved in a number of forms and functions, briefly described in the following subsections.

6.4.2 INSTRUCTION-LEVEL PARALLELISM

Superscalar architectures enable multiple operations to be launched by a single instruction issue. This is achieved through the incorporation of multiple arithmetic logic units (ALUs), including both floating-point and integer/logical functional units, among others. Additional single-instruction multiple data units may be included to perform the same operations on multiple data values from the same instruction. Known as ILP, this provides among the finest-grain parallelism available to a processor core, and for special cases it can have a dramatic impact on total throughput. Unfortunately, experience over more than two decades shows that in general such peak capabilities are rarely exhibited while still adding complexity, overhead, and power demand to the advanced designs.

6.4.3 BRANCH PREDICTION

The problem with conditional branch instructions is discussed in Section 6.4.1. To eliminate bubbles caused by the delay between determining the Boolean value of the predicate and committing the virtual address of the next instruction to be executed, a statistical approach known as "branch prediction" is employed. As the name implies, upon a branch instruction being issued, the hardware makes a guess as to which of the two alternative instructions that may be followed will be issued. There is a long history of techniques to do this, and further reading on this topic is found in the bibliography [2–6]. But for this discussion the key idea is that depending on the role of the particular branch prediction, one of the two paths is more likely. For example, if a branch is used at the bottom of a loop, it is far more likely that the predicate will redirect the execution flow to the top of the loop rather than immediately continuing on. If a branch is associated with error handling, it is highly unlikely that this path will be pursued and more likely that the next instruction to be issued will be part of the regular computation stream. There will always be cases where the wrong choice is made, so the hardware architecture has to be capable of rolling back the computation to take the other path; this itself is a large body of architecture lore. Some codes, like system software, are very heavy with branches, and in such cases branch prediction architecture support can go a long way in improving efficiency.

6.4.4 FORWARDING

Key to the concept of the execution pipeline is that the time to issue successive instructions is potentially far shorter than the time to completion through the many stages of the pipeline. It is possible that two succeeding instructions may impose one or more precedence constraints, such that the second instruction requires as arguments the result value of the preceding (first) instruction issued. Usually an instruction will acquire its operands from the core's register set. But in the condition described there will not have been enough time for the resulting value of the first instruction to be calculated and written back into the register bank before the second instruction would ordinarily read the same value from the register in which this intermediate value resides. The solution is "forwarding". Forwarding means added data transfer channels that move data from downstream execution pipeline segments to the appropriate upstream segment, making the argument value available in time for the instructions to follow more closely in succession. Combined with compiler reordering where necessary gaps can be filled with one or more unrelated instructions, pipeline stages can be filled and bubbles eliminated through forwarding.

6.4.5 RESERVATION STATIONS

Different operations take different amounts of time to complete, and the execution pipeline becomes multipath with shorter links in a simple Boolean logic operation than for a floating-point multiply. If strict ordering were preserved, i.e., the order of completion was forced to be identical to the order of issue, the rate of instruction processing would be constrained by the slowest operations with repeated stalls of backstream instructions. This problem is addressed by reservation stations, a concept dating back to the late 1960s, and the ideas of data flow in the 1970s. A reservation station is a special-purpose buffer register, invisible to the user, which temporarily holds a previous result value. Its special feature is that it "knows" what follow-on instructions require the captured value, and those instructions know the corresponding reservation station(s) from which to acquire their argument values. If the instruction tries to get the operand value before it is available in the designated reservation station, the instruction will be delayed at the reservation station but will not impede the progress of the execution pipeline. There are many alternative architecture methods by which this complex out-of-order scheduling mechanism can be achieved (often referred to as the "Tomasulo algorithm"), but in every case the use of reservation stations permits substantial flexibility in operation of the execution pipeline and greater efficiency.

6.4.6 MULTITHREADING

So far the discussion of the processor core's execution pipeline assumes a single stream of instructions, each with one or more associated operations. While these can prove complex in detail, they still are based on the original von Neumann concept of a single program counter (or instruction pointer) that is incremented for each instruction issue except for branch instructions. This is a clean and elegant approach but suffers from a number of edge conditions, such as those previously discussed. Many of these problems are due to the interrelationships among adjacent or neighboring instructions of a single instruction stream. One way to address this challenge in a single processor core was introduced by Burton Smith in the 1980s: the concept of "multithreading". In its simplest version, multithreading incorporates multiple instruction streams or threads routed through sets of multiple instruction pointers and their associated register sets. The rest of the execution pipeline is shared, and a round-robin instruction issue scheduler selects each successive instruction fetch from different threads. This hides the latency of the execution pipeline and, if sufficient threads are employed, the latencies to main memory as well.

BURTON SMITH AND THE MTA

Photo by Dimitrij Krepis via Wikimedia Commons

Burton Smith is a leading computer architect and is considered the father of multithreading architecture, for which he was awarded the Eckert-Mauchly Award and the Seymour Cray Award. As a cofounder of Denelcor and later the founder of Tera Computer Company Smith led the commercialization of multithreaded architecture. In 2000 Tera became Cray, with the merger of the Cray Research business unit of Silicon Graphics. Burton Smith was the chief architect of the Tera MTA (multithreaded architecture), a breakthrough design that continues to inform high performance computer development. Burton Smith became a technical fellow of Microsoft in 2005, where he remains to this day advancing future technologies and computing concepts.

The MTA-1 was deployed at the San Diego Supercomputer Center; the initial system was unique in that it was implemented using very high-speed logic based on gallium arsenide. This architecture incorporated four processors each with 128 independent register sets and program counters, permitting a total of 512 threads to be executed simultaneously. Each processor integrated a high-speed arithmetic processing unit to which its local threads could apply operations to be performed, thus sharing the ALU for maximum utilization, efficiency, and performance. The MTA's strength was in its ability to hide memory access latencies from the arithmetic units and adjust to asynchronies of operation. This eliminated the needs for data caches, precluding the complexities and costs of achieving consistency among them. Empty/full bits on every word and a use of tagged memory enabled fine-grain synchronization. Other tags made possible control semantics such as futures, among others. The MTA-1 prototype was followed by a much less expensive and more densely packed CMOS version, the MTA-2, with further advances leading to the Cray XMT System in 2009.

6.5 MEMORY HIERARCHY

The "memory wall", alternatively termed the "von Neumann bottleneck", recognizes the mismatch between the peak demand rate of the processor socket for data access and the possible delivered throughput and latency of the main memory technology, principally semiconductor DRAM. As demonstrated in Fig. 6.6, performance gain for processors increased on average by 60%/year, while that of main memory experienced only about a 9%/year improvement. Over time this has led to a two order of magnitude difference between processor speeds and memory speeds. To address this challenge, and indeed move even further into the domain of secondary storage and beyond, computer architecture in general and SMP architecture in particular have evolved a hierarchical structure of a sequence of layers of storage components with increasing density and capacity in one direction of the hierarchy, and greater access speed including higher bandwidth and lower latency in the other direction.

6.5.1 DATA REUSE AND LOCALITY

Fundamental to the success of this memory architecture is the strategy of data reuse through locality. If a value of a variable is used by a program repeatedly and frequently, storing it in a very high-speed memory device very close to the processor core will deliver near-peak performance. This is "temporal locality", which reflects the property of data that associates the probability of usage with recent prior usage. High temporal locality suggests that a particular variable is accessed frequently in a moderate period of time. Low temporal locality indicates that a variable is probably only used once or a couple of times in the moderate contiguous period, if accessed at all. A second form of locality often exploited is "spatial", which indicates an association of locality among adjacent or near neighbors in contiguous address space. High spatial locality suggests that the probability of a variable (virtually addressed value) being accessed is higher if one of its adjacent or neighboring variables has been recently accessed. These two forms of locality concerning the reuse patterns of virtually addressed

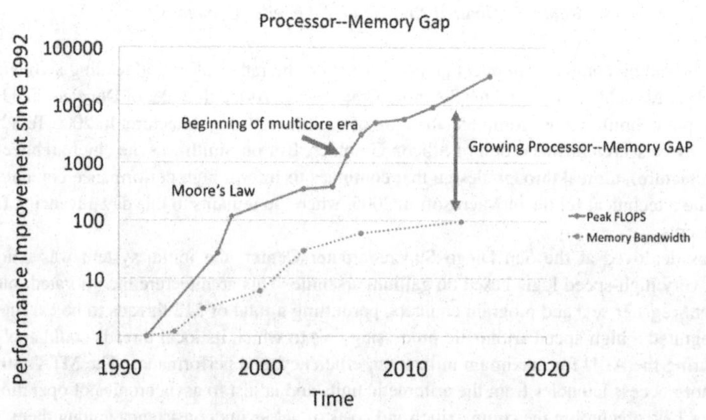

FIGURE 6.6

Performance gains for processors increased by four orders of magnitude while main memory experienced an improvement of only two orders of magnitude during the same period of time.

variables provide the foundations for the structure and operation of the memory hierarchy to mitigate the effects of the discrepancies between bandwidths and latencies of processor and memory technologies.

The second factor of practical concern is the tradeoff relationships between the characteristics of storage capacity per unit area, cycle time of access, and power consumption. In Chapter 17, it is shown that diverse on enabling technologies it is shown that diverse data storage technologies vary in terms of these parameters. In general, faster memory technologies take up more room on a semiconductor die or other medium for the same amount of storage while consuming greater power. It is impractical to create a main memory layer that is big enough to hold all the software and data required for a given user application while running fast enough to keep the processor cores fully utilized at their peak instruction issue throughput.

6.5.2 MEMORY HIERARCHY

The conventional way for modern computing architectures, including SMP systems, to address these tradeoffs through exploitation of data locality is in the structure of the memory hierarchy, also known as the memory stack.

As shown in Fig. 6.7, the memory hierarchy or stack consists of layers of memory storage technology, each with different tradeoffs between memory capacity, costs, and cycle times, which reflect bandwidths and latencies. By far the slowest but also the highest capacity is the use of tape archival storage, often consisting of possibly thousands of tape modules physically stored in a robotic library with total capacities approaching exabytes. But in an unloaded system access to stored data could take upwards of a minute, even though the cost of a megabyte is a fraction of a cent. Tape robots provide part of mass storage called "tertiary storage"; another part of mass storage is secondary storage made up of hard-disk drives (HDDs). Disks, like tapes, use a magnetic storage medium. But unlike tapes, which present one long serial stream of storage that can take a long time to go from one end to the other, data on disks are laid out in concentric rings (called "cylinders") that spin on an axis. A radial arm moving in and out across the spinning disk selects the appropriate cylinder and waits for the required data to come around to be detected by the arm's head. A typical disk drive may hold several terabytes, deliver data at a peak streaming rate of 300 MB/s, and impose an overall access time of around 10 ms. While this is 100,000 times longer than access to main memory, it may hold 1000 times as much stored data and exhibit a latency 10,000 times shorter than tape drives. A third technology recently introduced commercially, nonvolatile random access memory, is increasingly being employed as a partial replacement for disk drives for much faster response than disks but slower than main memory. Mass storage is usually presented to the user in the form of logical data modules called files, and directories that hold files as well as other directories.

At the other (top) end of the memory hierarchy are the processor core registers that operate at the speed of the clock rate and support multiple access ports allowing multiple reads and writes into/out of the register banks in each instruction cycle. While operating at native processor speeds, registers take up a lot of room and consume significant energy per cycle. Registers also exhibit their own address space not associated with the memory address namespace. The instruction-set architecture (ISA) is logically structured such that data explicitly moves between identified registers and the variables in the main memory.

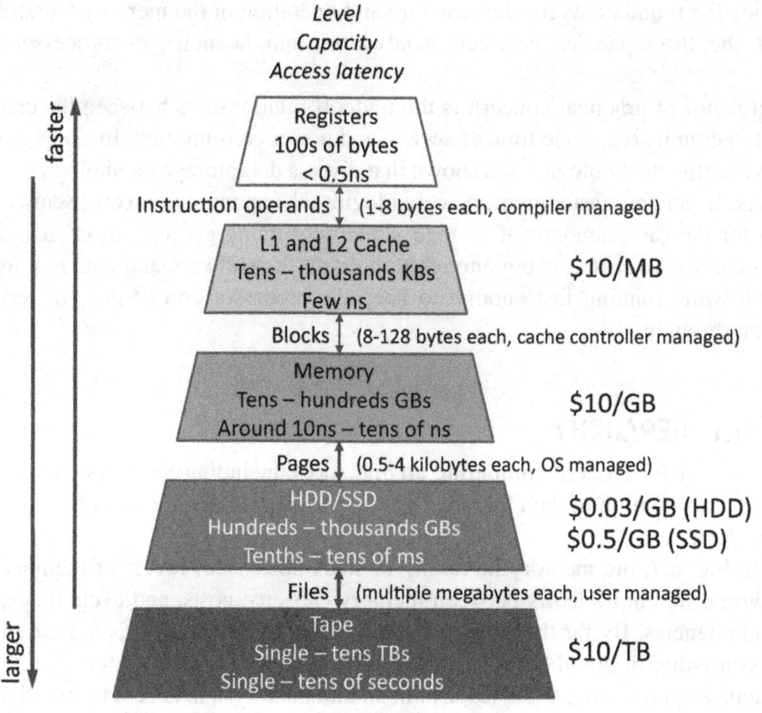

FIGURE 6.7

The memory hierarchy delineated by memory capacity, cost, and cycle times.

Courtesy David A. Patterson

The main memory is provided by DRAM semiconductor devices. Many such components are mounted on personal computer cards plugged into sockets compliant with industry-standard interfaces. As much as 4 gigabytes of memory per processor core for an SMP is often provided, although this can drop to as low as 1 gigabyte per core depending on the number of cores per socket. But access times from register to DRAM can be between 100 and 200 clock cycles, far too much for effective computing.

Between processor core registers and SMP main memory modules is a cache system to impedance match between these two extremes in timing and bandwidth. Logically the cache system is transparent to the user, in that it is not separately addressable but instead accepts memory access requests. If the variable address requested by a core has a copy of the variable value somewhere within its cache, the cache provides that value in the case of a load operation to the designated core register. If a copy does not exist, the cache system automatically passes the request to the main memory to perform the data access. Where data locality applies, a cache "hit" is likely and the access time will be that of high-speed cache rather than the slower main memory, which can be as much as two orders of magnitude faster.

In a modern SMP the cache is usually not a single layer of higher-speed memory, but rather multiple layers to find an optimal balance of speed and size. Typically there are three layers: L1, L2, and L3. L1 is the fastest and smallest, and usually consists of two separate caches: one for data and the other for instructions to provide enough peak bandwidth. L2 is slower but much larger, and like L1 is made from SRAM circuits. The L3 cache is much larger than the lower-layer caches, but is slower.

Unlike the first two, L3 is usually a separate chip of DRAM rather than SRAM circuits to achieve the greatest density.

A simple hierarchical structure would provide each core with its own separate L1, L2, and L3 caches. However, often multiple cores are working on the same set of data, and the maximum amount of data in a layer could be increased by allowing more than one core to share at least some of the cache. Typically the L1 cache is not shared due to the need for maximum individual bandwidth. Also typically the L3 cache is shared among the processor cores or some subset of them. L2 caches may be either dedicated to a single core or shared among two or more cores. Part of the tradeoff is about bandwidth and possible contention for cache access among sharing cores.

6.5.3 MEMORY SYSTEM PERFORMANCE

It is clear that the time to access a value from a specified variable in the memory system will vary dramatically depending on a number of factors, most specifically where the closest copy of the value is in the memory hierarchy. While analyzing such a complex memory architecture can be very complicated due to the number of levels, the overheads involved, issues of contention, and so forth, a simplified version of the problem still exposes the principal tradeoffs and shows how dramatically the average memory access time can change depending on the hit rates to cache as a consequence of locality. For this purpose, the cache is assumed to be a single intermediate layer between processor core registers and main memory. Without a detailed queuing analysis or similar in-depth model, operational metrics are adopted to capture the specific properties of the architecture and application memory access profile, plus a quality metric of performance. An analytical model is derived to show the sensitivity between delivered performance and the effectiveness of caching.

The quality metric of choice in this case is *CPI* or cycles per instruction. Time to solution, T, is proportional to cycle time, T_{cycle}, and the number of instructions to be executed for a user task, I_{count}. Because the purpose of this analysis is to expose the implications of memory behavior, the instruction count is partitioned between those instructions associated with the number of register-to-register *ALU* instructions, I_{ALU}, and the number of memory access instructions, I_{MEM}. For each of these two classes of instructions there is a separate measure of cycles per instruction, one for the register-to-register *ALU* operation, CPI_{ALU}, and one for the memory instructions, CPI_{MEM}. The total value for time, I_{count}, and *CPI* can be derived from the breakdown between *ALU* and memory operations according to Eqs. (6.10)–(6.12).

$$T = I_{count} * CPI * T_{cycle} \tag{6.10}$$

$$I_{count} = I_{ALU} + I_{MEM} \tag{6.11}$$

$$CPI = \frac{I_{ALU}}{I_{count}} * CPI_{ALU} + \frac{I_{MEM}}{I_{count}} * CPI_{MEM} \tag{6.12}$$

The full set of parameters is defined as:

T, total execution time; T_{cycle}, time for a single processor cycle; I_{count}, total number of instructions; I_{ALU}, number of ALU instructions (e.g., register to register); I_{MEM}, number of memory access instructions (e.g., load, store); *CPI*, average cycles per instruction; CPI_{ALU}, average cycles per ALU instruction; CPI_{MEM}, average cycles per memory instruction; r_{miss}, cache miss rate; r_{hit}, cache hit rate; $CPI_{MEM-MISS}$, cycles per cache miss; $CPI_{MEM-HIT}$, cycles per cache hit; M_{ALU}, instruction mix for ALU instructions; and M_{MEM}, instruction mix for memory access instructions.

The idea of an instruction mix simplifies representation of this distinction between ALU and memory operations, providing ratios of each with respect to the total instruction count.

In addition, the parameter that expresses the effect of data reuse is defined as the hit rate, r_{hit}, which establishes the percentage of time that a memory request is found in the cache. The opposite of this parameter can be useful: $r_{miss} = (1 - r_{hit})$. One last distinction is made for CPI_{MEM} depending on whether a hit or a miss occurred. These represent the costs, measured in number of cycles of memory instruction access times, depending on whether there was a hit or a miss at the cache. $CPI_{MEM\text{-}HIT}$ is a fixed value of the number of cycles required for an access that is served by the cache, and $CPI_{MEM\text{-}MISS}$ is the cost in cycles of going all the way to main memory to get a memory request serviced in the case of a cache miss. The relationships among these distinguishing parameters are demonstrated in Eqs. (6.13)–(6.17), associating them with the definition of full execution time.

Instruction mix:

$$M_{ALU} = \frac{I_{ALU}}{I_{count}} \tag{6.13}$$

$$M_{MEM} = \frac{I_{MEM}}{I_{count}} \tag{6.14}$$

$$M_{ALU} + M_{MEM} = 1 \tag{6.15}$$

Time to solution:

$$CPI = (M_{ALU} * CPI_{ALU}) + (M_{MEM} * CPI_{MEM}) \tag{6.16}$$

$$T = I_{count} * [\, (M_{ALU} * CPI_{ALU}) + (M_{MEM} * CPI_{MEM})] * T_{cycle} \tag{6.17}$$

Finally, the values for CPI_{MEM} and T as functions of r_{miss} are presented in Eqs. (6.18) and (6.19). It may appear peculiar that the coefficient of $CPI_{MEM\text{-}HIT}$ is not r_{hit}. This is because the cost of getting data from or to the cache occurs whether or not a miss occurs.

$$CPI_{MEM} = CPI_{MEM-HIT} + r_{miss} * CPI_{MEM-MISS} \tag{6.18}$$

$$T = I_{count} * [(M_{ALU} * CPI_{ALU}) + M_{MEM} * (CPI_{MEM-HIT} + r_{miss} * CPI_{MEM-MISS})] * T_{cycle} \tag{6.19}$$

This shows the effect of the application-driven properties, including I_{count}, M_{MEM}, and r_{miss}. Architecture-driven properties are reflected as T_{cycle}, $CPI_{MEM\text{-}MISS}$, and $CPI_{MEM\text{-}HIT}$ in determining the final time to solution, T.

Example

As a case study, a system and computation are described in terms of the set of parameters presented above. Typical values are assigned to these to represent conventional practices, architectures, and applications. These are shown below.

I_{count}	$=1E11$
I_{MEM}	$=2E10$
CPI_{ALU}	$=1$
T_{cycle}	$=0.5$ ns
$CPI_{MEM-MISS}$	$=100$
$CPI_{MEM-HIT}$	$=1$

The intermediate values for instruction mix are computed as follows:

$$I_{ALU} = I_{count} - I_{MEM} = 8E10$$

$$M_{ALU} = \frac{I_{ALU}}{I_{count}} = \frac{8E10}{1E11} = 0.8$$

$$M_{MEM} = \frac{I_{MEM}}{I_{count}} = \frac{2E10}{1E11} = 0.2$$

This example shows the impact of the cache hit rate on the total execution time, which can prove to be one of the most important determining factors of application time to solution and one of which the user has to be aware as data layout is considered. Two alternative computations are considered. The first is favorable to a cache hierarchy (this example simplifies, with only one layer) with a hit rate of 90%. With this value established, the time to solution can be determined as shown in Eqs. (6.20)–(6.22).

$$r_{hit\ A} = 0.9 \tag{6.20}$$

$$CPI_{MEM\ A} = CPI_{MEM-HIT} + r_{MISS\ A} * CPI_{MEM-MISS} = 1 + (1 - 0.9) * 100 = 11 \tag{6.21}$$

$$T_A = 1E11 * [(0.8 * 1) + (0.2 * 11)] * 5E10 = 150\ \text{s} \tag{6.22}$$

But if the cache hit rate is lower, in this case 50%, a recalculation with this new value shows a dramatic reduction of performance, as shown in Eqs. (6.23)–(6.25).

$$r_{hit\ A} = 0.5 \tag{6.23}$$

$$CPI_{MEM\ B} = CPI_{MEM-HIT} + r_{MISS\ B} * CPI_{MEM-MISS} = 1 + (1 - 0.5) * 100 = 51 \tag{6.24}$$

$$T_B = 1E11 * [(0.8 * 1) + (0.2 * 51)] * 5E10 = 550\ \text{s} \tag{6.25}$$

The difference is more than a factor of 3× performance degradation, just because of the change in the cache hit rate.

6.6 PCI BUS

The explosion of the personal computer market initiated in the late 1970s created a growing need for high performance industry-standard interfaces that would enable portability, reusability, and upgradeability of peripherals and custom expansion boards. While initially this void was filled by IBM's industry-standard architecture (ISA) bus, the bulkiness of its connector, low data bandwidth, poor expandability (limited number of interrupts and direct memory access channels), and cumbersome configurability forced the manufacturers to look for improved solutions. IBM's follow-up to ISA, the Micro Channel Architecture, did not gain widespread popularity due to being a proprietary standard that required licensing fees. Broad industry response resulted in the development of stopgap implementations such as extended ISA and Video Electronics Standards Association local bus, the latter of which was primarily used to satisfy the bandwidth requirements of newer graphics cards. The true breakthrough was the work of Intel's Architecture Development Laboratory that resulted in the specification of Peripheral Component Interconnect (PCI) in 1992 [7]. The PCI bus in somewhat modified form may still be found on some motherboards manufactured today.

The PCI bus operates independently from a processor's native memory bus and requires a bridge circuit to provide memory-mapped access from the CPU, as shown in Fig. 6.8. More than one bus may be supported via additional bridges. PCI originated as a parallel multidrop 32-bit bus in which multiple devices connect electrically to the single instance of control and data lines. Its signaling, timing, transaction protocol, mechanical connector properties, and power management have been defined and extended in a series of specifications, the last of which was version 3.0 released in 2004. The clocking frequency was originally set at 33 MHz for a peak bandwidth of 132 MB/s. Subsequent standard releases permitted a faster 66 MHz clock and added a 64-bit data bus option for peak data bandwidth of 533 MB/s. The signal levels were also reduced from 5 V to 3.3 V to reflect the prevailing trends in chip I/O standards and lower the required bus driver power levels. Extended PCI, later introduced to optimize certain aspects of PCI functionality in servers, increased the clock to 266 and 533 MHz, resulting in a maximum transfer rate of 4266 MB/s. To prevent potential card damage by using an incompatible implementation, these options were tied to differently keyed connectors (Fig. 6.9). A short-lived variant of PCI with a dedicated CPU-to-GPU (graphics processing unit) bus was called the Accelerated Graphics Port and featured its own connector type, incompatible with PCI.

To address several shortcomings of the conventional PCI bus architecture (poor scaling in a number of devices, interrupt sharing, an explosion in the number of pins, poor power characteristics of single-ended I/O, limited bandwidth scalability, and access synchronization issues), the PCI Special Interest Group, including among others Intel, Hewlett–Packard, Dell, and IBM, adopted in 2002 a new design called PCI Express (PCIe), with the system schematic shown in Fig. 6.10. Electrically, PCIe is a descendant of Intel's 3GIO (third-generation I/O) initiative that utilized multiple serial links operating

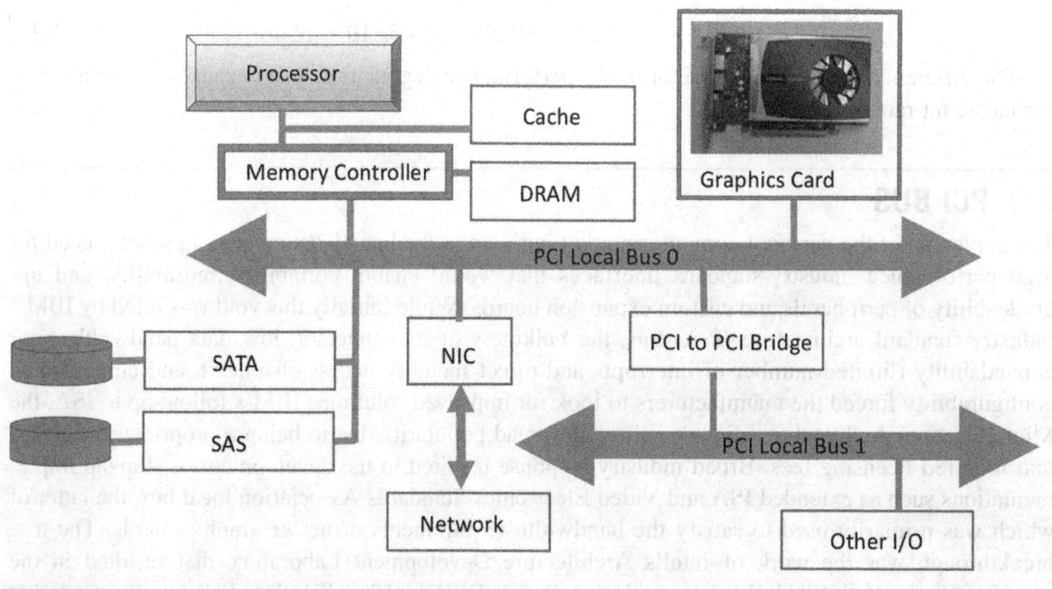

FIGURE 6.8

Layout of a system equipped with multiple PCI buses.

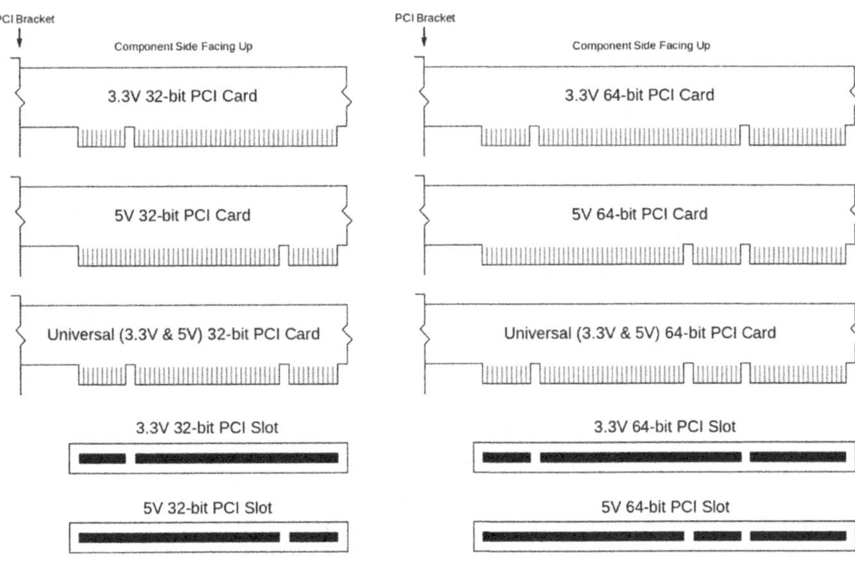

FIGURE 6.9

Connectors supporting different PCI variants.

Image via Wikimedia Commons

at 2.5 Gbps each. The links use low-voltage differential signaling, giving them very good noise immunity and reducing their electromagnetic interference (EMI) levels compared to single-ended operation. High bandwidth of a single link brings a much-needed reduction in the number of required pins: full-duplex connection requires only a pair of wires for transmit and another pair for the

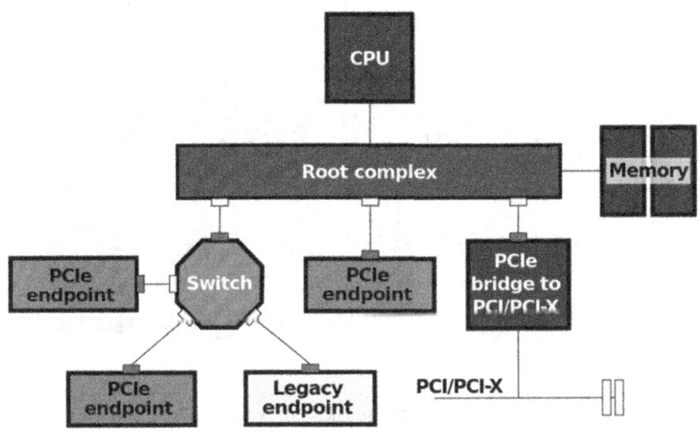

FIGURE 6.10

Diagram of a PCIe-equipped system.

By Mliu92 via Wikimedia Commons

receive function. Scaling to the desired bandwidth is accomplished by adding more links, called "lanes" in PCIe vernacular. Specifications permit up to 32 lanes per card slot, although practical implementations rarely exceed 16 lanes.

Three major revisions of PCIe specifications were released. The first defined operation at nominal 2.5 Gbps with 8 b/10 b encoding (each 8 bits of input data is converted into a 10-bit symbol on wire) for an effective peak of 250 MB/s per link. PCIe 2.0 increased the signaling rate to 5 Gbps per link, doubling the peak data bandwidth. Version 3.0 improved the encoding efficiency by using a 128 b/130 b scheme and further increased the wire rate to 8 Gbps, thus yielding 984.6 MB/s peak per lane, or 15.754 GB/s in aggregate when using a 16-lane device. Unlike conventional PCI, PCIe slots of different generations are backwards compatible, thus enabling the use of older cards in newer machines. PCIe permits plugging cards with fewer lanes into connectors providing more lanes; the inverse is also true as long as the connector can physically accept a card. It is also capable of sustaining the operation (at reduced bandwidth) even when some of the physical links fail. Fig. 6.11 compares sizes of PCIe connectors in various configurations.

PCIe connectors provide 12 V and 3.3 V supply voltages that may be used to power the connected cards. Slot-powered operation limits the power draw to only 25 W per board, which is insufficient to sustain the functioning of more demanding devices, such as GPUs. Such devices instead incorporate dedicated six-pin and eight-pin power connectors that plug into power supply harnesses to provide additional 75 W and 150 W circuits, respectively.

In terms of the protocol, PCIe inherits many properties of the original PCI. The communication is packet based. Each packet is either a posted request (writes data to target space), a nonposted request (initiates a read from the target), completion (carries the data read from the target space), or a

FIGURE 6.11

Comparison of PCIe slots with different lane counts (from the top: ×4, ×16, ×1, ×16) with a conventional PCI connector (bottom).

Via Wikimedia Commons

message that signals a specific event or supports a vendor-defined function. The elementary unit of transfer is a *double word* of 32bits. The transaction layer uses three or four double-word-long headers followed by the payload, which may contain up to 1024 double words (4 KB) of data. Larger data transfers must be split into multiple packets. The data-link layer wraps the transaction data with the packet sequence number and cyclic redundancy code sum used by the receiver to verify the packet integrity. The packets act on memory and I/O spaces (each can be independently configured to use 32- or 64-bit addresses) or the dedicated configuration space. PCIe devices may define up to six distinct read–write memory or I/O regions (fewer if 64-bit addressing is used) with different aperture (active address range) sizes, and a separate optional expansion read-only memory (ROM) space. The latter is used to provide device-specific information or, on compatible Intel platforms, to store additional boot code.

Today, PCIe is a dominant standard for attaching and high performance communication with expansion boards on different machines that may use a processor architecture other than the original Intel ×86 variant. The PCIe specifications are continuously updated and refined to reflect modern technological trends. The next revision of the standard, version 4.0, is expected to be finalized in 2017.

6.7 EXTERNAL I/O INTERFACES

The key I/O interfaces of an SMP are the network interface controllers, including Ethernet and IB, SATA for mass storage devices, JTAG for low-level hardware interface, and USB for connecting peripheral devices like keyboards. This section explores each in detail.

6.7.1 NETWORK INTERFACE CONTROLLERS

The two most common network interface controllers appearing in clusters in the Top 500 list of June 2016 were Ethernet and IB. The following subsections give a brief overview of these network interface controllers.

6.7.1.1 Ethernet

Named after a supposed medium for light propagation that was incorrectly thought to exist by many 19th century scientists, Ethernet is a standardized computer networking technology originally developed at Xerox's Palo Alto Research Center in 1973 by Robert Metcalfe, David Boggs, Chuck Thacker, and Butler Lampson [8]; it has since become ubiquitous. The Institute of Electrical and Electronics Engineers (IEEE) produced the official Ethernet standard 802.3 in 1983 and the technology continues to develop, reaching bandwidths of 100 Gbps.

Ethernet operates by breaking a stream of data into frames, with a preamble and start frame delimiter and ending with a frame check sequence. In the standard IEEE 802.3 Ethernet specification, the minimum frame size was 64 bytes and the maximum was 1518 bytes (since expanded to 1522 bytes). The preamble consists of 7 bytes followed by a single byte as a start frame delineator. The frame itself has a header containing the destination and source encoded in 48-bit addresses known as media access control (MAC) addresses. The frame data follows this header and is terminated by the frame check sequence. On Gigabit Ethernet networks jumbo frames of up to 8960 bytes can be used which bypass the standard Ethernet maximum of 1522 bytes.

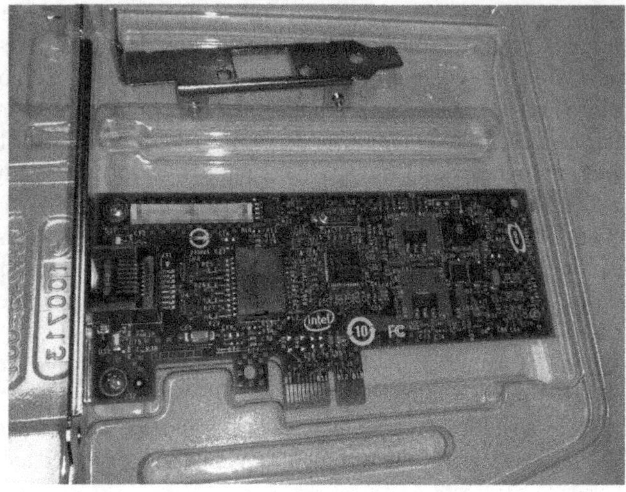

FIGURE 6.12

A Gigabit Ethernet network interface card.

By Dsimic via Wikimedia Commons

The state of the art for Ethernet is currently 100 Gbps. In the June 2017 Top 500 list of supercomputers, Gigabit Ethernet is featured in 207 systems and is the most common internal system interconnect technology in the list [9]. Examples of Gigabit Ethernet cards and switches are shown in Figs. 6.12 and 6.13.

FIGURE 6.13

The internals of a Gigabit Ethernet switch.

By Dsimic via Wikimedia Commons

6.7.1.2 InfiniBand

IB is an alternative to Ethernet for computer networking technology and originated in 1999. Unlike Ethernet, IB does not need to run networking protocols on the CPU; these are handled directly on the IB adapters. IB also supports remote direct memory access between nodes of a supercomputer without requiring a system call, thereby reducing overhead. IB hardware is produced by Mellanox and Intel, with IB software developed through the OpenFabrics Open Source Alliance [10].

The state of the art for IB transfer rates is the same as the fastest transfer rate supported by the PCIe bus (25 Gbps for enhanced data rate). In the June 2017 Top 500 list of supercomputers, IB technology is the second most-used internal system interconnect technology, appearing in 178 systems [9]. Examples of IB cards and a port are shown in Figs. 6.14 and 6.15.

6.7.2 SERIAL ADVANCED TECHNOLOGY ATTACHMENT

SATA is a computer interface and communication protocol introduced in 2003. Its specifications are currently developed by the independent, nonprofit Serial ATA International Organization led by multiple industry partners, including dominant computing systems and storage manufacturers. It is used primarily to provide connectivity to mass-storage devices. SATA replaces the older parallel ATA (PATA) technology that was characterized by lower data transfer bandwidths, bulky ribbon cables frequently obstructing air flow in the node's case, and lack of proper support for hot-swapping of I/O

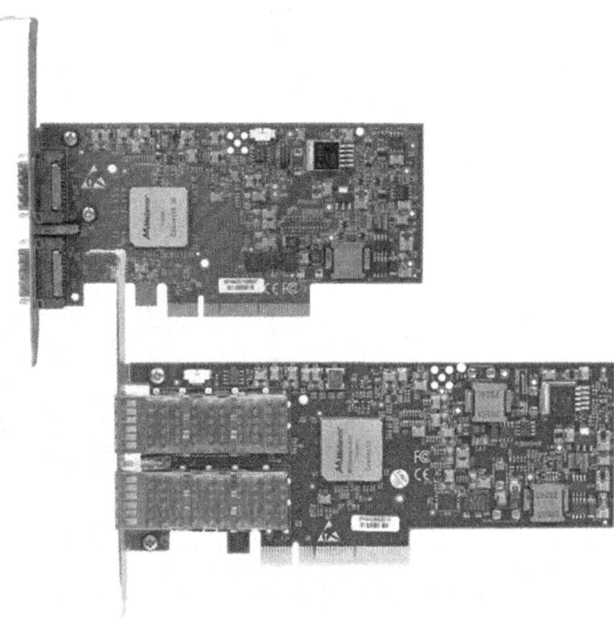

FIGURE 6.14

Mellanox IB cards.

Image courtesy Mellanox Technologies

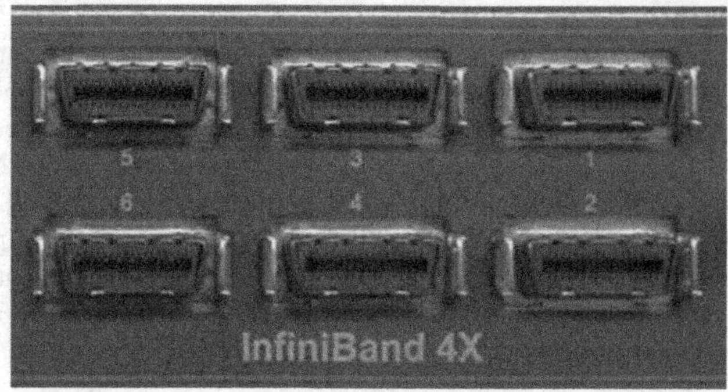

FIGURE 6.15

InfiniBand port.

By おむこさん志望 via Wikimedia Commons

devices. SATA interfaces may be found on most modern internal (i.e., housed inside the computer enclosure and therefore nonportable) HDDs, SSDs, and optical drives (CD-ROM, DVD-ROM, BD-ROM and their data-writer equivalents).

SATA supports only point-to-point topology between storage devices and controllers or port multipliers. SATA data connectors, shown in Fig. 6.16, contain only 7 pins compared to 40 mandated by PATA: one pair of wires for data transmission, a second pair of wires for data reception, and three ground connections. Data transmission is performed over high-speed serial links that use similar technology to PCIe and share many of the same quality characteristics with it. Serial links also take advantage of matched impedance cables, guaranteeing signal integrity over distances of at least 1 m. The power connectors utilize a 15-pin arrangement that provides ground reference and the 3.3, 5, and 12 V supply voltages needed by most of the attached devices to operate, and may also control

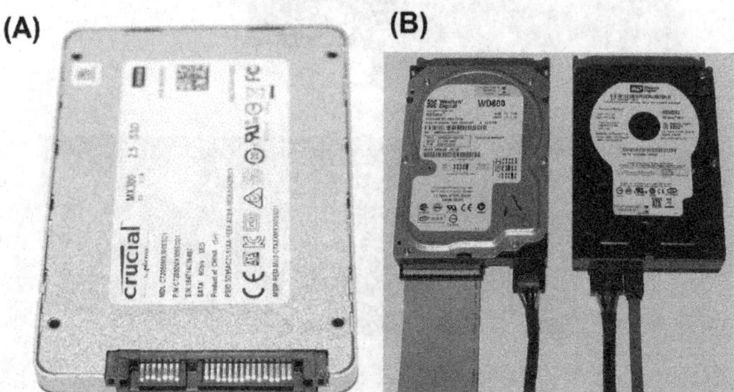

FIGURE 6.16

SATA connectors: (A) data (left, shorter) and power (right, longer) headers located on a 2.5" solid-state drive, and (B) older Parallel ATA cabling (left) contrasted with SATA (right).

staggered spin-up functionality. The latter is particularly useful in storage nodes populated with potentially dozens of disk drives, as enabling all of them at once would put a considerable strain on power supply during the power-up cycle, possibly reducing its useful lifetime. Both types of connectors use a two-phase mating sequence to ensure that the ground connection is made first and eliminate the possibility of unpredictable floating potentials during drive removal or insertion when the system is powered up. Most of the computer motherboards manufactured today support multiple SATA data ports (typically two to eight), while common power supplies provide multiple SATA-compatible hookups.

The first revision of SATA specifications supported a 1.5 Gbps signaling rate, resulting in a maximum peak data transfer rate of 150 MB/s. With the increases in HDD media speeds and the introduction of solid-state storage, this proved to be a serious performance bottleneck, and the next revisions, SATA 2.0 and 3.0, increased the raw signal rate to 3 and 6 Gbps, respectively. Modern chipsets are capable of detecting device speeds through autonegotiation and are backwards compatible with older drives. Early SATA 2.0 implementations, however, may require that the device is explicitly configured to the correct interface speed by setting a jumper on configuration pins and in some cases also by forcing proper basic input/output system settings. The newer SATA revisions also support native command queueing (NCQ), which may drastically improve the performance of I/O-intensive multitasking workloads by reordering the requests at physical block level, resulting in an overall shorter travel distance for the disk head. Other extensions included introduction of isochronous quality of service for periodically scheduled data accesses, host-side support for NCQ processing, and better power management. The specifications have been twice revised since (version 3.1 in 2011 and 3.2 in 2013), and defined additional interfaces, capabilities, and power management functions:

- mSATA interface for mobile devices
- M.2 small form factor standard
- microSSD standard for connectorless single-chip embedded storage
- "zero-power" state for idling optical drives
- TRIM command for SSDs that optimizes allocation of no longer used blocks on the device
- universal storage module for cable-free docking of portable storage modules
- required link power management, DevSleep, and transitional energy reporting for additional power savings
- rebuild assist that speeds up data reconstruction in redundant arrays of independent disks
- performance optimizations for solid-state hybrid drives
- signaling speed increase to 16 Gbps with a corresponding peak data rate of nearly 2 GB/s.

Besides the originally defined SATA data ports for internal I/O devices, several other form factors specified by the standard are already in widespread use or gaining popularity. The external SATA (eSATA) connector shown in Fig. 6.17 has been developed to provide connectivity to external storage devices. It features more robust connector and permits longer cables (up to 2 m) thanks to changes in required signal voltage levels. It is also shielded to reduce EMI emissions. eSATAp, or *powered* SATA, attempts to solve one of main shortcoming of eSATA, namely the necessity to provide a separate power source (and therefore an additional cable) to the external device. While not fully standardized yet, it aims to provide 5 and 12 V supply voltages as well as SATA and USB 2.0 data lines.

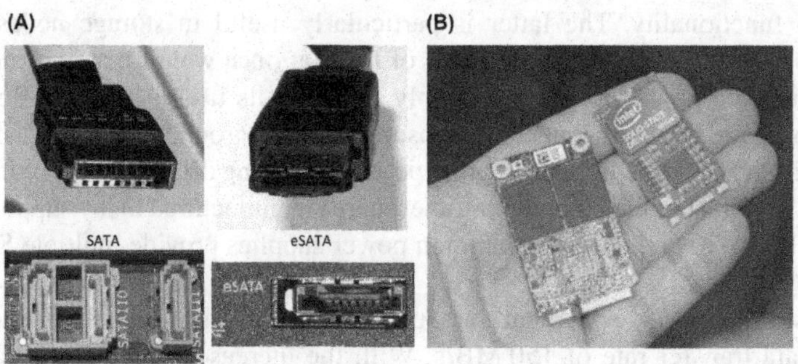

FIGURE 6.17

SATA interface variants: (A) eSATA compared to SATA; (B) mSATA (left) and M.2 (right) devices.

(B) Photo by Anand Lal Shimpi via Wikimedia Commons

Mini-SATA (mSATA) and its next revision, M.2 interfaces (Fig. 6.17B), are used where preservation of small form factor is important. They find applications in settop boxes and ultrathin laptops, but typically require a properly designed system board that is equipped with the correct connector and allows sufficient installation space.

A companion specification to SATA is the Advanced Host Controller Interface (AHCI) developed by Intel (currently at revision 1.3.1). It describes an implementation-independent, register-level interface between the host controller hardware and system software. The specification allows system programmers to support correctly additional hardware features such as NCQ and hot-swapping of I/O devices. AHCI is supported by default by many popular operating systems, such as Windows, Mac OS, and Linux.

6.7.3 JTAG

JTAG is a low-level hardware interface specified by IEEE Standard 1149 [11]. It takes its name from the Joint Test Action Group, which in the mid-1980s set out to develop verification and test methods for electronic circuits. While most casual computer users are never likely to have an opportunity to use JTAG directly, it is broadly adopted by the industry for postproduction printed circuit board testing (detection of shorts, mismatched and detached pins, "stuck" bits, in-silicon logic defects, and so on). As the density of integrated circuits increased, it quickly became uneconomical to provide explicit test points on board for all supported features. Additionally, JTAG permits in-circuit debugging of embedded applications by being able to access most if not all of the device register state, including the status of I/O pins. Coupled with the built-in self-test functionality commonly implemented by manufacturers in most large-scale integration and VLSI logic circuits, JTAG may identify many chip failure modes before allowing them to enter the supply chain. Since it can directly manipulate the device hardware state, JTAG is also occasionally used to perform firmware updates in cases when more user-friendly options may not be available or desirable.

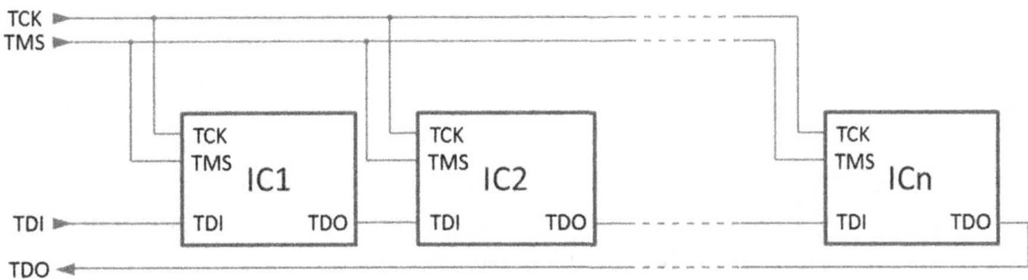

FIGURE 6.18

JTAG chain with n devices. Integrated circuit (IC) blocks represent individual integrated circuits that may be located on single or multiple printed circuit boards.

JTAG functionality relies on the presence of four signals: TCK (test clock), TDI (test data in), TDO (test data out), and TMS (test mode select). Optionally the interface may also contain a TRST (test reset) signal to perform reset of the test logic. To lower the required pin count, multiple JTAG-equipped devices may be daisy-chained as illustrated in Fig. 6.18. The test data and instructions are clocked in serially through the TDI line and output via TDO at the rising edge of the TCK (clock) signal. Beyond a few standard mandated exceptions, instruction semantics are implementation dependent. The level of the TMS pin influences the performed control function depending on the internal control state. Neither the JTAG connector nor its clock frequency is standardized; the latter may range from single to multiple 10s of MHz. The host may enable a bypass operation in any device on a chain, thus avoiding full communication with it if not required. A variant of JTAG permits a two-wire interface using only the TCK and TMSC (test serial data) signals, as described by the IEEE 1149.7 revision of the standard. The update addresses one of the common problems of the daisy-chained JTAG: to operate, all devices in the chain have to be powered up. IEEE 1149.7 also permits a star topology to be realized.

All JTAG implementations must support the test access port (TAP) with the TCK, TMS, TDI, and TDO pins, TAP controller, at least a two-bit wide instruction register, a one-bit bypass register, and a boundary scan register (one bit or more). Optionally, a 32-bit long IDCode register may also be exposed so that individual devices in the chain may be identified by the host. The instruction and data registers form parallel data paths that share the data input TDI as well as the output TDO. The TAP controller embeds a predefined state machine with 16 states. The transitions between states are performed in accordance with the TMS value during active clock edge. Individual states may force normal operation, invoke test functions defined by the contents of the instruction register, pause testing, and perform capture, update, or logical shift of instruction or data register contents. The required instructions for all implementations include device bypass and boundary scan support (state sampling, register load, and internal and external test execution).

Practical implementations frequently extend the basic JTAG instruction set and test range using custom chip-specific logic. For this reason vendors provide specialized software tools (command line and GUI based) that directly support native capabilities of the implementation without requiring the hardware engineer or system programmer to be familiar with the low-level details.

6.7.4 UNIVERSAL SERIAL BUS

Besides high performance components, computers need to communicate with relatively low-speed attached peripheral devices such as keyboards and printers. While these needs have been addressed in the past by a number of both specialized (such as IBM's PS/2 connector for mouse and keyboard) and industry-standard (e.g., serial and parallel communication ports) interfaces, their usefulness was limited when new types of attached devices became available. Among the shortcomings of previous solutions were bulky connectors, reduced interchangeability and interoperability, lack of an option to provide power to the attached devices, minimal or no ability to retrieve the type and operating parameters of connected peripherals, limited support for automatic configuration, no straightforward way to expand the number of available access ports, and, in some cases, insufficient communication speeds.

The USB standard [12] introduced in the mid-1990s successfully resolved these issues. It is currently guided by USB Implementers Forum Inc., a nonprofit corporation involving representatives of 894 hardware and software companies, including among others Intel, Hewlett−Packard, NEC, Renesas, Samsung, ST Microelectronics, Infineon, Philips, Sony, Apple, and Microsoft. The standard has been designed with low cost and simplicity as the primary features. The USB standard defines the architecture, data-flow model, mechanical and electrical properties of connectors and cables, signaling and physical layer, power supply and management, and transaction protocols. It is currently implemented in many categories of peripheral devices, including keyboards, mice, printers, scanners, cameras, mobile phones, media players, mass storage, modems, network adapters, game controllers, and more. The standard underwent updates in three major revisions that successively increased the communication bandwidth, detailed new connector types, defined multihost communication mode (USB On-The-Go), and specified additional power management and battery-charging protocols. The most recent version 3.1 was released in 2013.

USB provides a bidirectional communication link that originally operated at 1.5 Mbps ("low-speed") and 12 Mbps ("full-speed") signaling rates. Due to only one differential pair of wires dedicated to data transfer (the other two pins being ground and +5 V supply rail), the communication only supported half-duplex mode. The USB 2.0 update in 2000 increased the raw data rate to 480 Mbps ("hi-speed" mode), but due to protocol overheads the sustained data rate achieved was only 25−40 MB/s, i.e., less than 70% of the peak. USB 3.0 introduced "superspeed" of up to 5 Gbps, signified by blue-colored receptacles. Some USB 3.0 connectors are backwards compatible with USB 2.0, and the increased data rates are achieved by using an additional four pins (two differential line pairs for transmit and receive, thus permitting full-duplex operation) on the opposite side of the connector. In USB 3.1, doubling the maximal signal rate to 10 Gbps required introduction of an entirely new connector format, Type-C. An overview of various USB connectors and receptacles is presented in Fig. 6.19. The specification limits the cable length of low-speed devices to 5 m, full-speed devices to 3 m, and 5 m for hi-speed devices. USB 3.0 currently does not impose cable length constraints.

USB uses a tiered star topology with a single host at the top level, shown in Fig. 6.20. To overcome the limited number of host ports, multiple hubs may be inserted to add additional tier levels for up to seven tiers total and a maximum of 127 USB devices. Functionally, each USB device conforms to the same organizational scheme. Individual logical subdevices are called *functions* and communicate with the host via *pipes*. Pipes are logical channels that connect the host with an *endpoint* of a specific subdevice. A maximum of 16 input and 16 output endpoints per device are permitted. Endpoints are initialized in a process called *enumeration* (performed right after device

FIGURE 6.19

Comparison of common USB connector types (plugs on top, receptacles on bottom).

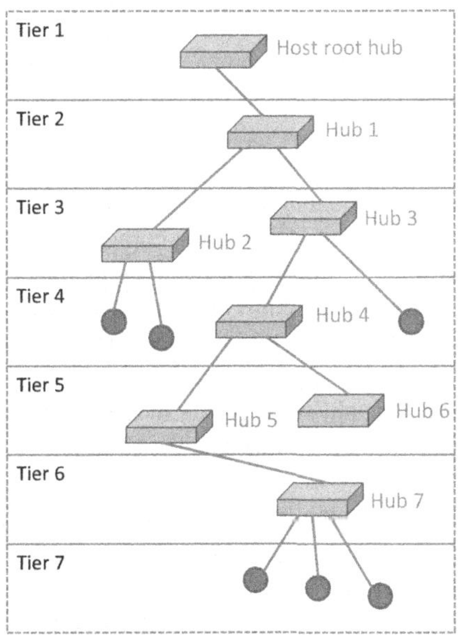

FIGURE 6.20

USB devices connected in multitiered topology.

power-up) and stay assigned as long as the device is connected. Pipes convey messages and streams: the first are relatively short commands that generate status response, while the latter are unidirectional and support *isochronous* (repeated communication with guaranteed bandwidth), *interrupt* (bounded latency communication), or *bulk* (asynchronous communication that may use the remaining link bandwidth) transfers. USB distinguishes several device classes, such as printer or mass storage, to facilitate loading the appropriate driver software on the host. Common features shared by devices in the same class are frequently supported by the operating system without the need for device-specific manufacturer software.

USB makes provisions for powering or charging peripheral devices through the same socket that facilitates the data transfer. Separate 5 V power and ground lines are included for that purpose. Nominally the current draw has to be negotiated with the host, and is limited to 100 mA for low-power devices (0.5 W) and 500 mA for high-power devices (2.5 W). These limits have been raised for superspeed devices to 150 and 900 mA, respectively. Unfortunately, not all devices comply with the specifications and draw more current than permitted, which on occasion may lead to their erratic behavior. The proliferation of mobile gadgets prompted the creation of a new port type, a *charging port*, which must deliver at least 1.5 A of current. It exists in a version that supports data communication (*charging downstream port*) and one that does not (*dedicated charging port*). A separate specification, *USB Power Delivery*, intends to extend this support to other devices such as laptops or hard drives by providing six power profiles to supply up to 100 W at three voltage levels using a dedicated power configuration protocol.

6.8 SUMMARY AND OUTCOMES OF CHAPTER 6

- The most widely used form of a high performance computer is the symmetric multiprocessor (SMP) architecture.
- SMPs are also referred to as *shared-memory* (SM) machines or *cache-coherent* computers.
- SMP architecture integrates a number of processor cores with a single shared main memory system by means of a common interconnection network.
- The symmetric multiprocessing attribute requires that copies of main memory data values that are held in caches for fast access must be consistent (cache coherency).
- Every SMP has multiple I/O channels that communicate with external devices (outside the SMP), user interfaces, data storage, system area networks, local area networks, and wide area networks, among others.
- A fundamental consequence of Amdahl's law is that independent of the size of the accelerator's peak performance gain, g, the sustained performance is bounded by the fraction, f, of the original code that can be accelerated.
- Defining characteristics of processors include the number of cores per socket, the size and interconnectivity of the cache levels (usually two or three levels), the clock rate of the core, the number and type of arithmetic logic units per core (ILP), the die size (between one and four square centimeters), the feature size, and the delivered performance for one or more standardized benchmarks.
- The pipeline logic structure is a general way of exploiting a form of very fine-grain parallelism, as each of the pipeline stages is operating simultaneously.

- Multithreading incorporates multiple instruction streams or threads, through sets of multiple instruction pointers and their associated register sets.
- The "memory wall" recognizes the mismatch between the peak demand rate of the processor socket for data access and the possible delivered throughput and latency of the main memory technology, principally semiconductor DRAM.
- The memory hierarchy or stack consists of layers of memory storage technology, each with different tradeoffs between memory capacity, costs, and cycle times which reflect bandwidths and latencies.
- In a modern SMP the cache is usually not a single layer of higher-speed memory but rather multiple layers to create an optimal balance of speed and size.
- PCI Express is a dominant standard for attaching and high performance communication with expansion boards on different machines that may use processor architecture other than the original Intel ×86 variant.
- The two most ubiquitous network interface controllers are Gigabit Ethernet and IB.
- SATA is used primarily to provide connectivity to mass-storage devices.
- JTAG is broadly adopted by the industry for postproduction printed circuit board testing.
- The USB standard provides a relatively low-speed method for communication with attached peripheral devices.

6.9 QUESTIONS AND EXERCISES

1. List and describe the components of an SMP node. Where applicable, name their most significant operational parameters and the units in which they are measured. Give approximate values these parameters may assume in common server hardware.
2. Expand and define each of the following acronyms. What are their application domains?
   - SMP
   - ILP
   - CPI
   - MAC
   - PCIe
   - SATA
   - USB
3. Why is standardization of I/O and expansion buses important? Provide examples.
4. You are an IT specialist at a small computational research institution. The scientists require a peak 100 Tflops machine to conduct their studies. The approved vendor offers two units rack-mount nodes with two CPU sockets that may accommodate either 12-core processors clocked at 3.4 GHz or 20-core processors operating at 2.5 GHz frequency. Each core can perform four floating-point operations per clock cycle. Given that there is 32U space for nodes available in each rack, answer the following.
   a. Which type of processor would you recommend to minimize the floor space occupied by racks?
   b. How many racks are needed to reach the required peak throughput?
   c. With all racks filled, what is the final peak computational throughput of the machine?

5. A sequential version of a simulation takes 90 min to compute 10,000 iterations. Each iteration can be accelerated using multiple threads of execution, but the overhead of assigning work to the threads is 100 ms. If the sequential setup of the application takes 10 min regardless of the number of iterations subsequently executed, how many cores are needed to bring the execution of a program performing 1000 iterations down to 12 min? What maximum speedup is possible assuming unlimited execution resources?
6. Execution of a 1,000,000-instruction program takes 2.5 ms on a 2.5 GHz core. The hardware monitor reports a cache miss ratio of 6% for the application. Main memory access takes on average 80 ns, while cache access has a latency of 800 ps. Given that all ALU instructions are executed effectively in a single clock cycle, calculate the following.
   a. The fraction of application instructions that performed ALU operations.
   b. If the core has a 16 KB cache and doubling the cache size decreases the miss rate by 1% for that particular application, what would be the required cache size (in powers of 2) to cut the execution time in half?
   c. What would the program runtime and resulting speedup be if all accessed data fits in the cache?

REFERENCES

[1] M.S. Papamarcos, J.H. Patel, A low-overhead coherence solution for multiprocessors with private cache memories, in: ISCA '84 Proceedings of the 11th Annual International Symposium on Computer Architecture, 1984.

[2] J. Wu, J.R. Larus, Static branch frequency and program profile analysis, in: MICRO 27 Proceedings of the 27th Annual International Symposium on Microarchitecture, 1994.

[3] T.-Y. Yeh, Y.N. Patt, Two-level adaptive training branch prediction, in: MICRO 24 Proceedings of the 24th Annual International Symposium on Microarchitecture, 1991.

[4] C.-C. Lee, I.-C.K. Chen, T.N. Mudge, The bi-mode branch predictor, in: MICRO 30 Proceedings of the 30th Annual ACM/IEEE International Symposium on Microarchitecture, 1997.

[5] S. McFarling, Combining Branch Predictors, 1993. WRL Technical Note TN-36.

[6] D.A. Jimenez, C. Lin, Neural methods for dynamic branch prediction, ACM Transactions on Computer Systems (TOCS) 20 (4) (2002) 369–397.

[7] PCI-sig Specifications, 2017 [Online]. Available: http://pcisig.com/specifications/.

[8] R.M. Metcalfe, D.R. Boggs, Ethernet: distributed packet switching for local computer networks, Communications of the ACM 19 (7) (1976) 395–404.

[9] TOP500 Highlights – June 2017, 2017 [Online]. Available: https://www.top500.org/lists/2017/06/highlights/.

[10] OpenFabrics Alliance, 2017 [Online]. Available: https://www.openfabrics.org/.

[11] IEEE Standards Association, 1149.1-2013-IEEE Standard for Test Access Port and Boundary-scan Architecture, 2013 [Online]. Available: http://standards.ieee.org/findstds/standard/1149.1-2013.html.

[12] USB-IF, Universal Serial Bus Revision 3.1 Specification, July 26, 2013 [Online]. Available: http://www.usb.org/developers/docs/usb_31_062717.zip.

CHAPTER

THE ESSENTIAL OPENMP

7

CHAPTER OUTLINE

7.1 INTRODUCTION

OpenMP is an application programming interface (API) to support the shared-memory multiple-thread form of parallel application development. "OpenMP" stands for "open multiprocessing" [1]. It greatly simplifies the development of multiple-threaded parallel programming compared to, for example, low-level operating system (OS) support services for threads and shared memory. OpenMP incorporates separate sets of bindings for the sequential programming languages Fortran, C, and C++. It gives easy

High Performance Computing. https://doi.org/10.1016/B978-0-12-420158-3.00007-1

access to the resources of the general class of symmetric multiprocessor (SMP) computers for parallel applications.

This chapter describes the syntax constructs related to the C programming language bindings. For those unfamiliar with C programming, a tutorial, "The Essential C", is offered in the appendix of this textbook. OpenMP provides extensions to C in the form of compiler directives, environment variables, and runtime library routines to expose and execute parallel threads in the context of shared memory. A principle of the design philosophy is to permit incremental changes to sequential C code for ease of use and natural migration from initial C-based applications to parallel programs. In so doing it provides a practical and powerful means of parallel computing, admittedly within the scalability limits of the SMP class of parallel computers.

OpenMP is among the most widely used parallel programming APIs. However, it is limited in scalability to hardware system architectures providing near uniform memory access (UMA) to shared memory. This chapter provides an introductory treatment to the essentials of OpenMP and how to program in parallel with it. Although it is an initial coverage assuming no prior experience with parallel programming, this chapter provides all the necessary concepts and semantic constructs to enable the development of useful real-world applications. This presentation is primarily focused on release 2.5, which is core to later releases and is probably the most widely used version as well as most broadly supported.

Shared-memory parallel architectures were first developed in the 1980s and a number of APIs were devised to assist in programming these. The OpenMP specification standard process began in 1997 based on this prior work and an early draft of such an interface, ANSI X3H5, was released in 1994. OpenMP evolution is overseen by the OpenMP Architecture Review Board, consisting of industry and government partners. The first C-based specification, C/C++ 1.0, was released in 1998, followed by C/C++ 2.0 in 2002. C and Fortran specifications have been released together since 2005, with OpenMP 2.5, 3.0, and 3.1 released in 2005, 2008, and 2011, respectively. The most recent version 4.5, released in 2015.

7.2 OVERVIEW OF OPENMP PROGRAMMING MODEL

OpenMP provides a shared-memory multiple-threads programming model. It assumes underlying hardware support for efficient management of shared memory, including virtual addresses and cache coherency among processor cores and across multiple sockets. This is the principal defining facet of the SMP class of parallel computers. All processor cores have direct access to all memory shared within the system. A simple but illustrative representation of the class of parallel computers suitable for OpenMP programming is shown in Fig. 7.1. The key elements are the processor cores, P, that perform the concurrent threaded computing, the memory banks, M, that are equally accessible by the threads, and the connectivity between both P and M elements that enables the shared-memory architecture and execution models.

7.2.1 THREAD PARALLELISM

Threads are the principal means of providing parallelism of computation. A thread is an independently schedulable sequence of instructions combined with its private variables and internal control. Usually there are as many threads allocated to the user computation as there are processor cores assigned to the computation. However, this is not required. Threads are divided among the master

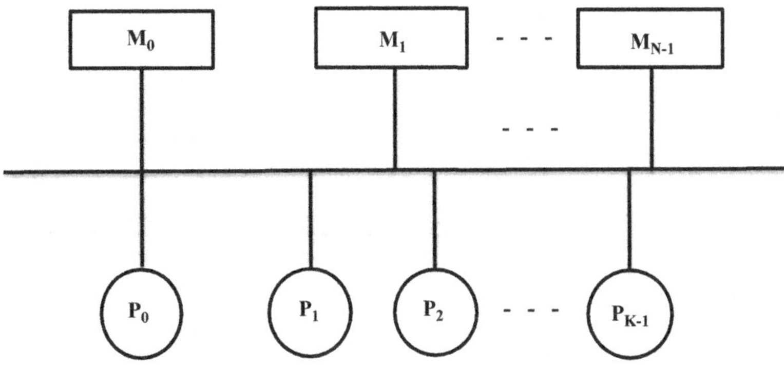

FIGURE 7.1

Shared-memory multiprocessor.

thread and the worker threads. The single master thread exists for the lifetime of the computation, from its initiation to its termination. Sometimes the master thread is the only thread being performed at one time. The worker threads provide additional paths of concurrency of execution for performance gain. Worker threads are controlled by the master thread and are delineated by OpenMP directives. Like the number of threads, how the threads are scheduled is determined by environment variables and can be static or dynamic.

OpenMP supports the fork-join model of parallel computing. At particular points in the execution the master thread spawns a number of threads and with them performs part of the program in parallel. The point of initiation of multiple worker threads is referred to as the *fork*. Usually all these threads perform their calculations separately, and when they reach completion they wait for the other threads to finish as well. This is the *join* of the parallel threads, and the default at the join is an implicit barrier synchronization. All the threads must complete before computation is continued beyond that point of control. An OpenMP parallel program mostly consists of a sequence of such fork–join worker and master thread parallel segments separated by lone sequential master thread segments, as shown in Fig. 7.2. Segments of concurrent master/worker threads often have all the threads the same, differentiated only by the values of their private variables. This is the single-program, multiple data (SPMD) model. Alternatively, the concurrent threads may each execute different code blocks, separately delineated by appropriate directives. In either case, join synchronization at the end of the concurrent threads is enforced unless explicitly avoided through added directives for this purpose. The figure illustrates this parallel control flow. The horizontal axis represents time from left to right, while the vertical access shows work in terms of one or more concurrent threads. The single lowest line is the master thread that continues from the beginning to the end of the OpenMP program. At key fork points multiple threads are launched for work that can be performed concurrently. These threads may be somewhat irregular, in that they do not execute exactly the same work even if their code is the same. When all the concurrent threads have completed at the join synchronization point, the computation can proceed; in each case by the master thread alone until the next thread fork is encountered.

OpenMP permits the representation of nested parallelism, such that inner fork–join segments of parallel threads can themselves be embedded into threads of outer parallel thread segments. However, while the syntax is supported and will execute correctly, not all implementations will take advantage of this additional parallelism and may treat it as sequential code, one inner thread after another. An

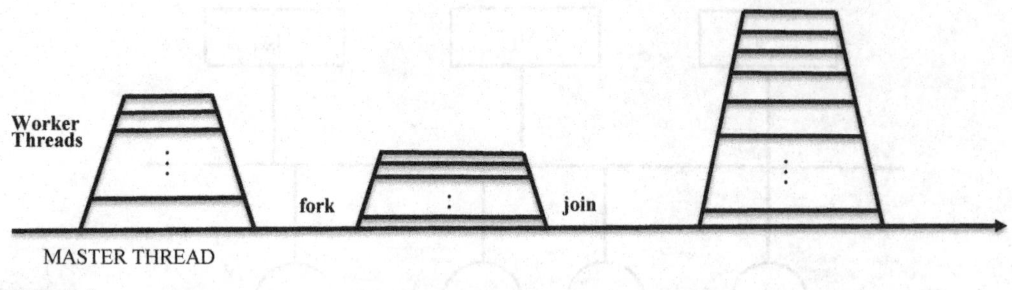

FIGURE 7.2

Fork–join model of master/worker threads.

example of nested parallelism is illustrated in Fig. 7.3. Again, the lower horizontal line represents the master thread, with time increasing from left to right. First a set of worker threads is created when the master thread encounters a forking point of parallelism; this is the *outer fork*. Each of these outer threads then separately encounters its own *inner fork* to create a second level of parallel threads, giving more concurrency for scalability. The inner threads of each outer thread then synchronize with their respective matching inner join, after which the outer thread proceeds until it encounters the outer join synchronization point with the other outer threads. The OpenMP scheduler uses this added parallelism to improve performance when possible.

7.2.2 THREAD VARIABLES

OpenMP is a shared-memory model allowing direct access to global variables by all threads of a user process. To support the SPMD modality of control where all concurrent threads run the same code block simultaneously, OpenMP also provides private variables. These have the same syntactical names, but their scoping is limited to the thread in which they are used. Private variables of the same name have different values in each thread in which they occur. A frequently occurring example is the use of index variables accessing elements of a vector or array. While all threads will use the same index variable name, typically "i", when accessing an element of the shared vector, perhaps "x[i]", the range of values of the index variable will differ for the separate concurrent threads. For this to be possible, the index variable has to be private rather than shared. In fact this particular idiom is so common that the default for such variable usage is private, although for most common variables the default is shared. Directive clauses are available for explicit setting of these properties of variables by users. Another variant on how variables may be used relates to reduction operators such as sum or product. In this specialized case the reduction variable is a mix of private and global, as discussed in detail in Section 7.5.

7.2.3 RUNTIME LIBRARY AND ENVIRONMENT VARIABLES

An OpenMP parallel application program consists of the syntax of the core language (i.e., Fortran, C, C++) with additional constructs to guide parallel threaded execution and set specific operational properties. These include environment variables, compiler directives, and runtime libraries. Environment variables define operational conditions and policies under which the executing OpenMP

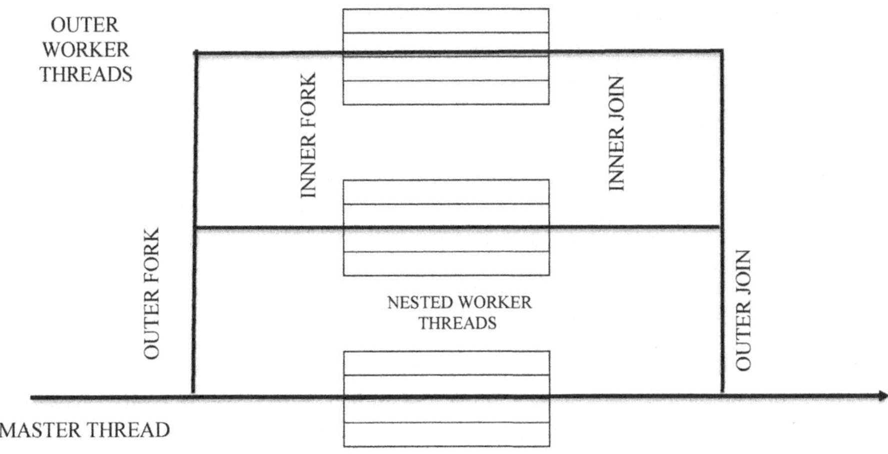

FIGURE 7.3

Nested parallel threads.

program will run. Their values can be set at the system shell through OS user interface commands; from within the program they can be accessed through runtime library routines. Compiler directives appear as comments, but through the OpenMP extensions, pragmas, are treated as commands to guide parallel execution. Additional functionality is provided through runtime library routines that help manage parallel programs. Many runtime library routines have corresponding environment variables that can be controlled by users. Examples include determining the number of threads and processors, scheduling policies to be used, and portable wallclock timing.

7.2.3.1 Environment Variables

OpenMP provides environment variables for controlling execution of parallel codes. These can be set from the OS command line or equivalent prior to execution of the application program, using export or setenv commands depending on the user shell. These variables have default settings, so they only have to be set explicitly if an optional value is required. There are four main environment variables.

OMP_NUM_THREADS controls the parallelism of the OpenMP application by specifying the number of threads to be used by the user program. This normally determines the number of cores allocated to the user program, but not always. When more threads are requested than available, they may be associated with OS Pthreads, requiring the OS to context switch adding additional overheads to the computing. The default option is system dependent. To set the value of this environment variable to 8 use the following bash command:

```
export OMP_NUM_THREADS=8
```

OMP_DYNAMIC enables dynamic adjustment of the number of threads for execution of parallel regions. Under certain conditions this provides a level of adaptability that makes optimal use of task granularity to minimize the effects of overhead and irregularity. However, it also incurs additional overhead within the runtime system and may not always improve performance. The default value for this environment variable is FALSE, which implies that the number of threads employed remains fixed at the value set in the environment variable OMP_NUM_THREADS. To change this to enable dynamic thread allocation, use the following bash command:

```
export OMP_DYNAMIC=TRUE
```

OMP_SCHEDULE manages the load distribution in loops such as the parallel for pragmas (discussed in Section 7.3.3). This environment variable sets the schedule type and chunk size for all such loops. The chunk size can be provided as an integer number. The default value for OMP_-SCHEDULE is 1. To set this two-tuple variable use the following form:

```
export OMP_SCHEDULE=schedule,chunk
```

OMP_NESTED permits nested parallelism in OpenMP applications. This may give the opportunity for more parallelism, which may increase scalability, but at the risk of finer granularity in the presence of fixed overheads, which may reduce efficiency. The default value for this Boolean environment value is FALSE, permitting only the top level of fork–join parallelism to be used. To set this environment variable to support multilevel parallelism, use the following form:

```
export OMP_NESTED=TRUE
```

7.2.3.2 Runtime Library Routines

Runtime library routines help manage parallel application execution, including accessing and using environment variables such as those above. Prior to using these routines in the code, the following *include* statement must be added:

```
#include <omp.h>
```

Two important routines allow the program to know how many threads are operating concurrently and identify a unique rank for each thread among the total set. The first function,

```
omp_get_num_threads()
```

returns the total number of threads currently in the group executing the parallel block from where it is called. Usually, this is a direct reflection of the environment variable OMP_NUM_THREADS.

The second important runtime routine,

```
omp_get_thread_num()
```

returns a value to each thread executing the parallel code block that is unique to that thread and can be used as a kind of identifier in its calculations. When the master thread calls this function, the value of 0 is always returned, identifying its special role in the computation. A call to this routine by a worker thread will return a value between 1 and the environment variable value OMP_NUM_THREADS -1.

7.2.3.3 Directives

OpenMP directives are a principal class of constructs used to convert initially sequential codes incrementally to parallel programs. They serve a multitude of purposes, primarily about controlling parallelism through delineation and synchronization. The following sections describe in detail the directives for parallelism, mutual exclusion of shared variables through synchronization, and reduction calculations. All directives take the following form:

```
#pragma omp <directive> <clauses> <statement/code block>
```

As shown in the examples, such directives may be treated one at a time in a nested organization, or in many cases combined to simplify textual presentation. The clauses permit optional conditions to be satisfied, like declaring the scope of a variable (e.g., private).

7.3 PARALLEL THREADS AND LOOPS

7.3.1 PARALLEL THREADS

In the tradition of C programming and the teaching thereof, the first program to present is "Hello World". Using OpenMP, a very simple parallel program can be constructed to print this statement by multiple threads. It requires only one OpenMP command,

```
#pragma omp parallel
```

to turn the classic sequential C code to a parallel code. This simplicity of transformation from serial to parallel is one of the hallmark strengths of OpenMP. Parallel Hello World is written as follows.

```
#include <stdio.h>
#include <omp.h>

int main() {
#pragma omp parallel
{
  printf("Hello World \n");
}

  return 0;
}
```

Code 7.1. Parallel Hello World example.

```
Hello World
Hello World
Hello World
Hello World
```

Output 1. The result from Code 7.1 when setting the environment OMP_NUM_THREADS to be 4.

That's it! When compiled and run, the result will be a succession of printed lines of text: Hello World. The number of such lines is determined by the environment variable OMP_THREAD_NUM.

The only difference between this and the conventional C version of this code is that in the parallel version is the single OpenMP directive: #pragma omp parallel is added. The effect of the parallel pragma is to fork the number of allocated threads, and for each such thread to execute the designated block of code. As a result every thread executes the printf statement once, each printing "Hello World". This admittedly rather useless code demonstrates the use and power of the parallel pragma, perhaps the most important directive in OpenMP. It creates the forks and subsequent joins of parallel threads throughout the program.

7.3.2 PRIVATE

In the simple version of Hello World, above, there is nothing to differentiate between the separate executed threads. For threads to become useful they need to support distinct work even if the code block is the same. Some local state for each thread is usually required, although there are some special cases (like reduction variables). The *private* clause within directives is the principal means of achieving this. It declares a variable within the code block to be local to each thread. By this means each thread has its own copy of the named variable, permitting each thread to have its own value, independent of the other threads executing the same code block.

```
#include <stdio.h>
#include <omp.h>
int main() {
  int num_threads, thread_id;
#pragma omp parallel private(num_threads, thread_id)
{
    thread_id = omp_get_thread_num();
    printf("Hello World. This thread is: %d\n", thread_id);
    if (thread_id == 0) {
    num_threads = omp_get_num_threads();
    printf("Total # of threads is: %d\n", num_threads);
    }
}
   return 0;
}
```

Code 7.2. An example hello world code where each OMP thread prints out its thread id.

```
Hello World. This thread is: 0
Total # of threads is: 4
Hello World. This thread is: 3
Hello World. This thread is: 1
Hello World. This thread is: 2
```

Output 2. The output from Code 7.2 with the environment OMP_NUM_THREADS set to be 4.

There are two variables, `num_threads` and `thread_id`, that are declared as private, and therefore separate copies of both are provided for each and every thread with the values potentially different. In this case `num_threads` is only used by the master thread, thread 0. The `omp_get_num_threads` runtime function is called only by the master thread. Each thread has its own copy of `thread_id`. The runtime function `omp_get_thread_num()` will return a different and unique value to each thread for the respective version of thread-id.

7.3.3 PARALLEL "FOR"

Among the most useful sources of parallelism is the distribution of loops among threads. In C, loops are defined by the "for" construct specifying the number of iterations of a code block through a designated range of an index variable local to that loop code. Here is a sequential code block to add two arrays together.

```
#include <stdio.h>
#include <stdlib.h>

int main (int argc, char *argv[])
{
  const int N = 20;
  int nthreads, threadid, i;
  double a[N], b[N], result[N];

  // Initialize
  for (i=0; i < N; i++) {
    a[i] = 1.0*i;
    b[i] = 2.0*i;
  }

  for (i=0; i<N; i++) {
    result[i] = a[i] + b[i];
  }

  printf(“ TEST result[19] = %g\n”,result[19]);

  return 0;
}
```

Code 7.3. Serial example of adding two arrays together.

```
TEST result[19] = 57
```

Output 3. The output from Code 7.3.

This program has three parts, like many real-world programs: initialization, calculation, and output. In this simple program most of the lines of text are dedicated to the declaration and initialization of program variables. Here these include integers N, nthreads, threadid, and i, as well as the double vectors a, b, and result. A for-loop is included to initialize the vector elements to (admittedly gratuitous) double values. The output of the computation is given by the single printf statement that sends the last element of the result vector to standard inout/output (usually the screen or a file).

This program can be readily converted to be executed in parallel to increase computational performance and reduce the time to solution. Three additions are required to transform the above program to parallel.

1. Include the OpenMP header.
2. Delineate the code block to be made parallel.
3. Specify the loop to be distributed among the concurrent threads.

The first two of these semantic constructs have already been discussed. The OpenMP libraries are incorporated through the command:

```
#include <omp.h>
```

The parallel code block is established through the directive:

```
#pragma omp parallel
{
...
}
```

The new construct is the `parallel for` instruction. This directive enables work sharing, where the total work of a loop is divided among the assigned threads. The effect is to divide the range of the private index variable of the for-loop into subranges, preferably of equal span, with one assigned to each of the parallel threads. Thus each thread is responsible for part of the total work of the loop; with all the threads working on their respective parts separately but at the same time, parallel computing is performed. Optimally, the speedup would be equal to the number of threads being used, but for a number of reasons (discussed later) it is infrequent that this level of scaling is fully realized. The `parallel for` directive is given as the following:

```
#pragma omp for
```

The parallel version of the vector addition example is presented in Code 7.4 with the additional OpenMP directive in lines 1, 17, and 20:

```
 1 #include <omp.h>
 2 #include <stdio.h>
 3 #include <stdlib.h>
 4
 5 int main (int argc, char *argv[])
 6 {
 7   const int N = 20;
 8   int i;
 9   double a[N], b[N], result[N];
10
11   // Initialize
12   for (i=0; i < N; i++) {
13     a[i] = 1.0*i;
```

```
14      b[i] = 2.0*i;
15    }
16
17 #pragma omp parallel
18   { // fork
19
20   #pragma omp for
21   for (i=0; i<N; i++) {
22      result[i] = a[i] + b[i];
23   }
24
25   } // join
26
27   printf(" TEST result[19] = %g\n",result[19]);
28
29   return 0;
30 }
```

Code 7.4. OpenMP parallel for version of Code 7.3. OpenMP additions are seen in lines 1, 17, and 20. The output of Code 7.4 is the same as Code 7.3, shown in Output 3.

While correct, the code above is a bit verbose. OpenMP allows some compression of code text by merging different directives where it makes sense. For example, the parallel and for directives can be combined into a single statement, as shown in Code 7.5:

```
#include <omp.h>
#include <stdio.h>
#include <stdlib.h>

int main (int argc, char *argv[])
{
  const int N = 20;
  int i;
  double a[N], b[N], result[N];

  // Initialize
  for (i=0; i < N; i++) {
     a[i] = 1.0*i;
     b[i] = 2.0*i;
  }

  #pragma omp parallel for
  for (i=0; i<N; i++) {
  result[i] = a[i] + b[i];
  }

  printf(" TEST result[19] = %g\n",result[19]);

  return 0;
}
```

Code 7.5. Combining the parallel and for directives into a single statement in Code 7.4

Notice that the braces are not required because a single statement now makes up the code block. To find out which thread executes which index of the vector addition, some additional statements are needed, as shown in Code 7.6.

```
#include <omp.h>
#include <stdio.h>
#include <stdlib.h>

int main (int argc, char *argv[])
{
  const int N = 20;
  int nthreads, threadid, i;
  double a[N], b[N], result[N];

  // Initialize
  for (i=0; i < N; i++) {
    a[i] = 1.0*i;
    b[i] = 2.0*i;
  }

#pragma omp parallel private(threadid)
 { // fork
 threadid = omp_get_thread_num();

 #pragma omp for
 for (i=0; i<N; i++) {
   result[i] = a[i] + b[i];
   printf(" Thread id: %d working on index %d\n",threadid,i);
 }

 } // join

 printf(" TEST result[19] = %g\n",result[19]);

 return 0;
}
```

Code 7.6. In this example of vector addition, the identity of the thread performing the operation for each index is printed to screen.

In Code 7.6 a new variable is introduced: threadid. It contains the OpenMP thread index and is initialized inside the OpenMP parallel region. Because it is declared outside the scope of the parallel region, it would by default be considered a global variable by OpenMP. Thus it is necessary to declare it as private in the clause following the OpenMP parallel pragma in line 17.

```
Thread id: 0 working on index 0
Thread id: 0 working on index 1
Thread id: 0 working on index 2
Thread id: 0 working on index 3
Thread id: 0 working on index 4
Thread id: 0 working on index 5
Thread id: 0 working on index 6
Thread id: 1 working on index 7
Thread id: 1 working on index 8
Thread id: 1 working on index 9
Thread id: 1 working on index 10
Thread id: 1 working on index 11
Thread id: 1 working on index 12
Thread id: 1 working on index 13
Thread id: 2 working on index 14
Thread id: 2 working on index 15
Thread id: 2 working on index 16
Thread id: 2 working on index 17
Thread id: 2 working on index 18
Thread id: 2 working on index 19
TEST result[19] = 57
```

Output 4. The output from Code 7.6 when using OMP_NUM_THREADS=3. The default thread scheduler in OpenMP will break the for-loop roughly into three equal pieces: thread 0 works on array indices 0 through 6, thread 1 works on array indices 7 through 13, and thread 2 works on array indices 14 through 19.

The behavior controlling which thread works on which index can be altered by using the schedule clause, as noted in Section 7.2.3.1. This is illustrated in Code 7.7.

```
#include <omp.h>
#include <stdio.h>
#include <stdlib.h>

int main (int argc, char *argv[])
{
  const int N = 20;
  int nthreads, threadid, i;
  double a[N], b[N], result[N];

 // Initialize
 for (i=0; i < N; i++) {
   a[i] = 1.0*i;
   b[i] = 2.0*i;
 }

```

```
int chunk = 5;

#pragma omp parallel private(threadid)
  { // fork
  threadid = omp_get_thread_num();

#pragma omp for schedule(static,chunk)
for (i=0; i<N; i++) {
   result[i] = a[i] + b[i];
   printf(" Thread id: %d working on index %d\n",threadid,i);
}

} // join

printf(" TEST result[19] = %g\n",result[19]);

return 0;
}
```

Code 7.7. An example of the schedule clause. Work in the for-loop will be statically divided into chunks of size 5.

```
Thread id: 0 working on index 0
Thread id: 0 working on index 1
Thread id: 0 working on index 2
Thread id: 0 working on index 3
Thread id: 0 working on index 4
Thread id: 0 working on index 15
Thread id: 0 working on index 16
Thread id: 0 working on index 17
Thread id: 0 working on index 18
Thread id: 0 working on index 19
Thread id: 1 working on index 5
Thread id: 1 working on index 6
Thread id: 1 working on index 7
Thread id: 1 working on index 8
Thread id: 1 working on index 9
Thread id: 2 working on index 10
Thread id: 2 working on index 11
Thread id: 2 working on index 12
Thread id: 2 working on index 13
Thread id: 2 working on index 14
TEST result[19] = 57
```

Output 5. Output from Code 7.7 when run using OMP_NUM_THREADS=3. The for-loop is statically divided into chunks of size 5 among three threads. Hence thread 0 operates on array indices 0–4 and 15–19, thread 1 operates on array indices 5–9, and thread 2 operates on array indices 10–14.

7.3.4 SECTIONS

OpenMP provides a second powerful method for specifying work sharing among parallel code blocks. The `sections` directive describes separate code blocks, each containing a different sequence of instructions, which may be performed concurrently. One thread is allocated to each code block. The full set of parallel blocks is initiated with the following directive:

```
#pragma omp sections
{ ... }
```

Within this structure is the set of nested code blocks, each begun by the directive:

```
#pragma omp section
{ <code block> }
```

with the exception of the first code block that does not require its own sections pragma (the sections pragma serves this second duty) heading. A simple example of a sections code block structure could look like this:

```
#pragma omp parallel
{
#pragma omp sections
 {
  {
   <1st parallel code block>
  }
  #pragma omp section
  {
   <2nd parallel code block>
  }
  #pragma omp section
  {
   <3rd parallel code block>
  }
 }
}
```

This nested structure of code blocks can be extended to represent as many distinct and concurrent blocks as necessary. But depending on the number of threads specified by the environment variable, not all of these may be executed simultaneously.

The example in Code 8 demonstrates the use of the sections and nested section directives to specify three separate code blocks to be executed concurrently. The three calculations determine statistics about a set of integer values, x. The first determines the minimum and maximum values of the set. The second computes the mean. The third computes the mean of the square of the values, which is used later to provide the variance.

```
#include <stdio.h>
#include <stdlib.h>
#include <omp.h>
```

```

int main()
{
  const int N = 100;
  int x[N], i, sum, sum2;
  int upper, lower;
  int divide = 20;
  sum = 0;
  sum2 = 0;

#pragma omp parallel for
  for(i = 0; i < N; i++) {
    x[i] = i;
  }


#pragma omp parallel private(i) shared(x)
{

// Fork several different threads
#pragma omp sections
  {
      {
        for(i = 0; i < N; i++) {
          if (x[i] > divide) upper++;
          if (x[i] <= divide) lower++;
        }
        printf(“The number of points at or below %d in x is %d\n”,divide,lower);
        printf(“The number of points above %d in x is %d\n”,divide,upper);
      }
#pragma omp section
      { // Calculate the sum of x
        for(i = 0; i < N; i++)
          sum = sum + x[i];
        printf(“Sum of x = %d\n”,sum);
      }
#pragma omp section
      {
        // Calculate the sum of the squares of x
        for(i = 0; i < N; i++)
          sum2 = sum2 + x[i]*x[i];

        printf(“Sum2 of x = %d\n”,sum2);
      }
  }
}
  return 0;
}
```

Code 7.8. Example of sections in OpenMP.

7.4 SYNCHRONIZATION

One strength of OpenMP is the sharing of global data among multiple concurrent threads. This "shared-memory" model presents a view of program data similar to that experienced with the use of conventional sequential programming interfaces like the C language. This is distinguished from "distributed-memory" models where special send–receive message-passing semantics are required to exchange values among concurrent processes, such as found in the message-passing interface programming libraries. But with this ease of use comes a serious challenge: control of the order of access to shared variables. This problem in a different form was encountered when the distinction between private and shared variables was made. By designating a variable as private, it was possible to avoid the out-of-order problem among multiple threads; here, copies of a named variable disassociated the accesses of separate threads. However, communication between or among threads through shared memory is a frequent and efficient means of computation cooperation, if appropriately coordinated. OpenMP incorporates semantic constructs to enable coordination in the shared use of global memory for the class of SMP parallel architectures.

On a shared-memory system communication between threads is mainly through read and write operations to shared variables. Where two threads are both reading the value of a shared variable, previously set, the order of accessing the variable by the threads is irrelevant; either thread can perform the read first, followed by the second thread. But if one thread is responsible for setting the value through a global write for the other thread to read and use, then clearly the order of access is important and failing to ensure proper order will likely result in an error. This can become more complex when more than two threads are involved.

Synchronization defines the mechanisms to help in coordinating execution of multiple parallel threads that use a shared context (shared memory) in a parallel program. Without synchronization, multiple threads accessing a shared-memory location may cause conflicts. This can occur by two or more threads attempting to modify the same location concurrently. It can also happen if one thread is attempting to read a memory location while another thread is updating the same location. Without strict control of ordering, a race condition may make the result of these actions nondeterminant; the result cannot be guaranteed always to produce the same answer. Synchronization helps to prevent such races and access conflicts by providing explicit coordination among multiple threads. These include implicit event synchronization and explicit protection synchronization directives.

Implicit synchronization determines the occurrence of an event across multiple threads. Barriers are a simple form of event synchronization in OpenMP to coordinate multiple threads such that they are aligned in time. A barrier establishes a point in a parallel program where each thread waits for all the other like threads to reach the same point in their respective execution. This ensures that all the computing threads have completed their computation prior to that specific instruction. Only after all threads have reached the barrier can any of them proceed.

Explicit synchronization directly controls access to a specific shared variable. This guarantees that access to the identified data location is limited to one thread at a time. This is particularly important when the thread needs to perform a compound atomic sequence of operations, such as a read–modify–write, on a data element without intrusion of another thread. While this does not fix the order of access, it does protect a variable until any one thread's activity associated with the variable has been completed without conflict. This class of synchronization constructs provides mutual exclusion.

7.4.1 CRITICAL SYNCHRONIZATION DIRECTIVE

The OpenMP pragma `critical` provides mutual exclusion for access to shared variables by multiple threads. It provides protection against race conditions and the minimum performance degradation in the case when all likely accesses to a given shared variable are from multiple concurrent threads of the same code sequence. The `critical` directive delineates a block of code that only one thread is permitted to execute at a time. Any global variable that is accessed within that sequence of instructions is protected from attempts by multiple concurrent executing threads of the same code block. Once one thread enters the critical region, the other threads have to wait until it has exited the region. The order in which the different threads perform the critical code block is undetermined; only the limit of one thread at a time entering and completing the specified code is guaranteed. The `critical` pragma permits atomic read–modify–write operation sequences to be safely conducted on a shared variable.

The `critical` pragma has the form:

```
#pragma omp critical
{
...
}
```

An example of its use to perform compound atomic operations safely is the following:

```
int n;
n = 0;
...
#pragma omp parallel shared(n)
{
#pragma omp critical /* delineate critical region */
 n = n + 1; /* increment n atomically */
} /* parallel end */
```

This simple code allows many threads to increment the shared variable n without the possibility of a race among them corrupting the resulting value. Independent of the order in which the critical regions of the separate threads are performed, the resulting value of n will be the same.

7.4.2 THE MASTER DIRECTIVE

The master directive provides another, and perhaps more simple, way of protecting a shared variable among threads to avoid races and possible corruption of result values. As the name implies, the directive gives total control to the master thread for a specified code block. Such a code block delineated by the master pragma is executed by only one thread, the master thread. When the master thread encounters the master directive, it proceeds to perform it like any other code. But when any thread other than the master thread (all the worker threads) reaches a master block, it does not execute it and skips over this part of the code. Thus this particular code block is only performed once, by the master thread. There is no possibility of a race condition because only one thread is allowed to access the global shared variables referred to within the master code block. There is no barrier implied by the master region. The worker threads that do not perform this code go right past it and continue without any delay caused by the master region. The master directive takes the following syntactical form:

```
#pragma omp master
{
... /* protected code block */
}
```

7.4.3 THE BARRIER DIRECTIVE

The barrier pragma puts the computation in a known control state. It synchronizes all the concurrent threads. When encountering a given barrier directive, all threads halt at that location in the code until all other threads have reached the same point of execution. Only when all the threads have reached the barrier can any of them proceed beyond it. Once all the threads have performed the barrier operation, they all continue with the computation after it.

The barrier operation is used to ensure that all the threads have completed the preceding computations no matter what order they are scheduled in or at what rate they are executing. An important purpose of this idiom is to implement the bulk synchronous parallel protocol, a very common form of parallel computation. With this approach, a set of threads reads from shared memory and performs the necessary arithmetic on their values. Then a barrier is performed. Only when all the threads have completed their computation and reached the barrier can they go ahead and write the resulting values back to the shared variables. In one form (there are several), after writing to shared memory every thread encounters a second barrier and again waits for all the other threads to complete their shared-memory write-back operation as well. Having safely performed all the writes, the threads can repeat the next step of the parallel calculation safely by reading the newly updated shared variables guaranteed to be correct because of the barriers. The barrier directive is:

```
#pragma omp barrier
```

7.4.4 THE SINGLE DIRECTIVE

The single directive combines a form of dynamic scheduling with synchronization. It expands the master pragma to permit any thread to perform the action, and combines this with an implicit barrier at the end. The delineated code block is executed by only one thread, like the master directive; but unlike master the executing thread can be any of the running threads, but only one of them. The first thread to reach the single pragma construct in its sequence of instructions will perform the designated code block. The remaining threads will not perform that code. But all the threads will encounter a barrier that blocks them from proceeding past the end of the single pragma code block until all of them have reached that point in their execution. Only after the thread executing the code designated by the single pragma has completed and exited that code can all the other threads continue. The single directive is:

```
#pragma omp single
{
... /* protected code executed by only one thread */
}
```

7.5 REDUCTION

Reduction operators are a means of bringing together a large number of values to produce a single result value. Familiar examples are numeric (integer or real) summation and logical OR over a range of variables. While this can be achieved through functions of more primitive operations, OpenMP (like other programming interfaces) provides a convenient way to accomplish reductions and in some cases to do so in parallel for performance speedup (over sequential implementations). The reduction pragma may take the following form:

```
#pragma omp reduction(op : result_variable)
{
result_variable = result_variable op expression
}
```

The reduction operator, *op*, is one of the following:

```
+, *, -, /, &, ^, |
```

The *result_variable* is of a scalar value, with one such element as a private variable for every thread.

```
#include <stdio.h>
#include <omp.h>

int main() {
  int i, n, chunk;
  float a[16], b[16], result;
  n = 16;
  chunk = 4;
  result = 0.0;


 for (i = 0; i < n; i++) {
   a[i] = i * 1.0;
   b[i] = i * 2.0;
 }

 #pragma omp parallel for default(shared) private(i) schedule(static, chunk) \
   reduction(+ : result)
   for (i=0; i < n; i++)
     result = result + (a[i] * b[i]);

 printf(“Result = %f\n”, result);
 return 0;
}
```

Code 7.9. Example of reduction.

```
Result = 2480.000000
```

Output 5. Output from Code 7.9.

7.6 SUMMARY AND OUTCOMES OF CHAPTER 7

- "OpenMP" stands for "open multiprocessing".
- OpenMP is an API for parallel computing that has bindings to programming languages such as Fortran and C.
- OpenMP supports programming of shared-memory multiprocessors, including SMP and distributed shared-memory classes of parallel computer systems.
- OpenMP supports the fork–join model of parallel computing. At particular points in the execution the master thread spawns a number of threads and with them performs a part of the program in parallel. The point of multiple worker thread initiation is referred to as the *fork*. Usually all these threads perform their calculations separately, and when they come to their respective completion they wait for the other threads to finish at the *join* of the parallel threads.
- OpenMP provides environment variables for controlling execution of parallel codes. These can be set from the OS command line or equivalent prior to execution of the application program.
- Runtime library routines help manage parallel application execution, including accessing and using environment variables such as those above. The library routines are provided in the omp.h file and must be included (`#include <omp.h>`) prior to using any of these routines.
- Threads are the principal means of providing parallelism of computation. A thread is an independently schedulable sequence of instructions combined with its private variables and internal control. Usually there are as many threads allocated to the user computation as there are processor cores assigned to the computation, although this is not required.
- `omp_get_num_threads()` returns the total number of threads currently in the group executing the parallel block from where it is called.
- `omp_get_thread_num()` returns a value to each thread executing the parallel code block that is unique to that thread and can be used as a kind of identifier in its calculations. When the master thread calls this function, the value of 0 is always returned, identifying its special role in the computation.
- OpenMP directives are a principal class of constructs used to convert initially sequential codes incrementally to parallel programs. They serve a multitude of purposes, primarily about controlling parallelism through delineation and synchronization.
- The parallel directive delineates a block of code that will be executed separately by each of the computing threads.
- The parallel for directive permits work sharing of an iterative loop among the executing threads, with one or more iterations performed by each thread.
- The private clause in a directive establishes that each thread has its own copy of a variable, and when accessing that designated variable will read or write its own private copy rather than a shared variable.
- The sections directive describes separate code blocks, each of a different sequence of instructions, which may be performed concurrently. There is one thread allocated to each code block.
- Synchronization directives define the mechanisms that help in coordinating execution of multiple parallel threads that use a shared context (shared memory) in a parallel program to preclude race conditions.

- The critical directive provides mutual exclusion of access to shared variables by permitting only one thread at a time to perform a given code block. When a thread enters the critical code section, all other threads that attempt to do so are deferred until the thread doing it has completed. Other threads are then free to execute the critical section of code themselves, but only one at a time.
- The master directive delineates a block of code that is only executed by the master thread, with all other threads skipping over it.
- The single directive delineates a block of code that is performed by only a single thread, but it can be any of the executing threads—whichever one gets to that code block first. All threads wait until the thread completing that code executes it.
- The barrier directive is a form of synchronization. When encountering a given barrier directive, all threads halt at that location in the code until all other threads have reached the same point of execution. Only when all the threads have reached the barrier can any of them proceed beyond it. Once all the threads have performed the barrier operation, they all continue with the computation after it.
- Reduction operators combine a large number of values to produce a single result value. A number of operations can be used for this purpose, such as + and | among others.

7.7 QUESTIONS AND PROBLEMS

1. Can you spot any mistakes in the following code? Please correct them.

```
#include <stdio.h>
#include <omp.h>

// compute the dot product of two vectors

int main() {
  int const N=100;
  int i, k;
  double a[N], b[N];
  double dot_prod = 0.0;

  // Arbitrarily initialize vectors a and b
  for(i = 0; i < N; i++) {
  a[i] = 3.14;
  b[i] = 6.67;
}

#pragma omp parallel
 {
 #pragma omp for
    for(i = 0; i<N; i++)
       dot_prod = dot_prod + a[i] * b[i]; // sum up the element-wise product of the two arrays
```

```
    }

    printf("Dot product of the two vectors is %g\n", dot_prod);

    return 0;
}
```

2. In line 23 of Code 7 in Section 7.3.3 the static scheduler was demonstrated. How would the output of this code change if the dynamic scheduler were used instead?
3. In Code 8 of Section 7.3.4 the sections pragma was introduced. What would happen to Code 8 if the number of OpenMP threads were fewer than the number of sections?
4. Write a matrix–vector multiply and parallelize with OpenMP directives.

REFERENCE

1. OpenMP, The OpenMP API Specification. [Online] http://www.openmp.org/specifications/.

CHAPTER

THE ESSENTIAL MPI

8

CHAPTER OUTLINE

High Performance Computing. https://doi.org/10.1016/B978-0-12-420158-3.00008-3

8.1 INTRODUCTION

A major form of high performance computing (HPC) systems that enables scalability is the distributed-memory multiprocessor. Both massively parallel processors (MPPs) and commodity clusters are examples of system-level architectures of this form. The distinguishing property of this important class of supercomputer is that the main memory of the system is partitioned into fragmented components, each associated with one or more processor cores and ancillary components that together comprise what has become casually referred to as a "node". Multiple nodes integrated by means of one or more interconnect networks constitute the full high performance computer. A distributed-memory system is such that a processor core is able to access the memory intrinsic to its resident node directly, but not the memory or the external nodes making up the total system. Exchange of data, cooperation and coordination of the tasks running on the separate nodes, and overall operation of the system as a single entity are achieved through the transfer of messages between nodes by means of the system area network tying all the pieces together. Logically this is achieved through the passing of messages between pair-wise executing processes, or sometimes among more than two processes at a time. The major advantage of the distributed-memory multiprocessor is its scalability. Within the constraints of power and cost, essentially any number of nodes can be incorporated within a single supercomputer. A somewhat more nuanced value is that the programmer is forced and therefore motivated to manage the program locality explicitly, making pieces of work fit within the confines of an individual node. This has resulted in a generation of scalable application software and libraries that has achieved a million times greater throughput performance than previous-generation computing models and architecture classes. How to use this successful class of high performance computer is the subject of this chapter, and the topic and means of doing so is the message-passing interface (MPI).

Over as many as 3 decades there have been many software application programming interfaces and implementation libraries that supported the communicating sequential processes model of computation, casually referred to as the "message-passing model". These were developed by industry, within academia, and from national labs and centers, among others. But by far the most significant has been MPI [1]. MPI was, and in its most recent versions still is, a community-driven specification. Starting in late 1992, representatives of industry, government, and academia began a community-led process to develop a standard programming interface based on principles first laid out by Anthony Hoare in the mid-1970s. The strength of this approach to community building was the ready acceptance of the result and the rapid development of useful applications. The weakness was that to achieve an agreed-upon initial standard, many more controversial semantics, constructs, and mechanisms were initially discarded for the sake of unity, resulting in a more simplistic and admittedly limited interface. However, in spite of such sacrifices of sophistication, this proved to be the right path for evolutionary progress that was much needed at the time. At the risk of hyperbole, there was probably no greater achievement of practical utility for the advancement of HPC than the development of MPI. Even in its most basic form, MPI has proven a powerful, flexible, and usable programming interface. With its hundreds of commands it deals with a rich and diverse set of circumstances, yet a very small subset of these is sufficient to write a wide array of parallel applications. This chapter presents only a small subset of the total set of possible commands, but in doing so gives the student a powerful set of tools for harnessing distributed-memory supercomputers and empowering the solution of computational end-user problems.

8.2 MESSAGE-PASSING INTERFACE STANDARDS

William D. Gropp. *Photo Courtesy NCSA*

William "Bill" Gropp is an American scientist who helped develop the MPI message-passing standard. He is also coauthor of the MPICH implementation of MPI. Apart from contributing to two very influential books, "Using MPI" and "Using MPI 2", he is also a designer of the widely used Portable, Extensible Toolkit for Scientific Computation library discussed in this textbook. Among his many honors, William Gropp received the IEEE Sidney Fernbach Award in 2008 "for outstanding contributions to the development of domain decomposition algorithms, scalable tools for the parallel numerical solution of partial differential equations (PDEs), and the dominant HPC communications interface".

From 1992 to 1994 a community representing both vendors and users decided to create a standard interface for message-passing calls in the context of distributed-memory parallel computers, principally early MPPs like the Intel Touchstone Paragon. MPI-1 was the result. From the very beginning it was "just" an application programming interface (API), not a language. This was achieved by adding constructs for parallelism, data exchange communication, synchronization, and collectives through bindings to existing conventional sequential programming languages—initially Fortran 77 and C. Language bindings permit the semantics and syntax of existing languages to be exploited from the frameworks of libraries for concurrency management. These bindings allowed the widest possible use of existing application kernels, compilers, and user skill sets while augmenting them with the needed concepts of communication frameworks for coordination, cooperation, and concurrency. The MPI standard can be found online [1].

Probably equally as important as the community-derived API was for the MPI was the first reduction to practice: the first reference implementation, called "MPI over CHameleon (MPICH)" and developed at Argonne National Laboratory [2]. This was delivered in 1995 and served as the template for the many other implementations of MPI to come afterwards. Led by William Gropp, the MPICH project provided both important experience in the implementation of MPI and a platform upon which the earliest practical applications were developed and run on the MPP systems of the time, such as the CM-5 (see Fig. 8.1).

Many lessons were learned about correctness, performance, portability, and user productivity. Another value of the MPI standard was that it provided a strong unifying formalism throughout the HPC community but permitted distinguishing opportunities for individual vendors like Cray, IBM, and Hewlett-Packard. Vendors were able to keep their own internals and optimizations behind the interface.

Since then MPI has matured and evolved. MPI-1.1 fixed bugs that were revealed in early experience and clarified issues where subtleties and ambiguities of semantics were exposed. This continued again through MPI-1.2 and new rewrites of MPICH to improve its efficiency and scalability vastly. MPI-2 was a new standard that significantly extended the utility and richness of MPI, including new datatype constructors, one-sided communication, a strong input/output (I/O) package, and dynamic processes. Additional bindings beyond the original ones were developed, including to Fortran 90 and to C++. Since then the MPI semantics have been yet again extended, in some cases extensively for the release of MPI-3, with MPI-4 actively under development in 2017. While tremendous advances have been made since the early formulation of MPI-1, the constructs comprising the foundations of MPI still

FIGURE 8.1

A connection machine 5 (CM-5) with 512 nodes and a theoretical maximum capability of 65.5 GFlops, operational between 1991 and 1997.

Photo by Austin Mills via Wikimedia Commons

provide a base-level set of interrelated concepts and constructs upon which to establish the means for parallel programming. It is from this initial starting point that this first tutorial in MPI programming is offered.

8.3 MESSAGE-PASSING INTERFACE BASICS

While the latest versions of MPI include literally hundreds of commands, a simple parallel program can be created using only three basic commands. This section describes how to do that. The bindings all assume the use of the C programming language, with which all examples and descriptions are presented.

8.3.1 MPI.H

Every MPI program must contain the preprocessor directive:

```
#include <mpi.h>
```

The mpi.h file contains the definitions and declarations necessary for compiling an MPI program. mpi.h is usually found in the "include" directory of most MPI installations. This directive can be positioned in any order with other directives, but must precede the beginning of the program with the main() call.

8.3.2 MPI_INIT

The part of the user application code that will contain function calls for MPI program constructs must begin with the single call to MPI_Init and expects arguments of the following form, returning an integer error value:

```
int MPI_Init(int *argc,char ***argv)
```

MPI_Init initializes the execution environment for MPI. This command has to be called before any other MPI call is made, and it is an error to call it more than a single time within the program. The number of arguments passed internally to all the parallel processes is pointed to by argc. The vector of the arguments' list is pointed to by argv, as is consistent with the C language and command-line argument variables passing. Every process launched by MPI_Init inherits copies of these two program argument variables and is achieved by the call:

```
MPI_Init(&argc,&argv);
```

prior to any of the other MPI calls within the application.

8.3.3 MPI_FINALIZE

In a sense, the other bookend to MPI_Init is the MPI_Finalize command. MPI_Finalize cleans up all the extraneous mess that was first put into place by MPI_Init. It brings to an end the computing environment for MPI. There are no arguments to this MPI service call, which has the following simple syntax:

```
MPI_Finalize();
```

This does not have to be the end of the entire program. Many other C statements can follow it. Also, its exact position in the code sequence is not particularly important as long as it comes after any other MPI commands in the program.

8.3.4 MESSAGE-PASSING INTERFACE EXAMPLE—HELLO WORLD

Somewhat sadly, there is a rite of passage that every neophyte programmer in just about any programming language has to go through: writing "Hello, World", a most trivial program first sketched out by Kernighan and Ritchie in their original book on C [3]. This is the most minimalist program one can imagine that actually works. Getting this far is a major milestone for a student, crossing the line from never having successfully written an actual computer program in the language of choice to being a programmer (sort of). So for the sake of tradition and with a justified nod to those giants who preceded us, here is "Hello, World" in MPI with C bindings.

```
#include <stdio.h>
#include <mpi.h>

int main(int argc,char **argv)
{
  MPI_Init(&argc,&argv);
  printf("Hello, World!\n");
  MPI_Finalize();
  return 0;
}
```

Code 8.1. A trivial example of "Hello, World" using MPI.

The example in Code 8.1 is compiled and run using the MPICH implementation of MPI on a Beowulf-class cluster, as follows.

```
> mpicc code1.c -o code1
> mpirun -np 4 ./code1
  Hello, World!
  Hello, World!
  Hello, World!
  Hello, World!
```

The *mpicc* compiler wrapper links in the appropriate MPI libraries and gives the path to the file location of the mpi.h header. *mpirun −np 4* launches four instances of the code executable in the runtime environment. While using *mpicc* and *mpirun* to compile and launch MPI applications is very common, they are not part of the MPI standard and the specific compile and launching approach may differ for different machines. For example, on a Cray XE6 MPP, Code 8.1 is compiled and launched as follows:

```
> cc code1.c -o code1
> aprun -n 4 ./code1
  Hello, World!
  Hello, World!
  Hello, World!
  Hello, World!
```

In this MPP case, the *cc* compiler wrapper links in the appropriate MPI libraries and finds the appropriate headers while the launch script *aprun* launches the four instances of the executable in the runtime environment.

The only work performed by Code 8.1, of course, is to print the character stream "Hello, World!" on the standard I/O device, which is the user's terminal screen. But unlike the equivalent sequential version of this simple program, this string will be printed multiple times; in fact, it will print out as many times as there are processes running under MPI at the same time. Although all output lines look the same (note that the \n character in line 7 of Code 8.1 causes a new line), the actual order in which they are output is unspecified. A later example is more revealing of this nondeterminacy. The resulting parallelism is a consequence of the pairing of the MPI_Init and MPI_Finalize calls. There is no interaction among the separate processes in this example, however. To get the different processes to interact, the concept of communicators is needed.

8.4 COMMUNICATORS

The "Hello, World" example in Code 8.1 is very simple. But it represents a broad range of parallel computing known as "throughput" computing, where every hardware node is running the same program but on different local data. This can be scaled to a very large degree, and additional examples are demonstrated in succeeding chapters. But the principal weakness of this limited form of processing is that the processes on different nodes run entirely independent of each other. It is a "share nothing" modality in which the outcome of any one of the concurrent processes can in no way be influenced by the intermediate results of any of the other processes. Without interprocess interaction, this type of computing only supports pure weak scaling or capacity computing, as described earlier. It cannot enable capability or coordinated computing, both of which are far richer in parallel computational forms and functions. Key to this advance is the means by which the concurrent processes can interact. And this is achieved through the concept and implementation of "communicators".

MPI programs are made up of concurrent processes executing at the same time that in almost all cases are also communicating with each other. To do this, an object called the "communicator" is provided by MPI. A communicator has its own address space and various properties. In particular, it encompasses a set of MPI processes as well as specific attributes. It is through the communicator that the processes of which MPI consists can communicate with other processes. A communicator consists of multiple coexisting MPI processes, so a process may be associated with more than one communicator at the same time. Thus the user may specify any number of communicators within an MPI program, each with its own set of processes. However, all versions of MPI provide one common communicator, "MPI_COMM_WORLD". This communicator contains all the concurrent processes making up an MPI program and does not have to be explicitly created by the programmer. For simplicity and ease of understanding, almost all examples presented in this book take advantage of MPI_COMM_WORLD, as it manages the communications between concurrent processes.

8.4.1 SIZE

A communicator embodies a number of attributes, many of which may be referenced by the user program. Among those most widely used is "size". This property, as its name implies, indicates some aspect of a communicator's scale, specifically related to processes. The size of a communicator is the number of processes that makes up the particular communicator. The following function call provides the value of the number of processes of the specified communicator:

```
int MPI_Comm_size(MPI_Comm comm, int *size)
```

The function name is "MPI_Comm_size", required to return the number of processes; *comm* is the argument provided to designate the communicator, recognizing that any process may be part of more than one communicator. The resulting value is returned to *size* within the process context. A typical statement for this purpose could be:

```
int size;
MPI_Comm_size(MPI_COMM_WORLD,&size);
```

This will put the total number of processes in the MPI_COMM_WORLD communicator in the variable size of the process data context. As this is the same for all processes of the communicator, their respective copies of the variable size will receive the same value.

8.4.2 RANK

A second widely used attribute of a communicator is identification of each of the processes within the communicator. Every process within the communicator has a unique ID referred to as its "rank". The

MPI system automatically and arbitrarily assigns a unique positive integer value, starting with 0, to all the processes within the communicator. The MPI command to determine the process rank is:

```
int MPI_Comm_rank (MPI_Comm comm, int *rank)
```

The function call "MPI_Comm_rank" indicates that the rank value of the calling process is to be returned to the process. The first argument, "comm", indicates the communicator to which the process belongs within which it requires its rank. The second argument, "rank", is the variable that will assume the value returned by the command. A typical statement for this purpose could be:

```
int rank;
MPI_Comm_size(MPI_COMM_WORLD,&rank);
```

In the case of the MPI_COMM_WORLD communicator, all the processes of the application will have a unique value of rank returned. Each process within this communicator when calling this function will receive a different value in its copy of the variable rank.

8.4.3 EXAMPLE

As a trivial case that nonetheless demonstrates the functionality of communicators and these simple but powerful commands, the following example is offered. This is a minor elaboration of the earlier and iconic "Hello, World" problem.

The purpose of this application program is for every process that exists within the MPI_COMM_WORLD communicator to identify itself by printing a statement to the standard output. The structure of this parallel program is the same as the previous, with the potentially interprocess communicating part of the code delimited by the pair of MPI_Init and MPI_Finalize commands. Between these two statements are the working parts of the program, such as the printf construct shown before. But added here are also the two service calls associated with the communicator: MPI_Comm_rank and MPI_Comm_size. The complete MPI code is given in Code 8.2.

```
#include <stdio.h>
#include <mpi.h>

int main(int argc,char **argv)
{
  int rank, size;
  MPI_Init(&argc,&argv);
  MPI_Comm_rank(MPI_COMM_WORLD,&rank);
  MPI_Comm_size(MPI_COMM_WORLD,&size);
  printf(" Hello from rank %d out of %d processes in MPI_COMM_WORLD\n",rank,size);
  MPI_Finalize();
  return 0;
}
```

Code 8.2. Example where each process prints its rank and the MPI_COMM_WORLD communicator size.

This code is compiled and executed on a Beowulf-class cluster as follows:

```
> mpicc code2.c -o code2
> mpirun -np 4 ./code2
  Hello from rank 0 out of 4 processes in MPI_COMM_WORLD
  Hello from rank 2 out of 4 processes in MPI_COMM_WORLD
  Hello from rank 3 out of 4 processes in MPI_COMM_WORLD
  Hello from rank 1 out of 4 processes in MPI_COMM_WORLD
```

Code 8.2 illustrates the use of the two most common calls related to communicators. The two commands bracket by MPI_Init and MPI_Finalize are the MPI_Comm_rank (line 8), which determines the ID of the process, and the MPI_Comm_size (line 9), which finds the number of processes. In both cases they refer to the MPI_COMM_WORLD communicator as specified as the first operand in each of the two calling sequences. The second argument in each case indicates the process variable in which the related integer value is put. The printf I/O service call not only outputs the string "Hello" but also prints out two integers, one for the process rank which is unique for each process and the other giving the size of the MPI_COMM_WORLD communicator in terms of the number of processes it contains. The size for all processes is the same. The order of printing the output is undetermined, as mentioned before. With each process uniquely identified within the communicator, it is now possible to begin sending messages between processes.

8.5 POINT-TO-POINT MESSAGES

Among its most important functionalities, MPI manages the exchange of data between processes within a selected communicator. The medium of this exchange is referred to as messages. Messages provide point-to-point communication from a source process to a corresponding destination process, each with its own unique rank by which it is identified. In its simplest form, two commands are required to achieve the passing of a message. The sending of the message from the source process is accomplished by a send command. The receiving of the message by the corresponding destination process is accomplished by a recv command. Messages are matched between the two commands. While there are a number of variants of both the send family and the recv family of commands, the most basic of these are MPI_Send and MPI_Recv.

The message specification can be considered as a combination of the connection and the data of the message. The connection describes the points forming the communication. These include the following.

1. The source process rank.
2. The destination process rank.
3. The communicator of which both processes are a part.
4. The tag, which is a user-controlled value that can be used to discriminate among a set of possible messages between the same two processes.

8.5.1 MPI SEND

The send function is used by the source process to define the data and establish the connection of the message. The send construct has the following syntax:

```
int MPI_Send (void *message, int count, MPI_Datatype datatype, int dest, int tag,
MPI_Comm comm)
```

There are six arguments to the MPI_Send call to provide this information. The first three operands establish the data to be transferred between the source and destination processes. The first argument points to the message content itself, which may be a simple scalar or a group of data. The message data content is described by the next two arguments. The second operand specifies the number of data elements of which the message is composed. These are all the same in form. The third operand indicates the data type of the elements that make up the message (see next subsection). These three values give the data to be moved by the message. The connection of the message is established by the second three operands: the rank of the destination process, the user-defined tag field, and the communicator in which the source and destination processes reside and for which their respective ranks are defined.

8.5.2 MESSAGE-PASSING INTERFACE DATA TYPES

MPI defines its own data types. This might appear redundant, as programming languages like C explicitly define data types as well. But for the sake of robustness where different processes may be written in different languages or run on different kinds of processor architectures, MPI makes explicit what is intended. Like other interfaces, MPI provides a set of primitive data types. More complex structured data types can be user defined, as is shown in a later subsection. The most common primitive data types are presented in Table 8.1, along with the C data type equivalents.

8.5.3 MPI RECV

The MPI_Recv command mirrors the MPI_Recv command to establish a connection between the source and destination processes within the specified communicator. Like the send command (MPI_Send), the receive command (MPI_Recv) describes both the data to be transferred and the connection to be established. The MPI_Recv construct is structured as follows:

```
int MPI Recv (void *message, int count, MPI_Datatype datatype, int source, int tag,
MPI_Comm comm, MPI_Status *status)
```

The information provided to describe the data to be exchanged is represented in a form similar to the operands of the MPI_Send command. The message itself is placed in a buffer variable, designated

Table 8.1 Some of the Basic MPI Data Types and Their C Data Type Equivalent

MPI Data Type	C Data Type Equivalent
MPI_CHAR	signed char
MPI_SHORT	signed short int
MPI_INT	signed int
MPI_LONG	signed long int
MPI_UNSIGNED_CHAR	unsigned char
MPI_UNSIGNED_SHORT	unsigned short int
MPI_UNSIGNED	unsigned int
MPI_UNSIGNED_LONG	unsigned long int
MPI_FLOAT	float
MPI_DOUBLE	double
MPI_LONG_DOUBLE	long double
MPI_BYTE	No direct equivalent but like unsigned char; just 1 byte

here as "message". The number of data elements making up the full message is given by the integer count. The data type of the element of the message is one of the MPI data types defined in the previous subsection or a user-defined data type (described later).

The connection information of the MPI_Recv command is similar but not identical to that of the MPI_Send command. The source field designates the rank of the process sending the message. As before, a tag variable is given for a user-defined integer that is provided in the Send command and can be extracted for user code manipulation by the receiving process. As in all cases, the communicator in which both processes reside is specified. A final argument variable, "status", is included as the final operand of MPI_Recv. This is a record of two fields about the actual message received: the first indicates the process rank from which the message was actually received, and the second field provides the tag.

8.5.4 EXAMPLE

Code 8.3 presents a third example based on "Hello, World" to illustrate MPI commands, in this case the send and receive commands. This example expands our experience in three important ways.

1. It shows the syntactical details for setting up the information, including declarations for the MPI commands to be used.
2. It illustrates an important idiom related to how to control concurrent execution and the idea of the manager—worker form of computing using MPI.
3. It solves the problem of the previous examples that we have seen with the nonsequential printf commands.

```
#include <stdio.h>
#include <stdlib.h>
#include <mpi.h>
#include <string.h>

int main(int argc,char **argv)
{
  int rank, size;
  MPI_Init(&argc,&argv);
  MPI_Comm_rank(MPI_COMM_WORLD,&rank);
  MPI_Comm_size(MPI_COMM_WORLD,&size);

  int message[2];  // buffer for sending and receiving messages
  int dest, src;  // destination and source process variables
  int tag = 0;
  MPI_Status status;

  // This example has to be run on more than one process
  if ( size == 1 ) {
    printf(" This example requires more than one process to execute\n");
    MPI_Finalize();
    exit(0);
  }

  if ( rank != 0 ) {
   // If not rank 0, send message to rank 0
    message[0] = rank;
    message[1] = size;
    dest = 0;  // send all messages to rank 0
    MPI_Send(message, 2,MPI_INT,dest,tag,MPI_COMM_WORLD);
  } else {
  // If rank 0, receive messages from everybody else
   for (src=1;src<size;src++) {
     MPI_Recv(message,2,MPI_INT,src,MPI_ANY_TAG,MPI_COMM_WORLD,&status);
     // this prints the message just received. Notice it will print in rank
     // order since the loop is in rank order.
     printf("Hello from process %d of %d\n",message[0],message[1]);
   }
  }

  MPI_Finalize();
  return 0;
}
```

Code 8.3. "Hello" example where all processes with ranks greater than 0 send their rank and size to the process with rank 0 for printing.

```
> mpicc code3.c -o code3
> mpirun -np 4 ./code3
  Hello from process 1 of 4
  Hello from process 2 of 4
  Hello from process 3 of 4
```

Much of this example is similar to the previous ones shown in this chapter. Commands such as MPI_Init, MPI_Finalize, MPI_Comm_rank, and MPI_Comm_size are all the same in their usage. And as in the other examples, the communicator used is MPI_COMM_WORLD. But at this point the similarities end.

The biggest difference is the important idiom of manager—worker organization, in which one process, the manager, coordinates the execution of the other processes, the workers. Sometimes the manager is referred to as the "root" process. All processes, whether root or worker, receive and execute the same process code (procedure). Thus it is within the user code itself that the distinction between manager and worker has to be prescribed. In this example, the manager is assumed to be of rank $= 0$ and the workers are identified as $1 < \text{rank} < \text{size} - 1$. Hence the code is separated between manager and workers by the conditional on line 24. If true, a message array of size 2 is populated with the rank and size variables. The message is then sent using the MPI_Send command to the destination process (line 28), which is always rank 0 in this case.

The magic occurs in the body of code executed by the root process within the otherwise bounded sequence in line 30. The ordered iterative loop embodied by the for block (line 32) accepts messages using the MPI_Send command in rank-ordered fashion and prints them out in that order, guaranteeing the sequence of outputs. The control by the root process makes certain that the output information from the worker processes is presented in a deterministic form, i.e., a rank-ordered list. This is an important idiom of control in MPI using the manager—worker paradigm. Because only one message is sent from each nonroot process, the MPI_Recv command is told to ignore the tag with the useful MPI_ANY_TAG field (line 33).

8.6 SYNCHRONIZATION COLLECTIVES

While point-to-point communication is the backbone of MPI management of data exchange, additional communication constructs that involve more processes at one time are a powerful addition to simplifying MPI programming and improving performance efficiency. These are referred to as "collective operations" or simply "collectives".

8.6.1 OVERVIEW OF COLLECTIVE CALLS

A communication pattern that encompasses all processes within a communicator is known as "collective communication". One of the important aspects of a communicator is the set of processes within an MPI program to which the programmer wants to apply collective operators, and this may not be all the processes used by the program as a whole. MPI has several collective communication calls. The most frequently used are synchronization collectives, communication collectives, and reduction collective operators. Synchronization collective operations bring all the processes of a communicator up to a known place in the control flow even though their separate processes are executing asynchronously, some further ahead than others. Communication collectives exchange data in different patterns among more than two (point-to-point) processes within a communicator. Reduction collective operators act as a common communicative operator across versions of the same variable of all the processes. The next subsection briefly describes the simplest of synchronization collectives, the global barrier.

8.6.2 BARRIER SYNCHRONIZATION

The MPI_Barrier command creates, as the name implies, a point of barrier synchronization among all the processes of the specified communicator. This command has a simple syntax of a single operand:

```
int MPI_Barrier (MPI_Comm communicator)
```

The `communicator` is the communicator of the processes engaged in the synchronization. The barrier requires that all the processes reach that point in their respective code, and then wait for all the other processes of the communicator to do the same before proceeding with their separate computations. Thus all processes block at the point of the barrier until they determine that all other processes are there as well.
Fig. 8.2 illustrates the barrier operation.

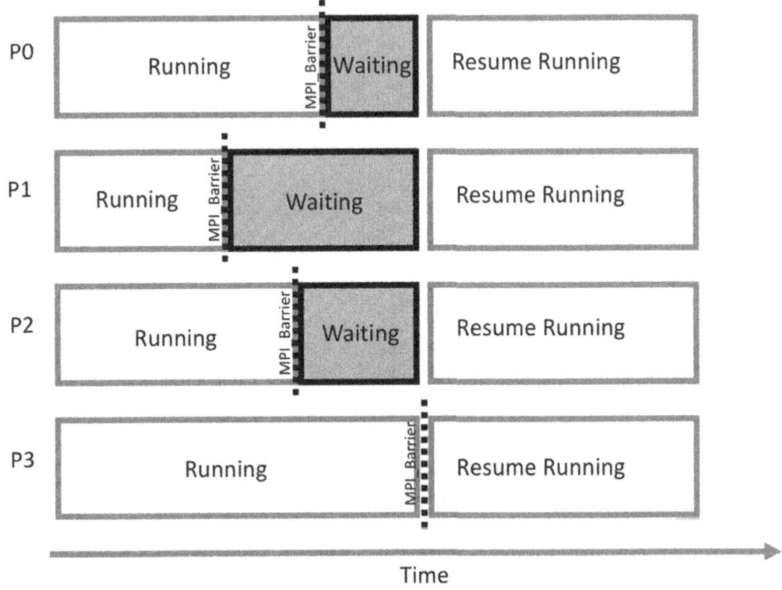

FIGURE 8.2

An illustration of the MPI_Barrier operation. Processes P0 through P3 enter the point of barrier synchronization at different times and potentially in unpredictable order. None of the processes proceeds beyond this point in the computation until all the processes reach this point. Only then do the four processes continue on to their next operations. In this way, all processes can be assured that the others have completed the necessary work. This can be an important condition to avoiding a number of different failure modes resulting from the uncertainty imposed by asynchronous operation.

8.6.3 EXAMPLE

A somewhat artificial example of the use of the MPI_Barrier collective command is presented below to demonstrate it syntax. This is an extension of the "Hello, World" example. It is also an opportunity to introduce another occasionally useful MPI instruction, MPI_Get_processor_name, which gives access to the actual hardware for purposes of identification. Depending on the MPI implementation, this might simply be the output from *gethostname* or may be something more detailed.

```
#include <stdio.h>
#include <mpi.h>

int main(int argc,char **argv)
{
  int rank, size,len;
  MPI_Init(&argc,&argv);
  char name[MPI_MAX_PROCESSOR_NAME];

  MPI_Barrier(MPI_COMM_WORLD);

  MPI_Comm_rank(MPI_COMM_WORLD,&rank);
  MPI_Comm_size(MPI_COMM_WORLD,&size);
  MPI_Get_processor_name(name,&len);

  MPI_Barrier(MPI_COMM_WORLD);

  printf(" Hello, world! Process %d of %d on %s\n",rank,size,name);

  MPI_Finalize();
  return 0;
}
```

Code 8.4. Example of MPI_Barrier and MPI_Get_processor_name.

```
> mpicc code4.c -o code4
> mpirun -np 4 ./code4
  Hello, world! Process 2 of 4 on cutter01
  Hello, world! Process 3 of 4 on cutter01
  Hello, world! Process 0 of 4 on cutter01
  Hello, world! Process 1 of 4 on cutter01
```

The example code above inserts two synchronization points with the two highlighted instances of the MPI_Barrier command. The first is just before the conventional MPI commands getting the size of the MPI_COMM_WORLD communicator and the unique rank identifiers of the individual process within that communicator. The second barrier is just after the newly introduced MPI_Get_processor_name command. Every process is blocked at both points until all processes have arrived at the respective barrier.

The MPI_Get_processor_name reminds the student that there is a difference between the abstraction of the executing process and the physical processor core resource upon which the process is computing. This command, as the name implies, acquires the character string that MPI uses to represent each processor core uniquely. In the example above, this character string is simply the output from *gethostname* which was *cutter01*, the name of the compute node on which the example was run. MPI has a lot of special constants that describe key values of its operation. Here one is used to specify the greatest possible length of the character string representing the processor name. This constant is MPI_MAX_PROCESSOR_NAME, and is referred to near the beginning of the code where the variable "name" is declared as a character buffer.

8.7 COMMUNICATION COLLECTIVES

Communication collective operations can dramatically expand interprocess communication from point-to-point to n-way or all-way data exchanges. These commands can greatly simplify user programming and provide the opportunity for greater execution efficiency by telling MPI what one actually wants to happen. Communication collective operations are among the most powerful contributing capabilities of MPI for weaving many individual processes into a single scalable computation. While there are many variants of communication collectives, a few are very widely employed in support of parallel algorithms and are described in this section.

8.7.1 COLLECTIVE DATA MOVEMENT

Collective data movement relates to different patterns by which compound data may be exchanged among concurrent processes within a specific communicator. The requirements for these data distributions are a function of the parallel algorithms being employed and the degree to which intermediate results of any process need to be shared with one or more other processes to continue the evolving distributed computation. Such patterns can be diverse, but four basic patterns satisfy most algorithmic requirements of data exchange: broadcast, scatter, gather, and allgather. These are illustrated in Figs. 8.3–8.6.

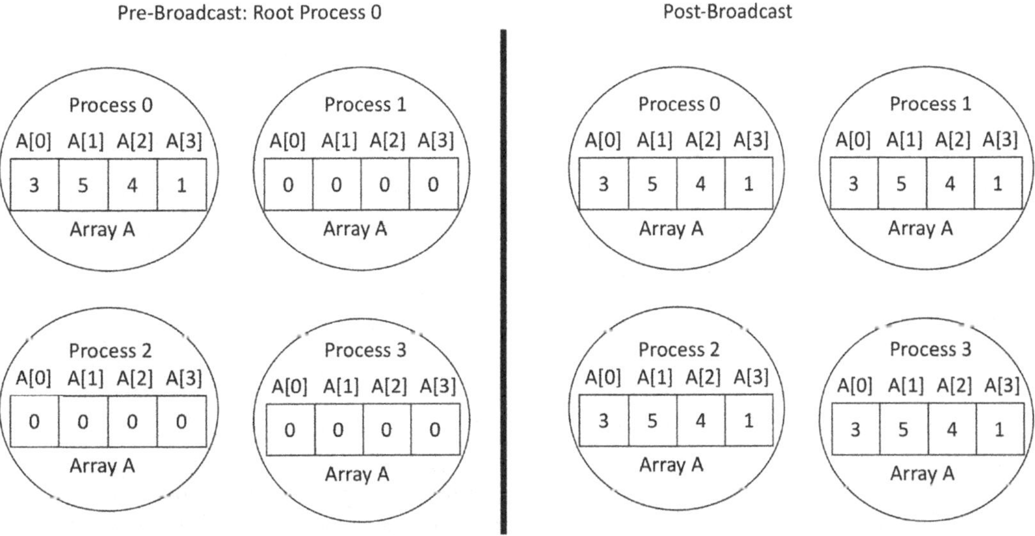

FIGURE 8.3

The broadcast operation. Broadcast shares a value or structure that exists within the context of one process with all the other processes of a communicator. In this example the root process, 0, shares the integer array A of length 4 with all the other processes.

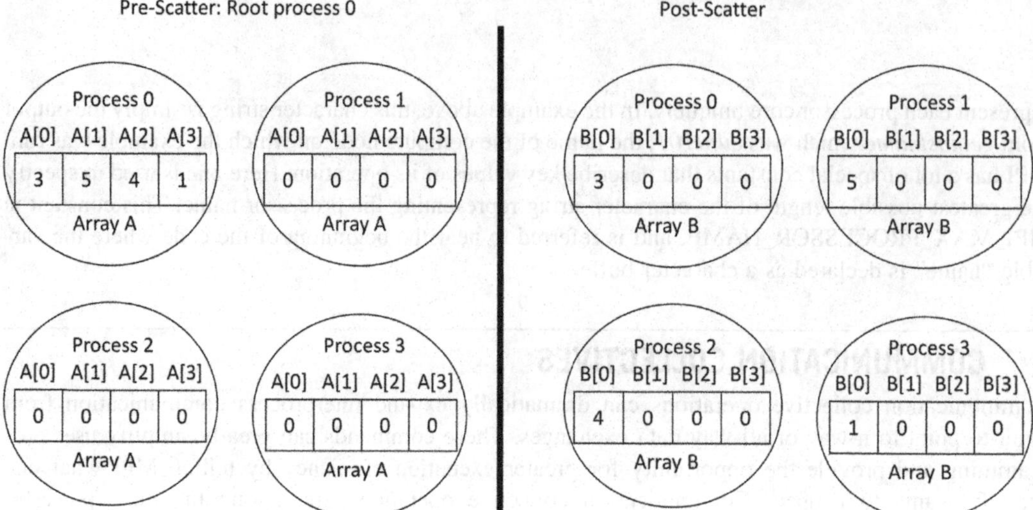

FIGURE 8.4

The scatter operation. The scatter collective communication pattern, like broadcast, shares data of one process (the root) with all the other processes of a communicator. But in this case it partitions a set of data of the root process into subsets and sends one subset to each of the processes. To be clear, each receiving process gets a different subset, and there are as many subsets as there are processes. In this example the send array is A and the receive array is B. B is initialized to 0. The root process (process 0 here) partitions the data into subsets of length 1 and sends each subset to a separate process.

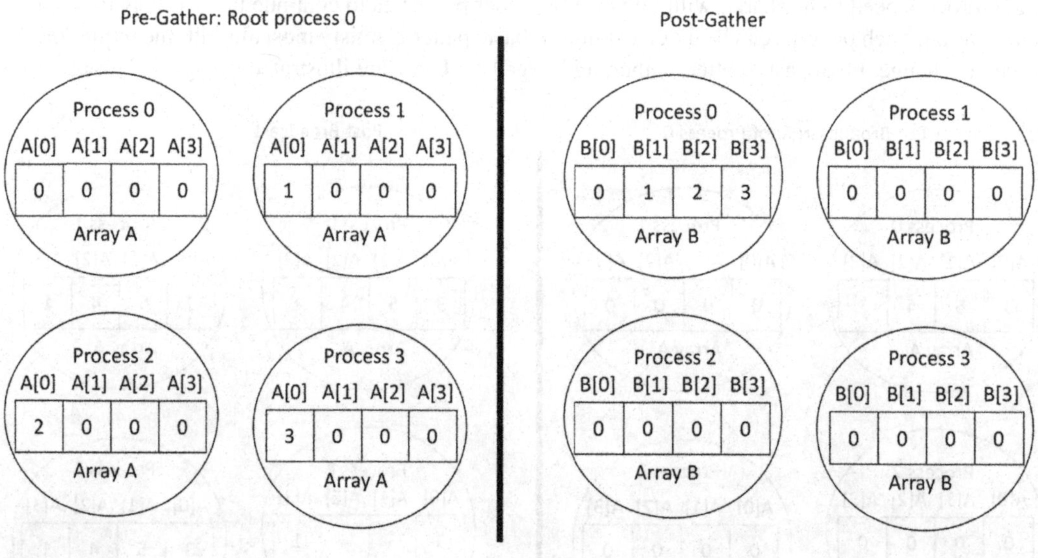

FIGURE 8.5

The gather operation. The gather collective communication pattern is, in a sense, the opposite of the scatter collective. In the case of the gather, as the name suggests, data from all the processes is sent to the root process, which is gathering up the data from the other processes. Of course, it is actually each process sending its respective designated data to the consumer process which organizes all the separate data partitions into one cumulative structure. In this example A is the send array and B is the receive array. B is initialized to 0 prior to the gather.

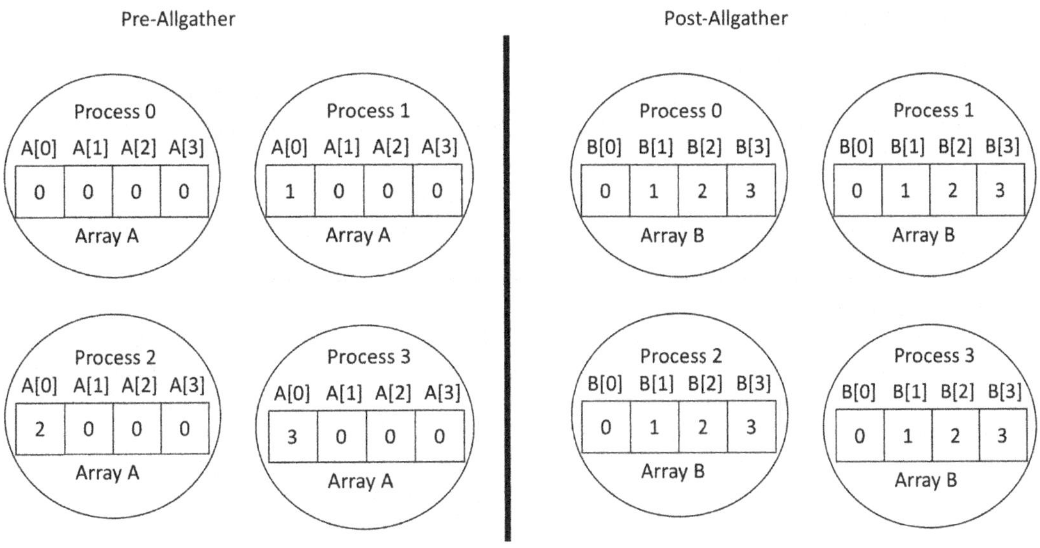

FIGURE 8.6

The allgather operation. This operation is equivalent to a gather operation followed by a broadcast of the array so that each process contains an identical receive array. In this example the A array is the send array and the B array is the receive array. B is initialized to 0.

Broadcast, illustrated in Fig. 8.3, shares a value or structure that exists within the context of one process with all the other processes of a communicator. As shown in the first diagram, the values in the A integer array in process 0 are copied to the equivalent arrays in all the other processes so they all have the same information. Broadcast, like other collective communications, provides the means by which the intermediate results of any one process are efficiently shared with all the other processes.

The scatter collective communication pattern, illustrated in Fig. 8.4, like broadcast shares data of one process with all the other processes of a communicator. But in this case it partitions a set of data of one process into subsets, and sends one subset to each of the processes. Each receiving process gets a different subset and there are as many subsets as there are processes. The process 0 has a set of data that is partitioned, in this case into four distinct partitions, A[0], A[1], A[2], and A[3], which is equal to the number of processes, processes 0 through 3 of the communicator. The first partition is returned to the source process, process 0. Data partition A[1] is sent to the second process, process 1. Partition A[2] is sent to process 2, and so on. In this way the original data in process 0 is distributed equally among all the processes of the communicator.

The gather collective communication pattern, illustrated in Fig. 8.5 is in a sense the opposite of the scatter collective. In the case of the gather, data from all the processes is sent to a particular process which is gathering up the data from the other processes. Of course, it is actually each process sending its respective designated data to the consumer process which organizes all the separate data partitions into one cumulative structure.

The extension of gather that makes it possible for all processes to use the results across the entire communicator is the allgather illustrated in Fig. 8.6. This is equivalent to first performing a gather of data from all the processes to a single receiving process and then broadcasting the accumulated data back to all the processes so that all processes have all of the resulting data.

8.7.2 BROADCAST

The broadcast communication collective operation is perhaps the simplest of the collectives, and among the most important as well. As described above, it permits a message incorporating data from a source process to be shared with all processes of a communicator. The syntax of the broadcast operation takes the following form:

```
Int MPI_Bcast (void *shared_data, int number, MPI_Datatype datatype,
 int source_process, MPI_Comm communicator)
```

The broadcast operation is achieved through the MPI_Bcast command in MPI. The operands define the form and source of the data to be sent to all the processes. The broadcast is performed within the scope of a communicator specified by the last argument, or the "communicator" of type MPI_Comm, and the broadcast data are sent to all the processes within it. The data come from a single process identified by its rank within the communicator by source_process (or root process), which is the penultimate argument of MPI_Bcast. Like many other message-passing commands, the data to be sent is determined by the first three arguments: the name of the variable pointing to the data buffer, here "shared_data" in the first argument, the type of data elements of which it is composed, here "datatype" of type MPI_Datatype in the third argument, and the "number" of elements of data type making up the data to be broadcast.

The equivalent MPI code to the broadcast illustrated in Fig. 8.3 is given in Code 8.5.

```
#include <stdio.h>
#include <mpi.h>

int main(int argc,char **argv)
{
 int rank, size,i;
 MPI_Init(&argc,&argv);
 MPI_Comm_rank(MPI_COMM_WORLD,&rank);
 MPI_Comm_size(MPI_COMM_WORLD,&size);

 int A[4];

 // Initialize array
 for (i=0;i<4;i++) {
   A[i] = 0;
 }

 int root = 0; // Define a root process

 if(rank == root) {
   //Initialize array A
   A[0] = 3;
   A[1] = 5;
   A[2] = 4;
   A[3] = 1;
 }
```

```
MPI_Bcast(A,4,MPI_INT,root,MPI_COMM_WORLD);

printf(" Rank %d A[0] = %d A[1] = %d A[2] = %d A[3] = %d\n",
          rank,A[0],A[1],A[2],A[3]);

 MPI_Finalize();
 return 0;
}
```

Code 8.5. An example of MPI_Bcast that corresponds to the illustration in Fig. 8.3.

```
> mpirun -np 4 ./code5
Rank 0 A[0] = 3 A[1] = 5 A[2] = 4 A[3] = 1
 Rank 2 A[0] = 3 A[1] = 5 A[2] = 4 A[3] = 1
 Rank 1 A[0] = 3 A[1] = 5 A[2] = 4 A[3] = 1
 Rank 3 A[0] = 3 A[1] = 5 A[2] = 4 A[3] = 1
```

8.7.3 SCATTER

The communication collective operation "scatter" distributes data of one process in separate parts to all the processes (including itself) within the scope of a communicator. The communicator of size processes disseminates the data of the source process in size-equal partitions. The distribution is in rank order across the set of processes and the linear dimension of the dataset. This is a particularly important construct for scalable matrices across a distributed-memory system.

The scatter operation is performed by means of the MPI_Scatter command. The operands define the form and source of the data to be sent. No destination identifier is required, as all processes are implicitly included as receiving part of the distributed data. The syntax of the scatter operation takes the following form:

```
int MPI_Scatter (void *send_data, int send_number, MPI_Datatype datatype,
void *put_data, int put_number, int source_rank, MPI_Comm communicator)
```

The scatter is performed within the scope of a communicator specified by the last argument, here "communicator" of type MPI_Comm, and the data is sent to all the processes within it. The data comes from a single process identified by its rank within the communicator by source_rank which is the penultimate argument of MPI_Scatter(). Like many other message-passing commands, the data to be sent is determined by the first three arguments: the name of the data, here "shared_data" in the first argument, the type of data elements of which it is composed, here "datatype" of type MPI_Datatype in the third argument, and the "send_number" of elements of data type making up the data to be distributed. Where the data is to be put at the receive processes is specified by put_data and the size of the data of the data type is given by the integer put_number. The equivalent MPI code to the scatter operation illustrated in Fig. 8.4 is given in Code 8.6.

```
#include <stdio.h>
#include <stdlib.h>
#include <mpi.h>

int main(int argc,char **argv)
{
  int rank, size,i;
  MPI_Init(&argc,&argv);
  MPI_Comm_rank(MPI_COMM_WORLD,&rank);
  MPI_Comm_size(MPI_COMM_WORLD,&size);

  if ( size != 4 ) {
  printf(" Example is designed for 4 processes\n");
  MPI_Finalize();
  exit(0);
 }

  // A is the sendbuffer and B is the receive buffer
  int A[4],B[4];

  // Initialize array
  for (i=0;i<4;i++) {
    A[i] = 0;
    B[i] = 0;
 }

  int root = 0; // Define a root process

  if (rank == root ) {
   // Initialize array A
    A[0] = 3;
    A[1] = 5;
    A[2] = 4;
    A[3] = 1;
 }

 MPI_Scatter(A,1,MPI_INT,B,1,MPI_INT,root,MPI_COMM_WORLD);

 printf(" Rank %d B[0] = %d B[1] = %d B[2] = %d B[3] = %d\n",
          rank,B[0],B[1],B[2],B[3]);

 MPI_Finalize();
 return 0;
}
```

Code 8.6. An example of MPI_Scatter that corresponds to the illustration in Fig. 8.4.

```
> mpirun -np 4 ./code6
 Rank 0 B[0] = 3 B[1] = 0 B[2] = 0 B[3] = 0
 Rank 2 B[0] = 4 B[1] = 0 B[2] = 0 B[3] = 0
 Rank 1 B[0] = 5 B[1] = 0 B[2] = 0 B[3] = 0
 Rank 3 B[0] = 1 B[1] = 0 B[2] = 0 B[3] = 0
```

8.7.4 GATHER

The communication collective operation "gather" is in some senses the opposite of the scatter operation described above. In this case every process of a given communicator sends its respective designated dataset to the same specified process. The syntax of the gather operation takes the following form:

```
int MPI_Gather (void *send_data, int send_number, MPI_Datatype send_datatype,
 void *put_data, int put_number, MPI_Datatype put_datatype, int destination_rank,
 MPI_Comm communicator)
```

The gather operation is done through the MPI_Gather command in MPI. The operands define the form and source of the data to be sent to the single receiving process and the form and destination of the data being received. The gather is performed within the scope of a communicator specified by the last argument, here "communicator" of type MPI_Comm, and the data is sent from all the processes within it to the single receiving process. The data comes from every process within the communicator. As before, the data to be sent is determined by the first three arguments: the name of the data, here "send_data" in the first argument, the type of the data elements of which it is composed, here "send_datatype" of type MPI_Datatype in the third argument, and the "send_number" of elements of data type making up the data to be distributed. Where the data is to be put at the receive process is specified by "put_data" of type "put_datatype", and the size of the data of data type is given by the integer "put_number". The process to which all the data across the processes is accumulated in the communicator is specified by the integer argument "destination_rank", which is the seventh operand. The equivalent MPI code to the gather operation illustrated in Fig. 8.5 is shown in Code 8.7.

```
#include <stdio.h>
#include <stdlib.h>
#include <mpi.h>

int main(int argc,char **argv)
{
 int rank, size,i;
 MPI_Init(&argc,&argv);
 MPI_Comm_rank(MPI_COMM_WORLD,&rank);
 MPI_Comm_size(MPI_COMM_WORLD,&size);

```

```
if ( size != 4 ) {
  printf(" Example is designed for 4 processes\n");
  MPI_Finalize();
  exit(0);
}

// A is the sendbuffer and B is the receive buffer
int A[4],B[4];

// Initialize array
for (i=0;i<4;i++) {
  A[i] = 0;
  B[i] = 0;
}
A[0] = rank;

int root = 0; // Define a root process

MPI_Gather(A,1,MPI_INT,B,1,MPI_INT,root,MPI_COMM_WORLD);

printf(" Rank %d B[0] = %d B[1] = %d B[2] = %d B[3] = %d\n",
             rank,B[0],B[1],B[2],B[3]);

MPI_Finalize();
return 0;
}
```

Code 8.7. An example of MPI_Gather that corresponds to the illustration in Fig. 8.5.

```
> mpirun -np 4 ./code7
 Rank 1 B[0] = 0 B[1] = 0 B[2] = 0 B[3] = 0
 Rank 2 B[0] = 0 B[1] = 0 B[2] = 0 B[3] = 0
 Rank 3 B[0] = 0 B[1] = 0 B[2] = 0 B[3] = 0
 Rank 0 B[0] = 0 B[1] = 1 B[2] = 2 B[3] = 3
```

8.7.5 ALLGATHER

The syntax of the MPI Allgather operation is nearly identical to that of the MPI gather operation, except that there is no longer any need to provide a destination rank because of the broadcast implicit in the allgather operation.

```
int MPI_Allgather (void *send_data, int send_number, MPI_Datatype send_datatype,
 void *put_data, int put_number, MPI_Datatype put_datatype, MPI_Comm communicator)
```

The equivalent MPI code to the allgather operation illustrated in Fig. 8.6 is shown in Code 8.8.

```
#include <stdio.h>
#include <stdlib.h>
#include <mpi.h>

int main(int argc,char **argv)
{
  int rank, size,i;
  MPI_Init(&argc,&argv);
  MPI_Comm_rank(MPI_COMM_WORLD,&rank);
  MPI_Comm_size(MPI_COMM_WORLD,&size);

  if ( size != 4 ) {
    printf(" Example is designed for 4 processes\n");
    MPI_Finalize();
    exit(0);
  }

  // A is the sendbuffer and B is the receive buffer
  int A[4],B[4];

  // Initialize array
  for (i=0;i<4;i++) {
     A[i] = 0;
     B[i] = 0;
  }
  A[0] = rank;

  int root = 0; // Define a root process

  MPI_Allgather(A,1,MPI_INT,B,1,MPI_INT,MPI_COMM_WORLD);

  printf(" Rank %d B[0] = %d B[1] = %d B[2] = %d B[3] = %d\n",
           rank,B[0],B[1],B[2],B[3]);

  MPI_Finalize();
  return 0;
}
```

Code 8.8. An example of MPI_Allgather that corresponds to the illustration in Fig. 8.6.

```
> mpirun -np 4 ./code8
 Rank 0 B[0] = 0 B[1] = 1 B[2] = 2 B[3] = 3
 Rank 1 B[0] = 0 B[1] = 1 B[2] = 2 B[3] = 3
 Rank 2 B[0] = 0 B[1] = 1 B[2] = 2 B[3] = 3
 Rank 3 B[0] = 0 B[1] = 1 B[2] = 2 B[3] = 3
```

8.7.6 REDUCTION OPERATIONS

Reduction collectives are similar to gather, but perform some sort of reducing operation on the gathered data such as calculating a sum, finding a maximum value, or performing some user-defined operation. Predefined reduction operations in MPI are given in Table 8.2.

The syntax for the reduction operation in MPI is as follows.

```
int MPI_Reduce (const void *send_data, void *put_data, int send_number,
 MPI_Datatype datatype, MPI_OP operation,int destination_rank, MPI_Comm communicator)
```

The first two arguments are the data sent to the reduction operation by each process and the location at the destination rank is specified by "put_data", both of type "datatype". The size of the data sent is given by the "send_number". The reduction operation is either one of those listed in Table 8.2 or user defined. An example of MPI_Reduce in a vector dot product calculation is presented in Code 8.9.

Table 8.2 Predefined Reduction Operations in MPI and Supported Predefined MPI Data Types

Predefined Reduction Operation	MPI Name	Supported Type
Maximum	MPI_MAX	MPI_INT, MPI_LONG, MPI_SHORT, MPI_FLOAT, MPI_DOUBLE
Minimum	MPI_MIN	MPI_INT, MPI_LONG, MPI_SHORT, MPI_FLOAT, MPI_DOUBLE
Summation	MPI_SUM	MPI_INT, MPI_LONG, MPI_SHORT, MPI_FLOAT, MPI_DOUBLE
Product	MPI_PROD	MPI_INT, MPI_LONG, MPI_SHORT, MPI_FLOAT, MPI_DOUBLE
Logical AND	MPI_LAND	MPI_INT, MPI_LONG, MPI_SHORT
Bit-wise AND	MPI_BAND	MPI_INT, MPI_LONG, MPI_SHORT, MPI_BYTE
Logical OR	MPI_LOR	MPI_INT, MPI_LONG, MPI_SHORT
Bit-wise OR	MPI_BOR	MPI_INT, MPI_LONG, MPI_SHORT, MPI_BYTE
Logical XOR	MPI_LXOR	MPI_INT, MPI_LONG, MPI_SHORT
Bit-wise XOR	MPI_BXOR	MPI_INT, MPI_LONG, MPI_SHORT, MPI_BYTE
Maximum value and location	MPI_MAXLOC	Pair data types: MPI_DOUBLE_INT (a double and an int), MPI_2INT (two ints)
Minimum value and location	MPI_MINLOC	Pair datatypes: MPI_DOUBLE_INT (a double and an int), MPI_2INT (two ints)

```
1 #include <stdlib.h>
2 #include <stdio.h>
3 #include <mpi.h>
4
5 int main(int argc,char **argv) {
6   MPI_Init(&argc,&argv);
7   int rank,p,i, root = 0;
8   MPI_Comm_rank(MPI_COMM_WORLD,&rank);
9   MPI_Comm_size(MPI_COMM_WORLD,&p);
10
11   // Make the local vector size constant
12   int local_vector_size = 100;
13
14   // compute the global vector size
15   int n = p*local_vector_size;
16
17   // initialize the vectors
18   double *a, *b;
19   a = (double *) malloc(
20        local_vector_size*sizeof(double));
21   b = (double *) malloc(
22        local_vector_size*sizeof(double));
23   for (i=0;i<local_vector_size;i++) {
24     a[i] = 3.14*rank;
25     b[i] = 6.67*rank;
26  }
27
28   // compute the local dot product
29   double partial_sum = 0.0;
30   for (i=0;i<local_vector_size;i++) {
31     partial_sum += a[i]*b[i];
32  }
33
34  double sum = 0;
35  MPI_Reduce(&partial_sum,&sum,1,
36          MPI_DOUBLE,MPI_SUM,root,MPI_COMM_WORLD);
37
38  if ( rank == root ) {
39    printf("The dot product is %g\n",sum);
40  }
41
42  free(a);
43  free(b);
44  MPI_Finalize();
45  return 0;
46 }
```

Code 8.9. Example of MPI Reduce which computes the dot product of two vectors. The two vectors here, a and b, are initialized arbitrarily (lines 23–26). The local dot product is computed in lines 29–32, and then the partial sum of the dot product from each process is summed using MPI_Reduce in lines 35–36. Note that the global vector sizes change as a function of the number of processes used, while the size of the vector segments local to the process remains constant as is done in weak scaling tests.

The companion to MPI_Reduce is MPI_Allreduce, which behaves the same as MPI_Reduce except that the result of the reduction is broadcast to all processes in the communicator. As such, the syntax for usage is nearly identical except that no "destination rank" input is needed since all ranks receive the result.

```
int MPI_Allreduce (const void *send_data, void *put_data, int send_number,
MPI_Datatype datatype, MPI_OP operation, MPI_Comm communicator)
```

```
#include <stdio.h>
#include <mpi.h>

int main(int argc,char **argv) {

  MPI_Init(&argc,&argv);
  int rank;
  MPI_Comm_rank(MPI_COMM_WORLD,&rank); // identify the rank

  int input = 0;
  if ( rank == 0 ) {
    input = 2;
  } else if ( rank == 1 ) {
    input = 7;
  } else if ( rank == 2 ) {
    input = 1;
  }
  int output;

  MPI_Allreduce(&input,&output,1,MPI_INT,MPI_SUM,MPI_COMM_WORLD);

  printf("The result is %d rank %d\n",output,rank);

  MPI_Finalize();

  return 0;
}
```

Code 8.10. An example of MPI_Allreduce. The sum of the input variable is computed and broadcast to all processes. If run on three processes or more, each process should have as output the value 10.

```
> mpirun -np 4 ./code10
The result is 10 rank 0
The result is 10 rank 1
The result is 10 rank 2
The result is 10 rank 3
```

8.7.7 ALLTOALL

There is an important extension to the MPI_Allgather pattern that frequently appears in scientific computations: the alltoall communication pattern. In this pattern, distinct data is sent to each of the receivers and each sender is also a receiver. When displayed as a matrix with rows representing processes and columns representing data partitions, the alltoall communication pattern looks exactly like the matrix transpose illustrated in Fig. 8.7.

The MPI_Alltoall operation has the following syntax:

```
int MPI_Alltoall (void *send_data, int send_number, MPI_Datatype send_datatype,
 void *put_data, int put_number, MPI_Datatype put_datatype, MPI_Comm communicator)
```

As an extension to MPI_Allgather, MPI_Alltoall takes the exact same arguments as MPI_allgather although the communication pattern is different, as illustrated in Fig. 8.7. The MPI version of the operation illustrated in Fig. 8.7 is shown in Code 8.11.

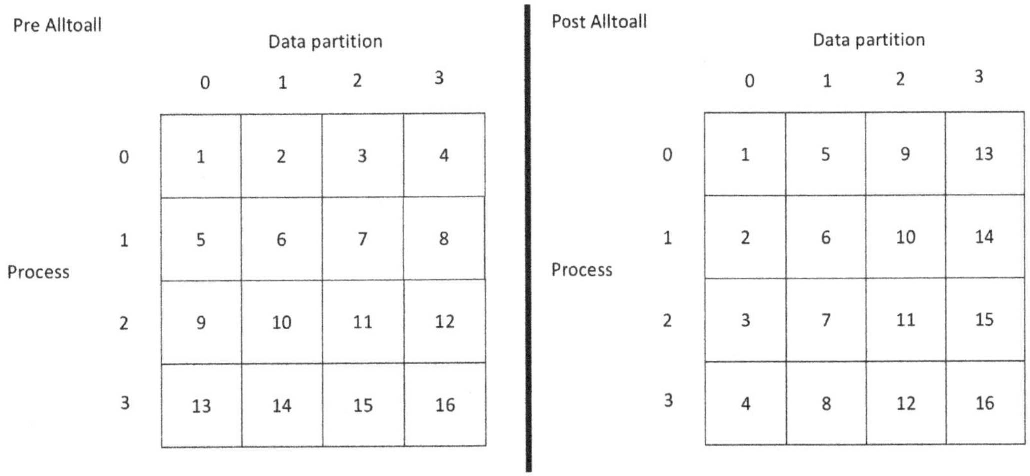

Pre Alltoall

Process \ Data partition	0	1	2	3
0	1	2	3	4
1	5	6	7	8
2	9	10	11	12
3	13	14	15	16

Post Alltoall

Process \ Data partition	0	1	2	3
0	1	5	9	13
1	2	6	10	14
2	3	7	11	15
3	4	8	12	16

FIGURE 8.7

The alltoall communication pattern extends allgather, where distinct data is sent to each receiver and each sender is also a receiver. The ith data partition is sent to the jth process. The communication pattern looks like a matrix transpose when listing the data in each process in rows and the data partitions on each process as the columns. In this example, each data partition on each process only contains a single integer and the number of processes has been limited to four to see the alltoall communication pattern better.

```
#include <stdio.h>
#include <stdlib.h>
#include <mpi.h>

int main(int argc,char **argv) {

  MPI_Init(&argc,&argv);
  int rank,size,i;
  MPI_Comm_rank(MPI_COMM_WORLD,&rank);
  MPI_Comm_size(MPI_COMM_WORLD, &size);

  if ( size != 4 ) {
    printf(" This example is designed for 4 proceses\n");
    MPI_Finalize();
    exit(0);
  }

  int A[4],B[4];

  for (i=0;i<4;i++) {
    A[i] = i+1 + 4*rank;
  }

  // Note that the send number and receive number are both one.
  // This reflects that fact that the send size and receive size
  // refer to the distinct data size sent to each process.
  MPI_Alltoall(A,1,MPI_INT,B,1,MPI_INT,MPI_COMM_WORLD);

  printf("Rank: %d B: %d %d %d %d\n",rank,B[0],B[1],B[2],B[3]);

  MPI_Finalize();

  return 0;
}
```

Code 8.11. The MPI example that corresponds to the illustration in Fig. 8.7.

```
> mpirun -np 4 ./code11
Rank: 0 B: 1 5 9 13
Rank: 1 B: 2 6 10 14
Rank: 2 B: 3 7 11 15
Rank: 3 B: 4 8 12 16
```

8.8 NONBLOCKING POINT-TO-POINT COMMUNICATION

The point-to-point communication calls introduced in Sections 8.5.1 and 8.5.3, MPI_Send and MPI_Recv, do not return from the respective function call until the send and receive operations have completed. While this ensures that the send and receive buffers used in the MPI_Send and MPI_Recv arguments are safe to use or reuse after the function call, it also means that unless there is a simultaneously matching send for each receive, the code will deadlock, resulting in the code hanging. This common type of bug is examined in Chapter 14. One way to avoid this is by using nonblocking point-to-point communication.

Nonblocking point-to-point communication returns immediately from the function call before confirming that the send or the receive has completed. These nonblocking calls are MPI_Isend and MPI_Irecv. They are used coupled with MPI_Wait, which will wait until the operation is completed. When querying whether a nonblocking point-to-point communication has completed, MPI_Test is often paired with MPI_Isend and MPI_Irecv. Nonblocking point-to-point calls can simplify code development to avoid such deadlocks more easily and also potentially enable the overlap of useful computation while checking to see if the communication has completed.

The syntax of each of these calls is the same as for the blocking calls except for the addition of a request argument and the elimination of the status output in the MPI_Recv arguments.

```
int MPI_Isend (void *message, int count, MPI_Datatype datatype, int dest, int tag,
 MPI_Comm comm, MPI_Request *send_request)
```

```
int MPI_Irecv (void *message, int count, MPI_Datatype datatype, int source, int tag,
 MPI_Comm comm, MPI_Request *recv_request)
```

Because both MPI_Isend and MPI_Irecv return immediately after calling without confirming that the message-passing operations have completed, the application user needs a way to specify when these operations must complete. This is done with MPI_Wait:

```
int MPI_Wait(MPI_Request *request, MPI_Status *status)
```

When MPI_Wait is called, the nonblocking request originating from MPI_Isend or MPI_Irecv is provided as an argument. The status that was previously provided directly from MPI_Recv is now supplied as an output from MPI_Wait.

Similar to MPI_Wait, MPI_Test can be paired with an MPI_Isend or MPI_Irecv call to query whether the message passing has completed while performing other work. MPI_Test shares similar syntax to MPI_Wait, adding only a flag that is set to true if the request being queried has completed.

```
int MPI_Test(MPI_Request *request, int *flag, MPI_Status *status)
```

An example of using nonblocking communication is presented in Code 8.12. In this example, the send commands are issued first, followed by the receive commands. If using blocking communication and sending a sufficiently large message this would normally result in a deadlock, but nonblocking communication avoids this pitfall.

```
#include <stdlib.h>
#include <stdio.h>
#include <mpi.h>

int main(int argc, char* argv[]) {
  int a, b;
  int size, rank;
  int tag = 0; // Pick a tag arbitrarily
  MPI_Status status;
  MPI_Request send_request, recv_request;

  MPI_Init(&argc, &argv);
  MPI_Comm_size(MPI_COMM_WORLD, &size);
  MPI_Comm_rank(MPI_COMM_WORLD, &rank);

  if (size != 2) {
    printf("Example is designed for 2 processes\n");
    MPI_Finalize();
    exit(0);
  }
  if (rank == 0) {
    a = 314159; // Value picked arbitrarily

    MPI_Isend(&a, 1, MPI_INT, 1, tag, MPI_COMM_WORLD, &send_request);
    MPI_Irecv (&b, 1, MPI_INT, 1, tag, MPI_COMM_WORLD, &recv_request);

    MPI_Wait(&send_request, &status);
    MPI_Wait(&recv_request, &status);
    printf ("Process %d received value %d\n", rank, b);

  } else {

    a = 667;

    MPI_Isend (&a, 1, MPI_INT, 0, tag, MPI_COMM_WORLD, &send_request);
    MPI_Irecv (&b, 1, MPI_INT, 0, tag, MPI_COMM_WORLD, &recv_request);

    MPI_Wait(&send_request, &status);
    MPI_Wait(&recv_request, &status);
    printf ("Process %d received value %d\n", rank, b);
  }

```

```
43 MPI_Finalize();
44 return 0;
45 }
```

Code 8.12. Example of nonblocking point-to-point communication. Process 0 sends the integer 314159 to process 1 while process 1 sends the integer 667 to process 0. The particular order of the listing of Isend and Irecv in lines 24–25 and 35–36 does not matter because the calls are nonblocking.

```
> mpirun -np 2 ./code12
Process 0 received value 667
Process 1 received value 314159
```

8.9 USER-DEFINED DATA TYPES

Application developers will frequently wish to create a user-defined data type built out of the predefined MPI types listed in Table 8.1. This is accomplished using MPI_Type_create_struct and MPI_Type_commit.

```
MPI_Type_create_struct(int number_items,
                       const int *blocklengths,
                       const MPI_Aint *array_of_offsets,
                       const MPI_Datatype *array_of_types,
                       MPI_Datatype *new_datatype_name)
```

```
MPI_Type_commit(MPI_Datatype *new_datatype_name)
```

Creating a user-defined data type consists of providing the number of different partitions of existing MPI data-type elements (*number_items*), three separate arrays of length *number_items* containing the number of elements per block, byte offsets of each block and the MPI data types of each block, and the new name for the user-defined type. This name is then passed as an argument to MPI_Type_commit, after which it can be used in all existing MPI functions.

An example of creating a user-defined data type from a C struct and broadcasting it to all processes is provided in Code 8.13. In this example, a C struct containing some typical variable names for a simulation is populated with values on process 0. The user-defined data type for this C struct, *mpi_par*, is created and committed on lines 38–39. The values for the structure are then broadcast to all other processes in line 41.

```
#include <stdio.h>
#include <stddef.h>
#include "mpi.h"

typedef struct {
  int max_iter;
  double t0;
  double tf;
  double xmin;
} Pars;

int main(int argc,char **argv) {

  MPI_Init(&argc,&argv);
  int rank;
  int root = 0; // define the root process
  MPI_Comm_rank(MPI_COMM_WORLD,&rank); // identify the rank

  Pars pars;
  if ( rank == root ) {
    pars.max_iter = 10;
    pars.t0 = 0.0;
    pars.tf = 1.0;
    pars.xmin = -5.0;
  }

  int nitems = 4;
  MPI_Datatype types[nitems];
  MPI_Datatype mpi_par; // give my new type a name
  MPI_Aint offsets[nitems]; // an array for storing the element offsets
  int blocklengths[nitems];

  types[0] = MPI_INT; offsets[0] = offsetof(Pars,max_iter);blocklengths[0] = 1;
  types[1] = MPI_DOUBLE; offsets[1] = offsetof(Pars,t0);blocklengths[1] = 1;
  types[2] = MPI_DOUBLE; offsets[2] = offsetof(Pars,tf);blocklengths[2] = 1;
  types[3] = MPI_DOUBLE; offsets[3] = offsetof(Pars,xmin);blocklengths[3] = 1;

  MPI_Type_create_struct(nitems,blocklengths,offsets,types,&mpi_par);
  MPI_Type_commit(&mpi_par);

  MPI_Bcast(&pars,1,mpi_par,root,MPI_COMM_WORLD);

  printf("Hello from rank %d; my max_iter value is %d\n",rank,pars.max_iter);

  MPI_Finalize();

  return 0;
}
```

Code 8.13. Example of creating and using a user-defined data type in an MPI collective.

```
> mpirun -np 4 ./code13
Hello from rank 0; my max_iter value is 10
Hello from rank 2; my max_iter value is 10
Hello from rank 1; my max_iter value is 10
Hello from rank 3; my max_iter value is 10
```

8.10 SUMMARY AND OUTCOMES OF CHAPTER 8

- There was probably no greater achievement of practical utility for the advancement of HPC than the development of MPI.
- MPI is a community-driven specification that continues to evolve.
- MPI is a library with an API, not a language.
- MPICH was the first reduction to practice the MPI standard.
- Key elements of MPI are point-to-point communication and collective communication.
- MPI has a set of predefined data types for use in library calls.
- Point-to-point communication calls are typified by the MPI_Send and MPI_Recv calls.
- Collective communication is typified by the broadcast, gather, and scatter operations.
- Important extensions of these collective operations are allgather, reduce, and alltoall.
- Nonblocking point-to-point communications are frequently used to simplify code development and avoid deadlocks.
- User-defined data types can be built up starting from existing MPI data types and used in MPI function calls.

8.11 EXERCISES

1. Modify Code 8.13 to send and receive the user-defined data type *mpi_par* multiple times between two processes. Add an integer to the Par struct to count how many times the data have been passed back and forth.
2. Modify Code 8.13 so that each process sends *mpi_par* to the process with rank + 2 and receives data from rank − 2. For example, if there were 16 processes, process 0 would send to process 2 and receive from process 14 while process 1 would send to process 3 and receive from process 15.
3. Write a distributed matrix−vector multiplication code using MPI. Use a dense matrix and a dense vector. Call C language Basic Linear Algebra Subprograms (CBLAS) on each process for the local matrix−vector multiplication.
4. Rewrite Code 8.11 using point-to-point communication. Generalize the code to run on an arbitrary number of processes. Compare the performance of MPI_Alltoall with your point-to-point communication implementation.

5. Rewrite Code 8.9 so that the global vector sizes stay the same as the number of processes varies. This will require changing the local vector size depending on the number of processes on which MPI is launched. Plot the time to solution for your code as a function of the number of processes for various global vector sizes.

REFERENCES

[1] MPI Forum, MPI Standardization Forum, [Online]. http://mpi-forum.org/.
[2] Argonne National Laboratory, MPICH, [Online]. www.mpich.org.
[3] B. Kernighan, D. Ritchie, The C Programming Language, Prentice Hall, s.l., 1988.

CHAPTER

PARALLEL ALGORITHMS

9

CHAPTER OUTLINE

9.1 INTRODUCTION

Modern supercomputers employ several different modalities of operation to take advantage of parallelism both to exploit enabling technologies and to contribute to achieving the highest performance possible across a wide spectrum of algorithms and applications. Three of these most common hardware architecture forms present in a supercomputer are single-instruction multiple data (SIMD) parallelism, shared memory parallelism, and distributed memory parallelism. Shared memory and distributed memory parallelism are subclasses of the multiple-instruction multiple data (MIMD) class of Flynn's computer architecture taxonomy.

Each of these modalities is present in a modern supercomputer. While the unifying theme of a parallel computer architecture is parallelism, the ways in which a parallel algorithm exploits physical parallelism in each of these modalities can differ substantially. Some parallel algorithms are better suited for one kind of parallelism versus another. Often a completely different parallel algorithm will be needed, depending on the targeted parallel computer architecture structure. Frequently a combination of all three will be necessary for a parallel algorithm to achieve the highest possible performance that a supercomputer can provide.

High Performance Computing. https://doi.org/10.1016/B978-0-12-420158-3.00009-5

Table 9.1 Examples of Generic Classes of Parallel Algorithms

Generic Class of Parallel Algorithm	Example
Fork–join	OpenMP parallel for-loop
Divide and conquer	Fast Fourier Transform, parallel sort
Halo exchange	Finite difference/finite element partial differential equation solvers
Permutation	Cannon's algorithm, Fast Fourier Transform
Embarrassingly parallel	Monte Carlo
Manager–worker	Simple adaptive mesh refinement
Task dataflow	Breadth first search

In 2004 an influential set of seven classes of numerical methods commonly used on supercomputers were identified [1]. These are known as the "seven dwarfs" or "seven motifs": dense linear algebra, sparse linear algebra, spectral methods, N-body methods, structured grids, unstructured grids, and Monte Carlo methods. These seven classes of algorithms represent a large segment of supercomputing applications today and many high performance computing (HPC) benchmarks are built specifically to target them. In addition to the original "seven dwarfs", researchers have added other important emerging classes of numerical methods found in supercomputing applications, including graph traversal, finite state machines, combinational logic, and statistical machine learning [2]. Optimally mapping these numerical methods to a parallel algorithm implementation is a key challenge for supercomputing application developers.

Several classes of parallel algorithms share key characteristics and are driven by the same underlying mechanism from which the parallelism is derived. Some examples of these generic classes of parallel algorithms include fork–join, divide and conquer, manager–worker, embarrassingly parallel, task dataflow, permutation, and halo exchange. Some examples of each class are listed in Table 9.1.

This chapter examines a wide variety of parallel algorithms and the means by which the parallelism is exposed and exploited. While the specific implementation of the algorithm for SIMD or MIMD parallel computer architectures will differ, the conceptual basis for extracting parallelism from the algorithm will not. The chapter begins by examining fork–join type parallel algorithms and an example from the divide-and-conquer class of parallel algorithms, parallel sort. Examples from manager–worker type algorithms and a specific subclass of it, embarrassingly parallel, are then examined. Halo-exchange parallel algorithm examples are examined also including the advection equation and sparse matrix vector multiplication. A permutation example of Cannon's algorithm and a task dataflow example of a breadth first search algorithm complete the chapter.

9.2 FORK–JOIN

The fork–join parallel design pattern is a key component of the OpenMP execution model presented in Chapter 7 and is frequently employed in programming models targeting shared memory parallelism. In

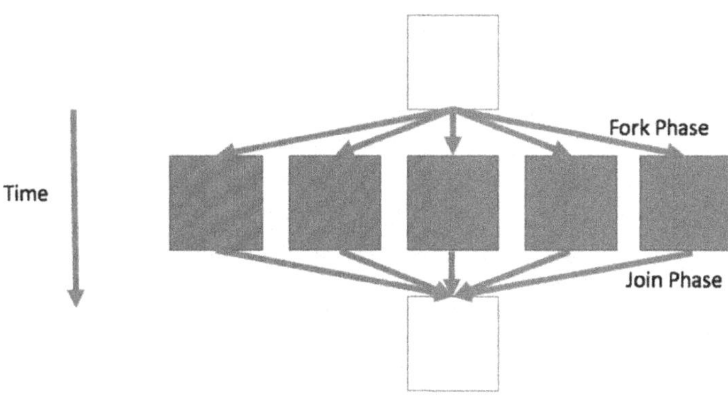

FIGURE 9.1

This is an illustration of the fork–join parallel design pattern frequently used in parallel algorithms intended for shared memory parallelism. The *empty boxes* indicate work that is serial (i.e., not parallelizable), while the *filled boxes* indicate work that can be performed concurrently. In the "fork" phase, concurrent operators known as threads (denoted here by the branching *lines*) are created to perform the concurrent work. In the "join" phase, the results of those concurrent operators are accumulated into a single resulting operator.

regions of a sequential algorithm where work can proceed concurrently, a group of lightweight concurrent operators, frequently called "threads", are created to perform that work. Once the work is completed, the results from each of these operators are accumulated during the "join" phase. This process is illustrated in Fig. 9.1.

The OpenMP parallel for-loop construct is a simple example of this type of parallel algorithm. Consider the example of parallel work sharing presented in Code 1. A previously initialized array b is added to another expression to initialize array a. Because each work element in the for-loop (see line 3) is independent of every other element, the work in this loop can proceed concurrently. Consequently, a parallel for-loop construct is added in line 1. Fig. 9.2 illustrates the fork–join behavior of the resulting concurrent operators.

```
1 #pragma omp parallel for
2   for (i=0;i<30;i++)
3     a[i] = b[i] + sin(i)
```

Code 1: An OpenMP example of fork–join for work sharing.

While the fork–join parallel design pattern is the main execution model for OpenMP, it is also found in other parallel programming models, especially those which target shared memory parallelism.

9.3 DIVIDE AND CONQUER

Algorithms denoted as "divide and conquer" break a problem into smaller subproblems which share similar enough algorithmic properties to the original problem that they can in turn also be subdivided. Using recursion, the larger problem is broken down into small enough pieces that it can

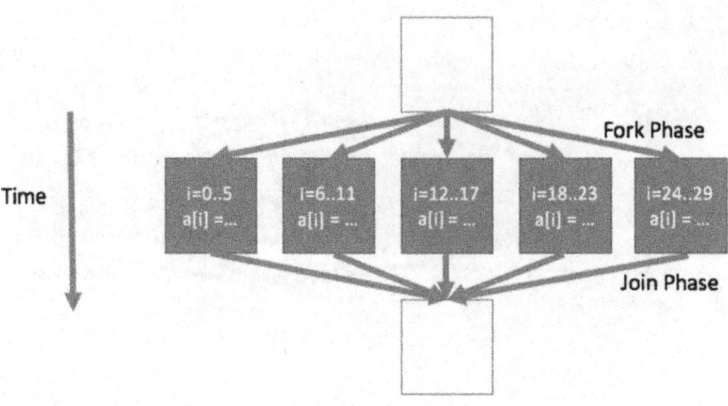

FIGURE 9.2

The resulting fork–join structure from the work-sharing example in Code 9.1 for five threads. Each concurrent operator performs an independent computation that is then joined into the final serial operator.

be easily solved with minimal computation. Because the original problem has been broken down into several smaller computations that are independent of one another, there is a natural concurrency for exploiting parallel computation resources. Frequently, divide-and-conquer type algorithms are also naturally parallel algorithms because of this concurrency and, like fork–join type algorithms, can perform very well on shared memory architectures. On distributed memory architectures, however, network latency and load imbalance can complicate the direct application of divide-and-conquer type algorithms.

One well-studied example of a divide-and-conquer algorithm with natural concurrency is quicksort [3]. As a sorting algorithm, it aims to sort a list of numbers in order of increasing value. To start, a random element of the array is selected to serve as a pivot point. Using this pivot, the rest of the list is divided into a list containing numbers smaller than the pivot and a list containing numbers larger than the pivot. This process is then repeated recursively for each of the two lists. Upon completion of recursion the resulting sorted child subproblems are concatenated for the final result. An example is given in Fig. 9.3.

The efficiency of the algorithm is significantly impacted by which element is chosen as the pivot point. If the array has N data items, the worst-case performance will be proportional to N^2; however, for most cases the performance is much faster, proportional to $N \log N$. Because the two branched lists in quicksort can be sorted independently, there is a natural concurrency of computation that can be used for parallelization. On a distributed memory architecture, exploiting this concurrency incurs a significant communication cost as sorted lists are passed from one process to another during recursion. This makes direct application of quicksort on a distributed memory architecture undesirable. However, a modification to the approach based on sampling can be made to improve this situation.

The regular sampling parallel sort algorithm is designed for better performance on distributed memory architectures with quicksort underlying the approach [4]. The algorithm is detailed below.

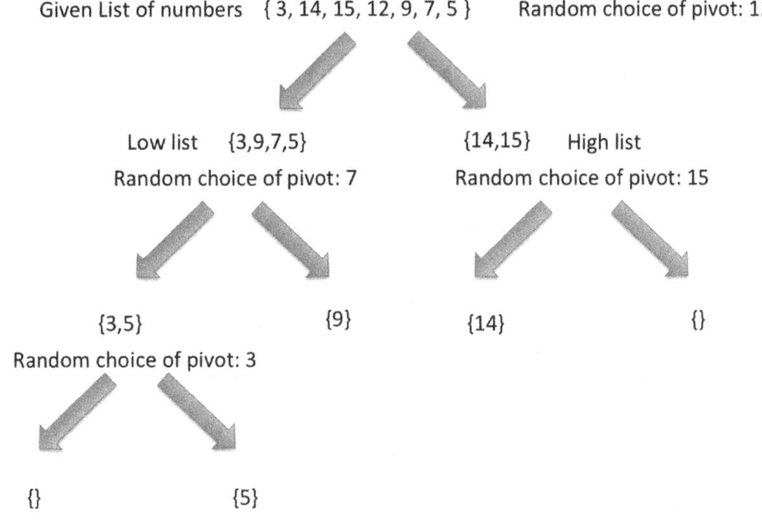

Concatenated result: {3,5,7,9,12,14,15}

FIGURE 9.3

Example of serial quicksort algorithm.

- An array of numbers to be sorted is distributed equally among *P* processes. Thus if the array size is *N*, each process will have *N*/*P* local elements.

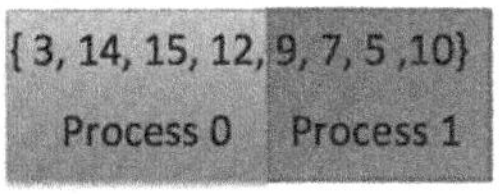

{ 3, 14, 15, 12, 9, 7, 5 ,10}
Process 0 Process 1

FIGURE 9.4A

- Each process runs sequential quicksort on its local data.

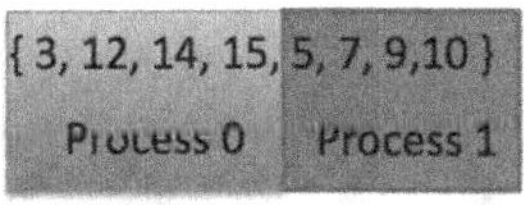

{ 3, 12, 14, 15, 5, 7, 9,10 }
Process 0 Process 1

FIGURE 9.4B

- The resulting sorted arrays are sampled at intervals determined by the global array size N and the number of processes P. Samples are taken at every N/P^2 location starting at 0, i.e.,: array element indices 0, N/P^2, $2N/P^2$, …, $(P - 1) N/P^2$ form the sample array from each local data.

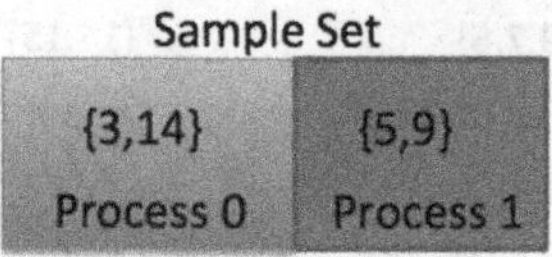

FIGURE 9.4C

- The resulting samples are gathered to a root process and sorted sequentially with quicksort.

FIGURE 9.4D

- Regularly sampled $P - 1$ pivot values computed from the sample set are broadcast to the other processes. Thus N/P^2, $2N/P^2$, …, $(P - 1) N/P^2$ indices form the sample $P - 1$ pivot points. In this example, the only pivot point broadcast is 9.

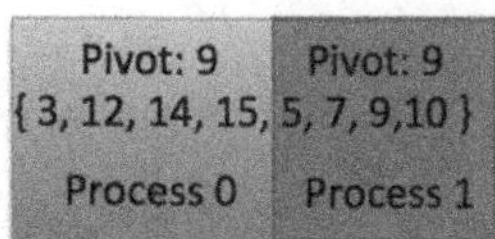

FIGURE 9.4E

- Each process divides its sorted segment of the array into P segments using the broadcast $P - 1$ pivot values.

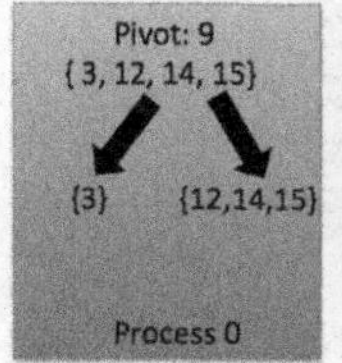

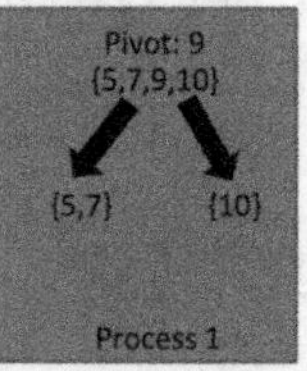

FIGURE 9.4F

- Each process performs an all-to-all operation on the P segments. Thus the ith process keeps the ith segment and sends the jth segment to the jth process.

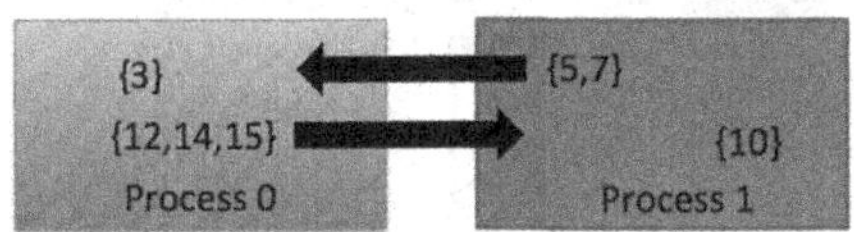

FIGURE 9.4G

- The arriving segments are merged into a single list and locally sorted.

Final result: {3,5,7,9,10,12,14,15}

FIGURE 9.4H

An example of this algorithm for $P = 2$ and $N = 8$ is illustrated in Fig. 9.4A–H.

9.4 MANAGER—WORKER

Manager—worker incorporates two different workflows in its execution: one intended for execution by just one process called the manager process, and another intended for execution by several other processes called worker processes. This approach has also historically been called "master—slave". Applications that are dynamic in nature frequently use this type of parallel design algorithm so that the manager process can coordinate and issue task actions to worker processes in response to changes in a simulation outcome. Many adaptive mesh refinement applications also use this parallel design algorithm because the meshes and data placement patterns change in response to a solution value. Such an adaptive mesh refinement is illustrated in Fig. 9.5. Manager—worker codes frequently take the form illustrated in Code 9.2, where an "if" statement distinguishes the workflow between manager and worker tasks.

```
if ( my_rank == master ) {
   send_action(INITIALIZE);

   for (int i=0;i<num_timesteps;i++) {
     send_action(REFINE);
     send_action(INTEGRATE);
     send_action(OUTPUT);
   }
} else {
  listen_for_actions();
}
```

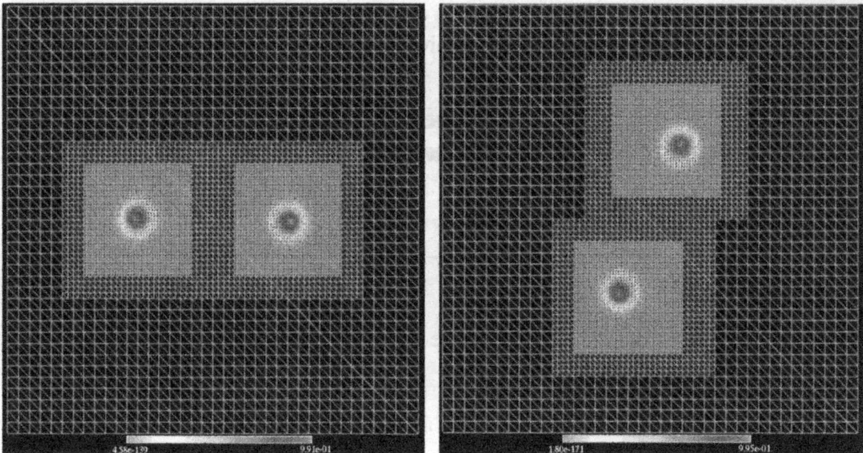

FIGURE 9.5

Example of a manager–worker adaptive mesh refinement code evolving a dynamic system of two compact objects orbiting each other. The meshes follow the orbiting compact objects as they move clockwise in the computational domain.

Code 9.2 is manager–worker example code adapted from the adaptive mesh refinement code used to generate Fig. 9.5. The manager process (called "master" in this example) directs the refinement characteristics and sends actions to worker processes that are always listening for additional instructions from the manager.

9.5 EMBARRASSINGLY PARALLEL

The term "embarrassingly parallel" is a common phrase in scientific computing that is both widely used and poorly defined. It suggests lots of parallelism with essentially no intertask communication or coordination, as well as a highly partitionable workload with minimal overhead. In general, embarrassingly parallel algorithms are a subclass of manager–worker algorithms. They are called embarrassingly parallel because the available concurrency is trivially extracted from the workflow. These algorithms sometimes require reduction operation at the end to gather the results into a manager process. While this does require some minimal coordination and intertask communication, these "almost embarrassingly parallel" algorithms are still generally referred to as embarrassingly parallel.

Monte Carlo simulations mainly fall into the category of embarrassingly parallel. Monte Carlo methods are statistical approaches for studying systems with a large number of coupled degrees of freedom, modeling phenomena with significant uncertainty in the inputs, and solving partial differential equations with more than four dimensions. Computing the value of π is a simple example.

- Define a square domain and inscribe a circle inside that domain.
- Randomly generate the coordinates of points lying inside the square domain; count the points that also lie in the circle.
- $\pi/4$ is the ratio of the number of points that lie in the circle to the total number of random points generated.

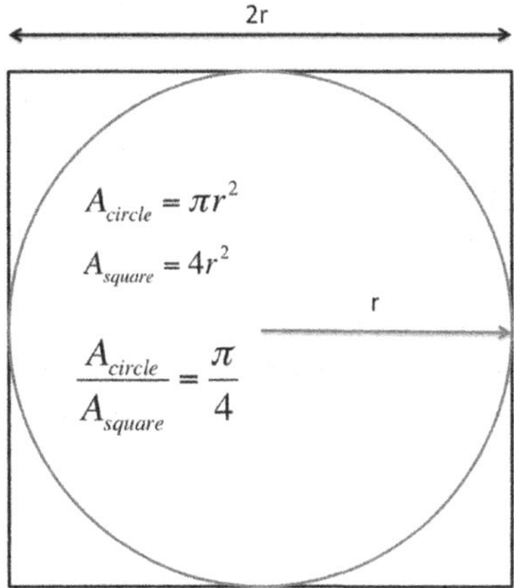

FIGURE 9.6

When generating random coordinates inside a square, the ratio of the number of points lying inside an inscribed circle to the total number of random points will be $\pi/4$.

The reasoning behind this algorithm is as follows. A circle with radius r inscribed in a square will have an area of πr^2 while the square will have an area of $(2r)^2 = 4r^2$, as seen in Fig. 9.6. The ratio of the area of the circle to the area of the square will also be the probability that a random point generated in the square lies in the circle. The ratio of these two areas is $\pi/4$.

The parallel version of this algorithm is illustrated in Fig. 9.7.

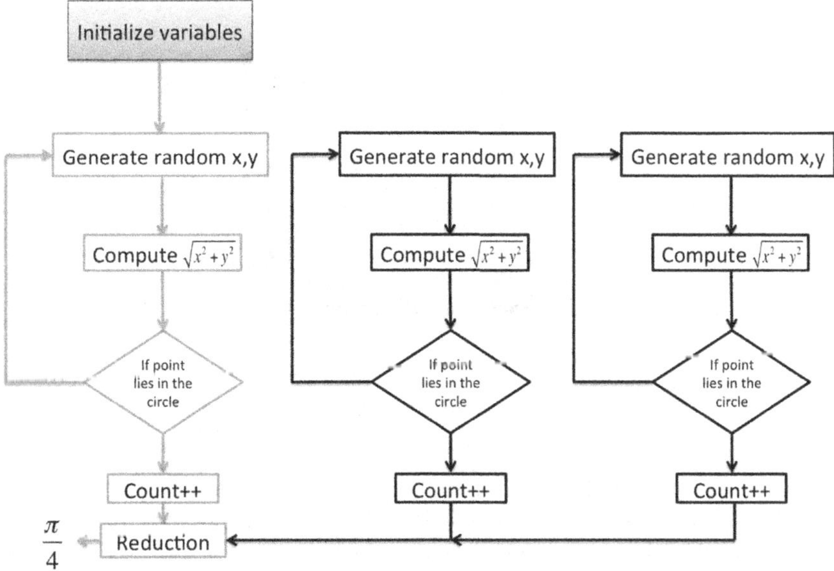

FIGURE 9.7

Embarrassingly parallel example: computing π using statistical methods. The manager is in light gray while the various workers are in black.

9.6 HALO EXCHANGE

Many parallel algorithms fall into a problem class where every parallel task is executing the same algorithm on different data without any manager algorithm present. This is sometimes referred to as the data parallel model. Data parallelism is frequently used in applications that are static in nature because a computational task can be mapped to particular subset of data throughout the life of the simulation. However, in all but the most simple of applications, some information in each data subset mapped to the parallel task has to be exchanged and synchronized for the application algorithm to function properly. This exchange of intertask information is called halo exchange.

As the name implies, a halo is a region exterior to the data subset mapped to a parallel task. It acts as an artificial boundary to that data subset and contains information that originates from the data subsets of neighboring parallel tasks. A halo is illustrated in Fig. 9.8.

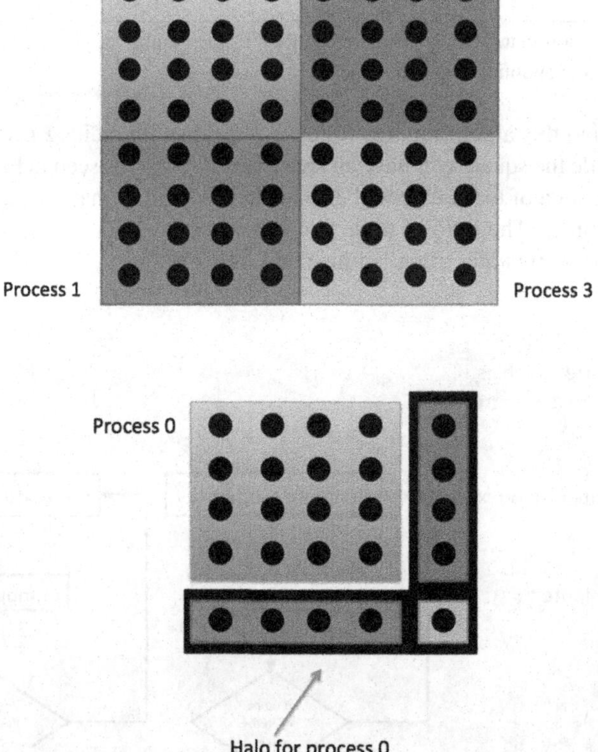

FIGURE 9.8

Illustration of a one-deep halo. In this illustration, various data points (colored dark) are split across four different processes (top figure). For each process there are two boundaries in the data that are interprocess boundaries. For process 0, these are the right and bottom edges of the square. A one-deep halo for process 0 (bottom figure) consists of those data points that are closest to the interprocess boundary of process 0 but not mapped to process 0.

Halo exchange enables each task to perform computations and update the subset of data mapped to that task while having access to any data necessary for such computations that may not be local. Halo exchange is extremely common in parallel toolkits for solving partial differential equations and in linear algebra computations. Two parallel algorithm examples are presented in this section using halo exchange: the advection equation and sparse matrix vector multiplication.

9.6.1 THE ADVECTION EQUATION USING FINITE DIFFERENCE

Wavelike phenomena permeate nature: examples include light, sound, gravitation, fluid flow, and weather, to name just a few. The study of wavelike phenomena is ubiquitous in supercomputing systems and is frequently modeled using a *partial differential equation*, or an expression involving derivatives taken against different independent variables. One of the simplest ways to solve these wavelike partial differential equations on a supercomputer is through the use of finite differencing and halo exchange. Finite differencing involves replacing the derivative expressions in the partial differential equation with approximations originating from estimating the slope between neighboring points on a uniform grid.

As an example of this parallel algorithm, consider the advection equation in Eq. (9.1).

$$\frac{\partial f}{\partial t} = -v\frac{\partial f}{\partial x} \tag{9.1}$$

This advection equation transports a scalar field $f(x, t)$ toward increasing x with speed v. The analytic solution to this partial differential equation is

$$f(x,t) = F(x - vt) \tag{9.2}$$

where $F(x)$ is an arbitrary function describing the initial condition of the system. So if the initial condition of the wavelike phenomenon for solution is

$$F(x) = e^{-x^2} \tag{9.3}$$

then the analytic solution to Eq. (9.1) would be

$$f(x,t) = e^{-(x-vt)^2} \tag{9.4}$$

as plotted in Fig. 9.9.

While the advection equation in Eq. (9.1) can be solved analytically with the solution shown in Fig. 9.9, a parallel algorithm based on halo exchange can be crafted to solve this equation numerically. The left- and right-hand partial derivatives in Eq. (9.1) are replaced with finite difference approximations to those derivatives:

$$\frac{f_i^{n+1} - f_i^n}{dt} = -v\frac{f_{i+1}^n - f_i^n}{dx} \tag{9.5}$$

where the field $f(x,t)$ has been discretized to a uniform mesh in which the x points are separated by distance dx and the time points are separated by time dt, with the subscript to f indicating the spatial location in that mesh and the superscript to f indicating the temporal location in that mesh. This is illustrated in Fig. 9.10.

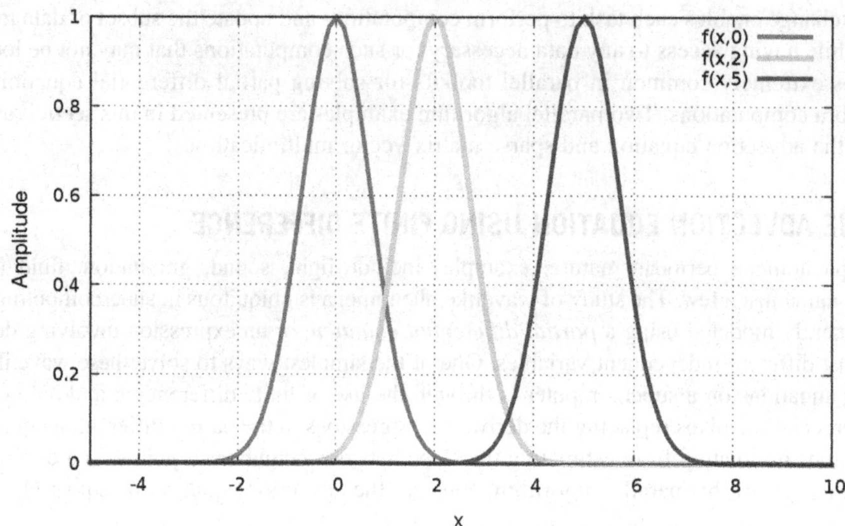

FIGURE 9.9

The solution to the advection equation given in Eq. (9.1) with the initial condition in Eq. (9.3) and velocity set to be 1. The solution at several times ($t = 0$, 2, and 5) is plotted. The scalar field is transported to the right as time increases.

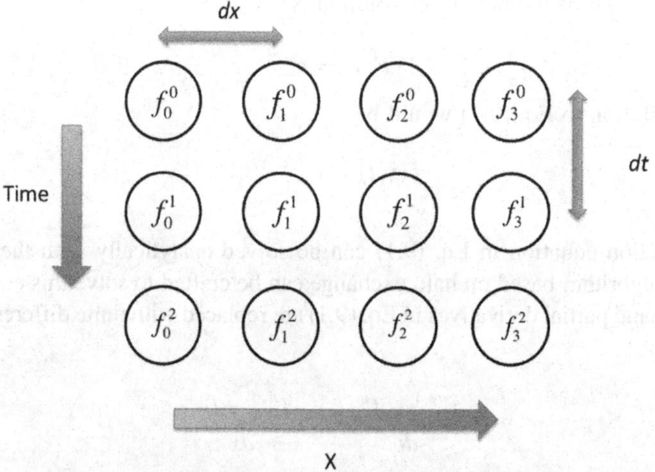

FIGURE 9.10

The scalar field values are assigned to discrete mesh points in time and space, with points separated from one another by value dx in the x direction and dt in the time direction. The superscript indicates the time index (0–2 in this illustration) and the subscript indicates the spatial index in the x direction (0–3 in this illustration).

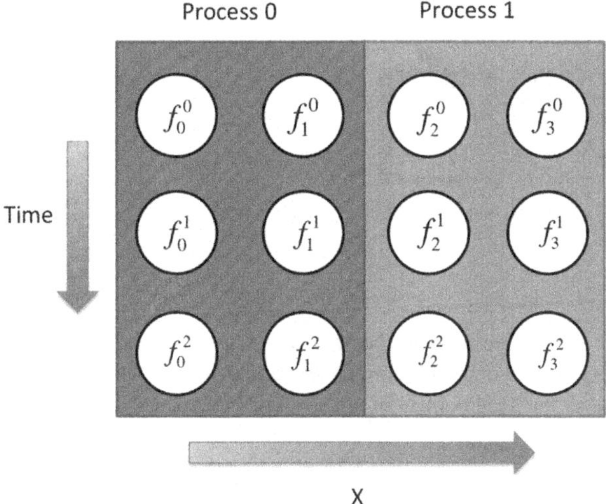

FIGURE 9.11

The discretized mesh is partitioned across several processes. As an example of a data parallelism, the same computation from the right-hand side of Eq. (9.6) is concurrently applied to different data in process 0 and 1 starting at the first row of values corresponding to the initial time.

Because the initial condition of the scalar field, f_i^0 or $f(x,0)$, is known, algebraic manipulation of Eq. (9.5) enables all future time values to be found iteratively using Eq. (9.6) provided that the right-hand side of the expression can be computed.

$$f_i^{n+1} = f_i^n - v\frac{dt}{dx}\left(\frac{f_{i+1}^n - f_i^n}{dx}\right) \tag{9.6}$$

To compute the right-hand side of Eq. (9.6) in parallel, the discretized mesh is partitioned across several processes, as illustrated in Fig. 9.11. This is an example of data parallelism where the same operation, computing the right-hand side of Eq. (9.6) in this case, is applied to different data spread across several processes.

To compute the right-hand side for the data in process 0, however, some information is needed from process 1. This information is provided through halo exchange, as illustrated in Fig. 9.12.

The parallel algorithm is summarized in Fig. 9.13.

9.6.2 SPARSE MATRIX VECTOR MULTIPLICATION

Parallel algorithms designed around halo exchange frequently show up not just in mesh-based solvers, as seen in Section 9.6.1, but also in sparse linear algebra operations such as the sparse matrix vector multiplication used in the high performance conjugate gradients (HPCG) benchmark presented in Chapter 4.

For a matrix of size $N \times N$ and vector of size N, matrix–vector multiplication is given by Eq. (9.7):

$$x_i = \sum_{j=0}^{N-1} A_{ij} b_j \tag{9.7}$$

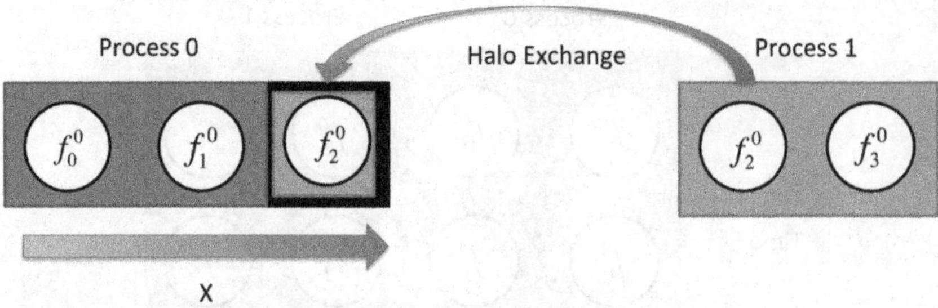

FIGURE 9.12

The information needed by process 0 to compute the right-hand side of Eq. (9.6) is provided from process 1 using halo exchange. The halo (highlighted in black) forms an artificial boundary so that the right-hand side of Eq. (9.6) can be computed entirely over the local domain of process 0 (colored dark gray).

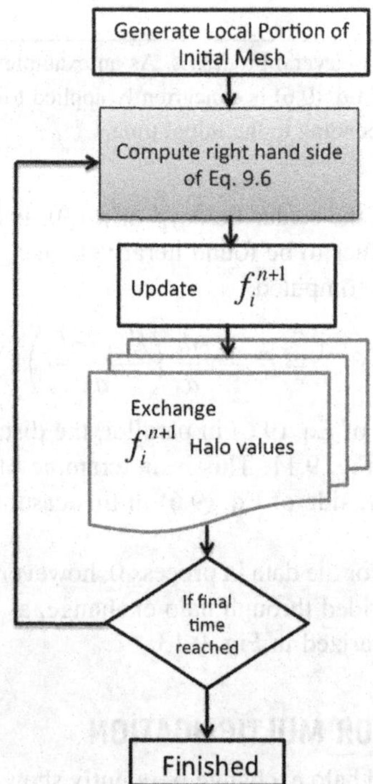

FIGURE 9.13

A parallel algorithm for the advection equation using halo exchange. Each process independently computes the same algorithm on different data, with halo exchange providing data needed from neighboring processes and serving as an interprocess boundary.

where A_{ij} is the (i,j)th element of the matrix, $i \in [0, N-1]$, and b_j is the jth element of the vector. For a sparse matrix, however, most A_{ij} values are zero, suggesting that memory would not need to be allocated for every (i,j)th element. In the case of the HPCG benchmark, the sparse matrix A uses *compressed sparse rows* format to store the nonzero values. Thus for each row, all nonzeros of that row are placed in contiguous memory and the offset of the column indices of each non-zero element are stored separately. To achieve data parallelism, the matrix and vector are partitioned into groups of rows assigned to each process, as illustrated in Fig. 9.14.

The compressed sparse format alters Eq. (9.7) to reflect that zeros are no longer stored nor manipulated:

$$x_i = \sum_{j=0}^{n_i} A_{ij} b_j \tag{9.8}$$

where n_i indicates the number of nonzeros for the ith row. Because the rows for both matrix A and vector b are partitioned across several processes, some information will need to be exchanged for Eq. (9.8) to be applied over each different set of data. This is illustrated in Fig. 9.15.

The data parallel model with halo exchange for sparse matrix vector multiplication is summarized in Fig. 9.16.

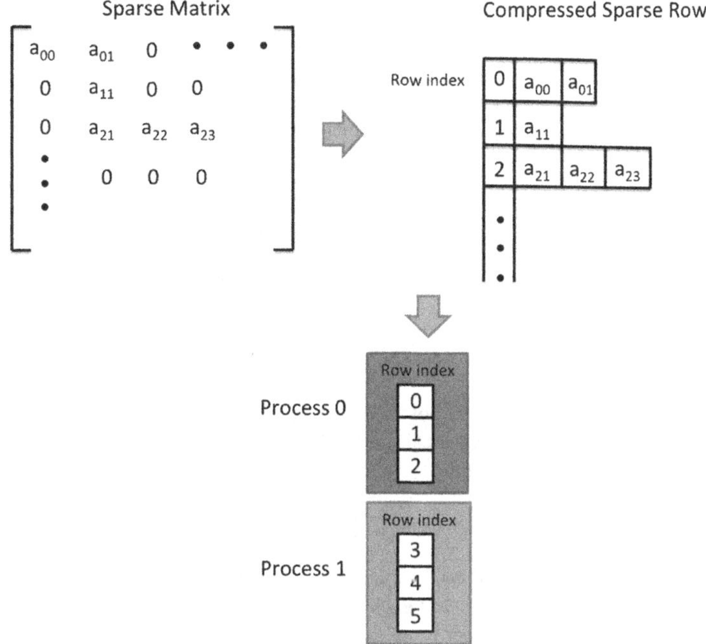

FIGURE 9.14

The zero entries of the sparse matrix are no longer stored in the compressed format, where a ragged array contains the only nonzero columns entries for each row. These rows are then partitioned across P processes.

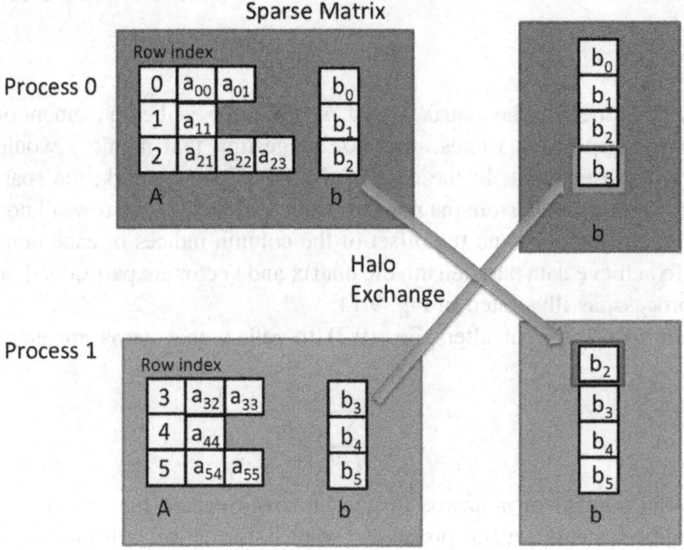

FIGURE 9.15

Illustration of the data parallel model with halo exchange for sparse matrix vector multiplication. Process 0 requires element b_3 to be available to compute Eq. (9.8), while process 1 requires element b_2. Once these vector elements are exchanged, indicated by the *arrows*, each process is able to compute Eq. (9.8) independently with local data.

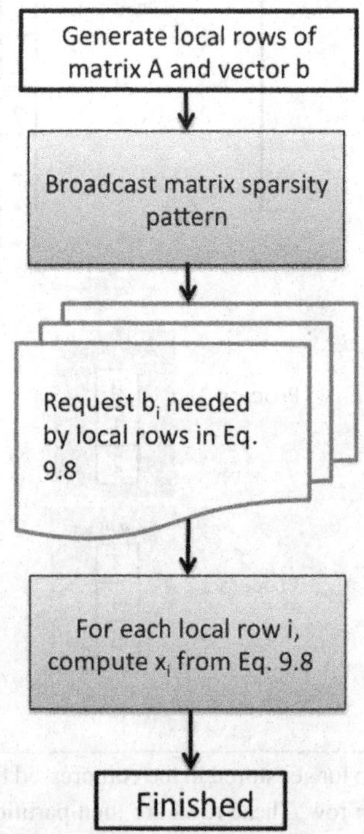

FIGURE 9.16

Summary of sparse matrix vector multiplication using a compressed sparse row format for a data parallel model with halo exchange. The halo-exchange phase is indicated in red (gray in print version).

9.7 PERMUTATION: CANNON'S ALGORITHM

Among algorithms which rely upon a data parallelism approach where the same algorithm is applied to different data to extract concurrency, a certain subclass of problem relies upon permutation routing operations to perform all-to-all operations iteratively. This type of parallel algorithm is very frequent used in applications requiring a linear algebra transpose operation or some type of matrix–matrix multiplication. In this section, one such example is explored: Cannon's algorithm for dense matrix–matrix [5].

In computational linear algebra, algorithms involving matrix operations are frequently divided into two classes: sparse and dense. Sparse matrices refer to those matrices that are dominated by zeros and generally employ some type of compression algorithm so that the zero entries are neither stored nor operated on. Dense matrices are those which are dominated by nonzero entries. Cannon's algorithm is a matrix–matrix multiplication algorithm for distributed memory parallelism designed for dense matrices, and relies heavily on permutation routing.

Matrix–matrix multiplication for two $N \times N$ matrices A and B is summarized in Eq. (9.9)

$$C_{ij} = \sum_{k=0}^{k=N-1} A_{ik} B_{kj} \tag{9.9}$$

where the subscripts indicate the row and column index of the matrix entry. To create a parallel algorithm for Eq. (9.9), a good place to start is a block algorithm that distributes subblocks of A, B, and C among processes where each subblock is of size $N/\sqrt{P} \times N/\sqrt{P}$ and P is the number of processes. This is illustrated in Fig. 9.17.

For example, computing the subblock C_{11} of the matrix–matrix product of $A \times B$ requires computing several serial matrix–matrix products each of size $N/\sqrt{P} \times N/\sqrt{P}$, as illustrated in Fig. 9.18.

For this block partitioning approach, matrix–matrix multiplication becomes a matter of orchestrating the communication and computation of the various serial subblock matrix–matrix products. This is the heart of Cannon's algorithm.

Initially the subblocks are mapped to each process, as illustrated in Fig. 9.19.

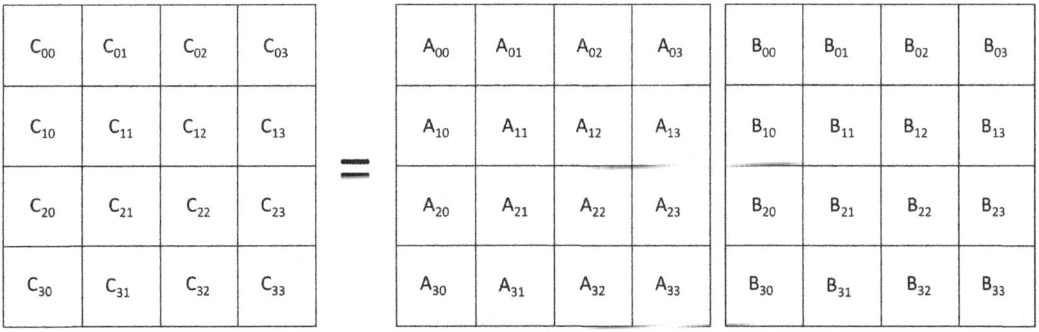

FIGURE 9.17

The global $N \times N$ matrices A and B are partitioned into P subblocks so that each subblock is of size $N/\sqrt{P} \times N/\sqrt{P}$. In this illustration, $P = 16$. Each process holds only one subblock.

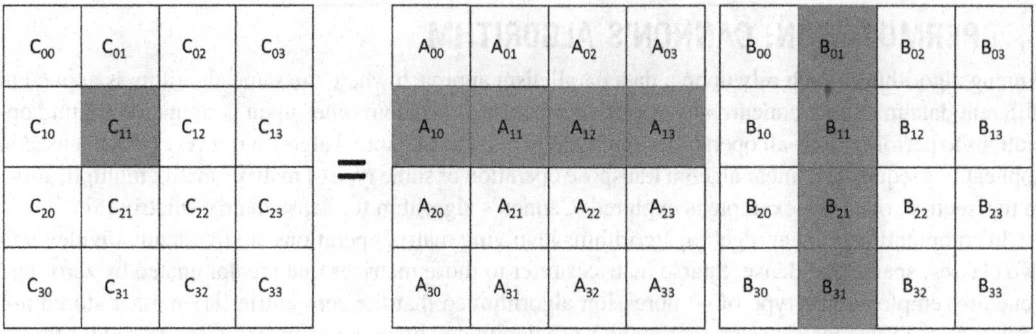

$$C_{11} = A_{10}B_{01} + A_{11}B_{11} + A_{12}B_{21} + A_{13}B_{31}$$

FIGURE 9.18

To compute the C_{11} subblock of the matrix–matrix product of $A \times B$, several matrix–matrix products of the highlighted subblocks must be computed. However, one block is assigned to each process, and only subblocks A_{11} and B_{11} are local to the process where C_{11} resides. All others subblocks must be communicated.

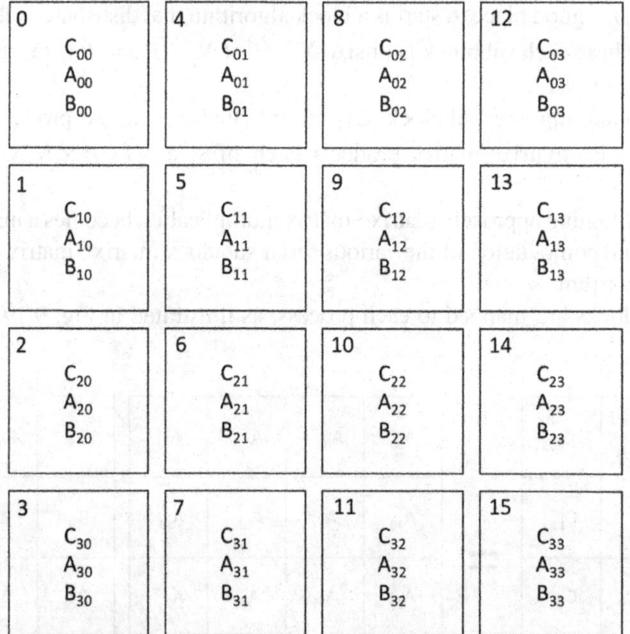

FIGURE 9.19

The subblocks are each mapped to a process for distributed memory parallelism. The process number is indicated in the upper left-hand corner in this illustration.

To set up Cannon's algorithm, the A subblocks are shifted to the left while the B subblocks are shifted up, as illustrated in Figs. 9.20 and 9.21.

The memory layout after the set-up permutations is shown in Fig. 9.22.

Cannon's algorithm consists of moving matrix subblocks so that for each iteration k from 0 to 3 matrix subblocks $A_{i,(i+j+k)}$ and $B_{(i+j+k),j}$ are located on the same process as C_{ij}. For each iteration, the partial sum in Eq. (9.10) is accumulated to C_{ij}:

$$C_{ij} += A_{i,(i+j+k)} B_{(i+j+k),j} \tag{9.10}$$

where each subblock matrix–matrix multiplication uses Eq. (9.9) to compute the matrix–matrix product. The sums in Eq. (9.10), $i + j + k$, are modulus $\sqrt{P}$ (4 in this example). Thus if $(i + j + k) = 6$, the index in the matrix would become 2.

For $k = 0$, Cannon's algorithm has already been set up. For example, in Fig. 9.22 matrix C_{31} is located in the same process as matrix A_{30} and B_{01}. For every subsequent iteration of k, the A matrices have to be shifted once left and the B matrices have to be shifted up once to satisfy the condition of Eq. (9.10) and compute the partial sum. This is illustrated in Fig. 9.23.

After $\sqrt{P}$ iterations of k, the matrix–matrix product has been computed. The resulting matrices for each of the k iterations for the example are shown in Fig. 9.24. Cannon's algorithm is summarized in Fig. 9.25.

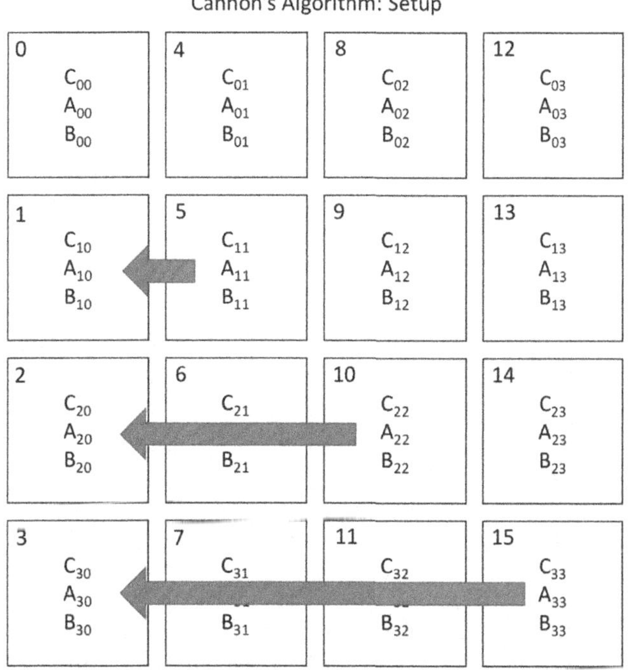

FIGURE 9.20

The A subblocks are permuted to the left to set up Cannon's algorithm.

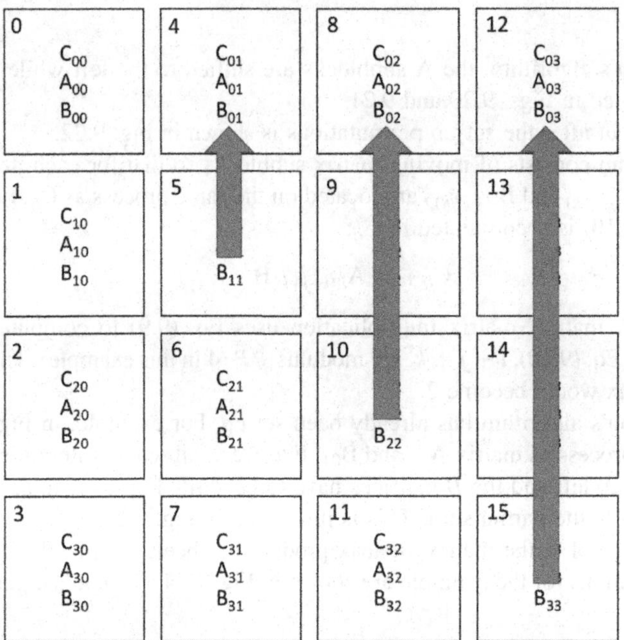

FIGURE 9.21

The B subblocks are permuted up to set up Cannon's algorithm.

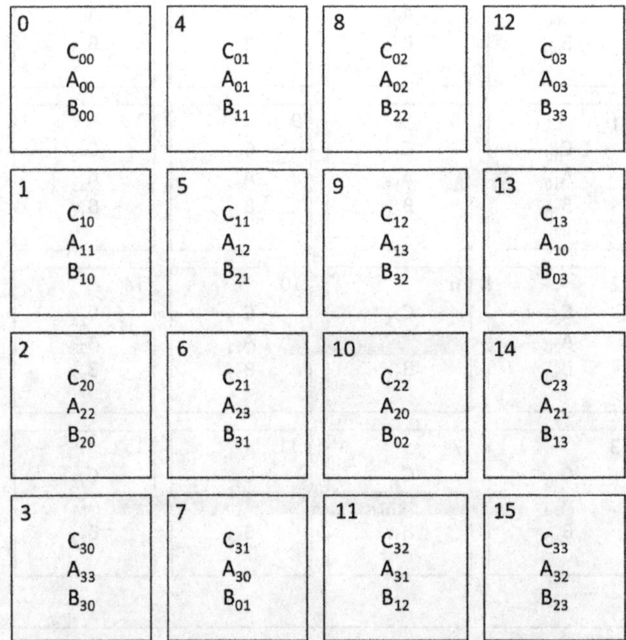

FIGURE 9.22

The layout of the matrix subblocks after performing the permutations illustrated in Figs. 9.19 and 9.20. This completes the set up of Cannon's algorithm.

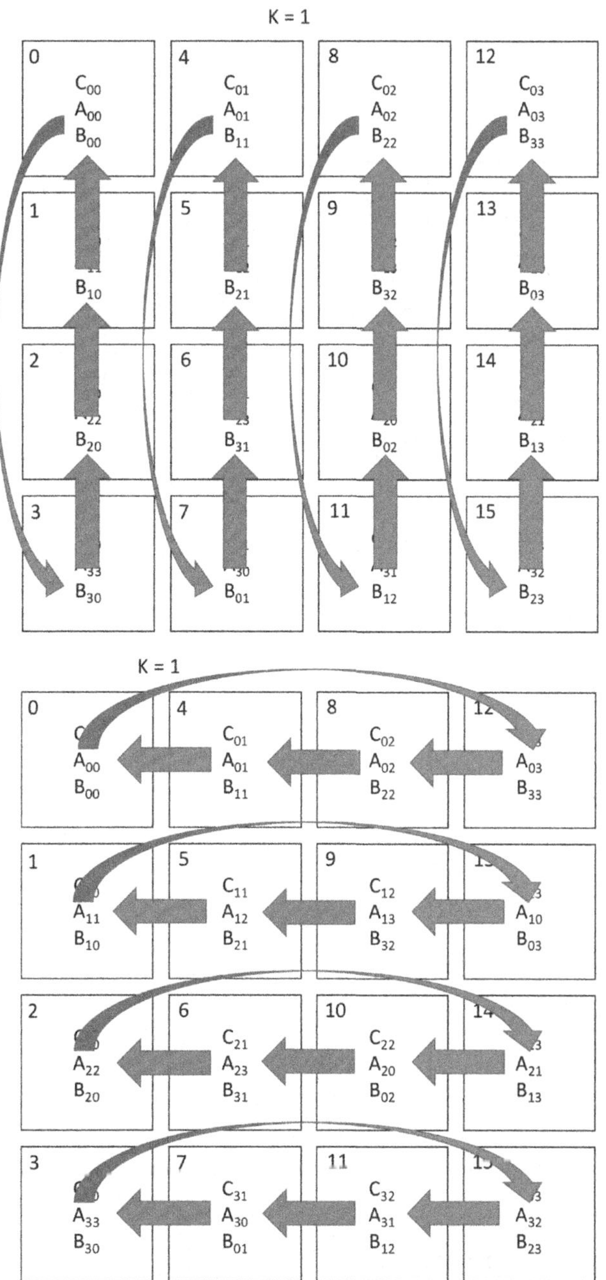

FIGURE 9.23

For each subsequent iteration of k, the B matrices are shifted up and the A matrices are shifted to the left to fulfill the condition for Eq. (9.10).

K = 0

0 C_{00} A_{00} B_{00}	4 C_{01} A_{01} B_{11}	8 C_{02} A_{02} B_{22}	12 C_{03} A_{03} B_{33}
1 C_{10} A_{11} B_{10}	5 C_{11} A_{12} B_{21}	9 C_{12} A_{13} B_{32}	13 C_{13} A_{10} B_{03}
2 C_{20} A_{22} B_{20}	6 C_{21} A_{23} B_{31}	10 C_{22} A_{20} B_{02}	14 C_{23} A_{21} B_{13}
3 C_{30} A_{33} B_{30}	7 C_{31} A_{30} B_{01}	11 C_{32} A_{31} B_{12}	15 C_{33} A_{32} B_{23}

K = 1

0 C_{00} A_{01} B_{10}	4 C_{01} A_{02} B_{21}	8 C_{02} A_{03} B_{32}	12 C_{03} A_{00} B_{03}
1 C_{10} A_{12} B_{20}	5 C_{11} A_{13} B_{31}	9 C_{12} A_{10} B_{02}	13 C_{13} A_{11} B_{13}
2 C_{20} A_{23} B_{30}	6 C_{21} A_{20} B_{01}	10 C_{22} A_{21} B_{12}	14 C_{23} A_{22} B_{23}
3 C_{30} A_{30} B_{00}	7 C_{31} A_{31} B_{11}	11 C_{32} A_{32} B_{22}	15 C_{33} A_{33} B_{33}

K = 2

0 C_{00} A_{02} B_{20}	4 C_{01} A_{03} B_{31}	8 C_{02} A_{00} B_{02}	12 C_{03} A_{01} B_{13}
1 C_{10} A_{13} B_{30}	5 C_{11} A_{10} B_{01}	9 C_{12} A_{11} B_{12}	13 C_{13} A_{12} B_{23}
2 C_{20} A_{20} B_{00}	6 C_{21} A_{21} B_{11}	10 C_{22} A_{22} B_{22}	14 C_{23} A_{23} B_{33}
3 C_{30} A_{31} B_{10}	7 C_{31} A_{32} B_{21}	11 C_{32} A_{33} B_{32}	15 C_{33} A_{30} B_{03}

K = 3

0 C_{00} A_{03} B_{30}	4 C_{01} A_{00} B_{01}	8 C_{02} A_{01} B_{12}	12 C_{03} A_{02} B_{23}
1 C_{10} A_{10} B_{00}	5 C_{11} A_{11} B_{11}	9 C_{12} A_{12} B_{22}	13 C_{13} A_{13} B_{33}
2 C_{20} A_{21} B_{10}	6 C_{21} A_{22} B_{21}	10 C_{22} A_{23} B_{32}	14 C_{23} A_{20} B_{03}
3 C_{30} A_{32} B_{20}	7 C_{31} A_{33} B_{31}	11 C_{32} A_{30} B_{02}	15 C_{33} A_{31} B_{13}

FIGURE 9.24

The distribution of the subblock matrices for each iteration of Cannon's algorithm for the example presented in Fig. 9.18.

9.8 TASK DATAFLOW: BREADTH FIRST SEARCH

The breadth first search algorithm is used for traversing graph data structures and is a key component of the Graph500 benchmark discussed in Chapter 4. A particular root vertex is given to the algorithm to start traversing the graph data structure. Each adjacent vertex to the root is then traversed and so on, thereby establishing the level (or distance) of every vertex from the root. An illustration is provided in Fig. 9.26.

While any parallel algorithm can be expressed as a graph of dependencies, many algorithms that explore graphs themselves are naturally expressed as task dataflow to maximize concurrency.

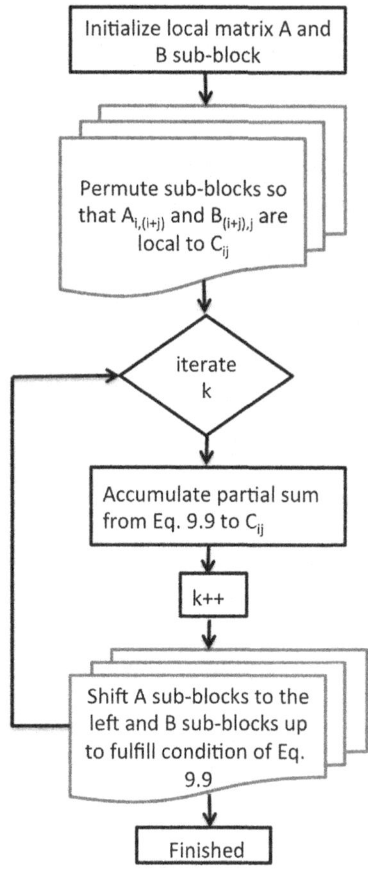

FIGURE 9.25

Summary of Cannon's algorithm for dense matrix–matrix multiplication.

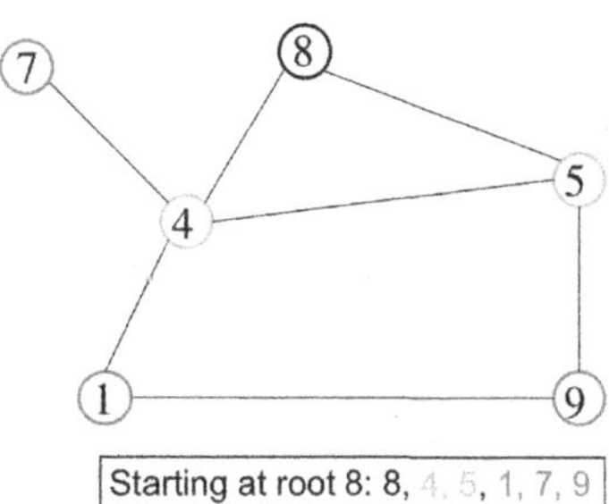

FIGURE 9.26

Example of the breadth first search traversal of this graph data structure starting at vertex 8. The adjacent vertices to the root are 4 and 5, colored light gray. The adjacent vertices to those are 1, 7, and 9, colored dark gray. *Lines* connecting the vertices are called edges.

The standard parallel breadth first search algorithm is illustrated as follows.

- Each vertex list is partitioned by process with its edge list (Fig. 9.27).

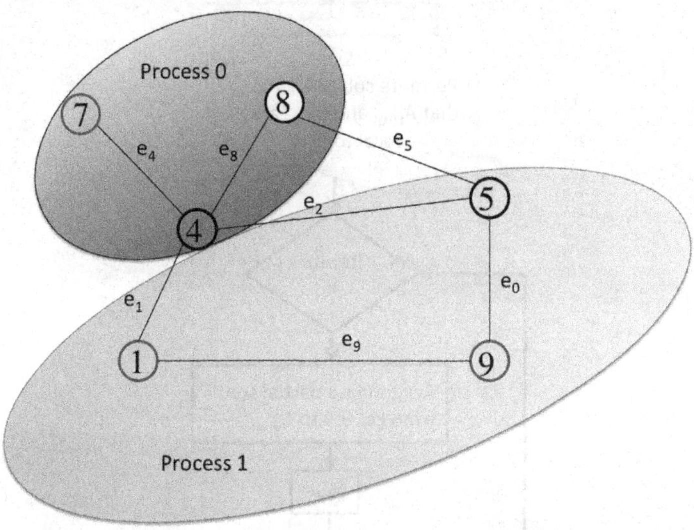

FIGURE 9.27

Partitioning the vertex list by process.

- For each vertex, associate a parent vertex and a binary flag indicating if the vertex has been visited (Fig. 9.28).

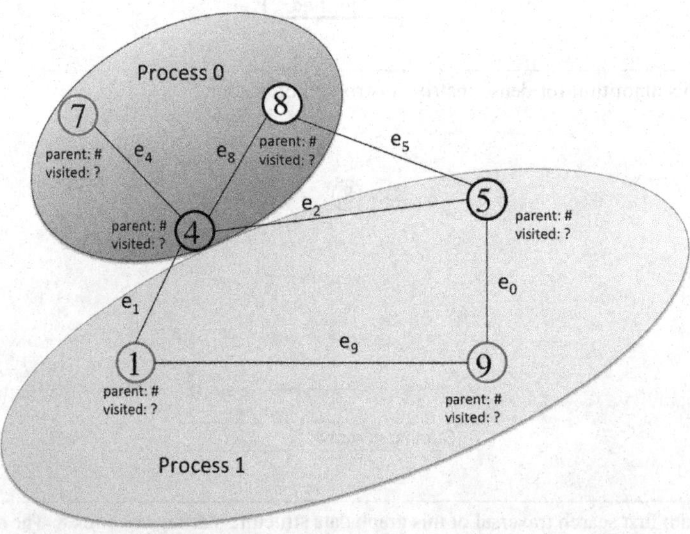

FIGURE 9.28

Adding parent vertex data and a bit to indicate if the vertex has been visited.

- In each process, scan if new vertices are visited (Fig. 9.29).

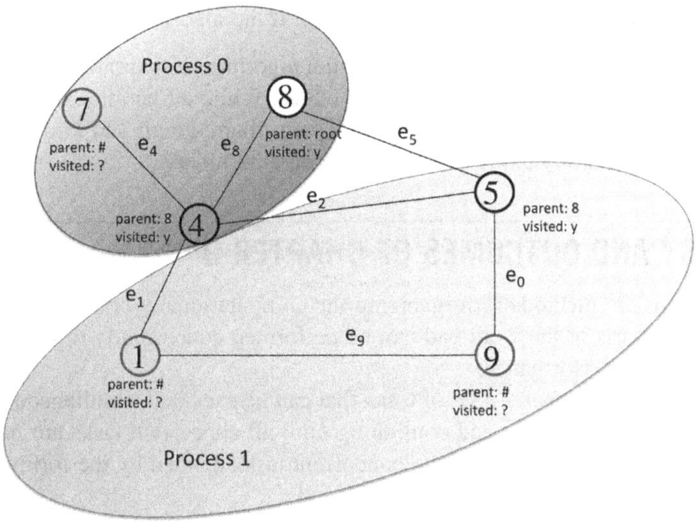

FIGURE 9.29

Each process scans if a vertex has been visited. In process 1, the scan finds that vertex 5 has been visited with parent vertex 8; in process 0, the scan finds that vertex 4 has been visited.

- For each process and each new vertex visited, follow the edge list; if the vertex is unvisited, set the parent and set to visited (Fig. 9.30).

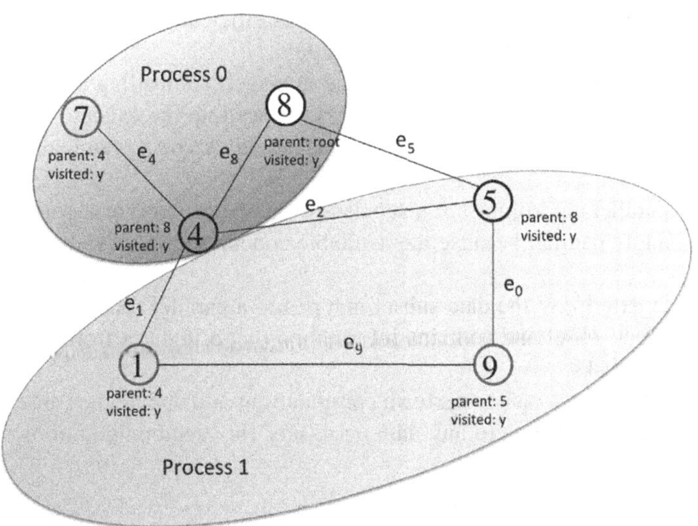

FIGURE 9.30

The edge lists for vertex 4 and vertex 5 are traversed by process 0 and process 1, respectively. Vertices 1, 7, and 9 are visited and marked accordingly. Only adjacent vertices to 4 and 5 are traversed to ensure level-wise iteration.

- Level-wise iteration is enforced with two global barriers per level, thereby ensuring no out-of-order traversals occur between processes.
- Perform an all-reduce operation at the checks to see if the algorithm has finished.

The concurrency of this breadth first search parallel algorithm is naturally tied to the edge list and the traversal tasks that result from traversing these edges. While all parallel algorithms presented in this chapter could be recast as task dataflow parallelism, many graph and knowledge management applications tend to be naturally expressed using this parallel model.

9.9 SUMMARY AND OUTCOMES OF CHAPTER 9

- Parallel algorithms are methods for organizing the computational work of a given application such that multiple parts of the workload can be performed concurrently to reduce the time to solution and increase performance.
- Fork–join parallelism delineates a set of tasks that can be executed simultaneously, beginning at the same starting point, the fork, and continuing until all concurrent tasks are finished having reached the join point. Only when all the concurrent tasks defined by the fork–join have been completed will the succeeding computation proceed.
- Fork–join parallelism is often used to divide instances of a given loop among multiple physical execution resources. This is referred to as "loop parallelism".
- Divide-and-conquer parallelism divides a large problem into two or more smaller problems that can be performed concurrently. Each of the smaller problems may be further subdivided to produce yet more parallel actions of even smaller work. This recursive dividing of work repeatedly into ever smaller subtasks increases the application parallelism until the smallest resulting tasks are trivial to perform.
- Quicksort is an example of a divide-and-conquer algorithm for ordering data.
- The regular sampling parallel sort algorithm improves efficiency and scalability for distributed computing, still borrowing from the quicksort method.
- Manager–worker workflow has one process, the manager, controlling the remaining worker processes, which exhibit the parallelism required to speed up the execution of the total workload. With a central control process, load balancing can be dynamically adapted to evolving data states.
- Embarrassingly parallel algorithms are a subclass of manager–worker algorithms. They are called embarrassingly parallel because the available concurrency is trivially extracted from the workflow.
- A halo is a region exterior to the data subset mapped to a parallel task. It acts as an artificial boundary to that data subset and contains information that originates from the data subsets of neighboring parallel tasks.
- Halo exchange enables each task to perform computations and update the subset of data mapped to that task while having access to any data necessary for such computations that may not be local.

- Sparse matrix calculations exploit arrays (e.g., vectors) that are mostly populated with elements of value zero and where only a relatively small number of the elements are nonzero. Sparse data structures compress the matrix by only storing the nonzero elements, thereby permitting much larger matrices to be represented than the main memory of a computer could otherwise store.
- Task dataflow algorithms represent the precedent constraints among subtasks by their dependencies in the form of a directed acyclic graph. This establishes which tasks must be completed prior to initiating a succeeding task.

9.10 EXERCISES

1. Implement the regular sampling parallel sort algorithm using a message-passing interface (MPI). Plot the time to solution as a function of the number of processes. Include the performance using serial quicksort as a comparison.
2. Compute the Mandelbrot set using MPI with a manager–worker algorithm. Produce a picture of the Mandelbrot set and of the speeding up as a function of the number of processes.
3. Using MPI, write a distributed sparse matrix vector multiplication based on halo exchange of the dense vector. Use the Fluorem/HV15R matrix from the SuiteSparse Matrix Collection [6] and generate a random dense vector. Plot the time to solution of the sparse matrix vector multiplication as a function of the number of processes. Include the memory bandwidth performance for the machine on which you run as given by the HPC Challenge memory bandwidth benchmark.
4. Implement the advection equation using finite difference as illustrated in this chapter using MPI. Plot the solution as a function of time and indicate in the plot which process calculated which point in the solution.
5. Explore the numerical methods identified in the "seven dwarfs". For each numerical method, list the different parallel algorithms that have been historically applied for solving the method. List the reasons that make it difficult to identify the best parallel algorithm for a numerical method.

REFERENCES

[1] P. Colella, Defining Software Requirements for Scientific Computing, 2004.

[2] K. Asanovic, et al., The Landscape of Parallel Computing Research: A View from Berkeley, Electrical Engineering and Computer Sciences, University of California at Berkeley, Berkeley, 2006. TR# UCB/EECS-2006-183.

[3] Wikipedia, Quicksort, [Online]. https://en.wikipedia.org/wiki/Quicksort.

[4] M. Quinn, Parallel Programming in C with MPI and OpenMP, McGraw Hill Education, London, 2008 (Chapter 14).

[5] Wikipedia, Cannon's Algorithm, [Online]. https://en.wikipedia.org/wiki/Cannon%27s_algorithm.

[6] SuiteSparse Matrix Collection: Fluorem/HV15R, [Online]. https://www.cise.ufl.edu/research/sparse/matrices/Fluorem/HV15R.html.

CHAPTER

LIBRARIES

10

CHAPTER OUTLINE

10.1 INTRODUCTION

Computational science applications use a significant amount of the available high performance computing (HPC) resources. A typical breakdown of the types of computational science research areas represented on HPC resources is presented in Fig. 10.1. This summary of HPC allocations originates from the Extreme Science and Engineering Discovery Environment (XSEDE) virtual system [1], which integrates 12 very large HPC resources for use in peer-reviewed research.

High Performance Computing. https://doi.org/10.1016/B978-0-12-420158-3.00010-1

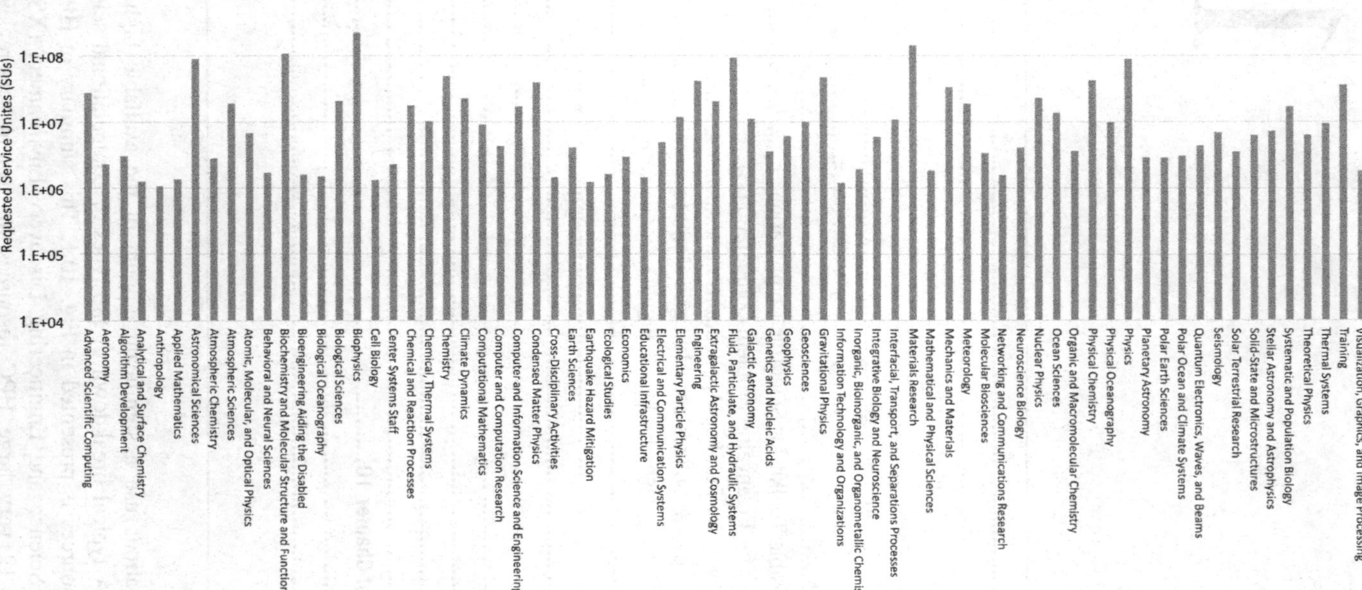

FIGURE 10.1

Extreme Science and Engineering Discovery Environment (XSEDE) allocation summary for 2015 indicating the number of service units (SUs) allocated to various research areas. Only research areas with allocations exceeding 1 million SUs are listed here. An SU is defined locally on each supercomputer, but is generally the walltime in hours multiplied by the number of cores used for a simulation. Thus a simulation requiring 64 cores that ran for 1 h would be charged 64 SUs. The research areas receiving the most HPC time from XSEDE in 2015 were biophysics and materials research.

While these applications are used in a wide variety of very different disciplines, their underlying computational algorithms are frequently very similar to one another. As a consequence, several software libraries have been developed for HPC resources to fill a specific computing need, so application developers do not have to waste time redeveloping supercomputing software that has already been developed elsewhere. Subsequently, these libraries end up becoming required software dependencies across many user applications, and their performance and usage become critically important for an application's performance. Libraries targeting numerical linear algebra operations are the most common, given the ubiquity of linear algebra in scientific computing algorithms. Other libraries target operations like input/output (I/O), fast Fourier transform (FFT), the finite element method, and solving ordinary differential equations. These libraries have generally been highly tuned for performance, often for more than a decade, making it difficult for the casual application developer to match a library's performance using a homemade equivalent. On account of their ease of use and their highly tuned performance across a wide range of HPC platforms, the use of scientific computing libraries as software dependencies in computational science applications has become widespread.

Apart from acting as a repository for software reuse, libraries serve the important role of providing a knowledge base for specific computational science domains. These libraries become community standards and serve as ways for members of the community to communicate with one another. This chapter explores some of the most widely used libraries in computational science and their characteristics on HPC resources. An abbreviated list of some of the most important libraries for scientific computing is found in Table 10.1. Each of the application domains in Table 10.1 is explored in the following sections.

10.2 LINEAR ALGEBRA

Numerical linear algebra is a key component to a large number of HPC applications, and libraries that provide numerical algorithms for solving sets of linear equations are among the most widely used on modern supercomputers. This is illustrated in part in Fig. 10.2, where a small sample of widely used

Table 10.1 Some Widely Used Libraries on HPC Systems and Their Associated Application Domains

Application Domain	Widely Used Libraries on HPC Systems
Linear algebra	BLAS [2], Lapack [3], ScaLapack [4], GNU Scientific Library [5], SuperLU [6], PETSc [7], SLEPc [8], ELPA [9], Hypre [10]
Partial differential equations	PETSc [7], Trilinos [11]
Graph algorithms	Boost Graph Library [12], Parallel Boost Graph Library [12]
Input/output	HDF5 [13], Netcdf [14], Silo [15]
Mesh decomposition	METIS [16], ParMETIS [17]
Visualization	VTK [18]
Parallelization	Pthreads, MPI, Boost MPI [12]
Signal processing	FFTW [19]
Performance monitoring	PAPI [20], Vampir [21]

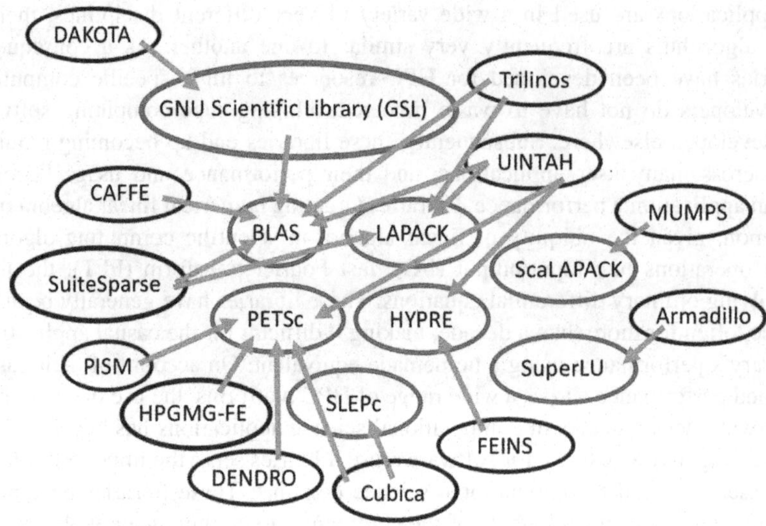

FIGURE 10.2

A small sample of core linear algebra libraries (blue [dark gray in print versions]) and a small sample of widely used application frameworks with dependencies on these libraries (red [black in print versions]). The dependencies (sometimes optional) are indicated by *green arrows* (light gray in print versions). The most fundamental libraries, basic linear algebra subprograms (BLAS), the linear algebra package (Lapack), and the portable, extensible toolkit for scientific computation (PETSc), show up very frequently as application dependencies. The application frameworks represented here include the Dakota software toolkit [22], the Caffe deep-learning framework [23], the SuiteSparse suite of sparse matrix algorithms [24], the parallel ice sheet model [25], the finite element high performance geometric multigrid benchmark [26], the Dendro suite of parallel algorithms [27], the Cubica toolkit for subspace deformations [28], the finite element incompressible Navier–Stokes solver [29], the Armadillo C++ linear algebra library [30], the multifrontal massively parallel sparse direct Solver [31], the UINTAH software suite [32], and the Trilinos project [11].

application frameworks is listed along with their dependencies on some of the key linear algebra libraries explored in this chapter. In addition to application frameworks, numerical linear algebra is a principal component of many of the key HPC benchmarks. For instance, seven of the HPC benchmarks explored in Chapter 3 deal with numerical linear algebra performance—highly parallel Linpack, DGEMM, high performance conjugate gradients, conjugate gradient, BT, SP, and lower/upper (LU)—reflecting the impact this discipline has on HPC.

This section explores several types of numerical linear algebra libraries, including very low abstraction level serial libraries like BLAS [2], higher abstraction level parallel libraries with extensive sparse matrix support like PETSc [7], and very high abstraction level domain-specific language libraries like MTL4 [33] and Blaze [34].

10.2.1 BASIC LINEAR ALGEBRA SUBPROGRAMS

Photo by Pierre Lescanne via Wikimedia Commons

John Backus was the cocreator of the first practical and widely used computer programming language, Fortran. In 1953 he assembled and led a team of 10 researchers at IBM whose task was to find an approach that would simplify the programming of computers while permitting proper structuring of the executable code to make it more understandable to other programmers. In times when computers were predominantly coded in machine language targeting a specific architecture that demanded a thorough understanding of machine internals, this was a truly groundbreaking development. The Fortran language, short for formula translator, was released in 1957 and combined elements of algebra and English language. This high-level language and its compiler (originally written in 25,000 lines of code) enabled practical portability and platform independence of computer programs. While Fortran syntax and concepts have been updated several times since its inception, it remains one of the most common programming languages in supercomputing and has an extensive set of software libraries supporting many domains of computational science.

John Backus is also known for developing the Backus–Naur Form (BNF), a metalanguage for expressing context-free grammars. For this contribution he was honored with the Association for Computing Machinery Turing Award in 1977. BNF is commonly used to describe the syntax of various programming languages, communication protocols, file formats, and others. Backus helped develop the influential ALGOL programming language that introduced many important procedural programming concepts; the original ALGOL variant has been fleshed out in BNF. His later work on the FP language and its descendant FL inspired broader research in functional programming.

For his achievements, John Backus was awarded an IBM Fellowship in 1963; he also received a National Medal of Science in 1975, the Harold Pender Award in 1983, and the Charles Stark Draper Prize in 1993.

BLAS provides a standard interface to vector, matrix–vector, and matrix–matrix routines that have been optimized for various computer architectures. In addition to the reference implementation [2], which provides both Fortran 77 and C interfaces, and the Automatically Tuned Linear Algebra Software project [35], which also has a BLAS implementation, there are multiple vendor-provided BLAS libraries optimized for their respective hardware. Finally, the Boost libraries [12] provide a C++ template class with BLAS functionality called uBLAS.

BLAS design and implementation was handled by Charles Lawson, Richard Hanson, F. Krogh, D.R. Kincaid, and Jack Dongarra beginning in the 1970s; the genesis of the idea for BLAS is credited to Lawson and Hanson while they were working at NASA's Jet Propulsion Laboratory [36]. BLAS development coincided with development of the Linpack package introduced in Chapter 3. Linpack was the first major package to incorporate the BLAS library.

The first BLAS routines developed were limited to vector operations, including inner products, norms, adding vectors, and scalar multiplication, and are typified by the operations of Eq. (10.1),

$$y = \alpha x + y \tag{10.1}$$

where x, y are vectors and α is a scalar value. These vector–vector operations are referred to as BLAS Level 1. At the time the fastest supercomputer in the world was the Control Data Corporation (CDC)-7600 (shown in Fig. 10.3), which had such a small cache size that matrix operations were not possible, thereby limiting the first BLAS routines to vector operations. The CDC-7600 further motivated the BLAS creators to focus on developing a portable linear algebra interface so that others would not have to compile assembly code by hand to utilize the CDC-7600's capabilities fully.

In 1987, about 10 years after BLAS Level 1 was released, routines for matrix–vector operations became available, followed by matrix–matrix operations in 1989. These later additions are the Level 2 (matrix–vector) and Level 3 (matrix–matrix) BLAS operations, typified by Eqs. (10.2)–(10.3).

$$y = \alpha Ax + \beta y \tag{10.2}$$

$$C = \alpha AB + \beta C \tag{10.3}$$

FIGURE 10.3

A section of the CDC-7600. The CDC-7600 could achieve up to 36 Mflops and was the fastest computer available from 1969 to 1975.

Photo by Jitze Couperus via Wikimedia Commons

BLAS matrix−vector operations are illustrated in Eq. (10.2), where x and y are vectors and α and β are scalars. BLAS matrix−matrix operations are illustrated in Eq. (10.3), where A, B, and C are matrices and α and β are scalars.

Each routine in BLAS has a specific naming convention that specifies the precision of the operation, the type of matrix (if any) involved, and the operation to perform. BLAS is natively written in Fortran 77, but C bindings to BLAS are available via CBLAS and are used in this chapter for illustration. For BLAS Level 1 operations there is no matrix involved and so the naming convention for each routine begins with *cblas_* after which a precision prefix is placed before the operation name. The core BLAS precision prefixes are summarized in Table 10.2. While these are the core precision prefixes, some BLAS operations support mixed precisions, resulting in combinations of the listed prefixes.

BLAS Level 1 operations can be subdivided into four different subgroups: vector rotations (Table 10.3), vector operations without a dot product (Table 10.4), vector operations with a dot product (Table 10.5), and vector norms (Table 10.6).

BLAS Level 2 and Level 3 operations involve matrices, and indicate the type of matrix they support in their name. Levels 2 and 3 names are of the form *cblas_*pmmoo, where the p indicates the precision, mm indicates the matrix type, and oo indicates the operation. Possible matrix types are listed in Table 10.7. Apart from general matrices, all other matrix types come in three storage scheme flavors: dense (default), banded (indicated by a "b" in the name), and packed (indicated by a "p" in the name). Dense storage schemes are either row-based or column-based storage in a continuous memory array. Packed storage schemes hold matrix values that are packed by rows or columns in a one-dimensional array, while band storage is applied to sparse matrices where the nonzero entries lie in diagonal bands. An example of a banded matrix is a tridiagonal matrix which has nonzero column entries at the $i - 1$, i, and $i + 1$ columns for the *ith* row. In band storage for a banded matrix, the diagonal bands to the left of the main diagonal ("subdiagonals") and diagonal bands to the right of the diagonal ("superdiagonals") are placed in a two-dimensional (2D) array.

BLAS Levels 2 and 3 operations are summarized in Table 10.8.

As an example, the name of the BLAS Level 3 routine *cblas_dgemm* indicates that this routine will perform a double-precision dense matrix−matrix multiplication. DGEMM is also the name for the matrix−matrix multiplication benchmark in the HPC Challenge suite introduced in Chapter 4.

Table 10.2 Precision Prefixes Used by BLAS Routines

Prefix	Description
s	Single precision (float), 4 bytes
d	Double precision (double), 8 bytes
c	Complex (two floats), 8 bytes
z	Complex∗16 (two doubles), 16 bytes

Some BLAS operations support mixed precision operations resulting in combinations of the following prefixes as well.

Table 10.3 BLAS Level 1 Rotation Operations

Name	Description	Supported Precisions
rotg	Computes parameters for a Givens rotation; that is, given scalars a and b, compute c and s so that $\begin{pmatrix} c & s \\ -s & c \end{pmatrix}\begin{pmatrix} a \\ b \end{pmatrix} = \begin{pmatrix} r \\ 0 \end{pmatrix}$ where $r = \sqrt{\lvert a\rvert^2 + \lvert b\rvert^2}$	s,d
rot	Applies the Givens rotation; that is, provided two vectors as input, x and y, each vector element is replaced as follows: $x_i = cx_i + sy_i$ $y_i = -sx_i + cy_i$ where c and s are the parameters for the Givens rotation (see rotg)	s,d
rotmg	Computes the 2×2 modified Givens rotation matrix $H = \begin{pmatrix} h_{11} & h_{12} \\ h_{21} & h_{22} \end{pmatrix}$ That is, given scaling factors d_1 and d_2 with Cartesian coordinates (x_1,y_1) of an input vector, compute the modified Givens rotation matrix H such that $\begin{pmatrix} x_1 \\ 0 \end{pmatrix} = H \begin{pmatrix} x_1\sqrt{d_1} \\ y_1\sqrt{d_2} \end{pmatrix}$	s,d
rotm	Applies the modified Givens rotation; that is, provided two vectors, x and y, compute: $\begin{pmatrix} x_i \\ y_i \end{pmatrix} = \begin{pmatrix} h_{11} & h_{12} \\ h_{21} & h_{22} \end{pmatrix}\begin{pmatrix} x_i \\ y_i \end{pmatrix}$ where h_{ij} are the elements of the modified Givens rotation matrix (see rotmg)	s,d

Table 10.4 BLAS Level 1 Vector Operations Without a Dot Product

Name	Description	Supported Precisions
swap	Swaps vectors $x \leftrightarrow y$	s,d,c,z
scal	Scales a vector by a constant $y = \alpha y$	s,d,c,z,cs,zd
copy	Copies a vector $y = x$	s,d,c,z
axpy	Updates a vector $y = \alpha x + y$	s,d,c,z

Note that the scal operation supports mixed precisions, where the α single-precision or double-precision constant can be multiplied by a complex vector.

Table 10.5 BLAS Level 1 Vector Operations Involving a Dot Product

Name	Description	Supported Precisions
dot	Dot product $x^T y$	s,d,ds
dotc	Complex conjugate dot product $x^h y$	c,z
dotu	Complex dot product $x^T y$	c,z
sdsdot	Dot product plus a scalar $\alpha + x^T y$	sds

Table 10.6 BLAS Level 1 Vector Operations Involving a Norm

Name	Description	Supported Precisions
nrm2	Compute the 2-norm $\|x\|_2 = \sqrt{\sum \lvert x_i \rvert^2}$	s,d,sc,dz
asum	Compute the 1-norm $\|x\|_1 = \sum \lvert x_i \rvert$	s,d,sc,dz
i_amax	Compute the ∞-norm $\|x\|_\infty = \max(\lvert x_i \rvert)$	s,d,c,z

Table 10.7 Matrix Types Supported in BLAS Levels 2 and 3

Matrix Type	Description
General: ge,gb	General, nonsymmetric, possibly rectangular matrix.
Symmetric: sy,sb,sp	Symmetric matrix. This is a special class of square matrix that is equal to its own transpose. So for matrix A with elements a_{ij}, a symmetric matrix would have elements which satisfy $a_{ij} = a_{ji}$.
Hermitian: he,hb,hp	Hermitian matrix. This is a special class of square matrix that is equal to its own Hermitian conjugate. So for matrix A with elements a_{ml}, matrix A is Hermitian if all elements satisfy $a_{ml} = \overline{a_{lm}}$ where the overbar is the complex conjugate.
Triangular: tr,tb,tp	Triangular matrix. This is a special class of square matrices where all the entries above the diagonal are zero (lower triangular) or all the entries below the diagonal are zero (upper triangular).

Table 10.8 BLAS Levels 2 and 3 Operations

Name	Description
mv	Matrix–vector product
sv	Solve matrix (only for triangular matrices)
mm	Matrix–matrix product, $C = \alpha AB + \beta C$ where A, B, C are matrices and α, β are scalars
rk	Rank-k update, $C = \alpha A A^T + \beta C$ where A, C are matrices and α, β are scalars
r2k	Rank-2k update, $C = \alpha AB^T + \overline{\alpha} BA^T + \beta C$ where A, B, C are matrices and α, β are scalars

The *cblas_dgemm* routine takes 14 arguments, shown here:

```
void cblas_dgemm(const enum CBLAS_ORDER Order, const enum CBLAS_TRANSPOSE TransA,
                 const enum CBLAS_TRANSPOSE TransB, const int M, const int N,
                 const int K, const double alpha, const double *A,
                 const int lda, const double *B, const int ldb,
                 const double beta, double *C, const int ldc);
```

- *Order* indicates the storage layout as either row major or column major. This input is either *CblasRowMajor* or *CblasColMajor.*
- *TransA* indicates whether to transpose matrix *A*. This input is either *CblasNoTrans*, *CblasTrans*, or *CblasConjTrans*, indicating no transponse, transpose, or complex conjugate transpose, respectively.
- *TransB* indicates whether to transpose matrix *B*. Acceptable options are the same as those listed for *A*.
- *M* indicates the number of rows in matrices *A* and *C*.
- *N* indicates the number of columns in matrices *B* and *C*.
- *K* indicates the number of columns in matrix *A* and the number of rows in matrix *B*. This is the shared index between matrices *A* and *B*.
- *alpha* is the scaling factor for *A***B*.
- *A* is the pointer to matrix *A* data.
- *lda* is the size of the first dimension of matrix *A*.
- *B* is the pointer to matrix *B* data.
- *lbd* is the size of the first dimension of matrix *B*.
- *beta* is the scaling factor for matrix *C*.
- *C* is the pointer to matrix *C* data.
- *ldc* is the size of the first dimension of matrix *C*.

An example of matrix–matrix multiplication is provided in Fig. 10.4. In this example a 3×3 matrix–matrix product is computed.

$$\begin{pmatrix} 47.1 & 56.52 & 65.94 \\ 131.88 & 169.56 & 207.24 \\ 216.66 & 282.6 & 348.54 \end{pmatrix} = \begin{pmatrix} 0 & 1 & 2 \\ 3 & 4 & 5 \\ 6 & 7 & 8 \end{pmatrix} \begin{pmatrix} 0 & 3.14 & 6.28 \\ 9.42 & 12.56 & 15.7 \\ 18.84 & 21.98 & 25.12 \end{pmatrix}$$

```c
#include <stdio.h>
#include <stdlib.h>
#include <cblas.h>

int main()
{
  double *A, *B, *C;
  int m = 3; // square matrix, number of rows and columns
  int i,j;

  A = (double *) malloc(m*m*sizeof(double));
  B = (double *) malloc(m*m*sizeof(double));
  C = (double *) malloc(m*m*sizeof(double));

  // initialize the matrices
  for (i=0;i<m;i++) {
    for (j=0;j<m;j++) {
      A[j + m*i] = j + m*i;  // arbitrarily initialized
      B[j + m*i] = 3.14*(j + m*i);
      C[j + m*i] = 0.0;
    }
  }
  double alpha = 1.0;
  double beta = 0.0;

  cblas_dgemm(CblasRowMajor, CblasNoTrans, CblasNoTrans,
              m, m, m, alpha, A, m, B, m, beta, C, m);

  for (i=0;i<m;i++) {
    for (j=0;j<m;j++) {
      printf(" A[%d][%d]=%g ",i,j,A[j+m*i]);
    }
    printf("\n");
  }

  for (i=0;i<m;i++) {
    for (j=0;j<m;j++) {
      printf(" B[%d][%d]=%g ",i,j,B[j+m*i]);
    }
    printf("\n");
  }

  for (i=0;i<m;i++) {
    for (j=0;j<m;j++) {
      printf(" C[%d][%d]=%g ",i,j,C[j+m*i]);
    }
    printf("\n");
  }


  free(A);
  free(B);
  free(C);
  return 0;
}
```

FIGURE 10.4

Example of multiplying two 3 × 3 matrices using *cblas_dgemm*.

10.2.2 LINEAR ALGEBRA PACKAGE

Lapack [3] was developed by a collaboration between Jack Dongarra, James Demmel, and others, and provides driver routines designed to solve complete problems such as a system of linear equations, eigenvalue problems, and singular value problems. It also provides computational routines that can perform specific tasks like LU or Cholesky factorization. Certain auxiliary routines are provided for common subtasks. Lapack requires BLAS Level 2 and Level 3 functionality, and it supersedes the Linpack library. Unlike Linpack, which also required BLAS but which targeted vector machines with shared memory, Lapack is designed around the cache-based memory hierarchies found on modern supercomputers. It was initially written in Fortran 77, but switched to Fortran 90 in 2008. A C interface to Lapack is provided by using Lapacke [37].

The naming scheme for Lapack routines is similar to BLAS. All routines are in the form of XYYZZZ, where X is the data type (one of s, d, c, or z, as in Table 10.2), YY is the type of matrix, and ZZZ is the computation performed. Lapack matrix types share all the BLAS matrix types in Table 10.7 and use the same names. Lapack has some additional matrix types, including unitary matrices and symmetric positive definite matrices among others. Like BLAS, Lapack provides support for dense, banded, and packed storage formats, but not for general sparse matrices. Driver routines are summarized in Table 10.9. Expert versions of some of these drivers are available by appending an *x* to the name; these versions provide more functionality but also generally require more memory. In some cases multiple driver routines are available to solve the same problem type reflecting different underlying algorithms.

Table 10.9 Lapack Driver Routines

Driver Name	Description
SV	Solver for system of linear equations: $Ax = b$
LS, LSY, LSS, LSD	Solver for linear least squares problems: minimize x in $\|b - Ax\|_2$ where A is not necessarily a square matrix, generally with more rows than columns as would occur in an overdetermined system of linear equations.
LSE	Linear equality-constrained least squares problems: minimize x in $\|c - Ax\|_2$ subject to the constraint that $Bx = d$ where A is an $m \times n$ matrix, c is a vector of size m, B is a $p \times n$ matrix, and d is a vector of size p, where $p \leq n \leq m + p$.
GLM	General linear model problems: minimize x in $\|y\|_2$ subject to the constraint that $d = Ax + By$ where A is a $m \times n$ matrix, B is a $n \times p$ matrix, d is a vector of size n, and $m \leq n \leq m + p$.
EV, EVD, EVR	Symmetric eigenvalue problems: find eigenvalues λ and eigenvectors k where $Ak = \lambda k$ for a symmetric matrix A.
ES	Nonsymmetric eigenvalue problems: find eigenvalues λ and eigenvectors k where $Ak = \lambda k$ for a nonsymmetric matrix A.
SVD, SDD	Compute the singular value decomposition of $m \times n$ matrix A: $A = UDV^T$ where matrices U and V are orthogonal and D is a diagonal real matrix of size $m \times n$ containing the singular values of matrix A.

Some of these drivers also comes in an expert flavor accessible by appending an X to the name. The expert flavor provides additional functionality but also generally requires more memory. In some cases, multiple drivers are available to solve the same problem type using different algorithms.

While Lapack is written in Fortran, C bindings are available through the Lapacke library which comes with Lapack. Fortran routines in Lapack can be called directly from C code, but the C bindings simplify code portability. The naming convention for Lapacke remains the same as Lapack but prefixes *LAPACKE_* to each routine. An example solving a system of linear equations in double precision is given in Fig. 10.5. This example solves the linear system:

$$\begin{pmatrix} 1 & 3 & 2 \\ 4 & 1 & 9 \\ 5 & 7 & 2 \end{pmatrix} x = \begin{pmatrix} -1 \\ -1 \\ 1 \end{pmatrix}$$

There are eight arguments to the dgesv routine:

```
lapack_int LAPACKE_dgesv( int matrix_layout, lapack_int n, lapack_int nrhs,
                          double* a, lapack_int lda, lapack_int* ipiv,
                          double* b, lapack_int ldb );
```

```
#include <stdio.h>
#include <lapacke.h>

int main (int argc, const char * argv[])
{
   double A[3][3] = {1,3,2,4,1,9,5,7,2};
   double b[3] = {-1,-1,1};
   lapack_int ipiv[3];
   lapack_int info,m,lda,ldb,nrhs;
   int i,j;

   m = 3;
   nrhs = 1;
   lda = 3;
   ldb = 1;

   // Solve the linear system
   info = LAPACKE_dgesv(LAPACK_ROW_MAJOR,m,nrhs,*A,lda,ipiv,b,ldb);

   // check for singularity
   if (info > 0 ) {
     printf(" U(%d,%d) is zero! A is singular\n",info,info);
     return 0;
   }

   // print the answer
   for (i=0;i<m;i++) {
     printf(" b[%i] = %g\n",i,b[i]);
   }

   printf( "\n" );
   return 0;
}
```

FIGURE 10.5

Example of Lapack DGESV general matrix solve ($Ax = b$) with one right hand side vector, b. Here the C bindings to Lapack (Lapacke) are used.

- *matrix_layout* specifies the whether the matrix comes in row-major or column-major form. Acceptable inputs are either LAPACK_ROW_MAJOR or LAPACK_COL_MAJOR.
- *n* indicates the size of the square matrix.
- *nrhs* indicates the number of right-hand-side vectors on which to perform the solve. dgesv can solve multiple right-hand sides in each call.
- *a* is the matrix.
- *lda* is the size of the first dimension of the matrix.
- *ipiv* is a vector of size *n* containing the pivot points.
- *b* is the right-hand-side vector.
- *ldb* is the size of the first dimension of the right-hand-side vector.

10.2.3 SCALABLE LINEAR ALGEBRA PACKAGE

The scalable linear algebra package (ScaLapack) [4] is the HPC equivalent of Lapack and shares much of the same interface. It is built on message passing, and relies on a parallel version of BLAS called PBLAS that accompanies the library. The relationship between ScaLapack and PBLAS is analogous to the dependency of Lapack on BLAS Levels 2 and 3 routines. Like Lapack, support is available for dense and banded matrices but not general sparse matrices. Matrices are decomposed in a 2D block-cyclic distribution across processes for use on distributed-memory architectures. The 2D block-cyclic distribution decomposes the matrix into 2D blocks of size $m_{block} \times n_{block}$ which are then mapped on to the processes.

10.2.4 GNU SCIENTIFIC LIBRARY

The GNU scientific library (GSL) [5] provides a wide array of linear algebra routines, including an interface to BLAS for C and C++. Unlike the other libraries described so far, support for general sparse matrices is provided in GSL, along with support iterative solvers for sparse systems of linear equations.

As an example of the GSL interface to dgemm is shown in Fig. 10.6.

10.2.5 SUPERNODAL LU

Supernodal LU (SuperLU) [6] is a library for direct solves of general sparse systems of equations through LU decomposition on HPC systems. It supports shared-memory and distributed-memory architectures as well as accelerator architectures such as graphics processing units (GPUs). Like Lapack and ScaLapack, it can solve multiple right-hand-side vectors in a single call for improved efficiency. The right-hand-side vectors are assumed to be dense, while the matrix must be square and is assumed to be sparse (dominated by zero entries). SuperLU consists of three libraries:

- Sequential SuperLU, like Lapack, is designed for sequential execution on processors with cache-based memory hierarchies.
- Multithreaded SuperLU is designed for SMP architectures.
- Distributed SuperLU is designed for distributed-memory architectures. Some routines in this library support hybrid computer architectures incorporating multiple GPUs.

```
#include <stdio.h>
#include <gsl/gsl_blas.h>

int main (void) {
  double a[] = { 0,1,2,
                 3,4,5,
                 6,7,8 };

  double b[] = { 0,    3.14, 6.28,
                 9.42, 12.56,15.7,
                 18.84,21.98,25.12 };

  double c[] = { 0.00, 0.00, 0.00,
                 0.00, 0.00, 0.00,
                 0.00, 0.00, 0.00 };

  gsl_matrix_view A = gsl_matrix_view_array(a, 3, 3);
  gsl_matrix_view B = gsl_matrix_view_array(b, 3, 3);
  gsl_matrix_view C = gsl_matrix_view_array(c, 3, 3);

  // Compute C = A B

  gsl_blas_dgemm (CblasNoTrans, CblasNoTrans,
                  1.0, &A.matrix, &B.matrix,
                  0.0, &C.matrix);

  printf (" %g, %g, %g\n", c[0], c[1],c[2]);
  printf (" %g, %g, %g\n", c[3], c[4],c[5]);
  printf (" %g, %g, %g\n", c[6], c[7],c[8]);

  return 0;
}
```

FIGURE 10.6

An example of using the BLAS dgemm routine in GSL. The example from Fig. 10.4 is redone here using GSL. The interface to dgemm in GSL simplifies things considerably; the number of arguments is only 7 instead of 14.

SuperLU complements ScaLapack, in that it provides a high performance direct solver for general systems of sparse linear equations whereas ScaLapack provides high performance direct solver support for dense and banded systems of linear equations.

10.2.6 PORTABLE EXTENSIBLE TOOLKIT FOR SCIENTIFIC COMPUTATION

PETSc [7] was started in 1991 and led by William Gropp, with the goal of providing a suite of data structures and routines to aid application scientists in solving partial differential equations on HPC resources. As the discretization of partial differential equations often results in a very large system of sparse linear equations, PETSc provides a large suite of parallel iterative linear equation solvers. These solvers are principally Krylov subspace solvers like the generalized minimum residual (GMRES) method and CG. PETSc also provides simple interfaces for application-specific linear solver preconditioners, including domain decomposition type preconditions like additive Schwartz

Table 10.10 A Small Sample of Distributed Vector Operations in PETSc

Vector Function Name	Description
VecAXPY(Vec y, PetscScalar alpha, Vec x)	$y = \alpha x + y$
VecAYPX(Vec y, PetscScalar alpha,Vec x)	$y = x + \alpha y$
VecPointwiseMult(Vec w, Vec x, Vec y)	$w_i = x_i * y_i$
VecMax(Vec x, PetscInt *p, PetscReal *r)	Returns the maximum value, $r = \max(x_i)$, and its location
VecCopy(Vec x,Vec y)	$y = x$
VecShift(Vec x, PetscScalar s)	$x_i = s + x_i$
VecScale(Vec x, PetscScalar alpha)	$x = \alpha x$

type and others. PETSc provides support for distributed matrices and vectors where each process locally owns a subvector of contiguous data. Selected distributed vector operations in PETSc are listed in Table 10.10. PETSc employs message-passing interface (MPI) for communication on distributed-memory architectures.

PETSc interfaces with a large number of other widely used libraries and forms one of the core libraries found on a supercomputer. Libraries which interface with PETSc include Hypre [38], SLEPc [8], Uintah [32], Sundials [39], Trilinos [11], SuperLU [6], SAMRAI [40], and TAU [41]. An application using PETSc was awarded the Gordon Bell Prize in 1999 [42].

10.2.7 SCALABLE LIBRARY FOR EIGENVALUE PROBLEM COMPUTATIONS

The scalable library for eigenvalue problem computations (SLEPc) [8] is an extension of PETSc and complements ScaLapack in providing an HPC library for solving very large sparse eigenvalue problems with both real and complex numbers. Like PETSc, it is built on the MPI library and shares much in common with PETSc. SLEPc is similar in function to the Fortran 77-based ARPACK software [43], which is also designed to solve large eigenvalue problems using message passing. SLEPc provides a transparent interface to ARPACK.

10.2.8 EIGENVALUE SOLVERS FOR PETAFLOP-APPLICATIONS

For many scientific computing applications such as quantum chemistry, computing the eigenvalues and eigenvectors of Hermitian matrices is a key computational kernel. The Eigenvalue SoLvers for Petaflop-Applications (ELPA) [9] created by the ELPA consortium is free software designed for highly scalable eigenvalue and eigenvector computations on Hermitian matrices. ELPA uses BLAS, Lapack, the basic linear algebra communication subroutines [44], ScaLapack, and MPI. ELPA is widely used in the materials science community on HPC resources via the density functional theory toolkit VASP [45].

10.2.9 HYPRE: SCALABLE LINEAR SOLVERS AND MULTIGRID METHODS

The Hypre library [38] provides a set of highly scalable preconditioners for systems of linear equations, as well as scalable iterative solvers and algebraic multigrid algorithms that have found broad usage in the HPC community. Hypre uses MPI for communication and interfaces with the PETSc library. Like PETSc, it also provides support for distributed vectors and matrices.

10.2.10 DOMAIN-SPECIFIC LANGUAGES FOR LINEAR ALGEBRA

The complexity of using linear algebra library routines like those in BLAS, Lapack, or PETSc has motivated in part the development of several higher-level abstraction interfaces so that application developers can develop distributed linear algebra applications using code that is very simple to read. The MATLAB® framework [46] is a proprietary example of such an approach, but is not competitive in terms of performance with the libraries presented in this section. A template library which achieves comparable performance with PETSc for sparse linear algebra operations but retains the look and feel of the original mathematical notation of linear algebra is MTL4 [33]. An example of MTL4 is shown in Fig. 10.7: it creates a Laplacian matrix, computes a sparse matrix−vector multiplication, and then performs a linear solve using a Krylov solver. The output from this code is shown in Fig. 10.8. The MPI distributed-memory version of the example MTL4 code in Fig. 10.7 is shown in Fig. 10.9. Another library with a similar goal to MTL4 is Blaze [34]. These two are a small sample of the many libraries available that aim to address the growing need in linear algebra libraries for both HPC capability and an intuitive interface to simplify application development.

10.3 PARTIAL DIFFERENTIAL EQUATIONS

PETSc [7], mentioned in Section 10.2.6 is one of the most important toolkits for solving systems of partial differential equations. Beyond supporting distributed vectors and matrices as well as distributed Krylov subspace methods like GMRES and CG, PETSc provides ordinary differential equation integrators and nonlinear solvers, including Newton-based methods.

A second widely used library for solving systems of partial differential equations is the Trilinos project [11]. Trilinos is a collection of libraries spread across 10 different capability areas, each with a direct impact on applications targeting the solution of partial differential equations. These capability areas range from the standard scalable linear algebra support to nontraditional parallel programming environments to provide portability across multiple HPC architectures while leveraging architecture-dependent system capabilities.

10.4 GRAPH ALGORITHMS

Sparse graph algorithms such as the breadth first search explored in Chapter 9 form a crucial component in many core HPC algorithms, such as shortest path problems, PageRank, and network flow problems. Three libraries available for high performance graph algorithms are the Parallel Boost Graph Library (PBGL) [12], Combinatorial BLAS [47], and Giraph [48]. PBGL extends the Boost Graph Library for HPC and provides a large number of graph algorithms for distributed-memory architectures. Combinatorial BLAS is another parallel graph library which provides linear algebra primitives for graphs and also targets distributed-memory architectures.

```
0001 #include <iostream>
0002 #include <boost/numeric/mtl/mtl.hpp>
0003 #include <boost/numeric/itl/itl.hpp>
0004
0005
0006 int main(int argc, char* argv[])
0007 {
0008     using namespace mtl;
0009
0010     mtl::par::environment        env(argc, argv);
0011
0012     // Use compressed sparse row format for sparse matrix element storage
0013     typedef matrix::compressed2D<double>     matrix_type;
0014
0015     typedef mtl::vector::dense_vector<double>    vector_type;
0016
0017     matrix_type A;
0018
0019     int n = 100;
0020     laplacian_setup(A,n,n);
0021
0022     vector_type x(num_rows(A),1.0),b;
0023
0024     // Sparse matrix vector multiplication
0025     b = A * x;
0026
0027     // Compute the two norm
0028     double mbnorm = two_norm(b);
0029     printf(" b vector l2norm %10.2f\n",mbnorm);
0030
0031     // reset x vector to be zero
0032     x= 0;
0033
0034     // Solve for x in Ax=b using a Krylov solver, BiCGStabilized.
0035     // Use the ILU_0 preconditioner
0036     itl::pc::ilu_0<matrix_type>        P(A);
0037     itl::cyclic_iteration<double> iter(b, 500, 1.e-8, 0.0, 5);
0038     bicgstab_2(A, x, b, P, iter);
0039
0040     // Print an element of x (should be one)
0041     printf(" x[1] = %g (should be one)\n",x(1));
0042
0043     return 0;
0044 }
```

FIGURE 10.7

A sparse linear algebra example using MTL4. This code stores a matrix in compressed sparse rows format (line 13), creates a Laplacian matrix (line 20), creates two vectors (a and b) (line 22), initializes vector x to be one (line 22), computes the sparse matrix vector product of A∗x (line 25), resets x to be zero (line 32), and solves Ax=b (line 38).

10.5 PARALLEL INPUT/OUTPUT

Parallel I/O libraries provide high performance output to a single file to avoid the problems associated with nonparallel I/O, including poor performance and creating a large number of individual files each

```
 b vector l2norm      20.20
iteration 0: resid 13.0643
iteration 5: resid 0.272981
iteration 10: resid 0.11331
iteration 15: resid 0.00256046
iteration 20: resid 4.89401e-05
iteration 25: resid 4.90882e-06
finished! error code = 0
26 iterations
7.61006e-08 is actual final residual.
3.76754e-09 is actual relative tolerance achieved.
Relative tol: 1e-08  Absolute tol: 0
Convergence:  0.474244
 x[1] = 1 (should be one)
```

FIGURE 10.8

Output from the MTL4 example in Fig. 10.7.

written by a single process that must be combined in postprocessing. Common libraries used for HPC I/O include the Network Common Data Form (NetCDF) [49] and the Hierarchical Data Format (HDF5) [50].

NetCDF is a portable format to represent scientific data and has been used extensively in climate modeling, satellite data processing, and geological institutes. NetCDF files are self-describing, portable across hardware architectures, and directly appendable. However, one of the most appealing properties of this data form is that it is archivable, meaning backward compatibility with earlier versions of NetCDF data is supported.

The HDF library was first created in 1988 at the National Center for Supercomputing Applications at the University of Illinois at Urbana–Champaign and, like NetCDF, provides a self-describing, portable data format. HDF5 is the most recent version of the format and provides support for parallel I/O. HDF5 parallel I/O is built on top of the MPI I/O functionality. An example using the HDF5 library to write an array of particle data to a file in HDF5 format is provided in Fig. 10.10.

The HDF5 library also provides a series of tools for examining HDF5 format data, including the tools *h5ls* and *h5dump*. *h5ls* is analogous to the Unix *ls* command and enables the user to query the HDF5 namespace in the same way *ls* queries the Unix file system directory. Executing *h5ls* on the "particles.h5" output file produced in Fig. 10.10 results in the following output:

Particle/data   Dataset{15}

The *h5dump* utility will dump to screen the data stored in the hdf5 file. The small portion of output resulting from executing *h5dump* on the "particles.h5" file in Fig. 10.10 is shown in Fig. 10.11.

The Silo library [15] developed at Lawrence Livermore National Laboratory uses lower-level I/O libraries such as HDF5 and portable binary database [51] to simplify implementation of parallel I/O schemes and output for scientific computing applications. Its application programming interface (API) supports output types common to scientific computing, including adaptive mesh refinement and unstructured grids in both 2D and 3D. As an example of simple parallel I/O of a 2D structured unigrid quad mesh, Fig. 10.12 shows how one might use Silo for distributed output. In this example each MPI process holds a local 2D mesh for output, but the number of I/O ranks can be varied by the user. If the

```
0001 #include <iostream>
0002 #include <boost/mpi.hpp>
0003 #include <boost/numeric/mtl/mtl.hpp>
0004 #include <boost/numeric/itl/itl.hpp>
0005
0006
0007 int main(int argc, char* argv[])
0008 {
0009     using namespace mtl;
0010
0011     mtl::par::environment        env(argc, argv);
0012     boost::mpi::communicator       world;
0013
0014     typedef matrix::distributed<compressed2D<float> >  matrix_type;
0015     typedef mtl::vector::distributed<dense_vector<double> >  vector_type;
0016
0017     matrix_type A;
0018
0019     int n = 100;
0020     laplacian_setup(A,n,n);
0021
0022     vector_type x(num_rows(A),1.0),b;
0023
0024     // Sparse matrix vector multiplication
0025     b = A * x;
0026
0027     // Compute the two norm
0028     double mbnorm = two_norm(b);
0029     printf(" b vector l2norm %10.2f\n",mbnorm);
0030
0031     // reset x vector to be zero
0032     x= 0;
0033
0034     // Solve for x in Ax=b using a Krylov solver, BiCGStabilized.
0035     // Use the ILU_0 preconditioner
0036     itl::pc::ilu_0<matrix_type>      P(A);
0037     itl::cyclic_iteration<double> iter(b, 500, 1.e-8, 0.0, 5);
0038     bicgstab_2(A, x, b, P, iter);
0039
0040     // Print an element of x (should be one)
0041     printf(" x[1] = %g (should be one)\n",x(1));
0042
0043     return 0;
0044 }
```

FIGURE 10.9

A version of the serial MTL4 code from Fig. 10.7 for running on a distributed-memory supercomputer using MPI is shown here. The matrix and vector types in lines 14–15 have been changed to distributed, and the print output has been restricted to rank 0 (lines 29, 43). All other pieces of the example code remain the same as in the serial version.

number of MPI ranks is greater than the number of I/O ranks, some MPI processes will write to the same file. For instance, if the number of I/O ranks specified by the user is one, all data for each MPI rank will be written to a single file. When datasets are written to multiple files, metadata connecting each file is also written so that a visualization tool can read the separate files as if they were one file.

```
#include <hdf5.h>
#include <math.h>

// particle data structure
typedef struct particle3D {
  double x, y, z;    // coordinates
} particle_t;

#define PARTICLE_COUNT 15

int main(int argc, char **argv)
{
  // declare and initialize particle data
  particle_t particles[PARTICLE_COUNT];
  for (int i = 0; i < PARTICLE_COUNT; i++) {
    double t = 0.5*i;
    particles[i].x = cos(t);
    particles[i].y = sin(t);
    particles[i].z = t;
  }

  // create HDF5 type layout in memory
  int mtype = H5Tcreate(H5T_COMPOUND, sizeof(particle_t));
  H5Tinsert(mtype, "x coordinate", HOFFSET(particle_t, x), H5T_NATIVE_DOUBLE);
  H5Tinsert(mtype, "y coordinate", HOFFSET(particle_t, y), H5T_NATIVE_DOUBLE);
  H5Tinsert(mtype, "z coordinate", HOFFSET(particle_t, z), H5T_NATIVE_DOUBLE);

  // create data space
  hsize_t dim = PARTICLE_COUNT;
  int space = H5Screate_simple(1, &dim, NULL);

  // create new file with default properties
  int fd = H5Fcreate("particles.h5", H5F_ACC_TRUNC, H5P_DEFAULT, H5P_DEFAULT);
  // create data set
  int dset = H5Dcreate(fd, "particle data", mtype, space, H5P_DEFAULT,
H5P_DEFAULT, H5P_DEFAULT);
  // write the entire dataset and close the file
  H5Dwrite(dset, mtype, H5S_ALL, H5S_ALL, H5P_DEFAULT, particles);
  H5Fclose(fd);
}
```

FIGURE 10.10

Example of use of the HDF5 library for output in the HDF5 format. This example outputs an array of particle information to a file called "particles.h5" and places this data in the dataset called "particle data". The HDF5 namespace resembles a file system directory, where HDF5 groups are analogous to directories and HDF5 datasets are analogous to files.

10.6 MESH DECOMPOSITION

One of the most important and widely used libraries for partitioning a finite element mesh across multiple processes is the METIS family of graph and hypergraph partitioning software, consisting of METIS [16] and its parallel MPI based counterpart called ParMETIS [17]. An example of mesh

```
HDF5 "particles.h5" {
GROUP "/" {
   DATASET "particle data" {
      DATATYPE  H5T_COMPOUND {
         H5T_IEEE_F64LE "x coordinate";
         H5T_IEEE_F64LE "y coordinate";
         H5T_IEEE_F64LE "z coordinate";
      }
      DATASPACE  SIMPLE { ( 15 ) / ( 15 ) }
      DATA {
      (0): {
            1,
            0,
            0
         },
      (1): {
            0.877583,
            0.479426,
            0.5
         },
```

FIGURE 10.11

Output from executing h5dump on the "particles.h5" output by the code in Fig. 10.10.

partitioning using the Trilinos library is shown in Fig. 10.13. These partitioning software tools are ubiquitous in simulations with unstructured meshes in order to decompose the mesh across multiple MPI processes.

10.7 VISUALIZATION

One of the most important libraries for HPC users is the Visualization Toolkit (VTK) [18]. It provides hundreds of visualization algorithms, enabling application developers to create their own visualization tools. It includes support for scalars, vectors, and tensors as used in contours, streamlines, and hyperstreamlines, respectively. VTK also supports distributed-memory parallel processing using MPI and multithreaded parallel processing for SMP architectures. An example of the VTK in use is the ParaView visualization tool, discussed in Chapter 12.

10.8 PARALLELIZATION

The most important parallelization library for distributed-memory architectures is the MPI library. There are multiple vendor and open-source implementations of MPI. A C++ friendly interface MPI is available via Boost.MPI [12]. For SMPs the most important parallelization libraries are OpenMP and Pthreads.

10.9 SIGNAL PROCESSING

Among libraries providing discrete Fourier transform capability, the FFTW ("fastest Fourier transform in the West") is one of the most widely used. It was developed at the Massachusetts Institute of

```
0001 #include <stdio.h>
0002 #include <stdlib.h>
0003 #include <assert.h>
0004 #include <math.h>
0005 #include <string.h>
0006 #include <mpi.h>
0007
0008 // Silo output headers
0009 #include <silo.h>
0010 #include <pmpio.h>
0011
0012 void DumpDomainToFile(DBfile *db, float *field, int myRank,int nx,int ny);
0013 void DumpMetaData(DBfile *db, PMPIO_baton_t *bat, char basename[], int
numRanks);
0014 void *Test_PMPIO_Create(const char *fname, const char *dname, void *udata);
0015 void *Test_PMPIO_Open(const char *fname, const char *dname, PMPIO_iomode_t
ioMode, void *udata);
0016 void Test_PMPIO_Close(void *file, void *udata);
0017
0018 int main(int argc,char *argv[])
0019 {
0020
0021   int numRanks, myRank;
0022   MPI_Init(&argc, &argv) ;
0023   MPI_Comm_size(MPI_COMM_WORLD, &numRanks) ;
0024   MPI_Comm_rank(MPI_COMM_WORLD, &myRank) ;
0025
0026   // The total number of files to write out
0027   int numfiles = 4;
0028   if ( numfiles > numRanks ) numfiles = numRanks;
0029
0030   // The local structured mesh size of each rank
0031   int nx = 50;
0032   int ny = 50;
0033
0034   // The data to write
0035   float *field;
0036   field = (float *) malloc(sizeof(float)*nx*ny);
0037
0038   // Specify some initial data
0039   for (int i=0;i<nx*ny;i++) {
0040     field[i] = myRank*3.14;
0041   }
0042
0043   // The silo library handler
0044   DBfile *db;
0045
0046   // the output filename
0047   char basename[32];
0048   sprintf(basename,"output_file.000.pdb");
0049
0050   // the subdirectory where the data is written
0051   char subdirName[32];
0052   sprintf(subdirName,"data_%d",myRank);
0053
```

FIGURE 10.12

Example of parallel I/O using the Silo library and the portable binary database as the low-level I/O library. Each MPI rank has its own unique 2D data that needs to be output. The number of files written by the code is decided by the user by changing the variable "numfiles" in line 27. Changing this variable can change the time it takes to write the output. The optimal performance will change depending on the file system in the supercomputer, but is generally somewhere between the two extremes of having each MPI process write its own file and having all MPI processes write to just one file. Regardless of the number of files written, however, visualization tools like VisIt (discussed in Chapter 12) can read and tie the separate output files together using the metadata added in line 84.

```
    if ( numRanks > 1 ) {
      // Set up baton passing
      // Three handler routines control the parallel creation, opening, and closing of the files.
      // These are named here: Test_PMPIO_Create, Test_PMPIO_Open, Test_PMPIO_Close
      // They are defined at the end.
      PMPIO_baton_t *bat = PMPIO_Init(numfiles, PMPIO_WRITE,MPI_COMM_WORLD,10101,
                                      Test_PMPIO_Create,
                                      Test_PMPIO_Open,
                                      Test_PMPIO_Close,
                                      NULL);

      // Determine the I/O rank
      int myiorank = PMPIO_GroupRank(bat,myRank);

      char fileName[64];

      // If I/O rank is 0, the filename is as specified
      // Otherwise, give the filename an integer suffix
      if (myiorank == 0) {
        strcpy(fileName, basename);
      } else {
        sprintf(fileName, "%s.%03d", basename, myiorank);
      }

      // Wait for the turn to write data to the file
      db = (DBfile*)PMPIO_WaitForBaton(bat, fileName, subdirName);

      DumpDomainToFile(db, field, myRank,nx,ny);

      if (myRank == 0) {
        // Dump necessary metadata
        DumpMetaData(db, bat, basename, numRanks);
      }

      // Finish writing, give someone else a turn to write
      PMPIO_HandOffBaton(bat, db);

      PMPIO_Finish(bat);
    } else {
      // Only one rank in this case, no parallel I/O needed
      int             driver=DB_PDB;
      db = (DBfile*)DBCreate(basename, 0, DB_LOCAL,"test data", driver);
      if (db) {
         DumpDomainToFile(db, field, myRank,nx,ny);
         DBClose(db);
      }
    }

    free(field);

    MPI_Finalize();
    return 0;
```

FIGURE 10.12 Cont'd

```
}

void DumpDomainToFile(DBfile *db, float *field, int myRank,int nx,int ny)
{

  // allocate the coordinate arrays
  float *nodex,*nodey;
  nodex = (float *) malloc(nx*sizeof(float));
  nodey = (float *) malloc(ny*sizeof(float));
  int dimensions[2];
  dimensions[0] = nx;
  dimensions[1] = ny;

  float *coordinates[2];
  const char *coordnames[2];

  coordnames[0] = "x";
  coordnames[1] = "y";

  // Give the local data some x and y coordinates
  for (int i=0;i<nx;i++) {
    nodex[i] = 0.1*(myRank*nx + i);
  }
  for (int i=0;i<ny;i++) {
    nodey[i] = 0.1*(myRank*ny + i);
  }
  coordinates[0] = nodex;
  coordinates[1] = nodey;

  static char     meshname[] = {"mesh"};
  DBPutQuadmesh(db,meshname,coordnames,coordinates,
                dimensions,2,DB_FLOAT,DB_COLLINEAR,NULL);

  char fname[80];
  sprintf(fname,"testvar");

  DBPutQuadvar1(db, fname, meshname,field,
         dimensions,2,NULL,0,DB_FLOAT,DB_NODECENT,NULL);

  free(nodex);
  free(nodey);

  return;
}

void DumpMetaData(DBfile *db, PMPIO_baton_t *bat,
                         char basename[], int numRanks)
{

  // We only write out on variable in this example, called "testvar"
  int numvars = 1;
  char vars[numvars][32];
  sprintf(vars[0],"testvar");
```

FIGURE 10.12 Cont'd

```
// These objects provide the metadata needed to tie together
// data from multiple files
// the 'multi' objects tell us where the mesh and variables are written
// in the files directory
char **multi_mesh;
char ***multi_var;
multi_mesh = malloc(numRanks*sizeof(char*));
multi_var = malloc(numvars*sizeof(char**));
for(int v=0 ; v<numvars ; ++v) {
   multi_var[v] = malloc(numRanks*sizeof(char*));
}

// the 'type' objects tell us the type of mesh and variables written
int *typemesh;
int *typevar;
typemesh = malloc(numRanks*sizeof(int));
typevar = malloc(numRanks*sizeof(int));

// We start from the root directory in the silo file
DBSetDir(db, "/");

// Specify the type of mesh and variable being written
for(int i=0 ; i<numRanks ; ++i) {
  multi_mesh[i] = malloc(64*sizeof(char));
  typemesh[i] = DB_QUADMESH;
  typevar[i] = DB_QUADVAR;
}
for(int v=0 ; v<numvars ; ++v) {
  for(int i=0 ; i<numRanks ; ++i) {
    multi_var[v][i] = malloc(64*sizeof(char));
  }
}

// Indicate where in the file hierarchy to write the mesh and data
for(int i=0 ; i<numRanks ; ++i) {
  int iorank = PMPIO_GroupRank(bat, i);
  if (iorank == 0) {
    snprintf(multi_mesh[i], 64, "/data_%d/mesh", i);
    for(int v=0 ; v<numvars ; ++v) {
snprintf(multi_var[v][i], 64, "/data_%d/%s", i, vars[v]);
    }

  } else {
    snprintf(multi_mesh[i], 64, "%s.%03d:/data_%d/mesh",
             basename, iorank, i);
    for(int v=0 ; v<numvars ; ++v) {
       snprintf(multi_var[v][i], 64, "%s.%03d:/data_%d/%s",
                basename, iorank, i, vars[v]);
    }
  }
}

// write out the metadata
DBPutMultimesh(db, "mesh", numRanks, (const char**)multi_mesh, typemesh,
NULL);
```

FIGURE 10.12 Cont'd

```

    for(int v=0 ; v<numvars ; ++v) {
       DBPutMultivar(db, vars[v], numRanks, (const char**)multi_var[v], typevar, NULL);
    }

    for(int v=0; v < numvars; ++v) {
      for(int i = 0; i < numRanks; i++) {
        free(multi_var[v][i]);
      }
      free(multi_var[v]);
    }

    // Clean up
    for(int i=0 ; i<numRanks ; i++) {
      free(multi_mesh[i]);
    }
    free(multi_mesh);
    free(multi_var);
    free(typemesh);
    free(typevar);

    return;
  }

  void *Test_PMPIO_Create(const char *fname,
                    const char *dname,
                    void *udata)
  {
     // This is where the file is created.
     // We overwrite ("clobber") any existing files with the same name that might
     // be in the way
     int              driver=DB_PDB;
     DBfile* db = DBCreate(fname, DB_CLOBBER, DB_LOCAL, NULL, driver);

     // All data is placed in the dname subdirectory.
     if (db) {
       DBMkDir(db, dname);
       DBSetDir(db, dname);
     }
     return (void*)db;
  }

  void *Test_PMPIO_Open(const char *fname,
                  const char *dname,
                  PMPIO_iomode_t ioMode,
                  void *udata)
  {
    // This is where we open the file for appending to each.
    DBfile* db = DBOpen(fname, DB_UNKNOWN, DB_APPEND);
```

FIGURE 10.12 Cont'd

```

    // All data is placed in the dname subdirectory.
    if (db) {
      DBMkDir(db, dname);
      DBSetDir(db, dname);
    }
    return (void*)db;
}

void Test_PMPIO_Close(void *file, void *udata)
{
   // Here the file is closed
   DBfile *db = (DBfile*)file;
   if (db)
     DBClose(db);
}
```

FIGURE 10.12 Cont'd

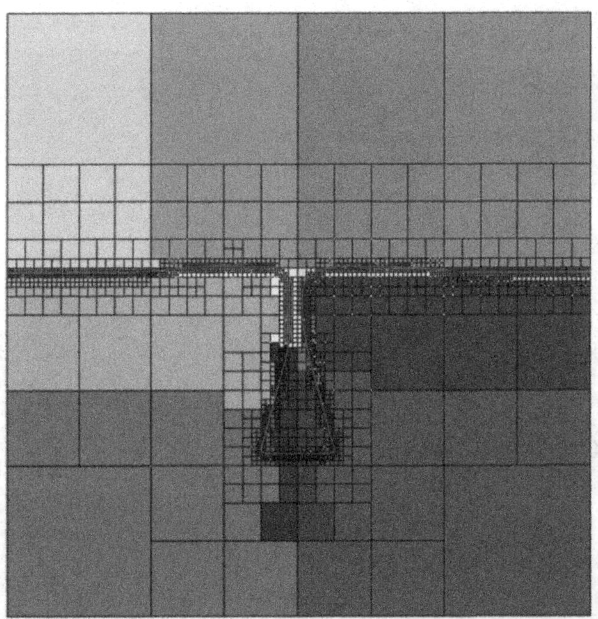

FIGURE 10.13

Example of partitioning algorithm using the Zoltan library. The different regions indicate the different partitions of the mesh domain.

Courtesy Lawrence C Musson at Sandia National Laboratories

Technology by Matteo Frigo and Steven Johnson, and provides discrete sine/cosine transform, discrete Fourier transform, and Hartley transform. It is optimized for speed by means of a special-purpose codelet generator called "genfft", which actually produces the C code that is used. FFTW supports SMP architectures with threads and distributed-memory architectures with MPI. It is used in two

```
#include <fftw3-mpi.h>
#include <stdlib.h>
# include <stdio.h>
#include <sys/stat.h>
#include <fcntl.h>
# include <time.h>
#include <math.h>

int main(int argc, char **argv){
  const ptrdiff_t N0 = 8589934592; // 2^33
  fftw_plan plan;
  fftw_complex *data;
  ptrdiff_t alloc_local, local_n0, local_0_start,local_no,local_o_start, i, j;
  MPI_Init(&argc, &argv);
  fftw_mpi_init();

  // This tells us the local size for each process
  alloc_local = fftw_mpi_local_size_1d(N0, MPI_COMM_WORLD,FFTW_FORWARD,
FFTW_ESTIMATE,
                        &local_n0, &local_0_start,&local_no,&local_o_start);

  // Allocate the data
  data = (fftw_complex *) fftw_malloc(sizeof(fftw_complex) * alloc_local);

  // This creates the plan for the forward FFT
  plan = fftw_mpi_plan_dft_1d(N0, data, data, MPI_COMM_WORLD, FFTW_FORWARD,
FFTW_ESTIMATE);

  // Initialize the input complex data to some random numbers between 0 and 1
  for (i = 0; i < local_n0; ++i) {
    data[i][0]= rand() / (double)RAND_MAX;
    data[i][1]= rand() / (double)RAND_MAX;
  }
  // Compute an unnormalized forward FFT
  fftw_execute(plan);

  // Clean up
  fftw_destroy_plan(plan);
  fftw_free(data);
  MPI_Finalize();
  return 0;
}
```

FIGURE 10.14

Example parallel one-dimensional discrete Fourier transform using FFTW with MPI.

widely distributed molecular dynamics toolkits, NAMD [52] and Gromacs [53]. An example of a parallel one-dimensional complex discrete Fourier transform using FFTW is shown in Fig. 10.14.

10.10 PERFORMANCE MONITORING

The Performance API (PAPI) [20] provides tools for performance measurement and portable access to hardware performance counters for monitoring software performance. For many users the PAPI performance counters most frequently encountered are those which measure the L1 data cache misses

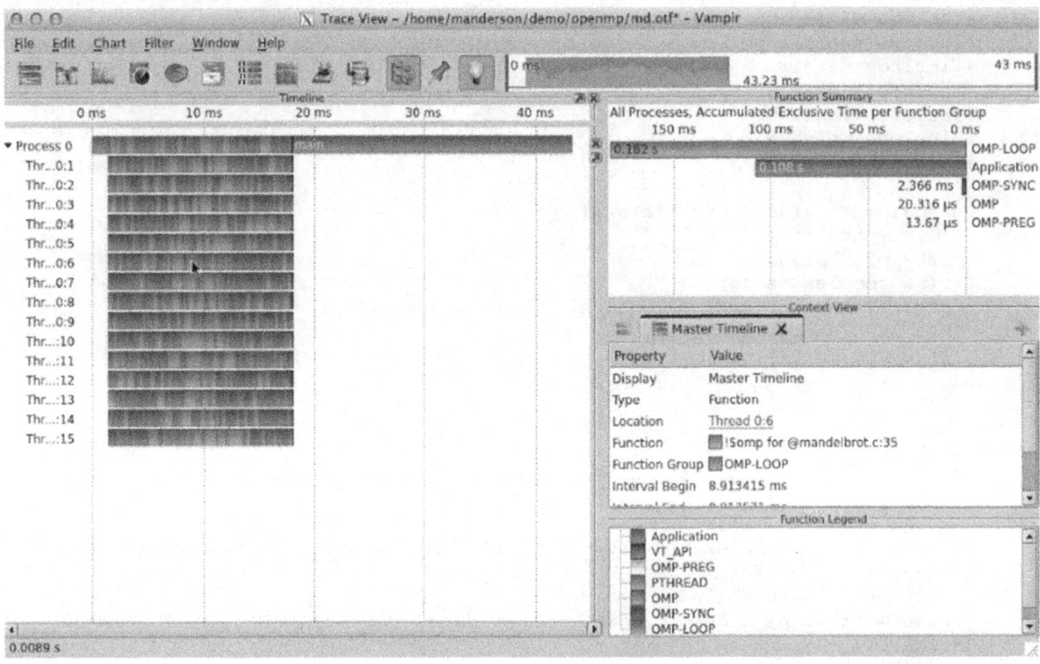

FIGURE 10.15

Performance-monitoring timeline of an OpenMP code run using 16 OpenMP threads within the VampirTrace framework. The timeline of execution for each thread is shown on the left, while the time summary of application functions and OpenMP looping is shown on the upper right. Context information for a region in the execution timeline can be examined, and is shown on the lower right above the function legend.

(*PAPI_L1_DCM*), the L2 data cache misses (*PAPI_L2_DCM*), and the number of floating-point operations executed (*PAPI_FP_OPS*). The PAPI library provides an important tool for users to diagnose performance issues via hardware counters from the bottom up in a portable way.

Other performance-monitoring tools like VampirTrace [21] can interface with PAPI as well as instrument MPI, OpenMP, and Compute Unified Device Architecture codes to provide a timeline of execution complete with messages and threads, illustrated in Fig. 10.15 using the Vampir performance-visualization tool.

10.11 SUMMARY AND OUTCOMES OF CHAPTER 10

- Several software libraries have been developed for HPC resources to fill specific computing needs, so application developers do not have to waste time redeveloping supercomputing software that has already been developed elsewhere.
- Apart from acting as a repository for software reuse, libraries serve the important role of providing a knowledge base for specific computational science domains.

- Libraries become community standards and serve as ways for members of the community to communicate with one another.
- BLAS provides a standard interface to vector, matrix–vector, and matrix–matrix routines that have been optimized for various computer architectures.
- BLAS Level 1 involve vector operations. The naming scheme is a *cblas_* after which a precision prefix is placed before the operation name. Operations include dot products, norms, and rotations, among others.
- BLAS Levels 2 and 3 operations involve matrices and incorporate the type of matrix they support in their name. Levels 2 and 3 names take the form *cblas_pmmoo*, where the p indicates the precision, mm indicates the matrix type, and oo indicates the operation.
- Lapack incorporates BLAS Levels 2 and 3 to provide full problem drivers such as eigenvalue problems and linear solvers. A high performance version of Lapack is available: ScaLapack.
- Multiple additional widely used libraries exist which specifically target HPC resources. This chapter summarizes 25 such mature libraries to give a small sampling of what is currently available.

10.12 EXERCISES

1. Explore the performance of matrix–matrix multiplication using the BLAS Level 3 dgemm routine for increasingly larger matrix sizes. Start with a randomly generated dense 3×3 matrix and incrementally increase the matrix size. For timing comparison, compute the matrix–matrix multiplication yourself just using for-loops without any BLAS calls for each matrix size explored. For each matrix size, which performs better, and by how much? Produce a plot comparing the time to solution for matrix–matrix multiplication with and without BLAS for each matrix size explored.
2. Using the DLATMR routine in Lapack to generate random square test matrices, compute the vector $b = Au$ where u is a vector whose elements are all 1 and A is the random matrix. Then use Lapack to solve the linear system $Ax = b$ for x. Check the solution to be sure that all elements of x are 1 after the solve. Produce a plot of the performance for solving $Ax = b$ for a wide variety of matrix sizes, beginning with 3×3 and exploring both symmetric and nonsymmetric test matrices.
3. Use PETSc and MPI to compute the sparse matrix vector product of a matrix and vector with randomly generated elements on a distributed-memory architecture. Select several sparse matrices to explore from the Matrix Market repository [54], and plot the time to solution as a function of the number of MPI processes used for the solve.
4. Write a code using the HDF5 library to read in the *particles.h5* file that is generated by running the code in Fig. 10.10.
5. Modify the FFTW code in Fig. 10.14 to compute the backward transformation, and then compare the input data prior to the forward transformation against the data that has gone through the forward and backward transformation.
6. Extend the Silo I/O example in Fig. 10.12 to support parallel 3D I/O. Test it by having each MPI rank write 3D data to file, instead of just 2D data as was done in Fig. 10.12.

REFERENCES

[1] XSEDE, Extreme Science and Engineering Discovery Environment, [Online]. www.xsede.org.
[2] BLAS (Basic Linear Algebra Subprograms), [Online]. http://www.netlib.org/blas/.
[3] LAPACK — Linear Algebra PACKage, [Online]. http://www.netlib.org/lapack/.
[4] ScaLAPACK — Scalable Linear Algebra PACKage, [Online]. http://www.netlib.org/scalapack/.
[5] GSL – GNU Scientific Library, [Online]. https://www.gnu.org/software/gsl/.
[6] SuperLU developers, SuperLU, [Online]. http://crd-legacy.lbl.gov/~xiaoye/SuperLU/.
[7] PETSc Team, Portable, Extensible Toolkit for Scientific Computation, [Online]. https://www.mcs.anl.gov/petsc/.
[8] Universitat Politècnica de València, SLEPc, the Scalable Library for Eigenvalue Problem Computations, [Online]. http://slepc.upv.es/.
[9] Max Planck Computing and Data Facility, Eigenvalue SoLvers for Petaflop-Applications, [Online]. https://elpa.mpcdf.mpg.de/.
[10] Center for Applied Scientific Computing, Lawrence Livermore National Laboratory, Hypre, [Online]. http://acts.nersc.gov/hypre/.
[11] The Trilinos Project, The Trilinos Project, [Online]. trilinos.org.
[12] Boost.org, Boost Home Page, [Online]. www.boost.org.
[13] The HDF5 Group, The HDF5 Home Page, [Online]. https://support.hdfgroup.org/HDF5/.
[14] NetCDF, Network Common Data Form Home page, [Online]. http://www.unidata.ucar.edu/software/netcdf/.
[15] Lawrence Livermore National Laboratory, Silo: A Mesh and Field I/O Library and Scientific Database, [Online]. https://wci.llnl.gov/simulation/computer-codes/silo.
[16] G. Karypis, METIS – Serial Graph Partitioning and Fill-reducing Matrix Ordering, [Online]. http://glaros.dtc.umn.edu/gkhome/metis/metis/overview.
[17] ParMETIS – Parallel Graph Partitioning and Fill-reducing Matrix Ordering, [Online]. http://glaros.dtc.umn.edu/gkhome/metis/parmetis/overview.
[18] The Visualization Toolkit, [Online]. http://www.vtk.org/.
[19] fftw.org, FFTW, [Online]. http://www.fftw.org/.
[20] The University of Tennessee, Performance Application Programming Interface, [Online]. http://icl.cs.utk.edu/papi/.
[21] GWT-TUD GmbH, VAMPIR, [Online]. www.vampir.eu.
[22] Sandia National Laboratories, Dakota – Algorithms for Design Exploration and Simulation Credibility, [Online]. https://dakota.sandia.gov/.
[23] Berkely Vision and Learning Center, Caffe – Deep learning framework, [Online]. http://caffe.berkeleyvision.org/.
[24] T.A. Davis, SuiteSparse: A Suite of Sparse Matrix Software, [Online]. http://faculty.cse.tamu.edu/davis/suitesparse.html.
[25] PISM Team, PISM: Parallel Ice Sheet Model, [Online]. http://www.pism-docs.org/wiki/doku.php.
[26] M. Adams, J. Brown, J. Shalf, B. Van Straalen, E. Strohmaier, S. Williams, High-Performance Geometric Multigrid, [Online]. https://hpgmg.org/fe/.
[27] R. Sampath, S. Adavani, H. Sundar, I. Lashuk, G. Biros, Dendro: Parallel Algoritms for Multigrid and AMR Methods on 2:1 Balanced Octrees, IEEE, Austin, Texas, 2008. SC.
[28] T. Kim, Cubica: A Toolkit for Subspace Deformations, [Online]. https://www.mat.ucsb.edu/~kim/cubica/.
[29] R. Schneider, FEINS: Finite Element Incompressible Navier-Stokes Solver, [Online]. http://www.feins.org.
[30] C. Curtin, Sanderson, Ryan, Armadillo: C++ Linear Algebra Library, [Online]. http://arma.sourceforge.net/.
[31] MUMPS: A MUltifrontal Massively Parallel Sparse Direct Solver, [Online]. http://mumps.enseeiht.fr/.

[32] C-SAFE and SCI, University of Utah, Uintah Software Suite, [Online]. http://uintah.utah.edu/.
[33] SimuNova, MTL4, [Online]. http://www.simunova.com/mtl4.
[34] K. Iglberger, et al., Blaze, [Online]. https://bitbucket.org/blaze-lib/blaze.
[35] Automatically Tuned Linear Algebra Software (ATLAS), [Online]. http://math-atlas.sourceforge.net/.
[36] J. Dongarra, [interv.] Thomas Haigh, April 26, 2004.
[37] netlib.org, LAPACKE, [Online]. http://www.netlib.org/lapack/lapacke.html.
[38] Lawrence Livermore National Laboratory, HYPRE, [Online]. http://computation.llnl.gov/projects/hypre-scalable-linear-solvers-multigrid-methods.
[39] SUNDIALS: SUite of Nonlinear and Differential/ALgebraic Equation Solvers, [Online]. http://computation.llnl.gov/projects/sundials.
[40] SAMRAI: Structured Adaptive Mesh Refinement Application Infrastructure, [Online]. http://computation.llnl.gov/projects/samrai.
[41] University of Oregon, TAU: Tuning and Analysis Utilities, [Online]. http://www.cs.uoregon.edu/research/tau/home.php.
[42] SC2000, Past Gordon Bell Award Prize Winners, [Online]. http://www.sc2000.org/bell/pastawrd.htm.
[43] Rice University, ARPACK software, [Online]. http://www.caam.rice.edu/software/ARPACK/.
[44] J. Dongarra, R.C. Whaley, Basic Linear Algebra Communication Subprograms, [Online]. http://www.netlib.org/blacs/.
[45] G. Kresse, et al., The Vienna Ab Initio Simulation Package, [Online]. https://www.vasp.at/.
[46] Mathworks, MATLAB, [Online]. https://www.mathworks.com/products/matlab.html.
[47] A. Azad, et al., Combinatorial BLAS, [Online]. http://gauss.cs.ucsb.edu/~aydin/CombBLAS/html/index.html.
[48] Apache, Apache Giraph, [Online]. http://giraph.apache.org/.
[49] Unidata, Network Common Data Form (NetCDF), [Online]. http://www.unidata.ucar.edu/software/netcdf/.
[50] The HDF Group, HDF5, [Online]. https://support.hdfgroup.org/HDF5/.
[51] S. Brown, PDBLib User's Manual, [Online]. https://wci.llnl.gov/codes/pact/pdb.html.
[52] Theoretical and Computational Biophysics Group, UIUC, NAMD: Scalable Molecular Dynamics, [Online]. http://www.ks.uiuc.edu/Research/namd/.
[53] Gromacs Project, Gromacs, [Online]. http://www.gromacs.org/.
[54] National Institute of Standards and Technology, The Matrix Market, [Online]. http://math.nist.gov/MatrixMarket/.

CHAPTER

OPERATING SYSTEMS

11

CHAPTER OUTLINE

11.1 INTRODUCTION

A supercomputer is manifest visibly as a large room filled with many rows of many racks of many nodes of many cores, combined with the loud noise of myriad fans moving tons of air for cooling. But from the perspective of most users, who never actually see the physical high performance computing (HPC) system, the supercomputer is most readily viewed as the operating system (OS) and the user interface to it. In day-to-day usage patterns with a supercomputer, the OS gives the sense that it is the supercomputer itself. The OS owns the supercomputer.

An OS is a persistent program that controls the execution of application programs, as illustrated in Fig. 11.1. It is the primary interface between user applications and system hardware. The primary

High Performance Computing. https://doi.org/10.1016/B978-0-12-420158-3.00011-3

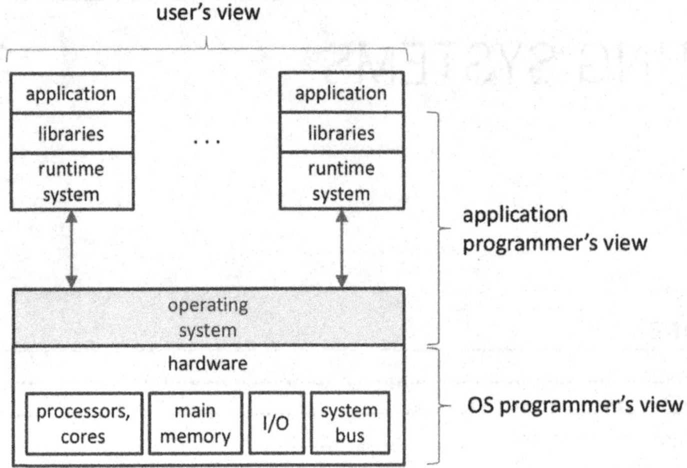

FIGURE 11.1

The primary functionality of the OS is to exploit the hardware resources of one or more processors, provide a set of services to system users, and manage secondary memory and I/O devices, including the file system.

functionality of the OS is to exploit the hardware resources of one or more processors, provide a set of services to system users, and manage secondary memory and input/output (I/O) devices, including the file system. The OS objectives are convenience for end users, efficiency of system resource utilization, reliability through protection between concurrent jobs, and extensibility for effective development, testing, and introduction of new system functions without interfering with ongoing service. The OS is one of the key layers in the total computer system stack, as illustrated in Fig.11.1.

Resources managed by the OS are the processors and their integrated cores, the main memory of the systems out of which the cores work, I/O modules, and the system bus. Processors within the same system may be of different classes, such as conventional processors (e.g., Xeon), lightweight cores (e.g., PHI), and graphics processing unit accelerators. Managing main memory is challenging, as it involves both the memory hierarchy and the virtual address space. Main memory usually refers to the banks of dynamic random access memory (DRAM) directly connected to the processors, but it also includes data movement between the main memory and the intervening cache hierarchy (two to four layers) and in the other direction to secondary storage. Memory objects are virtually addressed and the translation between virtual and physical addresses is the responsibility of the OS, including their placement in main memory and secondary storage. The I/O modules have diverse subsystems, including secondary storage and the file system hierarchy, communications equipment such as wide area networks, and terminals for user interactive control. The system bus provides communication between the processors, memory, and I/O.

The OS incorporates all services and facilities of a supercomputer.

- It holds the local directory and files system.
- It controls the allocation of the hardware resources.

- It governs the scheduling of user jobs.
- It stores temporary results.
- It provides many of the high-level programming tools and functions.
- It exports the user interface to the system for all user commands.
- It protects user programs from errors caused by other running applications.
- It supports user access to system I/O, networks, and remote sites.
- It provides firewalls for security of operation and data storage.

The OS performs all of these purposes and more to make a convenient, reliable system which delivers efficient and scalable performance. OS structures and interfaces can be complex, large, and complicated to use or program. The purpose of this chapter is to highlight specific capabilities, structures, and functionality that relate to effective HPC operation and use. It does not give exhaustive coverage of the entire OS, as the user is unlikely to encounter most of these aspects. An appendix, "The Essential Linux", describes the interface syntax that the user is likely to need in performing the hands-on examples and exercises. This chapter presents key aspects to understand the operation and use of the HPC OS, including:

- OS structures and services
- process management
- parallel threads
- memory management
- modern OS, Unix, and Linux.

11.2 OPERATING SYSTEM STRUCTURES AND SERVICES

OSs can be described in a number of ways. One is to represent the OS components and their interconnections, describing the data and control flow. Another way is to describe the services that are performed by the components comprising the OS. A third approach is to define the interface semantic constructs employed by users and programmers. This section introduces these ideas of OS structures and the services they provide.

11.2.1 SYSTEM COMPONENTS

OSs are complex software packages consisting of many separate but interrelated components. These components individually or in combination achieve the functions and deliver the services required by the users directly or for system management and control. While the OS may differ from machine to machine with low-level variation of means and methods, essentially all mainstream HPC OSs share the same major components. The following are representative of what one is likely to find in any of these computers.

11.2.2 PROCESS MANAGEMENT

User and system programs that are executing are made up of instances called "processes", which are instantiations of program procedures (code text). Many processes may operate concurrently under a single OS, so the OS incorporates a major component responsible for managing them. The process management component controls the full lifecycle of a process running on the system hardware. It creates and ultimately terminates all the processes, whether provided by the end user or part of the functioning system itself. Throughout the lifecycle of a process, this component manages its scheduling of operation and allocation of processor resources, suspending and resuming processes as required to optimize a selected objective function for system operation. Processes can communicate among themselves, with the output results of one conveyed to the input of another. The process management component enables the paths of communication between processes (e.g., sockets). The control flow between processes requires process synchronization and variables supervised by this component. In addition, the processor resource allocation to processes is handled by the process management component.

11.2.3 MEMORY MANAGEMENT

By some measures, including cost, an HPC system is mostly data storage. Program data must reside within the memory system, which seen from the architecture perspective is a multilevel hierarchy including registers, buffers, and three layers of cache: main memory, which may be distributed among all nodes, secondary storage, which is still primarily hard disks but increasingly includes nonvolatile semiconductor storage technology, and tertiary storage employing tape cassettes and drives for archival storage. The tradeoffs of all these layers are speed of access and cost of capacity, with reliability and energy also being important. The OS is responsible for data allocation to memory resources and migration between levels. Memory management is also responsible for address translation between the virtual address blocks of program data, called pages, and blocks of physical storage, called frames. The OS manages the page table that maps the page numbers to the frame numbers. In case that a particular page is not in memory, that is a page fault occurs, the OS has to swap the frame from secondary storage into main memory and update the page table accordingly prior to the related process continuing.

11.2.4 FILE MANAGEMENT

The OS is responsible for users' data and programs organized in files through a hierarchy of named directories. The file system managed by the OS presents this abstraction of the system to the user, and includes many more functions and used services. The system supports nonvolatile storage; that is, the information does not go away when the associated processes terminate. Ordinarily the file system resides on secondary storage, which is primarily hosted by hard-disk drives. However, newer systems may include nonvolatile random access memory (NVRAM) semiconductor devices for lower power consumption and faster response, sometimes dedicated to metadata for large graph structures. In the case of laptops, pads, and phones, solid-state devices made from these components may constitute all the file system. File management may also involve tertiary storage in the form of tape robots. The cost per byte of such storage is much lower than the cost for other forms, with much higher density, and it is therefore are perfect for archival storage of files. Initial access times can be measured in minutes, however, so the OS supports the user's file management system across a complex multilevel storage system, and possibly mounts external file systems as well for even greater data storage space.

11.2.5 I/O SYSTEM MANAGEMENT

The OS is responsible for managing all sources and destinations of data flow in and out of the computer it supports. The file system is just one example of the I/O system employing secondary storage. Users are most familiar with the standard I/O that gives them direct interactive access with the system by a minimalist command-line interface or the increasingly common windows-based graphical interfaces. Web browsers access the internet through additional I/O devices (e.g., Ethernet) from which much of the external data is acquired, also supported by the OS I/O management. For clusters and massively parallel processors, at the lowest level the system area network (e.g., Infiniband) for each node is the I/O channel that connects it to all the other system nodes comprising the total supercomputer and again managed by the OS I/O system. Many other devices are also supported, as described in the Chapter 6 on architecture. Some of these are for maintenance and are not visible to the users; others are as simple as switches and lights.

11.2.6 SECONDARY STORAGE MANAGEMENT

As mentioned, the OS is responsible for secondary storage. Usually comprising many hard-disk drives, but possibly also some solid-state NVRAM, secondary storage delivers high density and nonvolatility for long-term storage. The OS may manage access to local disks for each node or a separate part of the system of disks connected by a storage area network such as a redundant array of independent disks configuration (there are several) for higher access bandwidth and greater reliability through redundancy of storage. While secondary storage is important to users in its OS support for file systems, it also provides other services. Virtual memory, in which pages of data for a process may be temporarily stored in secondary storage, gives the impression of larger memory capacity, although the data pages are actually distributed between physical main memory and secondary storage. The OS also uses secondary storage to buffer processes for future scheduling, or sometimes when swapping jobs in and out of memory systems. In all these cases and more, the OS is responsible for managing secondary storage, providing interfaces to it, and including services.

11.3 PROCESS MANAGEMENT

A process is a program or subprogram in execution. It is a unit of work within the system that is performed to completion. A program is a passive entity; principally a block or blocks of binary code produced by a compiler from a high-level representation of an application to the low-level machine-interpretable form for machine execution. A process is the instantiation of a program within a computer as an active entity of work in progress. It consumes resources and combines program blocks with data representing both its current operating state and the information upon which the program is to operate. The OS is responsible for process management: where the data elements of the process are, its current control state and intermediate values, and how the process is related to both its parent (calling) process and possibly its child processes (those which it has called). This section introduces the elements and mechanisms of OS process management.

A process needs resources to accomplish its task(s): both hardware functionality and logical objects defining the state and direction of the process. A process needs to have allocated to it such hardware as one or more central processing units (CPUs), memory for both data being processed and program blocks, access to I/O ports and devices, and files in mass storage where input data to start the program, output data to store the process results, and possibly additional storage for intermediate results are handled.

The logical resources that ultimately specify the process include a number of data objects. The program counter points to the next instruction to be executed (an address) within the program code block. The code section itself describes the operations of the process to be performed. The process stack contains localized data of direct importance to the process specification and intermediate values, including such things as return addresses upon completion. The data section contains the global variables of the user computation. When the process terminates, all the reusable resources allocated to it are reclaimed by the OS for use by future processes.

Section 11.4 introduces the idea of a thread, which is itself an executable within the context of a process. If the process has only one thread, it includes only a single program counter defining the location of the next instruction to be performed. It is possible for a process to have more than one active thread, in which case the process contains multiple program counters; one counter for each operating thread.

A modern system, whether an enterprise server or a basic laptop, has a number of concurrent processes operating at the same time. Some are user processes, possibly in support of applications with multiple users; others are system processes providing services directly in response to user application requests or to support the management of system resources. Curiously, one process is responsible for the management of all these processes. These OS process management tasks are discussed in the following subsections.

11.3.1 PROCESS STATES

At any one time each activated process managed by the OS exists in one of a number of states, depending on its current condition and activity. These process states are mutually exclusive and collectively exhaustive, in that they fully describe the possible lifecycles of a given process. Different OSs are distinguished in part by the possible process states each supports and employs in guiding the evolution of its constitutive processes, but they exhibit many similarities. Here a relatively simple machine in a fully functional state is considered to illustrate OS-supported process states, as shown in the diagram below. All OSs will include these states or multiple states. For example, the Linux OS presented in Appendix B has a more diverse state structure, but all the states in this diagram can be mapped on top of the Linux state diagram.

When a new process is initiated for the first time for a specified program, it enters into the *new* state among the process states. In this state the process is being created and the necessary memory objects fully designing the process are being allocated and populated. When this has been accomplished, the process transitions into the *ready* state. In a symmetric manner, when the process has completed all work associated with it and deposited its results in the appropriate locations for future use, it enters the *terminated* state. Once in this state, the process is known to have finished execution. At this point the OS modifies its control tables to eliminate the context of the process and reclaim the physical and logical resources associated with the process.

The *running* state of the process is that condition under which the process is actually executing its instructions on the data associated with it. When running, the process is making progress toward completion of its workload. If in this state it reaches the point of completion, it transitions to the terminated state as described above. However, it is possible that other events will occur and require the process to suspend temporarily and resume at a later time. One of these circumstances can be an asynchronous external interrupt. An interrupt is a signal from any of several sources indicating that another process has immediate priority, such as an OS service routine that must be engaged for the system as a whole to progress. An interrupt will cause the current process in the running state to exit the processing resources (e.g., CPU) and transit to the *ready* state. Alternatively, if a process in the running state experiences a need to delay because of a wait event or an I/O request that may take tens of milliseconds, then if the process remained in the running state it would waste precious computing resources due to the delay caused by these conditions. Instead, the process will transition from the running state to its *waiting* state.

The waiting state is that condition of the process assumed when it is unable to proceed immediately with its execution because of a delay of a pending service, access such as I/O requests to mass storage, or a need for user input. Once entered, a process remains in the waiting state until the source of the delay is cleared by some external action (e.g., the arrival of the data requested from secondary storage). In this way other processes can enter the running state and take advantage of the processor resources for greater efficiency of system usage. When the delaying condition is satisfied and the process can proceed forward, it is unlikely that the computing resources are immediately available as one or more other processes are likely to be actively using them. Thus the process that had been in the waiting state transitions to the *ready* state of the process lifecycle. The OS draws upon the processes in the ready state to select the next process to be placed in the running state. Many processes may be pending in the running state, waiting for their turn to begin executing either for the first time after originating from the new state or resuming, having previously been in the running state at some time in the past. It is typical for a process to cycle back and forth among the three states, ready, running, and waiting, prior to completing its workload and finally entering the terminated state. In this way the user gets the impression that any number of processes are computing concurrently, when in fact they are time-sharing the physical resources but switching states so quickly that they all appear to be making progress towards their end computational goals.

11.3.2 PROCESS CONTROL BLOCK

Each process being managed by an OS is represented by a dedicated data structure referred to as a "process control block" (PCB). Like the process state machine, the PCB will vary from OS to OS. However, there are a minimum number of basic parameters common to the PCBs of all OSs. The PCB contains the data that specifies the existence of a particular process and the information necessary to permit the process to make forward progress.

From the previous subsection, it is clear that the process state is a critical parameter determining the modality of a process at any point in time and thus the possible states to which it may transit. The PCB contains a field that specifies an encoding of all possible process states, and holds the value associated with the state of the process as the process evolves throughout its lifecycle.

Calling parent process pointer provides the link to the active process that was responsible for the instantiation of the current process represented by the PCB. This pointer link is either the name of the parent or calling process (*process number*) or the virtual address of the PCB of the parent process. The process number is an arbitrary positive integer that is unique among all processes running in the system at any one time. The process pointers combined with the PCBs of an entire program form a tree describing the operating state of the program (user or system), with the PCBs as the vertices (nodes) of the tree and the pointers as the links. The next instruction to be executed by the process is represented in the PCB by the *program counter*. This can either be the virtual address of the next instruction or a combination of the virtual address of the program code block and the offset within the code block of the next instruction. This is updated, often incremented, after every instruction issue.

Registers are the highest level of the memory hierarchy (or lowest, depending on how you draw it) and hold the most important values of a process execution at any one time. Registers have their own namespace (register number) and update their value contents through load and store instructions. When a process is suspended (to either waiting or ready state), the values of the physical registers must be copied to the PCB, from which the registers can be restored when the process restarts in the running state. The other main data of the process is stored in main memory. It may include a stack frame assigned to the process and the blocks of main memory that it uses and possibly shares with other processes. Because the process data is in main memory, it does not need to be copied in the PCB; but the locations of such data may be required, including pointers to the head of the associated data blocks and the limits of those blocks and the stack frame.

Other information that is usually incorporated in a PCB specification includes accounting details associated with the program system resource usage, such as CPU utilization, memory capacity employed, secondary file storage space, priority, user information, and other characterizing data. In addition, the PCB holds information about the process related to the I/O devices allocated to it, including a list of all the open files it is currently accessing. With the PCB, a process can be restarted from any of its passive states to the running state at any time.

11.3.3 PROCESS MANAGEMENT ACTIVITIES

The OS is responsible for a number of services associated with all the processes active in the system. Implicit in these services is the simple overarching task of keeping track of all the active processes on the system and the resources of the physical system (e.g., CPUs, memory blocks, files, etc.) that are allocated to the processes. Foremost among these management activities is the creation and termination of processes—both user and system types. The creation of a process, that is its instantiation, is in response to a call either by the system (including user command-line requests) or the user program giving initial data. A new PCB is produced by the OS for instantiation of the specific process, with fields filled as previously discussed. Other resources such as additional memory blocks, file accesses, and I/O sockets may also be allocated. The termination of a process by the OS involves the deletion of the PCB and other assigned resources to free them up for future computations.

To achieve higher efficiency by making better use of the physical resources of the computer system, the OS supports process context switching. This requires suspending and resuming a process. A process can be suspended for a number of reasons. One is multiprogramming, where one or a few computing resources are shared by a much larger number of active processes so all of them are operating concurrently, making progress toward their conclusion in sufficiently small time steps such that the user experiences a sense of continued operation, but the time steps are large enough to avoid the deleterious effects of the overhead time associated with the action of context switching. Another important factor motivating context switching is the avoidance of resource blocking in the presence of operations imposing extended delays. Such waiting times can greatly degrade the efficiency of system usage. This is predominantly associated with I/O tasks, such as reading a file from secondary storage or waiting for real-time user input from a standard I/O. Operations like this can take hundreds of milliseconds or multiple seconds depending on the specific nature of the requests and contention for shared resources by other processes. When a process is so engaged, the OS relinquishes its dedicated computing resources (e.g., processor core), putting the process state in memory while simultaneously allocating those same resources to another pending process waiting for access to make progress. Upon completion of the delaying service request of the original process, the OS resumes activation of the process in its turn, based on scheduling mechanisms and policies (discussed below).

Processes often work together, cooperating on a single program and sometimes sharing mutable data and other resources. To do so correctly they must occasionally synchronize, so computational work is done in the right order. For example, if two processes share information in memory, they must coordinate to ensure that one does not read data until the other has written it (read-before-write hazard), or conversely that one does not write to a memory location until the other process has accessed it (write-before-read hazard). The OS supports synchronization mechanisms such as barriers, semaphores, and mutexes, among others, by which two or more processes may order their respective computations to avoid these possible hazards.

Processes may directly communicate with each other, passing or exchanging messages or data streams. Mechanisms for conducting such message passing between concurrent processes are provided by the OS, including the user interface calls that give control to the user program. Sockets are one example of the class of constructs used for this purpose, and are found in many but not all modern OSs. This is one case where multiprogramming becomes critical. If one process is active (occupies the processor) but requires a message from another process that is suspended, without appropriate OS control a deadlock condition could occur, precluding forward progress.

11.3.4 SCHEDULING

At the heart of the process management services supported by the OS and described in earlier sections is the cross-cutting functionality of process scheduling: the determination of what processes are given the necessary physical resources to run and when they are allocated. With a number of processes active (running, pending, or suspended) at any one time and fewer executing resources than processes, this selection and control function is actually very difficult to perfect and has been the subject of countless research and engineering undertakings over many decades.

The job queue holds all processes, whatever their states, and any new process entering the system is put in the job queue by the OS. Only upon termination is a process eliminated from the job queue. At any one time a process may be ready for execution or waiting for an I/O device service call. The job queue consists of a number of subqueues (this varies somewhat among different OSs) in which processes may be temporarily held until specific requirements are satisfied. A representative structure of the job queue may include the following.

- Ready queue—holds pointer to PCBs of processes pending execution.
- Child queue—holds processes (PCB pointers) waiting for their respective child processes to terminate.
- Interrupt queue—includes processes waiting for interrupts to occur.
- Multiprogramming queue—processes that have used up their last timeslice and must delay a minimum amount of time prior to resuming execution.
- I/O queues—a queue for each I/O device holding PCBs of processes requiring that device.

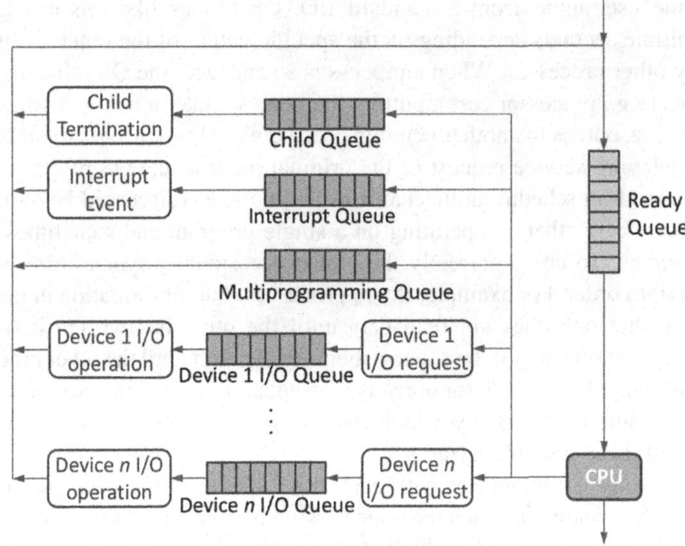

FIGURE 11.2

The job queue holds all processes, whatever their states, and any new process entering the system is put in the job queue by the OS. A representative job queue may include a ready queue, child queue, interrupt queue, multiprogramming queue, and I/O queues.

These are illustrated in Fig. 11.2. The OS is responsible for managing these (and potentially other) subqueues as part of the job queue structure. Each queue usually has two pointers, one to the head of the queue and one to its tail, if a first-in, first-out policy is employed, but other queue organizations are possible, such as a stack (last in, first out). The OS transfers the pointer to a process PCB from one queue to another as its condition state is altered.

The process scheduler incorporates a job scheduler where a job may comprise multiple processes. When many more jobs and their component processes exist than there are execution resources (e.g., processor cores), with total memory requirements that exceed the capacity of the physical memory (a common situation for a typical server), then many or perhaps a majority of the jobs must be spooled to secondary storage (typically hard disks) and only individually migrated to main memory when ready to be executed.

Typically, three job schedulers are employed to manage scheduling within the context of this memory hierarchy.

- Long-term scheduler—identifies processes or jobs from the spooler in mass storage to swap them into main memory in preparation for execution. Responsible for maintaining a balanced set of jobs, some I/O bound and some compute bound, to maintain even flow in all queues.
- Short-term scheduler—chooses the next process to be allocated computing resources for execution from those residing in the ready queue.
- Medium-term scheduler—swaps jobs or processes from main memory back into the mass-storage spooler when the priority of job ordering demands that main memory be freed up so new jobs can be included in the execution stream. Thus jobs may have to be swapped back on to the spooler on occasion.

As previously discussed, context switching is an OS function that moves a process state in and out of the execution resources. Specifically, when the short-term scheduler is preparing to execute a process that is in the ready queue, the OS must first copy the state of the prior process that had been using the resources intended for the new process into the first process' PCB. Then the context of the new process in its PCB is loaded into the execution resources, such as processor registers.

11.4 THREADS

Threads present another level of parallelism control within a process. While processes are said to provide coarse-grain parallelism, threads provide the means of realizing medium-grain parallelism, which may give more parallelism, better scalability, and possibly shorter time to solution. Sometimes threads are referred to as "lightweight processes", but this text avoids this, as there are specific distinctions between threads and processes that distinguish their usage and effects. Finally, processes and threads map very nicely on to modern architectures using many nodes, each with a number of processor cores. A process can occupy a full node of cores with threads running on individual cores.

The thread state is reminiscent of that of a process included in the PCB, but is generally less complex. The thread state will include:

- a designator of the process of which it is a part
- a program counter indicating the next instruction to be executed by the thread
- a stack pointer to the frame of the pages directly related to the thread
- register contents.

This context data must be swapped in and out of the hardware resources as one thread is replaced by another in the executing processor cores.

There are two general categories of threads. Threads directly managed by the OS, as discussed above, are known as "kernel threads". The OS allocates specific kernel threads to underlying hardware processor cores. Because the OS is involved in the direct manipulation of the kernel thread, the overhead of its management is significant, even if less than the management of processes. The other kind is the "user thread", sometimes referred to as "runtime threads". These are not directly managed by the OS but rather by a runtime software system in user space. The overheads are smaller and the runtime system knows more about what the user job wants to do and how to do it better. The relationship between the two kinds of threads is that the runtime system allocates user threads to individual kernel threads. Usually (but not always) there is one kernel thread instantiated by the OS for each processor core. Except in the case of interrupts or multiprogramming, the kernel thread stays relatively static in this mapping, so few context switches of kernel threads are required. The runtime system allocates the kernel threads made available to it to the user threads for which it is responsible. There are several ways that it can do this, illustrated in Fig. 11.3. For example, all user threads may be assigned to a single kernel thread, sharing it one at a time. This is known as "all to one". In this case no parallelism is exploited within the application, but rather the kernel threads are running different jobs for job parallelism. A second case is when the runtime system may simply assign one user thread to each of multiple available kernel threads. In this case overheads are low and parallelism is exploited but no dynamic control is used, as might be necessary with irregular user threads. This is known as "one to one". The most general form of mapping of user threads to kernel threads is when the set of user threads is dynamically and possibly adaptively assigned to kernel threads as the workload requires and kernel threads become available. The policy guiding such a "many-to-many" strategy can become quite complex and is a subject of continued study.

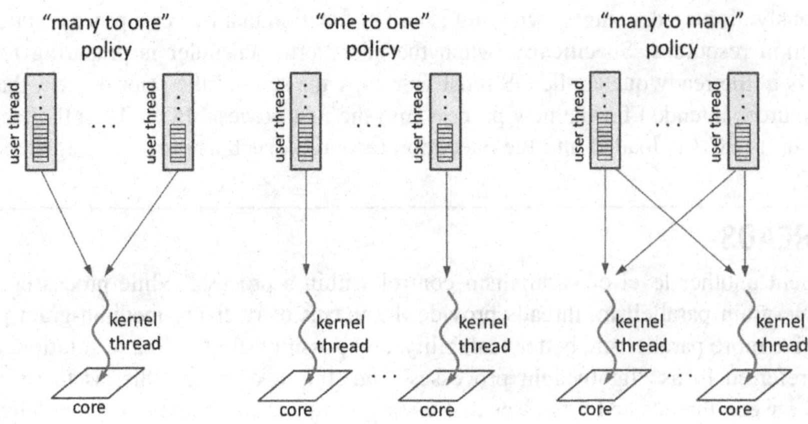

FIGURE 11.3

The runtime system allocates the kernel threads made available to it to the user threads for which it is responsible in several different ways.

11.5 MEMORY MANAGEMENT

While it may appear from the preceding text that the most important responsibility of the OS is management of execution resources and scheduling of jobs, processes, and threads on them, it can be argued that the management of the memory hierarchy is equally important and if anything more complex and demanding of OS functionality. Part of this is due to the disparity between the clock rates of the processor cores (complementary metal-oxide semiconductor technology) and the main memory (DRAM technology), which is between one and two orders of magnitude. With the separation of processor logic and main memory banks (the von Neumann bottleneck), full time to completion of memory access by cores can be between 100 and 200 processor core cycles. As discussed in Chapters 2 and 6 on architecture, modern computers and HPC systems incorporate multiple levels of storage to mitigate the latencies and bandwidth constraints imposed by this structure, and these are managed in part by the OS.

Memory management controls what data is in the main memory and registers at any particular time. Such data is usually stored in secondary storage organized in directories, files, and special blocks employed by the virtual memory page backing store. The OS ensures that all data needed for a scheduled process is in the main memory, as well as instructions for the executing code. The OS memory management subsystem maintains the tables (reference tables) that map the virtually addressed pages (discussed later) to the physical pages of memory and provide means for virtual address (to physical) translation. Memory management is an important part of achieving high utilization of the processor cores by maintaining the right data most likely to be accessed in the main memory. To achieve these goals, the OS memory management supports a multiplicity of activities, including control of allocation of physical memory to instantiated processes and deciding which memory pages should be swapped between memory and secondary storage to assign and reacquire memory space. Throughout these activities the OS must maintain its ability to support virtual address translation. This section expands on some of these key points.

11.5.1 VIRTUAL MEMORY

Virtual memory is a powerful abstraction for naming memory blocks independent of their physical location, supported by the OS. It is implemented by the memory management part of the OS. Virtual memory controls the relationship and mapping of the logical (virtual) address of a page of data to the location of physical data storage, which can be either main memory or secondary storage (e.g., hard disks). The implementation of virtual memory over the history of computing has yielded several important advantages over direct user control of physical memory. Originally, with the amount of main memory being relatively small, the use of mass storage to give the appearance of a larger storage space than just the physical memory greatly simplified the programmer's task while allowing portability of code across systems of different scale, type, and generation. Over time and the use of multiprogramming and multitasking where a multitude of processes and jobs would be being performed concurrently, virtual memory systems provided protection of memory usage by different processes, giving each process its own virtual address structure and making sure that one process did not interfere with the data in another process. Virtual memory also allowed the OS to overlap the sequence of different processes, so while one process is executing another process memory content can be read into memory and possibly a previous process results are read at the same time, thus minimizing the lag between the execution of successive jobs.

11.5.2 VIRTUAL PAGE ADDRESSES

There are a number of ways to organize data for use and storage. Among these is the simple concept of a "page", which is a fixed-length contiguous block of data that can be mapped on to an equivalent-sized block of physical memory or similar space on secondary storage. Paging allows a process to consist of a collection of fixed-size blocks. Each page has a virtual address. Every unit of data (i.e., bytes, words) within a page is identified by the virtual address of the page, and by an offset index from the starting location of the page to the position of the data within the page. The virtual address of the page is simply a page number. The virtual address of the page, once assigned by the OS, remains a constant independent of whether the virtually addressed page is stored in main memory or secondary storage. The medium-term scheduler may cause a page and other pages related to a process to swap in and out of secondary storage from main memory. A virtual page may reside in different physical memory pages throughout the computation, as determined by the OS memory management function.

11.5.3 VIRTUAL ADDRESS TRANSLATION

The OS incorporates a *page table* which is central to the method for associating virtual page addresses (or page numbers) to physical locations within the main memory or secondary storage. The page table has one entry per page. This entry is determined by the assigned page number as an offset within the page table (the value of the offset cannot exceed the length of the page). The page table entry for a particular virtual page stores the memory frame number of a page frame (or physical page) within the main memory. A request to memory for data can always be located through the page table. When the virtual page migrates in physical space, its respective entry in the page table is updated by the OS.

While this works logically and is a necessary component of OS memory management, it alone is insufficient to deliver performance. Every access request using the page table requires an OS function call, which is quite time consuming. For each instruction issue, which is about every processor core cycle, there must be a load of the instruction from the memory system. In addition, operational data needs to be loaded in the order of a quarter of the time (this varies per application workload). So the page table alone is inadequate to provide performance-oriented memory access in a virtually paged system.

The translation lookaside buffer (TLB), illustrated in Fig. 11.4, is an architecture means to deliver much of this needed performance, at least under favorable conditions. The TLB is a special-purpose cache that provides high-speed mapping of virtual page numbers to main memory frame numbers for recently used stored data. This in turn delivers very fast data access for memory loads and stores. Like a cache, the TLB exploits temporal locality where the physical addresses of recently used virtual pages are stored. The TLB has an associative access hardware that enables fast address translation and thus data access. Of course, regular data and instruction L1 caches provide most data access requests in one or two cycles as well, so on a good day (microcycle) virtually addressed data can be loaded in one or two cycles. Only when there is a TLB miss, when a particular virtual page number is not found in the TLB, does a page table access take place, with its significant overhead. In this case the OS accesses the page table, determines the correct frame number, and updates the TLB, at which point the memory access can continue as usual.

It is possible when locating a virtual page as a physical frame in main memory that there is no matching memory frame associated with the desired virtual page. This is referred to as a "page fault". It is a function of the OS to attempt to minimize page faults, as the cost of encountering one can be

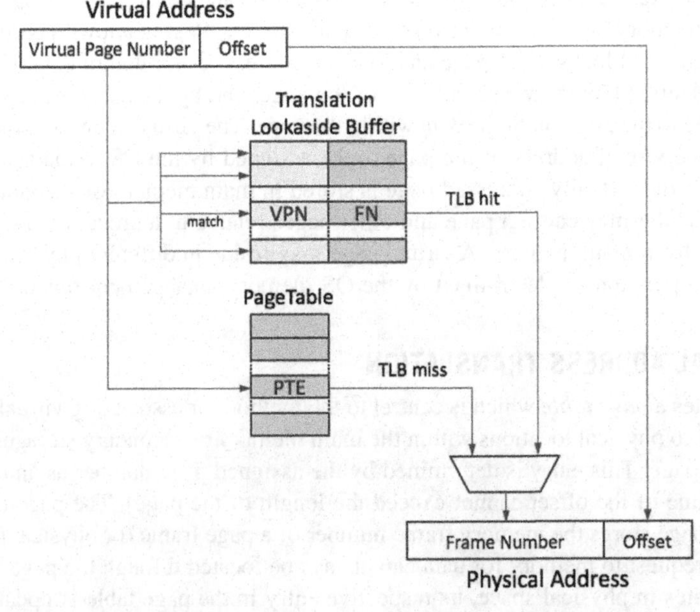

FIGURE 11.4

The translation lookaside buffer (TLB) is a special-purpose cache that operates to provide high-speed mapping of virtual page numbers to main memory frame numbers for recently used stored data.

significant. The combination of OS overheads and the transfer of a frame from secondary storage to main memory can take tens to hundreds of milliseconds. The OS bringing frames in from secondary storage when needed is known as *demand paging*. OS policies are applied to minimize the page faults. But programmers can help the system operate more efficiently in this regard by constructing workflows such that they take best advantage of data reuse and thereby limit the TLB misses, cache misses, and page faults.

Virtual-memory OSs provide a seamless way to take advantage of secondary storage without explicit user intervention through process and page swapping. In terms of user productivity this can be a very good thing; in terms of system performance it can be a very bad thing. The OS provides a powerful functionality in the form of a directory and file system that enable users to store and manage their data in a nonvolatile form. Indeed, a user's perspective of a supercomputer is largely enabled by the file system through the user interface, whether command line or point-and-click windows. The OS file system is so important to HPC that Chapter 18 is dedicated to this capability.

11.6 SUMMARY AND OUTCOMES OF CHAPTER 11

- The OS owns the supercomputer.
- An OS is a persistent program that controls the execution of application programs. It is the primary interface between user applications and system hardware.
- The primary function of the OS is to exploit the hardware resources of one or more processors, provide a set of services to system users, and manage secondary memory and I/O devices, including the file system.
- Resources managed by the OS are the processors and their integrated cores, the main memory of the systems out of which the cores work, I/O modules, and the system bus.
- User and system programs that are executing are made up of instances called "processes", which are instantiations of program procedures.
- Many processes may be operating concurrently under a single OS.
- OS memory management is responsible for address translation between the virtual addresses blocks of program data, called pages, and blocks of physical storage, called frames.
- The OS is responsible for the users' data and programs, organized in files through a hierarchy of named directories.
- The OS is responsible for managing all sources and destinations of data flow in and out of the computer it supports.
- The OS is responsible for a number of services associated with all the processes active in the system.
- At the heart of the process management services supported by the OS is the cross-cutting functionality of process scheduling: the determination of what processes are provided the necessary physical resources to run and when are they allocated.
- Threads present another level of parallelism control within a process.
- Virtual memory is a powerful abstraction for naming of memory blocks independent of their physical location, supported by the OS.
- The OS incorporates a page table, which is central to the method for associating virtual page addresses (or page numbers) to physical locations within the main memory or secondary storage.

11.7 EXERCISES

1. Explain the differences between a TLB miss, a cache miss, and a page fault. What are the performance consequences of each?
2. What is the purpose of the virtual memory address?
3. What types of processes are kept in the ready queue? Which types of processes are not in the ready queue?
4. What is the difference between OS threads and processes? Can processes be preempted? Can threads be preempted? Are threads confined to a process?
5. Is the PCB affected by a thread context switch? Explain.

CHAPTER

VISUALIZATION

12

CHAPTER OUTLINE

12.1 INTRODUCTION

Supercomputer applications frequently produce enormous amounts of output data that must be analyzed and presented to understand the application outcome and draw conclusions on the results. This process, frequently referred to as "visualization", can itself require supercomputing resources and is a fundamental modality of supercomputer usage.

Some of the principal reasons for visualizing data resulting from running an application on a supercomputer include debugging, exploring data, statistical hypothesis testing, and preparing presentation graphics. In some cases the output from running an application on a supercomputer will be something as simple as a single file with comma-separated values. However, it is much more likely that the output will be in a special parallel input/output (I/O) library format, like one of those mentioned in Chapter 10, to manage and coordinate the simultaneous output from multiple compute nodes to a single file.

This chapter discusses four key foundational concepts frequently needed as part of high performance computing (HPC) visualization: streamlines, isosurfaces, volume rendering through ray tracing, and mesh tessellations. Visualization is then practically explored through the use of five different visualization tools that are frequently used in the context of HPC: Gnuplot [1], Matplotlib [2], the Visualization Toolkit (VTK) library [3], ParaView [4], and VisIt [5]. Three of these tools (VTK, ParaView and VisIt) already incorporate the ability to use distributed memory parallel processing to accelerate the visualization process itself.

High Performance Computing. https://doi.org/10.1016/B978-0-12-420158-3.00012-5

12.2 FOUNDATIONAL VISUALIZATION CONCEPTS

Among the most frequently used concepts in scientific visualization are streamlines, isosurfaces, volume rendering through ray tracing, and mesh tessellations. Streamlines, like those illustrated in Fig. 12.1, take a vector field as input and show curves that are tangent to the vector field. Streamlines may be thought of as showing the trajectory that a massless particle would travel in the input vector field. While the starting point for each streamline can be specified explicitly, it is more common to use random starting points seeded inside a small geometric object like a sphere or a cube.

An isosurface, illustrated in Fig. 12.2, is a surface that connects points which have the same value. Isosurfaces are frequently used in medical visualization to extract surfaces that have the same density, like that seen in a 3D ultrasound. An isosurface is the 3D analogue to a contour line in two-dimensional (2D) visualizations.

Volume rendering through ray tracing, illustrated in Fig. 12.3, is where for each pixel a ray is used to sample the volume through which it passes. Based on a provided color transfer function, the ray is shaded while an opacity function alters the transparency of the data in the volume. This type of volume rendering can reveal internal structures in data, and produce blurry or sharp edges depending on the opacity function chosen.

A mesh tessellation, seen in Fig. 12.4, is where a collection of data points and their connectivities to other data points are visualized through a set of polygons, frequently triangles or quadrilaterals in 2D and tetrahedra or hexahedra in 3D. The meshes often provide important statistical information about a simulation, including error bounds and mesh adaptivity, while also visually conveying the scale at which simulation features are resolved.

These foundational visualization concepts are usually not implemented directly by the application developer, but rather accessed in the context of an existing visualization toolkit or library. Some of the most common visualization toolkits and libraries for HPC are discussed in the following sections.

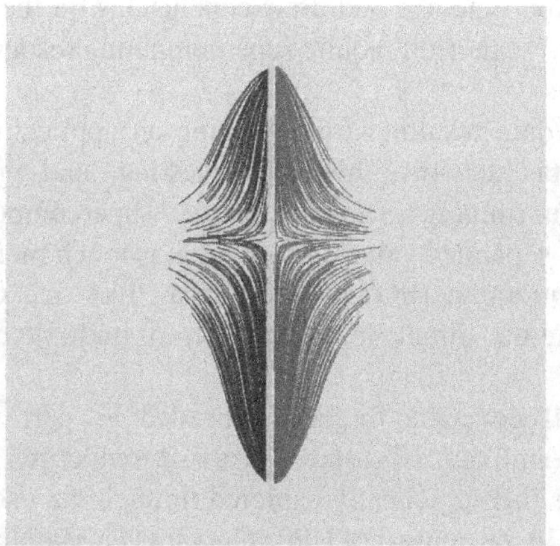

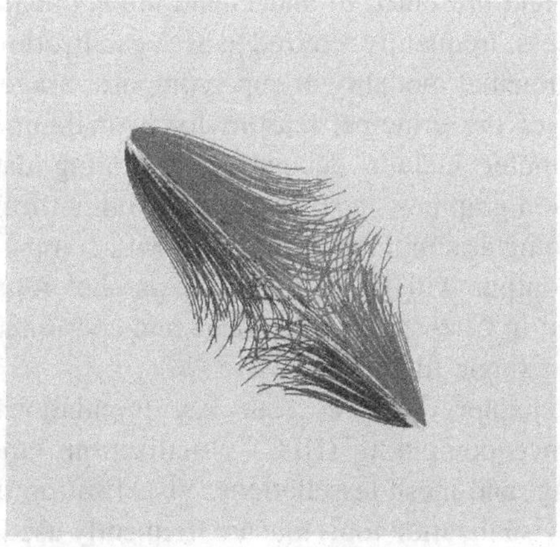

FIGURE 12.1

Streamline example using the gradient of the function $f(x,y,z) = 2550 \sin(100x) \sin(30y) \cos(40z)$ as input. Two different three-dimensional (3D) views are provided.

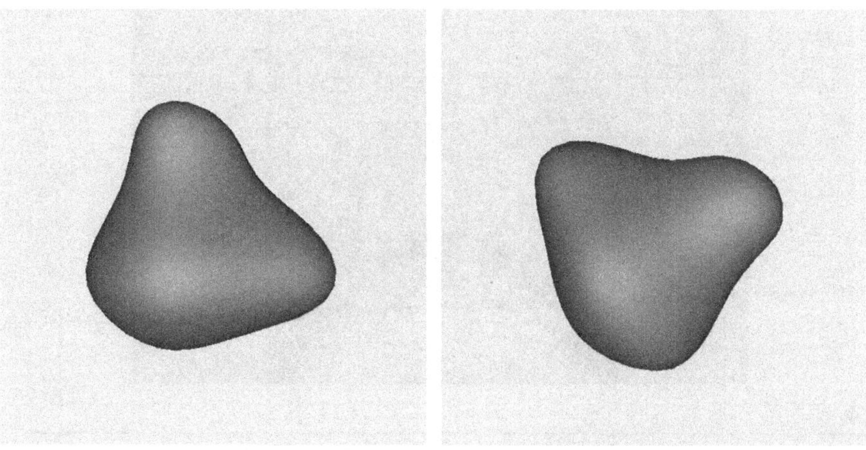

FIGURE 12.2

Isosurface example of the function $f(x,y,z) = 2550 \sin(10x) \sin(10y) \cos(10z)$ as input with the isosurface value set at 200. Two different 3-D views are provided.

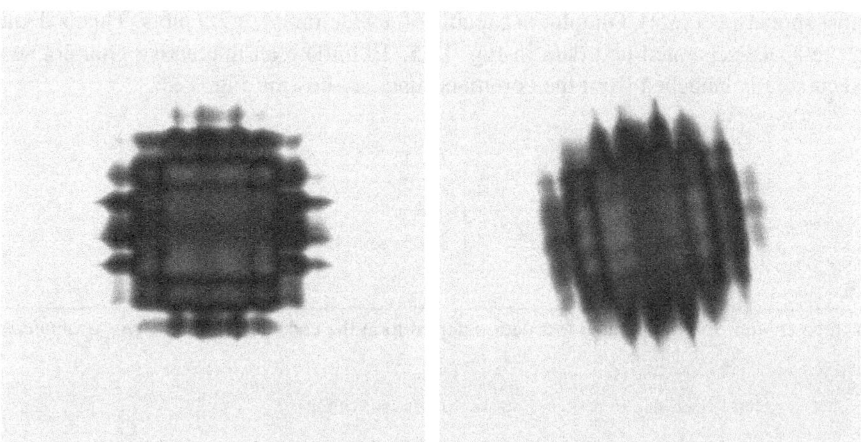

FIGURE 12.3

Example of low-resolution volume rendering of the function $f(x,y,z) = 2550 \sin(50x) \sin(50y) \cos(50z)$. The color and opacity map were chosen arbitrarily. Two different 3D views are provided.

12.3 GNUPLOT

Gnuplot [1] is a freely available and open-source command-line-driven visualization tool that includes support for both 2D and 3D plots. It has been around since 1986 and is found in most Linux distributions and on supercomputer login nodes. Several other independent applications use Gnuplot for

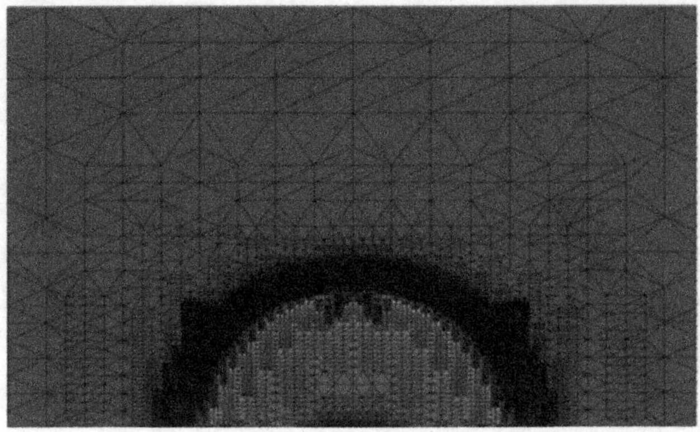

FIGURE 12.4

An example of a 2D mesh tessellation for an adaptive mesh shockwave simulation. The mesh, consisting of black lines, is visualized on top of a 2D color plot of the shockwave density.

graphics output, including GNU Octave [6], which features a high-level programming language very similar to Matlab [7].

Like most spreadsheet tools, Gnuplot is capable of a wide range of 2D plots. This is demonstrated here using the space-separated text data in Fig. 12.5. To initiate an interactive Gnuplot session, the *gnuplot* executable is launched from the command line, as shownin Fig. 12.6.

```
1 1 -1
2 2 -2
3 3 -3
4 4 -7
```

FIGURE 12.5

Example of three-column space-separated text data, referred to in the code examples as "*gnu_example.dat*".

```
[Matthews-MacBook-Pro-2:data andersmw$ gnuplot

        G N U P L O T
        Version 5.0 patchlevel 5    last modified 2016-10-02

        Copyright (C) 1986-1993, 1998, 2004, 2007-2016
        Thomas Williams, Colin Kelley and many others

        gnuplot home:     http://www.gnuplot.info
        faq, bugs, etc:   type "help FAQ"
        immediate help:   type "help"  (plot window: hit 'h')

Terminal type set to 'aqua'
gnuplot>
```

FIGURE 12.6

Launching an interactive Gnuplot session.

The *plot* command is the main command for 2D plots in Gnuplot, and takes the form of:

```
plot [ranges] <plot member> [, <plot member>, <plot member>]
```

If no ranges are specified, a default is computed based on the specific plot member. A plot member may be a predefined function like sin(x) or data read from a file, like that given in Fig. 12.5. Each plot member may have its plotting style altered using a predefined plotting style, such as *linespoints* or *circles*. Referring to the data in Fig. 12.5 as the file called "*gnu_example.dat*", three different ways of plotting with Gnuplot are illustrated in Figs. 12.7–12.9.

```
plot "gnu_example.dat" using 1:2 with linespoints
```

```
plot "gnu_example.dat" using 3:2 with linespoints
```

```
plot [0:4][-5:5] "gnu_example.dat" using 1:2 with linespoints title "data", sin(x)
title "sin(x)"
```

Gnuplot is also capable of 3D plots using the *splot* command, which shares most of the syntax of the 2D *plot* command. When plotting space-separated text data like that in Fig. 12.5, the first column gives the x values, the second the y values, and the third column is the value of the function at that point. An example of this is illustrated in Fig. 12.10.

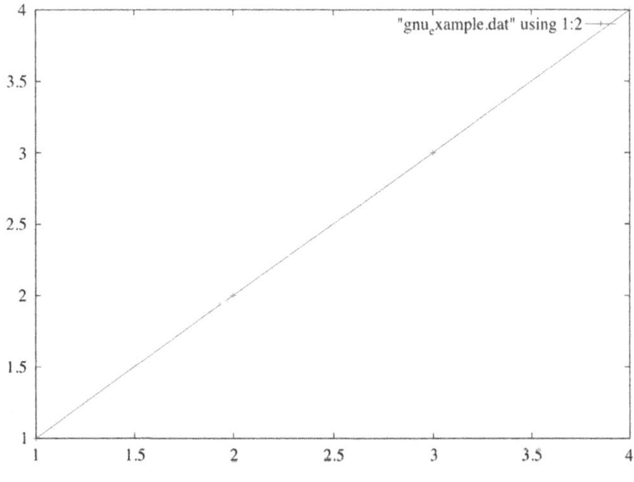

FIGURE 12.7

The first column of the data in Fig. 12.5 is used as the x values and the second column as the y values. Default ranges are generated.

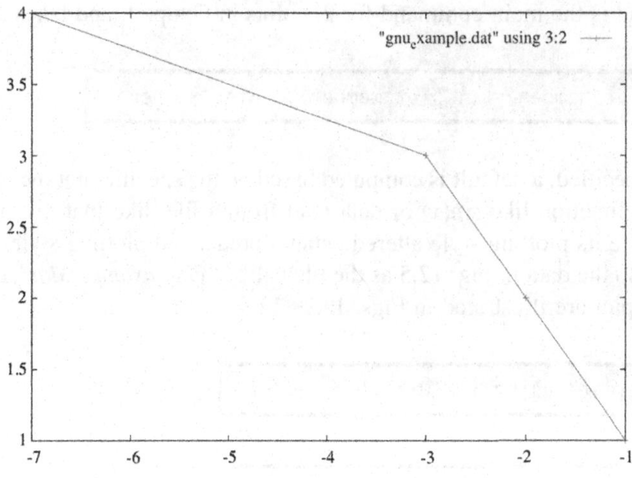

FIGURE 12.8

The third column of the data in Fig. 12.5 is used as the x values and the second column as the y values. Default ranges are generated.

```
splot "gnu_example.dat" with linespoints title "data", 10*exp(-(x-3)**2-(y-3)**2)
title "gaussian"
```

Among the many strengths of Gnuplot is the easy-to-use documentation accessed via the *help* command in interactive mode.

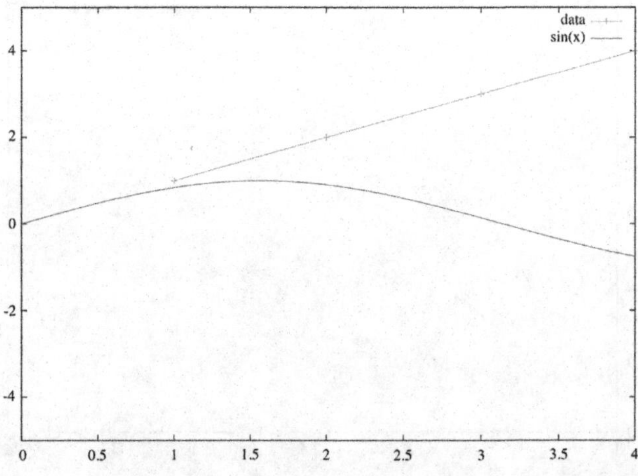

FIGURE 12.9

Plot containing the data from Fig. 12.5 as well as a plot of sin(x) with specified ranges.

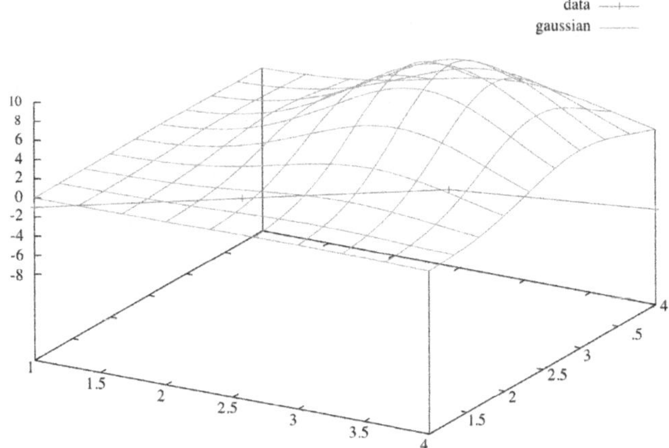

FIGURE 12.10

An example of a Gnuplot-generated 3D plot showing both the data in Fig. 12.1 and $f(x, y) = 10e^{-(x-3)^2-(y-3)^2}$.

12.4 MATPLOTLIB

Matplotlib [2] is a freely available and open-source Python language-based visualization tool with an interface that is similar to the look and feel of Matlab. It relies upon the NumPy extension to Python as a required dependency for array and matrix support. Like Gnuplot, Matplotlib is frequently found already installed on many supercomputers and is easily integrated into existing HPC application code bases for application-specific visualizations. Python is frequently used in scientific visualization, and in the case of Matplotlib using Python is a requirement. While the Python syntax is fairly simple and intuitive, a quick overview is given in an online guide [8].

In interactive mode, Matplotlib is initialized by launching Python and loading NumPy and Matplotlib, as illustrated below:

```
$ python
>>> import matplotlib.pyplot as plot
>>> import numpy
```

Once Matplotlib has been started in interactive mode, the data in Fig. 12.5 can be plotted interactively in a way analogous to that used with Gnuplot in Fig. 12.7. The Matplotlib example is shown in Fig. 12.11.

```
>>> data = numpy.loadtxt(“gnu_example.dat”,skiprows=0)
>>> xvalues = data.T[0]
>>> yvalues = data.T[1]
>>> l1, = plot.plot(xvalues,yvalues)
>>> plot.show()
```

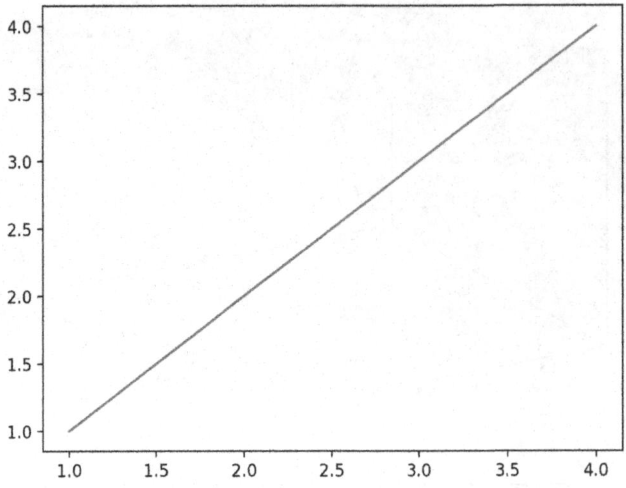

FIGURE 12.11

An interactive plot of the first and second columns of the data in Fig. 12.5 using Matplotlib. This is analogous to the Gnuplot version shown in Fig. 12.7. The text file "*gnu_example.dat*" is read into the data variable using the loadtxt method from NumPy. The data is rotated upon read-in so the data variable is transposed using the "T" operation and the columns are loaded into variables *xvalues* and *yvalues* for plotting.

Matplotlib easily integrates with the data-storage libraries explored in Chapter 10, including HDF5 and netCDF through their respective Python bindings. Data can then be easily manipulated using NumPy and plotted using Matplotlib. This is illustrated in Fig. 12.12.

In Fig. 12.12 the HDF5 dataset that was illustrated in Chapter 10 Fig. 10.7, *particles.h5*, is read into Python and the *x* and *y* values of the particles are plotted using Matplotlib. To do this, the Python bindings to HDF5 are loaded using the *import h5py* command in addition to loading Matplotlib and NumPy, as illustrated in the python script in Code 12.1.

```
import h5py
import numpy as np
import matplotlib.pyplot as plot

f = h5py.File("particles.h5","r")
dataset = f["particle data"]
xvalues = np.zeros(dataset.shape) #initializing memory
yvalues = np.zeros(dataset.shape) #initializing memory
for idx,item in enumerate(dataset):
  xvalues[idx] = item[0]
  yvalues[idx] = item[1]

l1, = plot.plot(xvalues,yvalues)
plot.show()
```

Code 12.1. Python code to plot the *x* and *y* values of the particle data stored in the "*particles.h5*" file created in Chapter 10.

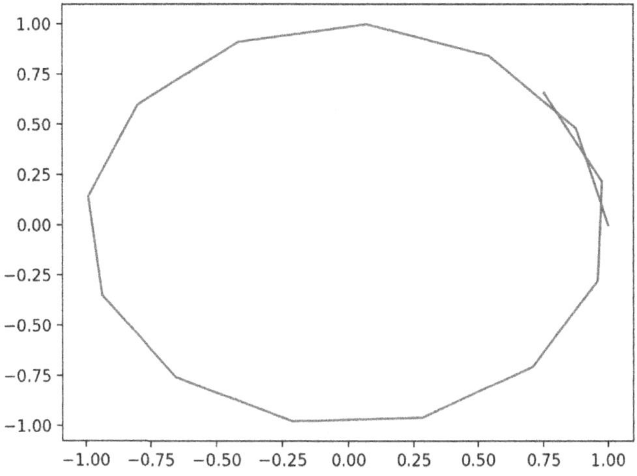

FIGURE 12.12

Matplotlib plotting the *x* and *y* coordinates of the particles data written in HDF5 format in Fig. 10.7 of Chapter 10. Matplotlib integrates well with the parallel I/O libraries discussed in Chapter 10.

The HDF5 file can then be loaded using the *h5py.File* method. A specific dataset in the file can be accessed by using the dataset name as a key to the file; in this case the dataset name is "particle data". A list of all datasets present in an HDF5 file can be found using the *h5ls* utility as well. The values in the dataset are copied to the appropriate *xvalues* and *yvalues* NumPy arrays and plotted, just as was done in Fig. 12.11.

Like Matlab, Matplotlib provides a number of tools for visualizing sparse matrices. One of the most common of these is the ability to plot the sparsity pattern of a matrix. This is illustrated in Code 12.2 and Fig. 12.13 for the matrix "*bcspwr06.mtx*" from the Matrix Market collection [9], using the matrix market reader provided in the SciPy ecosystem [10].

```
1 import scipy.io as sio
2 from matplotlib.pyplot import figure, show
3 import numpy
4
5 A = sio.mmread("bcspwr06.mtx");
6
7 fig = figure()
8 ax1 = fig.add_subplot(111)
9
10 ax1.spy(A,markersize=1)
11 show()
```

Code 12.2. Python script illustrating the ability to plot the sparsity pattern of a matrix. The matrix in this case, *bcspwr06.mtx*, comes from the Matrix Market collection [9]. The resulting sparsity pattern plot, producing using the spy method in line 8, is shown in Fig. 12.13.

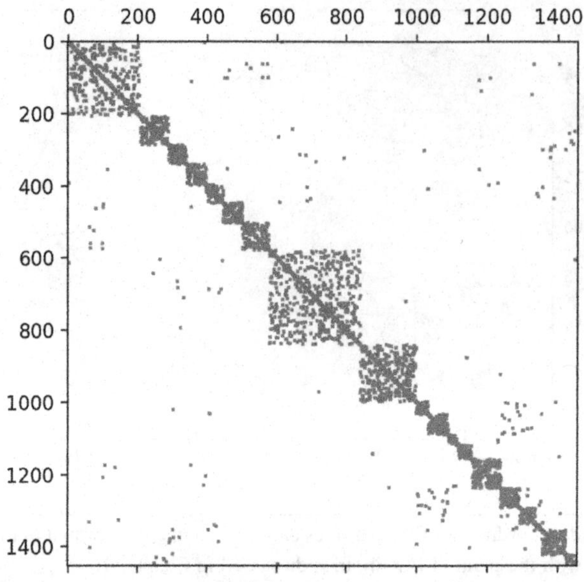

FIGURE 12.13

The sparsity pattern of a matrix plotted using Code 12.2.

Unlike Gnuplot, Matplotlib itself does not support 3D surface plots or other 3D-type visualizations. However, there are extension modules that can enable 3D plotting using Matplotlib, including mplot3d [11]. Matplotlib plots are also capable of integration within one of the most important and widely used libraries for 3D computer graphics, the VTK.

12.5 THE VISUALIZATION TOOLKIT

One of the most important open-source visualization libraries for HPC users is the VTK [3]. The VTK provides many 3D visualization algorithms, parallel computing support, and interfaces to interpreted languages like Python, which are used as examples in this section. The VTK is also used in several full visualization tools, including ParaView and VisIt, which are illustrated later in this chapter.

The most recent release of VTK is 8.0 and is conceptually laid out around the idea of a data pipeline incorporating maps with keys and values for passing information through the pipeline, objects for storing source data, algorithms, and filters, and a class for connecting together and executing the pipeline. In VTK terminology, "mappers" convert data into graphics primitives while "actors" alter the visual properties of those graphics. The example shown in Fig. 12.14 and Code 12.3 reads the HDF5 data "*particles.h5*" from Chapter 10 and plots a line in 3D through the points in the HDF5 dataset using VTK.

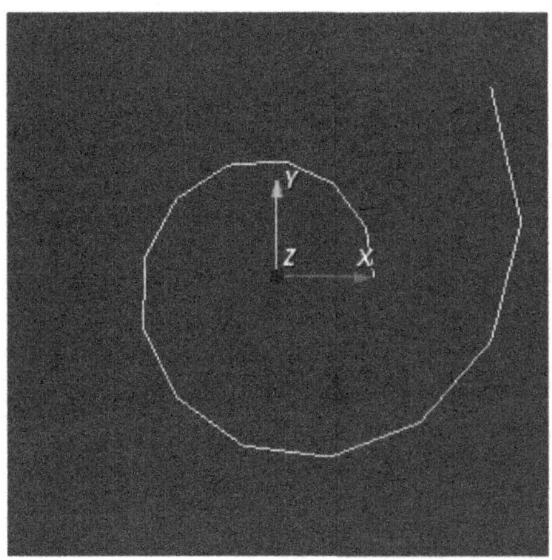

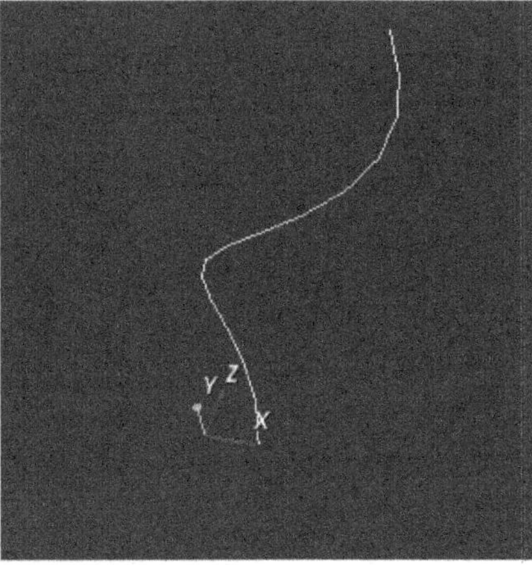

FIGURE 12.14

Two 3D plots of the particle locations found in *particles.h5* from Chapter 10 using VTK. The corresponding code for this visualization is found in Code 12.3.

```
import h5py     # the HDF5 Python interface
import vtk     # the VTK Python interface
f = h5py.File("particles.h5","r")  # read in the file "particles.h5"
dataset = f["particle data"]  # access the dataset "particle data" in "particles.h5"
points = vtk.vtkPoints()
points.SetNumberOfPoints(dataset.shape[0])  # create a list of points for particle locations
for idx,item in enumerate(dataset):
points.SetPoint(idx,dataset[idx][0],dataset[idx][1],dataset[idx][2]) # assign values

lines = vtk.vtkCellArray()
lines.InsertNextCell(dataset.shape[0])
for idx in range(0,dataset.shape[0]):  # assign the connectivity between the points
lines.InsertCellPoint(idx)

polygon = vtk.vtkPolyData()  # create a polygon geometric structure
polygon.SetPoints(points)
polygon.SetLines(lines)

polygonMapper = vtk.vtkPolyDataMapper()  # map the polygonal data to graphics
polygonMapper.SetInputData(polygon)
polygonMapper.Update()

axes = vtk.vtkAxesActor()     # create some axes
polygonActor = vtk.vtkActor()     # Manage the rendering of the mapper
polygonActor.SetMapper(polygonMapper)
```

```
renderer = vtk.vtkRenderer()      # The viewport on the screen
renderer.AddActor(polygonActor)
renderer.AddActor(axes)
renderer.SetBackground(0.1, 0.2, 0.3)

renderer.ResetCamera()

renderWindow = vtk.vtkRenderWindow()
renderWindow.AddRenderer(renderer)

interactive_ren = vtk.vtkRenderWindowInteractor()  # enable interactivity with visualization
interactive_ren.SetRenderWindow(renderWindow)
interactive_ren.Initialize()
interactive_ren.Start()
```

Code 12.3. A Python script to read in and visualize the 3D trajectory of the particle data stored in *particles.h5* from Chapter 10 using VTK. The resulting visualization is seen in Fig. 12.14.

All other major scientific visualization components are available in VTK. Isosurfaces of 3D data can be produced using vtkContourFilter, as illustrated in Fig. 12.15. In VTK, filters like vtkContourFilter are optionally applied in the pipeline before applying mappers and actors, as illustrated in Code 12.4.

FIGURE 12.15

An isosurface in VTK using Code 12.4.

```
1 import vtk # the VTK Python interface
2
3 rt = vtk.vtkRTAnalyticSource()  # data for testing
4
5 contour_filter = vtk.vtkContourFilter()  # isosurface filter
6 contour_filter.SetInputConnection(rt.GetOutputPort())
7 contour_filter.SetValue(0, 190)
8
9 mapper = vtk.vtkPolyDataMapper()
10 mapper.SetInputConnection(contour_filter.GetOutputPort())
11
12 actor = vtk.vtkActor()
13 actor.SetMapper(mapper)
14
15 renderer = vtk.vtkRenderer()
16 renderer.AddActor(actor)
17
18 renderer.SetBackground(0.9, 0.9, 0.9)
19
20 renderWindow = vtk.vtkRenderWindow()
21 renderWindow.AddRenderer(renderer)
22 renderWindow.SetSize(600, 600)
23
24 interactive_ren = vtk.vtkRenderWindowInteractor()  # enable interactivity with
   visualization
25 interactive_ren.SetRenderWindow(renderWindow)
26 interactive_ren.Initialize()
27 interactive_ren.Start()
```

Code 12.4. Example isosurface using the ContourFilter filter; the value of the isosurface is set at line 7. Test data was provided using vtkRTAnalyticSource in line 3. The resulting visualization is shown in Fig. 12.15.

One way to execute volume rendering through ray tracing in VTK is using the SmartVolume-Mapper class illustrated in Code 12.5 and Fig. 12.16. In this example, a color transfer function and an opacity map are passed as properties to shade the rays appropriately as they pass through the volume.

```
import vtk

rt = vtk.vtkRTAnalyticSource()
rt.Update()

image = rt.GetOutput()
range = image.GetScalarRange()

mapper = vtk.vtkSmartVolumeMapper()     # volume rendering
mapper.SetInputConnection(rt.GetOutputPort())
```

```
11 mapper.SetRequestedRenderModeToRayCast()
12
13 color = vtk.vtkColorTransferFunction()
14 color.AddRGBPoint(range[0], 0.0, 0.0, 1.0)
15 color.AddRGBPoint((range[0] + range[1]) * 0.75, 0.0, 1.0, 0.0)
16 color.AddRGBPoint(range[1], 1.0, 0.0, 0.0)
17
18 opacity = vtk.vtkPiecewiseFunction()
19 opacity.AddPoint(range[0], 0.0)
20 opacity.AddPoint((range[0] + range[1]) * 0.5, 0.0)
21 opacity.AddPoint(range[1], 1.0)
22
23 properties = vtk.vtkVolumeProperty()
24 properties.SetColor(color)
25 properties.SetScalarOpacity(opacity)
26 properties.SetInterpolationTypeToLinear()
27 properties.ShadeOn()
28
29 actor = vtk.vtkVolume()
30 actor.SetMapper(mapper)
31 actor.SetProperty(properties)
32
33 renderer = vtk.vtkRenderer()
34 renderWindow = vtk.vtkRenderWindow()
35 renderWindow.AddRenderer(renderer)
36
37 renderer.AddViewProp(actor)
38 renderer.ResetCamera()
39 renderer.SetBackground(0.9, 0.9, 0.9)
40 renderWindow.SetSize(600, 600)
41
42 interactive_ren = vtk.vtkRenderWindowInteractor()
43 interactive_ren.SetRenderWindow(renderWindow)
44 interactive_ren.Initialize()
45 interactive_ren.Start()
```

Code 12.5. Example volume rendering using VTK. Test data was provided using vtkRTAnalyticSource at line 3. Opacity and color map settings were made based on the image scalar range. The resulting visualization is shown in Fig. 12.16.

Streamlines in VTK are accomplished using the StreamTracer class. Streamlines require vector data as input, but VTK also provides a means to take a gradient of scalar data and then assign output as a vector which can be visualized as a streamline. This entire pipeline is demonstrated in Code 12.6 and Fig. 12.17. The starting point for a single streamline can be specified, as illustrated in the comment on line 31 of Code 12.6, or a streamline seed region can be created for starting multiple streamlines, as illustrated in lines 23–27.

FIGURE 12.16

An example volume rendering in VTK using Code 12.5.

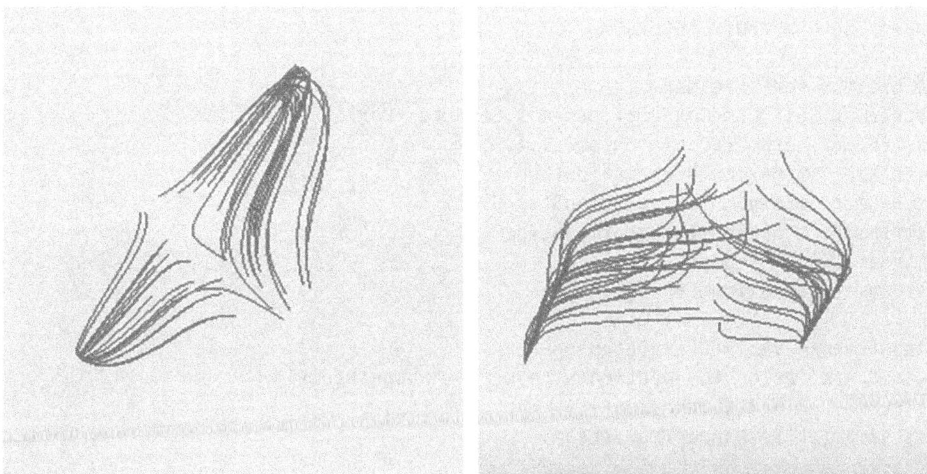

FIGURE 12.17

Streamlines in VTK using the gradient of the data shown in Figs. 12.15 and 12.16. The code that produced these streamlines in VTK is shown in Code 12.6.

```
import vtk

rt = vtk.vtkRTAnalyticSource()  # data for testing
rt.Update()

#calculate the gradient of the test data
gradient = vtk.vtkImageGradient()
gradient.SetDimensionality(3)
gradient.SetInputConnection(rt.GetOutputPort())
gradient.Update()

# Make a vector
aa = vtk.vtkAssignAttribute()
aa.Assign("SCALARS","VECTORS","POINT_DATA")
aa.SetInputConnection(gradient.GetOutputPort())
aa.Update()

# Create Stream Lines
rk = vtk.vtkRungeKutta45()
streamer = vtk.vtkStreamTracer()
streamer.SetInputConnection(aa.GetOutputPort())

# seed the stream lines
seeds = vtk.vtkPointSource()
seeds.SetRadius(1)
seeds.SetCenter(1,1.1,0.5)
seeds.SetNumberOfPoints(50)

# options for streamer
streamer.SetSourceConnection(seeds.GetOutputPort())
#streamer.SetStartPosition(1.0,1.1,0.5)
streamer.SetMaximumPropagation(500)
streamer.SetMinimumIntegrationStep(0.01)
streamer.SetMaximumIntegrationStep(0.5)
streamer.SetIntegrator(rk)
streamer.SetMaximumError(1.0e-8)

mapStream = vtk.vtkPolyDataMapper()
mapStream.SetInputConnection(streamer.GetOutputPort())
streamActor = vtk.vtkActor()
streamActor.SetMapper(mapStream)

ren = vtk.vtkRenderer()
renWin = vtk.vtkRenderWindow()
renWin.AddRenderer(ren)
iren = vtk.vtkRenderWindowInteractor()
iren.SetRenderWindow(renWin)
```

```
48
49 ren.AddActor(streamActor)
50 ren.SetBackground(0.9,0.9,0.9)
51 renWin.SetSize(300,300)
52 iren.Initialize()
53 iren.Start()
```

Code 12.6. Example code using vtkRTAnalyticSource to create streamlines with VTK. The gradient of the test data is computed in lines 7–10; the gradient is then assigned as vector data for use by the vtkStreamTracer filter for producing streamlines. The starting points for the streamlines are produced from point sources in a sphere computed in lines 24–27. A single starting point could also be assigned, as illustrated in the comment in line 31. The result from this code is seen in Fig. 12.17.

While the VTK library provides a complete visualization pipeline solution for HPC users, many users will prefer a turnkey visualization solution that is driven by a powerful graphical user interface (GUI) and is ready for supercomputing usage without having to write any code. Two widely used turnkey visualization tools that incorporate the powerful algorithms of VTK are ParaView and VisIt.

12.6 PARAVIEW

ParaView is an open-source HPC-capable turnkey visualization solution based on VTK. Like other visualization tools examined in this chapter, significant support for the Python language is provided, enabling control of ParaView from both a GUI or a script. Because ParaView is based on VTK, the naming of elements in the visualization pipeline follows that of the VTK API. ParaView has data readers for over 70 different data formats. An example dataset that comes with ParaView is shown in Fig. 12.18.

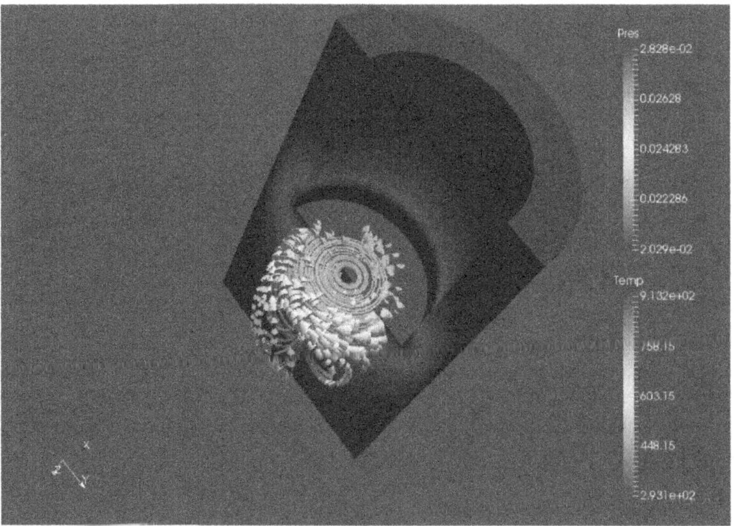

FIGURE 12.18

Example visualization that comes with ParaView illustrating streamlines with arrows and data slices.

12.7 VISIT

VisIt is another open-source HPC-capable turnkey visualization solution that uses VTK for several visualization algorithms. VisIt is particularly well suited for *in situ* visualization which occurs while the supercomputing simulation that creates the data is ongoing. An example VisIt visualization is shown in Fig. 12.19, with a skewed color map to reveal features in the data that would not be otherwise apparent.

VTK accepts over a 100 different data input formats and provides a simple scripting interface as an alternative to using the GUI for creating visualization.

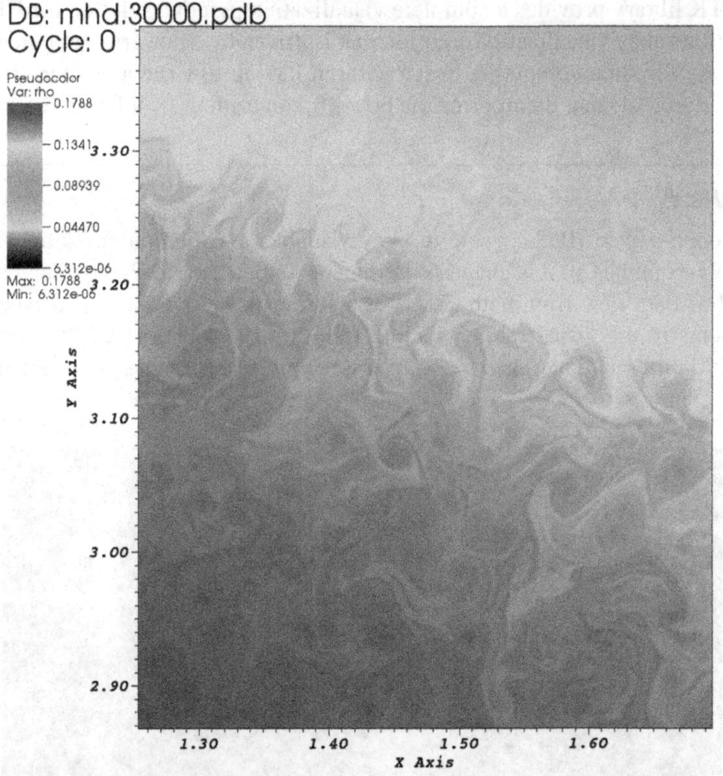

FIGURE 12.19

Example VisIt pseudo-color plot using a skewed color map to reveal a physical instability manifested as rolls in the data. The name of the visualized file appears in the upper left-hand corner, and the field variable name ("rho") is given above the color legend.

12.8 SUMMARY AND OUTCOMES OF CHAPTER 12

- Motivations for visualizing data include debugging, exploring data, statistical hypothesis testing, and preparing presentation graphics.
- Many scientific visualizations incorporate at least one of four foundational visualization concepts: streamlines, isosurfaces, volume rendering by ray tracing, and mesh tessellations.
- Streamlines take a vector field as input and show curves that are tangent to the vector field
- Isosurfaces are surfaces connecting data points which have the same value.
- Volume rendering by ray tracing casts rays through the data volume and samples the volume through which the rays pass.
- Mesh tessellations visualize data points and their connectivities to other data points using polygons.
- Gnuplot is a simple command-line visualization tool for 2D and 3D plots.
- Matplotlib is a Python-based visualization tool with easy integration to other libraries with Python bindings.
- VTK is an open-source collection of visualization algorithms for creating application-specific visualization solutions.
- ParaView and VisIt are turnkey visualization solutions incorporating VTK algorithms but providing a GUI and scripting interface for visualization.
- ParaView and VisIt already incorporate support for hundreds of widely used data formats on HPC systems.

12.9 EXERCISES

1. List all the factors that impact a decision to use a particular visualization approach for an HPC application. Create a table listing the trade-off space of the five visualization tools explored in this chapter.
2. Create a set of streamlines, isosurfaces, and volume renderings of the function $f(x,y,z) =$ 2550 sin $(50x)$ sin $(50y)$ cos $(50z)$ using the visualization tool of your choice.
3. Create a 2D dataset using the output library of your choice (i.e., HDF5, NetCDF, Silo, etc.) for the following function: $f(x,y) = e^{-x^2-y^2}$ where $x\in[-1,1]$ and $y\in[-1,1]$. Then, using the visualization library of your choice, read in this data and visualize it. Finally, compute the gradient of this data using the visualization tool you have chosen, and plot the result.
4. Visualization tools provide a large number of optional color legends. Why? In what circumstances is one color legend better than another?
5. Explore the parallel visualization capabilities of VisIt or Paraview by redoing problem 2 but using HPC resources. Produce a strong scaling plot showing the time to solution for the visualization as a function of the number of computing resources employed.

REFERENCES

1. Gnuplot homepage [Online], http://www.gnuplot.info/.
2. Matplotlib [Online], http://matplotlib.org/.
3. The Visualization Toolkit [Online], http://www.vtk.org/.
4. ParaView [Online], http://www.paraview.org/.
5. VisIt [Online], https://wci.llnl.gov/simulation/computer-codes/visit.
6. GNU Octave [Online], https://www.gnu.org/software/octave/.
7. MathWorks, MATLAB [Online], https://www.mathworks.com/products/matlab.html.
8. Python.org, Python Beginners Guide [Online], https://wiki.python.org/moin/BeginnersGuide/Programmers.
9. National Institute of Standards and Technology, Martrix Market Collection [Online], http://math.nist.gov/MatrixMarket/.
10. SciPy Developers, SciPy [Online], https://www.scipy.org/.
11. Matplotlib, mplot3d [Online], http://matplotlib.org/mpl_toolkits/mplot3d/.

CHAPTER

PERFORMANCE MONITORING 13

CHAPTER OUTLINE

13.1 INTRODUCTION

Performance monitoring is both an inherent and a key step in application development. The code development process does not stop when the program appears to be doing what it was designed to do and the generated results are validated for correctness. Even when the application has been tested using a broad range of input parameters and datasets as well as multiple supported computational modes stressing individual program features, there may still be hidden problems preventing it from executing at the smaximum performance permitted by the underlying platform. This is particularly important in parallel computing, where the impact of every inefficiency is effectively multiplied by the number of processor cores the application is running on. Besides increasing the time necessary to arrive at solutions, this may also have financial implications, since often the user is charged for computer use in proportion to the consumed aggregate machine time. One of the most important reasons for performance monitoring is therefore to verify that the application is not impacted by any obvious or easily preventable degradation factors. One way to confirm this is a simple sanity check: is the actual computation time in line with the processor speed and the estimated total number of operations that need to be performed? Is the communication phase taking longer than estimated given the message sizes transmitted by the application and network bandwidth? Fortunately, these questions may be

High Performance Computing. https://doi.org/10.1016/B978-0-12-420158-3.00013-7

answered by performing simple instrumentation of application code to measure the time required to execute the segments of the program involved. This is discussed in Section 13.2.

Even a simple measurement, such as capture of a timestamp, affects program execution due to greater than zero latency of the operation accessing the system timer and the nonzero resource footprint required to perform the operation. The more complex and frequent the measurements, the more overhead is introduced into program execution, potentially skewing the measurement results and in the worst case completely changing the application execution flow. The latter may be particularly damaging, since the identification of sections of code that need to be revised for performance improvement may be incorrect and cause additional programmer effort with little or no benefit. One way to alleviate this problem is to apply statistical sampling. Instead of registering every occurrence of an event in a program, a snapshot of program's state (sample) is taken at fixed intervals. The sampling period usually may be raised within a permitted range to increase the accuracy (again, at the cost of additional overhead) when there is a good possibility that some events were not accounted for, or lowered if the monitoring is discovered to be too intrusive or a coarse execution profile is sufficient. Another, albeit limited, way to lower instrumentation overheads is to use custom hardware to capture the events of interest. Modern CPUs implement dedicated registers that may be configured to count the occurrences of specific low-level events, such as branches, cache misses, instruction retirement, etc. Since the register updates are carried out entirely in hardware, executing software almost never sees the monitoring overhead. However, the consequence of hardware implementation is that the classes of supported events are predefined and cannot be extended or customized.

The remainder of this chapter discusses various performance monitoring tools commonly used to evaluate high performance computing workloads. Due to easier accessibility, broader portability, and no licensing costs, open-source tools are usually preferred. However, there are several useful proprietary tools that provide easy-to-use interfaces (especially those driven by a graphic user interface or GUI) and may leverage better technical expertise of hardware products than can be derived from publicly available documentation. While they will not be discussed in depth, they deserve a mention and are listed here to make the reader aware of other performance analysis options:

- Intel VTune Amplifier [1] is an integrated profiling environment targeting primarily Intel CPUs, including Xeon Phi. It can perform statistical hotspot analysis, thread profiling, and lock and blocking analysis, measure floating-point unit (FPU) utilization and Flops values, analyze memory and storage accesses, and trace computation offload to Graphics Processing Units (GPUs) via OpenCL. The tool integrates with Intel Parallel Studio XE and Microsoft Visual Studio, and supports programming languages such as C, C++, C#, Fortran, Java, Python, Go, and assembly. It is also capable of remote trace collection to enable monitoring of distributed applications such as a message-passing interface (MPI). Supported operating systems include Linux, Windows, and Mac OS X.
- CodeXL [2] is AMD's equivalent of VTune, providing an integrated suite of tools for performance analysis targeting x86-compatible CPUs as well as AMD GPUs and accelerated processing units (APUs) through the OpenCL Software Development Toolkit (SDK). It supports time-based profiling on CPUs, event-based profiling and instruction-based sampling on CPUs and APUs, and real-time power profiling including capture of CPU core clock frequencies, thermal trends, and P-states. CodeXL may be used as a standalone tool on Linux (Red Hat, Ubuntu, SUSE) and Windows, and is also available as an extension to Microsoft Visual Studio. While the source code is available through GitHub [3], much of the tool's core functionality relies on the proprietary AMD Catalyst software [4].

- The Nvidia CUDA Toolkit [5] includes a visual profiler (*nvvp*) that can be used to monitor and analyze the execution of parallel programs on Nvidia GPUs. Through collected traces, it gives the user an insight into program activity and the execution timeline decomposed into individual processing threads and workload phases. It also monitors memory usage (including unified memory on supporting architectures) as well as power consumption, clock speed, and thermal conditions. The tool has an option to analyze Pthread behavior on the host CPU as well as OpenACC applications (this requires a PGI compiler). Profiling may also be enabled from the command line using the *nvprof* utility. The toolkit is available for Linux, OS X, and Windows.

13.2 TIME MEASUREMENT

Execution time is one of the critical metrics of application performance and of primary importance to both application developers and end users. Its measurement may be carried out at the whole-program level as well as for selected sections of the monitored application. Each of these scenarios requires a different approach. The measurement of duration of application execution should typically be synchronized with the wall clock time to establish a common reference permitting meaningful comparisons with results obtained on other platforms and environments. This is particularly important when application execution takes a significant amount of time, potentially counted in days or months. Most computer system clocks are periodically synchronized over the network to a common high-accuracy standard, typically derived from an atomic clock using protocols such as Network Time Protocol (NTP) [6]. This provides sufficiently good average accuracy in the long term, although it does not avoid the issue of local clock jitter. It is also affected by the characteristics of the clock adjustment algorithm: if the measurement happens when the system clock's value is updated to match the standard, potentially a large skew may be introduced to the result. Most implementations tend to tune the system clock gradually by small amounts, thus alleviating the problem of a measured value being dependent on the time when the act of measurement is being performed.

Most Unix systems provide several utilities to access the wall clock time from the command line. One is the *date* program that outputs the current date and time with accuracy down to single seconds. It may be used in batch job scripts to provide coarse timestamps for the start and end times of application execution (or any intermediate phases as long as they are represented by separate applications). Its output will be captured in a file storing the standard output stream of the job's execution shell for future inspection. An example output of the command as invoked from the shell prompt is:

```
> date
Sun, Feb 05, 2017 6:17:33 PM
```

The date command also accepts custom date format specification as a command-line argument in case the default form shown above is not acceptable.

Since resolution at the full-second level may not be sufficient for short-running applications, more precise measurements can use the *time* utility that may be available as a bash shell built-in command or a standalone system program. It has to be followed by a correctly formed command line fully describing the application with its options and command-line arguments. The specified application will immediately be spawned as specified, while the timing utility captures several key characteristics of its execution. For example:

```
> /usr/bin/time dd if=/dev/zero of=/dev/null bs=4096 count=1M
1048576+0 records in
1048576+0 records out
4294967296 bytes (4.3 GB, 4.0 GiB) copied, 0.482873 s, 8.9 GB/s
0.37user 0.10system 0:00.48elapsed 100%CPU (0avgtext+0avgdata 415744maxresident)k
0inputs+0outputs (1643major+0minor)pagefaults 0swaps
```

The above times the execution of the *dd* program (available on any Linux distribution and used to copy and convert file data) that transfers 4 GB of zero-filled data to a null device. Note that the first three lines contain output from the *dd* utility itself. In this case, the program execution took 0.48 s (as given by the elapsed time entry), of which 0.37 s were spent executing user code and 0.1 s system (or kernel) code. The reported system and user times do not necessarily have to add to the elapsed time value. This is because program execution may be stalled, e.g., waiting for user input, completion of input/output (I/O) operations, or other external events. If the program could not fully utilize the allocated processor core(s), the reported utilization (as a percentage of the CPU) may be lower than 100%. Note that multithreaded programs may report values greater than 100%, since the displayed user and system times are the aggregate values over all compute threads spawned by the application.

The time utility also reports other details of program execution that may be helpful in analyzing the application's behavior. One of them, following the timings, provides information about memory resources allocated by the application. The first number indicates the average size of memory used by program text (instruction pages), the second represents the average size of unshared program data, and the third shows the maximum size of physical memory (resident set) used by the application's process. These numbers are reported in kilobytes. The last line displayed by the time command lists the number of I/O operations performed by the program, the number of minor and major page faults, and how many times the process was swapped out from memory for disk. The difference between major and minor page faults is that the first involves access to a storage device required to retrieve the contents of memory page, while a minor fault only requires an update of a page table entry. Thus the cost of a major fault is typically substantially higher than that of a minor fault. Similarly to *date*, the output of the *time* command may be customized through the command-line option `-f` or `--format` to include additional parameters such as the number of involuntary and voluntary context switches, the number of messages in socket-based communication, the number of signals delivered to the process, and the exit status of the process. Note that the shell built-in *time* command reports only the user, system, and elapsed timings for the monitored program.

The timing utilities operating at the whole-application level are not useful for measuring duration of execution of individual functions or code segments. For that purpose, a number of timing functions accessing the system's high-resolution clock are used. Individual implementations of high-resolution timers may differ from system to system depending on the actual processor type and system configuration. Since the native interfaces exposed by such timers are often not compatible with each other, typically the most portable way to access them is to use POSIX clock functions. The most frequently used call, clock_gettime, obtains the value of time that has elapsed from some fixed reference point in the past, typically machine boot time. Its prototype looks as follows:

```
#include <time.h>
int clock_gettime(clockid_t id, struct timespec *tsp);
```

where id identifies one of the clocks available on the system and the structure to store the time data pointed to by tsp comprises two fields. The first of them, tv_sec contains the number of full seconds and the other, tv_nsec, stores the number of nanoseconds expressing the remaining fraction of a second for the measured time interval. Both of these fields are integers of sufficient size to store the required data, frequently equal to machine's native word size. The function returns zero on success. To verify the actual resolution of the accessed clock, POSIX provides the clock_getres function that takes the clock identifier argument and stores the measurement resolution value in a structure pointed to by tsp:

```
int clock_getres(clockid_t id, struct timespec *tsp);
```

For fine-granularity measurements, useful clock ids include CLOCK_MONOTONIC and CLOCK_MONOTONIC_RAW. Unlike the system wall clock, which may be subjected to coarse changes of value due to the administrator manually adjusting the system time, the monotonic clock is only affected by incremental adjustments performed by the time synchronization protocol in use (e.g., NTP). The raw monotonic clock has the same properties as the monotonic clock, but it is not affected by external time adjustment. The POSIX interface also supports other clocks of interest: CLOCK_BOOTTIME that is similar to the monotonic clock, but includes the time that elapsed while the system was suspended; CLOCK_PROCESS_CPUTIME_ID, which measures processor time consumed by all threads in the process it was called in; and CLOCK_THREAD_CPUTIME_ID for a processor time clock that is limited to the specific thread. Selection of the suitable clock should be performed in the context of application and type of measurement; for most performance measurements on an "always-on" platform, the monotonic clock is often sufficient as long as the overhead of several tens of nanoseconds per access is acceptable.

To take advantage of POSIX clocks, the user code needs to be explicitly instrumented with timing functions. To demonstrate this, a program performing matrix−vector multiplication with source code listed in Code 13.1 is used. The same code is subsequently subjected to analysis by other performance monitoring tools in the next sections of this chapter. The application allocates heap memory, initializes the matrix and multiplicand and product vectors (routine init, lines 6−15), performs the multiplication by invoking the CBLAS library function (refer to Chapter 11 for more details on BLAS) to compute dot products (mult function, lines 17−23), and verifies the result by performing an absolute value sum on the elements of the product vector (cblas_dasum in line 33). Both initialization and multiplication can be performed in row- or column-major fashion, potentially impacting the duration of computations. This is controlled by the second command-line argument (transposition flag); the first one specifies the size of the matrix. To gather the timing information, `clock_gettime` functions were added to the `main` function of the source as shown in Code 13.2 (only the instrumented section is provided; the starting part of the program preceding line 25 is unchanged). Code 13.2 also defines the `sec` function that is used to convert the contents of the `timespec` structure to a floating-point number of seconds, thus enabling a straightforward calculation of time intervals. Note that collection of timestamps is arranged with as little additional code as possible, and therefore the conversions of timing values to seconds and printout of final values are performed outside the timed regions.

```
 1 #include <stdio.h>
 2 #include <stdlib.h>
 3 #include <cblas.h>
 4 #include <time.h>
 5
 6 void init(int n, double **m, double **v, double **p, int trans) {
 7   *m = calloc(n*n, sizeof(double));
 8   *v = calloc(n, sizeof(double));
 9   *p = calloc(n, sizeof(double));
10   for (int i = 0; i < n; i++) {
11     (*v)[i] = (i & 1)? -1.0: 1.0;
12     if (trans) for (int j = 0; j <= i; j++) (*m)[j*n+i] = 1.0;
13     else for (int j = 0; j <= i; j++) (*m)[i*n+j] = 1.0;
14   }
15 }
16
17 void mult(int size, double *m, double *v, double *p, int trans) {
18   int stride = trans? size: 1;
19   for (int i = 0; i < size; i++) {
20     int mi = trans? i: i*size;
21     p[i] = cblas_ddot(size, m+mi, stride, v, 1);
22   }
23 }
24
25 int main(int argc, char **argv) {
26   int n = 1000, trans = 0;
27   if (argc > 1) n = strtol(argv[1], NULL, 10);
28   if (argc > 2) trans = (argv[2][0] == 't');
29
30   double *m, *v, *p;
31   init(n, &m, &v, &p, trans);
32   mult(n, m, v, p, trans);
33   double s = cblas_dasum(n, p, 1);
34   printf("Size %d; abs. sum: %f (expected: %d)\n", n, s, (n+1)/2);
35   return 0;
36 }
```

Code 13.1. Matrix–vector multiply code operating in row- and column-major modes.

```
#include <stdio.h>
#include <stdlib.h>
#include <cblas.h>
#include <time.h>

void init(int n, double **m, double **v, double **p, int trans) {
  *m = calloc(n*n, sizeof(double));
  *v = calloc(n, sizeof(double));
  *p = calloc(n, sizeof(double));
  for (int i = 0; i < n; i++) {
    (*v)[i] = (i & 1)? -1.0: 1.0;
    if (trans) for (int j = 0; j <= i; j++) (*m)[j*n+i] = 1.0;
    else for (int j = 0; j <= i; j++) (*m)[i*n+j] = 1.0;
  }
}

void mult(int size, double *m, double *v, double *p, int trans) {
  int stride = trans? size: 1;
  for (int i = 0; i < size; i++) {
    int mi = trans? i: i*size;
    p[i] = cblas_ddot(size, m+mi, stride, v, 1);
  }
}

double sec(struct timespec *ts) {
  return ts->tv_sec+1e-9*ts->tv_nsec;
}

int main(int argc, char **argv) {
  struct timespec t0, t1, t2, t3, t4;
  clock_gettime(CLOCK_MONOTONIC, &t0);
  int n = 1000, trans = 0;
  if (argc > 1) n = strtol(argv[1], NULL, 10);
  if (argc > 2) trans = (argv[2][0] == 't');

  double *m, *v, *p;
  clock_gettime(CLOCK_MONOTONIC, &t1);
  init(n, &m, &v, &p, trans);
  clock_gettime(CLOCK_MONOTONIC, &t2);
  mult(n, m, v, p, trans);
  clock_gettime(CLOCK_MONOTONIC, &t3);
  double s = cblas_dasum(n, p, 1);
  clock_gettime(CLOCK_MONOTONIC, &t4);
  printf("Size %d; abs. sum: %f (expected: %d)\n", n, s, (n+1)/2);
  printf("Timings:\n program: %f s\n", sec(&t4)-sec(&t0));
  printf("  init: %f s\n  mult: %f s\n  sum: %f s\n",
         sec(&t2)-sec(&t1), sec(&t3)-sec(&t2), sec(&t4)-sec(&t3));
  return 0;
}
```

Code 13.2. Instrumented section of the matrix multiplication code.

Execution of the instrumented code in row-major mode with matrix size 10,000 × 10,000 yields:

```
> ./mvmult 20000
Size 20000; abs. sum: 10000.000000 (expected: 10000)
Timings:
   program: 1.148853 s
      init: 0.572537 s
      mult: 0.576276 s
       sum: 0.000037 s
```

Doing the same using the less efficient column-major operation results in:

```
> ./mvmult 20000 t
Size 20000; abs. sum: 10000.000000 (expected: 10000)
Timings:
   program: 12.126625 s
      init: 4.343727 s
      mult: 7.782852 s
       sum: 0.000043 s
```

As can be seen, program execution in the transposed mode takes an order of magnitude longer. The change is attributed primarily to a substantial increase in execution time of initialization and multiplication subroutines that access the matrix data. The absolute sum performed in the verification phase takes roughly the same amount of time, since the layout of the input data (product vector) does not change.

13.3 PERFORMANCE PROFILING

13.3.1 SIGNIFICANCE OF APPLICATION PROFILING

The goal of profiling is to provide an insight into application execution that may help identify the potential performance problems. These may be related to the algorithmic code makeup, memory management, communication, or I/O. Profiling tools usually concentrate on *hotspot* analysis—that is, detection of the parts of code the program spends most of its time executing. This may lead to identification of bottlenecks, or those hotspots that have unduly adverse effects on the application's performance. A bottleneck is usually apparent as a throughput-limiting component in processing flow. Typically, both the predecessor and successor components of a bottleneck are capable of providing higher aggregate throughput than that of a bottleneck. Bottlenecks may sometimes be replaced by a less limiting implementation (optimized); this may cause a dominant program bottleneck to move to another location in the code. Note that not every hotspot is necessarily a bottleneck. Many tightly optimized numeric libraries, for example, will spend nearly all of their time performing FPU computations, but this does not mean they are inefficient (the evidence for this is provided when the machine reaches performance near its hardware peak or close to the theoretical throughput limit of the computational algorithm used). Profilers may record compute performance data at the system level (including all active processes, system daemons, and kernel code running on a node), the process level, where only data relevant to a specific process is collected, or at the level of individual threads of a process. Additionally, profiling may be restricted to a user space, a kernel space, or both. Profiling requires that the analyzed application is *instrumented*, or modified in a way that permits the profiler to access the required runtime information. This process may be more invasive (e.g., the programmer injecting the required function calls or macros in the relevant places of source code) or less so (linking with a profiling library or attaching an external profiler to an already running process). The former often occurs when the tracking of user-defined events is necessary.

Besides analysis of computational performance, profiling tools may monitor other characteristics of the executed programs. One is memory usage over the course of program execution. This may apply to the overall size of virtual memory allocated by the application, the amount of physical memory assigned to the program, the shared memory that may be accessible to other concurrently executing processes, and the sizes of the program's stack, data, and text segments. The other aspect is I/O, for which the profiler may record the number of I/O operations, the amount of data transferred to or from the secondary storage or buffer cache, achieved data bandwidth, number of files opened, and so on. Finally, communication profiling registers the number and size of messages sent, their destinations, latencies, and bandwidths. This can be further categorized by network type (Ethernet, InfiniBand, etc.), communication endpoint type (sockets, RDMA), or protocol used. Information collected during profiling may be used to classify a program or its individual subroutines as *CPU* (or *compute*) *bound*, where execution time is dominated by processor speed, *memory bound*, for which execution time is primarily dictated by the amount of memory needed to store the program's data structures, or *I/O bound*, where a dominant fraction of execution time is spent performing I/O operations. It is worth noting that the code characteristic may change as a result of optimization, e.g., from CPU bound to I/O bound.

13.3.2 ESSENTIAL *GPERFTOOLS*

The *time* utility discussed previously is an example of a simple profiler. Its usefulness is limited by reporting only the single average, cumulative, or maximum value of parameters of interest for the entire duration of program execution. This makes it impossible to pinpoint the moment in program execution when performance was degraded and cross-reference it to the responsible sections of source code.

Modern profiling tools attempt to address this issue. One of the commonly used profilers is available as a part of the *gperftools* [7] package. While originally named Google Performance Tools, the code is currently maintained by the community and distributed under the BSD license. It provides a statistical CPU profiler, *pprof*, and several tools based around the *tcmalloc* (thread-caching malloc) library. Besides offering an improved memory allocation library for multithreaded environments, *tcmalloc* library supports memory leak detection and dynamic memory allocation profiling. To illustrate the use of these features, the program from Code 13.1 was compiled using the command shown below (note the addition of `-lprofiler` to the command line). To permit access to the program's symbol table, a `-ggdb` option was specified as well:

```
> gcc -O2 -ggdb mvmult.c -o mvmult -lcblas -lprofiler
```

The *gperftools* CPU profiler does not require any changes to the source code, and after successfully linking the instrumented application may be executed. The location of the file containing the collected data must be specified using the CPUPROFILE environment variable, as demonstrated below:

```
> env CPUPROFILE=mvmult.prof ./mvmult 20000
Size 20000; abs. sum: 10000.000000 (expected: 10000)
PROFILE: interrupts/evictions/bytes = 115/0/376
```

The program execution proceeds as before, with the expected output appearing on the console. The only change is the final line, which confirms that the profiling indeed took place and collected 115 data samples. To display the obtained information, the `pprof` tool is used:

```
> pprof --text mvmult mvmult.prof
Using local file mvmult.
Using local file mvmult.prof.
Total: 115 samples
      58  50.4%  50.4%       58 50.4% ddot_
      57  49.6% 100.0%       57 49.6% init
       0   0.0% 100.0%       57 49.6% 0x00007f2c9485e00f
```

The produced output is organized in several columns. The first shows the sample count associated with each function. Whenever the profiler collects a sample, it records, among other things, the current address stored in the instruction pointer of the running program context. Subsequent analysis done by `pprof` assigns the collected addresses to individual program functions. This is shown in the second column. The result above indicates that practically the entire program time is spent in two functions, `ddot_` and `init`. While `init` may be found in Code 13.1, `ddot_` is a Fortran function indirectly called by CBLAS that computes the double-precision dot product. The third column lists the cumulative percentage of samples for all functions displayed so far. The fourth and fifth columns deal with the aggregate sample counts and percentages for the annotated function as well as all its callees. Hence the unnamed function in the last line is the likely ancestor of the `init` function; it might be related to an early setup code that executes before the invocation of `main`. Finally, the last column lists the affected function names, or if not available, the raw sampled addresses.

The default sampling frequency is 100 samples per second. This can be set to a custom value using the `CPUPROFILE_FREQUENCY` environment variable, although the maximum speed for most Linux platforms is limited to 1000 per second. Since the test application runs for only about a second, trying to increase the number of samples may offer additional insights:

```
> env CPUPROFILE=mvmult1K.prof CPUPROFILE_FREQUENCY=1000 ./mvmult 20000
Size 20000; abs. sum: 10000.000000 (expected: 10000)
PROFILE: interrupts/evictions/bytes = 1147/0/536
```

About 10 times as many samples were collected. Their analysis reveals the following:

```
> pprof --text mvmult mvmult1K.prof
Using local file mvmult.
Using local file mvmult1K.prof.
Total: 1147 samples
     576  50.2%  50.2%      576  50.2% ddot_
     571  49.8% 100.0%      571  49.8% init
       0   0.0% 100.0%      571  49.8% 0x00007f5fd0cda00f
```

It is apparent that most of the test application execution is indeed concentrated in the two functions identified before. However, `pprof` supports other analysis options that may be changes through command line switches:

- `--text` displays the profile in a plain-text form
- `--list=<regex>` outputs only data related to functions whose names match the provided regular expression
- `--disasm=<regex>` is like list, but performs disassembly of relevant section of the program while annotating each line with a sample count

- `--dot`, `--pdf`, `--ps`, `--gif`, and `--gv` generate annotated graphical representation of a call graph and output it to *stdout* in the requested format. Requires that the *dot* converter is installed in the system. The last option uses *gv* viewer to open a window with call graph visualization.

The default output of `pprof` is performed at function granularity, but sometimes it is useful to change this to avoid lengthy output or zoom in more closely on to the source of the problem. Adjustment options, in order of decreasing resolution, are:

- `--addresses` shows annotated code addresses
- `--lines` annotates source code lines
- `--functions` lists the statistics per function
- `--files` switches to whole-file granularity.

To see how the samples are distributed within the `init` function, one may apply the following command to the set of profiling data collected before (to save space, the produced output was truncated and removed lines were replaced with "`[...]`"):

```
> pprof --list=init --lines mvmult mvmult1K.prof
Using local file mvmult.
Using local file mvmult1K.prof.
ROUTINE ====================== init in /home/maciek/perf/mvmult.c
   571     571 Total samples (flat / cumulative)
[...]
     .       .    6: void init(int n, double **m, double **v, double **p,
int trans) {
     .       .    7:     *m = calloc(n*n, sizeof(double));
     .       .    8:     *v = calloc(n, sizeof(double));
     .       .    9:     *p = calloc(n, sizeof(double));
     .       .   10:     for (int i = 0; i < n; i++) {
     1       1   11:       (*v)[i] = (i & 1)? -1.0: 1.0;
     .       .   12:       if (trans) for (int j = 0; j <= i; j++) (*m)[j*n+i]
= 1.0;
   570     570   13:       else for (int j = 0; j <= i; j++) (*m)[i*n+j] =
1.0;
     .       .   14:     }
     .       .   15: }
[...]
```

Not unexpectedly, this shows that most initialization time is spent within the main loop. Of that, the inner loop performing initialization of matrix rows dominates the execution time, while the multi-plicand vector initialization is marginal by comparison. Since the sources of BLAS routines are not available, a disassembled code listing may be used to identify the fine-grain hotspots in that code (again, the output was shortened to the most interesting fragment):

```
> pprof --disasm=ddot_ mvmult mvmult.prof
Using local file mvmult.
Using local file mvmult.prof.
ROUTINE ====================== ddot_
   576      576 samples (flat, cumulative) 50.2% of total
[...]
    48       48            fcc0: movsd  -0x8(%rax),%xmm0
     9        9            fcc5: add    $0x28,%rax
     .        .            fcc9: add    $0x28,%rcx
    60       60            fccd: movsd  -0x20(%rax),%xmm2
    43       43            fcd2: mulsd  -0x30(%rcx),%xmm0
     .        .            fcd7: mulsd  -0x20(%rcx),%xmm2
     2        2            fcdc: addsd  %xmm0,%xmm1
    26       26            fce0: movsd  -0x28(%rax),%xmm0
     .        .            fce5: mulsd  -0x28(%rcx),%xmm0
     .        .            fcea: addsd  %xmm0,%xmm1
    81       81            fcee: addsd  %xmm2,%xmm1
    93       93            fcf2: movsd  -0x18(%rax),%xmm2
     9        9            fcf7: mulsd  -0x18(%rcx),%xmm2
     .        .            fcfc: movapd %xmm1,%xmm0
    57       57            fd00: movsd  -0x10(%rax),%xmm1
    13       13            fd05: mulsd  -0x10(%rcx),%xmm1
     .        .            fd0a: cmp    %rax,%rdx
     .        .            fd0d: addsd  %xmm2,%xmm0
    70       70            fd11: addsd  %xmm0,%xmm1
    65       65            fd15: jne    fcc0 <ddot_+0x110>
[...]
```

It is not difficult to guess that the annotated instructions are performing the arithmetic operations (scalar double-precision multiplication and addition) and managing the data movement between memory and floating-point registers (here denoted as %xmm with a numeric suffix). The listed code segment captures the innermost loop, as evidenced by the backward conditional branch in the last line. The overhead of memory access is comparable to the cost of computation. The fact that only scalar arithmetic operations were used indicates an optimization opportunity, since the dense algebra algorithms frequently benefit from SIMD support available on modern CPUs. Further investigation reveals that CBLAS was linked to the reference BLAS library rather than to of any of the optimized versions.

For completeness, profile data of the transposed case sampled at 100 samples/second is available below. While the program's execution is still confined to the same functions as before, the ratio of data timing has changed: initialization is less affected by column-major layout. At this point it is difficult to ascertain the reason for the difference in performance based solely on CPU profile data.

```
> pprof --text mvmult mvmult_trans.prof
Using local file mvmult.
Using local file mvmult_trans.prof.
Total: 13577 samples
    9240  68.1%  68.1%      9240  68.1% ddot_
    4335  31.9% 100.0%      4335  31.9% init
       2   0.0% 100.0%         2   0.0% ddotsub_
       0   0.0% 100.0%      4335  31.9% 0x00007f6440b6900f
```

One of *gperftools* features is the ability to detect memory leaks. To enable this functionality, it is necessary to link the application with the *tcmalloc* library or set the environment variable `LD_PRELOAD` to `libtcmalloc.so`. Before launching the application, the leak detector needs to be informed about the flavor of checking that should be performed. This is accomplished by storing one of the keywords (`minimal`, `normal`, `strict`, or `draconian`) in the `HEAPCHECK` environment variable. They differ in scope and level of detail performed by the heap allocation checker; for most purposes `normal` mode is sufficient. The compilation command line and results of the instrumented program execution are shown below.

```
> gcc -02 mvmult.c -o mvmult -lcblas -ltcmalloc
> env HEAPCHECK=normal ./mvmult 20000
WARNING: Perftools heap leak checker is active -- Performance may suffer
tcmalloc: large alloc 3200000000 bytes == 0xe9e000 @ 0x7f887688eae7
0x4009b1 0x400b95
Size 20000; abs. sum: 10000.000000 (expected: 10000)
Have memory regions w/o callers: might report false leaks
Leak check _main_ detected leaks of 3200160000 bytes in 2 objects
```

Since the program in Code 13.1 performs explicit memory allocation in `init` and that memory is never freed, the heap checker reports a leak at the end of `main`. Note that *tcmalloc* prints statements whenever large amounts of memory are allocated.

The tool may also profile memory management, similarly to CPU profiling. In this case the source code needs to be explicitly instrumented: a `HeapProfilerStart` function has to be inserted before the profiled section of code, and a `HeapProfilerStop` function must be added at the end. The first function takes one argument describing the file name prefix used to store the profiling data (since multiple files may be generated, each has a unique number and ".prof" extension added automatically). The prototypes of these functions are defined in the header file "gperftools/heap-profiler.h". The profiler's behavior may be adjusted through dedicated environment variables, detailed below.

- HEAP_PROFILE_ALLOCATION_INTERVAL: each time the specified number of bytes is allocated the profile data is stored in file. Allocation interval defaults to 1 GB.
- HEAP_PROFILE_INUSE_INTERVAL: as above, but the profile is written every time the total memory use by the program increases by the specified value, defaulting to 100 MB.
- HEAP_PROFILE_TIME_INTERVAL: stores data for every time period in seconds (default: 0).
- HEAP_PROFILE_MMAP: in addition to the usual C and C++ memory allocation calls such as `malloc`, `calloc`, `realloc`, and `new`, `this` also profiles `mmap`, `mremap`, and `sbrk` calls. By default it is disabled (false).
- HEAP_PROFILE_ONLY_MMAP: constraints the profiling to only `mmap`, `mremap`, and `sbrk` functions; the default value is false.
- HEAP_PROFILE_MMAP_LOG: enables logging of `mmap` and `munmap` calls; default is false.

To illustrate the use of the memory profiler, the following sequence of commands compiles the instrumented application (the file prefix was set to "mvmult") and launches it with profiling enabled. The threshold is set to a low value to capture all allocation calls.

```
> env HEAP_PROFILE_ALLOCATION_INTERVAL=1 ./mvmult_heap 20000
Starting tracking the heap
tcmalloc: large alloc 3200000000 bytes == 0x2258000 @ 0x7fd915a2eae7
0x400a71 0x400c55
Dumping heap profile to mvmult.0001.heap
(3051 MB allocated cumulatively, 3051 MB currently in use)
Dumping heap profile to mvmult.0002.heap
(3051 MB allocated cumulatively, 3051 MB currently in use)
Dumping heap profile to mvmult.0003.heap
(3052 MB allocated cumulatively, 3052 MB currently in use)
Dumping heap profile to mvmult.0004.heap
(3052 MB allocated cumulatively, 3052 MB currently in use)
Size 20000; abs. sum: 10000.000000 (expected: 10000)
```

After the program execution completes, four data dump files may be found in working directories named from "mvmult.0001.heap" to "mvmult.0004.heap". The pprof may display the information in one of four modes determined by the additional command-line switch:

- `--inuse-space:`—shows the number of megabytes currently in use (the default)
- `--inuse-objects`—shows the number of objects in use
- `--alloc_space`—shows the number of allocated megabytes
- `--alloc-objects`—shows the number of allocated objects.

Thus to display the allocated data captured by the last sample, the following command is used:

```
> pprof --text --alloc_space mvmult_heap mvmult.0004.heap
Using local file mvmult_heap.
Using local file mvmult.0004.heap.
Total: 3052.1 MB
  3052.1 100.0% 100.0%    3052.1 100.0% init
     0.0   0.0% 100.0%       0.0   0.0% __GI__IO_file_doallocate
     0.0   0.0% 100.0%       0.2   0.0% 0x00000000c0e19fff
     0.0   0.0% 100.0%    3051.9 100.0% __libc_csu_init
```

While the *gperftool* suite directly supports profiling of individual applications, it is also possible to use it for inspection of MPI programs. Since application performance data must be written to a specific file, one way to avoid collisions is to make sure that each monitored MPI process is assigned a different file. This is accomplished by adding the following statement to the application's source at a point following `MPI_Init` invocation:

`ProfilerStart(`*filename*`);`

The prototype of this function is available in `gperftools/profiler.h` along with other calls that may be helpful to control the profiler's operation. The *filename* parameter must be a different string for each MPI process. This is typically arranged by deriving it from the rank of the process within `MPI_COMM_WORLD`. For example:

```
int rank;
MPI_Comm_rank(MPICOMM_WORLD, &rank);
char filename[256];
snprintf(filename, 256, "my_app%04d.prof", rank);
ProfileStart(filename).
```

13.4 MONITORING HARDWARE EVENTS

13.4.1 PERF

The *perf* framework [8], also referred to as *perf_events*, is a performance monitoring tool and event tracer closely integrated with the Linux OS kernel. Its primary functionality is based on the *sys_perf_event_open* [9] system call introduced in the 2.6 series of Linux. The system call enables access to special-purpose registers of the CPU that may be configured to collect the counts of specific hardware-level events. These events may vary from processor to processor, but their main categories include the following:

- Cache related: misses and references issued. These may be further grouped by cache level (L1 through L3), cache type (instruction and data), and access type (loads and stores).

- Translation lookaside buffer related. These may also be subdivided into instruction and data categories, and by access type (load/store).
- Branch statistics. These include counts of overall branch occurrences and missed branch target loads.
- Instructions and cycles. *Perf* can provide the number of executed instructions or the count of CPU cycles that occurred during program execution.
- Stalled or idle cycles. These further subdivide into front-end and back-end stalls. The first indicates inability to fill completely the available capacity of the first stages of the execution pipeline, and may be caused by instruction cache or translation lookaside buffer (TLB) misses, mispredicted branches, or unavailability of translation into microoperations for specific instruction(s). The back-end issues may be caused by interinstruction dependencies (e.g., a long-latency instruction delaying the execution of other dependent instructions, such as division) or availability of memory units.
- Node-level statistics: prefetches, loads and stores, and misses. Prefetch misses are counted separately to avoid false inflation of statistics describing actual data accesses generated by the monitored code.
- Data collected by the processor's performance management unit (PMU). These counters provide the aggregate values for the whole CPU, including primarily *uncore*-related events. Uncore is a term coined by Intel to describe segments of CPU logic that are not parts of the core execution pipeline and thus are shared by the cores. They include memory controllers and their interfaces, a node-level interconnect bus that provides NUMA functionality, last-level cache, a coherency traffic monitor, and power management.

The *perf* tool also provides access to many software-level kernel events that may be of great use for performance analysis. They comprise counts of context switches, context migrations, data alignment faults, major, minor, and aggregate page faults, accurate time measurements, and custom events defined using the Berkeley Packet Filter framework. The complete list of events supported on the local system is obtained with:

```
> perf list
```

Perf may be invoked in several modes of operation selected by the first argument on the command line. The frequently used commands are:

- `stat`, which executes the provided application with arguments while collecting the counts of specified events or a default event set
- `record`, which enables per thread, per process, or per CPU profiling
- `report`, which performs analysis of data collected by `records`
- `annotate`, which correlates the gathered profiling data to assembly code
- `top`, which displays the statistics in real time using format resembling that of the Unix *top* utility for visualization of process activity
- `bench`, which invokes a number of predefined kernel benchmarks.

To test this functionality in practice, we can profile the test application shown in Code 13.1. The result for row-major (nontransposed) mode is presented below.

```
> perf stat ./mvmult 20000
Size 20000; abs. sum: 10000.000000 (expected: 10000)

 Performance counter stats for './mvmult 20000':

      1219.404556      task-clock (msec)          #    1.000 CPUs utilized
                1      context-switches           #    0.001 K/sec
                0      cpu-migrations             #    0.000 K/sec
          781,490      page-faults                #    0.641 M/sec
    3,898,266,727      cycles                     #    3.197 GHz
    2,283,166,328      stalled-cycles-frontend    #   58.57% frontend
cycles idle
    1,372,252,385      stalled-cycles-backend     #   35.20% backend
cycles idle
    3,764,331,355      instructions               #    0.97  insns per
cycle
                                                  #    0.61  stalled cycles
per insn
      495,220,268      branches                   #  406.116 M/sec
          815,338      branch-misses              #    0.16% of all
branches

      1.219967824 seconds time elapsed
```

Invoking the same for a column-major layout produces the following.

```
 Performance counter stats for './mvmult 20000 t':

     12212.530334      task-clock (msec)          #    1.000 CPUs utilized
               11      context-switches           #    0.001 K/sec
                0      cpu-migrations             #    0.000 K/sec
        1,213,417      page-faults                #    0.099 M/sec
   42,933,883,759      cycles                     #    3.516 GHz
   39,567,001,587      stalled-cycles-frontend    #   92.16% frontend
cycles idle
   37,181,761,140      stalled-cycles-backend     #   86.60% backend
cycles idle
    6,077,067,370      instructions               #    0.14  insns per
cycle
                                                  #    6.51  stalled cycles
per insn
      918,790,187      branches                   #   75.233 M/sec
        1,276,503      branch-misses              #    0.14% of all
branches

     12.213751102 seconds time elapsed
```

Besides the duration of program execution, there are several other noticeable differences between the two modes of operation. Firstly, the number of front-end and back-end stalls is significantly increased. The effective number of stalls per instruction is an order of magnitude higher. The instruction throughput per cycle is also much lower. This suggests that serious inefficiencies are introduced in the processing pipeline. Curiously, despite using nearly identical algorithms, the number of executed instructions is 60% greater for the column-major case. The code also encounters a much higher number of page faults in that mode.

Since the types of executed instructions are likely similar for both cases, the increased number of stalls may indicate caching issues. The higher count of page faults might also suggest TLB problems. To confirm this, the codes are reexecuted with custom selection of events. Note that *perf* may accommodate a greater number of events in a single invocation than available hardware slots in the processor using a technique called *multiplexing*. It means that at any given moment only a subset of requested events is configured on the processor; this subset is periodically replaced with one that contains other requested events. This is repeated cyclically to permit all specified events to be active for an approximately equal share of time during application execution. The additional options that may be passed to *perf* invocation are listed below.

- `-e` *event* [`:`*modifier*][`,`*event*[`:`*modifier*]]...

  Explicitly specifies the kinds of monitored events. Each event name may be followed by one or more modifiers, such as `u` for measuring only the events when the application executes in user mode or `k` when it is in kernel mode (and others which are not relevant here).

- `-B`

  Separates groups of every three digits in numbers by commas for easier readability.

- `-p` *pid*

  Instead of directly launching an application, the profiler attaches to an existing process with the specified *pid*.

- `-r` *integer*

  Repeatedly runs the command, collecting the aggregate statistics. The result shows the mean values for each event and deviation from the mean.

- `-a`

  Forces *perf* to collect data for all CPUs, including profiles of other applications running at the same time. The default is to monitor only the specified application's threads.

To put this into practice, the code was run again with monitoring of cache misses and TLB load misses enabled:

```
> perf stat -B -e cache-misses,dTLB-load-misses,iTLB-load-misses ./mvmult
20000
Size 20000; abs. sum: 10000.000000 (expected: 10000)

 Performance counter stats for './mvmult 20000':

        29,307,244      cache-misses
         3,121,156      dTLB-load-misses
             4,224      iTLB-load-misses

       1.227144489 seconds time elapsed
```

And in transposed version:

```
Performance counter stats for './mvmult 20000 t':

       79,004,606      cache-misses
      405,044,765      dTLB-load-misses
           33,124      iTLB-load-misses

     12.185000849 seconds time elapsed
```

The collected data shows a significant increase for all three figures. Particularly damaging is the two orders of magnitude jump in data-TLB misses. This is caused by strided access to matrix elements; the consecutive references not only touch different cache lines but involve different memory pages (eight-byte entries with 20,000 element stride are effectively separated by 160 KB, which is far greater than the default page size of 4 KB). This emphasizes the importance of selecting algorithms that exhibit good spatial locality of access.

To verify that the change is caused by different data layouts used by the main compute functions, the performance data was recorded in sampling mode using the command shown below. The `-F` option controls the sampling frequency; in this case 1000 samples per second are requested.

```
> perf record -F 1000 -e cache-misses,dTLB-load-misses,iTLB-load-misses
./mvmult 20000 t
Size 20000; abs. sum: 10000.000000 (expected: 10000)
[ perf record: Woken up four times to write data ]
[ perf record: Captured and wrote 0.834 MB perf.data (17,967 samples) ]
```

The collected information may be analyzed using the "`perf report`" command. The most significant excerpts of the result are listed below.

```
# Samples: 6K of event 'cache-misses'
# Event count (approx.): 78141963
#
# Overhead  Command  Shared  Object   Symbol
# ........  .......  .......  ......  ..............................
#
    33.64%  mvmult   libblas.so.3.6.0 [.] ddot_
    27.12%  mvmult   [kernel.vmlinux] [k] clear_page
    24.04%  mvmult   mvmult           [.] init
     6.73%  mvmult   [kernel.vmlinux] [k] _raw_spin_lock
     3.93%  mvmult   [kernel.vmlinux] [k] page_fault
[...]
# Samples: 10K of event 'dTLB-load-misses'
# Event count (approx.): 405199968
#
# Overhead  Command  Shared  Object   Symbol
# ........  .......  .......  ......  ....................................
#
    99.03%  mvmult   libblas.so.3.6.0 [.] ddot_
     0.63%  mvmult   [kernel.vmlinux] [k] page_fault
     0.14%  mvmult   [kernel.vmlinux] [k] handle_mm_fault
[...]
# Samples: 1K of event 'iTLB-load-misses'
# Event count (approx.): 33857
#
# Overhead  Command  Shared  Object   Symbol
# ........  .......  ......  ...........
.........................................
#
    15.57%  mvmult   libblas.so.3.6.0 [.] ddot_
     8.86%  mvmult   libcblas.so      [.] cblas_ddot
     6.16%  mvmult   mvmult           [.] init
     5.97%  mvmult   [kernel.vmlinux] [k] cpumask_any_but
     5.74%  mvmult   [kernel.vmlinux] [k] page_fault
     5.54%  mvmult   [kernel.vmlinux] [k] notifier_call_chain
     4.62%  mvmult   [kernel.vmlinux] [k] flush_tlb_mm_range
     4.57%  mvmult   libcblas.so      [.] ddotsub_
     3.27%  mvmult   [kernel.vmlinux] [k] smp_apic_timer_interrupt
     2.90%  mvmult   [kernel.vmlinux] [k] apic_timer_interrupt
     2.33%  mvmult   [kernel.vmlinux] [k] update_vsyscall
     2.10%  mvmult   mvmult           [.] mult
[...]
```

As can be seen, the `ddot_` function is the primary contributor of cache and TLB misses. A large percentage of cache misses are also caused by the kernel's page-clearing function, most likely called as a consequence of using the `calloc` function to allocate the memory for matrix and vectors. Not surprisingly, the `init` function is the source of a significant fraction of cache misses.

Unlike *gperftools*, *perf* can only record the performance data in a file with a fixed name. This makes it harder to analyze the performance of all component processes comprising an MPI application. The workaround on a machine with dedicated local storage partitions (e.g., in `/tmp`) could be by starting the application in node-exclusive mode (one process per node) after changing the working directory to one on the local file system. After the application terminates, the generated data files may be copied (and renamed) for analysis to a shared file system using *scp*. If all component processes of the application execute a similar workload, it may suffice to set up monitoring for only one of them, as described in Section 3.5.2.2. The approximate counts for the whole application are then derived by multiplying the single process count by the number of executed MPI processes. Note that monitoring of arbitrary rank can also be arranged by subdividing the processes into correctly sized groups using the `-np` *n* option to *mpirun*, while remembering that they have to add up to the total count of processes required by the application and only one instance may invoke *perf*.

13.4.2 PERFORMANCE APPLICATION PROGRAMMING INTERFACE

The Performance Application Programming Interface (PAPI) [10] is a performance monitoring toolkit developed at the University of Tennessee Innovative Computing Laboratory. It provides C and Fortran library and header files containing prototypes of functions that may be used to instrument user applications. The application programming interface (API) categories comprise library initialization and shutdown, event description and translation between symbolic event names and their codes, creation and manipulation of event sets, starting and stopping of event counters, retrieval, accumulation, resetting, and initialization of counter values, system parameter queries, and various timing functions. The package also provides a number of practical utilities.

- `papi_avail` prints the symbolic names of *preset* events annotated with availability flags on the local systems and noting whether they are counted directly or derived by using more than one counter. Using option `-a` limits the display only to events locally available.
- `papi_native_avail` similarly displays so-called *native* events, which typically comprise uncore and node-level events.
- `papi_decode` outputs more detailed event descriptions in comma-separated values (csv) format.
- `papi_clockres` determines the practical resolution of various time and cycle measurement interfaces.
- `papi_cost` checks the latency of invocation of various API functions in different configurations.
- `papi_event_chooser` prints out events that may be added without conflict to a set containing events specified by the user.
- `papi_mem_info` shows the local machine cache and TLB hierarchy information.

PAPI events are less portable across processor architectures than those exposed by the *perf* tool. The user always needs to confirm whether a specific event is available on the target platform by using `papi_avail` or `papi_native_avail`. Due to the growing complexity of microprocessor designs, the interpretation of seemingly the same events may change even between different iterations of the same architecture. On the other hand, PAPI may be used to instrument the application in precise locations of the code and enables use of events that are normally not supported by *perf*.

To showcase the use of the interface, Code 13.1 was instrumented with two counters that tally the occurrences of double-precision operations, but one counts instances of all floating-point operations converted to scalar operations (`PAPI_DP_OPS`) and the other counts all vector operations (`PAPI_VEC_DP`). The counters are activated just before initialization (line 45) and their values are retrieved after return from the `init`, `mult`, and `cblas_dasum` functions (lines 48, 50, and 52). To guard against silent failures, a PAPI_CALL macro was defined in lines 25–30 to verify that called PAPI routines are completed successfully. As before, only the modified portion of the source code is provided (not counting the inclusion of the PAPI header, `papi.h`, in the top section of the source file) in Code 13.3.

```
1  #include <stdio.h>
2  #include <stdlib.h>
3  #include <cblas.h>
4  #include <time.h>
5  #include <papi.h>
6
7  void init(int n, double **m, double **v, double **p, int trans) {
8    *m = calloc(n*n, sizeof(double));
9    *v = calloc(n, sizeof(double));
10   *p = calloc(n, sizeof(double));
11   for (int i = 0; i < n; i++) {
12       (*v)[i] = (i & 1)? -1.0: 1.0;
13       if (trans) for (int j = 0; j <= i; j++) (*m)[j*n+i] = 1.0;
14       else for (int j = 0; j <= i; j++) (*m)[i*n+j] = 1.0;
15   }
16 }
17
18 void mult(int size, double *m, double *v, double *p, int trans) {
19 int stride = trans? size: 1;
20   for (int i = 0; i < size; i++) {
21     int mi = trans? i: i*size;
22     p[i] = cblas_ddot(size, m+mi, stride, v, 1);
23 } }
24
25 #define PAPI_CALL(fn, ok_code) do { \
26   if (ok_code != fn) { \
27     fprintf(stderr, "Error: " #fn " failed, aborting\n"); \
28     exit(1); \
29   } \
30 } while (0)
31
```

```
#define NEV 2

int main(int argc, char **argv) {
  int n = 1000, trans = 0;
  if (argc > 1) n = strtol(argv[1], NULL, 10);
  if (argc > 2) trans = (argv[2][0] == 't');

  int evset = PAPI_NULL;
  PAPI_CALL(PAPI_library_init(PAPI_VER_CURRENT), PAPI_VER_CURRENT);
  PAPI_CALL(PAPI_create_eventset(&evset), PAPI_OK);
  PAPI_CALL(PAPI_add_event(evset, PAPI_DP_OPS), PAPI_OK);
  PAPI_CALL(PAPI_add_event(evset, PAPI_VEC_DP), PAPI_OK);
  double *m, *v, *p;
  PAPI_CALL(PAPI_start(evset), PAPI_OK);
  init(n, &m, &v, &p, trans);
  long long v1[NEV], v2[NEV], v3[NEV];
  PAPI_CALL(PAPI_read(evset, v1), PAPI_OK);
  mult(n, m, v, p, trans);
  PAPI_CALL(PAPI_read(evset, v2), PAPI_OK);
  double s = cblas_dasum(n, p, 1);
  PAPI_CALL(PAPI_stop(evset, v3), PAPI_OK);
  printf("Size %d; abs. sum: %f (expected: %d)\n", n, s, (n+1)/2);
  printf("PAPI counts:\n");
  printf(" init: event1: %15lld event2: %15lld\n", v1[0], v1[1]);
  printf(" mult: event1: %15lld event2: %15lld\n", v2[0]-v1[0], v2[1]-v1[1]);
  printf(" sum: event1: %15lld event2: %15lld\n", v3[0]-v2[0], v3[1]-v2[1]);
  return 0;
}
```

Code 13.3. Instrumented section of Code 13.1 for collection of floating-point operation counts using PAPI.

For correct compilation, the program must be linked with the PAPI library, as shown below.

```
> gcc -O2 mvmult_papi.c -o mvmult_papi -lcblas -lpapi.
```

Running the instrumented program produces the following output.

```
> ./mvmult_papi 20000
Size 20000; abs. sum: 10000.000000 (expected: 10000)
PAPI counts:
  init: event1:              0  event2:        0
  mult: event1:      804193640  event2:        0
   sum: event1:          20276  event2:        0
```

Since the reference BLAS implementation does not use vector floating points, the count of vector operations stays at zero. The theoretical count of scalar operations should be $20{,}000^2$ for multiplication and 20,000∗19,999 for addition, for a grand total of 799,980,000 in the `mult` function and 19,999 operations (since the absolute value computation requires only clearing the sign bit) in `cblas_dasum`. The counters consistently register higher values, most likely due to speculative execution.
After replacing the reference BLAS library by a highly optimized Intel Math Kernel Library [11] that takes advantage of vector instructions supported by the target machine, the application was reexecuted to produce the following values.

```
PAPI counts:
 init: event1:           0  event2:         0
 mult: event1:  1055372246  event2: 527686123
  sum: event1:       24674  event2:     12337
```

The count of vector operations was roughly half of the scalar figure. This indicates that the library selected the use of vector instructions with two floating-point numbers per instruction. Indeed, the machine on which the test was performed supports Streaming SIMD Extensions (SSE) instruction set with up to two operands per vector. As a result of this change, the execution time dropped from 1.22 s to 1.08 s.

13.5 INTEGRATED PERFORMANCE MONITORING TOOLKITS

Software application components do not operate independently: not only do they have to share various system resources, such as processor cores, memory, storage, and network bandwidth, but they must also coexist with the periodically executing operating system threads, service daemons, and other applications. While the last issue is mitigated to some extent by properly configured job managers that schedule new processes on shared resources only when permitted by the owner of the already executing job on the node, the resultant application performance is the outcome of multiple factors, frequently acting against each other. To gain more complete understanding of an application's behavior, it therefore makes sense to create performance monitors that combine various aspects of application profiling in a single package that permits easy visualization and comparison of performance data.

One such tool is the Tuning and Analysis Toolkit (TAU) [12] developed at the Performance Research Laboratory at the University of Oregon and distributed under the BSD license. TAU may be used in single-node and distributed environments, including 32-bit and 64-bit Linux clusters, ARM platforms, Windows machines, Cray computers running Compute Node Linux, IBM BlueGene and POWER families on AIX and Linux, NEC SX series, and AMD, Nvidia, and Intel GPUs as well as a number of older architectures. In addition to instrumentation (for profiling or tracing), measurement, analysis, and visualization, it is capable of managing performance information databases and performing data mining functions. For graphical display of collected data TAU provides a Java-based *paraprof* visualization tool. Supported languages include C, C++, Fortran, UPC, Python, Java, and Chapel.

Event types recognized and captured by TAU include *interval* and *atomic* events. Interval events have defined start and end points. The statistics derived from interval event measurement may be *inclusive*, where outer intervals include event counts or timing collected for all nested intervals, or *exclusive*, when the resultant data shows only values for event counts or times that are relevant solely to the specified interval but excludes the statistics for all its "children" intervals. Interval metrics are monotonic—they may only increase during program execution (e.g., when a monitored function is reinvoked). Atomic events capture momentary metric values related to computation state at predefined trigger points. They may vary throughout the execution of the application. TAU captures them as a total (cumulative) value, minimum, maximum, average, and number of samples collected. The user-defined events may be of both interval and atomic kinds. In addition, execution context may be attached to atomic events to determine the calling path taken.

TAU supports three instrumentation methods that differ in level of their provided features.

- **Source-level** instrumentation is the most flexible method. This is the only mode supporting insertion of user-defined probes. Using this method permits exclusion of regions of code that are not critical for program performance or otherwise not interesting from the output. It also allows profiling of various low-level events, such as loops or program phases. This is accomplished by static analysis of source code using the Program Database Toolkit (PDT) package, creating a modified copy of sources, and compilation of the instrumented code.
- **Library-level** instrumentation is employed in cases when sources are not available, for example when monitoring of external or system libraries is needed. It applies wrapper libraries that may be used with static or dynamic libraries under investigation. In both cases symbol rewriting techniques are used (such as weak symbols for static libraries and library preloading for dynamic libraries) that redefine functions associated with specific identifiers, thus permitting interception of user calls and insertion of appropriate monitoring code.
- **Binary code** instrumentation requires *Dyninst* [13], developed by the Paradyn Tools Project. While the least invasive of all the described methods, it does not support many features available using other instrumentation approaches. Binary instrumentation is performed by rewriting binary application code, hence it may be used with already linked applications and without requiring any access to source files.

To demonstrate necessarily only a very few options from TAU's broad palette of supported configurations and measurements, Code 13.1 has been transformed using PDT-driven source instrumentation and compiled using the following command:

```
> taucc -tau:verbose -tau:pdtinst -optTauSelectFile=select.tau mvmult.c -O2
-o mvmult -lcblas -lm
```

While not required by the application, math library (`-lm`) had to be added to the command line to avoid linker complaints. TAU installation may support several different configurations involving on occasion options that may not be specified at the same time. The conflicts are avoided by encoding such configurations into separate Makefiles with names suffixed with the applicable configuration options. To point the TAU compiler toward the most relevant option, a suitable environment variable needs to be set:

```
> export TAU_MAKEFILE=/opt/tau/x86_64/lib/Makefile.tau-memory-phase-papi
-mpi-pthread-pdt
```

Of course, the installation path and the actual Makefile name have to be modified as appropriate on the local host.

The compilation command presented above illustrates simple selective instrumentation defined in the file `select.tau`. Its content is as follows.

```
BEGIN_EXCLUDE_LIST
void cblas_dasum(int, double *, int)
END_EXCLUDE_LIST

BEGIN_FILE_EXCLUDE_LIST
*.so

END_FILE_EXCLUDE_LIST
BEGIN_INSTRUMENT_SECTION
loops file="mvmult.c" routine="mult"
memory file="mvmult.c" routine="init"
END_INSTRUMENT_SECTION
```

This instructs TAU to exclude `cblas_dasum` (which earlier measurements showed to be nonessential to program performance) from profiling, as well as all dynamic libraries (since they contain system-level CBLAS and BLAS routines that are not the subject of investigation). TAU is also supposed to provide loop-level instrumentation in the `mult` function and memory instrumentation in `init`. Note that the wildcard character for function specification is "#" to avoid confusion with pointer syntax.

To collect data during the application's execution, TAU needs additional guidance on whether to profile or trace the application, what execution parameters to capture, and what type of hardware events should be collected. This is accomplished via environment variables, e.g.:

```
> TAU_METRICS=TIME
> TAU_PROFILE=1
```

The TAU_METRICS variable may contains several metric identifiers, including preset and native PAPI event names, separated by colons. After execution of the instrumented program is complete, a number of `profile.x.y.z` files, where x, y, and z are numbers corresponding to nodes (MPI ranks), contexts, and thread numbers, may be found in the execution directory. The graphical analysis tool, *paraprof*, may then be invoked to visualize the stored data—the main view window is shown in Fig. 13.1.

File Options Help

- Applications
  - Standard Applications
    - Default App
      - Default Exp
        - perf/maciek/home/
          - TIME

TrialField	Value
Name	perf/maciek/home/
Application ID	0
Experiment ID	0
Trial ID	0
CPU Cores	4
CPU MHz	3193.000
CPU Type	Intel(R) Xeon(R) CPU X5672...
CPU Vendor	GenuineIntel
CWD	/home/maciek/perf
Cache Size	12288 KB
Command Line	./mvmult 20000
Executable	/home/maciek/perf/mvmult
File Type Index	1
File Type Name	TAU profiles
Hostname	iugis
Local Time	2017-02-13T17:20:18-05:00
Memory Size	24733500 kB
Node Name	iugis
OS Machine	x86_64
OS Name	Linux
OS Release	4.8.17-gentoo
OS Version	#1 SMP PREEMPT Wed Jan ...
Starting Timestamp	1487024418598913
TAU Architecture	default
TAU Config	-prefix=/home/maciek/packa...
TAU Makefile	/home/maciek/packages/tau-...
TAU Version	2.26
TAU_BFD_LOOKUP	on
TAU_CALLPATH	on
TAU_CALLPATH_DEPTH	2
TAU_CALLSITE_LIMIT	1
TAU_COMM_MATRIX	off

FIGURE 13.1

Main window of *paraprof* analysis GUI.

At the same time *paraprof* opens a second window that visualizes execution phases (see Fig. 13.2).

Moving the mouse cursor over bars representing execution phases provides additional data, while the right-click opens context menus for additional actions. TAU GUI supports many more data views, including histograms, derived metrics, and three-dimensional profiling graphs. Additionally, the data may be presented in text format using the *pprof* utility. The reader is strongly encouraged to explore these options to gain more familiarity with the tool.

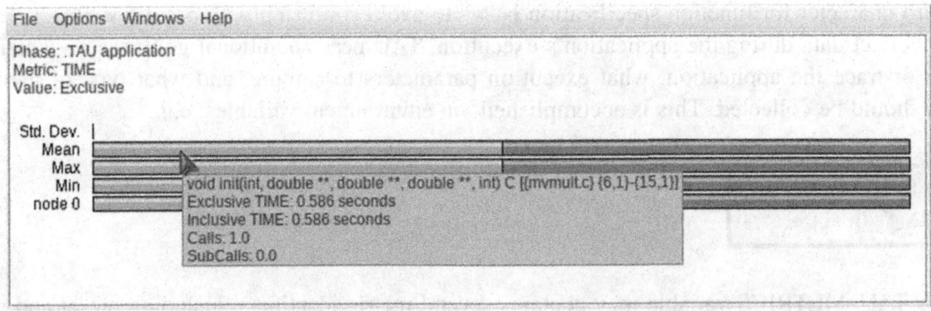

FIGURE 13.2

Paraprof execution-phase window.

13.6 PROFILING IN DISTRIBUTED ENVIRONMENTS

The *gperftools* and *perf* profilers discussed previously were originally developed for use with sequential codes, although there are somewhat more complex ways of using them with parallel programs. TAU, depending on configuration, may be capable of monitoring sequential, OpenMP, and MPI applications. However, there are several software tools explicitly designed for performance monitoring and profiling in distributed environments, including Scalasca [14], VampirTrace [15], and MPE2 [16]. As representative of the capabilities of these tools, this section explores VampirTrace profiling for distributed environments.

VampirTrace is an open-source performance monitoring infrastructure targeting high performance computing (HPC) applications. It provides a means for easily adding timing measurement function calls and performance counters to an application as part of instrumentation. Instrumentation in VampirTrace may be automatic or manual, and can be driven by the choice of programming model (MPI, OpenMP, CUDA, OpenCL, or hybrid), by a third-party package like TAU or Dyninst, or by using the VampirTrace API to insert measurement function calls manually to regions of interest in an HPC application. The output from VampirTrace instrumentation is in an open-source format, called the Open Trace Format, which is readable and analyzable through multiple tools including the proprietary Vampir graphical toolkit. VampirTrace itself is included as part of recent releases of OpenMPI and is frequently found already available on many supercomputers.

For most HPC applications developers, the quickest way to use VampirTrace for performance monitoring is to compile an application using the VampirTrace compiler wrappers: vtcc for C, vtcxx for C++, and vtfort for Fortran. The pingpong.c code illustrated in Code 13.4 is used as an example for MPI code, and the forkjoin.c code illustrated in Code 13.5 as an example for OpenMP code.

```
#include <stdio.h>
#include <stdlib.h>
#include <unistd.h>
#include "mpi.h"

int main(int argc,char **argv)
{
  int rank,size;
  MPI_Init(&argc,&argv);
  MPI_Comm_rank(MPI_COMM_WORLD,&rank);
  MPI_Comm_size(MPI_COMM_WORLD,&size);

  if ( size != 2 ) {
    printf(" Only runs on 2 processes \n");
    MPI_Finalize(); // this example only works on two processes
    exit(0);
  }

```

```
  int count;
  if ( rank == 0 ) {
    // initialize count on process 0
    count = 0;
  }
  for (int i=0;i<10;i++) {
    if ( rank == 0 ) {
      MPI_Send(&count,1,MPI_INT,1,0,MPI_COMM_WORLD); // send "count" to rank 1
      MPI_Recv(&count,1,MPI_INT,1,0,MPI_COMM_WORLD,MPI_STATUS_IGNORE); // receive it back
      sleep(1);
      count++;
      printf(" Count %d\n",count);
    } else {
      MPI_Recv(&count,1,MPI_INT,0,0,MPI_COMM_WORLD,MPI_STATUS_IGNORE);
      MPI_Send(&count,1,MPI_INT,0,0,MPI_COMM_WORLD);
    }
}

if ( rank == 0 ) printf("\t\t\t Round trip count = %d\n",count);

 MPI_Finalize();
}
```

Code 13.4. MPI pingpong.c code for illustrating MPI instrumentation using VampirTrace.

```
#include <omp.h>
#include <unistd.h>
#include <stdio.h>
#include <stdlib.h>
#include <math.h>

int main (int argc, char *argv[])
{
  const int size = 20;
  int nthreads, threadid, i;
  double array1[size], array2[size], array3[size];

  // Initialize
  for (i=0; i < size; i++) {
    array1[i] = 1.0*i;
    array2[i] = 2.0*i;
  }

```

```
  int chunk = 3;

#pragma omp parallel private(threadid)
  {
  threadid = omp_get_thread_num();
  if (threadid == 0) {
    nthreads = omp_get_num_threads();
    printf("Number of threads = %d\n", nthreads);
  }
  printf(" My threadid %d\n",threadid);

  #pragma omp for schedule(static,chunk)
  for (i=0; i<size; i++) {
    array3[i] = sin(array1[i] + array2[i]);
    printf(" Thread id: %d working on index %d\n",threadid,i);
    sleep(1);
  }

  } // join

  return 0;
}
```

Code 13.5. Example forkjoin.c code for illustrating instrumentation in OpenMP using VampirTrace.

When compiling C-language-based MPI code with the VampirTrace compiler wrappers, the MPI wrappers can be specified to the VampirTrace wrapper using the `-vt:cc` flag:

```
vtcc -vt:cc mpicc pingpong.c
```

Alternatively, the MPI libraries can be linked in without using the MPI compiler wrapper:

```
vtcc pingpong.c -lmpi
```

Note that in the latter approach the user may have to specify to the compiler where to find the MPI header file (mpi.h) and the MPI library.

While in principal using the VampirTrace compiler wrapper is enough to trigger automatic instrumentation for either MPI, OpenMP, or hybrid MPI+OpenMP applications, it is sometimes necessary to specify the programming model explicitly to the compiler using the `-vt:mpi`, `-vt:mt`, or

`-vt:hyb` specifications for MPI, OpenMP, and MPI+OpenMP applications respectively. For example, the pingpong.c MPI code (Code 13.4) could be compiled with MPI instrumentation as follows:

```
vtcc -vt:cc mpicc -vt:mpi pingpong.c
```

Likewise, the forkjoin.c OpenMP code in Code 13.5 could be compiled as follows:

```
vtcc -vt:cc gcc -vt:mt -fopenmp forkjoin.c
```

In this OpenMP example, the choice of the underlying compiler was explicitly set to be the GNU compiler (gcc) and the OpenMP library was enabled using the `-fopenmp` flag.

Once the codes are compiled using the VampirTrace compiler wrappers, they are executed just as they would normally be. However, upon completion of execution, an Open Trace Format file with the name of the code executable will appear in the execution directory. This file contains the measurement information provided by the instrumentation. There are several tools which can read the Open Trace Format file: Figs. 13.3 and 13.4 show Open Trace Files using the Vampir visualizer for the MPI pingpong.c code and the OpenMP forkjoin.c code, respectively.

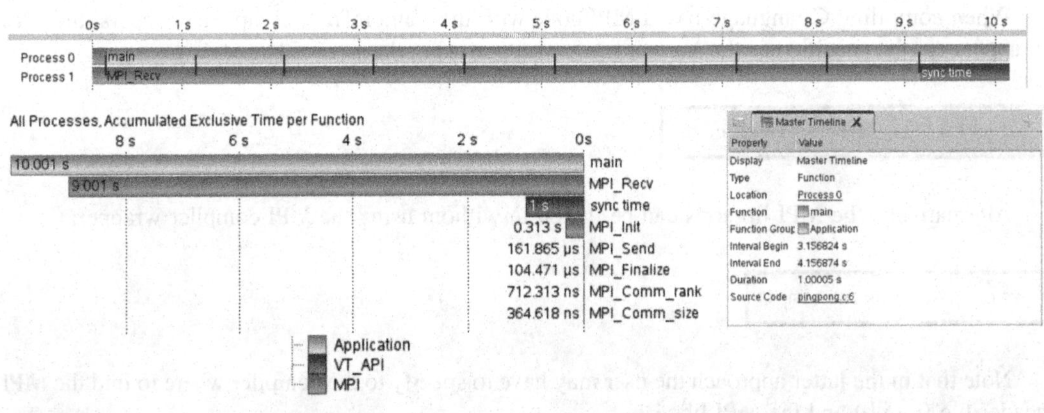

FIGURE 13.3

Instrumentation results from the pingpong.c MPI code (Code 13.4). A phase diagram shows the amount of time spent in application-level code (green (light gray in print versions)), MPI code (red (gray in print versions)), and time associated with the VampirTrace API. The information is shown both individually for each process as a function of time and cumulatively for the entire execution. In the top phase plot where information is shown individually for each process, the messages passed between the processes are illustrated using black lines. Portions of this phase plot can be highlighted and explored in detail with more information on the selected computational phase appearing in the context view labeled "Master Timeline".

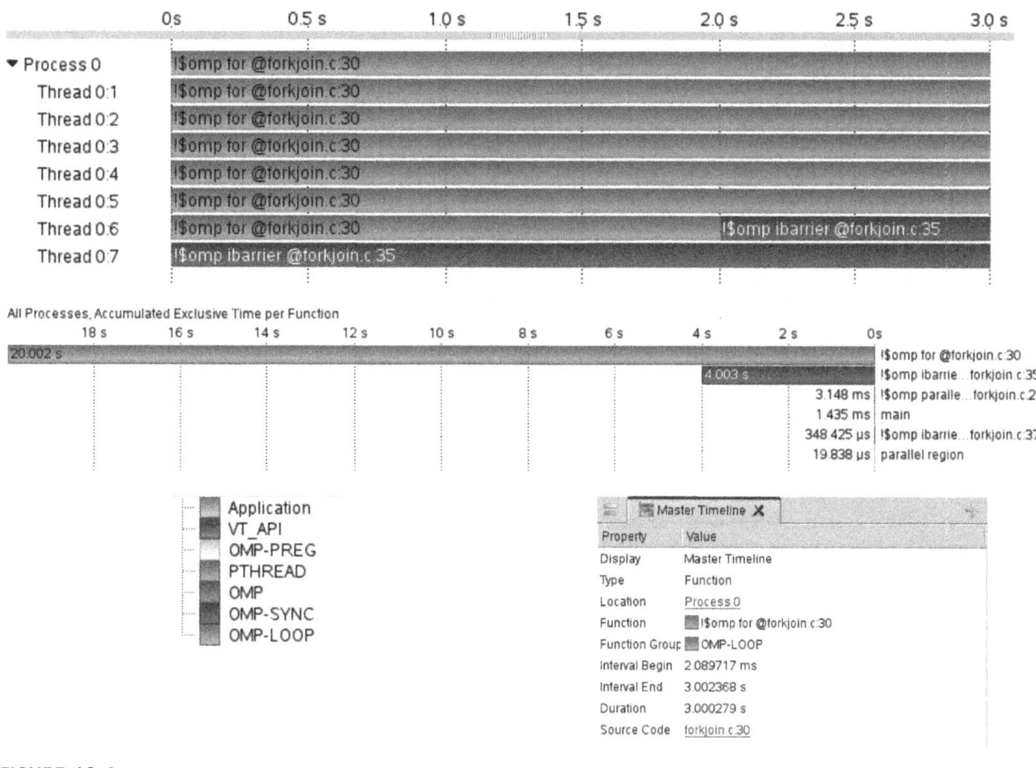

FIGURE 13.4

Instrumentation results from the forkjoin.c OpenMP code (Code 13.5) run using eight OpenMP threads. A color-coded computational phase diagram reveals most of the application time spent in the OpenMP loop, except for thread 7 which was idle throughout the computation. The cumulative time spent in each color-coded phase is also reported. Individual phase segments in each thread can be highlighted with more information appearing in the context view labeled "Master Timeline".

Apart from automatic instrumentation based on the programming model, VampirTrace can provide instrumentation via TAU, Dyninst, or manually inserting VampirTrace API calls to the code. These options are specified to the VampirTrace compiler wrapper as follows:

```
vtcc -vt:inst tauinst (For automatic TAU instrumentation)
vtcc -vt:inst dyninst (For automatic Dyninst instrumentation)
vtcc -vt:inst manual (For exclusive manual instrumentation)
```

Manual instrumentation in VampirTrace requires placing two API calls in regions of interest in a source code, VT_USER_START("<user-chosen name>") and VT_USER_END("<user-chosen name>"), and compiling with the flag `-DVTRACE`. To illustrate this, the pingpong.c code (Code 13.4) is modified to add these calls in Code 13.6.

```
1  #include <stdio.h>
2  #include <stdlib.h>
3  #include <unistd.h>
4  #include "mpi.h"
5  #include "vt_user.h"
6
7  int main(int argc,char **argv)
8  {
9    int rank,size;
10   MPI_Init(&argc,&argv);
11   MPI_Comm_rank(MPI_COMM_WORLD,&rank);
12   MPI_Comm_size(MPI_COMM_WORLD,&size);
13
14   if ( size != 2 ) {
15     printf(" Only runs on 2 processes \n");
16     MPI_Finalize(); // this example only works on two processes
17     exit(0);
18   }
19
20   int count;
21   if ( rank == 0 ) {
22     // initialize count on process 0
23     count = 0;
24   }
25   for (int i=0;i<10;i++) {
26     if ( rank == 0 ) {
27       MPI_Send(&count,1,MPI_INT,1,0,MPI_COMM_WORLD); // send "count" to rank 1
28       MPI_Recv(&count,1,MPI_INT,1,0,MPI_COMM_WORLD,MPI_STATUS_IGNORE); // receive it back
29       VT_USER_START("sleep section");
30       sleep(1);
31       VT_USER_END("sleep section");
32       count++;
33       printf(" Count %d\n",count);
34     } else {
35       MPI_Recv(&count,1,MPI_INT,0,0,MPI_COMM_WORLD,MPI_STATUS_IGNORE);
36       MPI_Send(&count,1,MPI_INT,0,0,MPI_COMM_WORLD);
37     }
38   }
39
40   if ( rank == 0 ) printf("\t\t\t Round trip count = %d\n",count);
41
42   MPI_Finalize();
43 }
```

Code 13.6. The pingpong.c code (Code 13.4) has been modified here for manual instrumentation. The VampirTrace API header ("vt_user.h") has been added in line 5 and the calls to VT_USER_START and VT_USER_END have been added surrounding the sleep function call in line 30. The section has been labeled "sleep section".

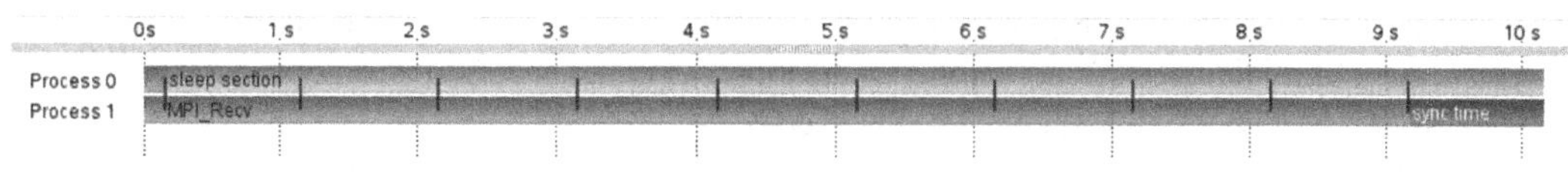

FIGURE 13.5

The computational phase plot for Code 13.6 with manual instrumentation along with compiler instrumentation of the MPI calls. The phase plot is now annotated not only with MPI calls but also with the manually instrumented "sleep section" which appears in the computational phases of process 0.

Code 13.6 can be compiled just as before, but with the `-DVTRACE` flag so that the manually added VampirTrace API calls will be recorded. In this example it is beneficial to combine the manual instrumentation with the MPI instrumentation automatically provided by the compiler, so the `-vt:inst` *manual* specification is not included in the compile command (it would otherwise override all compiler instrumentation):

```
vtcc -vt:cc mpicc -DVTRACE pingpong.c
```

The resulting computational phase plot for each process of Code 13.6 shown in Fig. 13.5 is now annotated with the manually instrumented computational phases labeled "sleep section" as well as the compiler-instrumented MPI phases.

13.7 SUMMARY AND OUTCOMES OF CHAPTER 13

- Performance monitoring is closely associated with application development and optimization. It detects the most frequently executed sections of code and measures the application's resource footprint.
- The act of measuring disturbs the measured system. Performance monitors employ minimally intrusive solutions to collect the performance metrics, leveraging dedicated low-overhead implementations such as hardware event counters whenever available.
- Monitored programs need to be instrumented, i.e., modified through insertion of suitable measurement and result collection functions. This may be accomplished at source level using compiler techniques, at library level by instrumentation, or at executable level. Each of these mechanisms differs in the degree of user involvement, measurement scope and precision, supported features, and intrusiveness.
- One of the fundamental metrics is time. Its measurement may be invoked from the command line using the *time* system utility or by instrumenting an application with timestamp collection functions such as *clock_gettime*.
- Profiling is one of the elementary techniques of performance monitoring. It is used to identify a program's execution hotspots and potentially capture other runtime metrics, such as memory size, communication parameters, and I/O activity. They may be used to classify the program as compute bound, memory bound, or I/O bound.

- Hotspots are parts of code the program spend most of the time executing. Bottlenecks are hotspots that have unduly adverse effects on the application's performance. Program optimization may relocate the bottleneck to another part of the code.
- One of the commonly used general-purpose profilers is provided by the *gperftools* suite. It can detect hotspots and memory management issues without modifications to the source code.
- The *perf_events* and *PAPI* packages are commonly used interfaces accessing hardware event counters. The first may be used from the command line, while the second enables instrumentation of arbitrary application sections.
- *TAU* is an example of an integrated profiling environment that supports multiple instrumentation modes, collection of execution profiles with multiple parameters, custom user probes, performance database management, and both text- and GUI-driven data analysis. It also interoperates with other tools using shared data formats.
- VampirTrace is one of the broadly used distributed profilers that is particularly useful for MPI and OpenMP (or hybrid) program tracing to capture program execution phases and communication activity. The generated traces may be displayed in a proprietary Vampir visualizer or exported to open-source tools such as TAU.

13.8 QUESTIONS AND PROBLEMS

1. Discuss differences between hotspots and bottlenecks. Provide examples to illustrate your answer.
2. Why do hardware event counters often provide a better insight into runtime behavior of an application? What are their limitations?
3. Write a program that estimates the overhead of time measurement using POSIX clocks. Make sure you collect numbers for both "hot" (i.e., initialized) and "cold" (uninitialized) cache scenarios.
4. Consider the following program:

```
#include <stdio.h>

int main() {
   long sum = 0;
   for (int i = 0; i < 1000000; i++)
      if (i&1 != 0) sum += 3*i;
   printf("sum=%ld\n", sum);
   return 0;
}
```

Instrument the for-loop using PAPI to count all conditional branches and taken conditional branches. Estimate the counts and verify your numbers by executing the instrumented code. How do the values change when the program is compiled with optimizations enabled compared to the unoptimized version? Why?
Note: to explain the discrepancies, it may be helpful to look at the generated assembly code. For gcc it can be done using the command:

```
gcc -S -fverbose-asm program.c
```

The resultant assembly listing annotated with variable names will be placed in the file `program.s`.

5. Profiling a program with the *perf* tool produces the following output:

```
Performance counter stats for './a.out':
      14207.022284      task-clock:u (msec)          #   1.000 CPUs utilized
                 0      context-switches:u           #   0.000 K/sec
                 0      cpu-migrations:u             #   0.000 K/sec
            10,301      page-faults:u                #   0.725 K/sec
    50,036,833,663      cycles:u                     #   3.522 GHz
    49,799,684,446      stalled-cycles-frontend:u    #  99.53% frontend
cycles idle
    46,725,530,082      stalled-cycles-backend:u     #  93.38% backend cycles
idle
     1,059,912,928      instructions:u               #   0.02  insn per cycle
                                                     #  46.98  stalled cycles
per insn
       115,260,873      branches:u                   #   8.113 M/sec
            55,407      branch-misses:u              #   0.05% of all
branches
      14.208427535 seconds time elapsed
```

What may be inferred about the code based on the above statistics?

6. Why might correlating different types of metrics supported by tools such as TAU be useful to program optimization? Provide examples.
7. An MPI program that makes a frequent use of MPI_Allreduce calls achieves poor parallel execution performance. Its developer suspects that this is due to load imbalance between the cores. How would you confirm her/his theory using VampirTrace?

REFERENCES

[1] Intel VTune Amplifier 2017, Intel Inc, 2017 [Online]. Available: https://software.intel.com/en-us/intel-vtune-amplifier-xe.

[2] CodeXL Web Page, Advanced Micro Devices, Inc., 2016 [Online]. Available: http://gpuopen.com/compute-product/codexl/.

[3] CodeXL GitHub Repository, 2017 [Online]. Available: https://github.com/GPUOpen-Tools/CodeXL.

[4] AMD Catalyst Software Web Page, Advanced Micro Devices Inc, 2017 [Online]. Available: http://www.amd.com/en-gb/innovations/software-technologies/catalyst.

[5] Nvidia CUDA Toolkit Web Page, Nvidia Inc, 2017 [Online]. Available: https://developer.nvidia.com/cuda-toolkit.

[6] D.A. Mills, Computer Network Time Synchronization: The Network Time Protocol, CRC Press, 2006, p. 304 p.

[7] Gperftools Wiki Page, Github, February 2017 [Online]. Available: https://github.com/gperftools/gperftools/wiki.

[8] perf: Linux profiling with performance counters, September 28, 2015 [Online]. Available: https://perf.wiki.kernel.org/index.php/Main_Page.
[9] PERF_EVENT_OPEN Manual Page, January 10, 2015 [Online]. Available: http://web.eece.maine.edu/~vweaver/projects/perf_events/perf_event_open.html.
[10] Performance Application Programming Interface, University of Tennessee, February 2017 [Online]. Available: http://icl.cs.utk.edu/papi/.
[11] Intel Math Kernel Library (Intel MKL), Intel Inc, 2017 [Online]. Available: https://software.intel.com/en-us/intel-mkl.
[12] TAU Reference Guide, University of Oregon, November 11, 2016 [Online]. Available: https://www.cs.uoregon.edu/research/tau/tau-referenceguide.pdf.
[13] Paradyn/Dyninst Web Page, University of Meryland and University of Wisconsin Madison, [Online]. Available: http://www.dyninst.org/.
[14] Scalasca Web Page, Juelich Forschungszentrum, Technische Universitaet Darmstadt, German Research School for Simulation Sciences, [Online]. Available: http://www.scalasca.org/.
[15] VampirTrace Web Page, Centre for Information Services and High Performance Computing (ZIH), Dresden University, 2016 [Online]. Available: https://tu-dresden.de/zih/forschung/projekte/vampirtrace.
[16] Performance Visualization for Parallel Programs web page, Laboratory for Advanced Numerical Software at ANL, [Online]. Available: http://www.mcs.anl.gov/research/projects/perfvis/software/index.htm.

CHAPTER

DEBUGGING

14

CHAPTER OUTLINE

14.1 INTRODUCTION

Frequently high performance computing (HPC) practitioners encounter anomalies in application execution that arise from a wide variety of origins, including hardware failures, programming errors, software technical errors, or even the unlikely case of a cosmic ray flipping a bit and interfering with the computation. Tracking the origin of such application execution anomalies is difficult even when using just a simple desktop or laptop computer. On an HPC resource, resolving such an anomaly in an application is compounded many times by the complex interplay between the multiple network, memory, and library components of the supercomputer and the different execution modalities employed. This chapter introduces several techniques and tools for debugging an HPC application and explores several of the more common types of bugs the practitioner will encounter, including deadlocks, races, memory leaks, segmentation faults, and invalid references, among others.

High Performance Computing. https://doi.org/10.1016/B978-0-12-420158-3.00014-9

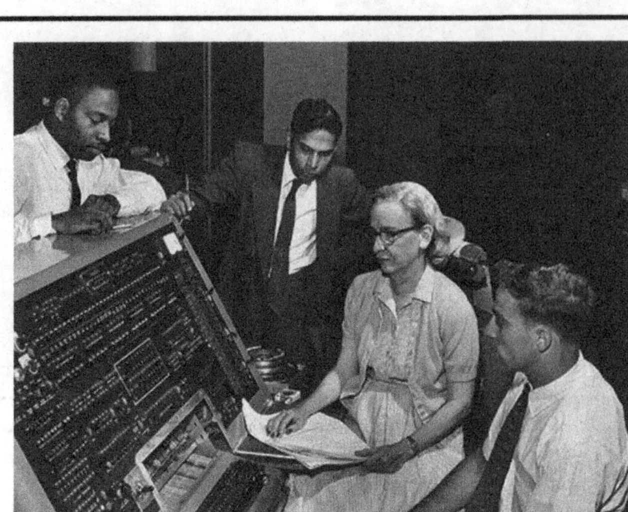

Grace Brewster Murray Hopper seated at the input console for the UNIVAC I. *Photo by Smithsonian Institution via Wikimedia Commons*

Grace Brewster Murray Hopper was a mathematics professor who became a US Navy rear admiral and strongly promoted and influenced the development of higher-level programming languages at a time when most programming was done in nonportable, machine-specific languages. In addition to her programming language and compiler work, which served as the genesis of the common business-oriented language (COBOL), she was a senior developer on the first commercial electronic computer, the UNIVAC 1. In her own words, "the most important thing I've accomplished, other than building the compiler, is training young people". Among numerous other accolades, Grace Hopper received the highest civilian award of the United States, the Presidential Medal of Freedom, posthumously in 2016.

Historically debugging is popularly associated with Grace Hopper, who discovered a moth interfering with a computer's operation while working on the Harvard Mark II electromechanical computer in 1947. The moth was placed in the group's logbook with the caption "First actual case of bug being found", as seen in Fig. 14.1. In a similar story that slightly predates Grace Hopper's experience, mathematician Norbert Wiener was called to diagnose the anomalous behavior of the automatic fire control of a warship gun during World War II. After hearing a description of the specific short circuits that occurred at certain gun muzzle positions, he correctly predicted that a dead mouse would be found in the device and the specific location where it would be found [1].

Not entirely unlike these famous cases of literal debugging, debugging an application on a high performance computer frequently requires a fairly detailed view of the supercomputer software and hardware stack to diagnose the anomaly properly. There are a wide variety of tools that can assist in diagnosing a problem. This chapter begins by introducing the use of the GNU debugger (GDB) and the Valgrind instrumentation framework, and mentioning some of the more prevalent commercial debugger tools. The chapter then uses the tools to explore a series of common bugs found in message-passing interface (MPI) and OpenMP codes. It finishes by enumerating a list of common compiler flags and messages that are helpful in debugging applications, and some available system monitor approaches to debugging.

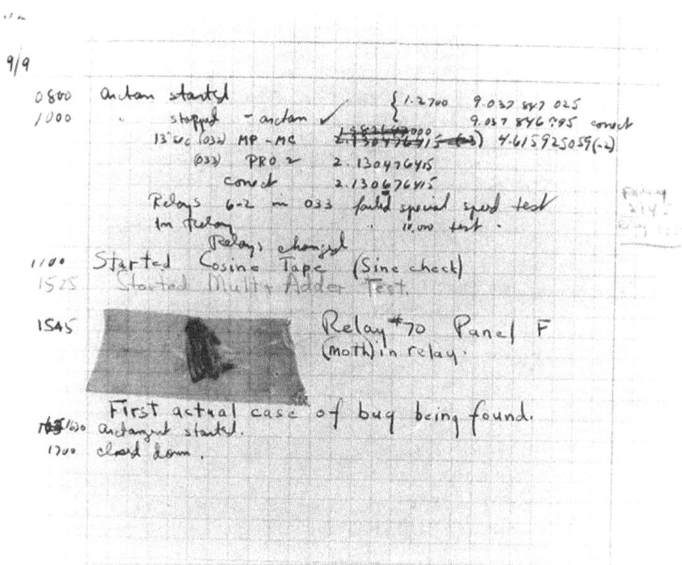

FIGURE 14.1

An example of literal debugging from the Harvard Mark II as recorded by Grace Hopper—a moth found in the machine has been taped to the logbook.

Photo courtesy: Naval Surface Warfare Center, Dahlgren, VA, 1988 via Wikimedia Commons

14.2 TOOLS

The complexity of debugging a code has motivated the development of multiple open-source and proprietary tools to assist the programmer in stepping through a code in execution and enabling the placement of breakpoints where the execution is paused and the memory can be viewed. The most common open-source debugging tools are serial in nature; however, they can be adapted for debugging in parallel, as shown later in this chapter. There are also several commercial debuggers specifically targeting parallel execution on a high performance computer; these are often made available to supercomputing users by system administrators, although the license cost per node may limit the scale at which a commercial debugger can be used. This section introduces two open-source and freely available debugging tools, the GDB and the Valgrind instrumentation framework, and gives some information on a subset of the more common commercial parallel debuggers available.

14.2.1 THE GNU DEBUGGER

The GDB is one of the commonest open-source debuggers available. One commercial debugger (Allinea DDT [2]) even uses the GDB as its engine. The GDB is a command-line debugger invoked on Linux and Unix systems using the command:

gdb <executable name> where the angled brackets are substituted for the executable intended for debugging. This section explores a small but important subset of GDB functionality that is used for the

```
#include <stdlib.h>
#include <stdio.h>

int main(int argc,char **argv) {
  int i;
  // Make the local vector size constant
  int local_vector_size = 100;

  // initialize the vectors
  double *a, *b;
  a = (double *) malloc(
       local_vector_size*sizeof(double));
  b = (double *) malloc(
       local_vector_size*sizeof(double));
  for (i=0;i<local_vector_size;i++) {
    a[i] = 3.14;
    b[i] = 6.67;
  }
  // compute dot product
  double sum = 0.0;
  for (i=0;i<local_vector_size;i++) {
    sum += a[i]*b[i];
  }
  printf("The dot product is %g\n",sum);

  free(a);
  free(b);
  return 0;
}
```

FIGURE 14.2

The example code dotprod_serial.c for exploring the GNU debugger.

debugging examples later in this chapter. To help illustrate GDB commands and usage, the example code of Fig. 14.2 is used. When running GDB on an executable, it is important to let the compiler know that the executable will be used for debugging. This is done by using the "-g" flag when compiling.

14.2.1.1 Break Points

One of the most useful commands in GDB is for setting a break point. A break point is an interruption in the execution of a code, enabling the user to examine the program's state at that moment. There are several ways to set a break point with the GDB, including specifying a function name, line number, file name and line number, a conditional, or even a memory address. Using the code from Fig. 14.2, several of these options are explored in Table 14.1, assuming that the code has been compiled with debug information enabled using the −g flag and the GDB has already started on the executable as indicated.

Information on each of the break points can be queried from the gdb command line using the command *info breakpoints*, as seen in Fig. 14.3. When calling *info breakpoints*, seven quantities are reported: the identifier of the break point, the type of break point, the disposition of the break point, whether or not the break point is enabled, the memory address of where the break point is in the

Table 14.1 Examples of Different Ways to Set a Break Point Using the Code in Fig. 14.2 as an Example

Break Point Command Type	gdb Breakpoint Command	Description
Break by function	break printf	Pauses the execution at line 24
Break by line number	break 17	Pauses the execution at line 17
Break by line number and filename	break dotprod_serial.c:17	Pauses the execution at line 17
Break by conditional	break dotprod_serial.c:16 if i==4	Pauses the execution at line 16 when i equals 4

```
(gdb) info breakpoints
Num     Type           Disp Enb Address            What
1       breakpoint     keep y   0x0000000000400450 <printf@plt>
2       breakpoint     keep y   0x00000000004005ef in main at dotprod_serial.c:17
3       breakpoint     keep y   0x00000000004005ef in main at dotprod_serial.c:17
4       breakpoint     keep y   0x00000000004005cf in main at dotprod_serial.c:16
        stop only if i==4
(gdb)
```

FIGURE 14.3

Information on all the break points in Table 14.1 set for the code in Fig. 14.2.

program, and where the break point is in terms of the file name and line number. While only break points have been discussed up to this point, two similar types of pausing points, called watch points and catch points, are discussed in the following subsection.

The disposition of a break point indicates whether it will be deleted when reached, or kept. This is often useful when setting a break point inside a for-loop so that the same break point is not repeatedly hit. A break point can be disabled by using the *disable* command followed by the break point identifier. For example, entering *disable 2* in the command line would disable break point number 2. It can be reenabled by using the command *enable* 2. Break points can be deleted altogether by using the *delete* command followed by the break point identifier. The disposition of a break point can also be changed by using the *enable* command. For example, if break point number 3 should be disabled after being hit once, the command *enable once 3* is used. To set a break point with the disposition to be deleted when hit, the *tbreak* command is used following the syntax of Table 14.1. These four useful break point commands, *enable, disable, delete,* and *tbreak*, are illustrated in Fig. 14.4.

While the setting of the break point by itself is frequently useful in helping to deduce control flow, it is usually most useful in examining the variables at that moment in the program's state. This can be done using the *print* command, illustrated in Fig. 14.5. Note that for the execution to begin after setting the break point in Fig. 14.5, the command *run* must be issued. Once the break point is reached, the execution will pause and the variables can then be examined via *print*.

14.2.1.2 Watch Points and Catch Points

Watch points and catch points are similar in nature to break points, but are conditional upon some variable being written to or some prespecified event like catching a C++ exception. To set a watch

```
(gdb) disable 2
(gdb) enable once 3
(gdb) delete 1
(gdb) info breakpoints
Num     Type           Disp Enb Address            What
2       breakpoint     keep n   0x00000000004005ef in main at dotprod_serial.c:17
3       breakpoint     dis  y   0x00000000004005ef in main at dotprod_serial.c:17
4       breakpoint     keep y   0x00000000004005cf in main at dotprod_serial.c:16
        stop only if i==4
(gdb) tbreak dotprod_serial.c:24
Temporary breakpoint 5 at 0x40067b: file dotprod_serial.c, line 24.
(gdb) info breakpoints
Num     Type           Disp Enb Address            What
2       breakpoint     keep n   0x00000000004005ef in main at dotprod_serial.c:17
3       breakpoint     dis  y   0x00000000004005ef in main at dotprod_serial.c:17
4       breakpoint     keep y   0x00000000004005cf in main at dotprod_serial.c:16
        stop only if i==4
5       breakpoint     del  y   0x000000000040067b in main at dotprod_serial.c:24
(gdb)
```

FIGURE 14.4

Beginning with the break points in Fig. 14.3, the commands disable, enable, delete, and tbreak are used to alter the enablement of a break point, disposition of a break point, deletion a break point, and setting of a temporary break point, respectively.

```
(gdb) tbreak 17
Temporary breakpoint 1 at 0x4005ef: file dotprod_serial.c, line 17.
(gdb) run
Starting program: /home/andersmw/learn/a.out

Temporary breakpoint 1, main (argc=1, argv=0x7fffffffdfc8) at dotprod_serial.c:17
17            b[i] = 6.67;
(gdb) print i
$1 = 0
(gdb) print a[i]
$2 = 3.1400000000000001
(gdb) print b[i]
$3 = 0
(gdb)
```

FIGURE 14.5

Example of using a temporary break point at line 17 of Fig. 14.2 and then examining the values of the variables inside the break point. Notice that the a[0] element has been initialized while the b[0] element has not yet been initialized, indicating that the break point pauses before the specified break point line is executed.

point, the command *watch* followed by the expression to watch is entered into the gdb command line. For example, to watch for changes to the value of the sum variable in Fig. 14.2, the command *watch sum* would be issued to the gdb command line once the variable sum was in the current context at line 20. This is illustrated in Fig. 14.6. Information on watch points can be obtained issuing the *info watchpoints* command illustrated in Fig. 14.7.

```
(gdb) b 20
Breakpoint 1 at 0x40061b: file dotprod_serial.c, line 20.
(gdb) r
Starting program: /home/andersmw/learn/a.out

Breakpoint 1, main (argc=1, argv=0x7fffffffdfb8) at dotprod_serial.c:20
20          double sum = 0.0;
(gdb) watch sum
Hardware watchpoint 2: sum
(gdb) continue
Continuing.
Hardware watchpoint 2: sum

Old value = 6.9533558074263132e-310
New value = 0
main (argc=1, argv=0x7fffffffdfb8) at dotprod_serial.c:21
21          for (i=0;i<local_vector_size;i++) {
(gdb) continue
Continuing.
Hardware watchpoint 2: sum

Old value = 0
New value = 20.9438
main (argc=1, argv=0x7fffffffdfb8) at dotprod_serial.c:21
21          for (i=0;i<local_vector_size;i++) {
(gdb)
```

FIGURE 14.6

A demonstration of setting a watch point on the variable sum from Fig. 14.2. A break point is set at line 20 so the variable is in the current memory context. Then the watch point is issued using issuing the command "watch sum". Each time the sum variable is written to, the execution will pause. The "continue" command is used to resume execution. The watch point is hit twice in this example. The abbreviations for "break", "b", and "run", "r", are also used. Command abbreviations are included in the GDB cheat sheet.

```
(gdb) info watchpoints
Num     Type           Disp Enb Address            What
2       hw watchpoint  keep y                      sum
        breakpoint already hit 2 times
(gdb)
```

FIGURE 14.7

Information on watch points can be obtained issuing the "info watchpoints" command.

14.2.1.3 Back Trace

When the execution has paused in the debugger, an overview of the callers leading to the present point in the execution can be revealed using the *back trace* command. As the example in Fig. 14.2 only has one call (main), any back trace using that example would only give one frame, or call stack member. To better illustrate the back trace command, the example of Fig. 14.2 is modified to include another function as seen in Fig. 14.8.

```
0001 #include <stdlib.h>
0002 #include <stdio.h>
0003
0004 void initialize(double *a, double *b,int local_vector_size)
0005 {
0006   int i;
0007   for (i=0;i<local_vector_size;i++) {
0008     a[i] = 3.14;
0009     b[i] = 6.67;
0010   }
0011 }
0012
0013 int main(int argc,char **argv) {
0014   int i;
0015   // Make the local vector size constant
0016   int local_vector_size = 100;
0017
0018   // initialize the vectors
0019   double *a, *b;
0020   a = (double *) malloc(
0021        local_vector_size*sizeof(double));
0022   b = (double *) malloc(
0023        local_vector_size*sizeof(double));
0024
0025   initialize(a,b,local_vector_size);
0026
0027   // compute dot product
0028   double sum = 0.0;
0029   for (i=0;i<local_vector_size;i++) {
0030     sum += a[i]*b[i];
0031   }
0032   printf("The dot product is %g\n",sum);
0033
0034   free(a);
0035   free(b);
0036   return 0;
0037 }
```

FIGURE 14.8

Example code for exploring the back trace command.

By setting a break point at line 8 in the initialize function of Fig. 14.8, the call stack for that point in the execution can be revealed using the back trace command, as shown in Fig. 14.9.

The call stack can be traversed using the *up* and *down* commands, enabling the user to exit or enter function calls and examine the variables and memory in those calls. The up and down commands, illustrated in Fig. 14.10, can be followed by a number to traverse several call stack frames with a single command.

14.2.1.4 Setting a Variable

Using GDB it is possible to set a variable during execution and continue execution using that variable. This capability is achieved using the *set* command, illustrated in Fig. 14.11. After setting a break point

```
(gdb) break 8
Breakpoint 1 at 0x40059e: file dotprod_serial.c, line 8.
(gdb) run
Starting program: /home/andersmw/learn/a.out

Breakpoint 1, initialize (a=0x601010, b=0x601340, local_vector_size=100)
    at dotprod_serial.c:8
8           a[i] = 3.14;
(gdb) backtrace
#0  0x000000000040059e in initialize (a=0x601010, b=0x601340, local_vector_size=100)
    at dotprod_serial.c:8
#1  0x0000000000400643 in main (argc=1, argv=0x7fffffffdfb8) at dotprod_serial.c:25
(gdb)
```

FIGURE 14.9

Illustration of the back trace command for showing the call stack. A break point is set in the code from Fig. 14.8 at line 8 and the code is executed to that point. Issuing the back trace command reveals a call stack with two frames: the execution frame in the initialize function (frame #0), and the calling frame (frame #1) back to the main routine.

```
(gdb) backtrace
#0  0x000000000040059e in initialize (a=0x601010, b=0x601340, local_vector_size=100)
    at dotprod_serial.c:8
#1  0x0000000000400643 in main (argc=1, argv=0x7fffffffdfb8) at dotprod_serial.c:25
(gdb) up
#1  0x0000000000400643 in main (argc=1, argv=0x7fffffffdfb8) at dotprod_serial.c:25
25          initialize(a,b,local_vector_size);
(gdb) list
20          a = (double *) malloc(
21               local_vector_size*sizeof(double));
22          b = (double *) malloc(
23               local_vector_size*sizeof(double));
24
25          initialize(a,b,local_vector_size);
26
27          // compute dot product
28          double sum = 0.0;
29          for (i=0;i<local_vector_size;i++) {
(gdb) down
#0  initialize (a=0x601010, b=0x601340, local_vector_size=100) at dotprod_serial.c:8
8           a[i] = 3.14;
(gdb) list
3
4         void initialize(double *a, double *b,int local_vector_size)
5         {
6           int i;
7           for (i=0;i<local_vector_size;i++) {
8             a[i] = 3.14;
9             b[i] = 6.67;
10          }
11        }
12
(gdb)
```

FIGURE 14.10

Example of traversing the call stack frames using the up and down commands. Beginning with the back trace from Fig. 14.9, the up command is issued moving the debugger context outside the initialize function to the main routine at line 25 of Fig. 14.8. The "list" command is useful in printing a few lines of the source code from the current context to screen. The down command is then issued and the debugger context is returned to the initialize function.

```
(gdb) break 17
Breakpoint 1 at 0x4005ef: file dotprod_serial.c, line 17.
(gdb) run
Starting program: /home/andersmw/learn/a.out

Breakpoint 1, main (argc=1, argv=0x7fffffffdfb8) at dotprod_serial.c:17
17          b[i] = 6.67;
(gdb) set var i=99
(gdb) continue
Continuing.
The dot product is 0
[Inferior 1 (process 12264) exited normally]
(gdb)
```

FIGURE 14.11

After setting a break point inside the initialization for-loop in the code from Fig. 14.2, the value of the variable i is set to 99, forcing the loop to exit when execution is resumed. Using the "set var" command, the execution can be steered inside the debugger.

inside the initialization *for*-loop in the code from Fig. 14.2, the value of the variable *i* is set to 99, forcing the loop to exit when execution is resumed. Using the "set var" command, the execution can be steered inside the debugger.

14.2.1.5 Threads

For multithreaded applications such as OpenMP, the GDB enables switching context between threads as well as applying debugger commands to all threads. The *info threads* command will list the threads along with a thread identifier. The debugger can switch between threads by issuing the *thread* command followed by the thread identifier.

To explore the thread debugging functionality in GDB, the OpenMP dot product example in Fig. 14.12 is used. The environment variable OMP_NUM_THREADS is set to four and the GDB is started in the normal way: *gdb <executable name>*. Stepping through the code and examining the private variables of each thread is illustrated in Fig. 14.13. A break point is placed at line 23 of the code in Fig. 14.12. The debugger notifies the user of the creation of three additional threads upon running, making a total of four threads as expected. Once at the break point, the command "*info threads*" lists the threads available. When issuing "*info threads*", the asterisk that appears next to the thread number indicates which thread context is active in the debugger. The private variable *i* is printed for each thread and the debugger context is switched between the threads using the "thread" command.

14.2.1.6 GDB Cheat Sheet

A brief summary of some of the more important GDB commands is listed in Table 14.2, along with their functions and abbreviations.

14.2.2 VALGRIND

The Valgrind tool suite [3] provides several very important tools for debugging applications, especially in the context of memory errors and thread data races. The suite consists of the tools shown in Table 14.3.

```
#include <stdio.h>
#include <omp.h>

int main ()
{
  const int n = 30;
  int   i,chunk;
  double a[n], b[n], result = 0.0;

  /* Some initializations */
  chunk = 5;
  for (i=0; i < n; i++) {
      a[i] = i * 3.14;
      b[i] = i * 6.67;
  }

#pragma omp parallel for         \
     default(shared) private(i) \
     schedule(static,chunk)     \
     reduction(+:result)

    for (i=0; i < n; i++)
        result += (a[i] * b[i]);

  printf("Final result= %f\n",result);
}
```

FIGURE 14.12

OpenMP dot product code to illustrate the GDB capability with threads.

Like the GDB, it is best practice to compile the executable with debugging information using the −g flag to provide the most information. Valgrind usage is simple: the executable is passed to Valgrind after passing the desired suite tool or check to perform. For example, the command

valgrind −tool=helgrind <program executable> would run the Helgrind tool for finding data race conditions on a specified program executable, such as an OpenMP code. If no tool is specified, Valgrind will run the Memcheck tool. Memcheck is one of the most widely used tools for identifying memory errors.

14.2.3 COMMERCIAL PARALLEL DEBUGGERS

There are a number of commercial parallel debuggers providing debugging support for C, C++, and Fortran-based codes for a wide variety of programming models and hardware architectures, including general-purpose graphics processing units and many integrated core architectures. A list of some of the more widely used parallel commercial debuggers available is provided in Table 14.4.

Each of the debuggers in Table 14.1 has a graphical user interface (GUI) for examining the state of each process or thread in a parallel execution. Several provide detection for memory leak or other memory errors. It is also common now to provide a replay capability whereby the execution state of the entire program is recorded for later playback. This can be especially useful in debugging the

```
(gdb) break 23
Breakpoint 1 at 0x40093c: file dotproduct.c, line 23.
(gdb) run
Starting program: /home/andersmw/learn/a.out
[Thread debugging using libthread_db enabled]
Using host libthread_db library "/lib/x86_64-linux-gnu/libthread_db.so.1".
[New Thread 0x7ffff73d1700 (LWP 44176)]
[New Thread 0x7ffff6bd0700 (LWP 44177)]
[New Thread 0x7ffff63cf700 (LWP 44178)]

Breakpoint 1, main._omp_fn.0 () at dotproduct.c:23
23              result += (a[i] * b[i]);
(gdb) info threads
  Id   Target Id         Frame
  4    Thread 0x7ffff63cf700 (LWP 44178) "a.out" main._omp_fn.0 () at dotproduct.c:23
  3    Thread 0x7ffff6bd0700 (LWP 44177) "a.out" main._omp_fn.0 () at dotproduct.c:23
  2    Thread 0x7ffff73d1700 (LWP 44176) "a.out" main._omp_fn.0 () at dotproduct.c:23
* 1    Thread 0x7ffff7fdc7c0 (LWP 44172) "a.out" main._omp_fn.0 () at dotproduct.c:23
(gdb) print i
$1 = 0
(gdb) thread 2
[Switching to thread 2 (Thread 0x7ffff73d1700 (LWP 44176))]
#0  main._omp_fn.0 () at dotproduct.c:23
23              result += (a[i] * b[i]);
(gdb) print i
$2 = 5
(gdb) thread 3
[Switching to thread 3 (Thread 0x7ffff6bd0700 (LWP 44177))]
#0  main._omp_fn.0 () at dotproduct.c:23
23              result += (a[i] * b[i]);
(gdb) print i
$3 = 10
(gdb) thread 4
[Switching to thread 4 (Thread 0x7ffff63cf700 (LWP 44178))]
#0  main._omp_fn.0 () at dotproduct.c:23
23              result += (a[i] * b[i]);
(gdb) print i
$4 = 15
(gdb) 
```

FIGURE 14.13

GNU debugger using threads. The code in Fig. 14.12 is executed in the GDB, where the environment OMP_NUM_THREADS is set to be four.

so-called Heisenbugs, which disappear when attempting to trap them. The startup options for TotalView include both a replay capability and memory debugging, as seen in Fig. 14.14. The entire program state can be viewed and toggled between each process or thread, as illustrated for TotalView in Fig. 14.15.

Commercial parallel debuggers provide excellent debugging support, but often at a significant license cost that becomes prohibitive as the number of nodes increases. For this reason, supercomputing centers frequently have an upper limit on the number of nodes across which such commercial debuggers will function. Application users debugging on scales above this limit will often have to revert to some of the other tools discussed in this chapter.

Table 14.2 Brief Summary of Some Major GDB Commands

Command	Abbreviation	Function
Run	r	Begins execution in the debugger
continue	c	Continues execution in the debugger after a pause
quit	q	Quits the debugger
break	b	Sets a break point
watch		Sets a watch point
backtrace	bt	Prints the call stack
set variable	set var	Sets a variable value
thread	t	Switches to a different thread identifier
list	l	Lists source code near the present stopping point

Table 14.3 Tools in the Valgrind Tool Suite

Tool	Description
Memcheck	Reports memory errors, including memory leaks and access to memory that is not yet allocated
Cachegrind	Identifies the number of cache misses
Callgrind	Extends cachegrind with some additional information
Massif	Heap profiler
Helgrind	Debugger for finding data race conditions
DRD	Multithread debugging for C and C++ programs

Table 14.4 Some of the More Widely Used Parallel Commercial Debuggers

Commerical Debugger	Notable Capabilities
TotalView [4]	Support for OpenMP, MPI, OpenACC, CUDA
Allinea DDT [2]	Support for OpenMP, Pthreads, MPI, CUDA
Intel Parallel Debugger [5]	Support for multicore debugging

14.3 DEBUGGING OPENMP EXAMPLE: ACCESSING AN UNPROTECTED SHARED VARIABLE

One of the most common errors made by OpenMP programmers is accessing an unprotected shared variable; an example is shown in Fig. 14.16. A correct version of this example is given in Fig. 14.17.

If the code in Fig. 14.16 is run using Valgrind, the data race on the variable *sum* is immediately identified:

valgrind –tool=helgrind ./a.out

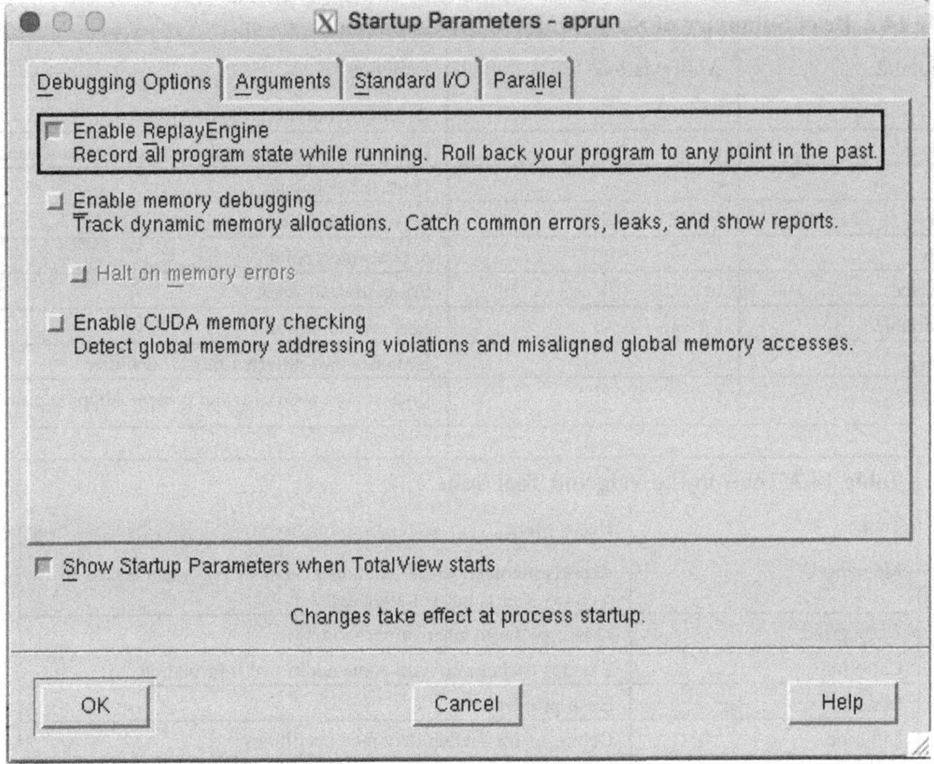

FIGURE 14.14

Startup options for a two-process MPI SendRecv example using TotalView. Important options include enabling replay and memory debugging.

Valgrind produces a warning of a data race in the code *bug.c* (Fig. 14.16); this warning is shown in Fig. 14.18, and it even correctly indicates the line number where the problem occurs. This experiment could also have been conducted using the GDB to observe the race condition as different threads attempt to write to the variable *sum* concurrently.

14.4 DEBUGGING MPI EXAMPLE: DEADLOCK

A common error in MPI programming is a deadlock, where competing requests completely impede their fulfillment and the program cannot proceed. An example is given in Fig. 14.19, and the situation is rectified in Fig. 14.20. Deadlocks like this can be difficult to debug, as they result in the program execution hanging without error message or additional output.

This deadlock can be easily identified using a debugger. Although the GDB is a serial debugger, one simple and straightforward way to debug this parallel application is to launch the GDB for each process. There are two ways to do this.

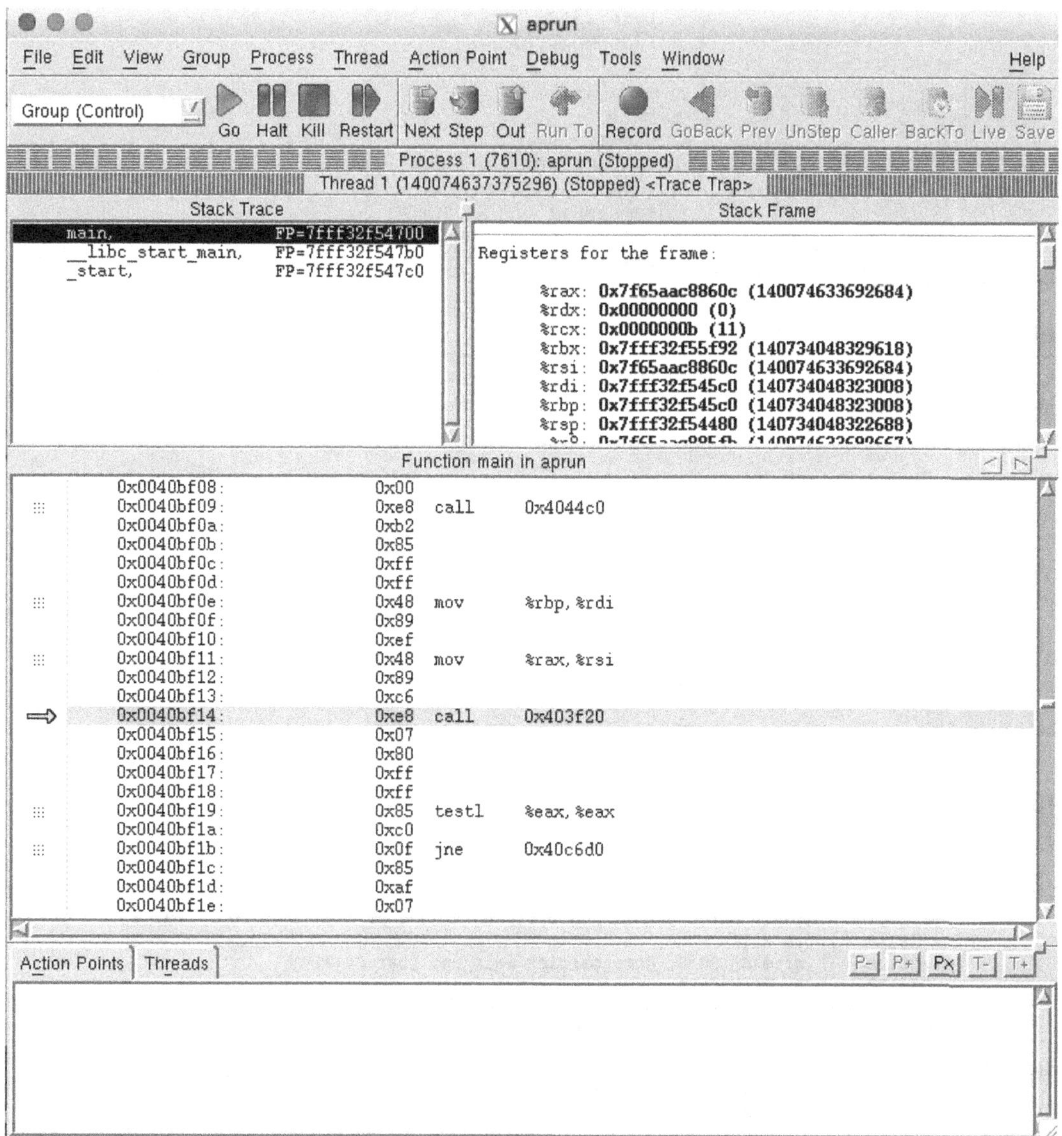

FIGURE 14.15

The TotalView GUI for examining and stepping through the program state on each process or thread.

The first approach involves launching an xterm window for each process and using the debugger in each to investigate the problem. This is illustrated in Fig. 14.21. While this will work on some clusters, many are not configured to allow xterm windows to be launched from the compute nodes.

The second approach does not require launching an xterm window and will work on nearly all clusters. However, it requires adding a few lines of code to what is being debugged. This additional

```
#include <stdio.h>
#include <omp.h>

int main () {
  int i;
  int sum = 0;
#pragma omp parallel for
  for (i=0;i<100;i++) {
    sum += i;
  }
  printf(" Result sum=%d\n",sum);
}
```

FIGURE 14.16

Example of unprotected access of a shared variable: bug.c. The shared variable is “sum”, and running this with more than one OpenMP thread will result in both incorrect and inconsistent results.

```
#include <stdio.h>
#include <omp.h>

int main () {
  int i;
  int sum = 0;
#pragma omp parallel for reduction(+:sum)
  for (i=0;i<100;i++) {
    sum += i;
  }
  printf(" Result sum=%d\n",sum);
}
```

FIGURE 14.17

Corrected version of the code in Fig. 14.16.

```
==30110== Possible data race during write of size 4 at 0x5845800 by thread #1
==30110== Locks held: none
==30110==    at 0x4E4E638: gomp_barrier_wait_end (bar.c:40)
==30110==    by 0x4E4C681: gomp_team_start (team.c:805)
==30110==    by 0x4E48999: GOMP_parallel (parallel.c:167)
==30110==    by 0x400725: main (bug.c:7)
```

FIGURE 14.18

Output from Valgrind when debugging the code bug.c in Fig. 14.16.

code prints the process identifier (PID) for each process to allow the GDB to be attached to that process. A “while” loop is added to pause the execution of the code until a debugger can be attached to each process. The deadlock code modified for debugging with the GDB is presented in Fig. 14.22; the code that has been added is seen in lines 17–24.

To debug in parallel with the GDB, the code in Fig. 14.22 is run as normal on two processes, i.e., mpirun −np 2<executable name>. The PIDs then print and the execution will pause, as illustrated in Fig. 14.23.

```
#include <stdio.h>
#include <stdlib.h>
#include <mpi.h>

int main(int argc, char* argv[]) {
  const int n = 10000;
  int *x, *y, nprocs,proc_id,i;
  int tag1 = 19;
  int tag2 = 20;
  MPI_Status status;
  MPI_Request send_request, recv_request;

  MPI_Init(&argc, &argv);
  MPI_Comm_size(MPI_COMM_WORLD, &nprocs);
  MPI_Comm_rank(MPI_COMM_WORLD, &proc_id);

  x = (int *) malloc(sizeof(int)*n);
  y = (int *) malloc(sizeof(int)*n);

  // this example only works on two processes
  if (nprocs != 2) {
    if (proc_id == 0) {
      printf("This only works on 2 processes\n");
    }
    MPI_Finalize();
    return 0;
  }

  if (proc_id == 0) {
    // only process 0 does this part
    for (i=0;i<n;i++) x[i] = 314159;

    MPI_Send(x, n, MPI_INT, 1, tag2, MPI_COMM_WORLD);
    MPI_Recv(x, n, MPI_INT, 1, tag1, MPI_COMM_WORLD,&status);

    printf(" Process %d received value %d\n",proc_id,x[0]);
  } else {

    MPI_Send(y, n, MPI_INT, 0, tag1, MPI_COMM_WORLD);
    MPI_Recv(y, n, MPI_INT, 0, tag2, MPI_COMM_WORLD,&status);
  }

  free(x);
  free(y);

  MPI_Finalize();
  return 0;
}
```

FIGURE 14.19

Example of a deadlock: two competing MPI_Send requests block the communication progress and the execution hangs.

Once the PIDs are known, the GDB can be attached to each process. This is done by logging on to the node(s) where the processes are waiting and launching the GDB for each PID waiting on that node, as illustrated in Fig. 14.24.

[andersmw@cutter: ~$ gdb attach 17331

[andersmw@cutter: ~$ gdb attach 17332

```
#include <stdio.h>
#include <stdlib.h>
#include <mpi.h>

int main(int argc, char* argv[]) {
  const int n = 10000;
  int *x, *y, nprocs,proc_id,i;
  int tag1 = 19;
  int tag2 = 20;
  MPI_Status status;
  MPI_Request send_request, recv_request;

  MPI_Init(&argc, &argv);
  MPI_Comm_size(MPI_COMM_WORLD, &nprocs);
  MPI_Comm_rank(MPI_COMM_WORLD, &proc_id);

  x = (int *) malloc(sizeof(int)*n);
  y = (int *) malloc(sizeof(int)*n);

  // this example only works on two processes
  if (nprocs != 2) {
    if (proc_id == 0) {
      printf("This only works on 2 processes\n");
    }
    MPI_Finalize();
    return 0;
  }

  if (proc_id == 0) {
    // only process 0 does this part
    for (i=0;i<n;i++) x[i] = 314159;

    MPI_Send(x, n, MPI_INT, 1, tag2, MPI_COMM_WORLD);
    MPI_Recv(x, n, MPI_INT, 1, tag1, MPI_COMM_WORLD,&status);

    printf(" Process %d received value %d\n",proc_id,x[0]);
  } else {

    MPI_Recv(y, n, MPI_INT, 0, tag2, MPI_COMM_WORLD,&status);
    MPI_Send(y, n, MPI_INT, 0, tag1, MPI_COMM_WORLD);
  }

  free(x);
  free(y);

  MPI_Finalize();
  return 0;
}
```

FIGURE 14.20

A corrected version of the deadlock in Fig. 14.19.

Note that there is no need to attach the debugger to the process in the same directory as in the original executable. This will start a GDB for each process. Each process will still be in the *while* loop in line 23 of Fig. 14.22, so it will be necessary to change the value of the "*i*" variable to proceed with the debugging. Running *back trace* in one of the debuggers shows that the "*i*" variable is not in the current call stack frame, but two frames above the current execution frame. This is shown in Fig. 14.24.

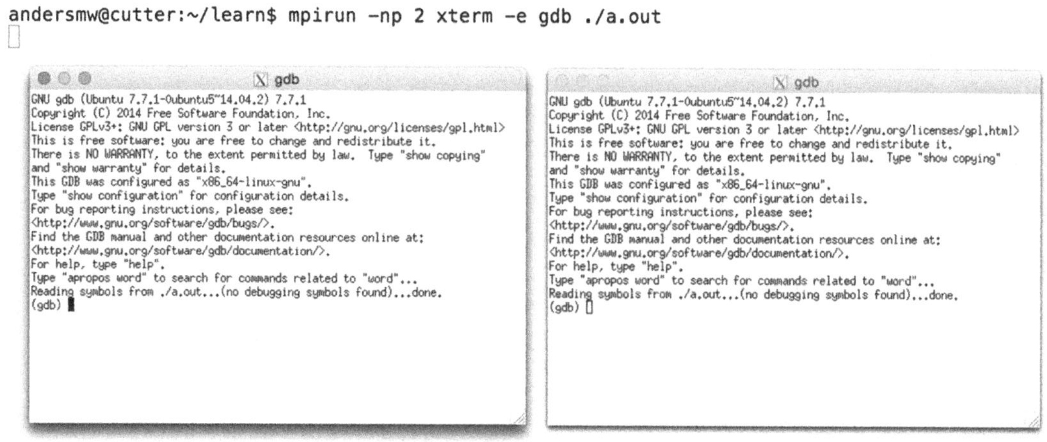

```
andersmw@cutter:~/learn$ mpirun -np 2 xterm -e gdb ./a.out
```

```
gdb
GNU gdb (Ubuntu 7.7.1-0ubuntu5~14.04.2) 7.7.1
Copyright (C) 2014 Free Software Foundation, Inc.
License GPLv3+: GNU GPL version 3 or later <http://gnu.org/licenses/gpl.html>
This is free software: you are free to change and redistribute it.
There is NO WARRANTY, to the extent permitted by law.  Type "show copying"
and "show warranty" for details.
This GDB was configured as "x86_64-linux-gnu".
Type "show configuration" for configuration details.
For bug reporting instructions, please see:
<http://www.gnu.org/software/gdb/bugs/>.
Find the GDB manual and other documentation resources online at:
<http://www.gnu.org/software/gdb/documentation/>.
For help, type "help".
Type "apropos word" to search for commands related to "word"...
Reading symbols from ./a.out...(no debugging symbols found)...done.
(gdb)
```


```
gdb
GNU gdb (Ubuntu 7.7.1-0ubuntu5~14.04.2) 7.7.1
Copyright (C) 2014 Free Software Foundation, Inc.
License GPLv3+: GNU GPL version 3 or later <http://gnu.org/licenses/gpl.html>
This is free software: you are free to change and redistribute it.
There is NO WARRANTY, to the extent permitted by law.  Type "show copying"
and "show warranty" for details.
This GDB was configured as "x86_64-linux-gnu".
Type "show configuration" for configuration details.
For bug reporting instructions, please see:
<http://www.gnu.org/software/gdb/bugs/>.
Find the GDB manual and other documentation resources online at:
<http://www.gnu.org/software/gdb/documentation/>.
For help, type "help".
Type "apropos word" to search for commands related to "word"...
Reading symbols from ./a.out...(no debugging symbols found)...done.
(gdb)
```


FIGURE 14.21

Example of launching two serial debuggers via xterm to debug the deadlock in Fig. 14.19. While this will work on some clusters, many will not be configured to allow this type of operation.

To set the "*i*" variable to some value other than 0 and thereby break out of the *while* loop in line 23, the debugger frame is changed to frame #2 and the "*i*" is set to 1 using the *set variable* command in GDB. This is done in both debugger command lines, and is illustrated in Fig. 14.25.

The code is now running in parallel within two different instances of the GDB. Generally it is best practice to set any desired break points prior to issuing the *continue* command in Fig. 14.25. However, in this deadlock example the debugger will be used to establish why the code hangs by simply stopping the execution of both debuggers using *control-c* and then issuing the *back trace* command in each debugger, as illustrated in Fig. 14.26.

The back traces from both debugger instances gives the call stacks for the two hanging processes, indicating that they are both waiting on account of blocking send calls resulting in a deadlock.

The debugger allows the MPI application developer to query the behavior of a parallel application directly, place break points and watch points, and traverse the call stack and memory to diagnose problems quickly at large scales. While in this example a GDB was attached to each process, this is probably not feasible when debugging with thousands of processes. In such a case the debugger can be attached to only a relevant subset of processes by appropriately modifying the code inserted to print out PIDs and wait, as shown in lines 17–24 of Fig. 14.22.

14.5 COMPILER FLAGS FOR DEBUGGING

Compiler warnings are a significant resource to assist in debugging an application. Specific command-line options for the compiler can be used to check for common mistakes programmers make. In Table 14.5 a summary of command-line options for the GNU, Intel, LLVM, and PGI compilers is presented, along with the associated action they invoke in the context of debugging.

```
0001 #include <stdio.h>
0002 #include <stdlib.h>
0003 #include <mpi.h>
0004
0005 int main(int argc, char* argv[]) {
0006   const int n = 10000;
0007   int *x, *y, nprocs,proc_id,i;
0008   int tag1 = 19;
0009   int tag2 = 20;
0010   MPI_Status status;
0011   MPI_Request send_request, recv_request;
0012
0013   MPI_Init(&argc, &argv);
0014   MPI_Comm_size(MPI_COMM_WORLD, &nprocs);
0015   MPI_Comm_rank(MPI_COMM_WORLD, &proc_id);
0016
0017   // Wait for attach
0018   i = 0;
0019   char hostname[256];
0020   gethostname(hostname, sizeof(hostname));
0021   printf("PID %d on %s ready for attach\n", getpid(), hostname);
0022   fflush(stdout);
0023   while (0 == i)
0024       sleep(5);
0025
0026   x = (int *) malloc(sizeof(int)*n);
0027   y = (int *) malloc(sizeof(int)*n);
0028
0029   // this example only works on two processes
0030   if (nprocs != 2) {
0031     if (proc_id == 0) {
0032       printf("This only works on 2 processes\n");
0033     }
0034     MPI_Finalize();
0035     return 0;
0036   }
0037
0038   if (proc_id == 0) {
0039     // only process 0 does this part
0040     for (i=0;i<n;i++) x[i] = 314159;
0041
0042     MPI_Send(x, n, MPI_INT, 1, tag2, MPI_COMM_WORLD);
0043     MPI_Recv(x, n, MPI_INT, 1, tag1, MPI_COMM_WORLD,&status);
0044
0045     printf(" Process %d received value %d\n",proc_id,x[0]);
0046   } else {
0047
0048     MPI_Send(y, n, MPI_INT, 0, tag1, MPI_COMM_WORLD);
0049     MPI_Recv(y, n, MPI_INT, 0, tag2, MPI_COMM_WORLD,&status);
0050   }
0051
0052   free(x);
0053   free(y);
0054
0055   MPI_Finalize();
0056   return 0;
0057 }
```

FIGURE 14.22

Deadlock example modified for attaching to the debugger. Lines 17–24 have been added to print the PIDs and then wait for the debugger to be attached to those processes.

```
andersmw@cutter:~/learn$ mpirun -np 2 ./a.out
PID 17331 on cutter ready for attach
PID 17332 on cutter ready for attach
```

FIGURE 14.23

Running the code in Fig. 14.22 results in the PIDs for the processes printing to screen. The execution then pauses due to the "while" loop in line 23 of Fig. 14.22.

```
(gdb) backtrace
#0  0x00007fa6cebcbdfd in nanosleep () at ../sysdeps/unix/syscall-template.S:81
#1  0x00007fa6cebcbc94 in __sleep (seconds=0)
    at ../sysdeps/unix/sysv/linux/sleep.c:137
#2  0x0000000000400c55 in main (argc=1, argv=0x7ffe6f24c2d8) at deadlock.c:24
```

FIGURE 14.24

The call stack upon attaching the GDB to one of the PIDs. Note that the call frame where the "*i*" variable and *while* loop are found is frame #2, or two frames up from the execution frame (frame #0).

```
(gdb) up 2
#2  0x0000000000400c55 in main (argc=1, argv=0x7ffe6f24c2d8) at deadlock.c:24
24              sleep(5);
(gdb) list
19          char hostname[256];
20          gethostname(hostname, sizeof(hostname));
21          printf("PID %d on %s ready for attach\n", getpid(), hostname);
22          fflush(stdout);
23          while (0 == i)
24              sleep(5);
25
26          x = (int *) malloc(sizeof(int)*n);
27          y = (int *) malloc(sizeof(int)*n);
28
(gdb) set var i=1
(gdb) continue
```

FIGURE 14.25

The variable "*i*" is set to 1 to break out of the *while* loop, pausing execution in the code of Fig. 14.22. This is done by changing the execution frame to be where the variable "*i*" is in the current context ("up 2"), resetting "*i*" to be 1 ("set var i=1"), and resuming execution.

14.6 SYSTEM MONITORS TO AID DEBUGGING

Many clusters employ monitoring software to inspect the status of node hardware and obtain information about the currently executing workload. The former may be as simple as verification that the node is responsive to remote commands, but may also include measurement of temperatures of critical components (they typically rise under increased load) or even access to low-level built-in sensors that monitor other physical aspects of the hardware (supply voltages, fan speeds, etc.). The latter is primarily concerned with the utilization of available central processing units (CPUs) (see Fig. 14.27), but

MPI Process 0

```
^C
Program received signal SIGINT, Interrupt.
0x00007fa6cebd62a7 in sched_yield () at ../sysdeps/unix/syscall-template.S:81
81      ../sysdeps/unix/syscall-template.S: No such file or directory.
(gdb) backtrace
#0  0x00007fa6cebd62a7 in sched_yield () at ../sysdeps/unix/syscall-template.S:81
#1  0x00007fa6c93da772 in psmi_mq_wait_internal (do_lock=0, status=0x0, ireq=0x7ff
e6f24bde8) at psm_mq.c:279
#2  0x00007fa6c93da772 in psmi_mq_wait_internal (ireq=0x7ffe6f24bde8)
    at psm_mq.c:314
#3  0x00007fa6c93bd61f in amsh_mq_send (len=40000, ubuf=0x153c6a0, tag=20, flags=<
optimized out>, epaddr=0x1517498, req=0x7fa6cf551ef0, mq=0x14c3468)
    at am_reqrep_shmem.c:2799
#4  0x00007fa6c93bd61f in amsh_mq_send (mq=0x14c3468, epaddr=0x1517498, flags=<opt
imized out>, tag=20, ubuf=0x153c6a0, len=40000) at am_reqrep_shmem.c:2847
#5  0x00007fa6c93daa4b in __psm_mq_send (mq=<optimized out>, dest=<optimized out>,
 flags=<optimized out>, stag=<optimized out>, buf=<optimized out>, len=<optimized
out>) at psm_mq.c:393
```

MPI Process 1

```
^C
Program received signal SIGINT, Interrupt.
0x00007f1c104ef690 in __psmi_poll_internal (ep=0x1ebf538,
    poll_amsh=poll_amsh@entry=1) at psm.c:499
499     }
(gdb) backtrace
#0  0x00007f1c104ef690 in __psmi_poll_internal (ep=0x1ebf538, poll_amsh=poll_ams
h@entry=1) at psm.c:499
#1  0x00007f1c104ed7a6 in psmi_mq_wait_internal (do_lock=0, status=0x0, ireq=0x7
ffcffbfeac8) at psm_mq.c:279
#2  0x00007f1c104ed7a6 in psmi_mq_wait_internal (ireq=0x7ffcffbfeac8)
    at psm_mq.c:314
#3  0x00007f1c104d061f in amsh_mq_send (len=40000, ubuf=0x1f0a280, tag=429496731
5, flags=<optimized out>, epaddr=0x1e6b2e8, req=0x7f1c16664ef0, mq=0x1e88458)
    at am_reqrep_shmem.c:2799
#4  0x00007f1c104d061f in amsh_mq_send (mq=0x1e88458, epaddr=0x1e6b2e8, flags=<o
ptimized out>, tag=4294967315, ubuf=0x1f0a280, len=40000)
    at am_reqrep_shmem.c:2847
#5  0x00007f1c104eda4b in __psm_mq_send (mq=<optimized out>, dest=<optimized out
>, flags=<optimized out>, stag=<optimized out>, buf=<optimized out>, len=<optimi
zed out>) at psm_mq.c:393
```

FIGURE 14.26

The back trace from both debugger instances after pausing execution via control-c to find out why the program is hanging. The call stacks for both processes indicate that they are both waiting (frames #1 and #2) on account of blocking send calls resulting in a deadlock.

may also provide other important statistics such as fraction of workload spent executing in user and system modes, amount of used and free memory, volume of data transferred in input/output operations, network traffic level, available disk space, and others. The monitoring relies on lightweight daemons executing in the background on every node that sample and collect the required information at regular intervals (e.g., every minute). This information is aggregated on a dedicated server and available to users through a commonly accessible interface, such as a webpage. Commonly used system monitors include Nagios [6] and Ganglia [7].

Table 14.5 Command-Line Options Used for Debugging for GNU, Intel, LLVM, and PGI Compilers

Action	Gcc	icc	clang	pgcc
Enable pointer bounds checking (R)	-fcheck-pointer-bounds	-check-pointers-mpx=rw		-Mbounds
Enable address sanitizer (R)	-fsanitize=address		-fsanitize=address	
Enable thread sanitizer (R)	-fsanitize=thread		-fsanitize=thread	
Enable leak sanitizer (R)	-fsanitize=leak		-fsanitize=leak	
Enable undefined behavior sanitizer (R)	-fsanitize=undefined		-fsanitize=undefined	
Enable all common warning types (S)	-Wall	-Wall	-Wall	-Minform=warn
Warn if the code does not strictly comply with ANSI C or ISO C++ (S)	-pedantic		-pedantic	-Xa
Warn on use of uninitialized variables (S)	-Wuninitialized	-Wuninitialized	-Wuninitialized	
Warn when local variable shadows another variable (S)	-Wshadow	-Wshadow	-Wshadow	
Warn if comparison between signed and unsigned integer may produce wrong result (S)	-Wsign-compare	-Wsign-compare	-Wsign-compare	
Warn if undefined identifier is used in preprocessor directive (S)	-Wundef		-Wundef	
Warn when undeclared function is used or declaration does not specify a type (S)	-Wimplicit	-Wmissing-declarations -Wmissing-prototypes	-Wimplicit	

ANSI, American National Standards Institute.

Note: Actions annotated with (R) denote that error conditions are indicated during runtime, while (S) produces a warning during static analysis of the code (compilation). Options in shaded cells do not accurately reflect the semantics of the Gcc option in the same row.

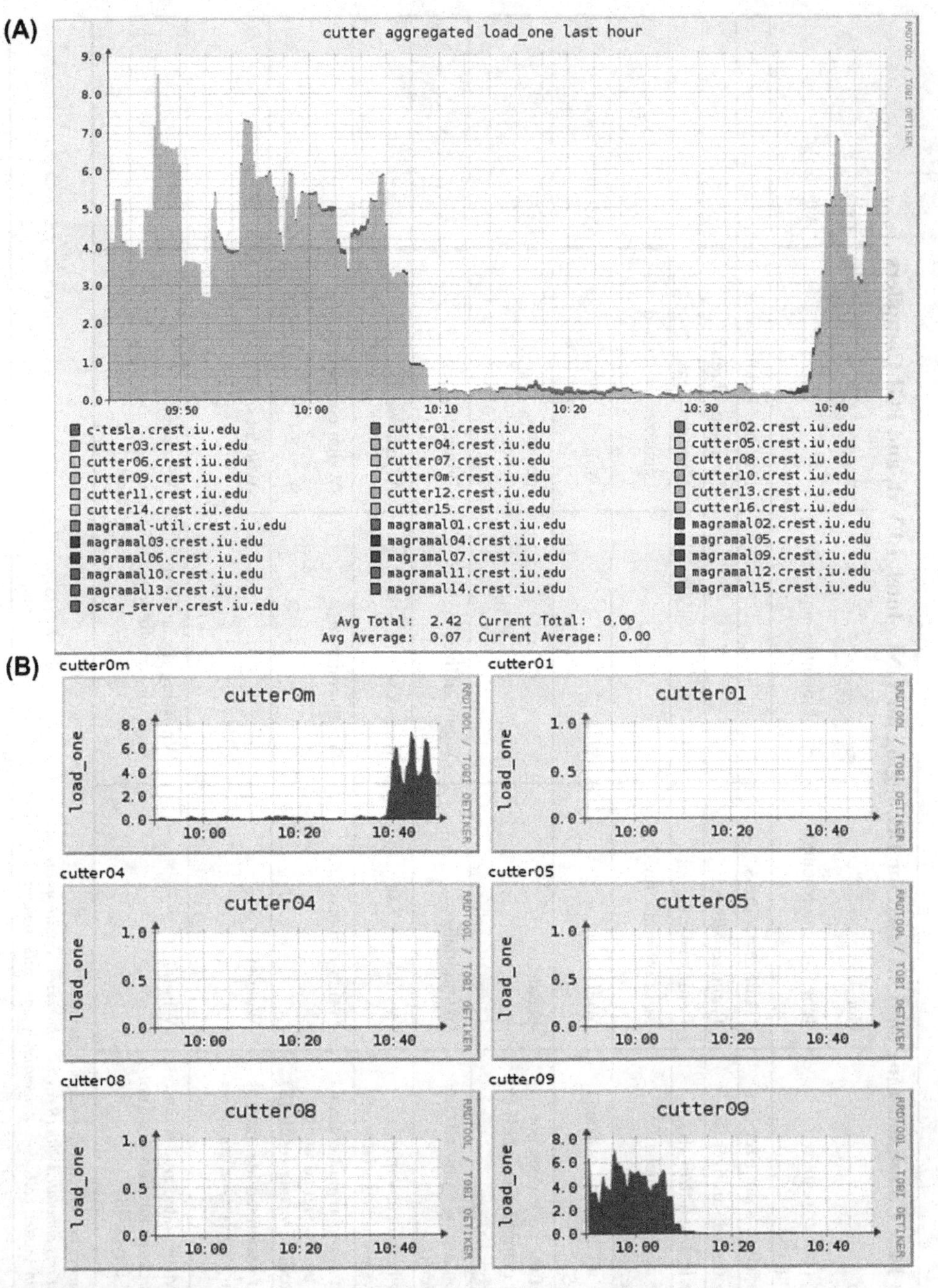

FIGURE 14.27

Example snapshot of processor load produced by Ganglia and presented as (A) composite graph for all monitored nodes and (B) individual nodes (only a fragment shown due to space constraints).

Since sampling is performed at a relatively coarse resolution to minimize the impact of monitoring on the primary workload execution, only limited analysis is possible. However, coupling the execution of a debugged application with a graphical representation of system status may frequently provide clues that would be otherwise difficult to obtain. Any load imbalances during application execution are immediately visible. If the load is expected to be uniform by algorithm design but in reality is asymmetric, this immediately identifies locations (nodes) that require closer inspection. This may arise from logical flaws in the code, but may also be caused by an incorrectly terminated job that previously executed on the same node or a system service that got out of control. Threads stuck in a spin lock usually exhibit CPU load close to 100%, while idling threads (such as those waiting for tasks to execute) have a minimal CPU utilization. Large load changes observed in multithreaded programs may suggest incorrectly designed critical sections or improper locking mechanisms. Monitoring memory usage may explain random performance fluctuations caused, for example, by approaching the point of exhaustion of physical memory. While a debugger will certainly catch a failed memory allocation call, it often will not be able to establish whether the failure occurred after prolonged execution with a large memory footprint or was a result of a spurious allocation request. Observation of network traffic may help identify undesirable hotspots for algorithms with an expectation of uniform communication patterns. While many of the system-monitor-inspired approaches are related to performance debugging, harnessing them for conventional debugging may help focus on the true cause of faults faster. They also provide much-needed sanity checks to verify that the startup environment for application execution matches the programmer's expectations.

14.7 SUMMARY AND OUTCOMES OF CHAPTER 14

- Tracking the origin of a parallel application execution anomaly on a supercomputer is generally much more difficult than debugging a serial application.
- Debugging an application on a high performance computer frequently requires a fairly detailed view of the supercomputer software and hardware stack to diagnose the anomaly properly.
- Several open-source and commercial debugging tools and suites have been developed to assist the debugging process.
- There are several commercial parallel debuggers which support MPI and OpenMP codes.
- There are several open-source serial debuggers and tool suites which can be used to debug MPI and OpenMP codes. In the case of MPI, they may require attaching several serial debuggers to a simulation.
- The GDB provides multiple tools for debugging a code and enabling the user to step through the code and call stack, as well as viewing variables and changing their values.
- The GDB also provides support for debugging codes with multiple threads.
- The Valgrind suite of tools provides six major tools for debugging applications, including rectifying data races and memory leaks.
- Multiple serial debuggers can be attached to an MPI execution to conduct parallel debugging.
- There is significant compiler support for debugging through specific flags to enable pointer bounds checking and other memory checking.
- System monitors provide an independent way to examine program execution and match that to the programmer's expectations.

14.8 EXERCISES

1. The following code allocates and initializes a two-dimensional array for a send buffer in connection with an MPI code. However, it has memory problems: an invalid write and a memory leak. Use Valgrind to identify and fix the invalid write and memory leak.

```
#include <stdio.h>
#include <stdlib.>

int main(int argc,char **argv) {

  int comm_count = 20;
  int numfields = 10;
  int length = 159;

  double **send_buffer = (double **) malloc(comm_count*sizeof(double *));
  for (int p=0;p<comm_count;p++) {
    send_buffer[p] = (double *) malloc(numfields*length*sizeof(double));
  }

  // Copy data into the send buffer
  for (int p=0;p<comm_count;p++) {
    for (int fields=0;fields<numfields;fields++) {
      for (int i=0;i<=length;i++) {
        send_buffer[p][i + length*numfields] = 3.14159;
      }
    }
  }

  return 0;
}
```

2. The following code uses OpenMP to compute $a_3 = sin(a_1 + a_2)$ where a_1, a_2, a_3 are arrays of length 20.

```
#include <omp.h>
#include <unistd.h>
#include <stdio.h>
#include <stdlib.h>
#include <math.h>

int main (int argc, char *argv[])
{
 const int size = 20;
 int nthreads, threadid, i;
```

```
11   double array1[size], array2[size], array3[size];
12
13   // Initialize
14   for (i=0; i < size; i++) {
15     array1[i] = 1.0*i;
16     array2[i] = 2.0*i;
17   }
18
19   int chunk = 3;
20
21 #pragma omp parallel private(threadid)
22   {
23   threadid = omp_get_thread_num();
24   if (threadid == 0) {
25     nthreads = omp_get_num_threads();
26     printf("Number of threads = %d\n", nthreads);
27   }
28   printf(" My threadid %d\n",threadid);
29
30   #pragma omp for schedule(static,chunk)
31   for (i=0; i<size; i++) {
32     array3[i] = sin(array1[i] + array2[i]);
33     printf(" Thread id: %d working on index %d\n",threadid,i);
34     sleep(1);
35   }
36
37   } // join
38
39   return 0;
40 }
```

Run the code using four OpenMP threads. Use the GDB to perform the following operations. Put a hardware watch point on the variable *nthreads*. Which thread ID stops at this hardware watch point? Does the debugger thread ID correspond to the *threadid* variable in line 23 of the code?

3. The following code creates a new communicator, and within that communicator sends its rank to its new communicator neighbor. However, it has a bug. This code works properly when run on between one and four processes, but hangs when using anything more than four processes. Use the tools and techniques from the chapter to debug why this code fails on five or more processes. Then fix the problem.

```
#include <mpi.h>
#include <stdio.h>
#include <stdlib.h>

```

```
int main(int argc,char *argv[])
{
 int myid,numprocs;

 MPI_Init(&argc,&argv);
 MPI_Comm_size(MPI_COMM_WORLD,&numprocs);
 MPI_Comm_rank(MPI_COMM_WORLD,&myid);

 int color = myid%2;
 MPI_Comm new_comm;
 MPI_Comm_split(MPI_COMM_WORLD,color,myid,&new_comm);

 int new_id,new_nodes;
 MPI_Comm_rank(new_comm,&new_id);
 MPI_Comm_size(new_comm,&new_nodes);

 printf(" Rank %d Numprocs %d New id %d New nodes %
 d\n",myid,numprocs,new_id,new_nodes);

 int right = (new_id + 1) % new_nodes;
 int left = new_id - 1;
 if (left < 0)
  left = new_nodes - 1;

 int buffer[2],buffer2[2];
 MPI_Status status;
 buffer[0] = myid;
 buffer[1] = rand();

 MPI_Sendrecv(buffer, 2, MPI_INT, right, 123,
   buffer2, 2, MPI_INT, right, 123, new_comm, &status);

 printf(" Rank %d received %d\n",myid,buffer2[0]);

 MPI_Finalize();
 return 0;
}
```

4. The following code hangs when run on two processes.

```
#include <stdlib.h>
#include <stdio.h>
#include "mpi.h"

```

```
5 int main(int argc, char* argv[]) {
6   const int n = 100000;
7   int x[n], y[n], np, id,i;
8   int tag1 = 19;
9   int tag2 = 20;
10  MPI_Status status;
11
12  MPI_Init(&argc, &argv);           /* Initialize MPI */
13  MPI_Comm_size(MPI_COMM_WORLD, &np); /* Get number of processes */
14  MPI_Comm_rank(MPI_COMM_WORLD, &id); /* Get own identifier */
15
16  /* Check that we run on exactly two processes */
17  if (np != 2) {
18   if (id == 0) {
19     printf("Only works on 2 processes\n");
20   }
21   MPI_Finalize();      /* Quit if there is only one process */
22   exit(0);
23  }
24
25  if (id == 0) {   /* Process 0 does this */
26    for (i=0;i<n;i++) x[i] = 314159;
27
28    MPI_Send(&x, n, MPI_INT, 1, tag2, MPI_COMM_WORLD);
29    MPI_Recv(&x, n, MPI_INT, 1, tag1, MPI_COMM_WORLD,&status);
30
31    printf(" Process %d received value %d\n",id,x[0]);
32  } else {
33    for (i=0;i<n;i++) y[i] = 137035;
34    MPI_Send(&y, n, MPI_INT, 0, tag1, MPI_COMM_WORLD);
35    MPI_Recv(&y, n, MPI_INT, 0, tag2, MPI_COMM_WORLD,&status);
36  }
37
38   MPI_Finalize();
39   exit(0);
40 }
```

a. Why does it hang?

b. When size of variable n in line 6 is changed to be much smaller, the code does not hang any more. Try this: set $n = 10$ in line 6. What does process 0 print to screen? Why?

c. Why does the code not hang when variable n is small?

d. Fix the problem so that the code works for any n size. What prints to screen as the result now? Why?

REFERENCES

[1] F. Conway, J. Siegelman, Dark Hero of the Information Age: In Search of Norbert Wiener, The Father of Cybernetics, s.l., Basic Books, 2006.

[2] Allinea, Allinea DDT, [Online]. http://www.allinea.com/products/ddt.

[3] Valgrind Tool Suite, [Online]. valgrind.org.

[4] RogueWave Software, TotalView for HPC, 2016 [Online]. http://www.roguewave.com/products-services/totalview.

[5] Intel, Intel Parallel Debugger Extension, [Online]. https://software.intel.com/en-us/articles/parallel-debugger-extension.

[6] Nagios: The Industry Standard in IT Infrastructure Monitoring, [Online]. https://www.nagios.org.

[7] Ganglia Monitoring System, [Online]. http://ganglia.info/.

CHAPTER

ACCELERATOR ARCHITECTURE 15

CHAPTER OUTLINE

15.1 INTRODUCTION

The design of the modern processor involves multiple trade-offs focused on optimizing the functionality, performance, energy consumption, and manufacturing cost. The final product is a compromise between the supported feature set, physical constraints, and a projected retail price. Since CPUs must execute a very broad range of workload types, their instruction sets are as generic as possible to enable reasonable performance for most applications. While additional specialized function units could be and sometimes are incorporated on processor dies to enable hardware support for specific computation types, this increases the final chip and case size. The function units may also require additional input/output (I/O) pins for dedicated communication links or memory banks, and increased

High Performance Computing. https://doi.org/10.1016/B978-0-12-420158-3.00015-0

die size results in greater probability of the occurrence of manufacturing defects. All these factors have nonlinear effects on the final product price, which often renders such enhancements prohibitive.

Practical accelerators explore different functionality, power requirements, and resultant price points to offer complementary features to existing processors, albeit without trying to optimize execution performance for all anticipated application profiles. In high performance computing (HPC) accelerators are typically employed to increase the computational throughput (most often expressed in terms of floating-point operations per second), although at a cost of programmability. Control logic used by accelerators is often incompatible with the existing processor instruction set architecture (ISA), forcing the application developers to invest their time in mastering custom programming languages, language extensions, or wrapper libraries provided by the vendor to enable access to accelerator features. More often than not, naïve usage of accelerators without a working knowledge of their control and data paths and other details of internal architecture does not yield the desired results expected by interpolation from raw peak performance of the underlying hardware modules and general application traits measured on conventional processors. Thus programming of such *heterogeneous systems* that include accelerators working side by side with regular processors still presents many challenges to the uninitiated.

To improve portability, accelerators are frequently attached to the remainder of the system using industry-standard interfaces, such as Peripheral Component Interconnect (PCI) Express [1] (see Fig. 15.1). This permits the incorporation of accelerated hardware in practically any machine that is equipped with such an interface, has sufficient power budget to supply energy to the accelerator, and,

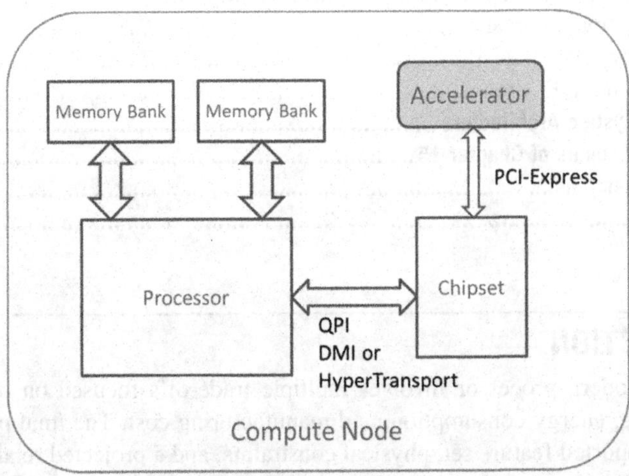

FIGURE 15.1

Typical placement of an accelerator in a conventional compute node. Modern processors often incorporate Peripheral Component Interconnect (PCI) Express endpoints on the die, thereby not relying on the chipset as a necessary component to achieve accelerator connectivity.

of course, has enough physical space within its enclosure to host the accelerator physically. The latter is often associated with additional infrastructure requirements, for example efficient removal of the excess heat generated by the added hardware. Separating the accelerator subsystem from the particular implementation of the compute node offers additional advantages. First, the accelerators may be upgraded to newer, higher-performance revisions without the need to modify other hardware components of the compute node. And second, accelerators may be implemented using their own optimized ecosystem to provide the highest levels of performance. While conventional processors are often limited by the aggregate memory bandwidth to stream input operands and computation results efficiently, accelerators may leverage optimized memory components that offer higher bandwidths.

Unfortunately, the separation of the two functional domains by a standard bus also introduces a number of significant limitations to control transfer and access of the results that the accelerators produce. The conventional processor predominantly plays the role of master control entity in heterogeneous systems, hence arbitrary postprocessing of results or supplying them as an input to a variety of I/O operations (such as saving to secondary storage) still requires the transfer of computed data from the accelerator memory to the main memory on the node. While there are solutions that utilize the bus mastering capabilities of accelerators to forward the computed datasets directly to the network interface controller (NIC) memory, to be later sent to a remote node without involvement of the main processor, this requires precise integration of all involved components and cooperation of their drivers. Due to the relatively high latency of PCI Express turnaround (request submission and result readout), the offload of computational tasks is a high-overhead operation in both direct memory access (DMA) and programmed I/O (PIO) mode. This effectively sets a lower bound on the granularity of tasks submitted to the accelerator; in many cases short tasks are performed faster by the main processor unless they can be coalesced into larger chunks to take advantage of the PCI Express bandwidth.

The primary focus of this chapter is the graphics processing unit (GPU) as an exemplar of accelerator architecture that significantly evolved from previous solutions, sometimes being drastically different in terms of both capabilities supported and integration with the remainder of the system. Currently, GPUs are one of the most common accelerator types employed in HPC. They provide a compelling balance between peak processing rates, supported hardware features, and energy usage. The next section provides a brief history of early accelerators, starting with coprocessors and peripheral-like floating-point units (FPUs). It further describes one of the more popular custom double-precision floating-point accelerators employed in supercomputing, made by the now-defunct company ClearSpeed. The following sections delineate the fundamental functions and development of graphics processors, leading to a discussion of modern GPU architecture. The conscientious reader may inquire why Intel's Xeon Phi (previously known as "Many Integrated Core" or MIC) is not a subject of this chapter. While this design is commonly identified with accelerators, it is actually a derivative of the traditional x86 architecture that aggregates an increased number of simplified processor cores with attached single-instruction multiple data (SIMD) units. The current revision of this product, dubbed "Knights Landing," is employed as the main processing unit in a compute node in many supercomputing systems, demonstrating that it is in fact the next step in conventional CPU development.

15.2 A HISTORIC PERSPECTIVE

Photo by Don Armstrong via Wikimedia Commons

The Connection Machine 2 (CM-2) was a rare example of a practical—if only for a short period—large scale SIMD supercomputer. Launched by the Thinking Machines Corporation (TMC) in 1987, it featured 65,536 "single-bit" processing elements with 4Kbit memory each arranged in a hypercube topology. Teams utilizing the CM-2 won the prestigious Gordon Bell prize for both the best performance on a single computer (6 GFlops achieved in seismic data processing problem) and the most price-performance efficient computation (sustained 400 MFlops per $1 million in oil reservoir modeling) in 1989.

The original design of the Connection Machine was based on the PhD thesis of MIT graduate W. Daniel Hillis, who later co-founded TMC with Sheryl Handler. His primary idea was to create a computer inspired by the structure of brain, containing a large number of densely connected simple processors that work on a single task. The development efforts were aided by Nobel Prize laureate in physics Richard Feynman, who contributed, among other concepts, an improved algorithm to calculate logarithms and analysis of router buffering for the hypercube interconnect. A full-scale CM-2 consisted of eight smaller "cubes," each populated with 16 logic boards (with 32 processing chips per board) and two I/O channels with peak throughput of 50 MB/s. The channels could be used for visualization output or data transfer to mass storage, called Data Vaults, each of which could hold 30 GB of data. The CM-2 hosted one Weitek 3132 FPU for every 32 processing elements that provided the numeric performance. Available programming languages included CM Fortran (Fortran77 with elements of Fortran90), C*, and *Lisp with the latter two being data-parallel extensions of conventional C and Common Lisp.

CM-2 enclosure design is considered to be one of the most unusual and visually engaging in the world of supercomputing. Conceived by Tamiko Thiel, it combines art and function. The activity of processing elements is directly represented on the front panel by dedicated red LEDs providing clues to the parallel operation of the machine.

The ILLIAC4. *Photo by Steve Jurvetson via Wikimedia Commons*

ILLIAC (Illinois Automatic Computer) denotes a series of machines designed and built at the University of Illinois. The ILLIAC IV incarnation of the series, shown above, was notable for being one of the earliest massively parallel processors. The building of ILLIAC IV was contracted by what was then ARPA in 1966 as a project under direction of prof. Daniel Slotnick. The original design called for a four quadrant machine, with 64 processing elements (PEs) per quadrant. Each PE was coupled with a memory (PEM) storing 2048 64-bit words. A PE contained four register arithmetic units that performed conventional operations on 64-, 32-, and 8-bit arguments using a 16 MHz clock. As processing elements did not include control flow logic, they executed the same instruction in lock-step as dictated by the shared control unit. Individual PEs could be enabled or disabled using so-called mode bits; this allowed a simple form of instruction predication. To facilitate data broadcasts and exchanges, ILLIAC provided a shared global data bus as well as interconnect supporting circular shifting of PE register contents among all PEs in the quadrant. The machine was delivered to NASA in 1972. Due to problems manufacturing the PE logic as LSI integrated circuits, only a single quadrant of the computer was completed using SSI and MSI technology. This resulted in much bigger size. The aggregate performance of ILLIAC IV with 64 PEs was approximately 200 MIPS with peak throughput of 205 double-precision MFlops for addition and 114 MFlops for multiplication.

Accelerators of various types and capabilities have long coexisted with and complemented general-purpose computing systems. However, accelerator portability and ease of integration with the rest of the systems commonplace today have not always been the case. This section presents a progression of earlier solutions, ranging from coprocessors to bus-attached accelerators that paved the path toward modern implementations. Each of these is illustrated with a brief discussion of accelerator functions, performance achieved, and operating modes relevant at the times they were utilized.

15.2.1 COPROCESSORS

Some of the earliest accelerators were coprocessors. Even though this technology dates back many decades, it still finds applications in many currently manufactured systems, albeit in a modified form compared to those earliest pioneering designs. Through evolutionary refinement of the applied solutions, it has also guided the introduction of modern accelerator devices that alleviate many limitations of their predecessors but at the same time retain most of their basic characteristics. Coprocessors were commonplace as standalone implementations from the 1970s through to the early 1990s, when the available scale of integration (expressed as the number of transistors or logic gates per die) used by the main processors' manufacturing process was insufficient to make the inclusion of all potentially useful functions cost effective. In this form they were available as special-purpose chips or modules that could be plugged into a dedicated socket in a target system. The most common application of the first coprocessors was high-speed computation on floating-point numbers, thus avoiding costly emulation of such arithmetic by fixed-point (integer) execution units of the primary processor. Besides providing FPU implementations, coprocessors were successfully employed in many other areas, including:

- I/O data transfer and processing, smart DMA
- media, with efficient encoding, decoding, and demultiplexing of audio and video streams
- cryptography, typically providing public-key operations, hashing algorithm implementations, and random number generation
- signal processing, incorporating fixed- or floating-point digital signal processing [2] units
- graphics, accelerating the memory-to-memory bit block transfers (BitBLTs) that gave rise to modern GPUs.

Currently coprocessors are frequently integrated on dies side by side with the main processor logic, a practice especially popular in systems on chip (SoC). Standalone implementations in the form of dedicated integrated circuits that are soldered on the motherboard are still common. Examples of both these approaches may be found in mass-produced consumer electronic devices, such as cellular phones and tablets.

As suggested by their name, coprocessors coexist with and are controlled by the primary processor in the system. This requires a specific arrangement of control, data, and/or address lines in cooperation with processor control logic. Coprocessors rely on the master processor to offload explicitly each work unit, which typically is a single instruction identified by a specially formed operation code. Completion of the offload triggers the processing of the received operation, and when done the coprocessor passes the result back to the processor. Individual implementations may vary, using different synchronization schemes between the processor and coprocessor, and also specifying whether the main processor may execute its own work while the coprocessor is busy. In general, the work performed by coprocessors has to be synchronized with the execution of the program on the main processor. Due to strong hardware dependencies, the portability of coprocessors between systems of different types is extremely limited, and typically involves only consecutive revisions of processors within the same family.

To illustrate the concept, two popular floating-point coprocessors broadly utilized in a large number of systems in the 1980s are discussed below. Each of them utilizes a slightly different offload mechanism.

15.2.1.1 *Intel 8087*

The Intel 8087 (Fig. 15.2) was the first incarnation of the numerical accelerator for the 8086 family of processors. Even though heavily influenced by the writings of William Kahan, a major contributor to the later standard for floating-point arithmetic, IEEE 754 [3], results of some operations do not conform to the standard's letter. The Intel 8087 was announced in 1980 as a 3 μm high-density metal-oxide semiconductor implementation using 45,000 transistors, making it capable of achieving 50 kFlops while dissipating a maximum of 2.4 W. It was an ambitious project: by contrast, the 8086 CPU totaled only approximately 29,000 transistors. The coprocessor had to run at the same speed as the main processor, and to support this was offered in five speed variants, ranging from 4 to 10 MHz. All revisions were housed in 40-pin dual in-line package cases and powered from 5°V rails. Besides Intel, the 8087 was manufactured by AMD and Cyrix Corporation, although in very limited quantities. A cloned version was also available in the Soviet Union.

As shown in Fig. 15.3, the coprocessor shared data and address lines with the main processor. Interaction with the coprocessor was controlled by additional queuing status lines QS*n*, request/grant strobes (RQ/GT) for memory access, and a BUSY signal indicating coprocessor availability. The offload sequence started with the main processor detecting the so-called "escape" instruction. This name was coined as a result of sharing the same bit pattern in the high bits by instruction opcode (binary "11011") with the ASCII code for the ESC (escape) symbol. If the operand identified by further bits of the two-byte opcode described a memory access, the processor calculated the effective address and performed a dummy memory read. At this point control was transferred to the coprocessor, which captured the memory address and data stored at that time on the related processor buses. The same address could have been used to store the result of the operation if so dictated by the intercepted FPU instruction. The coprocessor relinquished control back to the main processor after the operation execution was completed.

In theory the main processor was free to execute other (nonescaped) instructions while the coprocessor was busy. Since in practice this frequently led to crashes when both processors attempted to access one or both system buses concurrently, many assemblers automatically inserted an FWAIT instruction after every escaped instruction. This explicitly forced the main processor to wait until the coprocessor finished computation. The crashes could also happen if the coprocessor could not meaningfully decode the escaped instruction. Later 80x87 family designs removed this limitation by the processor explicitly handing the coprocessor instructions to execute, although at the penalty of increased latency.

FIGURE 15.2

Intel 8087 coprocessor in a 40-pin ceramic package.

Photograph by Dirk Oppelt via Wikimedia Commons

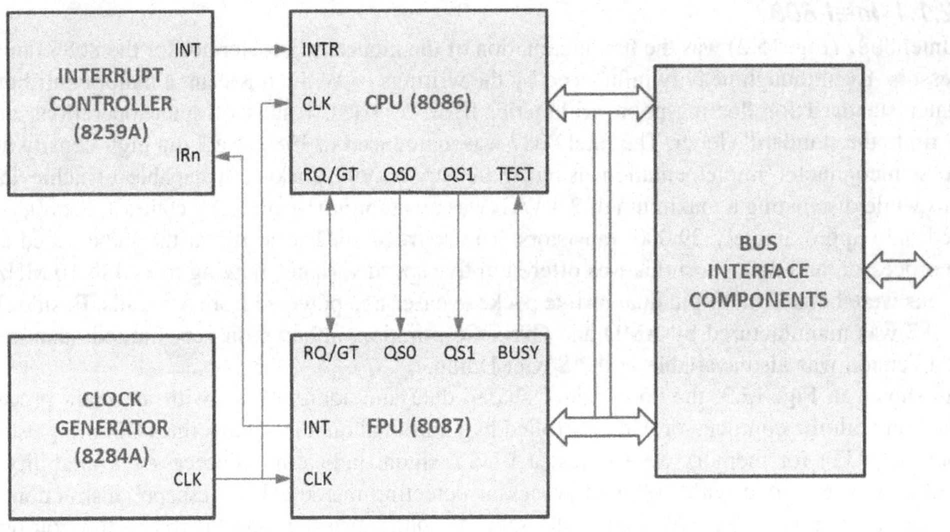

FIGURE 15.3

Typical components and simplified control connections of an 8086 system with an 8087 coprocessor.

Internally, the 8087 consisted of a control unit and a numeric execution unit connected through the microcode control unit and operand queue. The first unit contained the logic controlling the address, data, and status buses including the associated data buffer to hold memory-sourced operands or memory-targeted results, and 16-bit registers storing control and status words. The numeric execution unit housed a stack of eight 80-bit registers connected to 16-bit exponent and 64-bit fraction buses, corresponding to the components of the floating-point numbers. The first bus supplied the exponent module, while the second interconnected bus supplied the programmable shifter, arithmetic module, and a set of temporary registers. Interestingly, the 8087 instructions do not address the floating-point registers directly, instead treating them as an eight-level stack with the register ST(0) on top and ST(7) at the bottom. The calculations are performed by pushing the input operands on the stack, which are then popped by the actual instructions. Binary operations may implicitly consume the top two entries on the stack or use one register operand combined with a memory operand. The results may also be either pushed on the stack or stored in memory. Finally, the ST(0) register may be used as an accumulator, i.e., a register providing the input operand that is later rewritten by the result of the operation. Accumulator contents may also be exchanged with any of the seven remaining registers using dedicated instructions.

The Intel 8087 supported about 60 instruction types, including floating-point addition, subtraction, multiplication, division, comparison, square root, sine, cosine, tangent, arc tangent, product with base two logarithm result, sign change, absolute value, scaling, and rounding. In addition, it supported loads and stores of arguments with possible integer conversion, as well as the management of stack contents and status and control words. The recognized numeric types included 32-bit (single precision), 64-bit (double precision), and 80-bit (extended precision) floating-point numbers, 16-, 32-, and 64-bit signed binary integers, and 80-bit binary coded decimal (BCD) integers.

Further revisions of the 8087 included the 80187, 80287, and 80387, of which the latter was the first released Intel coprocessor conformant with the IEEE 754-1985 standard. This compatibility with the floating-point standard, later adopted by other manufacturers, helped achieve better portability of scientific codes. These designs featured improved clock speeds, a wider data bus, and extended functionality (such as other transcendental functions). Even though marketed as a coprocessor, the 80487SX chip released in 1991 actually contains a full 80486DX processor implementation with an FPU integrated on die, effectively ending the need for discrete numeric coprocessors. This is an early example of the FPU integration commonly seen in modern high performance CPUs.

15.2.1.2 Motorola MC68881

The Motorola MC68000 series of 32-bit processors were the main rival to Intel's 8086 line and provided core processing for many systems available during the heyday of 80x87, ranging from bargain desktops to high performance workstations. To remain competitive, Motorola decided to design a product with equivalent, if not improved, functionality. The result was the Motorola MC68881 family of FPU coprocessors introduced in 1984 (Fig. 15.4). Due to the later release date compared with the 8087, the Motorola coprocessor targeted processors with 32-bit data buses in the lineup, the MC68020 and MC68030. Earlier processors featuring 8- and 16-bit buses could access the FPU as a peripheral device using software emulation. While the full feature set was available, the operation rates in such a mode were slower. Interestingly, the upgrade of the main processor to a later revision (including a wider data bus) did not require changes to the executable code for continued use of the MC68881 in the same system.

The original FPU design contained 155,000 transistors using an high-speed complementary metal-oxide semiconductor process. It was available in several speed variants, with clock rates ranging from 12.5 to 25 MHz encased in two package types: a 68-pin plastic-leaded chip carrier and 68-pin pin-grid array (PGA). The fastest version could deliver up to 240 kFlops while dissipating only 0.75 W with a 5 V supply. The latency of simple register-to-register operations ranged from 40 clock cycles for

FIGURE 15.4

Motorola MC68881 arithmetic coprocessor in a PGA case.

Photograph by Dirk Oppelt via Wikimedia Commons

addition to 92 clock cycles for division in extended mode, while using special single-precision instructions resulted in 46 cycles for multiplication and 58 cycles for division.

Unlike the 8087, the Motorola coprocessor's control register space is memory mapped, simplifying control and instruction offload (see Fig. 15.5). Communication is accomplished through standard bus cycles and does not require the FPU and main processor to operate by the same clock (since the bus must accommodate devices with different timing characteristics). The coprocessor may utilize all the addressing modes supported by the CPU, although the effective addresses are computed on demand by the main processor. The main processor may view any of the eight 80-bit data registers in the coprocessor as if they were locally resident general-purpose registers, and access to them is symmetric (any instruction may use any register). Since the main processor uses a CPU address space function during coprocessor access, the FPU control registers do not overlap with instruction or data address spaces. A single CPU could control up to eight MC68881 FPUs.

Internally, the MC68881 included a bus interface unit, an execution control unit (ECU), and a microcode control unit (MCU). The first was responsible for communication with the main processor by providing several coprocessor control interface registers and 32-bit control, status, and instruction address registers. The actual 80-bit data registers were located in the ECU, which also contained a 67-bit arithmetic unit used for both significand and exponent calculations, a single-cycle barrel shifter, and constants read-only memory (ROM). The MCU included a clock generator, microcode sequencer, microcode ROM, and self-test circuitry.

Data formats supported by the MC68881 included 8-, 16-, and 32-bit long integers, single-, double-, and extended-precision binary floating-point numbers, and 96-bit packed BCD decimals (3-digit signed exponent and 17-digit significand). Internally, all operations were performed on extended-precision (80-bit) binary numbers with implicit conversion for single- and double-precision floating points, and packed BCD operands. The set of available operations comprised addition, subtraction, multiplication, division, modulo, remainder, compare, absolute value, negate, scale exponent, square root, sine, cosine, tangent, arc sine, arc cosine, arc tangent, hyperbolic sine, hyperbolic cosine, hyperbolic tangent, hyperbolic arc tangent, base 2, e, and 10 exponentiation, base 2, e, and 10 logarithm,

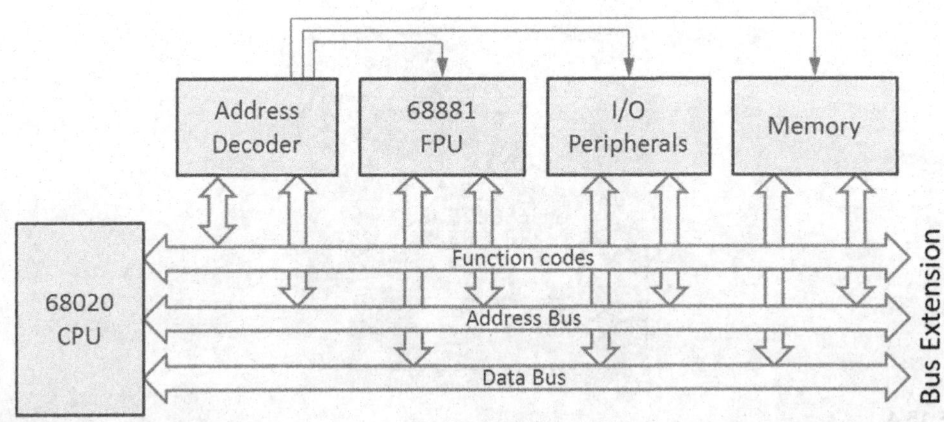

FIGURE 15.5

Placement of the floating-point coprocessor in a typical MC68000 system.

and integer part. The FPU conformed to the soon-to-be-published IEEE 754 standard in number formats, special value interpretation, and required operation accuracy.

The MC68881 was succeeded by an MC68882 unit that was capable of executing more than one floating-point operation at a time and performed faster conversions between external and internal number representations. Its performance exceeded 0.5 MFlops at 50 MHz. Starting with the MC68040 CPU, future revisions of the MC68000 series processors incorporated the FPU on die. The memory-mapped access featured by Motorola coprocessors may be perceived as a significant step toward unification of communication interfaces between the CPU and accelerator.

15.2.2 ACCELERATORS IN PROCESSOR I/O SPACE

Early microprocessors of the 1980s and early 1990s were limited in performance due both to clock rates and to logic complexity available from contemporary semiconductor fabrication facilities. This had a particular impact on compute intensive applications that demanded significant floating-point operations within their instruction mix. The Intel x86 architecture family and the Motorola MC68000 microarchitecture were important steps in increased microprocessor capabilities, but lagged behind in floating-point performance. This opened an opportunity for new markets in accelerator devices delivering external coprocessors for floating-point operations. The Weitek Corporation built a series of accelerators to operate in conjunction with other high-production microprocessors. These Weitek FPUs were configured to work with Intel i286, i386, and i486 processors. A variation of these architectures was developed to provide FPU capabilities for the MIPS architecture. Eventually units were developed that were compliant with the industry-standard interfaces of the time, including EISA and Video Electronics Standards Association Local Bus. But the advance of semiconductor technology ultimately made it possible for microprocessor vendors to include FPUs directly within their dies, eliminating the need for external floating-point accelerators.

Weitek FPUs operated as memory-mapped devices. To processors from the Intel x86 family they appeared as a memory segment in the upper portion of the address space. Communication with the device was performed by issuing memory move instructions. Since the pin layout of Weitek chips was largely incompatible with existing coprocessor sockets, the Weitek WTL 3167 released in 1989 had to include an interposition socket which provided a superset of 80,387 pins. Interestingly, instructions to execute were formed by concatenating 14 least-significant bits of address with three of four byte-enable signals. The WTL 3167 contained 32 single-precision registers which could be paired to provide up to 16 double-precision registers. The supported FPU capabilities were significantly less diverse than those of the i387 and included four basic arithmetic operations, square root, and multiply—accumulate in addition to data movement, format conversion, compare and test, and sign change instructions. What it might have lacked in functionality, however, it more than made up in speed. At the time, the WTL 3167 was the fastest FPU on the market, delivering 1.36 and 0.6 MFlops in single- and double-precision Linpack respectively, and 5.6 and 3.7 MFlops in single- and double-precision Whetstone benchmarks (25 MHz version). Power dissipation of the 25 MHz chip was less than 1.84 W. The WTL 3167 was manufactured in 16—33 MHz variants using a 121-pin ceramic PGA case. Its successor, the WTL 4167 (shown in Fig. 15.6), offered approximately three times better numeric performance, but was less successful due to later models of i486 CPUs including an on-die FPU and architectural modifications that made communication with the processor slower.

FIGURE 15.6

Weitek WTL 4167 FPU (PGA package).

By Konstantin Lanzet (CPU collection) via Wikimedia Commons

15.2.3 ACCELERATORS WITH INDUSTRY-STANDARD INTERFACES

As mentioned above, one way to achieve accelerator portability is to arrange for the underlying hardware design to use one of the commonly available hardware interfaces. The selected interface should match the characteristics of the accelerator, at least to provide acceptable access latency and required data transfer bandwidth. One of the most widespread interfaces today is PCI Express, a descendant of PCI bus, which existed in several variants over the past 2 decades and still may be found in some desktop computers. Its implementations varied in data bus width, clock speed, and voltage levels.

The exemplar of the PCI-attached HPC accelerator discussed in this section is an FPU array module manufactured by ClearSpeed. While there were other solutions oriented to provide similar capability, including but not limited to cards with the STI (Sony, Toshiba, and IBM) Cell Broadband Engine (also known as the Cell processor), ClearSpeed offered a more competitive combination of accuracy, throughput, energy use, and cost. While it was available, it was one of very few custom solutions offering true hardware-level support for double-precision floating-point computations. The main reason for its abandonment in HPC was the proliferation of cheaper GPUs that began to include double-precision FPUs.

The best-known ClearSpeed product is likely the Advance X620 card (Fig. 15.7 depicts a newer version of the accelerator called "Advance e710.") utilizing dual custom CSX600 processors. Introduced in 2005, it was capable of running at 250 MHz and delivering 50 GFlops in the double-precision general matrix multiplication benchmark with a power dissipation of 36 W per card (maximum thermal design power was 43 W). The Advance X620 used a PCI-X connector for peak data bandwidth of 1066 MB/s with a 133 MHz clock. The actual achieved DMA bandwidth was somewhat lower, at 750 MB/s. The Advance X620 provided 1 GB of error-correcting memory (512 MB per processor) to store user datasets. One of the unusual solutions employed by ClearSpeed was the adoption of field programmable gate array (FPGA) devices to implement glue logic between its CSX processors and the PCI-X bus. The Japanese cluster Tsubame, located at the Tokyo Institute of Technology, was populated

FIGURE 15.7

Clearspeed Advance e710 accelerator board incorporating a faster Peripheral Component Interconnect (PCI) Express interface and providing a peak performance of 96 Gflops.

Photo courtesy of Bibek Wagle

with these accelerators and reached the number seven spot in the November 2006 release of the Top 500 list.

The CSX600 processors were implemented using the IBM 130 nm eight-layer metal (copper) process on a 15 × 15 mm die. They included 128 million transistors and could reach sustained double-precision 33 GFlops with average power dissipation around 10 W. The processing power was provided by a multithreaded array processor consisting of multiple execution units and one control unit. The execution units were grouped in two parts: one processed the scalar data (the mono unit) and the other executed parallel workloads in synchronous SIMD mode (a poly unit composed of 96 processing elements or PEs). The instructions were fetched from a single instruction stream, decoded, and dispatched to the execution units (mono and poly) or I/O controllers. While the mono unit processed conditionals similarly to a regular reduced instruction set computer processor, the poly unit used "enable registers" to activate or disable the individual SIMD cores. Enable registers were organized as stacks on to which the results of tests may be pushed or popped, permitting efficient handling of nested conditions and loops. Each processing element had its own register file and access to 6 KB of local storage, with which it exchanged data through load and store instructions. Additionally, PEs could indirectly access operands stored in mono registers, as their values were broadcast to all PEs. The PEs could also communicate directly with their nearest left and right neighbors. Finally, the mono unit could transfer data between mono memory and poly memory using the PIO mode.

To facilitate programming of accelerators, ClearSpeed provided a parallel extension of the C language, Cn. It introduced a "poly" data type qualifier signifying that each PE would have its own replica of a variable stored at the same location in local memory. The company also distributed CSXL accelerated libraries that supported the Basic Linear Algebra Subprograms (linear algebra) interface and FFT (fast Fourier transforms, inverse transforms, and convolution functions).

15.3 INTRODUCTION TO GRAPHICS PROCESSING UNITS

GPUs are specialized computing devices that perform multiple processing functions associated with image generation. Due to the volume of computations required and their real-time nature, conventional CPUs cannot be successfully used for this task. The GPU moniker was coined by Nvidia Corporation in 1999, when it used this term to describe a line of its new graphics cards, GeForce256. The computational functions primarily apply to rendering of three-dimensional (3D) scenes, or, more accurately, generation of the perspective projection of 3D objects. They include distance-dependent scaling of object sizes (utilizing *perspective transformation*, possibly combined with other optical distortions), object occlusion (obstruction of view of objects further away by objects closer to the viewer), color and lighting (shading of the object's surface dependent on the object's assigned color and reflective properties, distance from light sources, and angles between the incident light rays and vectors normal to the object's surface). These operations involve small (typically 4×4) matrix—vector multiplications per vertex or dot product, scalar—vector product, and sum calculation of three-element vectors for color values. To make the rendered images more realistic, GPUs may perform *texture mapping* to enhance the look of the objects compared to a uniformly colored default, at the same time saving substantial computational effort. For example, the definition of a complex material such as marble would be excessive in terms of storage size and number of manipulated entities when using primitive, individually colored component objects. Instead, textures are simply two-dimensional (2D) images that are projected onto surfaces of major objects that define the viewed scene, avoiding costly setup and resulting computations. To enhance the realism of images further, GPUs support *bump mapping* that locally perturbs the normal to the surface in accordance with a specified algorithm to simulate fine relief, such as the surface of an orange or skin pores. *Environment-mapped bump mapping* extends the effect to provide the ability to emulate reflective objects, such as water with a wave pattern on its surface; the textures in this case are derived from the rendered scene contents (environment). To approximate reasonably some natural phenomena that are difficult to express using explicit object aggregations, such as fog or smoke, *volumetric rendering* techniques may be applied. They are also useful for visualization of 3D-sampled datasets projected onto a two-dimensional surface, for example obtained by the means of tomographic reconstruction (magnetic resonance imaging and computed tomography scans, among others). Hardware *tessellation* support is a relatively new addition to GPUs and controls the resolution of a vertex mesh representing an object; objects that are far away from the observer are automatically replaced by their planar or low-resolution 3D approximations, accelerating the computations. Finally, GPUs handle oversampling of final image data to avoid aliasing artifacts due to the discrete representation (image pixels) of a contiguous 3D domain. These manifest themselves as jagged or staircase-like object edges if they are not parallel to image boundaries.

Most GPUs approximate optic laws when generating images, due to the enormous amount of computations that would have to be done otherwise. While other complex rendering techniques, such as ray tracing [4] and radiosity [5], may produce nearly photorealistic quality, the resulting image-generation times of complex scenes on GPUs are still prohibitively long. This is especially cumbersome when trying to achieve smooth motion or animation as required in video games, scientific visualization, computer-aided design, and medical imaging. Additionally, GPUs must simplify object geometry to cope with a myriad of shapes available in nature. The visualized objects are approximated by meshes covering their exterior surfaces; the more intricate the shape, the higher the resolution of mesh needed. The scene is then rendered by performing computations on polygons connecting mesh nodes. Polygons are convenient for this task since they do not require much space for representation of their geometry: essentially just one 3D coordinate for each vertex. Furthermore, since a polygon's surface is flat, shading and lighting are uniform across the entire surface and have to be calculated only once independent of the polygon's size (flat shading model). Curved surfaces are approximated with a sufficient number of smaller polygons to provide a smooth look to the observer, referred to as the Gouraud shading model [6]. Additional visual improvements may be attained through extrapolation of vectors normal to the surface originally specified at the polygon's vertices (Phong shading [7]). Even though in that case shading has to be computed separately for each pixel, typically far fewer polygons are required to describe an object.

Fig. 15.8 illustrates the main geometric concepts involved in rendering 3D scenes. The resultant image is a projection of a portion of a 3D scene carved out by viewing the frustum out of a 3D space on a 2D viewing plane. The viewing frustum vertex coincides with the position of an observer or camera. Each picture element (pixel) is rendered as if an imaginary ray originating from the frustum vertex was cast through each pixel to find the nearest intersecting object in the scene. GPUs maintain *Z-buffers* mapping the intersection depths for each pixel (by convention, the Z axis is perpendicular to the image plane and signifies object depth). This information is used to perform *Z-culling*, or elimination of occluded pixels, thus avoiding unnecessary computations of their shading or texture. Commonly, there is also a clipping plane perpendicular to the Z axis in front of the viewer; scene elements with Z coordinates greater than that of the plane are not rendered, to avoid obstruction of the view by objects very close to the camera.

Three-dimensional scene rendering is a highly parallel task, and can be subdivided into a large number of concurrent computations operating on their own section of the image. GPUs provide extensive resources that perform concurrent 3D transformations of vertex coordinates and compute

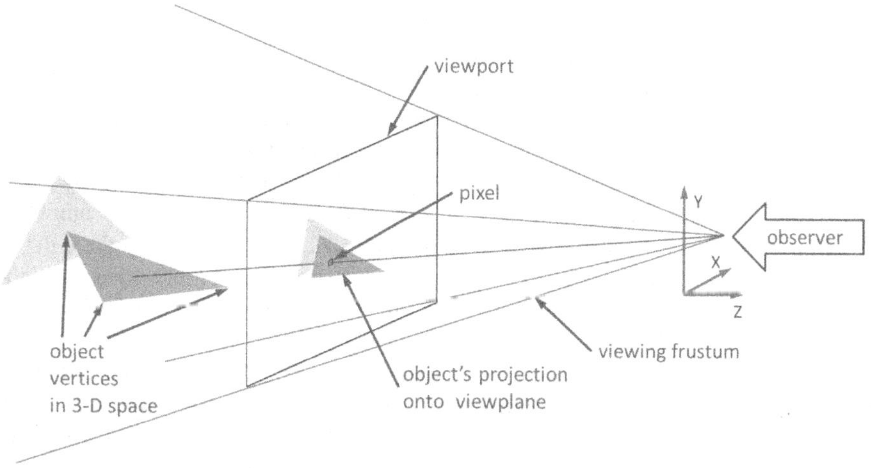

FIGURE 15.8

Primary components of a 3D scene rendered by a graphics processing unit.

color and intensity values for every pixel in a visual frame. To accomplish this, GPUs include a large number of FPUs and execution logic supporting a significant number of processing threads plus substantial memory bandwidth to feed the data at sustained high rates. The FPUs are optimized for single-precision arithmetic, as this level of accuracy is sufficient for most graphics operations, although they started to include double-precision hardware in late 2000s to extend the range of GPU applications to areas beyond computer graphics. To avoid prohibitive numbers of on-die instruction fetch, decode, and issue units, the execution resources are arranged in SIMD arrays that can be managed by fewer control units. To provide sufficient memory bandwidth, GPUs include on-board specialized memory modules that operate independently from the system's memory, typically GDDR SDRAM (graphics double data rate synchronous dynamic random access memory). Current GDDR5 revision can achieve aggregate streaming bandwidth of 480 GB/s using a 384-bit bus at 10 giga-transfers per second. This is an order of magnitude more compared to the peak bandwidth of memory modules supporting modern CPUs; the fastest available variant of the DDR4 technology delivers approximately 25 GB/s per channel. Besides memory bandwidth, metrics to measure GPU capabilities include processed polygons per second, texels (texture elements) per seconds, single- and double-precision Flops, and occasionally frame rate for some standardized rendering tasks.

15.4 EVOLUTION OF GRAPHICS PROCESSING UNIT FUNCTIONALITY

Early graphics processors primarily handled 2D aspects of image generation. The need to break away from text-based terminals was mainly caused by the increasing popularity of video games in 1970s. The video processors used at that time shared access to system memory with the main CPU, since using dedicated frame buffer storage was usually prohibitively costly. These chips controlled the generation of analog red, green, blue (RGB) video signals, accessed portions of memory containing display data for every scanline to be output, and were capable of manipulating overlay graphics (sprites) to emulate simple moving objects. One of the popular chips employed in Atari game consoles and later eight-bit computers was the ANTIC (alphanumeric television interface controller) video processor designed in 1978. It was one of the first programmable processors to execute so-called display lists—small programs that select a particular display mode (graphics or text with related resolution and color depth) or blank lines to be placed at arbitrary vertical segments of the screen. ANTIC was also capable of CPU-independent vertical and horizontal fine scrolling of screen sections, as well as interrupting the main processor based on reaching a specific entry in a display list. The latter function was used in games and demo programs to show simultaneously a greater number of colors than were allowed by any individual regular display mode, and was achieved by the CPU's interrupt handler dynamically reprograming color registers. ANTIC's sprite support provided four independent "players" and four "missiles" that could span the entire screen height. In connection with a sibling CTIA (color television interface adapter) chip, it could detect "collisions," i.e., pixel overlaps between sprites, as well as sprites and specified areas of background. The sprite defining bitmaps could be placed anywhere in a 16-bit address space. In text modes, ANTIC supported redefinable character sets. In addition, it provided readout of coordinates generated by light-pen hardware. But even though programmable, ANTIC ultimately lacked the capability to perform memory updates.

The introduction and subsequent popularization of the IBM PC in the beginning of the 1980s brought about a number of graphic card implementations compatible with the then-current ISA expansion bus. Some of the most notable were the CGA (color graphics adapter) based on the Motorola 6845 supporting 80 × 25 text mode and up to 640 × 200 pixel graphics mode with fixed two colors (or 320 × 200 pixel in four-color mode), the EGA (enhanced graphics adapter) introduced in 1984 that could display 16 simultaneous colors from a palette of 64 colors at a resolution of up to 640 × 350 pixels, and finally the VGA (video graphics array) appearing in 1987. The latter became a de facto standard and defined the minimum set of requirements for implementations of graphics circuitry that followed. It supported a frame size of 640 × 400 pixels with a 16-color palette or 320 × 200 pixels with 256 colors, any of which could represent an arbitrary 18-bit RGB value (6 bits per color component). Even though image resolution and color space substantially improved over time, most of these cards did not offer significant hardware acceleration of graphics operations. Some programming tricks coupled with use of multiple video memory pages enabled faster video-memory-to-video-memory copies (as opposed to using the system memory as an intermediary), faster single-color polygon fills, and double buffering.

Perhaps the first self-contained design to provide graphics support in hardware was the TMS34010 released in 1986 by Texas Instruments. It combined a general-purpose pipelined 32-bit CPU logic with additional logic to control screen refresh and timing as well as providing communication with a host system. The processor's instruction-set architecture directly supported operations on individual pixels and arrays of pixels of different sizes (bit-level addressable data fields), two operand raster operations (Boolean and arithmetic), X/Y addressing, window clipping and checking, pixel size transforms, transparency computation, and bit masking. The results of operations could be streamed to standard RAM through an autonomous memory controller that automatically performed the bit alignment and masking necessary to access data located at arbitrary bit boundaries. It also featured a write queue that enabled execution of subsequent graphics instruction without waiting for the memory operation of the previous instruction to finish.

The first widespread fixed-function 2D accelerator was the IBM 8514, which appeared in 1987. Despite many conveniences provided by the TMS34010 architecture, drawing algorithms still had to be developed in software. In contrast, the 8514 offered commands for line drawing, rectangle and area fills, block transfers (BitBLTs) using X and Y coordinates, and raster operations. As IBM never published the register interface documentation, the 8514 was subject to reverse engineering and cloning. The clones frequently improved on the original functionality (fewer or simpler algorithm parameters, deeper command queues, additional resolutions and color depths) and were offered at a lower price. Companies which developed their own versions of the 8514 logic include Chips&Technologies, Matrox, NEC, Tseng Labs, Paradise Systems, and most notably ATI with its line of Mach GPUs.

The efforts to develop specialized hardware for 3D geometry calculations also originated around the same time. Most notably, ideas behind the Stanford Geometry Engine [8] inspired the formation of Silicon Graphics, Inc. (SGI) and its extensive line of graphics workstations. At the height of their popularity, they featured MIPS CPUs and could process scenes at rates of hundreds of thousands (Indigo, announced in 1991) to more than 10 million (Onyx2, introduced in 1996) polygons per second. In the second half of the 1990s SGI faced strong competition from many newcomers to the market which offered either add-on 3D rendering cards (such as the Voodoo line from 3dfx Interactive) or combined 2D and 3D acceleration hardware (S3's ViRGE, ATI's Rage chips). By the end of the decade they typically supported 2D acceleration for line drawing, polygon fills, and BitBLTs. From the current viewpoint, the 3D rendering capabilities of that time were still quite rudimentary, but included

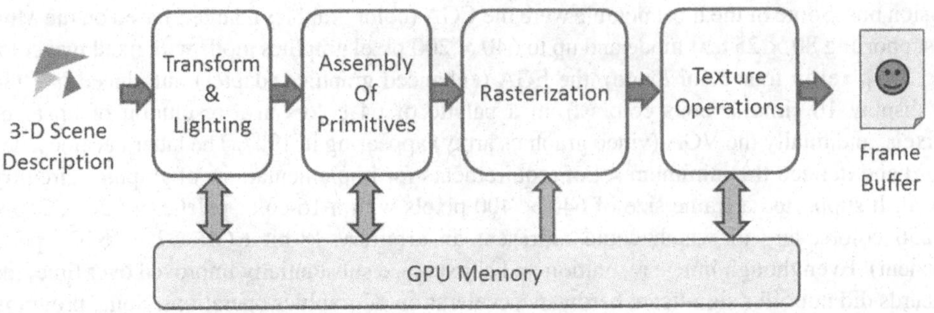

FIGURE 15.9

Main stages of the fixed-function rendering pipeline.

perspective transformation, flat and Gouraud shading, texture mapping and filtering, "multum in parvo" (much in little) mapping (precomputed antialiased sequence of images of decreasing size to increase the efficiency and quality of texture rendering), alpha blending (combination of translucent foreground with opaque background color), depth queueing, fogging, and Z buffering. Many implementations also started to include support for video stream decoding (primarily MPEG-1).

The next step-up in performance was the addition of hardware transform, clipping, and lighting acceleration, also known as T&L. This was originally introduced by the Nvidia GeForce256 in 1999 and soon mirrored by ATI's newly developed Radeon chip. Additionally, the Radeon R100/RV200 series featured a combination of texture compression, Z-buffer clearing, and hierarchical Z-buffer setup (collectively known as Hyper-Z) that increased the effective texture fill rate to as much as 1.5 Gtexels/s. Further GPU developments mainly resulted in increased versatility of shader[1] functions, introduced stencil buffers for more realistic shadows and reflections, antialiasing, high-definition video decode, and multiple screen support. This led to the first *programmable shaders*, promulgated with the release of the Nvidia GeForce3 series in which pixel colors could be determined by execution of a simple algorithm that potentially used multiple texture inputs. Similarly, vertex processing could also be performed by a short program. ATI's R300, marketed soon thereafter, featured programmable shaders with more flexible floating-point support and looping. It also supported anisotropic texture filtering and high dynamic range rendering. Further development of GPUs using fixed-function pipelines (illustrated in Fig. 15.9) essentially brought improvements in clock speed, number of processing elements, memory size, and speed, with some additional functional extensions such as antialiasing (image space oversampling that improves the look of edges), stencil buffers for more realistic shadows and fog, support for decoding additional video stream types (e.g., wmv), and the ability to drive multiple monitors. At that point, Nvidia and ATI effectively became the market leaders in GPU design, with the latter being purchased by AMD in 2006. Nvidia's GeForce7 series may serve as a representative device of that time, with impressive peak performance of 15.6 Goperations/s that enabled fill rates of 10.4 Gpixel/s, 15.6 Gtexel/s, and geometry throughput of 1.3 Gvertices/s using the

[1]The term shader was introduced by Pixar Animation Studios in the interface specification of their 3D rendering software, RenderMan.

G71 silicon revision clocked at 650 MHz. More powerful versions were produced by populating the graphics boards with two processing chips, but at the cost of nearly doubling the power consumption.

Even though the rendering throughput achieved was substantial, the fixed-function pipeline was in many ways limiting. The first programmable shaders helped, but were unable to generate new vertices algorithmically and apply more generic (or newly devised) classes of processing algorithms. The allocation of resources became more difficult to manage when the contents of the scene changed dynamically, and impacted processing efficiency caused by fixed resource ratios between individual stages of the pipeline. The next critical innovation was the introduction of *unified shaders*, which essentially behave as programmable processing elements that may assume each other's functions as directed by the programmer and are no longer rigidly assigned to a specific stage of processing pipeline (Fig. 15.10). The first GPUs providing this capability were Nvidia's GeForce8 and the AMD Radeon HD2000 series. The consequence of architectural enhancements was the continued generalization of GPU compute resources that eventually brought the first hardware supporting double-precision arithmetic, such as RV670 for AMD and GT200 for Nvidia (also known as the Tesla architecture), introduced respectively in 2007 and 2008, thus enabling their broader use for scientific applications. Some practitioners in the field emphasize this fact by using the GPGPU acronym for general-purpose computing on GPUs to distinguish this from purely graphics-related usage. Further microarchitecture optimizations included tessellation and better support for asynchronous processing, such as AMD's asynchronous computing engines with independent scheduling and work dispatch introduced in its Graphics Core Next (GCN) product family. GCN also features primitive discard accelerators which remove objects that are invalid or do not impact any pixels before they are sent to fragment shaders. It is worth noting that both companies differentiate their product lines into consumer market offerings that are primarily graphics oriented and have a lower price tag and GPGPU implementations that offer better stability and reliability at added cost. Table 15.1 presents a comparison of the current (at the time of writing) top-of-the-line products. Even though the

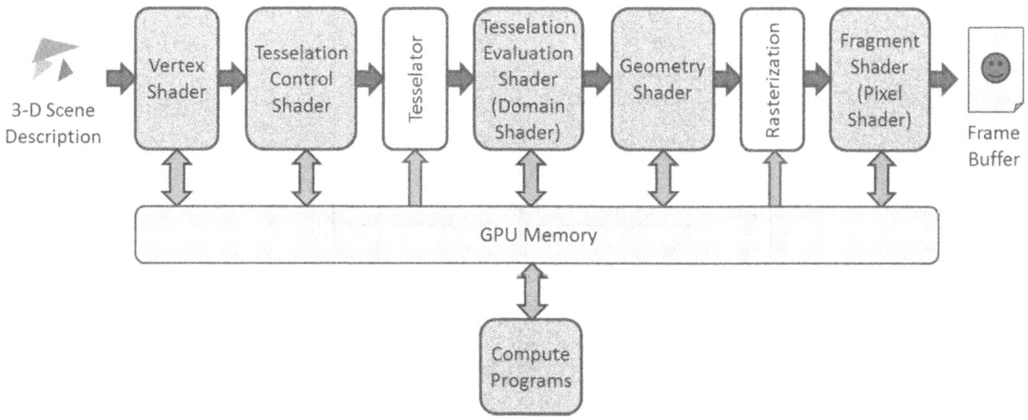

FIGURE 15.10

Primary components of a modern rendering pipeline. Blocks in blue (light gray in print versions) indicate parts of processing performed by the unified shaders.

Table 15.1 Comparison of Modern Graphics Processing Unit (GPU) Properties (Only Single-Chip GPU Implementations Considered)

Company	Product Name	Product Type	Transistor Count (Billion)	Base Clock (MHz)	Peak FP GFlops		Memory Bandwidth (GB/s)	Memory Bus Width	Max. Power (W)
					SP	DP			
AMD	Radeon R9 Fury X	GPU	8.9	1050	8601.6	537.6	512	4096	275
AMD	FirePro W9100	Accel.	6.2	930	5240	2620	320	512	275
Nvidia	GeForce GTX Titan X	GPU	8	1000	6144	192	336	384	250
Nvidia	K40	Accel.	7.1	745	5040	1680	288	384	235

Since the double-precision performance of the Maxwell GPU is only 1/32 that of single precision, the previous-generation model (Kepler) is reported in the "accelerator" rubric for Nvidia.

availability of floating-point operations is common in modern GPUs, special caution must be taken with respect to their accuracy (especially rounding), since not all GPUs support all IEEE 754 number postprocessing modes.

15.5 MODERN GRAPHICS PROCESSING UNIT ARCHITECTURE

This section discusses the details of the Nvidia Pascal architecture [9] as an exemplar of a modern general-purpose GPU designed primarily for use in HPC. The Pascal line of accelerators (hardware code name GP100) was announced in April 2016. It contains a number of solutions that improve the aggregate computational performance in various application areas, such as an increased number of 64-bit FPUs compared to single-precision FPUs and the addition of a "half-precision" (16-bit) number format that is expected to increase the effective processing bandwidth for certain artificial intelligence and deep-learning applications (specifically neural network training), sensor data processing, radio astronomy, and others. Pascal is the first GPU to feature the NVlink interconnect [10] that enables point-to-point communications between multiple GPUs and CPUs and GPUs. Such links will be included in IBM's POWER9 processors to facilitate high-bandwidth data streaming to the upcoming Volta GPUs currently under design by Nvidia and to be used as intranode interconnects in the future Department of Energy-commissioned supercomputers "Summit" and "Sierra" [11]. Pascal leverages second-generation stacked high-bandwidth memory (HBM2) [12], which shares the package with GPU logic to achieve substantially higher bandwidths and realize wider data paths than possible using the commonly available external GDDR5 [13] memory. Other improvements provide faster atomic operations and target both on-chip shared and DRAM memory and different modes of access. To support very large datasets, Pascal enables unified access to system memory, making it possible to share data between the GPU and CPU without the user explicitly initiating data movement operations. This is implemented through virtual memory demand paging capable of handling thousands of outstanding simultaneous page faults. As a result, Pascal delivers tremendous computational throughput, as illustrated in Table 15.2, along with other operational parameters.

15.5.1 COMPUTE ARCHITECTURE

A sketch of Pascal chip-level architecture is presented in Fig. 15.11. The largest portion of GP100 die is dedicated to streaming multiprocessors (SMs). A single GPU comprises a maximum of 60 SMs grouped in blocks of 10 per graphics processing cluster (GPC). Up to four SMs may be disabled as a result of manufacturing defects. As each GPC encapsulates all elements of the rendering pipeline, it effectively acts as a small, independent GPU. GPCs further subdivide into texture processing clusters, each containing two SMs. The remainder of the die is utilized by a shared 4 MB L2 cache that stores global datasets fetched from memory, eight HBM2 memory controllers with 512-bit wide buses, a third-generation PCI Express interface supporting 16 lanes, and four bidirectional NVlink controllers. Additionally, the GigaThread engine is responsible for global scheduling of thread blocks consisting of up to 1024 threads and related context switching. This constitutes the coarse level of workload scheduling, while the secondary part is performed by the individual SMs. Each thread block executes on the same set of assigned SMs, sharing access to caches and local data scratchpads. Thread blocks

Table 15.2 Significant GP100 Architecture Parameters

Parameter	Value
Technology node	TSMC 16 nm Fin-FET
Transistor count	15.3 billion
Die size	610 mm^2
Clock frequency	1328 MHz (1480 MHz boost)
Memory type	HBM2
Memory size	16 GB
Memory bus width	8 × 512 bits
Memory bandwidth	720 GB/s
Thermal design power	300 W
Resource Counts (Per GPU)	
Streaming multiprocessors	56 (max. 60)
CUDA cores	3584
Texture processing clusters	28
Texture units	224
Register file size	14336 KB
L2 cache size	4096 KB
FP32 CUDA cores	2584
FP64 CUDA cores	1792
Aggregate Performance	
Peak double precision	5.3 TFlops
Peak single precision	10.6 TFlops
Peak half precision	21.2 TFlops

further subdivide into "warps" consisting of up to 32 individual threads. Complete warps are dispatched on individual SMs.

The bulk of processing is performed by SMs, whose structure is shown in Fig. 15.12. Each SM contains 64 single-precision and 32 double-precision Compute Unified Device Architecture (CUDA) cores that are organized in two blocks, each with its own instruction buffer, thread scheduler, two dispatch units, and a 128 KB register file. The FP32 cores complete one single-precision or two half-precision operations every clock cycle; the issue rate for the FP64 cores is one instruction every two cycles. All floating-point logic supports subnormal arithmetic as well as fused multiply—add operations with optimized rounding that results in minimal precision loss. The SMs also include 16 load/store units, each of which computes one effective address per cycle, and 16 special-function units that execute fast approximate calculations such as reciprocal, square root, and some transcendental functions.

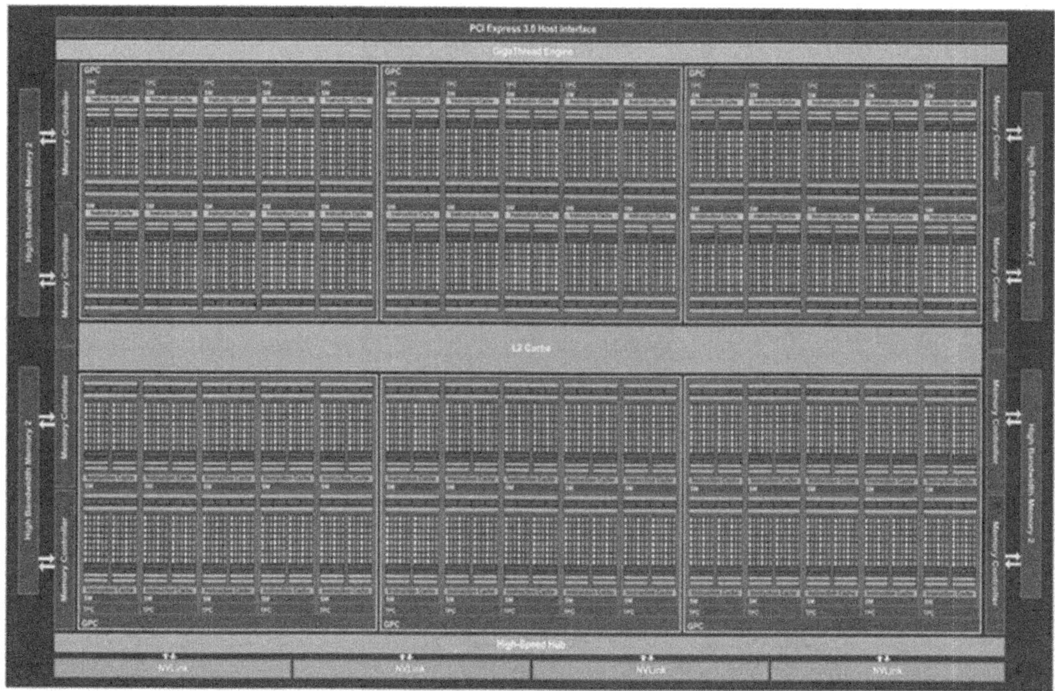

FIGURE 15.11

Pascal GP100 architecture diagram.

From NVIDIA

While the core count per SM has decreased compared to the previous generation Maxwell architecture, this produced more favorable resource ratios. Pascal compute cores have access to twice as many registers, can concurrently execute twice as many warps, may utilize 100% higher memory bandwidth, and have 33% greater shared memory capacity. The latter is available as 64 KB shared memory per SM. Shared memory provides access times comparable with register access, and acts as a software-managed data scratchpad.

Pascal improves atomic access to shared memory data, implementing native read–modify–write operations on 32-bit integers and by providing native compare-and-swap for both 32-bit and 64-bit data, in contrast to the lock–update–unlock algorithm used in previous-generation GPUs. Extending the previous capability of natively supporting atomic floating-point addition of single-precision numbers in global memory, GP100 can also perform atomic addition on double-precision operands. This operation may be performed on data accessible over PCI Express and NVlink. The rounding mode of floating-point addition has been upgraded to unbiased *round-to-nearest-even* mode instead of *round-to-zero*.

SMs feature dedicated 64 KB L1 data caches that operate independently from shared memories. This deviates from previous architecture revisions, in which the L1 cache and shared memory had to occupy the same memory block but adjustments of the fraction of its capacity dedicated to each were permitted. The data caches may double as texture caches when graphics workloads are executed. They

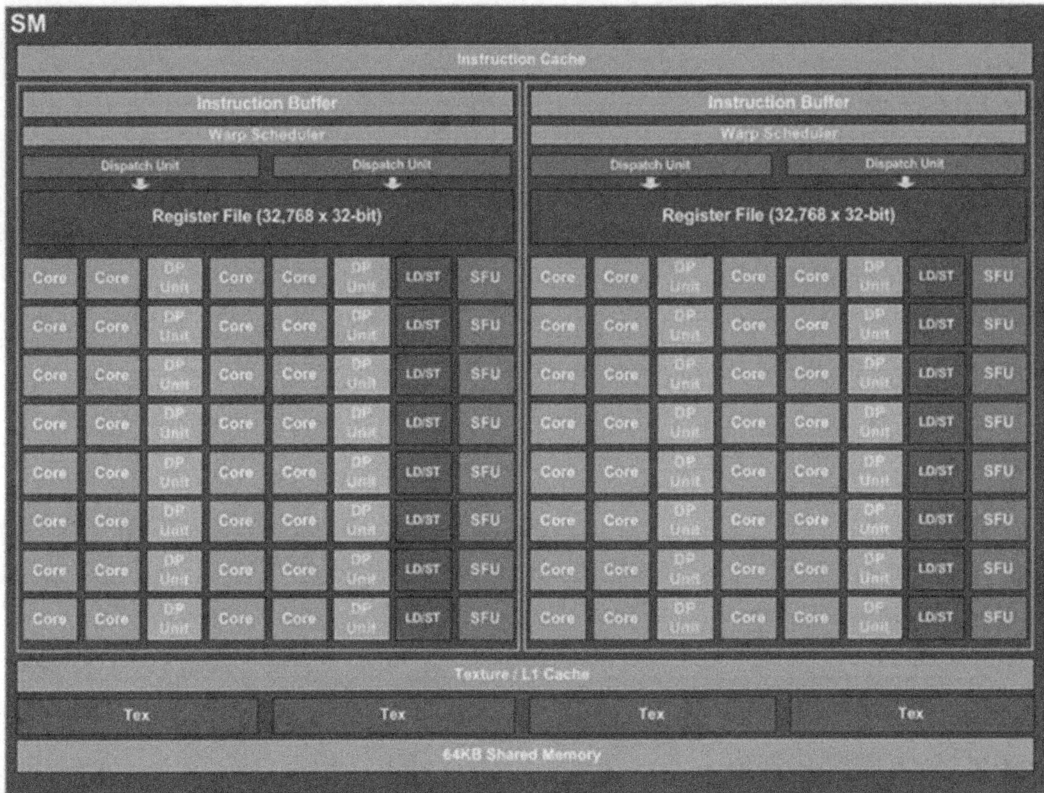

FIGURE 15.12

Organization of a single streaming multiprocessor.

From NVIDIA

also perform coalescing of data retrieved from global memory prior to their delivery to executing warps to achieve better sustained data bandwidth.

GP100 implements instruction-granularity preemption of compute kernels through which they may be arbitrarily interrupted and have their context relegated to GPU memory. This is in stark contrast to preemption at block granularity available in previous GPUs, which made them susceptible to become unresponsive while waiting for a single misbehaving task to complete. This made coexecution of compute and visualization kernels (which are strongly time constrained) very difficult. Fine-grain preemption also enables interactive debugging of applications on a GPU—a feature that previously was cumbersome to support and required explicit instrumentation of the debugged code by the compiler.

15.5.2 MEMORY IMPLEMENTATION

High aggregate processing rates of GPU execution resources can only be realized when matching data feed rates are provided. While conventional approaches relied on ever-wider and higher frequency implementations of "graphics" DRAM to cope with the increasing demand for bandwidth, the limitations of external memory modules required a less conventional solution. The Pascal architecture is the first Nvidia implementation that packages GPU logic together with memory. This is accomplished by using a passive silicon interposer that supports both the GPU die and multiple stacks of HBM2 memory attached to it through microbumps. The memory stacks may consist of up to 8 dies, each providing up to 8 Gbit of storage. Individual HBM2 dies interconnect using through-silicon via (TSV) [14]; a single 8 Gb die is said to contain as many as 5000 TSV connections. In GP100 each memory stack operates at 180 GB/s data bandwidth. Currently, GP100 ships with four four-level HBM2 stacks, each connected to two dedicated memory controllers over a 1024-bit bus yielding a total of 16 GB memory per accelerator. The whole arrangement is packaged in a single 55 × 55 mm ball grid array.

When using external memories, error detection and correction consume part of the memory capacity (storage of parity data) and require an additional logic stage that rebuilds the original data word. These respectively decrease the effective data bandwidth and increase access latency. The important benefit of HBM2 is that error correction is active at all times without imposing bandwidth penalty.

One of the main problems plaguing GPU programming is effective arrangement of data transfers between the CPU and GPU memories. As the local interconnect (typically a multilane PCI Express bus) is an order of magnitude slower than the aggregate bandwidth of GDDR RAM attached to GPU controllers and the size of GPU memory is often a small fraction of system memory, allocation of GPU memory and orchestrating data movement at the right time have a substantial impact on performance. The Pascal architecture supports a unified virtual address space through which the GPU can access all GPU and CPU memory present in the system. Unified memory, originally introduced in the CUDA6 programming model, can create a shared memory allocation that is accessible to both the CPU and the GPU via a single pointer. The use of this feature in the past was limited due to the need for synchronization of any portion of memory modified by the CPU before it could be used by kernels running on the GPU. Pascal supports page-faulting mechanisms that bring the necessary data pages into the accelerator's memory on demand; explicit offload of the entire dataset is no longer necessary. Moreover, the pages to be accessed may stay at their current location and be mapped in GPU address space for access over PCI Express or NVlink. Page migration is systemwide and symmetric: both the CPU and the GPU may request migration of pages from the CPU's or other GPUs' address spaces. The page-faulting mechanism also guarantees global memory data consistency. To reduce the translation lookaside buffer impact of GPU paging, large pages of up to 2 MB size are supported. These techniques allow oversubscription of physical memory on the GPU and permit fine-tuning of data movement performance through application programming interface (API) hints ("cudaMemAdvise").

15.5.3 INTERCONNECTS

A typical accelerated HPC system integrates multiple GPUs in a single node. While attaching the accelerator through a standard PCI Express bus is possible and convenient, it also introduces a serious communication bottleneck. To alleviate this issue, Nvidia included four NVlink controllers per GPU, each consisting of two unidirectional sublinks that provide data bandwidth of 20 GB/s. A single sublink aggregates eight differential pairs that operate at 20 Gbps each using Nvidia's high-speed signaling technology. Individual links may be combined ("ganged") to provide greater point-to-point bandwidth figures. To access processing components on the GPU, the links communicate

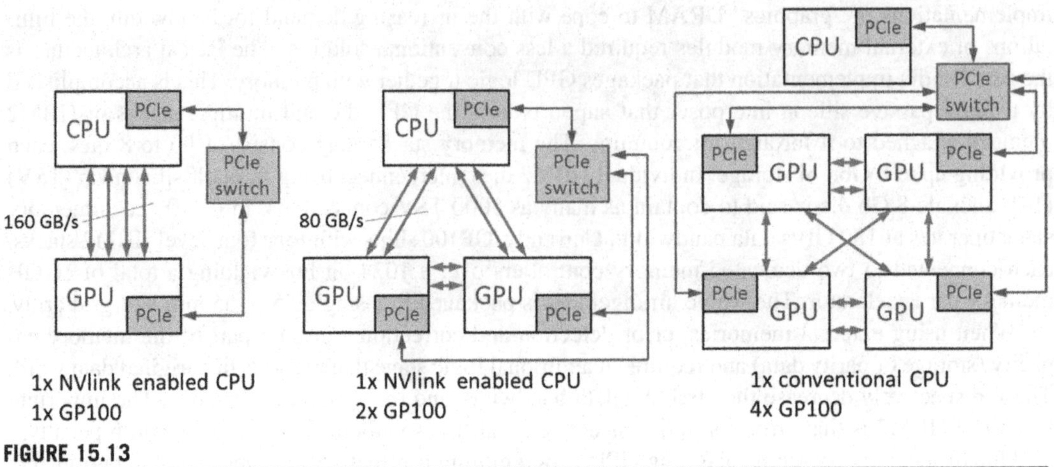

FIGURE 15.13

Some of the supported node topologies employing Pascal NVlink ganging.

through a high-speed hub that attaches directly to the internal GPU cross-bar switch. Integrated data movement infrastructure uses high-speed copy engines that are capable of saturating the link bandwidth.

The external link topologies include GPU to GPU and GPU to (properly equipped) CPU. Arbitrary link aggregations are possible to achieve higher communication bandwidths between any component pairs. Some of the possible layouts are illustrated in Fig. 15.13.

In addition to NVlink, GP100 integrates a 16-lane PCI Express 3.0 endpoint on the die. Besides enabling connectivity with processors not equipped with NVlink hardware, it may be used to perform I/O operations without CPU involvement through RDMA (remote DMA). This feature, named GPUDirect, permits various I/O devices such as NICs, InfiniBand adapters, and some solid-state devices to read from and write to GPU memory directly. This is particularly useful for distributed message-passing interface applications executing on the GPU, as it lowers the communication latency and eliminates the need for copying data to memory accessible to the main processor.

15.5.4 PROGRAMMING ENVIRONMENT

There are several general programming toolkits available for Nvidia GPUs, differing in level of attainable optimization and access to hardware features as well as program portability to other systems. The best level of compatibility is obtained using Nvidia's own CUDA API and compiler. Initial Pascal GPU support is included, starting with the compute capability 6.0 of the toolkit. CUDA works with C, C++ (using the Low Level Virtual Machine-based "nvcc" compiler), and Fortran (using a custom compiler from The Portland Group, Inc.) languages. The program sources in CUDA must be transformed to include certain attributes, such as "__global__" informing the compiler which functions are to be executed on GPUs instead of on the host computer, or "__shared__" to qualify the on-GPU storage type of variables. Kernel invocation requires special bracket syntax to specify the desired parallelization parameters. The syntax modifications are complemented with library calls that provide GPU memory allocation and copying, stream operations, atomics, event handling, and many other features. The main restriction of CUDA is its support of only Nvidia brand GPUs.

OpenACC (Open Accelerator) is another GPU programming model that builds on the directive (pragma) based syntax in C, C++, and Fortran popularized by OpenMP. This has a direct advantage of producing an equivalent sequential version of the executable from the same set of sources if OpenACC compilation is not enabled through a command-line option. OpenACC also includes an API to interact with multiple accelerator devices, perform memory allocation and data copying, and support asynchronous operation. As OpenACC primarily focuses on simplicity and portability, it may not benefit from all available architectural features and optimizations provided by individual GPUs.

OpenCL (Open Computing Language) is an effort to provide a unified programming environment for heterogeneous devices, including multicore CPUs, GPUs, digital signal processors, FPGAs, and other. It includes a C-like programming language, API, associated libraries, and runtime system. OpenCL uses a hierarchy of four models—platform model, memory model, execution model, and programming model—to define the basic properties, interactions, and rules guiding the execution of workloads in a heterogeneous environment. The framework extends the C language with additional types for vectors, pointers, floating points, images, matrices, and events; qualifiers for address space, functions, and access; and operator overloads for vector operations. It also provides an extensive library of mathematical, geometric, relational, vector, synchronization, memory, atomic, and image functions. OpenCL permits workloads to execute on the CPU and accelerators at the same time. Since the key focus of the framework is portability, certain performance sacrifices are expected, especially compared with native implementations such as CUDA.

15.6 HETEROGENEOUS SYSTEM ARCHITECTURE

The physical separation of CPU and GPU logic in the same system has both benefits and disadvantages. The implementation of each can be independently optimized (GPUs for scale, CPUs for thread performance), potentially using different manufacturing processes. They could be independently upgraded as long as the connectivity options (industry-standard buses, such as PCI Express shown in Fig. 15.14A) remain compatible across silicon generations. The resultant system topology is more flexible, as more GPUs can be added to the system to populate the available interconnect slots. The memory interfaces can be tailored to provide data feed bandwidths and access latencies matching the dominant processing characteristics of either component. It is also worth noting that many heterogeneous supercomputing installations, including those used to run applications that were recently awarded the Gordon Bell Prize, utilize discrete GPUs. However, since the computations in both domains proceed independently, there is always an associated overhead when the involved datasets must cross the domain boundary. As the available system interconnects operate at substantially slower rates than those of memory banks, data copying becomes detrimental to overall performance. Moreover, application programmers frequently need to anticipate and manage data movement so that it overlaps with the ongoing computations as much as possible. Note that the additions to Pascal GPUs

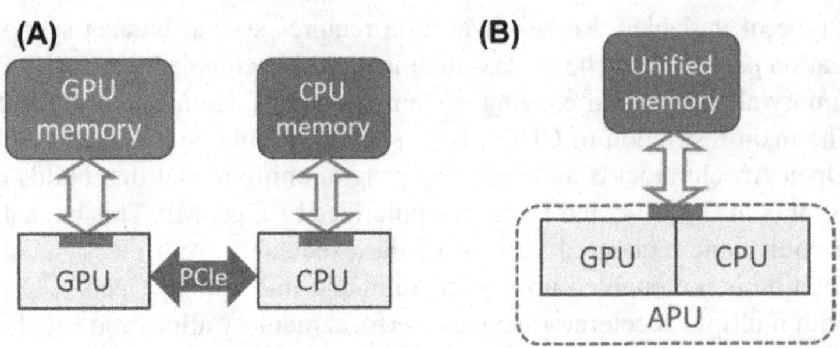

FIGURE 15.14

System structure with (A) discrete CPU and GPU and (B) HSA-enabled architecture.

discussed in the previous section cannot prevent data copies, and naïvely arranged on-demand page migration is still going to produce substantial delays between the first access causing a page fault and actual data availability in local memory. To alleviate these problems, AMD proposed the heterogeneous system architecture (HSA) that places cooperating hardware devices on the same bus and uses shared memory to physically colocate the processed datasets. This concept is illustrated in Fig. 15.14B.

The HSA specifications [15] are developed by the nonprofit HSA Foundation, whose members include a host of industrial and academic members, AMD, ARM, Texas Instruments, Samsung, Qualcomm, MediaTek, Imagination Technologies, and several US national laboratories. The HSA Foundation's goal is to reduce the programming complexity of systems incorporating heterogeneous components by providing ISA-independent runtime and system architecture APIs. The specification identifies two types of compute units: a latency compute unit (such as a CPU) and a throughput compute unit (TCU, such as a GPU). These components share cache-coherent virtual memory hardware implementing a unified virtual address space. As a result, cooperating devices utilize the same page tables, enabling data sharing simply by exchanging pointers and thus incurring no memory copy penalties. This is accomplished by custom memory management units that coordinate access to both coherent and noncoherent system memory. Support for page faulting eliminates the need for high-overhead driver-managed pinned memory pools. HSA also obviates high-overhead system calls by promoting user-level dispatch of work units to TCU queues. Further, it defines a mechanism by which TCU hardware may directly switch between individual application queues without operating system involvement, accomplishing faster scheduling that requires less power. The specifications do not define any custom or specific language for application programming, but instead attempt to leverage a number of existing high-level languages and programming models such as C++, Java, Python, C#, OpenMP, and OpenCL.

HSA is of primary interest to SoC design and programming, where efficiency and low power consumption are paramount. It is less likely to be applied to flagship GPUs, since colocation of different device types on the same die might take away resources and thus reduce the effective throughput of a TCU. A good example of mainstream HSA hardware is the AMD accelerated processing unit (APU) starting with Kaveri architecture. It combines a few x86_64-compatible processor cores with GPUs. An overview of their main parameters is presented in Table 15.3.

Table 15.3 Properties of Select HSA-Compliant AMD APUs

Architecture Code Name	Fabrication Process (nm)	Die Size (mm^2)	CPU			GPU		Memory Support	Max. TDP (W)
			Architecture	Clock (GHz)	Max. Cores	Clock (MHz)	Shaders		
Kaveri	28 nm	245	Steamroller	4.1/4.3	4	866	512	DDR3-2133	95
Carrizo	28 nm	245	Excavator	2.1/3.4	4	800	512	DDR3-2133	35
Bristol Ridge	28 nm	250	Excavator	3.8/4.2	4	1108	512	DDR4-2400	65

15.7 SUMMARY AND OUTCOMES OF CHAPTER 15

- Accelerators are hardware devices that speed up certain types of computation. While controlled and coordinated by the main processor in the system, they are capable of performing these computations independently.
- Accelerator implementations leverage different sets of trade-offs and design constraints, driven by the available technology in each time period. The technology determines the level of integration with the main CPU, work offload mechanisms, and the effective performance.
- The first floating-point accelerators were coprocessors. They operated in lock step with the primary CPU and required custom hardware interfaces to operate.
- Portability of accelerator functions across systems of different types is achieved through reliance on widely adopted industry standards as a communication interface between the main CPU and the accelerator.
- GPUs evolved to become the modern-era floating-point accelerators through continued unification of previously hardwired functions specialized to support the individual stages of the graphics rendering pipeline and explicit addition of other features required by HPC, such as double-precision floating point.
- Large-scale integration affording high transistor counts per chip enables additional performance and programmability optimizations by combining multiple traditionally separate devices on a single die.

15.8 PROBLEMS AND QUESTIONS

1. What motivated the introduction of accelerators in computing systems?
2. Briefly characterize the coprocessor-enhanced architecture. Which properties made coprocessors cumbersome to use? Given that modern CPU transistor budgets frequently go into billions, would it be worthwhile to revisit the concept and include specialized coprocessor logic on processor dies?
3. Which components of modern GPUs make them suitable for generic computing applications? Which architectural solutions may prevent them from reaching the peak processing throughput with arbitrary computing problems?
4. What are the benefits of using a unified memory system in HSA versus a discrete GPU and CPU approach? What are the drawbacks?
5. A floating-point accelerator with 256 FPUs clocked at 512 MHz and equipped with 512 MB of local memory is used to speed up the multiplication of two 16×16 K matrices containing double-precision floating-point numbers. The multiplication nominally takes 200 s on the host CPU. The accelerator is attached through a PCI Express bus with a sustained data transfer rate of 1 GB/s in each direction. Each of its FPUs performs a fused multiply–add operation within a cycle. Assuming that the overheads of local data movement and space required to store the executable code in the accelerator may be ignored, and the setup of data transfer between the CPU and the accelerator takes a negligible amount of time, calculate the following.

a. Matrix multiplication speed-up if executed only by the accelerator. Remember that the input matrices are originally stored in the host memory, thus the result matrix should be placed there as well.

b. With optimal workload distribution, how would the speed-up change if both accelerator and host CPU worked in tandem?

REFERENCES

[1] PCI Special Interest Group, PCI-Express Specifications Library, 2016 [Online]. Available: https://pcisig.com/specifications.

[2] S.W. Smith, The Scientist's and Engineer's Guide to Digital Signal Processing, California Technical Publishing, San Diego, 1997.

[3] 754-2008-IEEE Standard for Floating-Point Arithmetic, IEEE Computer Society, 2008.

[4] T. Whitted, An improved illumination model for shaded display, Communications of the ACM 23 (6) (1980) 343–349.

[5] C.M. Goral, K.E. Torrance, D.P. Greenberg, B. Battaile, Modeling the interaction of light between diffuse surfaces, Computer Graphics 18 (3) (1984) 213–222.

[6] H. Gouraud, Continuous shading of curved surfaces, IEEE Transactions on Computers C-20 (6) (1971) 87–93.

[7] B.T. Phong, Illumination for computer generated pictures, Communications of the ACM 18 (6) (1975) 311–317.

[8] J.H. Clark, The geometry engine: a VLSI geometry system for graphics, ACM Computer Graphics 16 (3) (1982) 127–133.

[9] Nvidia Corp, NVIDIA Tesla P100 (Whitepaper), 2016 [Online]. Available: https://images.nvidia.com/content/pdf/tesla/whitepaper/pascal-architecture-whitepaper.pdf.

[10] Nvidia Corp, Whitepeper: NVIDIA NVLink High-speed Interconnect: Application Performance, November 2014 [Online]. Available: http://info.nvidianews.com/rs/nvidia/images/NVIDIA%20NVLink%20High-Speed%20Interconnect%20Application%20Performance%20Brief.pdf.

[11] Nvidia Corp, Whitepaper: Summit and Sierra Supercomputers: An inside Look at the U.S. Department of Energy's New Pre-exascale Systems, November 2014 [Online]. Available: http://www.teratec.eu/actu/calcul/Nvidia_Coral_White_Paper_Final_3_1.pdf.

[12] JEDEC Solid State Technology Association, JESD235A: High Bandwidth Memory (HBM) DRAM, November 2015 [Online]. Available: https://www.jedec.org/standards-documents/results/jesd235.

[13] JEDEC Solid State Technology Association, JESD232A: Graphics Double Data Rate (GDDR5X) SGRAM Standard, August 2016 [Online]. Available: https://www.jedec.org/standards-documents/docs/jesd232a.

[14] B. Black, M. Annavaram, et al., Die stacking (3D) microarchitceture, in: Proceedings of the 39th Annual IEEE/ACM International Symposium on Microarchitecture, 2006.

[15] HSA Foundation, HSA Standards, 2016 [Online]. Available: http://www.hsafoundation.com/standards/.

CHAPTER

THE ESSENTIAL OPENACC 16

CHAPTER OUTLINE

16.1 INTRODUCTION

As discussed in Chapter 15, graphics processing units (GPUs) are currently one of the most dominant accelerator types employed in high performance computing. In contrast to conventional multicore processors, however, their programming is a much more complex task. The main reason for this stems from the relatively young age of GPU technology, resulting in a dearth of mature programming tools and environments. Various aspects of the technology are constantly being improved and modified, which further complicates the development of general-purpose programming approaches and compilers. Compared to conventional hardware, the accelerators also use a diametrically different execution model. While for many practical purposes each core on a multicore CPU could be considered a separate context of execution, the same is not true for a thread ensemble running on a GPU core. This is particularly apparent in cases of performance loss due to *branch divergence*, when a

High Performance Computing. https://doi.org/10.1016/B978-0-12-420158-3.00016-2

subset of threads follows a different code path than the others as a result of a conditional instruction. Conventional processor architecture in combination with an optimizing compiler makes many implicit components of program execution (register allocation, cache management, data consistency enforcement, optimization of branches, instruction reordering, speculative execution, and many others) transparent to the user, who is free to focus on fleshing out the essential program algorithms and data structures in a high-level programming language. In GPUs many details of the architecture still need to be explicitly addressed by a programmer who is interested in extracting the highest level of performance. Due to the much larger number of execution resources and also the stronger emphasis on parallelism, resource allocation and management become far more critical to achieving a good level of performance. These often have to take into account the physical structure, count, and resource limits on GPUs, especially if many computational kernels with different memory footprints and performance characteristics need to be scheduled concurrently. Since data locality references play a critical role in maximizing the performance and GPU memory capacity is traditionally undersized compared to that of the host machine, efficient scheduling of data offloads adds another dimension to the complexity of managing the computations on an accelerator. Note that offload speeds are usually constrained by the available bandwidth of the PCI Express bus, potentially resulting in significant latencies when transferring large amounts of data. To offer any advantage over a nonaccelerated model of computation, these costs would have to be amortized by performance gains over the entire course of an application execution. Moreover, the question of what is the right placement for a specific kernel in a heterogeneous architecture is not always easy to answer. It has to be weighed against the individual programmer's experience in GPU code development, familiarity with the architectural features of the target GPU, programming tools available, and ported algorithm characteristics. Even then it may turn out that due to unforeseen overheads or latencies the speed-up gained through execution on an accelerator does not present any practical advantage compared to conventional hardware. This directly affects programmers' productivity: their time would have likely been better spent developing and optimizing a multicore implementation of the algorithm, or even better linking with an optimized external library providing the required functionality. Finally, to take advantage of both worlds, one might attempt to balance the computation across all available execution resources in the system. While potentially yielding the best performance, this approach is also the most difficult to manage. Strong disparities between the execution environments involved make the predictable scheduling of computations very difficult to attain, save for the most trivial and well-characterized problems.

Initially, GPU programs leveraged three-dimensional graphics application programming interfaces (APIs) such as OpenGL [1] and DirectX [2] to perform operations on vectors and dense matrices, since these were natively supported by the graphics pipeline. One of the first algorithms accelerated on a GPU was matrix multiplication using 8-bit (with 16-bit internal precision) fixed-point arithmetic published in 2001 [3]. To trick the graphics hardware into performing the desired operations, the authors used two textures corresponding to the input matrices and mapped multiple copies of them on to the interior of a cube, keeping one parallel and the other perpendicular to the projection plane. The partial products obtained through multitexturing in modulate mode were summed on to the front face of the cube using blending in orthographic view (to avoid perspective distortions). The final result (image) was then retrieved using GPU-to-CPU memory copy. The reader will immediately notice that this method of performing computations is not very practical. To provide a more convenient programming environment, a number of custom interfaces specialized for GPUs and in some cases targeting general heterogeneous platforms were developed throughout the 2000s. As the feature sets of newer GPUs grew richer and after the introduction of new architectural capabilities (programmable shaders, double-precision floating points, support for dynamic parallelism, etc.), many of these interfaces were revised to include the appropriate support for added extensions. It is not uncommon for many of these APIs to undergo several specification revisions over the relatively short span of their existence, the newest of which frequently require recent versions of graphics hardware to provide the full set of operational features. A brief overview of several popular toolkits with different programming models, supported features, portability, and scope is presented below.

16.1.1 CUDA

This widespread proprietary GPU programming toolkit, originally known as the Compute Unified Device Architecture (CUDA) [4], only works with devices manufactured by Nvidia, including the GeForce, Quadro, and Tesla families. Frequently used high performance computing languages such as C, C++, and Fortran are supported through compiler extensions and a runtime library. For the C family of languages Nvidia provides `nvcc`, a low level virtual machine-based compiler, while Fortran support is available from the Portland Group's (PGI) CUDA Fortran compiler. The programming environment is supplemented by libraries optimized for specific tasks, such as fast Fourier transform computation, basic linear algebra subprograms, random number generation, dense and sparse solvers, graphs analytics, and game physics simulation. CUDA has several performance-oriented features that are typically not available through standard graphics-based interfaces, such as scattered memory reads, unified memory access, fast on-GPU shared memory access, improved speeds of offload and state retrieval, additional data types, mixed-precision computing, supplementary integer and bit-wise operations, and profiling support. As of June 2017, the most recent revision of the toolkit is 8.0.

16.1.2 OPENCL

Open Computing Language [5], initially released in 2009 by the non-profit Khronos consortium, is an open standard attempting to define a unified heterogeneous programing framework. It provides an API on top of the C language (ISO/IEC 9899:1999) and C++14 (starting with revision 2.2) that supports using the target device's memory and processing elements (PEs) for program execution. Execution in a heterogeneous environment places substantial constraints on language features that are permitted—for example, recursion, type identification, go-to statements, virtual functions, exceptions, and function pointers may not be used at all or only with severe limitations. Device vendors determine how and which PEs are actually offered to the user. OpenCL permits up to four levels of memory hierarchy to be implemented by the device: global memory (large, but with substantial latency), read-only memory (small and fast, but writable by the host only), local memory shared by a subset of PEs, and per PE private memory (e.g., registers). Corresponding qualifiers (`global`, `local`, `constant`, `private`) are integrated with the language and understood by the compiler when used in variable declarations. Functions executing on accelerators are marked with the `kernel` attribute and accept argument declarations tagged with the address space qualifiers listed above. Kernels defined as source code may be compiled in runtime by the appropriate online compiler if the platform is *full-profile* compliant; otherwise an offline, platform-specific compilation is used (*embedded profile*). Besides explicitly defined kernels, devices may provide built-in functions that are enumerated and offered by OpenCL. The framework supports execution synchronization at three levels: workgroup, subgroup, and command. Revision 2.2–3 of the OpenCL specification was released in May 2017.

16.1.3 C++ AMP

Developed by Microsoft, C++ Accelerated Massive Parallelism [6] is a compiler and set of extensions to C++ that enable the acceleration of C++ applications on platforms that support various forms of data-parallel execution. The accelerator does not necessarily have to be an external device such as a GPU; it could be integrated on the same die as the main CPU, or even be an extension of the main processor's industry-standard architecture, such as streaming single-instruction multiple data (SIMD) extensions or advanced vector extensions provided by some members of the ×86 processor family. Its device model assumes that the accelerator may be equipped with a private memory that is not accessible to the host, or that both host and device share the same memory. The C++ AMP runtime performs or avoids memory copies as required by a particular implementation. The framework defines two types of function restriction specifiers, `cpu` and `amp`, the latter of which marks the relevant code for execution on the accelerator. Functions tagged in this way must conform to the C++ subset that is permitted by the underlying hardware type. Accelerators are represented by `accelerator` objects with an associated logical *view* (more than one view per accelerator is possible) that implement command buffers for computational tasks to be processed by the accelerator. Commands may be submitted for execution immediately or deferred; completion of the accelerator workload may be synchronous (blocking) or asynchronous, using future-based markers for a single task or task group. Data types are based on n-dimensional arrays with related n-dimensional *extent* (determining array bounds) and *index* objects (referring to a specific element). To exercise control over data copying and caching with minimal overhead, *array views* are provided that permit access to a segment of a relevant array. Array views may be accessed locally or in a different coherence domain, implying the necessary data copies for the latter. C++ AMP also supports a range of atomic operations and a `parallel_for_each` construct to launch parallel operations. The current revision of the specification is v1.2, released in 2013.

16.1.4 OPENACC

The Open Accelerator framework [7], also known as "directives for accelerators," differs from the approaches described above in that it attempts to simplify the accelerator programming interface significantly, making code development for GPUs and other attached devices more approachable to a casual developer. It also focuses on better code and performance portability across different platforms. The initial OpenACC specification was created by PGI, CAPS Entreprise, Cray, and Nvidia in 2011. Since then the group has been joined by national labs and multiple industry and academic members, including AMD, Pathscale, and Sandia and Oak Ridge National Laboratories. Since the directive-based approach requires compiler support, commercial tools from PGI (support for multiple target platforms with OpenACC compatibility version 2.5) and Cray (for Cray systems only) are available. Several open-source compilers have also been developed, including OpenUH from University of

Houston [8], OpenARC provided by Oak Ridge National Laboratory [9], and GCC's experimental OpenACC v2.0a support starting with version 5.1, to be further refined in the GCC 6 release series. Since OpenACC resembles another directive-based parallel programming framework, OpenMP, it is expected that the two environments will eventually be combined and share a single programming specification. The most recent (October 2015) revision of the OpenACC API is 2.5. Its essential features are discussed in more detail in the remainder of this chapter.

16.2 OPENACC PROGRAMMING CONCEPTS

OpenACC supports offloading of designated parts of the program on to accelerator devices connected to the local host computer. Segments of code that may benefit from parallel execution must be explicitly identified by the programmer through relevant directives, or *pragmas* in C and C++, and specially formatted comments in Fortran. Automatic detection of the offloadable sections of program is not supported. The applied method is portable between different CPU types, supported accelerator devices, and underlying operating systems. The details of initialization of accelerator hardware and suitable functions responsible for parallel code execution, management of workload offload, and result retrieval from the accelerator are hidden from the programmer and performed implicitly by the compiler and runtime system. OpenACC currently does not support automatic workload distribution across multiple accelerator devices, even if such are available on the same host machine. Similarly to OpenMP, the directives are simply ignored if the relevant functionality is not supported or not enabled in the compiler.

The execution of the user application is controlled by the host, which nominally follows most of the control flow within the program and initiates transfer of work and data constituting the identified parallel regions to the accelerator. For these code segments, the host may be involved in the allocation of sufficient memory on the device to accommodate the computational kernel's dataset, performing the relevant data transfer between the host and accelerator memory (frequently over the direct memory access or DMA channel), sending the executable code, marshalling and forwarding the input arguments for the parallel region, queuing the code for execution, waiting for completion, and finally fetching the computation results and releasing the memory allocated on the device. Accelerators typically support several levels of parallelism: coarse grain, referring to parallel execution on multiple execution resources, fine grain, involving one of multiple threads within a PE, and function unit level, which exposes SIMD or vector operations within each fine-grain execution unit. In OpenACC these levels are matched respectively by *gang*, *worker*, and *vector* parallelism, as illustrated in Fig. 16.1. The accelerator device executes a number of gangs, each of which contains one or more workers. In turn, a worker may take advantage of available vector parallelism by executing SIMD or vector instructions.

Execution of a compute region on the accelerator starts in so-called *gang-redundant* (GR) mode, in which each gang has a single worker executing the same code. Once the control flow in the program reaches the region marked for parallel execution, the execution switches to *gang-partitioned* (GP) mode, where the work performed by different iterations of one loop or multiple loops is distributed across the gangs, but still with only one worker active in each gang. In both these scenarios program execution proceeds in *worker-single* mode; similarly, if only one lane of vector processing is used by the worker, the program operates in *vector-single* mode. If the parallel region or its section has been

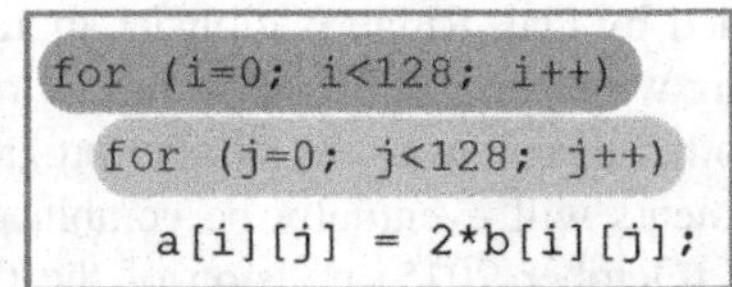

FIGURE 16.1

Example mapping of nested loop iterations on to OpenACC parallelism levels with 2 gangs, 4 workers, and 16 vector lanes. The numeric indices of the accessed matrix element in a specific iteration are shown in square brackets. In this case the outer loop is partitioned across gangs, while the inner loop iterations are divided among workers and vector lanes.

marked for worker-level work sharing, all workers in a gang are activated and the execution continues in *worker-partitioned* mode (WP). Note that parallel regions may enable GP and WP modes at the same time, which causes distribution of available work among all workers in all gangs. A similar distinction applies to vector parallelism: it may be enabled on a per loop or loop nest basis to partition the parallel operations across available SIMD or vector units, thus executing in *vector-partitioned* (VP) mode. VP mode for the specific portion of workload may be activated concurrently with any combination of gang and worker modes.

Explicit synchronization involving barriers or locks across gangs, workers, and vector operations is discouraged. Due to differences between OpenACC implementations and accelerator architectures, some of the gangs may not even begin to execute before others complete. A similar observation applies to workers and vector lanes: since scheduling of worker or vector operations is not always defined deterministically, a specific workload synchronization method that works on one accelerator architecture may lead to a deadlock on another.

Both hosts and accelerators use the concept of a thread, albeit with some differences. Host threads are closely tied to processor execution units, such as cores or hyperthread slots, depending on the actual architecture. What constitutes an accelerator core strongly depends on the accelerator type or even the particular implementation of the same device type. For example, AMD demarcates core boundaries on its GPUs differently from Nvidia. OpenACC defines the accelerator thread as a single lane of a single worker in a gang; this unambiguously corresponds to a single parallel execution context. Most accelerator threads can operate asynchronously from host threads. The framework permits submitting the work units to one or more *activity queues* on the device. Operations entered in a single queue will execute in submission order, but operations stored in different activity queues may execute in arbitrary order. The usage of other multithreading environments on the host, such as OpenMP, concurrently with OpenACC is generally unrestricted, although users should take care to avoid oversubscription of execution resources if OpenACC code regions are also scheduled to run on the host processors.

The conscientious OpenACC programmer must be aware of the consequences of the memory model exposed by the framework. Many accelerators, especially PCI Express attached GPUs, are equipped with separate memories from that of the host computer. It means that the host is incapable of directly accessing the device memory and, conversely, the device cannot efficiently access the host memory. Data movement between the two memory pools has to be orchestrated through other means, such as DMA. The programmer must take this into account when writing portable OpenACC code, since the overhead of scheduling and performing a data transfer between host and accelerator memory usually impacts the overall execution performance and may vary from instance to instance. When computing on a large amount of data, the programmer must also be aware of memory size limitations, which are typically much more restrictive on the accelerator side. The datasets accessed by the application must be appropriately partitioned into pieces that may individually fit in the device memory, in some cases imposing changes on the computational algorithm. Data structures containing raw pointers to data in the host memory may also have to be redesigned. Many GPUs utilize a weak memory model in which operations between accelerator threads are performed in arbitrary order unless synchronized by a memory fence, thus potentially producing different results for multiple runs of the same code. Similar considerations apply to unified memory architectures or those offering shared memory space between the host and the accelerator or multiple accelerators. Explicit synchronization to ensure that updates to shared data are fully carried out before they are accessed by the consumer entity is strongly recommended.

16.3 OPENACC LIBRARY CALLS

OpenACC provides a number of predefined values and library functions that may be invoked from user applications. Note that in general none of these functions is required to create fully functional OpenACC programs. They are used in situations when additional information has to be retrieved from the system or explicit management of runtime functions may yield better execution performance. Specifications subdivide the library interfaces into five major sections: definitions, device-oriented functions, asynchronous queue management, device functionality tests, and memory management. Since application of many of these requires an in-depth understanding of host–accelerator interactions, only a small subset of the available interfaces is discussed below.

Since actual OpenACC implementations may conform to different revisions of the specification, one of the macros provided by the OpenACC library may be used to test for the provided functionality. It is called `_OPENACC` and expands to a six-digit decimal number, in which the first four digits denote the year and the remaining two the month of the specification release date on which the library is based. The `_OPENACC` macro may be used to enable conditional compilation of code segments that rely on more recently introduced features.

The OpenACC library definitions comprise prototypes of runtime functions and internal data types used by the library that specifically describe runtime function arguments as well as enumerations that identify accelerator types or variants of asynchronous request queue management. The commonly used runtime calls include the following.

```
int acc_get_num_devices(acc_device_t devtype);
```

This returns the number of attached accelerator devices of the type specified by `devtype`. It must not be used inside parallel regions offloaded to an accelerator. Even though symbolic identifiers describing permitted `devtype` values may depend on the actual implementation, the standard recommends the following:

- `acc_device_nvidia` for Nvidia GPUs
- `acc_device_radeon` for AMD GPUs
- `acc_device_xeonphi` for Intel Xeon Phi processors.

```
acc_device_t acc_get_device_type();
```

This indicates the device type currently set as the target accelerator, and may return acc_device_none if the accelerator device has not been selected. Similar to `acc_get_num_devices`, it may not be called inside the accelerator region.

```
void acc_set_device_type(acc_device_t devtype);
```

This sets the type of device to be used as the accelerator for parallel regions of code. The device type is indicated by the input argument. Calling this function may result in undefined behavior (including program abort) if devices of the requested type are not available or the program was not compiled to support execution on the specified accelerator type. This function may not be called inside the accelerated region of code.

```
int acc_get_device_num(acc_device_t devtype);
```

The function returns the number (index) of the accelerator device of the specified type that will be used by the current thread to offload the parallel computations. As before, it may not be called inside the code region to be executed on the accelerator.

```
void acc_set_device_num(int n, acc_device_t devtype);
```

This defines which accelerator device of the specified type may be used to execute parallel regions by the current thread. If the value of `n` is negative, the implementation will select a default accelerator device. If `devtype` is zero, the specified number will be assumed for all attached accelerator types. Function execution may result in undefined behavior if `n` is greater than or equal to the number of devices available of the indicated type. Again, acc_set_device_nummay not be called from within the accelerated code region.

Example:

```
#include <stdio.h>
#include <openacc.h>

int main() {
  printf("Supported OpenACC revision: %d.\n", _OPENACC);

  int count = acc_get_num_devices(acc_device_nvidia);
  printf("Found %d Nvidia GPUs.\n", count);
  int n = acc_get_device_num(acc_device_nvidia);
  printf("Default accelerator number is %d.\n", n);

  count = acc_get_num_devices(acc_device_host);
  printf("Found %d host processors.\n", count);
  n = acc_get_device_num(acc_device_host);
  printf("Default host processor number is %d.\n", n);
}
```

Code 16.1. Example code illustrating the use of the OpenACC library functions.

The example program shown in Code 16.1 invokes several library functions and has been compiled to run on a Cray XK7 system containing AMD Opteron CPUs and Nvidia Kepler GPUs. Launching it on a node equipped with a single GPU prints the following:

```
Supported OpenACC revision: 201306.
Found 1 Nvidia GPU(s).
Default accelerator number is 0.
Found 1 host processors.
Default host processor number is 0.
```

The retrieved release date is June 2013, which corresponds to OpenACC specifications revision 2.0. All the following code examples presented in this chapter were executed in the same environment.

16.4 OPENACC ENVIRONMENT VARIABLES

Currently, OpenACC defines only three environment variables that may be used to modify the runtime behavior of applications.

- ACC_DEVICE_TYPE determines the default device type which will be used to accelerate the marked parallel regions of the code. This value is implementation dependent. For example, the PGI compiler permits the values of NVIDIA, RADEON, and HOST to signify respectively the selection of an Nvidia or AMD branded GPU as the target accelerator device or execution on the host processor. The program has to be compiled in a way that enables the use of multiple accelerator devices.

Example:

```
export ACC_DEVICE_TYPE=NVIDIA
./openacc_app
```

Or:

```
env ACC_DEVICE_TYPE=NVIDIA ./openacc_app
```

These will accelerate the "openacc_app" application using the available Nvidia GPU. Note that the actual command line used to invoke the application may be subjected to additional requirements imposed by the runtime environment on the target platform, in particular the job management subsystem.

- `ACC_DEVICE_NUM` is a nonnegative integer that identifies the physical accelerator device to be used. The number should not be greater than or equal to the number of the attached accelerator devices on the host node, otherwise the behavior is implementation dependent.

  Example:

```
export ACC_DEVICE_NUM=0
./openacc_app
```

  This will execute parallel regions of code on the first physical accelerator in the system. The second invocation form, as shown for ACC_DEVICE_TYPE, may also be used.

- `ACC_PROFLIB` selects the appropriate profiling library, if one is available on the target system.

  Example:

```
export ACC_PROFLIB=/usr/lib/libaccprof.so
./openacc_app
```

  This will profile the execution of parallel regions in the application "openacc_app."

16.5 OPENACC DIRECTIVES

The primary method of controlling the parallel execution of OpenACC programs is via *directives* interspersed within the source code of the program. In C and C++ the directives have the following format:

`#pragma acc` *directive-name [clause-list]*

Each directive line must be terminated with a new-line character. The initial # may be optionally preceded and followed by a white space. Note that the remainder of the directive (shown above in italics) is subjected to standard conventions governing C and C++ programs, such as macro substitution. It also means that it is case sensitive.
The following sections use the same syntax format as presented above. The required literals are entered in boldface, while symbolic names referring to various components of a directive are italicized. Optional syntax components are placed inside square brackets.

16.5.1 PARALLEL CONSTRUCT

The `parallel` directive is used to identify parallel execution regions. When the flow control in the program reaches the parallel directive, it creates one or more gangs to execute the following code region. The numbers of gangs, workers per gang, and vector lanes per worker remain constant throughout the execution of the parallel region. Initially all gangs begin the execution of the specified code in a GR mode, unless changed by the appropriate clause (see below). By default, the parallel execution is terminated by an implicit barrier at the end of the region, thus blocking the execution of the next segment of the program until all work in the parallel region is finished. Note that code inside the parallel region may not branch out or be entered as a result of an external branch. The syntax of the `parallel` construct is as follows:

`#pragma acc parallel`*[clause-list]*

structured-block

The structured-block is typically a section of the code delimited by curly braces that effectively determines the scope of the parallel region, but it could also be a single statement, such as a loop. Some of the most often used clauses in the `parallel` construct are as follows.

- `async`*[*`(`*integer-expression*`)`*]*
  This removes the synchronization barrier at the end of the parallel region, permitting the host processor to execute the nonaccelerated code concurrently with the offloaded parallel computations. Optionally, it may be paired with a nonnegative integer-valued argument that is later used in a corresponding `wait` clause (or directive) to ensure the host control thread blocks until the specific asynchronous computation is completed. The number can be thought of as the number of the activity queue to which the workload is submitted. Thus two regions with async clauses having the same argument will be executed in order on the accelerator.
- `wait`*[*`(`*integer-expression-list*`)`*]*
  This blocks the current host thread until the asynchronous workload units indicated by the argument values have been completed. The specified numbers should match the arguments passed to `async` clauses. If no arguments are listed, the control thread blocks until all submitted asynchronous work has been executed.

- `num_gangs(`*integer-expression*`)`
  The `num_gangs` clause is used to specify explicitly the number of gangs across which the workload is distributed. If absent, an implementation-specific default is used. Note that restrictions imposed by the target architecture may cause the implementation to choose a lower number of gangs than that requested.
- `num_workers(`*integer-expression*`)`
  Analogous to `num_gangs`, this clause requests the specific number of workers per gang used for execution of the parallel workload in WP mode. The default number of workers is chosen if not specified, in which case it is not guaranteed to be consistent between different parallel regions (marked by the `parallel` or `kernel` directives) invoked by the program. As mentioned above, the particular implementation may modify the number of workers due to architectural constraints.
- `vector_length(`*integer-expression*`)`
  This requests the specific number of vector lanes to be assigned to each worker for code segments annotated by the `vector` clause with the `loop` directive (discussed later). Due to the arrangement of execution resources, the implementation is free to choose a value that better matches hardware specifications.

In addition to these, data management clauses may be present; these are discussed in Section 16.5.3.

Example:

```
#include <stdio.h>

const int N = 1000;

int main() {
  int vec[N];
  int cpu_sum = 0, gpu_sum = 0;

  // initialization
  for (int i = 0; i < N; i++) vec[i] = i+1;

  #pragma acc parallel async
  for (int i = 100; i < N; i++) gpu_sum += vec[i];

  // the following code executes without waiting for GPU result
  for (int i = 0; i < 100; i++) cpu_sum += vec[i];

  // synchronize and verify results
  #pragma acc wait
  printf("Result: %d (expected: %d)\n", gpu_sum+cpu_sum, (N+1)*N/2);

  return 0;
}
```

Code 16.2. Example of concurrent GPU and CPU execution triggered by the async clause.

The example application listed in Code 16.2 sums all components of a 1000-element vector. The first 100 elements are added on a CPU, while the GPU asynchronously sums the remaining 900 numbers at the same time. Synchronization with the GPU is achieved in line 19 preceding the result output. It uses a `wait` directive and not a `wait` clause on a `parallel` directive, since the latter would require an executable workload to be specified. That way, the `printf` statement immediately following in line 20 is executed by the host. The `parallel` directive allows the user to define precisely the way in which the affected workload is parallelized, but by default it is not going to parallelize anything (the execution is started in GR mode). As there are no additional parallelization clauses specified in line 12, the compute region in line 13 is not going to be vectorized. Since the code does not use any OpenACC library calls or macros, it is not necessary to include the OpenACC header file. The program produces the following output:

```
Result: 500500 (expected: 500500)
```

16.5.2 KERNELS CONSTRUCT

The compiler encountering the `kernels` directive performs the analysis of marked sections of the code and converts these into a sequence of parallel kernels that will be executed in order on the accelerator device. The number of gangs and workers and vector size may be different for each such kernel. The workload subdivision is typically performed in a way that creates one kernel for each loop nest present in the code. The primary difference between the `kernels` construct and the `parallel` directive is that the latter relies on the programmer to configure various parameters that divide the workload across accelerated execution resources. Thus the use of the `kernels` directive is recommended for beginners to OpenACC programming, but it may not always yield the best-performing code. Its syntax is shown below:

`#pragma acc kernels` *[clause-list]*

structured-block

The `kernels` construct accepts `async` and `wait` clauses that behave as described for the `parallel` clause, as well as data management clauses (discussed further in Section 16.5.3). Similar restrictions to those of the **parallel** directive apply: the code may not branch out or into the accelerated region.

Example:

```
1  #include <stdio.h>
2
3  const int N = 500;
4
5  int main() {
6    //initialize triangular matrix
7    double m[N][N];
8    for (int i = 0; i < N; i++)
9      for (int j = 0; j < N; j++)
10       m[i][j] = (i > j)? 0: 1.0;
11
12   // initialize input vector to all ones
13   double v[N];
14   for (int i = 0; i < N; i++) v[i] = 1.0;
15
16   // initialize result vector
17   double b[N];
18   for (int i = 0; i < N; i++) b[i] = 0;
19
20   // multiply in parallel
21   #pragma acc kernels
22   for (int i = 0; i < N; i++)
23     for (int j = 0; j < N; j++)
24       b[i] += m[i][j]*v[j];
25
26   // verify result
27   double r = 0;
28   for (int i = 0; i < N; i++) r += b[i];
29   printf("Result: %f (expected %f)\n", r, (N+1)*N/2.0);
30 }
```

Code 16.3. Accelerated matrix–vector multiply using the `kernels` directive.

The program listed in Code 16.3 performs multiplication of a matrix and a vector, the dimensions of which are known at compile time and fixed. The accelerated region of code follows the `kernels` directive in line 22 and contains a loop nest: the outer loop iterates over matrix rows (index i) and the inner loop over the columns (index j). Unlike Code 16.2, the execution of the parallel region is synchronous (there is no `async` clause), meaning that the program will not proceed to result verification until the accelerated kernel computation is finished. The result of program execution is shown below:

```
Result: 125250.000000 (expected 125250.000000)
```

16.5.3 DATA MANAGEMENT

The resultant speed-up of an accelerated program strongly depends on the efficiency of data transfers between host and accelerator memories. In some cases, such as for AMD accelerated processing units, the accelerator shares the address space with the host processor. The overheads of communicating the data structures between the two components are minimal, as they are simply accomplished through pointer passing without any explicit data copies. If an accelerator needs to perform computation on certain elements of the data array, it only has to compute the resulting address of the data element based on the supplied pointer value, element index, and data type, and dereference it (fetch the desired element from memory), just as the host processor would. Unfortunately, many accelerator devices utilized in current supercomputing installations feature separate memory modules that necessitate explicit data transfers. Ideally, such transfers would be orchestrated without involving any unnecessary data or even entirely avoiding communication when not required. The first case is apparent when performing computation only on a subset of array or vector elements; copying the entire structure would only increase the latency data offload. The second scenario may arise when a dataset produced as a result of GPU computation would overwrite the contents of an array originally created on the host. Copying the initial state of such an array to the GPU before performing the accelerated computation is obviously unnecessary.

Unfortunately, due to the complexity of C and C++ code, static analysis of data access patterns by the compiler cannot always determine with certainty which portions of the affected data structures should be offloaded to the accelerator. OpenACC by default chooses correctness over efficiency and performs full bidirectional copies, i.e., transfer of the initial state of all involved data structures to the device before initiating accelerated computations and copying back the possibly updated state of involved datasets after the accelerated region's execution completes. Note that this is supported implicitly only when the dimensions of the involved arrays are known at compile time; for dynamically allocated arrays or arrays that are passed by pointer, it is a good idea to specify explicitly the ranges of data that should be offloaded to avoid potential out-of-bounds access errors during runtime. OpenACC implementations may further optimize (or even avoid) the data transfers if the accelerator is capable of accessing the host memory directly.

OpenACC provides the following clauses to control data copying between the host and accelerator memories.

- `copy(`*variable-list*`)`
  This makes data copies upon entry to and exit from the parallel region. First, for each variable specified in the variable list, the runtime system checks if the required data exists in the accelerator memory. If so, its reference count is incremented; otherwise a sufficient accelerator memory is allocated and a data copy from host memory to the allocated memory is arranged. The corresponding reference count for the data structure is set to one. On exit from the parallel region, the reference count is decremented. If it reaches zero, the corresponding data is copied back to the host memory and the allocated memory segment on the accelerator is deallocated.

- `copyin(`*variable-list*`)`
  This makes data copies upon entry to the parallel region. It behaves as a one-directional version of the `copy` clause. All operations specified for region entry in the `copy` clause are executed without modification. However, on exit from the parallel region the reference counts for all data structures specified in the variable list are decremented. If the count for a specific variable reaches zero, the corresponding device memory is deallocated, but no data transfer to host memory takes place.
- `copyout(`*variable-list*`)`
  This makes data copies upon exit from a parallel region. The `copyout` clause may be viewed as a complement to the `copyin` clause. Upon entry to the parallel region, if the data are already present in the accelerator memory, their reference counter is incremented. If not, the sufficient memory segment is allocated in the device memory and the reference count for it is set to one. The allocated memory is not initialized (and no data transfer takes place).
  Upon exit, the reference count for the involved data structures is decremented. If it reaches zero, the data are copied back to the host memory and the corresponding memory segment on the device is deallocated.
- `create(`*variable-list*`)`
  This creates a data structure on the accelerator to be used by local computation. The `create` clause never transfers any data between the host and accelerator memories. When the affected parallel region is entered and the data structure already exists in the device memory, the runtime increments the reference counter; otherwise a suitable amount of device memory will be allocated, with the reference count set to one. On exit the reference count is decremented, and if it reaches zero the corresponding memory is deallocated.

The *variable-list* specifier accompanying the clauses listed above contains identifiers of program variables that are subjected to data copy operations. The identifiers are separated by a comma (","). They may be optionally followed by a range specification consisting of a pair of square brackets per dimension, each enclosing the index range specification. The index range consists of two integer expressions separated by a colon (":"), with the first integer value denoting the starting index and the second value indicating the length (number of contiguous elements per dimension). If the first number is omitted, zero is assumed. The second number may be omitted if the size of the array is known at compile time, and implies that the full dimension is used. Thus `a[5:t]` describes the range of elements of vector `a` starting at index 5 and containing `t` elements, i.e., the sequence `a[5]`, `a[6]`, ..., `a[5+t-1]`. Analogously, `mat[:N][16:32]` refers to a rectangular segment of array `mat` that comprises 32-element-long fragments of its first N rows. Each such fragment starts at index 16. The entire dataset thus includes N × 32 array elements.

Thanks to compiler support, OpenACC supports several different ways in which arrays may be defined in C and C++ programs.

1. Statically allocated arrays with fixed bounds, such as:

```
int cnt[4][500];
```

   One important restriction related to specifying the data transfer range for statically allocated arrays is that it must identify a contiguous chunk of memory. Only the range specifier for the first dimension may describe a subset of elements, while the specifiers for the remaining dimensions must identify full bounds. Thus for the declaration above `cnt[2:2][:500]` (last two rows of matrix `cnt`) is legal, whereas `cnt[:4][0:100]` (first 100 columns of matrix `cnt`) is not.

2. Pointers to fixed-bound arrays:

```
typedef double vec[1000];
vec *v1;
```

3. Statically allocated array of pointers:

```
float *farray[500];
```

4. Pointer to array of pointers:

```
double **dmat;
```

Multidimensional array definitions may include mixed declarations involving static bounds and pointers. To follow the range specification constraints correctly in a general case, it may be helpful to realize that the runtime system will mirror the organization of the source data structures from the host on the accelerator, allocating pointers where necessary and filling in their values. Once the data structures are defined, modification of the embedded pointers on the host or device is discouraged. To demonstrate the application of improved data management techniques to Code 16.3, it is rewritten to support dynamically allocated arrays storing the main matrix data and input and output vectors. The result is listed in Code 16.4.

Example:

```
#include <stdio.h>
#include <stdlib.h>

int main(int argc, char **argv) {
  unsigned N = 1024;
  if (argc > 1) N = strtoul(argv[1], 0, 10);

  // create triangular matrix
  double **restrict m = malloc(N*sizeof(double *));
  for (int i = 0; i < N; i++)
  {
    m[i] = malloc(N*sizeof(double));
    for (int j = 0; j < N; j++)
      m[i][j] = (i > j)? 0: 1.0;
  }

  // create vector filled with ones
  double *restrict v = malloc(N*sizeof(double));
  for (int i = 0; i < N; i++) v[i] = 1.0;

  // create result vector
  double *restrict b = malloc(N*sizeof(double));

  // multiply in parallel
  #pragma acc kernels copyin(m[:N][:N], v[:N]) copyout(b[:N])
  for (int i = 0; i < N; i++)
  {
    b[i] = 0;
    for (int j = 0; j < N; j++)
      b[i] += m[i][j]*v[j];
  }

  // verify result
  double r = 0;
  for (int i = 0; i < N; i++) r += b[i];
  printf("Result: %f (expected %f)\n", r, (N+1)*N/2.0);

  return 0;
}
```

Code 16.4. Example OpenACC matrix−vector multiply with improved data transfers.

The size of the involved arrays may be defined (within reason) on the command line. To preserve the double-index notation when accessing the elements of matrix `m` rather than flattening it to a vector, it has been declared as a pointer to a vector of pointers to dynamically allocated rows (this corresponds to scenario 4 described above). The pointers are declared with the `restrict` attribute telling the compiler that it should not expect pointer aliasing and potentially leading to a better optimized code. Since both the input matrix `m` and vector `v` are not modified by the computation, they are declared in the `copyin` clause. Vector `b` does not need to be initialized from the host memory, since its entire content is overwritten by computation. It is therefore declared as a `copyout` variable. Since the accelerator can easily zero out individual elements of `b` before accumulating partial dot product values into it, this part of the computation has been explicitly moved to the accelerated region. Running the program with argument 2000 yields:

```
Result: 2001000.000000 (expected 2001000.000000)
```

16.5.4 LOOP SCHEDULING

The `loop` directive is one of the fundamental OpenACC constructs responsible for identifying and fine-tuning the parallelization of accelerated workloads. It may be specified either as a separate directive:

```
#pragma acc loop [clause-list]
for (...)
```

Or as a clause combined with a parent `parallel` or `kernels` directive. In any case, it applies to the for-loop immediately following the clause or directive. The available loop control clauses include the following:

- `collapse(`*integer-expr*`)`
  This specifies how many nested loop levels indicated by the argument value are affected by the scheduling clauses present in the directive. Normally only the nearest loop following the directive is considered. The argument must evaluate to a positive integer.
- `gang`
- `gang(`*[*`num:`*] integer-expr [, integer-expr...]*`)`
- `gang(static:`*integer-expr*`)`
- `gang(static:*)`

  This distributes iterations of the affected loop(s) across gangs created by the parent `parallel` or `kernels` directive.

When used with the `parallel` construct, the number of gangs is determined by the parent directive, hence only the static argument is permitted in one of the two forms listed above. It indicates the *chunk* size: a count of loop iterations that is used as a unit of workload assignment. Chunks are assigned to gangs in a round-robin fashion. If the last form of gang specification is used, chunk size is determined by implementation. It should be stressed that for correct results loop iterations must be data independent (except for the reduction clause described below), since the compiler is not going to perform the full code analysis, as when using the `kernels` directive.

If the `loop` clause is associated with the `kernels` construct, all forms are permitted with some restrictions. The first two variants may be specified only if `num_gangs` does not appear in the parent `kernels` construct. If used with a numeric argument, it specifies the number of gangs to be used for parallel execution of the loop. The meaning of the static argument is as described above for the `parallel` construct.

- `worker`
- `worker(`*[*`num:`*]integer-expr*`)`
  This causes the loop iterations to be distributed across the workers in a gang. When used with the `parallel` construct, only the first form is allowed. It causes the gang to switch to WP execution. The loop iterations must be data independent. When the parent directive is `kernels`, the form with an argument may be used only if `num_workers` was not specified in the parent construct. The expression must evaluate to a positive integer that indicates the number of workers per gang to be used.
- `vector`
- `vector(`*[*`length:`*]integer-expr*`)`
  This enables execution of loop iterations in vector or SIMD mode. The conditions of use are analogous to those of the `worker` clause, except that they apply to vector-level parallelism.
- `auto`
  This forces analysis of data dependencies in the loop to determine if it can be parallelized. It is implied in every `kernel` directive that does not contain the `independent` clause.
- `independent`
  This instructs the compiler to treat the loop iterations as data independent, thus enabling more possibilities for parallelization. It is implied for all `parallel` directives that do not specify `auto` clauses.
- `reduction(`*operator*`:`*variable*`[,`*variable...*`])`
  The reduction clause marks one or more of the specified variables as a participant in the reduction operation performed at the end of the loop. The variable may not be an array element or a structure member. The supported operators include `+`, `*`, `max`, `min`, `&`, `|`, `&&`, and `||` for sum, product, maximum, minimum, bitwise-and, bitwise-or, logical-and, and logical-or, respectively.

Example:

```
#include <stdio.h>

const int N = 10000;

int main() {
  double x[N], y[N];
  double a = 2.0, r = 0.0;

  #pragma acc kernels
  {
    // initialize the vectors
    #pragma acc loop gang worker
    for (int i = 0; i < N; i++) {
      x[i] = 1.0;
      y[i] = -1.0;
    }

    // perform computation
    #pragma acc loop independent reduction(+:r)
    for (int i = 0; i < N; i++) {
      y[i] = a*x[i]+y[i];
      r += y[i];
    }
  }

  // print result
  printf("Result: %f (expected %f)\n", r, (float)N);

  return 0;
}
```

Code 16.5. Example program using the `loop` directive with parallelism and reduction clauses.

The program listed in Code 16.5 showcases the use of the `loop` directive to perform accelerated vector scaling and accumulation reminiscent of the *daxpy* routine from the linear algebra package. For demonstration purposes, the initialization code has also been moved to the accelerator. It requests parallelization in WP mode with the default number of gangs and workers. The parallelization parameters of the computational loop are left to the discretion of the implementation. The loop is explicitly marked as data independent to promote this and avoid the compiler analysis which would be performed by default for the `kernels` construct (less sophisticated compilers may interpret the update of `y[i]` as data dependence). To verify the correctness of the result, a reduction clause is used that sums all elements of the result vector `y` into variable `r`. The generated output is given below:

```
Result: 10000.000000 (expected 10000.000000)
```

16.5.5 VARIABLE SCOPE

It should be apparent at this point that the OpenACC treatment of variables participating in the computation varies depending if they are loop indices or data structures and where they are declared in the code. Loop variables are considered private to each thread that executes loop iterations. Variables declared in a block of code that is marked for execution in VP mode are private to the thread that is associated with each vector lane. For code executed in WP vector-single mode the variables are private to each worker, but shared across vector lanes associated with that worker. Similarly, variables declared in a block marked for worker-single mode are private to the containing gang, but shared across the threads operating at worker and vector levels in that gang.

OpenACC defines a `private` clause that may be used to restrict the sharing of variables further. It may be declared alongside the `parallel` or `loop` directive, and accepts a list of variable names as argument. In the first case, a copy of each variable in the list is generated for each parallel gang. In the loop context, a copy of each variable is created for each thread associated with each vector lane (VP mode). In vector-single WP mode, a copy of every item in the list will be created and shared for each set of threads associated with vector lanes in each worker. Otherwise, a variable copy is created and shared across all vector lanes of every worker in each gang. A `firstprivate` variant of the `private` clause is also available for the `parallel` directive with the same access semantics, except the variable copies are additionally initialized to the value of the variables inherent to the first thread encountering the `parallel` construct during the code execution.

16.5.6 ATOMICS

Parallelization of code across multiple execution resources on occasion calls for synchronization of access to some data structures that should be carried out in predefined order. This is enforced by the `atomic` construct with the syntax described below:

`#pragma acc atomic` *[atomic-clause]*
    statement;

Supported atomic clauses include `read`, `write`, `update`, and `capture`, depending on the type of access synchronization. If a clause is absent, an `update` clause is assumed. The `read` clause is used to force atomic access to variables on the right-hand side of the equal sign in an assignment statement. Analogously, the `write` clause protects writes to variables on the left-hand side of the equal sign in assignments. The `update` clause enforces correct updates of values of variables that have to be performed using read–modify–write sequence of operations. Examples include prefix and postfix increment and decrement operators as well as updates in the form of *op*=, where *op* is a binary operator such as +, -, *, etc. The `capture` clause refers to assignment statements in which the right-hand side is an atomic update expression such as described for the `update` clause, while the left-hand side is a variable supposed to capture the original or final value of the atomically modified variable (depending on the operation type).

Example:

```
1  #include <stdio.h>
2
3  int main(int argc, char **argv) {
4    if (argc == 1) {
5      fprintf(stderr, “Error: file argument neede!\n”);
6      exit(1);
7    }
8    FILE *f = fopen(argv[1], “r”);
9    if (!f) {
10     fprintf(stderr, “Error: could not open file \”%s\“\n”, argv[1]);
11     exit(1);
12   }
13
14   const int BUFSIZE = 65536;
15   char buf[BUFSIZE], ch;
16   // initialize histogram array
17   int hist[256], most = -1;
18   for (int i = 0; i < 256; i++) hist[i] = 0;
19
20   // compute histogram
21   while (1) {
22     size_t size = fread(buf, 1, BUFSIZE, f);
23     if (size <= 0) break;
24     #pragma acc parallel loop copyin(buf[:size])
25       for (int i = 0; i < size; i++) {
26         int v = buf[i];
27         #pragma acc atomic
28         hist[v]++;
29     }
30   }
31   // print the first highest peak
32   for (int i = 0; i < 256; i++)
33     if (hist[i] > most) {
34       most = hist[i]; ch = i;
35   }
36   printf(“Highest count of %d for character code %d\n”, most, ch);
37
38   return 0;
39 }
```

Code 16.6. Example program showing the application of the `atomic` clause.

The program presented in Code 16.6 calculates a histogram of ASCII character occurrences in a file given as the command-line argument. The `atomic` directive in line 27 (implied `update` clause) ensures the correct increment of the histogram bin for a specific character. Running the code for file containing the first paragraph of the “*lorem ipsum*” text [10] produces:

```
Highest count of 68 for character code 32
```

16.6 SUMMARY AND OUTCOMES OF CHAPTER 16

- There are several programming environments for accelerators; they differ in approach, scope, supported features, and availability. The most commonly used include CUDA, OpenCL, OpenACC, and C++ AMP.
- OpenACC is a GPU and accelerator programming framework that attempts to simplify parallel programming and achieve better programmability by using a directive-based approach similar to OpenMP. It requires a specialized compiler capable of generating executable accelerator code following the static analysis of appropriately marked source code. Compilers with OpenACC support are available from PGI, Cray, and several open-source communities (OpenUH, OpenARC, and GCC).
- The main method of identifying potential parallel execution regions is through the addition of suitable "`#pragma acc`" directives in the relevant places in source code. In addition to directives, the execution of programs is affected by predefined library calls and environment variables.
- OpenACC programs rely on the host machine to initiate the program computations and offload the data and executable code to the accelerator at appropriate times. Accelerated code execution is by default synchronized with the execution of the nonaccelerated sections of the program on the host machine. Additional speed-up may be obtained by asynchronously coscheduling computations on the GPU with computations on the host processor.
- Performance gains in regions executed on the accelerator are realized through parallelization at three levels: gang, worker, and vector (from the coarsest to the finest grain). The programmer retains control of parameters influencing each level, although he/she may also select implementation defaults.
- There are two main compute directives: "`parallel`" and "`kernels`." The first forgoes much of the correctness analysis of the source code, relying on the programmer to verify data independence between concurrently executing accelerator threads. The second performs a thorough static analysis of the code, and allows vectorization and parallel execution only if it is safe to do so.
- Distribution of regular and nested loop iterations across the accelerated execution resources is one of the primary methods of increasing application performance gains. It is controlled by the `loop` clause, which also supports an accelerated set of reduction operations.
- Overall application performance depends on the efficiency of data transfers between accelerator and host memories. OpenACC supports additional control clauses to optimize this aspect of execution (`copy`, `copyin`, `copyout`, `create`).
- OpenACC provides simple mechanisms for synchronization of access to critical variables from multiple accelerator threads to ensure the correctness of program execution. Four modes of atomic access are supported: `read`, `write`, `update`, and `capture`.

16.7 QUESTIONS AND PROBLEMS

1. Characterize directive-based programming. How does it differ from using functionality provided by software libraries?

2. Write an OpenACC program to compute the approximation of the natural logarithm of 2 using the first 10,000,000 terms of Maclaurin expansion:

$$\ln(1+x) = x - \frac{1}{2}x^2 + \frac{1}{3}x^3 - \frac{1}{4}x^4 + \ldots$$

Make sure the generated accelerator code is parallelized.
3. Modify Code 16.6 to compute the frequency of alphabetic digraph (two-letter sequence) occurrence in a block of text. Ignore case sensitivity.
4. Write a simple OpenACC program that computes the average value of elements occupying the lower triangular part (i.e., all elements on and below the main diagonal) of a large square matrix. Is it possible to optimize the program so that:
   a. efficiency of data transfers is improved (by avoiding copying data not used by computation)?
   b. the work performed in each iteration is balanced across GPU threads?
   Implement optimizations that are possible. How do they affect performance? Test several different matrix sizes.
5. To debug an OpenACC program, the irrelevant portions of the code were removed, yielding the following:

```
#include <stdio.h>

const int N = 100, M = 200;

int main() {
  int m[N][M];
  for (int i = 0; i < N; i++)
    for (int j = 0; j < M; j++)
      m[i][j] = 1;

  #pragma acc kernels
  for (int i = 0; i < N; i++)
    for (int j = M-i; j < M; j++)
      m[i][j] = i+j+1;

  // verify result
  int errcnt = 0;
  for (int i = 0; i < N; i++)
    for (int j = 0; j < M; j++) {
      int expect = (j >= M-i)? i+j+1: 1;
      if (m[i][j] != expect) errcnt++;
    }
  printf("Encountered %d errors\n", errcnt);
  return errcnt != 0;
}
```

The code fails (produces a nonzero error count) when compiled with certain OpenACC compilers. What may be the reason for that? How may the errors be prevented?

REFERENCES

[1] Khronos Group, OpenGL: The Industry's Foundation for High Performance Graphics; Version 4.5 Specifications, Khronos Group, 2016 [Online]. Available: https://www.opengl.org/documentation/current_version/.

[2] Microsoft Corporation, Getting Started with DirectX Graphics, 2016 [Online]. Available: https://msdn.microsoft.com/en-us/library/windows/desktop/hh309467.

[3] E.S. Larsen, D. McAlister, Fast matrix multiplies using graphics hardware, in: Proceedings of Supercomputing 2001, 2001.

[4] Nvidia Corporation, CUDA Toolkit Documentation v8.0, September 27, 2016 [Online]. Available: http://docs.nvidia.com/cuda/.

[5] Khronos Group, The OpenCL Specification (provisional), Version 2.2, March 11, 2016 [Online]. Available: https://www.khronos.org/registry/cl/specs/opencl-2.2.pdf.

[6] Microsoft Corporation, C++ AMP: Language and Programming Model, v1.2, December, 2013 [Online]. Available: http://download.microsoft.com/download/2/2/9/22972859-15C2-4D96-97AE-93344241D56C/CppAMPOpenSpecificationV12.pdf.

[7] The OpenACC Application Programming Interface, Version 2.5, OpenACC-Standard.org, October, 2015 [Online]. Available: http://www.openacc.org/sites/default/files/OpenACC_2pt5.pdf.

[8] OpenUH – Open Source UH Compiler (Source Repository), 2015 [Online]. Available: https://github.com/uhhpctools/openuh.

[9] S. Lee, J. Vetter, OpenARC: extensible OpenACC compiler framework for directive-based accelerator programming study, in: WACCPD: Workshop on Accelerator Programming Using Directives in Conjunction with SC'14, 2014.

[10] Lorem Ipsum Generator, [Online]. Available: http://www.lipsum.com.

CHAPTER

MASS STORAGE

17

CHAPTER OUTLINE

17.1 INTRODUCTION

The storage subsystem is one of the key components of every computing platform. Although the organization, speed, capacity, and supported functions of storage vary depending on platform class, its presence is always required for computations to be carried out. In high performance computing (HPC) one can observe quite possibly the broadest variety of storage options and involved storage technologies as well as range of implementation scales. This chapter discusses the segment of storage

High Performance Computing. https://doi.org/10.1016/B978-0-12-420158-3.00017-4

technology and low-level techniques utilized to support the requirements of HPC systems reliably to preserve the high volume of computational state in the form of both scientific data and elements of the operating environment. The state retention must be persistent between the power cycles of the machine for it to be able to execute bootstrap procedures on restart, attain the correct operational status, and resume interrupted computational tasks. This part of the storage hierarchy is referred to as "mass storage" to reflect its capability to absorb large amounts of data. Mass storage is not concerned with volatile devices, such as main memory or processor registers. Besides input and output (I/O) datasets used by and produced as a result of computation, mass storage preserves the code (executables and libraries) necessary to run the operating system and its associated background management processes, configuration, and update scripts, as well as the user's and system administrator's tools and utilities. Finally, mass storage plays an integral role in checkpoint and restart of compute applications, alleviating the impact of temporal and system resource limits imposed on application execution.

Traditionally, the storage hierarchy is subdivided into four levels that differ in access latency and supported data bandwidth, with latencies increasing and effective transfer bandwidth dropping when moving away from the top level of the hierarchy. At the same time, storage capacity rapidly grows. The commonly recognized hierarchy levels are as follows.

- *Primary storage*, which comprises system memories, caches, and CPU register sets. This type of storage is predominantly volatile (loses data contents when powered off), with the exception of read-only memories (ROMs) that store firmware or CPU boot code. While there have been some efforts to utilize various types of nonvolatile random access memories (NVRAMs) as a part of the overall memory pool accessible to processors, their access latencies typically prohibit achieving good integration, requiring dedicated and nontransparent support from the operating system (OS) and applications. The data access latencies range from a single CPU clock cycle (a fraction of a nanosecond) for registers to several hundred cycles for dynamic memories in remote non-uniform memory access domains; the respective bandwidths span from over 100 GB/s (SIMD registers in a single core) down to a few GB/s per bank of double data rate memory (such as DDR3, still in use in many installations). Aggregate memory size in HPC ranges from a few tens of gigabytes for small nodes to hundreds of gigabytes for nodes dedicated to memory-intensive tasks.
- *Secondary storage* is the first level of storage that leverages mass-storage devices. Normally CPUs cannot directly access the secondary (or higher-level) storage and therefore transfers of data between primary and secondary storage have to be mediated by the OS and computer chipset. The granularity of data access is typically limited to fixed-size blocks, while most primary storage devices operate at byte resolution. The most commonly used technology in this tier are hard disk drives (HDDs), which offer the industry's best cost per unit of storage coupled with satisfactory reliability. Over the last decade, however, their dominance in the market has been slowly eroding due to the introduction of high-capacity solid-state storage. The random access latency of secondary storage media may be less than 100 μs for the fastest solid-state devices to as much as tens of milliseconds for HDDs. The bandwidths may range from just below 100 MB/s for slower HDDs to a single GB per second for solid-state devices. HDDs still maintain the lead in total capacity, with up to 10 TB per single device.
- *Tertiary storage* is distinguished from secondary storage in that it usually involves large collections of storage media or storage devices which are nominally in an inaccessible or powered-off state, but may be reasonably quickly enabled for online use. Activation is typically

accomplished by automated mechanisms such as robots that physically move the requested mass-storage medium from its assigned long-term retention slot to the specified online access device (drive). To lower contention between multiple users, tertiary storage equipment typically hosts several independent media drives that may be accessed concurrently. Examples of tertiary storage equipment include tape libraries and optical jukeboxes. Since the bandwidth of a single drive is often insufficient to sustain many concurrent I/O requests, the content of the selected medium is copied to secondary storage first (e.g., disk cache). The access latency to tertiary storage may be substantially greater than that of secondary storage, especially when multiple competing requests must be serviced. In a contention-free state it typically takes single tens of seconds for the robot to grab and mount the medium, and the achieved single-device bandwidths are comparable to those of secondary storage. The storage capacity of robotic jukeboxes may reach as much as multiple hundreds of petabytes.

- *Offline storage* requires human intervention to enable access to the storage medium. It is primarily employed to archive, frequently in a secure location off site, precious information. Since the storage unit is not under the direct control of any computer, this provides a much-needed "air gap" to protect the security, confidentiality, and integrity of the archives. Offline storage is in principle similar to tertiary storage, although lack of predictability related to medium load requests results in highly random latency figures and it may not be considered a practical high performance solution other than for some niche applications.

The design and deployment of supercomputing storage subsystems comes with their own set of challenges. The prevailing trends of the past few decades have shown steady increases not only in memory capacity due to Moore's law, but also in supercomputing platform scale expressed as number of nodes per machine. As the aggregate size of computed datasets is roughly proportional to the total system memory size, this has resulted in a superlinear increase in demand for mass-storage capacity. Moreover, each successive generation of dynamic random access memory (DRAM) improved data transfer bandwidth, thus enabling faster data creation rates. At the same time, I/O device bandwidth exhibited comparatively modest growth and over the last decade effectively leveled out. Storage capacity per device originally loosely followed Moore's curve, but suffered from highly limited growth rates throughout most of the 2010s. This resulted in a continuously increasing storage performance gap, and the time required to save or retrieve the data occupying a significant fraction of a machine's memory is rising as well. In extreme cases checkpoint or restart of large applications may take several hours.

The addition of global high-bandwidth networks, such as Internet2 [1], has enabled access to collections of data at remote sites as well as input data streaming. In many cases the expansion of the input dataset is reflected by the volume of generated output and/or intermediate data, additionally stressing the local storage subsystem. This is particularly relevant to a relatively new class of data-intensive applications collectively known as "Big Data" which, in addition to operating on large data volumes and requiring substantial processing speeds, are frequently hampered by intrinsic variety and irregularities of the processed data structures. As the storage capacity scales linearly with the number of I/O devices, support of large volumes of data results in I/O subsystems occupying a significant amount of floor space at data centers and drawing substantial amounts of electric power. Since the bulk of secondary storage capacity is provided by electromechanical devices such as disk drives, the data centers must install measures to deal with common device failures. Even though devoid of moving parts, solid-state storage devices are not immune to failures either, and these are exacerbated by dissipated heat and the number of data rewrites per device. To maintain the operation the centers must therefore provide redundant storage, further expanding the system's volume and energy requirements.

Efficient data transfer between the primary and other storage levels requires significant dedicated interconnect bandwidth. Unfortunately, large machine procurement practices at many institutions frequently focus on components directly related to computations, such as processors, memory, and network. Storage considerations are often secondary and based on poor analysis of requirements. This produces bandwidth-starved implementations with insufficient reliability and performance that, in some cases, share the I/O load with other components of the system (such as login nodes). While an increase in network switch capacity to provide the required bandwidth from compute nodes to mass storage may visibly impact the final system's cost, it will yield a better-balanced computing platform.

The challenges outlined above apply to many systems currently in service. While there is no single universal solution to address them, their impact may be alleviated through exploration of better I/O architectures, hardware-level solutions, and advances in the software stack. Architectural solutions may introduce additional intermediate hierarchy levels that provide high performance data sinks and sources in close vicinity to compute nodes. Such storage devices are capable of high-bandwidth communication with the nodes to satisfy the most urgent I/O requests with low latency, while constantly performing in the background slower data exchanges with larger storage devices located lower in the hierarchy. An example of this is the Cray burst buffer technology [2], which provides a number of nodes equipped with fast solid-state storage and regularly interspersed with other compute nodes. The burst buffer nodes have the benefit of the full Aries interconnect [3] bandwidth, but can also use a fraction of switch performance to interact with the storage servers. Hardware improvements are primarily focused on building more reliable, faster, and higher-capacity mass-storage devices. This is expected to lower power consumption, reduce the volume occupied by the secondary storage subsystem, and decrease the costs of ownership by requiring fewer spare storage devices to replace those that fail. An overview of these advances is discussed in the remainder of this chapter. Finally, software solutions arising from the design of better storage abstractions that embrace parallelism and asynchrony of access (such as the parallel file systems described in Chapter 18) can anticipate the I/O access patterns utilized by applications, fetch the required data ahead of time, and forward it to the memory of the prospective client, or provide smart checkpoint and restart that can gracefully overlap compute state management (saving, retrieval, transformation, compression) with ongoing computations. Software improvements may also directly address deficiencies or extend functionality of specific components in the system. For example, locating the data preprocessing and postprocessing engine on a storage node may conserve the network bandwidth required to ship the data between storage devices and compute nodes.

17.2 BRIEF HISTORY OF STORAGE

Technological progress brought dramatic improvements in both capacity and performance of mass-storage devices over the course of several decades. As illustrated in Fig. 17.1, starting with punched cards as the first external information store in the mid-1940s, through tape drives in the early 1950s, and continuing with HDDs from the mid-1950s to the present day, storage capacity grew an amazing 11 orders of magnitude. The increases in device storage capacity were reflected by the corresponding improvements in device I/O bandwidth (Fig. 17.2), which advanced six orders of magnitude over the same period. However, access latency improvements were far more modest, decreasing from single and tens of seconds for punched cards and tape to a few milliseconds in modern HDDs. Latency still remains one of the biggest performance bottlenecks plaguing most of the I/O devices in use today.

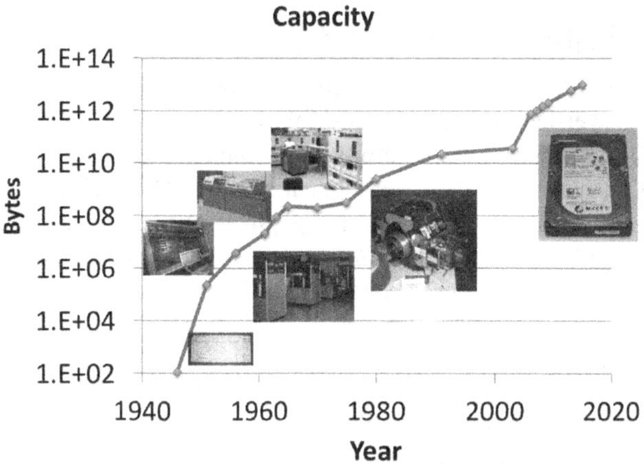

FIGURE 17.1

Increases in mass-storage capacity. Represented systems are a punch card on the ENIAC (1946), a Uniservo tape drive (1951), IBM 350 (1956), IBM 1301 (1961), IBM 1302 (1963), IBM 2314 (1965), IBM 3330 (1970), IBM 3350 (1975), IBM 3380 (1980), IBM 3390 (1991), Western Digital Raptor (2003), Seagate Barracuda 7200.10 (2006), HGST Deskstar 7K1000 (2007), Seagate Barracuda 7200.11 (2008), Western Digital WD20EADS (2009), HGST Ultrastar He6 (2013), and HGST Ultrastar He10 (2015).

Punchcard, UNIVAC I, and IBM 3380 photos by Arnold Reinhold via Wikimedia Commons. IBM 305 photo by US Army Red River Arsenal via Wikimedia Commons. IBM 2314 photo by Scott Gerstenberger via Wikimedia Commons

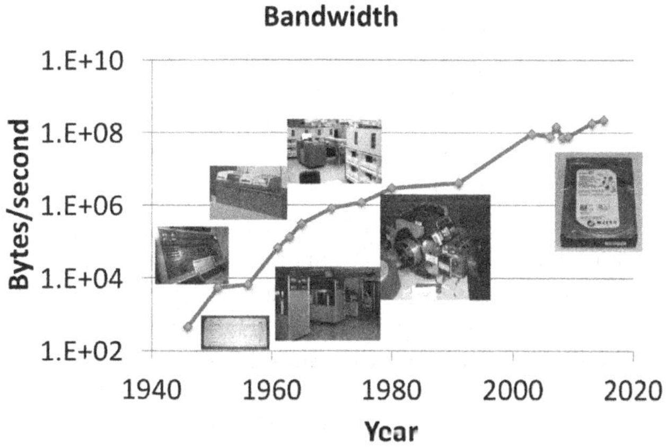

FIGURE 17.2

Improvements in I/O data access bandwidth. Represented systems include a punch card on the ENIAC (1946), a UNISERVO tape drive (1951), IBM 350 (1956), IBM 1301 (1961), IBM 1302 (1963), IBM 2314 (1965), IBM 3330 (1970), IBM 3350 (1975), IBM 3380 (1980), IBM 3390 (1991), Western Digital Raptor (2003), Seagate Barracuda 7200.10 (2006), HGST Deskstar 7K1000 (2007), Seagate Barracuda 7200.11 (2008), Western Digital WD20EADS (2009), HGST Ultrastar He6 (2013), HGSTUltrastar He10 (2015).

Punchcard, UNIVAC I, and IBM 3380 photos by Arnold Reinhold via Wikimedia Commons. IBM 305 photo by US Army Red River Arsenal via Wikimedia Commons. IBM 2314 photo by Scott Gerstenberger via Wikimedia Commons

17.3 STORAGE DEVICE TECHNOLOGY

As illustrated by the preceding section, the technology of hardware storage devices continuously evolved to support the ever-increasing demands for storage capacity and data access bandwidth. Currently the majority of storage systems utilize four main types of mass storage devices: HDDs, solid-state drives (SSDs), magnetic tapes, and optical storage. Although they serve largely the same purpose, they substantially differ in the underlying physical phenomena used to implement data retention as well their operational characteristics and cost. The fundamental properties and working principles of modern storage devices are discussed below.

17.3.1 HARD DISK DRIVES

HDDs have a long history as a data storage device in computing. Introduced in 1956, the first hard drive used in the IBM 350 RAMAC system [4] was approximately 68″ high, 60″ deep, and 29″ wide, and weighed approximately one ton. It contained 50 platters (disks serving as the recording medium for data) with a diameter of 24 in rotating at 1200 revolutions per minute (RPM). It stored 5 million six-bit characters that were transferred at a rate of 8800 per second. The successor drives appearing in the 1960s featured removable platter packs that could be moved between the different drive enclosures. Many improvements utilized by modern HDDs were developed in that decade, such as a multiple read–write head assembly that avoided the delay of head movement from one data platter to another, aerodynamic head design that permitted stable head operation in very close proximity to the recording medium, and the first voice–coil actuator. The introduction of the "Winchester" design in the early 1970s, using a dedicated portion of the media as a landing zone for read–write heads, marked the return to nonswappable platters (hence the occasionally used alternative name "fixed-disk drive"). The rotary actuator, a common component of modern HDDs, was developed by IBM in 1974 and used in its Gulliver [5] line of drives. The first disk drive approximating form factors broadly used today was released by Shugart Technology (now Seagate) in 1980; it featured 5.25″ housing, stored 5 MB of data, required an external controller board, and could be mounted inside larger personal computers such as the IBM PC [6]. Ongoing developments in this decade brought the familiar 1″ high 3.5″ (Conner Peripherals CP3022 storing 21 MB) and 2.5″ (PrairieTek 220 with a capacity of 20 MB) form factors. The 1990s brought many improvements in drive speed and capacity prompted by the development of partial response maximum likelihood (PRML) technology [7] (see below) for reliable decoding of weak signals retrieved from media and successive application of the giant magnetoresistive (GMR) [8] phenomenon to disk head design. Progress in storage areal density increase enabled a 1.8″ drive to be created in 1991 (Integral Peripherals 1820 with over 20 MB per disk), followed by IBM's 1″ Microdrive in 1999 that stored 340 MB of data. As the flash memory technology could not support competitive bit densities in that period, such miniature HDDs from multiple manufacturers were used as content storage for portable media players, among others the Apple iPod. At the same time, Seagate's Cheetah drives became one of the first to feature the record-breaking 10,000 RPM and later 15,000 RPM spindle speeds. Advances that followed after the year 2000 leveraged perpendicular magnetic recording to increase information density further on storage media, continuously increased embedded buffer memory size to permit better latency management, shifted to glass-based platter substrates, introduced helium as a cavity-filling gas to minimize energy loses due to rotating platter drag and turbulence, and used shingled magnetic recording. This continued technological progress has

FIGURE 17.3

Internal components of a hard disk drive (2 TB Seagate HDD).

resulted in hard drives being able to store more information per device, provide faster access to data, consume less energy per operation, and last longer in a production environment.

Modern HDDs are a marvel of materials, electrical, and mechanical engineering. Their principal internal components are annotated in Fig. 17.3. The information is recorded on one or both surfaces of a disc-shaped *platter*. While the base material for platters is typically glass due to several well-mastered technological processes that guarantee the maximum surface flatness, the platters may also be made of aluminum or ceramics. The platters are polished to a roughness of less than 1 Å (10^{-10} m) and covered with several thin (single nanometers) layers of various materials containing cobalt, iron, nickel, ruthenium, platinum, chromium, and their alloys that promote the formation of the required crystallographic structure with properly oriented magnetic domains. The resulting material exhibits high coercivity, which is the ability to retain the acquired magnetization in the presence of an external magnetic field. The deposition of individual layers is done using a process called magnetron sputtering. The platter also receives a protective carbon-based coating through ion-beam or plasma-enhanced vapor deposition. Finally, a lubricant coat is deposited on the active surfaces and bonded. Storage densities of media manufactured this way exceed 800 Gb per square inch. A typical HDD stacks several platters on the same axle (spindle) to achieve the desired total storage capacity. The spindle is a part of a direct-drive brushless motor that rotates at several thousand RPM (commonly used speeds are 3600, 4200, 5400, 7200, and occasionally 10,000 and 15,000 RPM). Data are retrieved from and written to the platters using multiple read—write heads mounted at the end of the actuator arm. The arm can move in an arc over the platters to be able to locate a specific data track; the information is stored on platters in the form of concentric circles, referred to as *cylinders* to emphasize the three-dimensional aspect of the data layout. The actuator motion is controlled by the so-called *voice coil*, named in analogy to a dynamic loudspeaker construction which has coils surrounded by permanent magnets which push the sound-generating membrane. Both mechanisms work due to Lorentz force causing the motion of a conductor in a magnetic field when electric current flows through it. While earlier implementations used stepper motors to move the heads, voice coils are a much more lightweight alternative and thus may achieve significantly faster movement at a lower energy profile.

Read–write heads are not attached directly to the actuator arms, but to *sliders*—tiny (that is, a fraction of millimeter in the longest dimension and weighing a fraction of a gram) aerodynamically shaped carriers that are responsible for maintaining the correct distance between the head and the spinning medium. Interestingly, no electrically powered techniques are used to stabilize the separation distance. Sliders are mounted on a gimbal assembly attached to the arm, and thus have some freedom of motion. Since the spinning platters force the boundary layer of air to move with them, this generates an aerodynamic force acting on the slider. The slider's surface consists of a number of patterns that generate both an air bearing with positive air pressure that pushes the slider away from the medium and a negative pressure area that pulls the slider closer to the surface. Since the relative linear motion of the slider with respect to the platter surface changes significantly for the inner and outer cylinders, the parameters of the slider's shape must be precisely calculated to provide nearly constant flight height in these conditions. In modern HDDs this distance is on the order of few nanometers.

Due to the precision involved, it is not difficult to see that foreign contaminants present a serious damage risk to HDDs. Most drives have ventilation outlets protected by additional filters to stop foreign matter. Some HDD versions are hermetically sealed and use inert gases such as nitrogen or helium to support their operation. Since debris may also be generated by nonfatal impacts of the slider with the medium, there is an additional built-in recirculation filter to contain the particulate matter. This works due to constant motion of the air propelled by the spinning platters.

Modern hard drives utilize multiple technologies to improve their access speeds and increase storage density. One breakthrough was the practical application of the GMR effect to the construction of read–write heads. A GMR head sandwiches a spacer of nonmagnetic metal between two layers of magnetic metal and adds a fourth antiferromagnetic layer to "pin" the magnetic orientation of the nearest magnetic layer. This structure, called a *spin valve*, demonstrates high sensitivity to weak magnetic fields (such as those recorded on the HDD medium) of the unpinned layer, resulting in substantial resistance changes following those of the external magnetic field. Besides information access, signals derived from the GMR head serve as a feedback to head movement servos, resulting in accurate positioning on top of the recorded track. Another critical technique is perpendicular recording, illustrated in Fig. 17.4. Due to the fundamental limit on magnetic domain size caused by the superparamagnetic effect, the traditional horizontal arrangement of domains results in poor utilization of the medium surface. Reorienting the domains vertically, which requires a specially formed recording medium via the multistage process mentioned above as well as the modification of the writing head's shape, produces increased bit density.

The peak media transfer speeds of current HDDs are in the order of 100–250 MB/s. In addition to user data, the recorded information contains error-correcting codes (ECCs) to detect and if possible correct any malformed data. The information in each track is subdivided into a number of sectors of constant size, each requiring an identifier, synchronization information, and an explicit gap separating it from its nearest neighbors. The standard for several decades was 512-byte sectors, but modern large-

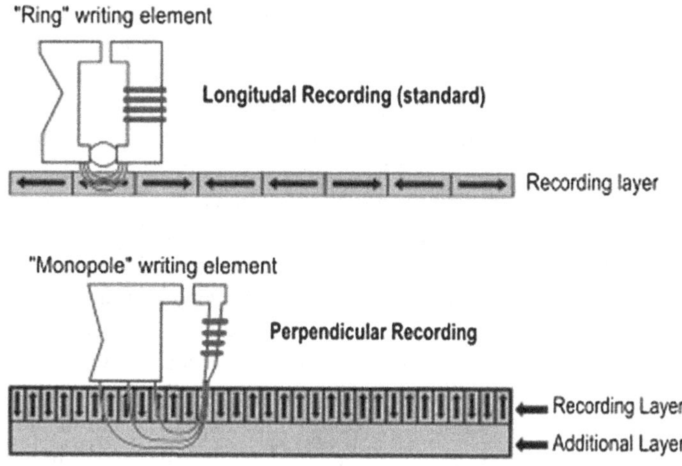

FIGURE 17.4

Bit density increase with perpendicular recording.

Diagram by Luca Cassioli via Wikimedia Commons, 2005

capacity drives forced manufacturers to migrate to 4096-byte sectors (called Advanced Format) to lower the spatial overheads of metadata, primarily ECCs, associated with each sector (see Fig. 17.5A). Older disks maintained a fixed number of sectors in each cylinder, hence producing a nonuniform recording density between the innermost and outermost tracks. Since the platters spin mostly at a constant rate, the solution was to introduce zone bit recording, illustrated in Fig. 17.5B. The platter surface is subdivided into concentric zones with different radii. Each zone features a specific number of sectors per track, thus allowing an increased number of sectors to be stored in the outer cylinders.

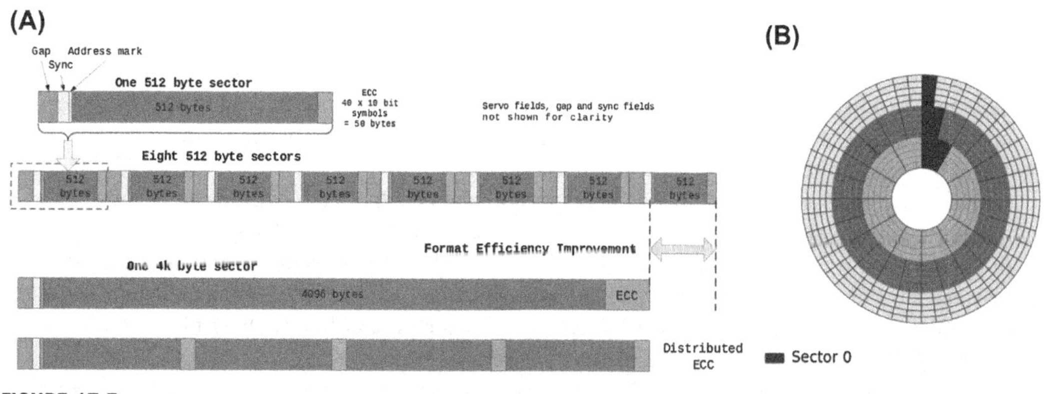

FIGURE 17.5

Physical information layout on HDDs: (A) advantage of larger sectors, (B) zone bit recording.

Diagrams by Dmitry Nosachev and Jan Schaumann via Wikimedia Commons

The continuing increases in bit density resulted in a smaller effective size of "bit area" and therefore weaker signals that still must be reliably detected. PRML is a signal processing technique responsible for boosting storage densities by as much as 40% while retaining a very high probability of correctly reconstructing the recorded information. In contrast to older methods relying on peak detection in read signal (which corresponds to points where the read head passes over domains, changing orientation of their magnetic field), PRML operates not only with weaker signals but signals where narrowly spaced domains may affect each other's magnetic field magnitude. The induced signals usually have too low an amplitude to register correctly with conventional peak detectors. PRML implementation consists of a variable-gain amplifier, an analog-to-digital converter, analog and digital filters, a clock recovery circuit, and finally a Viterbi [9] decoder running in real time analyzing serial input data streams at a rate of several gigabits per second. PRML inspired even more complex algorithms of signal reconstruction, such as the noise-predictive maximum likelihood [10] method.

Despite all the precautions, internal material imperfections and external shocks may eventually cause damage or otherwise degrade sections of recorded media. HDDs are manufactured with spare capacity that permits transparent remapping of damaged sectors. The only indication that this has happened is decreased sequential access performance; the sectors that were occupying the same physical track and could be read back-to-back during a single rotation of the platter may require additional head movement if they were migrated to different areas of the disk. Most drives available on the market are equipped with self-monitoring, analysis, and reporting technology (SMART) [11] that continuously monitors the health status of the device and may even warn the user ahead of time about an impending failure. While the interpretation details of individual values may be vendor specific, commonly reported parameters include start/stop count, spin-up time, seek and read error rates, total power-on hours, power cycle count, reallocated sector count, unrecoverable error count, command timeouts, current and highest recorded temperature, registered shock values, servo off-track errors, uncorrectable and failing sector count, total data read and written, and others. SMART is also capable of performing a variety of online and offline tests to verify the most visible problems related to drive operation.

Due to the nature of their implementation and their broad range of performance characteristics, HDDs are described using a number of parameters that help determine their usefulness for a specific application (Table 17.1). Many of these metrics also apply to other storage devices.

- *Storage capacity* is typically expressed in gigabytes or terabytes. Unlike memory capacities it is measured in powers of 10, hence 1 TB is 10^{12} bytes. HDD manufacturers tend to round this figure up. Note that due to storage of file system metadata, the data capacity available to users is 1%–5% less than the nominal capacity of the drive.
- *Seek time* (in milliseconds) expresses the duration taken by the read–write head to move to a specific cylinder. Average seek time is determined statistically as travel distances over one-third of all tracks on a disk. Of specific interest are also track-to-track latency (moving the head between adjacent tracks) and full-stroke latency, which involves travel between the innermost and outermost cylinders. They describe respectively the shortest and longest possible seek times.
- *RPM* is the number of rotations the platters perform in 1 min.
- *Rotational latency* (in milliseconds) describes the time required to position a specific sector under the read–write head. Average latency is typically given as the time it takes the drive to perform half a rotation of the platter, and is directly dependent on its RPM rating.

Table 17.1 Comparison of Characteristic Hard Disk Drive Properties From Several Manufacturers

Manufacturer and Drive	Capacity (TB)	Media Transfer Rate (MB/s)	Seek Time (ms)		RPM	Cache (DRAM/ flash) (MB)	MTBF (million hours)	Average Power (W)		UER	Acoustic Noise [dB(A)]		Form Factor (inches)	Market Segment
			Track to Track	Full Stroke				Seek	Idle		Seek	Idle		
WDC WD101KRYZ	10	249			7200	256/0	2.5	7.1	5.0	<1 in 10^{15}	36	20	3.5	Enterprise
WDC WD60EZRZ	6	175			5400	64/0		5.3	3.4	<1 in 10^{14}	28	25	3.5	Economy desktop
HGST HTS541010A9E680	1	124	1	20	5400	8/0		1.8	0.5		26	24	2.5	Mobile
Seagate ST10000VX0004	10	210				256/0	1	6.8	4.42	<1 in 10^{15}			3.5	A/V streaming
Seagate ST2000DX002	2	156	<9.5 (average)			64/8192		6.7	4.5	<1 in 10^{14}			3.5	Performance desktop

- *Access time* (in milliseconds) is the delay between the time a request for data is submitted by the host and the time data is returned by the drive. It is a compound metric involving a combination of rotational latency and seek time, typically determined through a synthetic benchmark that exercises various access scenarios.
- *Media transfer rate* (in megabytes per second) measures how fast the signal processing chain and controller can read the data from the platter.
- *Burst rate* (in megabytes per second) describes how fast the data may be transmitted between the host and the disk cache using transfers that do not exceed the cache capacity.
- *Areal density* (in gigabits per square inch) provides the achievable upper limit of information density per surface area on a recordable medium. Related metrics involving linear densities are tracks per inch and bits per inch.
- *Mean time between failures* (MTBF, in millions of hours) estimates a drive's resilience to nonrecoverable faults.
- *Uncorrectable error rate* (UER, no unit) estimates the probability of receiving data containing a hard error, i.e., an error that could not be either detected or fixed by the built-in ECC mechanisms or could not be corrected through operation retries.
- *Power consumption* (in watts) describes average energy requirements of a drive in several possible scenarios: during regular operation, during power-up (spin-up), while idle, and during standby. The latter may involve several levels of inactivity (sleep modes) that are particularly relevant to mobile and other battery-powered devices.
- *Acoustic noise* (in dB(A)) provides an upper bound on noise level produced by the device during active operation.
- *Shock resistance* (in g) describes a device's resilience to external mechanical impact. Typically two figures are given, for nonoperating and operating modes (the first is often orders of magnitude higher due to the robust protection mechanisms used in powered-off devices). The figures are often accompanied by test conditions specifying the shock duration or whether it was repeating.
- *Size* (in inches) provides mechanical dimensions of the drive so that proper enclosure may be adopted for its use.

17.3.2 SOLID-STATE DRIVE STORAGE

Advances in semiconductor technology enabled practical realization of high-capacity persistent storage in solid-state devices. The most broadly utilized SSDs today are the descendants of electrically erasable programmable read-only memory (EEPROM) technology, introduced by Toshiba in 1984. EEPROMs can store small amount of data using floating-gate metal oxide semiconductor (FGMOS) arrays. The FGMOS transistors are similar to regular field-effect transistors with oxide isolators, but they sandwich additional electrodes between the oxide layers above the channel. During the programming cycle (Fig. 17.6A), sufficiently high potential applied to the control gate causes the transistor to conduct. Applying a relatively high source-drain voltage causes some high-energy channel electrons to overcome the oxide barrier and "jump" to the floating gate in a process called hot electron injection. After the removal of programming voltage, the charge remains trapped on the floating electrode, thus creating an additional electric field that may modulate the width of the transistor's channel. By putting suitable voltages on the control gate and drain (much lower than those needed for programming), the channel source-drain resistance reflects the amount of charge stored on the floating

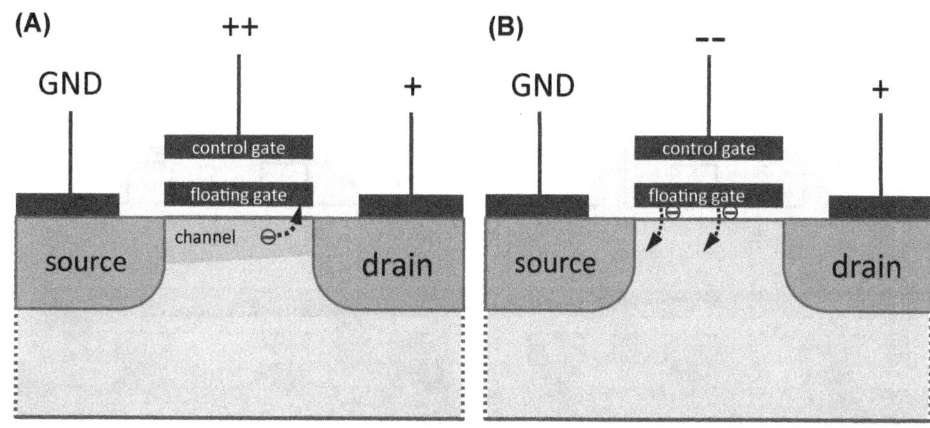

FIGURE 17.6

FGMOS transistor: (A) programming by hot electron injection and (B) erasing through quantum tunneling.

(B) From Smart Card Handbook, W. Rankl and W. Effing, third edition © 2002 Carl Hanser Verlag, München

gate. The erase process (Fig. 17.6B) requires negative voltage on the control gate and positive potential on the source and drain electrodes to cause Fowler–Nordheim tunneling of the trapped charge to the transistor body. Some variants of EEPROM used quantum tunneling for both programming and erasure. EEPROMs usually provide fine-grain access to storage, typically organizing data in groups equal in size to the width of a data bus (8 or 16 bits), but their capacities rarely exceed a few megabits. Early EEPROMs were frequently unable to support a fine-granularity erase function, instead supporting erasure of the entire chip or significant portions thereof. Future implementations alleviated this limit.

Increasing the device capacity necessitated reduction of the control structure and the number of internal connections, resulting in two dominant flash memory types: NOR and NAND. Their respective layouts are illustrated in Fig. 17.7. The names of flash configurations are derived from internal structures resembling that of NOR gate with a parallel arrangement of output n-type transistors and series connection of n-type transistors in the NAND gate. While the NOR configuration is nearly directly derived from the initial EEPROM structure, the NAND cell was proposed in 1987. Due to associated changes in storage transistor architecture (e.g., split gates and multiple-control gates) and their size, various flash operations became faster and more power efficient. This is particularly true for the erase operation, which could take as many as several seconds for EEPROMs but requires only a few tens of milliseconds for the NOR flash and single milliseconds for a NAND flash.

All flash memories are susceptible to several issues that negatively affect the reliability of general operation and data retention in the floating gate. The first is charge leakage, which may be caused by oxide (isolator) defects, electron detrapping, or contamination, in which positive ions present in the memory cell may in part offset the charge stored on the floating gate. The others are called *disturbs*, and may occur in neighboring cells that share some electrical connections with the cells that are programmed or erased (gate and drain disturbs). Moreover, as the electrical erase operation is not self-limiting, an extended erase cycle may leave a net-positive charge on the floating gate. This effect is

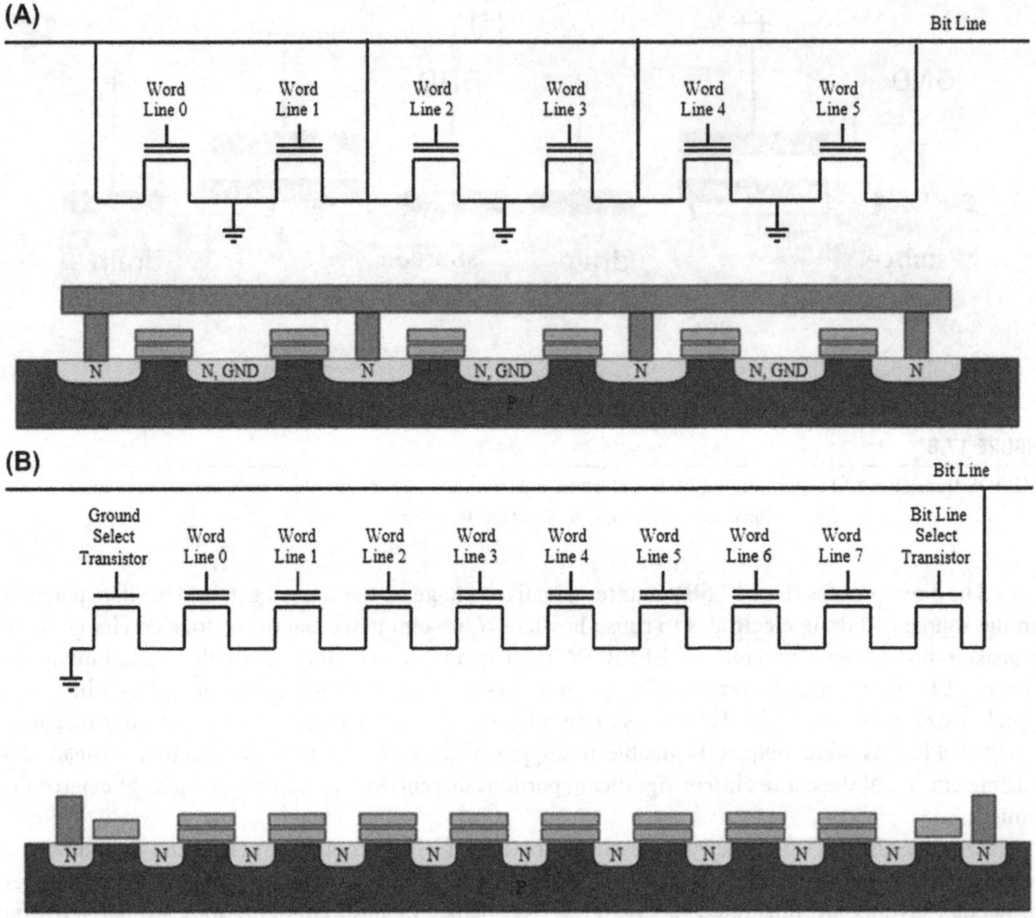

FIGURE 17.7

Storage cell connections and corresponding hardware implementation of (A) NOR flash memory and (B) NAND flash memory.

Both diagrams by Cyferz via Wikimedia Commons

called *overerasing*. The inverse phenomenon, *overprograming*, is also possible. The speed of various operations on flash storage is affected by its organization; the main features of NOR and NAND flash memories are compared in Table 17.2.

As can be seen, neither of the currently available flash technologies is ideal for mass storage. While the ability to manufacture high-capacity storage devices cheaply is paramount, selection of NAND memory is associated with serious drawbacks. The first is the relatively low number of update cycles that can be performed. Modern devices cope with this by application of wear-leveling algorithms that distribute the updates across all physical data blocks in a device by performing on-the-fly remapping of

Table 17.2 Comparison of Principal Properties of NOR and NAND Flash Memory

Property	NOR Flash	NAND Flash
Capacity	Low	High
Cost per bit	High	Low
Read speed	High	Medium
Write speed	Very slow	Slow
Erase speed	Very slow (10–100 s of ms)	Medium (single ms)
Erase cycles (endurance)	100,000–1,000,000	1000–10,000
Active power	High	Low
Standby power	Low	Medium
Random access	Easy	Hard
Block storage	Medium	Easy

logical addresses of rewritten blocks to physical addresses of the least utilized available blocks. This also means that many applications which take for granted multiple rewritability of stored data (such as when using HDDs) should not be used without caution. A good example is data wiping performed by repeated in-place overwriting of the file contents with pseudorandom data to prevent the reconstruction of its contents; due to wear leveling, it is completely ineffective in an SSD. The jury is still out on whether installation of a swap partition on a flash device is a good idea. It may substantially boost the performance compared to HDD-based solution; but while for relatively lightweight paging duties such an arrangement should not cause measurable problems, its use in severely memory-constrained systems may lead to premature failure of the flash drive.

Charge leakage is one of the main factors limiting the miniaturization of storage cells. Moreover, the amount of charge per cell cannot be decreased indefinitely. Thus in recent years the industry transitioned to encoding multiple bits per cell. Originally, NAND storage used single-level cell (SLC) implementation; commercial devices available today resort to multilevel cells (MLCs) with 2 bits per cell and even triple-level cells (TLCs) with 3 bits stored in a cell, thus representing eight data states. Sizes of cells used in MLC and TLC devices are somewhat larger than those of SLC to provide a reasonable margin of error despite leakage and disturbs. To ensure reliability, flash-based solid-state storage employs Bose–Chaudhuri–Hocquenghem codes [12] for error detection and correction. These enable correction of 24-bit errors in each 1024-bit sequence (two data sectors), with about 4% encoding overhead. Even then, endurance of TLC devices drops effectively to about 3000 erase cycles.

To operate correctly, SSDs require controller logic in addition to flash memory circuits. The controller interfaces to the host computer, typically using common high-bandwidth buses such as Serial AT Attachment, PCI Express (PCIe), or their variants (mini-PCIe, M.2, etc.). The controller must support a data buffer implemented in fast memory (DRAM) to cope with relatively slow performance of erase and write operations by individual chips. Since the storage pool is organized into multiple banks, the controller takes care of proper interleaving and overlap of the data accesses to extract maximum bandwidth from the pool. Mapping of logical to physical data blocks and wear leveling are also handled by the controller. Due to charge leakage, the read data has to be verified against ECC; if errors are detected, the corrected bit values are computed and written back to the storage. The controller may periodically check for data that has been residing a long time in storage without being accessed to ensure it is viable; this function is called data *scrubbing*. Finally, the controller takes care of block allocation for new data, in many cases interpreting block usage hints from the OS, such as TRIM commands.

Table 17.3 presents examples of commercially available SSD devices with their parameters. Unlike HDDs, SSDs do not have moving parts, hence there is no equivalent of RPM or seek time. However, since solid-state storage handles multiple short accesses with much better performance, the number of I/O operations per second (IOPS) is given. The limited rewrite count of a flash is reflected through the terabytes written (TBW) statistic, which estimates the total volume of data a drive is guaranteed to accommodate over its lifetime taking into account wear leveling. Alternatively, some manufacturers may specify diskful writes per day over the warranty period of the drive. Independent tests verify that most SDDs significantly exceed this parameter in typical usage environments, with the possible exception of applications in which the drive is updated in low temperatures (significantly below room temperature) and stored in powered-off state for extended time at an elevated temperature (e.g., 50°C). Fig. 17.8 shows photographs of the devices listed in Table 17.3.

17.3.3 MAGNETIC TAPE

Magnetic tape has a long history as a computer data storage medium. Having been used as secondary storage (manufactured by Uniservo) in UNIVAC in 1951, tape predates HDDs by approximately 5 years. It consisted of 0.5″ wide and 0.0015″ think nickel-plated phosphor bronze metal tape wound on open reels, was up to 1500 ft long, and recorded information at the density of 128 bits per inch. The sustained data bandwidth was 7200 characters per second. A single reel with tape weighed about 3 pounds.

Later developments introduced polymer-based tapes, such as cellulose acetate, incorporating ferrous oxides as the magnetic recording medium. The IBM 726 shown in Fig. 17.9A is the iconic example of mid-1950s tape storage technology. The data was recorded in seven parallel tracks (including one-bit parity for ECC) on tape that could be read forwards and backwards. The tape could start advancing or reach a full stop in much less than 10 ms thanks to an innovative “vacuum column” arrangement that avoided the use of slower conventional tape-tensioning mechanisms. The maximum per-reel capacity was about 2 million six-bit characters.

Besides increases in data density and length of tape stored on a reel, improvements in tape and deck technology brought more practical implementations of replaceable storage media. Instead of using independent reels, they were packaged into *tape cartridges* that combined reels, tape, and some elements of a guiding mechanism into a single enclosure. An example is IBM’s 3840 tape format (Fig. 17.9B) and its later derivatives. IBM’s compatible tape storage was also manufactured by other vendors, such as Fujitsu, M4 Data, StorageTek, VDS, and Overland Data. But a lack of widely accepted standards for tape storage resulted in a proliferation of mutually incompatible cartridge families, including DDS (digital data storage, from 1989), DAT (digital audio tape, originated in 2003), DLT (digital linear tape, 1984–2007), and finally LTO (linear tape-open, 2000–today). Example cartridges and supporting tape decks are shown in Fig. 17.10. There were several iterations of capacity and resultant cartridge formats within each family; with some exceptions (e.g., DLT value line, or DLT-V), the newer releases are explicitly not backwards compatible with the products of earlier generations in each product line.

Table 17.3 Examples of Currently Manufactured SSD Devices and Their Operational Properties

Manufacturer and Device	Capacity (GB)	Sequential Read (MB/s)	Sequential Write (MB/s)	Maximum 4 KB Random Reads (kIOPS)	Maximum 4 KB Random Writes (kIOPS)	Terabytes Written	MTTF (million hours)	Power (Active/ Idle) (W)	Memory Type	Interface
Crucial CT2050MX300SSD1	2050	530	510	92	83	400	1.5	0.15 (average)	3D TLC NAND	SATA 6 Gbps
Samsung MZ-V6P2T0BW	2048	3500	2100	440	360	1,200		(5.8/1.2)	48-layer MLC V-NAND	NVMe 1.1, PCIe 3.0 × 4
SanDisk SDFADCMOS-6T40-SF1	6400	2800	2200	285	385	22,000		25 (peak)	MLC	PCIe 2 × 8

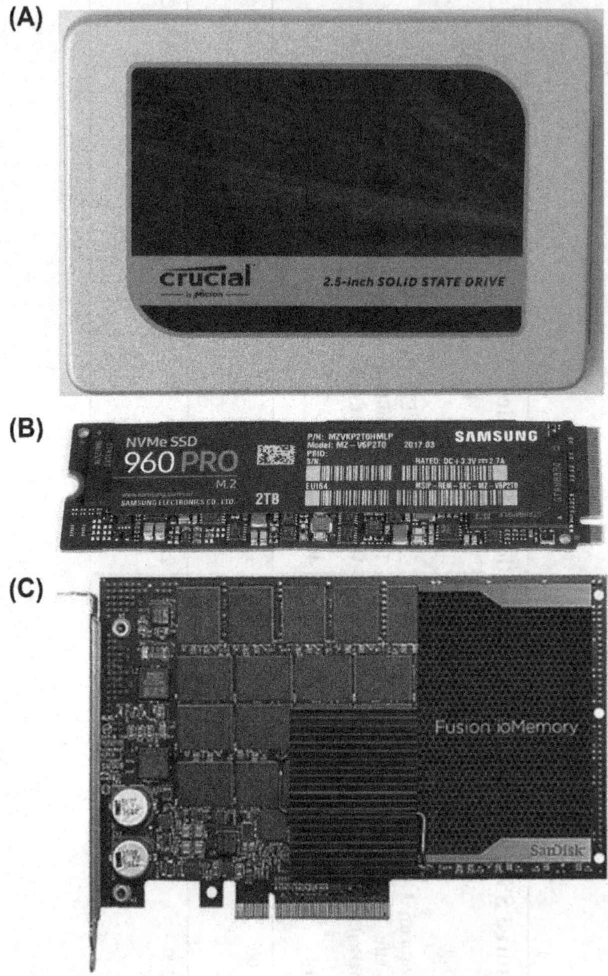

FIGURE 17.8

SSD examples: (A) Crucial MX300 series (2.5″ form factor), (B) Samsung 960 PRO series (M.2 form factor), and (C) SanDisk Fusion ioMemory SX350 series (8-lane PCI Express card).

(B) Photo by Dmitry Nosachev via Wikimedia Commons

The tape is a sequential-access medium, which means that it may require a comparatively lengthy time to locate a specific piece of data. The information on tape can be arranged in several ways. The earliest approaches used linear multitrack recoding, illustrated in Fig. 17.11A. In this mode, each read–write head records data lengthwise in a separate linear data track; the tracks are parallel to each other. As the bit density increased and track width decreased, linear-serpentine recording (Fig. 17.11B) permitted installation of several read–write heads side by side without loss of medium coverage. The head assembly moves across the width of the tape to start a new track in unrecorded space whenever

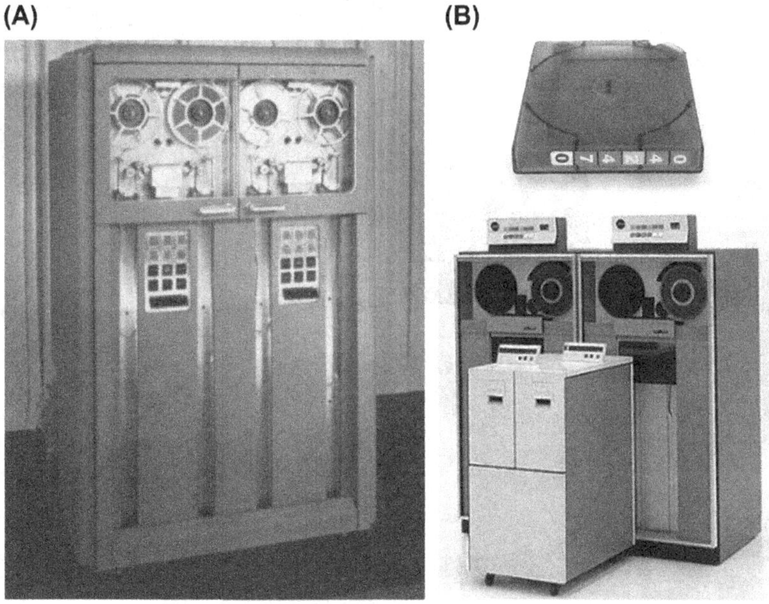

FIGURE 17.9

Advances in magnetic tape storage: (A) IBM 726 from 1951, (B) IBM 3480 format tape (top) and the corresponding deck subsystem (bottom) from 1984, with older 3480 system in the background.

(A) Courtesy of International Business Machines Corporation, © International Business Machines Corporation. (B) Bottom: Courtesy of International Business Machines Corporation, © International Business Machines Corporation

the tape reaches one of its ends. Helical recording, shown in Fig. 17.11C, arranges a large number of relatively short data tracks at an angle to the tape's edge. This last approach, resembling the recording technology used by tape-based camcorders and videocassette recorders, requires the use of a *scanning head* (a revolving drum which contains one or more heads along its circumference and is mounted at an angle to the tape's movement).

The longest-surviving technology still popular today is LTO, established in response to proprietary tape formats and developed by a consortium founded by Hewlett-Packard, IBM, and Quantum. Its current generation, LTO-7, supports up to 6 TB of data per cartridge packed on a 960 m long, 12.65 mm wide, and 5.6 μm thick tape. The tape substrate is polyester-based (polyethylene naphthalate), encasing particles of barium ferrite pigment as the active storage medium. The data is recorded in a linear-serpentine fashion on four data bands interleaved with five narrow servo (positioning) bands. Each data band is further subdivided into 28 wraps. There are 32 tracks per wrap (the same as the count of read–write elements in a head assembly), hence the total number of tracks stored on a tape is $4 \times 28 \times 32 = 3584$. The number of head passes required to fill the tape completely is a product of the data band count and the wrap count or 112; a data band is usually completely filled before the mechanism advances to the next band.

Table 17.4 compares operational parameters (only uncompressed data rates and capacities are reported) of some currently available tape decks. Their primary applications are backups and archivization of large datasets.

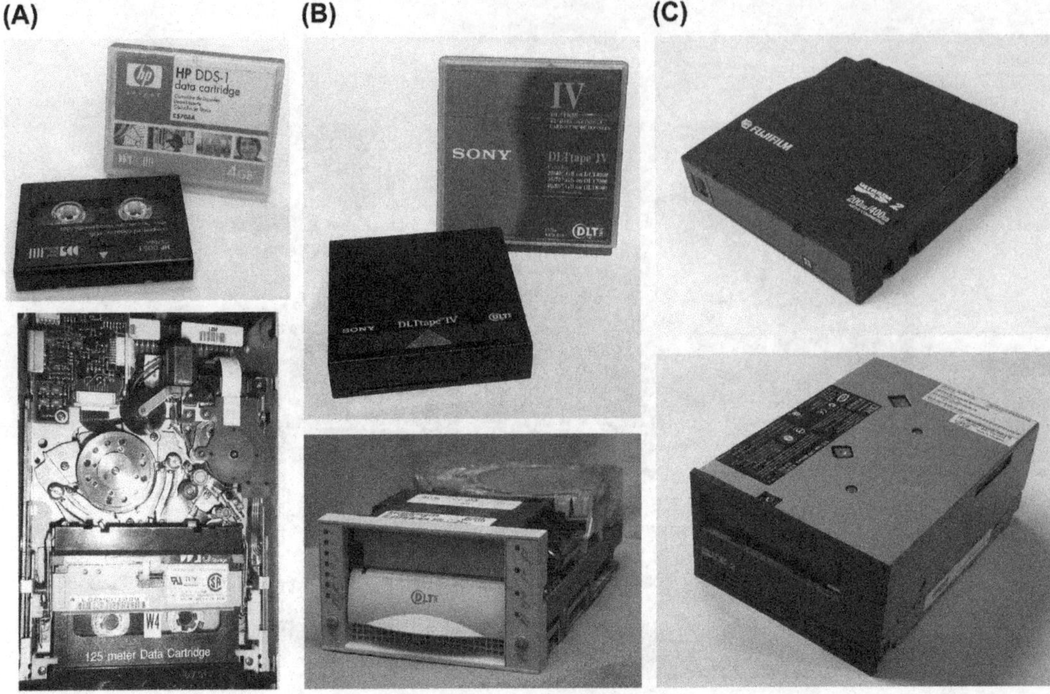

FIGURE 17.10

Comparison of dominant tape storage families: (A) DDS-1 (1989), (B) DLT-IV (1999), and (C) LTO-2 (2005). Data cartridges are shown on top and the corresponding tape decks at the bottom in each column.

(A) bottom photo by Adlerweb via Wikimedia Commons; (B) bottom photo by Christian Taube Chtaube via Wikimedia Commons; (C) Bottom and top figures by Austin Murphy via Wikimedia Commons

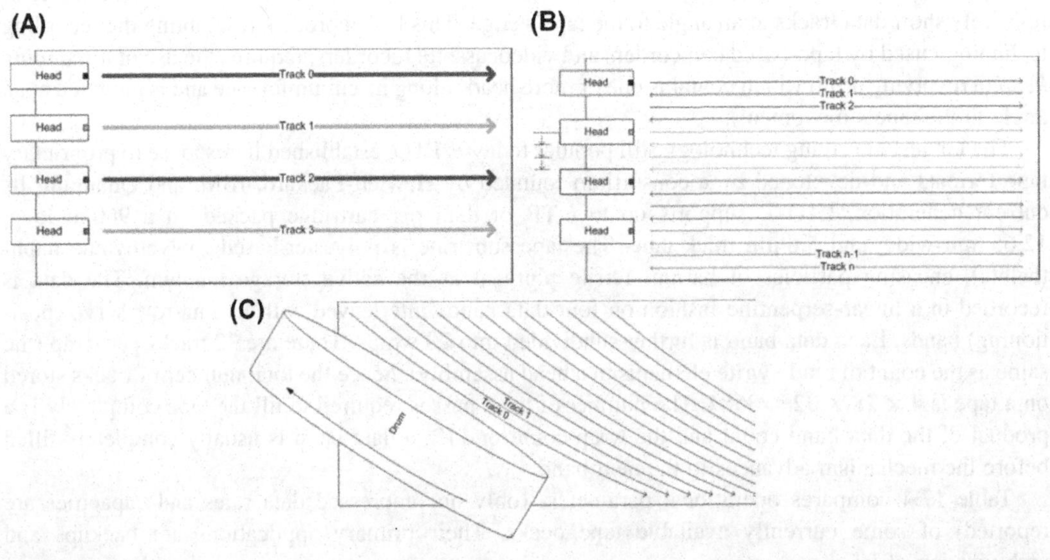

FIGURE 17.11

Tape-recording formats: (A) linear, (B) linear-serpentine, and (C) helical.

Diagrams by Kubanczyk at the English language Wikipedia

Table 17.4 Operational Parameters of Selected Tape Drives

Manufacturer and Drive	Capacity (TB)	Sustained Data Rate (MB/s)	High-Speed Search (m/s)	Maximum Operating Power (W)	Data Format	Cartridge Types Supported	Interface
IBM TS1150	Up to 10 (medium dependent)	360, 300	12.4	46	32-channel linear-serpentine	IBM 3592 Generations 3 and 4	8 Gbps fiber channel
HP Enterprise BB873A	Up to 6	300			32-channel linear-serpentine	LTO-7 (rewritable), LTO-6 (rewritable), LTO-5 (read only)	6 Gbps Serial Attached SCSI

17.3.4 OPTICAL STORAGE

While there were many attempts to apply optical means for storage and retrieval of digital information, none attained widespread popularity before the commercial release of the compact disc (CD) in 1982. The CD is the result of a collaboration between Philips and Sony, who jointly developed the Red Book CD digital/audio specifications and agreed to manufacture compatible hardware. Even though originally intended as a medium for music distribution, the CD was soon used to store photographs, graphics, artwork, sound samples, video, and, of course, data. As early versions did not support recording data, the information stored on the disks was read-only and inspired the CD-ROM moniker describing media carrying digital data. Starting in the 1990s and continuing to this day, CD-ROM and its derivatives are extensively used as an inexpensive medium to distribute software and other auxiliary data.

Physically, a CD is a 1.2 mm thick plastic disc with a diameter of 120 mm. The base material is polycarbonate with an impressed spiral pattern of elongated pits to encode the data. The data track is covered with a reflective metal layer (usually aluminum or occasionally gold) before sealing it with a protective layer of lacquer and artwork (Fig. 17.12B). The information is retrieved from the spinning disc using an infrared laser beam equipped with appropriate collimating optics and tracking mechanism (Fig. 17.12C). Most discs have just one active surface that is used to read the data, although there are variants with information recorded on both sides. A smaller 80 mm version of the disc called a mini-CD is also in circulation. While a conventional CD stores 74–80 min of audio or up to 700 MB of data, a mini-CD reduces this to up to 24 min of music and approximately 200 MB of data. On audio disc, two channels of sound are sampled at 44.1 kHz using linear 16-bit encoding (the complement integer of two) per sample per channel. The audio data is organized in 192-bit *frames*; each frame contains six interleaved audio samples from left and right channels. In addition to audio samples, frames incorporate ECC and synchronization data. Due to symbol transcoding to reduce the density of pits on the disc surface (eight-to-fourteen modulation code [13]), each frame effectively ends up occupying 588 bits on the disc. Frames are combined into *sectors*, each containing 98 frames or 2352 bytes of audio data. The sectors are assigned to *tracks* that correspond to individual songs on the

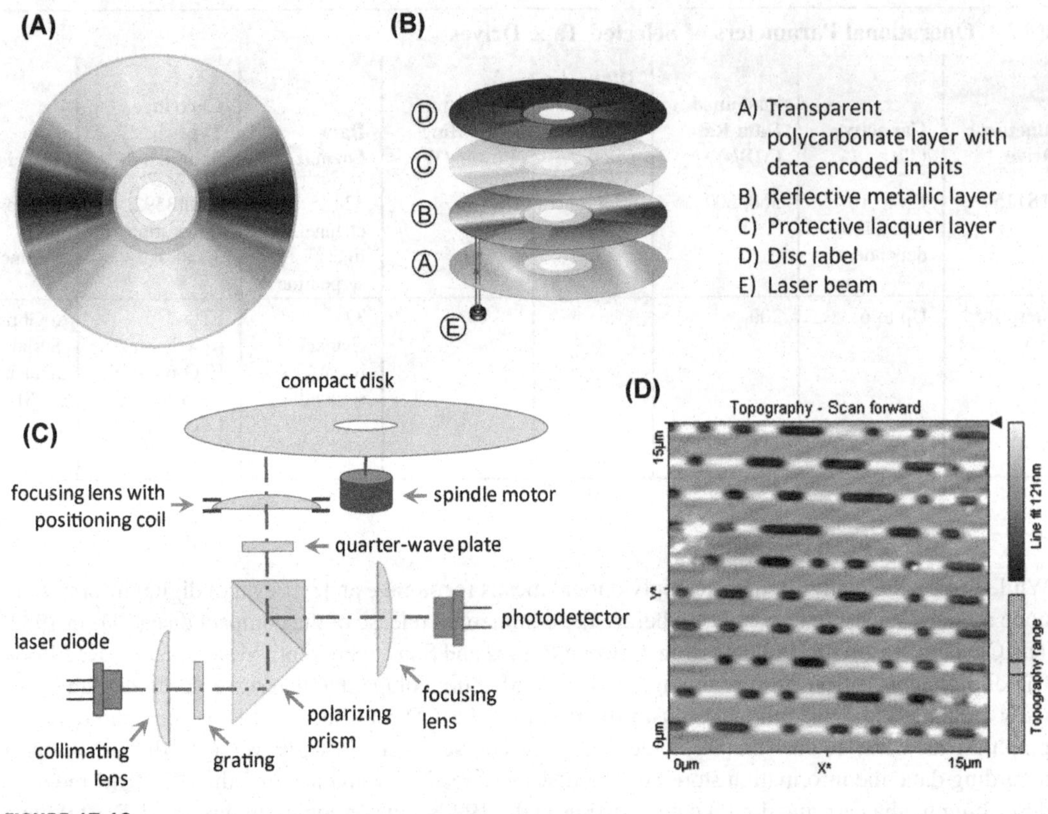

FIGURE 17.12

Compact disc: (A) medium, (B) component layers, (C) optical pickup mechanism, and (D) geometric properties of the data track.

(A) Image by Arun Kulshreshtha via Wikimedia Commons; (B) Image by Pbroks13 via Wikimedia Commons; (D) Image by Valacosa and Blair Lebert via Wikimedia Commons

CD; up to 99 tracks may be stored on one disc. The nominal data rate is 2 (channels) × 2 (bytes per sample) × 44,100 (samples per second) = 176.4 kB/s; this is equivalent to a throughput of 75 sectors per second. Data integrity is protected by cross-interleaved Reed–Solomon code (CIRC) [14], which adds one parity byte for every three bytes of data. CIRC is capable of correcting up to two full byte errors in each 32-byte block, or, due to interleaving of parity data with the neighboring blocks, it can fully correct up to 4000-bit-long error bursts corresponding to 2.5 mm in linear distance. This makes it a very effective solution to deal with scratches, particulate matter, and small stains on the disc surface.

For data storage, a CD-ROM retains the basic organization of information on the disc, but the effective number of data bytes per sector is reduced to 2048 (CD-ROM Mode 1) due to the stronger ECC schemes employed (audio data may be reconstructed to some extent by interpolation, but this is not true for arbitrary digital information). For some applications, like video, robust protection is less important than data density, hence CD-ROM Mode 2 specification permits 2336 data bytes per sector. The base data rate, referred to as 1× speed, is derived as the data throughput of 75 CD-ROM Mode 1 sectors per second or 153.6 kB/s. Many currently manufactured CD-ROM drives are capable of spinning the disc much faster than that, resulting in sustained transfer rates of 24×–48× and higher.

One of the main drawbacks of a CD-ROM is that its content is fixed at the factory, essentially precluding its use as a practical mass-storage medium. This has been addressed by CD-recordable (CD-R) and later CD-rewritable (CD-RW) formats, detailed by Orange Book specifications. Both retain the original form factor of the 120 mm disc. CD-R media replace data-defining pits with a fixed spiral "pregroove" to aid laser positioning and add a layer of organic dye between the polycarbonate substrate and reflective layer. During the write process, the laser power is modulated to affect ("burn") the organic dye, making it locally more opaque or absorptive. The read is performed at much lower beam power so the written data is not destroyed. As the mass-produced media adopt primarily three (cyanine, phtalocyanine, and azo) dyes of quite different properties, careful calibration of laser power is required ahead of data deposition. This process is aided by the additional information (absolute time in pregroove) stored on the blank disc in the pregroove outside the useful data area, which identifies media manufacturer as well as the recommended laser power. CD-R discs may be "burned" only once, but depending on the write mode selected it may be possible to add data at a later time to a disc that has not been "closed" (*track at once* mode as opposed to *disk at once* mode). Since some of the dyes are sensitive to ultraviolet light, ensuring proper storage conditions is strongly encouraged to achieve the desired information longevity. Good-quality CD-R media recorded in properly calibrated devices and stored in a dark location with stable temperature and humidity may last over 50 years without data loss; archival-quality discs using gold as the reflective layer may extend this to as much as 100 years. A National Institute of Standards and Technology study estimated the longevity of several tested media brands to be at least 30 years if kept at ambient temperature and controlled humidity conditions [15]. Rewritable discs utilize silver-indium-antimony-tellurium phase-change media that may alternate between crystalline and amorphous phases differing in reflectivity. Thus the composition of CD-RW discs is similar to that of regular CD-ROMs, but with a different material constituting the reflective layer. As the nominal reflectivity of phase-change media is much lower than that of aluminum or gold, the recorded CD-RW media may not always work correctly in older CD-ROM drives. CD-RW discs require even more precise control of laser power while writing than CD-R, and constrain both the upper and lower limits of data transfer rate while burning. Rewritable media endurance is commonly estimated at approximately 1000 rewrite cycles. Since CD-RW media can be updated and erased, *packet writing* mode has been developed to support changes to the stored information.

The maximum data capacity of a CD is insufficient to store a full-length movie in National Television System Committee resolution, even using a lossy compression such as MPEG-2. To cope with the growing demand for multimedia content and simultaneously increase the storage capacity of disc-based media, Philips, Sony, Toshiba, and Panasonic introduced the DVD (digital versatile disc, alternatively known as digital video disc) in 1995. While DVDs have the same external dimensions as CDs, the information is retrieved using a red laser of wavelength 650 nm, which permits reducing the gap between the consecutive windings of data "groove," thus making it much longer. DVDs may store data in one or two layers; this results in a total capacity of 4.7 GB or 8.5 GB per disc. The nominal (1×) data rate is 1385 kB/s; note that this reference speed for DVDs is substantially higher than that of CDs. Modern DVD-ROM drives may retrieve the data at a rate that is 8–20× greater than the base rate.

Similar to CDs, DVDs support recordable and rewritable variants. Due to "format wars" there are two recordable versions, DVD-R and DVD + R and two rewritable versions, DVD-RW and DVD + RW. The "-" and "+" formats are not directly compatible with each other, but most drive manufacturers release products that support both. Since the -R and -RW formats originally developed by Pioneer were released earlier, they are supported by more devices, especially standalone DVD video players. The "+" variants specified by Sony and Philips feature more robust error correction, hence they may be somewhat more suitable for data preservation. Additionally, the DVD-RAM (digital versatile disc-random access memory) format backed by Hitachi, Toshiba, Maxell, Samsung, LG, Panasonic, Lite-On, and Teac offers very good support for data updates (minimum of 100,000 rewrites at low speeds), protection, and retention. Unlike other recordable DVD discs, the DVD-RAM stores data in concentric tracks, similarly to HDDs, and therefore requires specialized drives.

Widespread adoption of high-definition (HD) video formats prompted the development of a suitable storage medium. Of two competing variants, HD-DVD and Blu-ray disc (BD), the latter ultimately emerged as a winner in 2008. Blu-ray media can store 25 GB per layer thanks to the availability of violet laser diodes operating at 405 nm wavelength. This permitted shrinking the track pitch further from 740 nm for DVDs to just 320 nm (Fig. 17.13). BD differs from other optical disc technologies in that the data tracks are much closer to the surface and thus are more vulnerable to scratches. A specially formulated hard-coat layer applied to the top surface alleviates the effects of mechanical impact. The 1× speed for Blu-ray is equivalent to real-time reproduction bandwidth for compressed 1080p video at 60 frames per second, and equals 4.5 MB/s. Practical speeds achieved by currently manufactured drives range from 4× to 16×. Data capacities per disc range from 25 to 50 GB for single-layer and dual-layer media to 100 GB (triple-layer) and 128 GB (quad-layer) BDXL discs. Example optical drive specifications are listed in Table 17.5.

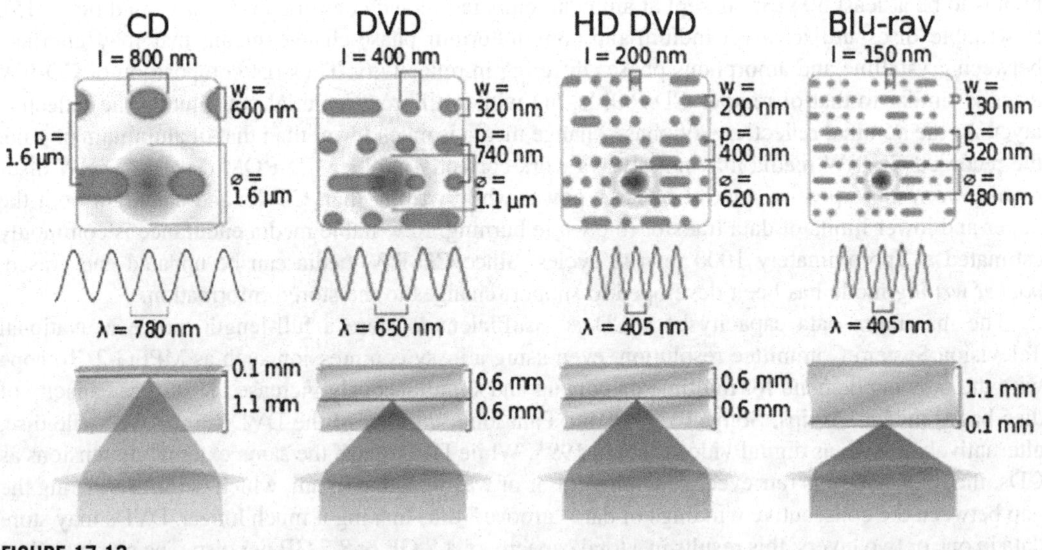

FIGURE 17.13

Comparison of optical format geometries (CD, DVD, HD-DVD, and Blu-ray). The listed parameters denote minimum feature length (l), track width (w), track pitch (p), laser beam diameter (φ), and wavelength (λ).

Diagram by Cmglee via Wikimedia Commons

Table 17.5 Parameters of a Typical Consumer-Grade Multiformat Optical Drive

Manufacturer and Drive	BD access Time (ms)	DVD access Time (ms)	CD access Time (ms)	Maximum Data Rate						Buffer Size (MB)	Interface
				BD Read	BD Write	DVD Read	DVD Write	CD Read	CD Write		
Lite-On iHBS312	250 (SL) 380 (DL)	150 (ROM) 160 (DL) 200 (RAM)	150	6× (RE DL) 8× (SL)	2× (rewrite) 8× (DL) 12× (SL)	16×	6× (rewrite) 12× (RAM) 16× (+R, −R)	48×	24× (−RW) 48× (−R)	8	SATA (internal)

17.4 AGGREGATED STORAGE

17.4.1 REDUNDANT ARRAY OF INDEPENDENT DISKS

Redundant array of independent disks (RAID; formerly redundant array of inexpensive disks, attributed to David Patterson, Garth Gibson, and Randy Katz of the University of California at Berkeley) attempts to address reliability issues of conventional mass-storage devices. All storage devices, including HDDs and SSDs, have a limited lifespan and undergo random mechanical or electrical failures. The consequence of a failure is usually loss of a portion or the whole amount of the data stored on the device. RAID works by extending the pool of drives containing actual data with additional devices. These *redundant* drives store information that is derived from the contents of other drives in the pool. By treating such a formed array of drives as a single, virtualized I/O device, the impact of individual component failures may be alleviated. However, RAID should never be considered a perfect or universal solution. It may mitigate component failures only to a certain extent, which is defined by RAID level, implementation, parameters of component drives, and even their fabrication characteristics. Since drives in an array are accessed in aggregate, in many cases RAID usage translates into improved data access performance compared to that of a single device. Here a number of commonly recognized RAID configurations are discussed, along with their main operational properties.

17.4.1.1 RAID 0: Striping

RAID 0 is not a proper RAID level, in that it does not provide any data redundancy should drive failures occur. It describes a configuration in which the data blocks are simply distributed (striped) across available disks in a round-robin fashion, as shown in Fig. 17.14. A *stripe* is a sequence of blocks spanning all disks in the array; for example, block 4—block 5—block 6 in the figure constitutes a stripe. An arbitrary number of disks may be arranged this way, but assuming that failure occurrences are independent and have exponential probability distribution, the reliability for the whole array including *d* data disks will be a fraction of that for a single drive:

$$MTBF_0 = \frac{MTBF_D}{d}$$

Thus building an array of four enterprise drives, each with a good MTBF rating of 1,200,000 h, will result in an MTBF for the array of 300,000 h—equivalent to an average consumer drive. With

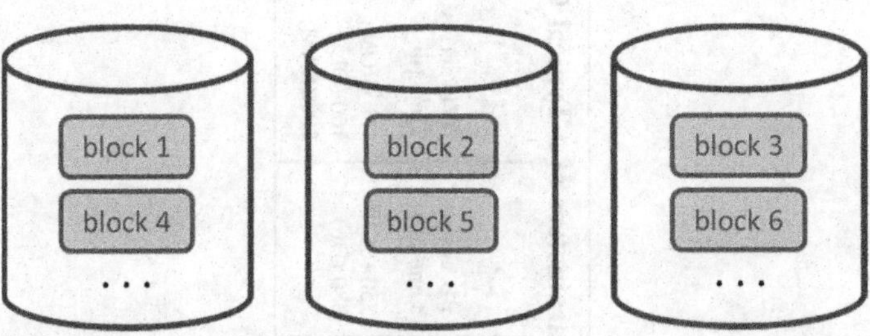

FIGURE 17.14

RAID 0 data layout.

independent controllers, data on the drive may be accessed concurrently, providing increased read and write bandwidths in proportion to the number of drives:

$$B_{R_0} = d \cdot B_{R_D}$$

$$B_{W_0} = d \cdot B_{W_D}$$

where B_{R_D} and B_{W_D} are respectively read and write bandwidths of a single drive.

Finally, the storage capacity of the whole array is a sum of the component drive capacities:

$$C_0 = d \cdot C_D$$

where C_D is the capacity of a single drive.

17.4.1.2 RAID 1: Mirroring

RAID 1 is the lowest RAID level supporting data protection (Fig. 17.15). This is accomplished by storing replicas of used data blocks that reside on the primary data drive on all other drives in the array (data mirroring). While there is no upper limit on the number of drives arranged in this fashion, typical installations use just one redundant drive (mirror) in addition to the primary drive. Hence the number of data disks is fixed at $d = 1$; assuming a general case with p mirror drives, a RAID 1 array can tolerate up to p concurrent drive failures without data loss. It is worthy of note that read accesses can take advantage of all I/O devices to issue concurrent requests, thus effectively matching the throughput of RAID 0 with the equivalent number of devices. Write operations, however, need to store data replicas on all mirror drives in addition to the "regular" data drive, effectively achieving the write throughput equivalent of a single drive. The resulting formulae are:

$$d = 1, \ p \geq 1$$

$$B_{R_1} = (p + 1) \cdot B_{R_D}$$

$$B_{W_1} = B_{W_D}$$

$$C_1 = C_D$$

Due to its simplicity, mirroring is frequently used by both hardware and software RAID implementations, but its biggest drawback is 50% (or higher) storage overhead.

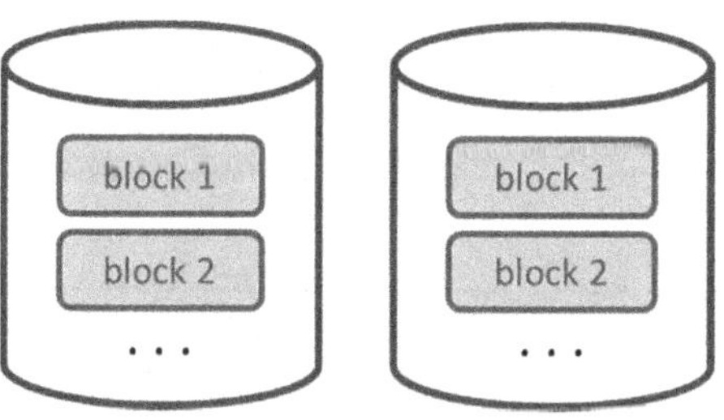

FIGURE 17.15

RAID 1 data layout.

17.4.1.3 RAID 2: Bit-Level Striping With Hamming Code

RAID 2 attempted to reduce spatial overheads caused by data mirroring by selecting a more efficient data protection code. Hamming code uses $p \geq 2$ code bits to protect each group of $d = 2^p - p - 1$ data bits against single bit errors, hence attaining $(2^p - p - 1)/(2^p - 1)$ efficiency or *code rate*. A RAID 2 array consists of *d* data drives and *p* parity (protection bits are calculated as parity for selected bits in the entire bit-stripe) drives. The minimum configuration consists of two parity drives and one data drive, although it has poor storage efficiency of 1/3; the efficiency vastly improves for larger ensembles. The drives have synchronized spindles, ensuring lock-step update and retrieval of each bit in individual stripes (denoted as a and b in Fig. 17.16). This arrangement is able to recover from a single device failure. Since hamming code can pinpoint the position of the erroneous bit in each stripe, RAID 2 is capable of detecting silent drive malfunctions in which the affected device may appear to work but returns invalid data. This property may also be used to correct occasional data errors on the fly due to the nonzero probability of uncorrectable read errors returned by individual disks. Due to the implementation complexity requiring specialized hardware controllers, RAID 2 is no longer used in practice. Its performance characteristic strongly depends on the implementation details, and hence is not analyzed here.

$$d = 2^p - p - 1, \quad p \geq 2$$
$$C_2 = d \cdot C_D$$

17.4.1.4 RAID 3: Byte-Level Striping With Dedicated Parity

RAID 3 further decreases the required number of redundant drives in the assembly. Unlike RAID 2, it performs byte-level striping. Just one extra drive ($p = 1$) is used to store the parity value for all bytes in the same stripe (Fig. 17.17). Since the parity alone cannot be used to identify a broken drive, RAID 3 recovery is activated after one of the devices overtly fails. In that case, the missing information (assuming the failed drive was not the parity drive) is reconstructed from parity information and the

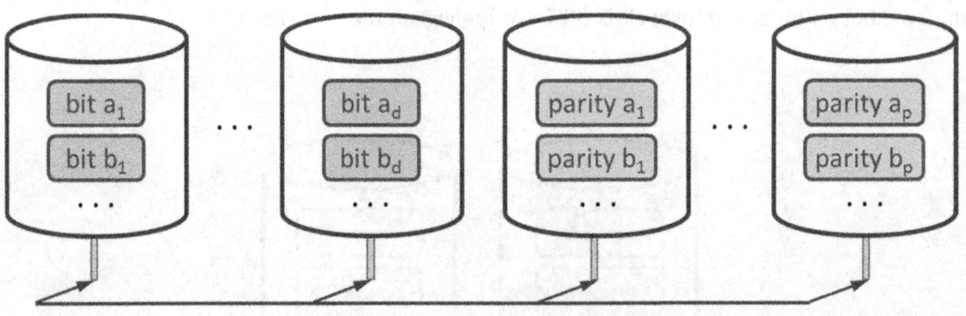

FIGURE 17.16

RAID 2 data layout.

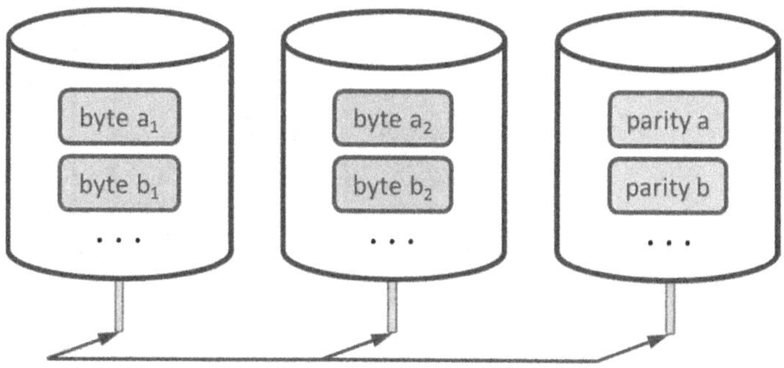

FIGURE 17.17

RAID 3 data layout.

remaining byte values in the corresponding stripe. Operation at byte granularity forced synchronized disk spindle control, similar to RAID 2. As RAID 3 does not offer specific advantages over higher RAID levels and requires specialized hardware support to work, it too was phased out from common usage. RAID 3 achieves good large-volume sequential read and write performance (see below), but lags for small or multiple simultaneous requests.

$$d \geq 2, \quad p = 1$$

$$B_{R_3} = d \cdot B_{R_D}$$

$$B_{W_3} = d \cdot B_{W_D}$$

$$C_3 = d \cdot C_D$$

17.4.1.5 RAID 4: Block-Level Striping With Dedicated Parity

RAID 4 (Fig. 17.18) eschews the fine-granularity synchronization of RAID 3, instead performing block-level striping across all data devices much like RAID 0. For recovery, one parity drive is used; its function is similar to the parity drive in RAID 3 except that parity information is computed on a per block basis. The minimum configuration consists of three devices (two data drives, one parity drive). The large request performance is good, since it can be satisfied with sequential access to multiple blocks on each data drive. Since the drives do not have to be synchronized, simultaneous small requests may be distributed over multiple devices, yielding improved IOPS figures.

$$d \geq 2, \quad p = 1$$

$$B_{R_4} = d \cdot B_{R_D}$$

$$B_{W_4} = d \cdot B_{W_D}$$

$$C_4 = d \cdot C_D$$

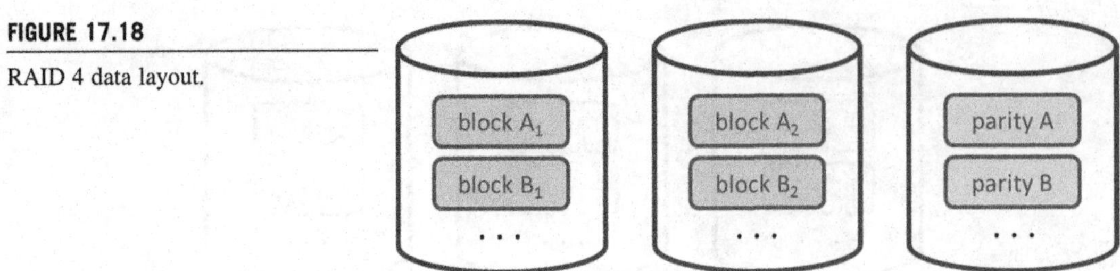

FIGURE 17.18

RAID 4 data layout.

17.4.1.6 RAID 5: Block-Level Striping With Single Distributed Parity

RAID 5 is one of the most commonly employed data protection schemes (Fig. 17.19). It shares many similarities with RAID 4 in terms of parity computation, access granularity, minimum configuration, and vulnerability to failures. The main difference is that there is no dedicated parity drive: the parity blocks are distributed in round-robin fashion across all participating devices. This modification enables the system to achieve high read bandwidths, effectively matching those of RAID 0 with an equal number of disks. The main issue of RAID 5 storage is its high vulnerability in a degraded state (i.e., after it has suffered drive failure). Even if the replacement drive is quickly furnished, the rebuild process for the whole array may take several hours. During that time the component drives are accessed at close to full bandwidth, exposing the remaining devices to increased stress levels. A second device malfunction during that time may effectively destroy the nonrebuilt fraction of data stored in the array.

$$d \geq 2, \quad p = 1$$

$$B_{R_5} = (d+1) \cdot B_{R_D}$$

$$B_{W_5} = d \cdot B_{W_D}$$

$$C_5 = d \cdot C_D$$

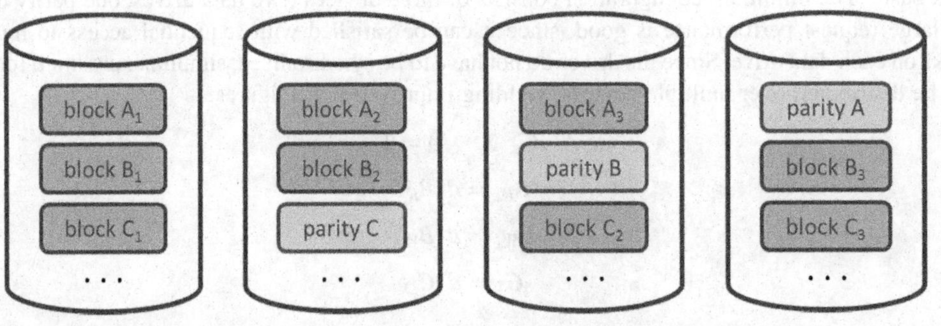

FIGURE 17.19

RAID 5 data layout.

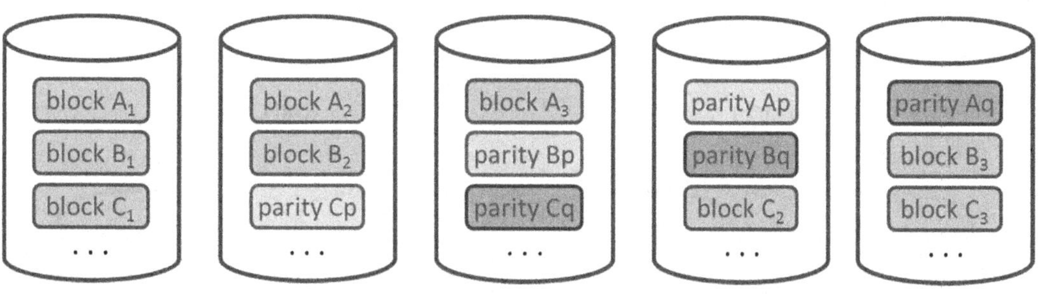

FIGURE 17.20

RAID 6 data layout.

17.4.1.7 RAID 6: Block-Level Striping With Dual Distributed Parity

To maintain array operation in a degraded state with no more than two failed drives, RAID 6 associates two parity drives with each group of data drives. Much like RAID 5, the parity blocks are distributed over all drives in the array. Parity information, denoted in Fig. 17.20 by indexes p and q, must be computed using different methods, e.g., conventional bitwise XOR on the original contents of the stripe and XOR on the stripe contents transformed by an irreducible binary polynomial selected using the Galois field [16] theory. Following a single drive failure, the array may be reconstructed using conventional parity, which is fast to compute. A double fault requires usage of both parity blocks per stripe or, if the simple parity block was stored on the faulty drive, the missing data may be recomputed from the available data blocks and the secondary parity information. The calculation of secondary parity is more involved, and may benefit from hardware implementation.

$$d \geq 2, \quad p = 2$$

$$B_{R_6} = (d+2) \cdot B_{R_D}$$

$$B_{W_6} = d \cdot B_{W_D}$$

$$C_6 = d \cdot C_D$$

17.4.1.8 Hybrid RAID Variants

The most common hybrid RAID configurations are illustrated in Fig. 17.21. RAID 10, also denoted RAID 1+0, combines data mirroring at a lower level and striping at a higher level. This provides the benefits of a simple-to-implement redundancy scheme (mirroring) with improved data access performance due to striping. The main drawback is the low storage utilization of 50%. The configuration shown in Fig. 17.21 can tolerate two drive failures (one per mirror group). This version of RAID is commonly implemented in hardware controllers, including low-cost solutions embedded in motherboard firmware. A variant of RAID 10 that improves storage utilization replaces the mirroring with RAID 5 at the lowest level, and is known as RAID 50. As the smallest number of devices supported by RAID 5 is three, the minimum layout of RAID 50 consists of six devices. In comparison to conventional RAID 5 with six devices, striping improves the write throughput, while the ability to tolerate one fault per redundancy group makes this arrangement substantially more resilient. Of course, either

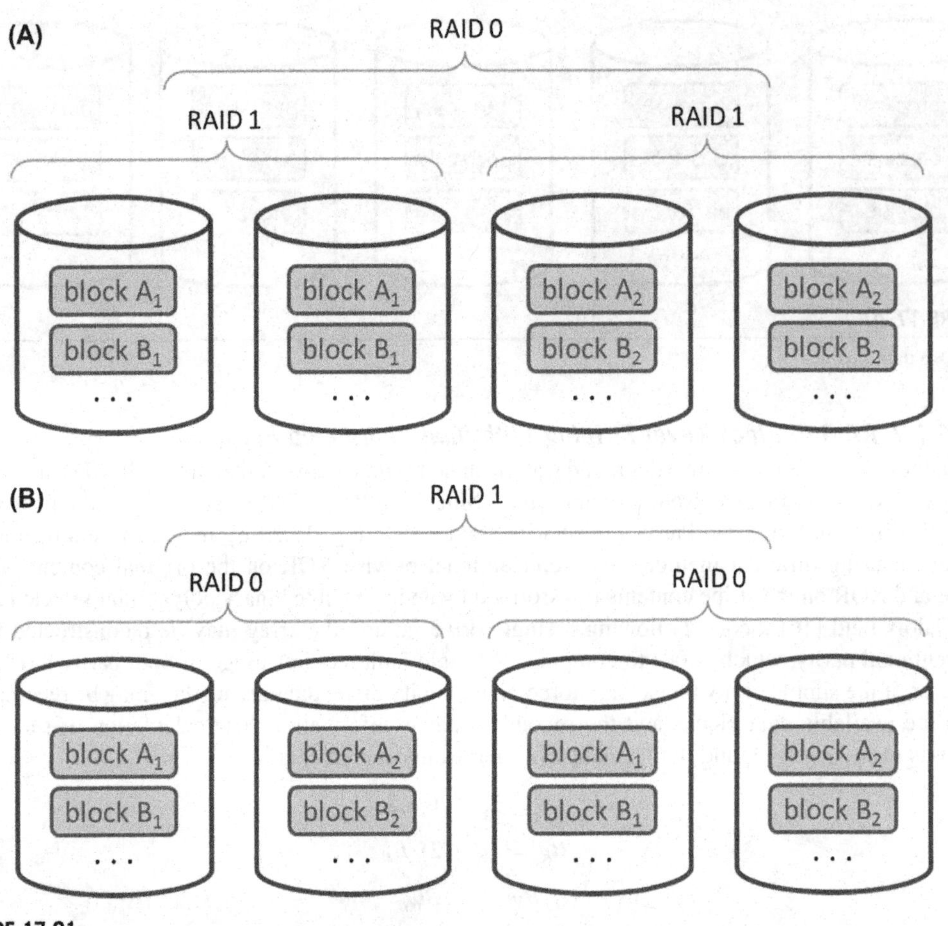

FIGURE 17.21

Diagram of data distribution: (A) RAID 10 (stripe of mirrors) and (B) RAID 01 (mirror of stripes).

RAID x0 configuration may include more than two components per stripe for further bandwidth boost, albeit at the cost of additional drives.

RAID 01 (or 0+1) has the same storage utilization, capacity, and access performance as RAID 10 with an equivalent number of mirrors and stripe units. However, while RAID 10 is still able to operate with one failed drive per mirror group, in RAID 01 loss of single drive equals the loss of the entire stripe. This has dramatic consequences for rebuild performance: RAID 10 can accomplish this by simply copying the contents of the remaining drive in its mirror group without disturbing other components of the array, while RAID 01 must pull the data from another functional mirror, interfering with its regular operation. RAID 01 has, however, practical applications when portions of the array are distributed over a network. Having a fully functional local RAID 0 setup is more important in the event of network outage than a mirror containing partial data.

Since the timely completion of array rebuild is often critical to stored data integrity, many RAID implementations include hot spares: idle drives that are connected to the controller, but do not actively share any part of the data. When a disk failure occurs, the controller may automatically switch to the replacement drive and start repopulating the array without having to wait for the system administrator. The failed drive may be pulled and replaced later at the operator's convenience.

Selection of component drives for the array has to be performed with special care. Good practice calls for verification that devices come from different fabrication batches to minimize the probability of correlated failures. Since malfunctions may also be related to other connected devices, avoiding sharing of critical components, such as power supplies, may prevent some failure modes. RAID-compatible drives typically support time-limited error recovery, which constrains the time spent by the drive on bad-sector recovery to prevent it from being marked by the RAID controller as unresponsive or faulty.

With high performance multicore processors being a common component of a node, many RAID modes do not require a specialized hardware controller to achieve good performance. Operating systems frequently offer optimized support for common levels (such as RAID 0, 1, 5, 6, and their hybrids) and sometimes nonstandard levels that nevertheless may provide well-performing redundant storage with less common drive counts and configurations. Software implementations may expose more configuration parameters, thus I/O benchmarking with different options is crucial to extracting maximum performance. They may, however, suffer from problems that are avoided by correctly designed hardware controllers; one such issue is the "write hole" caused by a system crash (e.g., due to power blackout) leaving parity information in an inconsistent state with the data on drives. Some file systems, such as ZFS developed by Sun Microsystems, support RAID-like data striping and protection without being vulnerable to this issue. Harnessing OS support to manage data integrity has additional benefits. Neither hardware controllers nor low-level software implementations are aware which portions of disk store the actual information, so upon failure the recovery algorithms must perform verification of data consistency on the entire drive, or at least the impaired partition. The same process guided by a file system's internal data structures may be far more efficient and focus only on the relevant areas of the disk. Prioritization is also possible, so the most critical file system metadata is recovered first. Since array rebuild places the system in a particularly vulnerable state, minimizing its duration additionally lowers the chances of unrecoverable failures.

17.4.2 STORAGE AREA NETWORKS

A storage area networks (SAN) provides a block-level storage abstraction over common networks (Fig. 17.22). Its purpose is to enable access to shared storage devices for multiple entities, including virtualized server pools or other hosts (e.g., related to management and monitoring infrastructure) attached to a common network. The shared storage devices may include HDDs or SSDs, optical jukeboxes, and tape silos. Clients connected to a correctly implemented SAN have an illusion of directly communicating with the attached storage devices, extracting close to the full available device bandwidth.

SANs offer many benefits to system administrators. Physical separation of servers and storage enables fast and independent replacement of failed components. Scaling in the number of storage devices as well as servers is usually easily accomplished. Application servers may directly boot from the attached drives, which minimizes the configuration time for newly added or replaced servers. Since

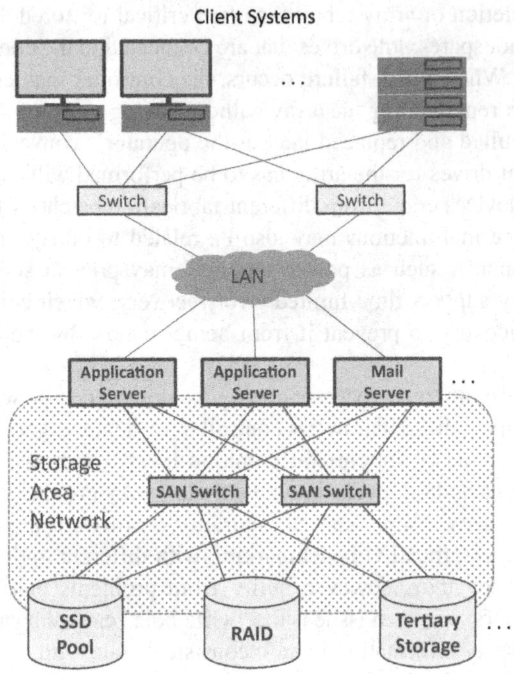

FIGURE 17.22

Example configuration of a storage area network.

the connecting network can span a large distance, significantly exceeding the length of interface link attaching individual storage devices, SANs are key to efficient disaster recovery. Storage contents can be replicated to different physical locations, with fast synchronization mechanisms already in place should major faults occur. SANs are frequently configured with multiple switches and redundant paths for increased reliability.

A SAN encapsulates lower-level access protocols to storage devices, such as SCSI (small computer system interface), in higher-level network protocols, primarily Ethernet, InfiniBand, and Fibre Channel (FC). The latter frequently utilizes optical fiber for connectivity, with communication rates between 1 and 128 Gbps. FC supports multiple topologies, including point to point, arbitrated loop, and switched fabric. Even though it has a reputation for being expensive and difficult to manage, it is often the preferred choice for SAN implementation. One of its main advantages is the asynchronous protocol design that is able to handle large numbers of data packets in a heavily loaded network. Different implementations of SANs utilize protocols that best fit the class of deployed network and low-level interfaces used by mass-storage devices. The number of combinations is quite large, but the dominant variants include FCP (Fibre Channel Protocol that encapsulates SCSI packets over FC), FCoE (Fibre Channel over Ethernet), HyperSCSI (SCSI over Ethernet), iFCP (FCP over IP), iSCSI (SCSI over Transmission Control Protocol/Internet Protocol (TCP/IP)), iSER (iSCSI extensions for RDMA in the InfiniBand network), SRP (a simpler SCSI RDMA protocol for transmitting SCSI over InfiniBand), AoE (ATA over Ethernet), and FICON (Enterprise Systems Connection over FC, used by mainframe machines).

17.4.3 NETWORK ATTACHED STORAGE

Network attached storage (NAS) is a common component of supercomputing installations. It provides centralized shared storage capability, frequently with very large capacity, to multiple hosts, specifically including compute and login nodes. While SANs provide shared access to mass storage at the device level, NAS operates at file-system level. The accessing clients use specifically designed libraries or kernel extensions to import data volumes hosted by NAS servers. Remote data shares may be mounted on the client side to provide practically identical application programming interfaces to those exposed by local file systems, such as Portable Operating System Interface I/O. The contents of remote data shares may be then accessed using standard utilities and libraries that have been developed to support "regular" files, effectively making the fact that the communication with the server and the data transfer are performed over the network completely transparent to the application.

NAS implementations utilize a handful of network file system protocols. The commonly used ones include Server Message Block (SMB), originally developed by IBM and Microsoft, Common Internet File System (CIFS), which is a more feature-rich version of SMB, Apple Filing Protocol (AFP), a proprietary protocol used by Apple File Service, and Network File System (NFS), which originated at Sun Microsystems. While the first two are usually found in Microsoft DOS and Windows-based environments, AFP is restricted to Apple products and NFS is broadly employed in the Unix world, including Linux. NFS is an open standard defined in the Internet Engineering Task Force/Internet Society Request for Comments and has open-source implementations. SMB functionality is available on Unix-compatible platforms thanks to the open-source SMB/CIFS reimplementation known as Samba. Finally, AFP is supported by the open source Netatalk project. All these protocols rely on TCP/IP for connectivity, although some SMB and NFS variants are capable of datagram-based communication (User Datagram Protocol).

A high performance NAS server, depicted in Fig. 17.23, derives from the architecture of a conventional compute node. The primary differences are possible inclusion of multiple network adapters to provide the necessary data bandwidth to clients and a substantially expanded storage pool. The latter usually requires multiple controller boards to provide the required number of ports for connecting the

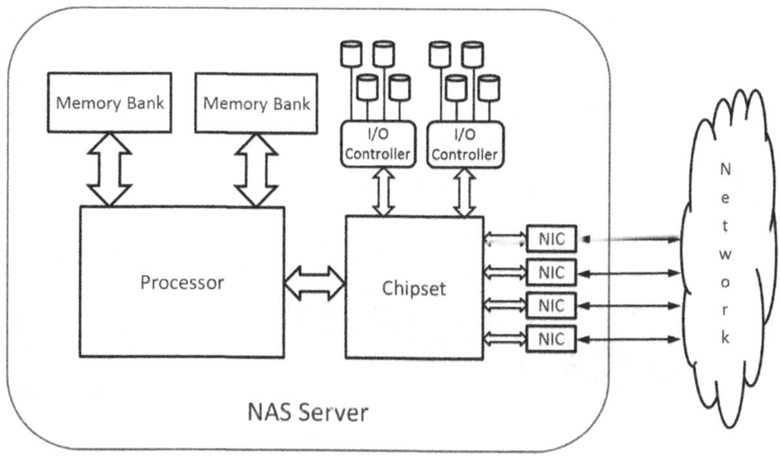

FIGURE 17.23

Simplified architecture of NAS server.

storage devices and optionally to incorporate hardware-level data protection, such as RAID. The server should have a sufficiently large memory pool to be able to accommodate a large number of outstanding I/O requests and efficiently buffer data. Due to the increased power draw caused by the large storage pool, a NAS server should also be equipped with redundant power supplies of appropriate rating and make allowance for sufficient case ventilation to evacuate the generated heat. Since a single server will eventually hit a performance barrier, a clustered NAS may be considered to enable capacity scaling. A clustered NAS takes advantage of distributed (Ceph, AFS, GFS, and others) or parallel (GPFS, Lustre, PANFS, OrangeFS, PVFS, and others) file systems to provide an abstraction of a single logical file system comprising all storage devices while enabling high-bandwidth access to file data and load distribution across the component servers.

17.4.4 TERTIARY STORAGE

Tertiary storage comprises high-capacity data archives designed to incorporate vast numbers of removable media, such as tapes or optical discs. The removable media are normally not stored in suitable drives but held in specially arranged retention slots, shelves, or carousels in an offline state. A tertiary storage platform may be perceived as a specialized type of NAS that uses additional robotic mechanisms to transfer media between their long-term storage locations and available drives without human intervention. To fulfill a client access request, a separate database that maintains the catalogue of archive contents must be consulted. As the tape library or optical jukebox cannot handle a large number of concurrent requests (there is only a limited number of tape or optical drives which operate at nominal data rates per device), the archive contents are typically copied to a data cache, for example a regular NAS server. Clients may then access the data at high speeds and possibly in parallel. The retrieved content is retained in the cache for as long as it is needed or until it is retired as an effect of the application of relevant data retention policies. Tertiary storage also performs periodic (or other policy-managed) scans of stored media to detect signs of content decay and possibly activate recovery procedures. Examples of two high-capacity tertiary storage systems, a tape library and an optical jukebox, are shown in Fig. 17.24 and compared in Table 17.6.

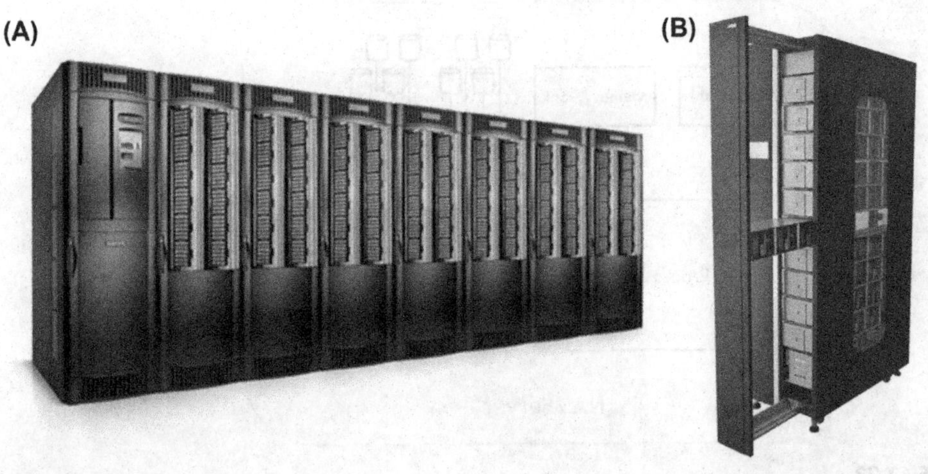

FIGURE 17.24

Tertiary storage platforms: (A) Quantum tape library, (B) BluRay optical jukebox.

Table 17.6 Properties of Selected High-Capacity Tertiary Storage Systems

Manufacturer	Product	Maximum Capacity (TB)	Media Slots	Media Type	Interface	Power
Quantum	Scalar i6000 tape library	180,090	12,006	LTO-7 cartridge	8 Gbps Fibre Channel	24 kVA
HIT Storage	HMS-5175 BluRay library	175	1750	100 GB BDTL disc	1 Gbps Ethernet	

17.5 SUMMARY AND OUTCOMES OF CHAPTER 17

- Mass storage enables computational state retention to be consistent between power cycles of the machine.
- The majority of storage systems utilize four main types of mass-storage devices: HDDs, SSDs, magnetic tapes, and optical storage. Although they serve largely the same purpose, they substantially differ in the underlying physical phenomena used to implement data retention as well their operational characteristics and cost.
- The storage hierarchy is subdivided into four levels that differ in access latency and supported data bandwidth, with latencies increasing and effective transfer bandwidth dropping when moving away from the top level of the hierarchy.
- Primary storage comprises system memories, caches, and CPU register sets.
- Secondary storage is the first level that leverages mass-storage devices. Normally, CPUs cannot directly access the secondary (or higher-level) storage and therefore transfers of data between the primary and secondary storage have to be mediated by the OS and computer chipset.
- Secondary storage capacity grew 11 orders of magnitude between the 1940s and 2016. Device I/O bandwidth advanced six orders of magnitude over the same period.
- The most commonly used technology in the secondary storage tier is HDDs, which offer the industry's best cost per unit of storage coupled with satisfactory reliability.
- Redundant array of independent disks (RAID) attempts to address reliability issues of conventional mass-storage devices.
- Tertiary storage is distinguished from secondary storage in that it usually involves large collections of storage media or storage devices which are nominally in an inaccessible or powered-off state, but may be reasonably quickly enabled for online use.
- Tertiary storage comprises high-capacity data archives designed to incorporate vast numbers of removable media, such as tapes or optical discs.
- Latency remains one of the biggest performance bottlenecks plaguing most of the I/O devices in use today.
- SANs provide a block-level storage abstraction over a common network. Their purpose is to enable access to shared storage devices for multiple entities, including virtualized server pools or other hosts attached to a common network. The shared storage devices may include HDDs and SSDs, optical jukeboxes, and tape silos.

- Network attached storage is a common component of supercomputing installations. It provides centralized shared storage capability, frequently with a very large capacity, to multiple hosts, specifically including compute and login nodes.

17.6 QUESTIONS AND PROBLEMS

1. What are the main storage-related challenges presented by large HPC systems? Elaborate.
2. Identify parameters the values of which may be used to classify an arbitrary HDD to one of the market segment categories mentioned in the last column of Table 17.1.
3. Your product development team has been tasked with design and implementation of an in-flight entertainment system for a large airliner. Your responsibility is to select a suitable lightweight storage device from several technologies discussed in the chapter. Justify your choice taking into account (1) cost, (2) reliability of operation, (3) required storage capacity, and (4) performance. When considering your choices, be mindful of the target operating environment for the system.
4. A 4096-node cluster runs large-scale simulations that are checkpointed every 2 h using burst buffers for intermediate I/O storage. The nodes are equipped with 64 GB memory each and the ratio of nodes to burst buffers is 16:1. Calculate:
   a. the minimum required capacity of each burst buffer to keep the checkpoint phase as short as possible
   b. the duration of a large simulation before device failures appear, given that the TBW metric of each burst buffer is 400.
5. A RAID6 system uses eight 4 TB drives, including the minimum required number of parity drives. Calculate the effective read and write data throughput for the array. What is its effective data capacity? How many drives would be needed to assemble a RAID10 system of equivalent capacity? How would the data throughputs change?
6. SAN and NAS are similarly sounding acronyms that may confuse novices in the field. What are the differences and advantages of each over the other? Provide primary examples of their application.
7. A particle detector generates data streams requiring an aggregate bandwidth of 4 TB/s in bursts of up to 1 min long. The streams are analyzed by a 2048-node system that extracts events of interest and compresses them, reducing the data volume to 1/100th of the original size. The events of interest are then archived on a dedicated robotic tape storage using LTO-7 tapes at a sustained rate of 250 MB/s per deck. Given that experiments (each producing a single burst of data) are performed at 1 h intervals and the tape change overhead is factored into sustained storage bandwidth, answer the following.
   a. How many tape decks working in parallel are necessary to accommodate the extracted event data without forced interruptions to the experiment schedule or additional intermediate data buffers?
   b. If the capacity of a tape cartridge is 6 TB, how many tapes are required to provide data storage for experiments performed over the span of 1 year? What is the estimated shelf volume required to archive all cartridges written in 1 year if the dimensions of a single cartridge are 102 mm × 105 mm × 21 mm?

c. Assuming that data processing requires a negligible amount of memory in addition to that needed to hold the input data, how much DRAM (in powers of 2) must each node be equipped with to avoid the use of intermediate data buffers?

REFERENCES

[1] Internet2 Home, 2017 [Online]. Available: http://www.internet2.edu.

[2] Cray XC40 DataWarp I/O Applications Accelerator, Cray Inc., 2014 [Online]. Available: http://www.cray.com/sites/default/files/resources/CrayXC40-DataWarp.pdf.

[3] B. Alverson, E. Froese, L. Kaplan, D. Roweth, Cray XC Series Network, 2012. WP-Aries01−1112.

[4] IBM Corp., RAMAC, The First Magnetic Hard Disk, [Online]. Available: http://www-03.ibm.com/ibm/history/ibm100/us/en/icons/ramac/.

[5] IBM 62GV/STC 8800 Super Disk, Wiki foundry, [Online]. Available: http://chmhdd.wikifoundry.com/page/IBM+62GV+%2F+STC+8800+Super+Disk.

[6] Computer History Museum, Seagate ST-506, [Online]. Available: http://s3.computerhistory.org/groups/ds-seagate-st-506.pdf.

[7] G.D. Forney Jr., Maximum-likelihood sequence estimation of digital sequences in the presence of inter-symbol interference, IEEE Transactions on Information Theory 18 (3) (1972).

[8] G. Binasch, P. Gruenberg, F. Saurenbach, W. Zinn, Enhanced magnetoresistance in layered magnetic structures with antiferromagnetic interlayer exchange, Physical Review B 39 (7) (1989) 4828−4830.

[9] A.J. Viterbi, Error bounds for convolutional codes and an asymptotically optimum decoding algorithm, IEEE Transactions on Information Theory 13 (2) (1967) 260−269.

[10] E. Eleftheriou, W. Hirt, Noise-predictive maximum-likelihood (NPML) detection for the magnetic recording channel, in: IEEE International Conference on Communications ICC'96, Dallas, TX, USA, 1996.

[11] International Committee for Information Technology Standards, 4.21 self-monitoring, analysis, and reporting technology (smart) feature set, in: Information Technology − AT Attachment 8-ATA/ATAPI Command Set (ATA8-ACS), T13/1699-D Revision 6a, American National Standards Institute, Washington, DC, USA, 2008.

[12] R.C. Bose, D.K. Ray-Chaudhuri, On a class of error correcting binary group codes, Information and Control 3 (1) (1960) 68−79.

[13] K.A. Immink, J.G. Nijboer, H. Ogawa, K. Odaka, Method of Coding Binary Data, USA Patent US 4501000 A, July 27, 1981.

[14] K. Odaka, Y. Sako, I. Iwamoto, T. Doi, L.B. Vries, Error Correctable Data Transmission Method, USA Patent US4413340 (A), November 1, 1983.

[15] The Library of Congress, National Institute of Standards and Technology, Optical Disc Longevity Study, Technology Administration, US Dept. of Commerce, 2007.

[16] H.M. Edwards, Galois Theory, Springer-Verlag, 1984.

CHAPTER

FILE SYSTEMS

18

CHAPTER OUTLINE

18.1 ROLE AND FUNCTION OF FILE SYSTEMS

The mass-storage devices discussed in Chapter 17 use only a limited number of data-access interfaces. They are closely related to the low-level protocols used for data transfers between the device and the system's memory, and to the physical data layout and storage partitioning permitted by the device. The stored data may only be accessed at predefined granularity dependent on the particular device, namely at the level of physical *blocks* (occasionally also referred to as *records* or *sectors*) that typically vary in

High Performance Computing. https://doi.org/10.1016/B978-0-12-420158-3.00018-6

size from 512 bytes to as much as 16 KB. Carrying out small modifications to stored data or appending information to it in smaller than block-sized amounts may require a sequence of multiple read and write operations. Such direct data accesses necessitate correct calculation of the physical addresses of relevant blocks. This computation in some cases may involve intrinsic parameters describing the storage geometry implemented by the device, such as the now-obsolete cylinder-head-sector schema utilized by older hard-disk drives. As many modern storage appliances in tandem with their operating system (OS) drivers attempt to hide the details of translation of logical block addresses to physical, device-specific locations as well as the remapping of damaged blocks, they provide only very limited means of keeping track of the allocation of the device's storage space or higher-level content management of utilized blocks. Furthermore, mass storage with asymmetric performance or protocol structures for different operation types, such as reading from and writing to optical discs, may require different strategies and scheduling to support these operations efficiently, placing the burden of encoding the related control algorithms and heuristics on the application writer. Even though direct access to the physical medium is on occasion necessary to extract a predictable level of performance from a storage device or ensure strict control of data state replication in some applications (virtual memory swap space, some database implementations), it is far too inconvenient for general use in multitasking and multiuser environments.

File systems provide an abstraction that addresses these issues and adds other usability and convenience features, including storage space management and organization, a consistent programming interface that is portable and mostly independent from the underlying mass-storage device types, and extensions that use functions of other system components through the same application programming interface (API). To achieve good performance and coordinate access to shared physical resources from multiple programs issued by multiple users, the file system code is usually integrated with the OS. As is explained in Section 18.2, certain elements of the file system programming interface may be also implemented at the runtime-system level, both to provide additional features and for efficiency. Additional storage is needed for *metadata*, or information that indicates various attributes of stored datasets, comprises file system data structures, and is used to manage the allocation of physical storage blocks. Because of that, the effective space available on a mass-storage device that implements a file system will typically be reduced by a few percent compared to its raw capacity. The most notable features commonly supported by file systems are as follows:

- *Organization.* The file system imposes a hierarchical layout using *directories* and *files* as its primary components. Directories serve as containers for other directories and files, while the files comprise the actual datasets written to or read from the mass storage. File systems rarely impose limitations on what kinds of information may be stored inside files; this is usually decided by the applications creating and accessing files. In many cases additional conventions and even software are required to decipher the actual contents of files, which otherwise may be viewed only as anonymous byte streams. Depending on the file system, file size is usually limited to a large value that rarely interferes with the practical aspects of file access. In most modern disk or solid-state device (SSD) file systems, that value is on the order of tens or hundreds of terabytes. Similarly, the directory space may have constraints, such as the maximum number of entries (files or directories) per directory it can accommodate, and possibly the total number of all directories and files coexisting in a single file system.

- *Namespace*. One of the most important usability aspects of a file system is the support of a naming scheme independent of the system architecture for stored information. All logical names of files and directories are expressed in the form of *paths*, or multicomponent strings in which each element names the containing directory ordered from the topmost in the hierarchy to the lowest level at the path's leaf component (which may be either a file or directory). Thus each file system component is uniquely identified by its symbolic name. While some details of path construction and how many roots, i.e., top-level hierarchy entry points, are supported differ between the individual file systems, the overall naming scheme conforms to the same common model across many implementations. One of the frequently used conventions to interpret the file contents relies on so-called *extensions*: a short suffix added to the file name and separated from it by an agreed character, typically a period. File system namespaces often support additional constructs, for example *links* that act as aliases for storable components. This permits the creation of alternative traversal paths that are not confined to the tree hierarchy and in some variants may even cross the file system boundary.
- *Metadata*. Due to the shared nature of file systems, access to certain datasets must be constrained to only preapproved users in the system. In Unix this is traditionally arranged at the level of the file or directory owner, a specific user group, and "others" (collectively all users known to the system). In each of these categories the access rights may be individually enabled or revoked for reading, writing, and executing a specific file system entry. Unix and compatible file systems may also specify additional flags, such as "sticky bits" (restricting file deletion only to the actual owner), *setuid* and *setgid* flags that elevate the effective execution privileges to those of the file's owner, or a flag that restricts the file's execution to specific users. Some implementations also support more fine-grained access schemes, such as access control lists (ACLs). They are more flexible than the default owner/group/others categories in that arbitrary permissions can be assigned to arbitrary users, albeit at the cost of additional space that may be required to store the list. Metadata are commonly used to describe other properties of files, most notably their size. Even though storage is allocated in blocks, file size is tracked with byte resolution (the last block of a file may be partially filled). File systems may combine several small files into a single block to conserve storage space. Note that large amounts of metadata remain opaque to the user, including the actual device block numbers allocated to the file as well as internal data structures that describe more complicated layouts, such as large files or files with "holes".
- *Programming interface (API)*. From the user's perspective, one of the fundamental operational properties of a file system is to permit creation of, writing to, and reading back the contents of files. This is accomplished through library calls that internally invoke the lower-level system functions. The files are identified by their symbolic names (paths) before the actual data access functions are enabled. This verifies that the target file exists and may be accessed by the requestor, and initializes the necessary data structures for access. It also relies on shorter and uniform file handles, eliminating the need to pass potentially highly variable file names to the data access functions. The API also allows specification of some metadata elements when new files are created. Besides file data access, the programming interface supports the manipulation of the storage hierarchy, such as directory traversal, file and subdirectory deletion, and creation of new subdirectories and links.

- *Storage space management.* As all physical devices have explicit capacity limits, the file system must carefully monitor the use of space in the storage medium, which may be shared potentially between millions of files and directories. Additionally, space for newly created files should be allocated in a way that ensures good access performance for the specific device type. Thus for standard hard-disk drives the file system typically strives to reserve the space for a file in continuous segments that reside on the same platter and cylinder, since sequential access offers the highest effective data bandwidth and latency. However, as the device becomes full, allocation in contiguous chunks may become more and more difficult (the available space becomes fragmented). Many modern file systems implement on-the-fly defragmentation algorithms, so performance degradation is not noticeable until the available capacity drops below a few percent (or even less in some cases). Other file systems may require explicit online or offline defragmentation to restore performance.
- *File system mounting.* Computers frequently utilize multiple storage devices at the same time. They can be made available for use at arbitrary points in time and not only during system initialization, as some of the storage media may be removable. This is performed in a process called *mounting*, in which the hierarchy defined by the imported file system is exposed to the OS and runtime environment. In single-namespace file systems utilized by some operating systems like Unix, this requires support to expand the existing name hierarchy. In such an OS the *mount points* under which the external file systems may be made accessible can conceivably be any existing directories. After the mount operation is completed, the imported file system hierarchy replaces the original layout extending below the mount point. Multiple file systems may be mounted at the same time, including nesting.
- *Special files.* The Unix environment is commonly known for implementing the "everything is a file" abstraction. This means the file system namespace may be used to provide access to other system entities and software constructs such as raw devices, named pipes, and sockets. The latter two enable interprocess communication as long as the interacting entities agree in advance on the name and type of the communication channel. While the communication uses the same API as that applied to transfer data to and from regular files, users must take care not to exceed the internal buffer capacity. Unfortunately, the elegance of the abstraction breaks when access to advanced features or adjustment of control parameters is necessary; in such cases the much-overloaded *fcntl* and *ioctl* interfaces are invoked to access the required functionality.
- *Fault handling.* As with any physical device, mass storage suffers from random failures. A properly designed file system can minimize the impact of these faults on stored data integrity. While device-related faults can range from individual bad blocks to whole devices, this does not exhaust the possible spectrum of failures. Due to data caching in memory and the need to perform multiple low-level updates even for a single logical access operation, commonly occurring problems are aborted write operations or destruction of unwritten data in memory caused by power fluctuations or system crashes due to other reasons. The data and/or metadata stored on disk may thus be left in inconsistent state and needing to be fixed before regular operation resumes. Many file systems deal with this by scanning the contents of data structures on the storage device during bootstrap and fixing incompatible entries using a dedicated utility program

(*fsck* in Unix). Such scan operations may be significantly accelerated when using an independent *journal*, or log of file system transactions that have to be carried out. While the file system check operation is not always able to recover all the data that were misplaced during a crash, it ensures that the loss is limited only to the data transferred during the failed operation and that stored metadata are consistent.

The landscape of currently available file systems covers many instances with different features and characteristics, deployment environments, target storage devices and media, and applications. There are file systems specifically optimized for use with hard-disk drives, SSDs, flash memories, tapes, and optical media. File systems may transparently support compression to save space and encryption to protect the confidentiality of the stored information. Pseudo file systems are used to expose details related to arbitrary installed devices and system data structures using familiar semantics (such as `procfs`, `sysfs`, and `devfs` in Linux). Particularly important to high performance computing (HPC) are distributed and parallel file systems, which support multiple clients communicating with storage devices over network or computer interconnects. However, unlike storage area networks (SANs), they do not share file contents at the physical block level but implement a service layer translating and executing received requests. Not all distributed file systems can necessarily provide high performance concurrent access to the same file from multiple clients, but instead focus on supporting the shared namespace and metadata and achieving significantly better throughputs when each client operates on its own disjoint set of files. This issue is better addressed by parallel file systems, making them more suitable for supercomputing applications which may read or write various sections of the same file or file set from multiple compute nodes. Note that this mode of operation is associated with several nontrivial challenges. Firstly, a parallel file system needs to employ appropriate mechanisms to accommodate multiple storage devices by distributing the contents of files over multiple disks or SSDs (striping). This is necessary to extract the required aggregate data throughput. The stripe unit has to be carefully chosen so as not to impose too high an overhead (small blocks) and not to destroy striping benefits for smaller files (large blocks). Secondly, the file system is expected to provide the abstraction of a single server to accessors: details of the underlying architecture, physical arrangement of supporting hosts and storage devices, fault-tolerance measures, file striping parameters, and many other aspects should be hidden from users who are not interested in optimizing the input/output (I/O) performance for specific applications. A familiar file access interface (such as Portable Operating System Interface or POSIX) may be provided to reduce the learning curve for new users and facilitate application porting. Thirdly, both metadata and data have to utilize appropriate consistency protocols, since there must be no discrepancies between file contents, sizes, and other attributes when simultaneously viewed by different nodes. While multiple readers of a file can easily be accommodated, the addition of even a single writer may complicate the way information is propagated to and possibly replicated on the participating nodes. Parallel file systems may also resort to relaxing access atomicity (i.e., the guarantee that no portion of data read or written in a single call is ever modified by an overlapping preceding or subsequent access) to be able to attain reasonable data throughput rates. Finally, the governing algorithms must scale to support not only a large number of concurrent accessors, possibly extending to the total number of compute nodes in the system, but also growing storage pools.

18.2 THE ESSENTIAL POSIX FILE INTERFACE

The POSIX standard [1] describes the elements of runtime API, shells, and utilities, specifying compatibility requirements for variants of the Unix operating system. The file I/O interface is part of the specification. The necessarily limited overview presented here focuses only on a subset of data transfer functions, with a few auxiliary calls that are frequently used in parallel programs. Directory access and manipulation, link creation, file deletion, and other namespace and metadata functions are not discussed, as they are rarely invoked directly from applications but instead are typically handled by job scripts using appropriate system utilities. File access functions come in two flavors: system calls and buffered I/O. Both are described below, along with usage examples and enumeration of their semantic differences.

18.2.1 SYSTEM CALLS FOR FILE ACCESS

System calls are used to invoke OS kernel functions directly. While all system calls typically share the same generic invocation format, a thin wrapper layer is additionally provided by the runtime library for user convenience and to facilitate first-level argument checking. Since system calls incur greater overheads than regular user–space function invocation, this interface should be used to transfer larger amounts of data (several memory pages or more) per call. The interfaces described below show function arguments and the necessary "include" files, defining their prototypes and optional argument macros. Since system calls are often used to access other entities in the system, such as terminals, pipes, or sockets, only semantics related to regular file access are discussed here.

18.2.1.1 File Open and Close

```
#include <sys/stat.h>
#include <fcntl.h>

int open(const char *path, int flags, ...);
```

```
#include <unistd.h>

int close(int fd);
```

The `open` call allocates an integer *file descriptor* that shall be used in all subsequent accesses to the file whose name is specified in the `path`. The descriptor returned is the lowest integer not currently used for file access by the calling process, and identifies the kernel data structure associated with the opened file. The `flags` argument consists of just one of `O_RDONLY`, `O_WRONLY`, and `O_RDWR` for read-only, write-only, and mixed read-and-write access respectively. The access mode flag can be bitwise or-ed with the arbitrary combinations of flags listed below.

- `O_APPEND` causes initial file offset to be set to the end of file instead of its beginning.

- O_CREAT creates the file if it does not exist, and is otherwise ignored as long as O_EXCL is not set. The file is created with access rights specified in the third argument that conform to conventional owner/group/other permissions.
- O_EXCL when used together with O_CREAT will cause the call to fail if the file exists. If the flag is specified without O_CREAT, the result is undefined.
- O_TRUNC truncates the existing file to zero length if the access mode is O_WRONLY or O_RDWR. Using this flag in read-only mode produces an undefined result.

The list of supported flags in the open call is fairly extensive and permits among other uses the specification of nonblocking accesses and synchronization of write operations. The description of their exact semantics is beyond the scope of this brief overview.

A successful open call returns a nonnegative integer that is a valid file descriptor. A negative one is returned on failure and a corresponding code is set in the global errno variable. Error causes include insufficient access or file creation rights, invalid path, exceeded maximum number of simultaneously opened files in the system, and requested file creation with an exclusive flag but the target file already exists. A failed open cannot modify an existing file status or create a new file.

The opened files may be closed by passing their descriptors to the close call. This causes deallocation of the file data structure and releases the file descriptor for reuse within the calling process.

18.2.1.2 Sequential Data Access

```
#include <unistd.h>

ssize_t read(int fd, void *buf, size_t n);
ssize_t write(int fd, void *buf, size_t n);
```

The read function attempts to read at most n bytes at the current offset from the file identified by fd into a user buffer pointed to by buf. Successful invocation returns the actual number of bytes stored in the user buffer. The call may return a value less than n if the number of bytes between the current offset associated with fd and the end of the file is smaller than the requested value. Partial read interrupted by a signal may also return fewer bytes than requested. A successful call will increase the file offset by the number of bytes transferred to the user buffer and update the file access time to the system time at which the access was carried out.

A negative return value indicates an error whose cause is identified in the global variable errno. Possible error causes include the use of an invalid file descriptor, exceeding the maximum offset, and a read operation that has been interrupted by a signal without having started yet.

The write call attempts to transfer n bytes provided in the user buffer pointed to by buf to a file identified by the descriptor fd. The position at which the data are stored in the file is determined by the current value of the file offset associated with the descriptor. If the offset of the last written byte is greater than the file length, the file length will be updated to the position of the last written byte increased by one. A successful call returns the actual number of bytes written; the internal file offset is incremented by this value and file's modification and status timestamps are updated as well. If the write would exceed the maximum file size limit or medium capacity, only the portion of user buffer that can be accommodated is written. Successful file updates are immediately visible to other accessors (including other processes); "read" from file locations affected by a successful write call will return the data transferred by that call. This data will persist only as long as there is no subsequent write call issued that would overwrite the data in the same position.

Similarly to "read", the write function returns −1 on error. The error causes resemble those of "read", with the addition of writes that would exceed the maximum file size without the possibility of performing a partial data transfer.

18.2.1.3 File Offset Manipulation

```
#include <unistd.h>

off_t lseek(int fd, off_t offs, int whence);
```

The lseek call is used to modify the file offset associated with the descriptor fd. The semantics of the call depend on the value of the whence parameter. The offset is directly set to offs value if whence is SEEK_SET. If whence is SEEK_CUR, the file offset is set to the sum of the current offset value and offs. Finally, for SEEK_END the resultant offset is the length of file plus offs. Note that the file offset can be advanced to point beyond the end of file; the unwritten segments of the file will read as zeros until they are overwritten. The call returns the updated offset value (measured from the beginning of the file) in bytes.

18.2.1.4 Data Access With Explicit Offset

```
#include <unistd.h>

ssize_t pread(int fd, void *buf, size_t n, off_t offs);
ssize_t pwrite(int fd, void *buf, size_t n, off_t offs);
```

The pread and pwrite calls provide explicit offset variants of the read and write functions. They save the explicit invocation of lseek when accesses at random locations in the file need to be performed. The value of the implicit file offset associated with the descriptor fd is not modified by the calls.

18.2.1.5 File Length Adjustment

```
#include <unistd.h>

int ftruncate(int fd, off_t len);
```

The ftruncate function sets the length of file identified by fd to len; the file must be opened for writing. The result may be the effective truncation of file length, in which case the data located at and after len offset will no longer be accessible to reads or file length increase, with the appended data segment reading as zero-filled. The ftruncate function does not modify the value of the file pointer associated with the descriptor fd.
The call returns zero on success or −1 on error.

18.2.1.6 Synchronization With Storage Device

```
#include <unistd.h>

int fsync(int fd);
```

The fsync function transfers all data and metadata associated with the file identified by fd to the underlying storage device. The call blocks until all data are transferred or an error occurs. On success zero is returned, otherwise it is −1.

18.2.1.7 File Status Query

```
#include <fcntl.h>
#include <sys/stat.h>

int lstat(const char *restrict path, struct stat *restrict buf);
int fstat(int fd, struct stat *restrict buf);
```

Both calls retrieve metadata of the file system entity identified either by path (lstat) or by the opened file descriptor fd (fstat) in a status structure pointed to by buf. They return a value of zero on success and −1 otherwise. Individual metadata entries are stored in different fields of struct stat, and include among others:

- **st_size**—size of file in bytes
- **st_blksize**—size of block used by file system in I/O operations
- **st_mode**—file type "sand" mode; if set, bit flags S_IRUSR, S_IWUSR, S_IRGRP, S_IWGRP, S_IROTH, and S_IWOTH identify enabled read and write access rights for user, group, and others in the system
- **st_uid**—user ID of file owner
- **st_gid**—group ID of file owner
- **st_atim**—time of last file access
- **st_mtim**—time of last modification of the file
- **st_ctim**—last status change time.

Code 18.1 shows an example code using a system call file interface to write a number of integers to a created (or truncated) file, flush it to persistent storage, and read back a smaller section of written file.

```
#include <stdio.h>
#include <stdlib.h>
#include <unistd.h>
#include <sys/stat.h>
#include <fcntl.h>

#define BUFFER_SIZE 4096
#define HALF (BUFFER_SIZE/2)

int main(int argc, char **argv)
{
  // initialize buffer
  int wbuf[BUFFER_SIZE], i;
  for (i = 0; i < BUFFER_SIZE; i++) wbuf[i] = 2*i+1;

  // open file, write buffer contents, and flush it to the storage
  // the file is accessible (read/write) only to the creator
  int fd = open(“test_file.dat”, O_WRONLY | O_CREAT | O_TRUNC, 0600);
  int bytes = BUFFER_SIZE*sizeof(int);
  if (write(fd, wbuf, bytes) != bytes) {
    fprintf(stderr, “Error: truncated write, exiting!\n”);
    exit(1);
  }
  fsync(fd);
  close(fd);

  // retrieve the second half of the file and verify its correctness
  int rbuf[HALF];
  fd = open(“test_file.dat”, O_RDONLY);
  bytes /= 2;
  if(pread(fd, rbuf, bytes, bytes) != bytes) {
    fprintf(stderr, “Error: truncated read, exiting!\n”);
    exit(1);
  }
  close(fd);

  for (i = 0; i < HALF; i++)
    if (wbuf[i+HALF] != rbuf[i]) {
      fprintf(stderr, “Error: retrieved data is invalid!\n”);
      exit(2);
  }
  printf(“Data verified.\n”);

  return 0;
}
```

Code 18.1. Example demonstrating the use of I/O system calls to create, write, and read data from a file.

18.2.2 BUFFERED FILE I/O

Buffered file access is implemented by the Unix runtime system library, `libc`. It introduces additional data buffers in the application's address space that may improve performance if frequent operations involving small amounts of data are performed. The buffers and their control parameters are not exposed directly to the application. Whenever possible, I/O calls issued by users are satisfied by copying the data between the user buffer in the application and the internal library buffer, thus avoiding the overhead of system calls. Occasionally system calls have to be issued to access the underlying physical storage, but their cost is amortized by transferring large amounts of data between the OS kernel and library buffers either by performing read-ahead for the input stream or waiting until the internal buffer is sufficiently filled before handing it off to the kernel. This interface is also known as the *streaming* interface (and related file description structures as *streams*), since the best performance is achieved during sequential access. As the buffering layer is not exposed to the kernel, the newly written file data may not be immediately visible to other accessors of the file in the system and are also more likely to be lost in a system crash.

This interface is part of the *stdio.h* chapter of the International Organization for Standardization (ISO)/International Electrotechnical Commission (IEC) C language standard [2] and is thus far more portable than functions based on system calls.

18.2.2.1 File Open and Close

```
#include <stdio.h>

FILE *fopen(const char *restrict path, const char *restrict mode);
int fclose(FILE *stream);
```

The `fopen` call opens or creates a file identified by `path` and associates it with a stream. The first character of the mode argument determines the file access mode and may be one of the following:

- "r" opens the file for reading
- "w" creates a file or truncates the file to zero length if it already exists and opens it for writing
- "a" creates or opens a file for write access at the end of file (append mode).

The mode string may also contain a "+" character which enables access in *update* mode, or both reading and writing performed in any order. The other characteristics defined by the first character of the mode string are preserved. If the file is used in update mode, the application must ensure that input and output operations are separated by a seek call, or, in case of reads following writes, `fflush`.

A successful call to `fopen` returns a valid stream pointer, or NULL otherwise.

The opened streams may be closed using the `fclose` function. The side-effect of close operation is propagation of the contents of data buffers to the file. Invocation of `fclose` causes the `stream` to be disassociated from the underlying file independently of return status. The function returns zero on success or EOF on failure. Common error causes include exceeding the file size or offset limit while attempting to flush the buffer contents to storage, exhausting the space available on the device, and receiving a signal while executing `fclose`.

18.2.2.2 Sequential Data Access

```
#include <stdio.h>

size_t fread(void *restrict buf, size_t size, size_t n, FILE *restrict stream);
size_t fwrite(const void *restrict buf, size_t size, size_t n, FILE *restrict stream);
```

The `fread` and `fwrite` functions are stream equivalents of `read` and `write` calls. They attempt respectively to read or write an integral number of elements, `n`, each of size `size bytes`, from an opened stream `stream` by transferring them from or to the user buffer pointed to by `buf`. Both functions return the number of elements successfully transferred. The return value may be less than `n` only if the end of the file has been encountered while reading or an error has occurred during writing. The file offset associated with the stream is increased by the number of bytes successfully transferred. If an error occurs, the value of offset for the file associated with the stream is unspecified.

18.2.2.3 Offset Update and Query

```
#include <stdio.h>

int fseek(FILE *stream, long offs, int whence);
long ftell(FILE *stream);
```

The `fseek` function sets the value of the file offset for a specified `stream` in accordance with the values of `offs` and `whence` arguments. The latter can be one of `SEEK_SET`, `SEEK_CUR`, and `SEEK_END`; their interpretation is the same as for `lseek`. Upon success, `fseek` returns zero or −1 on error. `fseek` causes the yet-unwritten buffered data to be propagated to the underlying file.
The `ftell` call returns the current value of the internal file offset associated with stream `stream` measured in bytes from the start of the file. The error is indicated by −1 as a return value. Note that `ftell` fails if the current offset cannot be correctly stored in a variable of `long` type.

18.2.2.4 Buffer Flush

```
#include <stdio.h>

int fflush(FILE *stream);
```

The `fflush` function forces the unwritten data stored in a buffer associated with a `stream` opened in write or update mode to be written to the underlying file. If the stream has been opened for reading, the call will set the offset of the underlying file to the current offset position of the stream. If the `stream` is a null pointer, the function will perform the described action for all opened streams. The call returns zero on success and EOF on error.

18.2.2.5 Conversion Between Streams and File Descriptors

```
#include <stdio.h>

FILE *fdopen(int fd, const char *mode);
```

```
#include <unistd.h>

int fileno(FILE *stream);
```

On occasion it may be useful to convert between streams and file descriptors to be able to invoke alternative interface functions. For example, the stream library does not provide any calls to force data propagation to the physical storage medium; this is typically handled by kernel functions. Similarly, switching to a buffered interface may be beneficial if large numbers of fragmented sequential I/O operations are to be carried out. Thus `fdopen` accepts an open file descriptor and mode string whose meaning is the same as for the `fopen` call, and creates and returns a corresponding stream descriptor. The supplied `mode` argument has to be compatible with the access mode of the file referred to by the descriptor `fd`. The offset of the returned stream will be set to the same value as that of the opened file indicated by `fd`. A failed call returns a null pointer.
The converse operation, `fileno`, extracts the descriptor of the underlying file from the specified stream structure, or returns −1 to indicate an error.

Code 18.2 presents a converted version of a program originally listed in Code 18.1 that uses a buffered I/O interface instead of system calls. While the transformation is obvious for most I/O functions used, one detail is particularly noteworthy. Since the `fflush` call native to the `stdio` library can only push the contents of stream buffers to the kernel, the actual propagation of dirty data to storage has to be performed by a system call (`fsync`). To provide the file descriptor expected as an input argument to that call, `fileno` is used to retrieve it from the stream descriptor (line 21).

```
1 #include <stdio.h>
2 #include <stdlib.h>
3 #include <unistd.h>
4
5 #define BUFFER_SIZE 4096
6 #define HALF (BUFFER_SIZE/2)
7
8 int main(int argc, char **argv)
9 {
10  // initialize buffer
11  int wbuf[BUFFER_SIZE], i;
12  for (i = 0; i < BUFFER_SIZE; i++) wbuf[i] = 2*i+1;
13
14  // open file, write buffer contents, and flush it to the storage
15  FILE *f = fopen("test_file.dat", "w");
```

```
    size_t count = BUFFER_SIZE;
    if (fwrite(wbuf, sizeof(int), count, f) != count) {
        fprintf(stderr, "Error: truncated write, exiting!\n");
        exit(1);
    }
    fflush(f); fsync(fileno(f));
    fclose(f);

    // retrieve the second half of the file and verify its correctness
    int rbuf[HALF];
    f = fopen("test_file.dat", "r");
    count /= 2;
    fseek(f, count*sizeof(int), SEEK_SET);
    if (fread(rbuf, sizeof(int), count, f) != count) {
        fprintf(stderr, "Error: truncated read, exiting!\n");
        exit(1);
    }
    fclose(f);

    for (i = 0; i < HALF; i++)
    if (wbuf[i+HALF] != rbuf[i]) {
        fprintf(stderr, "Error: retrieved data invalid!\n");
        exit(2);
    }
    printf("Data verified.\n");

    return 0;
}
```

Code 18.2. Equivalent program to Code 18.1 that uses the streaming I/O interface.

18.3 NETWORK FILE SYSTEM

The Network File System (NFS) is one of the oldest and at the same time one of the most broadly deployed distributed file systems in computing installations. Originally conceived at Sun Microsystems in 1984, it is currently an open standard that has spurred many implementations, including several open-source versions. Its main appeal is that a regular file system with access confined to a single host can be "exported" to permit remote access to its contents (files, directories, links, etc.) from multiple client machines. There are no significant restrictions regarding the properties of the underlying file system; any POSIX-compliant file system can be accessed via NFS and in some cases (e.g., new technology file system through the Microsoft Subsystem for Unix-based Applications) even file systems with incompatible interfaces are available. The remote file system can be transparently mounted at any place in the directory hierarchy and accessed as if it was local. Earlier revisions of NFS were frequently described as *stateless* protocols, since the server did not track clients which mounted the file system or which files were in use. This has the benefit of easy recovery after failures: the client must only retry the request until the server responds, but without renegotiating the connection and causing rebuild of the preexisting state or generating a new, incompatible state. While some persistent data structures had to be introduced to alleviate certain problems, the protocol attempts to limit the additional server-side state as much as possible. The NFS requests are self-contained, which makes the protocol very efficient.

NFS services can utilize both transmission control protocol (TCP) (connection-oriented) and user datagram protocol (UDP) (datagram based) messages. At the heart of the protocol stack is support for Remote Procedure Call (RPC), which permits sending requests from clients to a remote host, invocation of a function local to the host, and propagation of returned data and operation status in reply packets. Originally based on Sun RPC implementation, it is now defined by the Open Network Computing (ONC) RPC specification [3]. RPC implementation must uniquely specify the procedure to be called on the remote end, match the response messages to original requests, and define provisions for authenticating the requestor to service and vice versa. It also handles errors caused by protocol and version mismatch, unavailability of the requested procedure on the server, and authentication failures. Due to the requirement to support hosts with different data type properties and byte order, an external data representation [4] layer is used to serialize and retrieve the call arguments and other data that are conveyed as packet payloads. To support RPC, *port mapper* services on a dedicated port 111 must be configured on the participating machines. ONC RPC was relicensed in 2009 to use the standard three-clause Berkeley Software Distribution license.

The basic architecture of NFS is illustrated in Fig. 18.1. Before users are permitted to issue any data access requests, the remote file system has to be mounted on the client host. This is accomplished by the mount program parsing the name of the NFS server and asking it to provide the handle for the

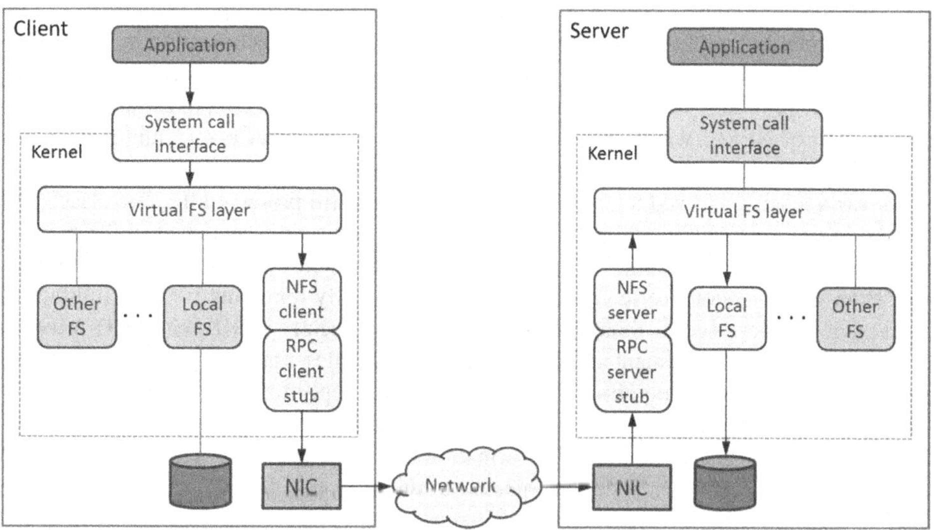

FIGURE 18.1

Architecture of Network File System and its integration with other kernel components in Linux. The arrows show the propagation of client requests to the server and remote file system. The virtual file system (VFS) layer provides an implementation-independent interface to access the underlying file system(s). The NFS client relies on the Remote Procedure Call (RPC) service to enable transparent invocation of file system functions on a remote node as requested by a client.

remote directory. If the requested directory exists and export is permitted, the server returns its handle. This causes the local kernel to access the virtual file system (VFS) layer and create a virtual node (vnode), or translation from a symbolic path to an arbitrary accessed file system object, for the remote directory. Among other things, vnodes store information about whether the target object is local or remote. Thus the subsequent open request for the remote file issued by the user finds the parent portion of the file's path that translates to vnode marked as remote, retrieves the stored server address, sends the *lookup* request to the server utilizing the RPC code stubs on client and server, and creates the opened file entry using the retrieved file attributes provided by the server. The corresponding descriptor index is then returned to the user program. The lookup procedure is used since the server does not execute a regular `open` call to avoid creation of state; as a result of using lookup a specially formed *handle* is returned that uniquely identifies the file to the server. Data access, such as read operations, proceeds similarly, except that since the client may be permitted to cache the file data locally in newer NFS revisions, a local cache lookup is performed to check if the data are available locally. NFS servers also use a simple strategy to deal with request duplication, such as that caused by packet retransmits due to network errors. This applies only to *nonidempotent* requests, i.e., those that would fail if retransmitted, such as directory or file removal. The servers maintain a *request replay cache* in which all nonidempotent requests are kept for a predetermined period; finding that a newly received request's transaction ID, source address, and port match one already in the cache will suppress its execution and cause the cached reply to be reemitted.

The first publicly released version of NFS was version 2 (NFSv2). Since it was developed in the late 1980s, it is considered dated by today's standards. For example, NFSv2 used 32-bit signed integers for file offsets, practically limiting access to the first 2 GB (gigabytes) of data per file. The size of the data payload per packet was limited to 8 KB; this, coupled with synchronous operation in which the server must complete a data write before issuing a reply to the client, caused poor write throughput. While asynchronous operation was possible, it gave rise to silent corruption of data in certain circumstances. Another problem of NFSv2 was lack of data consistency enforcement across multiple clients. File handles in this version were 32 bytes long.

NFSv3 was a much-improved revision of the protocol that still preserved the "stateless" design. It is still found in use today, although many data centers and institutions switched to the next version, which introduced some minimal state at the server to handle features that otherwise would have to be supported externally. Version 3 offered 64-bit offsets, practically removing file size limitations. The per-packet payloads increased to about 60 KB for UDP and typically 32 KB with TCP. A weak cache consistency scheme was implemented to detect changes to files made by other clients. This was achieved by injecting current file attributes into the server's reply to read and write requests; these could be used by the client to determine if its cached file data or attributes were stale. If this was the case, the client would discard the cached information and flush any dirty data to the server. While NFSv2 clients were interpreting mode flags passed to the `open` call directly to verify access permissions, NFSv3 made this a server's responsibility (using the `access` call), thus enabling correct access to file systems supporting ACLs from non-ACL-aware clients. The write performance was also improved by storing data sent in multiple data requests (while acknowledging each received packet) in memory and then committing all of them at once to disk.

The current revision of NFS was heavily influenced by the design of the Andrew File System [5] and Microsoft's Common Internet File System (CIFS) [6]. NFSv4 supports operations that inherently require server-side state, such as file locking. The new protocol is capable of byte-range locking that is lease based. Since clients may crash before releasing active locks, it forces them to stay in touch with the server for the duration of locked operations. Otherwise, the locks are revoked after preset timeout. A new approach to caching of file contents called *delegation* has been introduced. It permits a client to modify files locally in its own cache without communication with the server. Read delegation can be granted to multiple clients simultaneously, while write delegation may be permitted to only one client at a time. When a conflict is detected for the currently held delegation(s), they may be revoked using a callback mechanism. Version 4 improves overall response time by permitting compound RPCs, i.e., calls that combine several commonly executed request sequences (such as lookup, open, and read) into one. The security of operation and authentication has been substantially augmented through introduction of Kerberos 5 [7] and SPKM/LIPKEY [8]. The administrative overhead required to coordinate numeric user and group IDs across multiple hosts and to enforce conventional Unix permission flags is reduced thanks to the new ACL mechanism that interoperates with both POSIX (though not perfectly) and Windows ACLs, with user names expressed as strings. Finally, the NFSv4 protocol implements file migration and replication.

Despite these improvements, NFS best supports *session semantics*, in which clients have exclusive access to files and the updates to them are propagated on file close (session finish). Scenarios where multiple applications perform modifications of a shared file, such as appending to a shared log file, will not achieve good performance. While the optional parallel NFS extension introduced in the minor revision 4.1 [9] of the standard supports rudimentary parallel access semantics, these operations are better left to parallel file systems, two examples of which are discussed in the next sections.

18.4 GENERAL PARALLEL FILE SYSTEM

The General Parallel File System (GPFS) was developed by IBM and released commercially in the late 1990s. Its functionality has been influenced by the Tiger Shark file system [10] research project at IBM Almaden, oriented to provide high performance multimedia streaming. GPFS also incorporates design ideas from an earlier Vesta parallel file system designed by IBM [11]. It supports concurrent access from multiple clients to possibly multiple file system instances distributed over physical storage devices in the system. The storage devices can be either accessible via SAN or exported over network using higher-level protocols. The file placement optimizer is a feature that allows efficient GPFS operation in the "shared-nothing" cluster architecture frequently favored by "big data" applications. GPFS features data replication, providing high recoverability and availability, policy-based storage management, a global namespace that permits shared file access across different GPFS instances (called GPFS *clusters*) on wide area networks (WANs), and standard (including POSIX) file interfaces that support conventional OS file system utilities as well as execution of unmodified applications. Similarly to NFS, the latter is accomplished through kernel extensions that inject GPFS functionality into the VFS layer, making it appear to the kernel as another natively supported file system. The high level of performance is achieved by spreading data accesses across multiple storage devices (to obtain high aggregate data bandwidth), load balancing to eliminate storage hotspots, efficient support for concurrent reads and writes from multiple clients (even to the same files), a sophisticated token management system as a basis for distributed lock management and file data consistency, intelligent prefetching of file data recognizing sequential (forward and reverse) and various forms of strided I/O patterns, and the ability to specify multiple networks for communication between GPFS daemons.

Table 18.1 Selected Operational Parameter Limits of the Current Version of GPFS

Parameter	Design Limit	Tested Value
Number of joined nodes per cluster	16,384	9,620
Number of disks per cluster	2,048	Unknown
File size	2^{99} bytes	Approximately 18 PB
Number of files per file system	2^{64}	9,000,000,000

GPFS implementation of journaling (I/O transaction logging) improves the chances of recovery after system crashes. The architectural limits of the main operational parameters listed in Table 18.1 give an idea of the extent of scaling supported by GPFS. The most recent revision, GPFS v4.2, is available for AIX (Power processor), Windows, and Linux OS (x86 series processors). Since 2015 the IBM GPFS brand has been known as IBM Spectrum Scale.

The basic architecture of GPFS is illustrated in Fig. 18.2. The diagram shows two configurations, one with I/O nodes resembling a traditional network attached storage arrangement and separated from

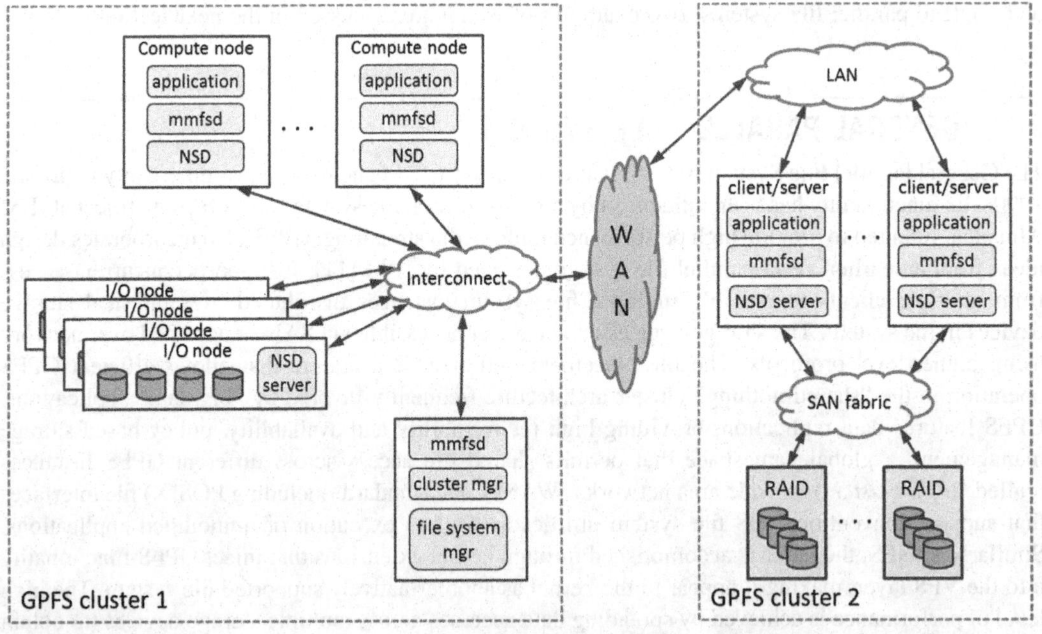

FIGURE 18.2

Some of the possible deployment configurations of GPFS: a network attached storage pool servicing a collection of client compute nodes on the left (GPFS cluster 1), and a server group managing SAN devices based on redundant array of independent disks on the right (GPFS cluster 2). Both clusters may communicate thanks to the shared WAN connection. Physical storage in both installations is abstracted through the Network Shared Disk (NSD) protocol. The core file system functionality is provided by the GPFS daemon, mmfsd, distributed across multiple computational resources in the system.

the compute nodes, and a second with nodes that provide storage server capabilities while also permitting client applications to run. The second configuration transparently integrates a SAN storage pool which may offer enhanced resilience in case of either disk or network link failures through redundant links exposed by the SAN fabric. Other configurations are also possible. Both GPFS instances (clusters) may interact thanks to the WAN connection. The storage devices in GPFS installations are abstracted via the Network Shared Disk (NSD) protocol. They provide cluster-wide naming and high-bandwidth access to disk data for all clients that have no physical access to the underlying storage. NSD *servers* are started on the storage-equipped nodes, thus exposing virtual storage connections to other NSD components. For robust resilience, each NSD component may be associated with up to eight NSD servers: if one server fails, the next one in the list takes over. Older revisions of GPFS executing on the IBM SP series of machines provided an analogous service using virtual shared disk entities that communicated using a proprietary IBM interconnect. The current NSDs relax this constraint to permit other network types, but still require that a high-speed network is present.

GPFS daemons (denoted *mmfsd* in the figure) implement the core functionality of GPFS, including support for all I/O operations and data buffer management. They are instantiated as multithreaded processes with a separate group of dedicated threads for high-priority requests. Multiple daemons may communicate with each other to coordinate changes in configuration and recovery, and to synchronize concurrent updates to the same data. GPFS daemons are responsible for allocation of disk space required by newly created files and when existing files need to be extended; management of directories, including creation of new directories, updating the contents of existing directories, and identification of directories with pending I/O operations; lock management to protect the integrity of both file data and metadata; starting the related I/O operations; and quota accounting. To optimize performance, the daemons take advantage of *pagepool*, a pinned memory region that contains data and metadata of selected files. It is used to support frequent writes that may be overlapped with the execution of applications and data that are frequently reused (but fit into pagepool), and to provide buffer space for data prefetch, thus accelerating the performance of large sequential reads. Nonpinned memory may be allocated from the kernel heap and is primarily used to hold control structures and vnode information related to in-kernel aspects of file system management. The in-daemon shared memory is used as *inode cache* (inodes, short for index-nodes, are internal data structures used by the file system to control file layout) and *stat cache* that contains a subset of attributes of the most recently accessed files and directories. The daemons may also allocate internal nonshared memory segments to support operation of file system manager functions (including token management).

The file system manager (one per file system, but possibly distributed across multiple nodes), which may run on a dedicated node or as part of a regular client node, supervises the operation of all nodes using the file system. It provides services oriented on file system configuration (expanding the storage pool, performing file system repairs, and adjustment of disk availability), storage space allocation, token management, and quota management. Token management is critical to concurrent operations performed on shared GPFS files. If the file system manager executes on multiple nodes, the load is distributed across all participating token management servers. Token services issue tokens that temporarily grant file access rights (read and write of file data and metadata) to token holders. This locking is done per byte range, thus permitting simultaneous read accesses to some portions of a file while enforcing a rigorous order of updates on portions of file that are targeted by writes without explicit serialization of all requests. Interaction with the token server happens the first time a node requests access to a file. After having been granted a read or write token, the client may perform compatible data accesses without further contact with the token manager. If the token server detects a conflicting access, it provides a list of all nodes holding tokens to the requested byte range. To avoid blocking the token server, it is the requesting client's responsibility to get the current token holders to relinquish them. As this must potentially wait for release of locks held on file, often the related pending I/O operations must be completed.

Each GPFS cluster has one associated cluster manager, elected by a quorum of the nodes constituting the cluster. The cluster manager keeps track of disk leases, monitors node failures and supervises recovery processes while ensuring that the necessary quorum of nodes exists to support the continued operation of the cluster, propagates configuration changes to remote nodes, chooses the file system manager node(s), and performs user identifier mapping from remote nodes.

Since concurrent write operations are often the source of conflicts when performed on shared files, it is educational to analyze the involved data and metadata paths (Fig. 18.3). A dirty block of data must be written when a system command requesting a flush of buffered data to storage has been invoked, a write in synchronous mode was called, the system needs to reuse buffers currently occupied by dirty data, a file token has been revoked, or the last byte of file block accessed sequentially has been written. Each open file in GPFS is associated with precisely one *metanode*, which is used to maintain metadata integrity. Typically the metanode is located on the host that had the file open for the longest period of

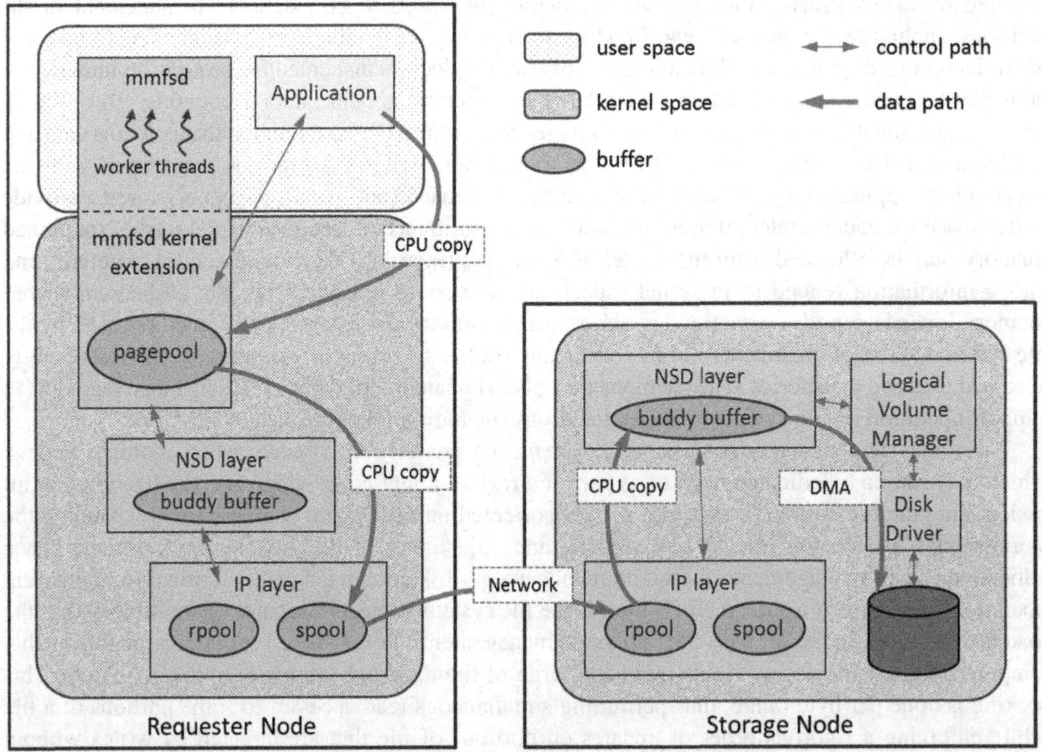

FIGURE 18.3

Data and control paths for execution of a remote write in GPFS.

time and functions as a synchronization point for file metadata for all nodes in the system. Both data and metadata are flushed as described in the following three scenarios of varying complexity:

1. *Buffer available in client memory.* This occurs if the buffer has been created for a previous write and the write token is still available. The contents of the application buffer are copied to the GPFS data buffer; at this point the write is complete from the application perspective. If the buffer flush conditions listed above are fulfilled, the daemon schedules an asynchronous buffer write to storage using one of its threads. This permits the write to overlap with application execution. The GPFS worker thread calls the NSD layer, causing the request to be broken up into chunks fitting message payloads and copied to the communication buffers in send pool. The list of destination I/O nodes is derived from file metadata. The data are transferred over the interconnect to the NSD server receive buffer pool. As soon as all packets are received, a buddy buffer is allocated to reassemble the write buffer contents. At this stage the related receive buffers in the NSD server are released and disk write is initiated. The latter may be delayed by a preconfigured time to permit coalescing with other neighboring write requests. Since the buddy buffer may not always be available, the request could remain queued with data stored in receive pool buffers until sufficient space is provided.
2. *Write token locally available, but data buffer absent.* This may happen if the buffer has been reused due to recent I/O activity or a previous write did not "touch" all data locations for which it obtained a token. Kernel code suspends the calling thread and instructs a daemon thread to obtain a buffer. If the write range covers the whole block (full overwrite), a new empty buffer is allocated. If the write affects a portion of a block and the remainder of the block exists, the remaining portion of the block is fetched and placed in the buffer. The call then proceeds as described in (1).
3. *Both data buffer and token are unavailable.* First a token for a specific byte range must be acquired. Based on the discovered I/O pattern, the byte range may be larger than the one requested by the application in anticipation of future requests, as long as no conflicts are detected with other accessors of the file. The token management may be forced to revoke the token currently owned by another node. After the token is obtained, processing progresses as delineated in (2).

As can be seen, parallel file systems provide much richer semantics and are more flexible in terms of supported file access patterns and data sharing than distributed file systems. Their algorithms are carefully designed to avoid communication and synchronization hotspots while maintaining high-bandwidth access to file data whenever possible, providing stronger guarantees of data integrity, and supporting the necessary level of fault resilience and availability. Of the top 10 machines on the Top 500 list, Cori at National Energy Research Scientific Computing Center, Mira at Argonne National Laboratory, and Piz Daint at Centro Svizzero di Calcolo Scientifico (Switzerland) use GPFS to manage respectively 30, 27, and 5.8 PB of storage.

18.5 LUSTRE FILE SYSTEM

Lustre is a parallel distributed file system originally released in 2003. Its name is derived from "Linux" and "clusters", indicating the intended target platforms for its deployment. Its development was initially carried out under the Department of Energy Accelerated Strategic Computing Initiative (ASCI) Path Forward [12]. Corporate ownership of the project and its code base changed hands several times and has included Sun Microsystems, Oracle, Whamcloud, and, since 2012, Intel.

Lustre provides a POSIX-compliant file system interface with atomic semantic support for most operations, thus avoiding data and metadata inconsistencies. It design is highly scalable, making it a preferred file system for HPC by supporting multiple tens of thousands clients, petabytes of storage, and I/O bandwidths reaching multiple hundreds of GB/s. Deployment of multiple clusters is simplified with Lustre, as it permits aggregation of both capacity and performance of multiple storage subsystems. The storage space and I/O throughput can be also dynamically increased by providing additional storage servers as needed. Lustre takes advantage of high performance networking infrastructure, such as low-latency communication and remote direct memory access (RDMA) over InfiniBand with OpenFabrics Enterprise Distribution (OFED) [13]. Lustre software enables the bridging of multiple RDMA networks and provides integrated network diagnostics. The file system supports high availability with multiple failover modes using shared storage partitions and interfacing with different high-availability managers. This implements automatic failovers with no single point of failure, as well as transparent application recovery. The chances of file system corruption are minimized through a multiple-mount protection feature. Particularly noteworthy is the online distributed file system check (LFSCK) that is capable of operating while the file system is in use to restore data consistency after a major file system error is detected. Security of operation is enforced by permitting TCP connections only on privileged ports and application of ACLs and extended attributes based on POSIX ACLs with custom additions, such as *root squash* (reduction of effective access rights for the remote superuser). Lustre uses a distributed lock manager (LDLM) to permit file locking with byte granularity as well as fine-grain metadata locks to permit concurrent operation of multiple clients on the same files and directories. File striping across physical storage devices permits the user to specify the layout parameters, which may be flexibly arranged at the level of a whole file system, a single directory, or individual files to match the needs of specific applications. Lustre is highly interoperable; it supports a dedicated MPI-IO abstract-device interface for I/O layer to provide optimized parallel I/O to message-passing interface (MPI) applications and permits exports of its files through commonly used distributed file system interfaces such as NFS and CIFS, enabling access to its files from non-Unix hosts. The Lustre code base compiles and runs on a variety of hardware platforms, including machines of different endianness and native data sizes, and transparently interfaces with older revisions of file system software. Lustre software is open sourced under the GNU public license 2.0 license; its current major revision is v2.8. Many of these features account for the popularity of Lustre deployment in HPC systems: as of November 2016 half the 10 fastest supercomputers on the Top 500 list (Tianhe 2, Titan, Sequoia, Oakforest-PACS, and Trinity) integrated Lustre as the main storage management layer.

A schematic view of Lustre architecture is shown in Fig. 18.4. The primary functional components of a Lustre system are as follows:

- *Management server* (MGS) is responsible for storing, managing, and supplying the configuration information to other Lustre components. It interacts with all targets (configuration providers) and clients (configuration accessors) in the system. While MGS typically works using a dedicated set of storage devices for independent operation, the storage could also share the physical devices present in the metadata server pool.
- *Management target* (MGT) provides storage space for the management server. Its space requirements rarely exceed 100 MB even in large-scale Lustre installations. While the performance of the underlying storage is not critical for the operation of the system

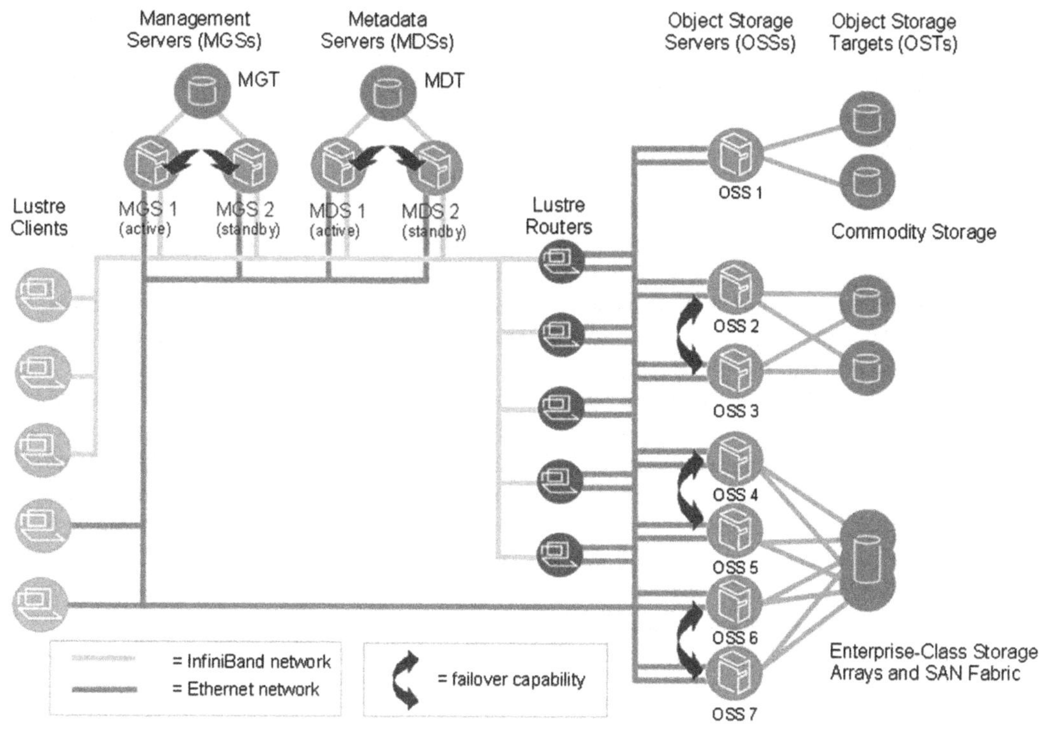

FIGURE 18.4

Layout of typical Lustre deployment at scale.

Image via Lustre.org

(seeks and writes of small amounts of data), its reliability is paramount. MGT may leverage redundant storage structures such as RAID1 to provide it. Multiple MDTs per system are supported.

- *Metadata server* (MDS) that is responsible for management of the names and directory contents. The namespace in Lustre may be distributed across multiple MDSs. Each MDS also handles network requests for one or more MDTs. MDS failovers are supported: a standby MDS assumes the functions of a failed active MDS.
- *Metadata target* (MDT) that stores various metadata, including directories, file names, permissions, and file layout information on physical storage associated with an MDS. There is nominally one MDT per file system, although recent revisions support multiple MDTs under the distributed namespace environment (DNE). The primary MDT comprises the root of the file system, while the additional MDSs with their own attached MDTs may hold various subdirectories. It is also possible to distribute the contents of a single directory across multiple MDT nodes, thus creating a *striped directory*. MDT storage usually accounts for 1%–2% of the total file system capacity.

- *Object storage server* (OSS) that services file data I/O requests and other network requests for one or more object storage target (OST). A common Lustre configuration involves an MDT on a dedicated hardware node, two or more OSTs on every OSS node, and an I/O client on every compute node of a system. The ratio of OSTs to OSSs typically varies between two and eight.
- *Object storage target* (OST) that manages physical storage for user file contents. The file data are contained in one or more objects, each of which is under control of a specific separate OST. The number of objects a file is divided into is configurable by the user. Single OST capacity is limited to 128 TB (256 TB on ZFS, an advanced file system originally developed at Sun Microsystems); the total file system capacity is the sum of capacities of all OSTs.
- *Clients* that execute the applications generating the I/O data. They may include conventional compute nodes, but also loosely associated desktops, workstations, or visualization servers that are permitted to mount the file system.
- *Lustre Networking* (LNET) that provides the communication infrastructure for the whole system. Its main features include concurrent access to and support of many common network types (IB/OFED, TCP variants, including GigE, 10GigE, and IPoIB, Cray Seastar, Myrinet MX, Rapid Array, and Quadrics Elan), RDMA (if available), routing between individual network segments, high availability, and recovery from network errors. LNET strives to achieve end-to-end communication bandwidth nearing the available peak bandwidth. Its software includes the higher-level code module and the underlying network driver (LND). The LNET layer is connectionless and asynchronous, leaving the verification of data transmission status to the connection-oriented LND. Bonding of multiple network interfaces for increased bandwidth is also supported.

The high-level organization of a file in Lustre is depicted in Fig. 18.5. The files are referred to by 128-bit file identifiers (FIDs) that consist of a unique 64-bit sequence number, a 32-bit object ID (OID), and a 32-bit version number. FID identifies an object in MDT whose extended attributes encode the layout information: one or more pointers to OST objects that contain the file data. Since the objects must be stored on different OSTs, the data are striped in a round-robin fashion across all OSTs (obviously, no striping is applied if only one OST is associated with the file). The number of stripes, stripe size, and target OSTs are user configurable. The default stripe count is one and the default stripe size is 1 MB. There may be up to 2000 objects per file. Since the client performing data I/O operations on a file must first fetch the layout extended attribute data from the MDT object identified by FID, further data transfers can be arranged directly between the client node and the related OSS nodes storing the file data.

Efficient synchronization of file operations in parallel file systems is a key factor in achieving a good level of performance. Lustre resources are associated with locks that may be local or global. LDLM is based on a locking algorithm utilized by VAX DLM [14]. To give the reader an idea of the complexity, a brief overview of the involved data structures and algorithms is presented below.

LDLM locks may exist in one of six modes.

- *Exclusive* mode requested by MDS before a new file is created.
- *Protective Write* mode issued by the OST to the client requesting a write lock.
- *Protective Read* mode granted by the OST to clients that need to read or execute files.
- *Concurrent Write* mode issued by the MDS to clients requesting write lock when opening a file.
- *Concurrent Read* mode associated with intermediate path traversal during path lookups and effected by the related MDS.
- *Null* mode.

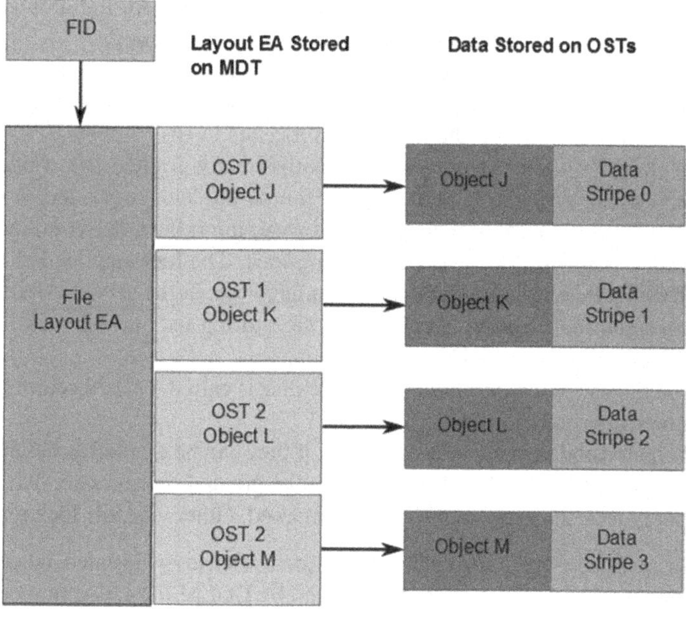

FIGURE 18.5

Lustre file layout.

In addition, Lustre defines four types of locks:

- *extent lock* for OST data protection
- *flock* required to support user space requests for file locking
- *inode bit lock* to protect metadata attributes
- *plain lock*, usually unused.

Lock management supports three types of callback functions. *Blocking callback* is invoked when a client requests a lock conflicting with the current one, giving the client an opportunity to renounce the lock or the lock is forcibly revoked. *Completion callback* is called when a requested lock is granted or a lock is converted to a different mode. Finally, a *glimpse callback* is used to provide certain information about file without releasing the held lock. LDLM also uses the concepts of *namespace* and *intent*. Each service in Lustre, such as OST, MDS, and MGS, is associated with a namespace. In turn, the intent is a small amount of data indicating that special processing must be invoked during the lock processing operation. Each namespace has potentially several different intent handlers to support that. The two fundamental operations, lock request and release, are controlled by precisely defined algorithms. Thus to obtain a lock, the following actions must occur.

1. A client locking service determines if the lock belongs to a local namespace. If it is local, the algorithm advances to (7).

2. A lock enqueue RPC is sent to LDLM on the appropriate server. An initial ungranted lock is created, with some fields initialized from data supplied by the request.
3. The enqueue step inspects if there is an intent set on the lock. If not, it invokes the policy function associated with the lock type. The policy function determines whether the lock may be granted or not. If the intent on the lock is set, the algorithm proceeds to (6).
4. The server then checks if there are any conflicts with already granted and waiting locks for the resource specified by the request. If no conflict is found, the lock is granted. A completion callback is invoked and the lock is acquired. Otherwise, the processing continues in (5).
5. A blocking callback is invoked for every conflicting lock. The lock may be held at the client, in which case an RPC request is emitted; otherwise, a flag is set at the server. After all the locks are scanned, the processed lock request is entered on the waiting list and the lock is returned to the client with its status set to "blocked".
6. After the lock intent is set, an appropriate intent handler is called. LDLM returns the result of the call without further interpretation.
7. Local locks are created and then enqueued to check if they can be granted as described above. This process continues without any RPCs. If the lock can be granted or errors are detected, the control returns immediately with the lock status correctly marked. Otherwise, the lock request is blocked.

Typically, locks in Lustre are held indefinitely. Lock release is initiated when another process requests a conflicting lock, a blocking callback is issued by LDLM, or a blocking callback is invoked on the client node. The lock cancellation proceeds as follows.

1. If the sum of active readers and writers is nonzero, it means that another process on the same client is using the lock and no action is taken. The lock owner(s) will eventually release it.
2. There are no readers or writers. A blocking callback is invoked with a flag indicating lock revocation.
3. If the lock is not in the local namespace, an RPC call is sent to the client containing a cancellation request. Otherwise, local cancellation is performed that takes the lock off all the lists.
4. All waiting locks on the resource are reevaluated.
5. If any of the waiting locks can be granted, they are moved to the granted lock list and a completion callback is invoked.

One of Lustre's strengths is fault management, which can be applied to most of its functional components. Two basic failover modes are available: active/passive and active/active. In the first configuration the active server processes client requests and provides resources, while the passive server stays idle. In case of active node failure, the passive server becomes active and takes over. The second scenario involves multiple active servers, each providing a subset of resources. If one fails, the remaining ones take over the failed node's resources. A variation of these schemes is also used to provide better utilization of system resources. For example, an idle server in active/passive configuration for one Lustre cluster may at the same time be the active server for another file system.

An overview of various operational parameters of the Lustre file system is presented in Table 18.2. Since the underlying file system can be selected by the system administrator as either *ldiskfs* (a modified and patched revision of the Linux *ext4* journaling file system) or ZFS, some of the absolute

Table 18.2 Select Operational Parameters of Lustre

Parameter	Design Target	Production Tested
Maximum file size	31.25 PB (ldiskfs) 16 TB (32-bit ldiskfs) 8 EB (ZFS)	Multiple TB
Maximum file count	32 billion (ldiskfs) 256 trillion (ZFS)	2 billion
Maximum storage space	512 PB (ldiskfs) 1 EB (ZFS)	55 PB
Number of clients	≤131,072	50,000+
Single-client I/O performance	90% network bandwidth	2 GB/s data I/O 1000 metadata ops/s
Aggregate-client I/O performance	10 TB/s	2.5 TB/s
OSS count	1000 OSSs, up to 4000 OSTs	450 OSSs with 1000 4 TB OSTs 192 OSSs with 1344 8 TB OSTs 768 OSSs with 768 72 TB OSTs
Single OSS performance	10 GB/s	6+ GB/s
Aggregate OSS performance	10 TB/s	2.5 TB/s
MDS count	≤256 MDTs, ≤256 MDSs	1 primary and 1 backup
MDS performance	50,000 create ops/s 200,000 stat ops/s	15,000 create ops/s 50,000 stat ops/s

Excerpted from Intel Corp., Lustre Software Release 2.x Operations Manual [Online]. Available: http://doc.lustre.org/lustre_manual.pdf.

limits listed depend on the file system type used. As Lustre continues to be deployed in installations of increasing scales and capacities, some of the listed configurations tested in production may be out of date by the time of publication.

18.6 SUMMARY AND OUTCOMES OF CHAPTER 18

- File systems provide an abstraction necessary to manage the information kept on mass-storage devices. They organize the information in a hierarchical layout, provide human-accessible namespace to identify individual stored entities uniquely, maintain attributes describing access permissions and various properties of individual entries, verify the consistency of stored information, provide fault-recovery mechanisms, and expose the user interface for access. File systems achieve these by defining and manipulating additional *metadata* that describes the layout and various properties of the stored raw data.
- Distributed file systems are file systems that are capable of handling I/O requests issued by multiple clients over the network. To manage the demands of scaling, they frequently span multiple server nodes while providing a "single view" access to the stored data and related namespace.

- Parallel file systems are distributed file systems that are specifically optimized to support concurrent file access efficiently from parallel applications. In particular, they implement synchronization mechanisms that permit the distributed application to operate on different sections of the same file or enable strided access for individual clients accessing the same file while preserving the consistency of data and metadata for multiple accessors.
- The POSIX standard defines a local file access interface in Unix environments. Two modes of access are commonly supported by the runtime library: one based on system calls and another on buffered file I/O (streams).
- NFS is one of the most frequently deployed distributed file systems in small and medium cluster environments. It permits the use of the POSIX interface and implements session semantics in which the clients most efficiently operate on disjoint files with updates propagated at the end session (file close). The available features and performance strongly depend on the installed NFS code revision and configuration.
- GPFS is a high performance proprietary parallel file system designed for scalability and high-bandwidth concurrent file access. It implements token-based locking of arbitrary shared file sections and synchronization techniques that identify concurrent file access conflicts and guarantee consistency of the affected data and metadata.
- Lustre is a high performance open-source parallel file system supporting multiple network types and host architectures. Due to its good performance, permissive licensing, and extensive list of features (dynamic expandability, multiple network support, RDMA, failover for multiple components, sophisticated distributed file lock management, POSIX and MPI-IO interfaces, NFS and CIFS export support, and many others), it is frequently used in large-scale cluster installations.

18.7 QUESTIONS AND PROBLEMS

1. Summarize the main challenges of creating efficient persistent data storage for an HPC system. How may they be solved?
2. What are the differences between system-call-based and streaming I/O interfaces in POSIX? What are their implications for file access performance?
3. Write a program that saves an array of 1000 double-precision floating-point numbers to a file using in-memory layout and an array of 1000 structures consisting of one character and one double-precision number to another file. Do the sizes of the generated files match the estimated values based on the sizes of the involved elementary data types multiplied by array size? If not, what is the reason for the discrepancy? Can the inefficiency (if any) be eliminated?
4. A computational scientist attempts to debug his stubbornly crashing MPI application. Due to a complicated sequence of events leading to the crash, he gets an idea to use a shared log file located on an NFS partition to store the information about the event occurrences on every node. When analyzing the file he begins to suspect that not all captured data were actually written to file. What may be the reason for that? How would you improve the reliability of logging the precrash data?

5. Consider the following code that prints array elements to a file and reads them back.

```
#include <stdio.h>

#define SIZE 512
#define FILENAME “myfile”

int main() {
   double data[SIZE], iodata[SIZE];
   for (int i = 0; i < SIZE; i++) data[i] = i+1/(double)(i+1);

   FILE *f = fopen(FILENAME, “w”);
   for (int i = 0; i < SIZE; i++) fprintf(f, “%lf\n”, data[i]);
   fclose(f);

   f = fopen(FILENAME, “r”);
   for (int i = 0; i < SIZE; i++) {
     fscanf(f, “%lf”, &iodata[i]);
     if (data[i] != iodata[i])
       printf(“ERROR: item %d should be %lf, got %lf\n”, i, data[i], iodata[i]);
   }
   fclose(f);
   return 0;
}
```

a. Is running the code going to produce any error messages? Why? Verify your answer by compiling and executing the program.
b. How would you fix the encountered problem(s)?
c. Based on this experience, would you recommend saving floating-point data as text? Justify your answer.

6. Contrast distributed and parallel file systems. Which solutions provided by the latter improve the efficiency of concurrent accesses to shared files?

REFERENCES

[1] IEEE and The Open Group, The Open Group Base Specifications Issue 7, IEEE Standard 1003.1–2008, 2016 Edition, [Online]. Available: http://pubs.opengroup.org/onlinepubs/9699919799.

[2] ISO/IEC 9899:201x C Language Standard Draft, April 12, 2011 [Online]. Available: http://www.open-std.org/jtc1/sc22/wg14/www/docs/n1570.pdf.

[3] IETF Network Working Group, RFC 5531: RPC: Remote Procedure Call Protocol Specification Version 2, May, 2009 [Online]. Available: https://tools.ietf.org/html/rfc5531.

[4] IETF Network Working Group, RFC 4506: XDR: External Data Representation Standard, May, 2006 [Online]. Available: https://tools.ietf.org/html/rfc4506.

[5] R.H. Arpaci-Dusseau, A.C. Arpaci-Dusseau, The Andrew File System (AFS), in: Operating Systems: Three Easy Pieces, Arpac-Dusseaui Books, 2014.
[6] Microsoft TechNet Library, Common Internet File System, Microsoft, [Online]. Available: https://technet.microsoft.com/en-us/library/cc939973.aspx.
[7] Kerberos: The Network Authentication Protocol, Massachusets Institute of Technology, November 16, 2016 [Online]. Available: http://web.mit.edu/kerberos/.
[8] IETF Network Working Group, RFC 2847: LIPKEY - A Low Infrastructure Public Key Mechanism Using SPKM, June, 2000 [Online]. Available: https://tools.ietf.org/html/rfc2847.
[9] IETF, RFC 5661: Network File System (NFS) Version 4 Minor Version 1 Protocol, January, 2010 [Online]. Available: https://tools.ietf.org/html/rfc5661#page-277.
[10] R.L. Haskin, F.B. Schmuck, The Tiger Shark File Syetem, in: Compcon '96: Technologies for the Information Superhighway, 1996.
[11] P.F. Corbett, D.G. Feitelson, The Vesta parallel file system, ACM Transactions on Computer Systems 14 (3) (1996) 225–264.
[12] G. Grider, The ASCI/DOD Scalable I/O History and Strategy, May, 2004 [Online]. Available: https://www.dtc.umn.edu/resources/grider1.pdf.
[13] OFED Overview, OpenFabrics Alliance, [Online]. Available: https://www.openfabrics.org/index.php/openfabrics-software.html.
[14] N.P. Kronenberg, H.M. Levy, W.D. Strecker, VAXclusters: a closely-coupled distributed system, ACM Transactions on Computer Systems 4 (2) (1986) 130–146.
[15] Intel Corp., Lustre Software Release 2.x Operations Manual, [Online]. Available: http://doc.lustre.org/lustre_manual.pdf.

CHAPTER

19 MAPREDUCE

CHAPTER OUTLINE

19.1 INTRODUCTION

MapReduce is a simple programming model for enabling distributed computations, including data processing on very large input datasets, in a highly scalable and fault-tolerant way. While the concept of MapReduce was motivated initially by functional programming languages like *LISP* with its *map* and *reduce* primitives, it is also closely related to the message-passing interface (MPI) concepts of *scatter* and *reduce* for distributed-memory architectures. However, unlike in MPI programming, the details of the underlying parallelization in MapReduce are hidden from the programmer, making it easier to use. MapReduce algorithms have been shown to scale from single servers all the way to hundreds of thousands of cores while at the same time delivering transparent fault tolerance to the end user. MapReduce was developed by Google [2], and the programming model has since been adopted by many software frameworks, libraries, and end users. Apache's open-source Hadoop framework [1] is one of several libraries which support MapReduce, and is used for the examples in this chapter.

19.2 MAP AND REDUCE

A *map* is a functional that executes a supplied function on all members of an input list. Because the map function only requires the input data member to execute, it can be run in parallel, providing a massive potential speed-up. The map function itself returns a set of two linked data items: a key for lookup and a value. The key can either be the output from the function or the input data element itself.

High Performance Computing. https://doi.org/10.1016/B978-0-12-420158-3.00019-8

For example, suppose the map function counts the number of characters of an input word, returning as a key the word length and returning as a value the input word. So if the word "computing" is supplied to the map function, it would return the key–value pair of "9:computing" where the key is "9", the length of the word "computing", and the corresponding value to the key is the input data element word, "computing". The keys from the output are then grouped by key after executing the map function on each data element. For example, if the same map function were executed on each word in the sentence "This is a book about high performance computing", the result of the map portion in MapReduce would be the groupings shown in Table 19.1.

The results of the map function and associated groupings are then passed to the *reduce* function. The reduce function takes as an argument a key and all values associated with that key. Like the map function, the reduce function can also be executed independently on each key and grouping of values, thereby enabling embarrassingly parallel execution. For example, suppose a crossword-puzzle designer would like to know the number of words with a length of four characters that occur in a large-input dataset. The reduce function in this case would simply count the number of grouped values associated with each key. Using the previous map function example, the output from the reduction function in this case would be as shown in Table 19.2.

In this example, there are three words with a length of four characters and the rest are all of length one.

From the user's perspective, some of the principal strengths of the MapReduce programming model are that the parallelization and fault-tolerance details of the MapReduce implementation are hidden from the user and only the map and reduce functions need to be supplied. Map and reduce functions themselves vary widely in complexity. The following subsections give some additional examples of map and reduce functions.

Table 19.1 Sample MapReduce Map Function Groupings

Key	Grouped Values
1	"a"
2	"is"
4	"this", "book", "high"
9	"computing"
11	"performance"

Table 19.2 Sample MapReduce Reduce Function Groupings

Key	Output From Reduce Function
1	1
2	1
4	3
9	1
11	1

19.2.1 WORD COUNT

Counting the number of times each word has been used in a body of text is the canonical didactic example for MapReduce. The map function returns as a key a single word and the associated value with the key is unity. For example, the result for this map function on the famous text from Shakespeare's *Hamlet*, "To be or not to be—that is the question", is as shown in Table 19.3.

Because the words "to" and "be" occur twice, the value of 1 is added to the grouped values twice (once per occurrence).

The reduce function simply sums up the grouped values for each key, as illustrated in Table 19.4.

Running this map and reduce function on the entire text of Shakespeare's *Hamlet* gives the word counts for some common words, as shown in Table 19.5.

19.2.2 SHARED NEIGHBORS

Finding shared neighbors in graph applications provides another good example of MapReduce functionality. A sample graph is shown in Fig. 19.1, where multiple vertices share the same neighbors. For example, in this graph vertex "0" shares a common neighbor with vertex "2"; this common neighbor is vertex "1". MapReduce can be used to find those shared neighbors.

Table 19.3 Sample MapReduce Word Counts

Key	Grouped Values
"to"	1, 1
"be"	1, 1
"or"	1
"not"	1
"that"	1
"is"	1
"the"	1
"question"	1

Table 19.4 Sample MapReduce Reduce Function Output

Key	Output From Reduce Function
"to"	2
"be"	2
"or"	1
"not"	1
"that"	1
"is"	1
"the"	1
"question"	1

Table 19.5 Sample MapReduce Word Counts

Key	Output From Reduce Function
"but"	269
"as"	222
"be"	210
"England"	21
"Norway"	13

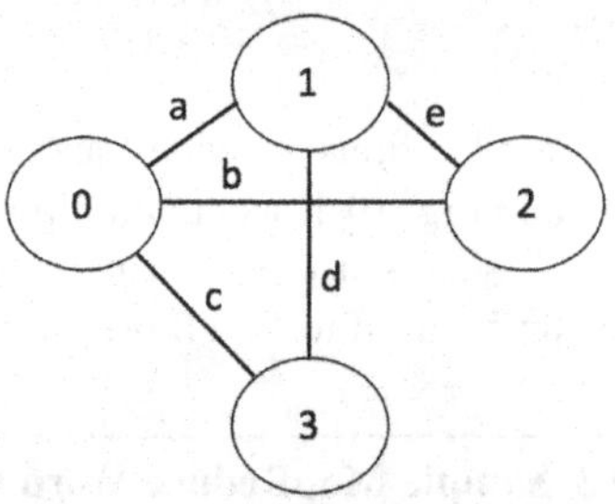

FIGURE 19.1

A small graph where the vertices share multiple neighbors. Vertices are listed as numbers (0–3) and edges are lower-case letters (a–e).

In this case, the map function returns each edge of a vertex as a key. The value for each key is the list of all the neighboring vertices to that vertex (Table 19.6).

This gives the group values shown in Table 19.7.

The reduce function returns the intersection of each key's grouped values, thereby revealing shared neighbors for each edge (Table 19.8).

This simple map and reduce operation reveals the shared neighbors between any two connected vertices. For example, vertices connect by edge "a" in Fig. 19.1 (vertices 0 and 1) also share two of the same neighbors, vertices 2 and 3.

19.2.3 K-MEANS CLUSTERING

K-means clustering partitions a data space into *k* clusters, each with a mean value. Each individual in the cluster is placed in the cluster closest to the cluster's mean value. K-means clustering is frequently

Table 19.6 Values of Vertices in Fig. 19.1

Vertex 0		Vertex 1		Vertex 2		Vertex 3	
Key	Values	Key	Values	Key	Values	Key	Values
a	1,2,3	a	0,2,3	e	0,1	c	0,1
b	1,2,3	d	0,2,3	b	0,1	d	0,1
c	1,2,3	e	0,2,3				

Table 19.7 Grouped Values of Vertices in Fig. 19.1

Key	Grouped Values
a	(1,2,3), (0,2,3)
b	(1,2,3), (0,1)
c	(1,2,3), (0,1)
d	(0,2,3), (0,1)
e	(0,2,3), (0,1)

Table 19.8 Shared Neighbors in Fig. 19.1 Revealed in MapReduce

Key	Output From Reduce Function
a	2,3
b	1
c	1
d	0
e	0

used in data analysis, and a simple example with five x and y value pairs to be placed into two clusters using the Euclidean distance function is given in Table 19.9.

To begin the clustering, two initial cluster points are supplied: (0,0) and (1,1). Using the Euclidean distance measure, $\sqrt{(x_1 - x_2)^2 + (y_1 - y_2)^2}$, each individual is assigned to the cluster nearest to the (x,y) pair, as summarized in Table 19.10.

The initial cluster points have moved from (0,0) to (0.1,0.3) and from (1,1) to (0.8,0.85). This same process can be repeated until the cluster mean values stop changing or a maximum number of iterations is reached.

In a MapReduce programming model, for a given (x,y) value pair the mapper iterates over each cluster's mean value and finds the cluster with the nearest distance to the (x,y) pair. It returns as a key the cluster and as a value the (x,y) pair (Table 19.11).

Table 19.9 Example of K-Means Clustering

Individual	(x,y) Pair
a	(0.1,0.3)
b	(1.1,0.4)
c	(0.8,0.7)
d	(1.2,1.2)
e	(0.1,1.1)

Table 19.10 Assignment of Cluster Members

Cluster 1		Cluster 2	
Members	**Mean *x,y* Value**	**Members**	**Mean *x,y* Value**
a	(0.1,0.3)	b,c,d,e	(0.8,0.85)

Table 19.11 MapReduce K-Means Clustering

Key	Grouped Values
1	(0.1,0.3)
2	(1.1,0.4), (0.8,0.7), (1.2,1.2), (0.1,1.1)

The reducer receives a list of (*x*,*y*) value pairs for each cluster and computes the new cluster mean value (Table 19.12).

This MapReduce operation can be performed iteratively until no more updates occur or a maximum number of iterations is reached.

19.3 DISTRIBUTED COMPUTATION

Distributed processing in MapReduce may be summarized in three phases: a map phase, a shuffle phase, and a reduce phase. These phases can be overlapped to some degree to improve efficiency. The map step applies the map function to data local to the processor. Input data for MapReduce is frequently stored in a distributed file system where data blocks are already shared between different linked storage devices, with some redundancy for fault tolerance. The map function does not operate on redundant copies. The shuffle step relocates the map output data based on the output key from the map function so that map output is grouped by output key. The reduce step applies the reduce function to the output data from the map function.

The map functions, like the reduce functions, can be executed concurrently giving a significant potential for speedup. However, efficient distributed MapReduce execution generally requires minimizing the movement of data. For example, it is more efficient for the nodes performing map functions to execute the map on blocks local to the node. Similarly, in the shuffle and reduce phases, the movement of data can be reduced by executing reduce functions on nodes where the map output data already resides.

Table 19.12 MapReduce Cluster Mean Values

Key	Output From Reduce Function
1	(0.1,0.3)
2	(0.8,0.85)

19.4 HADOOP

The Hadoop project by Apache [1] is an open-source implementation of the MapReduce programming model. It provides a distributed file system, job scheduling and resource management tools, including YARN (Yet Another Resource Negotiator), and MapReduce programming support. Historically, MapReduce applications in Hadoop are programmed using Java, although support for C++, Python, and a few other languages is also available.

The Hadoop distributed file system (HDFS) enables distributed file access across many linked storage devices in an easy way. It was motivated by the Google file system, which was instrumental in the original MapReduce programming model development [3]. Data in the distributed Hadoop file system is broken into blocks and distributed across the linked storage devices on the system. Blocks are generally replicated at least once to guard against storage or machine failures depending upon the fault-tolerance properties used when configuring Hadoop. File system commands are run on the Hadoop distributed file system using the *hdfs dfs* command. A summary of the most commonly used file system commands for hdfs dfs are listed in Table 19.13.

As an example, a text file of Shakespeare's *Hamlet* (*hamlet.txt*) stored in the local file system can be placed in HDFS as follows:

```
hdfs dfs -put hamlet.txt /hamlet
```

The contents of hdfs can be queried using the "ls" command on the "/" directory:

```
hdfs dfs -ls /
```

This file can now be used in conjunction with a MapReduce operation inside Hadoop.

As an example MapReduce application, the word count MapReduce from Section 19.2.1 is implemented in Hadoop using the Java programming language in Fig. 19.2. The mapper function, which returns a single word for the key and unity for a value, is illustrated in lines 69–82. The reducer, which returns the single word as a key and the sum of the grouped values provided from the mapper as a value, is illustrated in lines 87–98.

Table 19.13 Select Hadoop Distributed File System Commands

Select Hadoop Distributed File System Commands	Description
hdfs dfs −cat <filename>	Copies the specified filename to stdout.
hdfs dfs −ls	HDFS equivalent of Linux "ls" command.
hdfs dfs −mkdir <directory>	HDFS equivalent of Linux "mkdir" command
hdfs dfs −put <local files>... <destination>	Copy the source files to the destination path in HDFS
hdfs dfs −get <src> <destination>	Copy the source file to the local file system destination
hdfs dfs −rm <filenames>	Delete the specified files; only deletes files
hdfs dfs −rmr <directory name>	Delete the specified directory and all content

```
0001 import java.io.IOException;
0002
0003 // need StringTokenizer for space delimited input
0004 import java.util.StringTokenizer;
0005
0006 // Needed for filesystem path (lines 49-50)
0007 import org.apache.hadoop.fs.Path;
0008
0009 // Needed for providing job configuration
0010 import org.apache.hadoop.conf.Configuration;
0011
0012 // Needed for Hadoop data wrappers like Text and IntWritable
0013 import org.apache.hadoop.io.*;
0014
0015 // MapReduce
0016 import org.apache.hadoop.mapreduce.Mapper;
0017 import org.apache.hadoop.mapreduce.Reducer;
0018 import org.apache.hadoop.mapreduce.Job;
0019 import org.apache.hadoop.mapreduce.lib.input.FileInputFormat;
0020 import org.apache.hadoop.mapreduce.lib.output.FileOutputFormat;
0021
0022 public class HamletCounter {
0023
0024  public static void main(String[] args) throws Exception {
0025
0026    // check that two arguments are supplied:  the input data and output
location
0027    if (args.length != 2)
0028    {
0029      System.out.println("Takes two arguments: <data in> <result>");
0030      System.exit(0);
0031    }
0032
0033    // Set up the job configuration
0034    Configuration config = new Configuration();
0035
0036    // Give a name to the job:  "Counting Hamlet"
0037    Job job = new Job(config, "Counting Hamlet");
0038
0039    // Use Hadoop data types:  in both the mapper and the reducer
0040    //   the key is a string and the value is an int.  The Hadoop
0041    //   equivalents to string and int are Text and IntWritable, respectively.
0042    job.setOutputKeyClass(Text.class);
0043    job.setOutputValueClass(IntWritable.class);
0044
0045    // Give the job the names of the map and reduce classes
0046    job.setReducerClass(reducing.class);
0047    job.setMapperClass(mapping.class);
0048
0049    FileInputFormat.addInputPath(job, new Path(args[0]));
0050    FileOutputFormat.setOutputPath(job, new Path(args[1]));
0051
0052    // start
0053    job.waitForCompletion(true);
0054  }
```

FIGURE 19.2

Example code, HamletCounter.java, using Hadoop. The mapper is in lines 69–82 and returns each word as a key and unity as a value. The reducer is in lines 87–98 and returns the word as a key and the sum of the list of values it receives from the reducer.

```
public static class mapping extends Mapper<LongWritable, Text, Text,
IntWritable> {

    // IntWritable is the Hadoop version of an integer optimized for Hadoop
    private final static IntWritable unity = new IntWritable(1);

    // Usage of Hadoop data wrappers was set in lines 42-43
    // Use Text instead of Java's String class for output
    private Text single_word = new Text();

    // The Hadoop MapReduce framework calls map(Object, Object, Context)
    // The key is a LongWritable -- Hadoop's version of long
    // The value is a Text -- Hadoop's version of String
    // Context objects are used for writing output pairs from mappers and
reducers
    public void map(LongWritable key, Text val, Context output)
                                 throws IOException, InterruptedException {
      // Converting the input line of text from Hadoop's Text to a String
      String text_line = val.toString();

      // Split the line into space delimited
      StringTokenizer space_delimited = new StringTokenizer(text_line);
      while (space_delimited.hasMoreTokens()) {
        single_word.set(space_delimited.nextToken());

        // Here we write a single word as the key and give it a value of unity
        output.write(single_word, unity);
      }
    }
  }

  public static class reducing extends Reducer<Text, IntWritable, Text,
IntWritable> {

  public void reduce(Text key, Iterable<IntWritable> grouped_values, Context
output)
                                               throws IOException,
InterruptedException {
    int sum_of_times_word_is_used = 0;
    for (IntWritable single_value : grouped_values) {
      sum_of_times_word_is_used += single_value.get();
    }

    // Hadoop data wrappers are set to be used in lines 42-43 so the output
can't be an int;
    //  make it an IntWritable
    IntWritable total_times_word_used = new
IntWritable(sum_of_times_word_is_used);
    output.write(key, total_times_word_used);
    }
  }
}
```

FIGURE 19.2 Cont'd

The application requires two arguments: the input data file placed in HDFS and the output directory where results from the reducer will be written. The code is compiled using *javac* and the compiled classes are placed in a subdirectory called *build*:

```
mkdir build
javac -cp $(hadoop classpath) -d build HamletCounter.java
```

A Java archive file, *hamletcount.jar*, is then created using the compiled class files in the build directory in preparation for execution by Hadoop:

```
jar -cvf hamletcount.jar -C build
```

Hadoop then executes the Java archive file as follows:

```
hadoop jar hamletcount.jar HamletCounter /hamlet /hamlet_result
```

where */hamlet* and */hamlet_result* are the input and output arguments required by the program. The */hamlet* text was already added to HDFS and the output from the MapReduce execution will be written to the */hamlet_result* directory. This data can be retrieved from the distributed file system to the local file system using *hdfs dfs −get* as follows:

```
hdfs dfs -get /hamlet_result
```

This will copy the entire directory of */hamlet_result* to the local file system with the results of the word count for *Hamlet*.

19.5 SUMMARY AND OUTCOMES OF CHAPTER 19

- MapReduce is a simple programming model for enabling distributed computations, including data processing on very-large-input datasets in a highly scalable and fault-tolerant way.
- The details of the underlying parallelization in MapReduce are hidden from the programmer, thereby making it easier to use.
- A *map* is a functional that executes a supplied function on all members of an input list.
- The results of the map function and associated groupings are passed to the *reduce* function.
- The map functions, like the reduce functions, can be executed concurrently giving a significant potential for speed-up.
- Distributed processing in MapReduce may be summarized in three phases: a map phase, a shuffle phase, and a reduce phase.

- Efficient distributed MapReduce execution generally requires minimizing the movement of data.
- The Hadoop project provides an open-source implementation of the MapReduce programming model.
- Hadoop provides a distributed file system, job scheduling and resource management tools, and MapReduce programming support

19.6 EXERCISES

1. By either using the word counter map and reduce functions from Fig. 19.2 or creating your own, discover how many times the word Denmark is used in Shakespeare's *Hamlet*. Then find William Shakespeare's top 10 most used words by applying your word counter tool to all the works of Shakespeare.
2. Implement the map and reduce functions of the shared neighbor finder in the graph problems presented in Section 19.2.2. Apply this map–reduce operation to the IMDb movie database [4] to find the common costar links between 10 famous actors or actresses.
3. Implement the map and reduce functions of the K-means clustering algorithm presented in Section 19.2.3. Generate a random set of x and y points and execute K-means clustering on this set. Plot the time to solution as a function of set size.
4. Using a full Wikipedia dump [5] as input, find the 20 most common words in the 10 most widely spoken languages [6] (Mandarin, Spanish, English, Hindi, Arabic, Portugese, Bengali, Russian, Japanese, and Punjabi).

REFERENCES

[1] Apache, Apache Hadoop. [Online] http://hadoop.apache.org/.
[2] J. Dean, S. Ghemawat, MapReduce: simplified data processing on large clusters, in: OSDI'04: Sixth Symposium on Operating System Design and Implementation, s.n., San Francisco, 2004.
[3] S. Ghemawat, H. Gobioff, S.-T. Leung, The Google file system, in: 19th ACM Symposium on Operating Systems Principles, ACM, Lake George, NY, 2003.
[4] IMDb, Plain Text Data Files for IMDb FTP Site. [Online] ftp://ftp.fu-berlin.de/pub/misc/movies/database/.
[5] Wikipedia, Wikipedia Downloads. [Online] https://dumps.wikimedia.org/.
[6] List of Languages by Number of Native Speakers, Wikipedia. [Online] https://en.wikipedia.org/wiki/List_of_languages_by_number_of_native_speakers.

CHAPTER

CHECKPOINTING

20

CHAPTER OUTLINE

20.1 INTRODUCTION

Many high performance computing (HPC) applications take a very long time to run even when using a large number of concurrent compute resources. Examples of applications that have historically required very long runtimes on HPC resources include molecular dynamics simulations, fluid-flow simulations, astrophysical compact object merger simulations, and mathematical optimization problems. Apart from these, an application that does not strong scale very well may require large runtimes because it can only effectively use a limited number of compute resources and would see no time-to-solution benefit when adding more. Applications with long execution times run a significant risk of encountering a hardware or software failure before completion. Long execution times also frequently violate supercomputer usage policies where a maximum wallclock time limit for a simulation is established to accommodate a large number of users better. In either case, the consequences of having a job killed can be very significant and costly in terms of time lost and computing resources wasted. Checkpointing is one way to help mitigate this risk.

At designated points during the execution of an application on a supercomputer, the data necessary to allow later resumption of the application at that point in the execution can be output and saved. This data is called a checkpoint, and the resumption of application execution is called a restart. It is no surprise that checkpoint files can be extremely large. Beyond mitigating the cost of an execution failure during a simulation that runs for a long time, checkpoint files provide snapshots of the application at different simulation epochs, help in debugging, aid in performance monitoring and analysis, and can help improve load-balancing decisions for better distributed-memory usage. This chapter explores two different approaches to checkpointing frequently encountered in HPC: system-level approaches and application-level approaches.

High Performance Computing. https://doi.org/10.1016/B978-0-12-420158-3.00020-4

20.2 SYSTEM-LEVEL CHECKPOINTING

System-level checkpointing performs the checkpoint and restart procedures via a full memory dump. This type of checkpointing does not require any changes to the application to enable its use, and writing of the checkpoint may be triggered either by the system or by the user. Examples of such user-transparent approaches for HPC support include Berkeley Lab Checkpoint/Restart [1], Checkpoint/Restore in Userspace [2], and Distributed MultiThreaded CheckPointing (DMTCP) [3]. These system-level approaches are generally fully integrated with the resource management system on a supercomputer, including Simple Linux Utility for Resource Management (SLURM) and Portable Batch System (PBS), and provide checkpoint/restart support for multithreaded applications and distributed-memory applications based on the message-passing interface (MPI). They are fully transparent to the user, requiring no changes to an application code, although they generally require a preload library step and inputs to specify the checkpoint interval, checkpoint directory, and restart directory.

The key advantage of system-level checkpoint/restart approaches over application-level approaches is that they require no changes to the application source code. Additionally, many system-level approaches incorporate access to kernel resource information, such as process IDs, which can simplify restarting the application. However, because the system-level checkpointing strategy includes a full memory dump, the checkpoint files may be significantly larger than just saving the smallest amount of relevant information, as is done with an application-level approach.

As an example of interactive system-level checkpointing, the OpenMP code in Code 20.1 is used in conjunction with the DMTCP tool in this section.

```
#include <omp.h>
#include <unistd.h>
#include <stdio.h>
#include <stdlib.h>
#include <math.h>

int main (int argc, char *argv[])
{
  const int size = 20;
  int nthreads, threadid, i;
  double array1[size], array2[size], array3[size];

  // Initialize
  for (i=0; i < size; i++) {
     array1[i] = 1.0*i;
     array2[i] = 2.0*i;
  }

  int chunk = 3;

#pragma omp parallel private(threadid)
  {
  threadid = omp_get_thread_num();
  if (threadid == 0) {
```

```
25      nthreads = omp_get_num_threads();
26      printf("Number of threads = %d\n", nthreads);
27    }
28    printf(" My threadid %d\n",threadid);
29
30    #pragma omp for schedule(static,chunk)
31    for (i=0; i<size; i++) {
32      array3[i] = sin(array1[i] + array2[i]);
33      printf(" Thread id: %d working on index %d\n",threadid,i);
34      sleep(1);
35    }
36
37    } // join
38
39    printf(" TEST array3[199] = %g\n",array3[199]);
40
41    return 0;
42 }
```

Code 20.1. Example OpenMP code, checkpoint_openmp.c, for demonstrating system-level checkpointing. A "sleep" statement has been added to line 34 to add a pause to the execution after each thread performs the operation of line 32.

DMTCP provides several easy-to-use commands for transparent system-level checkpointing. The *dmtcp_coordinator* acts as a command-line interface to DMTCP for examining the checkpoint interval, accessing status messages, and forcing a manual checkpoint outside the specified checkpoint interval from the command line. The *dmtcp_coordinator* is launched in a separate terminal and awaits command-line input instructions and outputs status messages, as shown in Fig. 20.1.

```
andersmw@cutter:~/dmtcp-dmtcp-35386c2/bin$ ./dmtcp_coordinator
dmtcp_coordinator starting...
    Host: cutter (156.56.64.43)
    Port: 7779
    Checkpoint Interval: disabled (checkpoint manually instead)
    Exit on last client: 0
Type '?' for help.

?
COMMANDS:
  l : List connected nodes
  s : Print status message
  c : Checkpoint all nodes
  i : Print current checkpoint interval
      (To change checkpoint interval, use dmtcp_command)
  k : Kill all nodes
  q : Kill all nodes and quit
  ? : Show this message
```

FIGURE 20.1

The *dmtcp_coordinator* for status updates and interact with DMTCP via the specific commands listed here, including forcing a checkpoint outside the checkpoint interval by issuing the "c" command.

To checkpoint the code illustrated in Code 20.1, it is compiled just as if it were not being checkpointed:

```
gcc -fopenmp -O3 -o checkpoint_openmp checkpoint_openmp.c -lm
```

The math library ("-lm") is added for the sin(x) function used on line 32 of Code 20.1 and the executable is named "checkpoint_openmp".

The number of OpenMP threads is also set in the normal way through the environment variable OMP_NUM_THREADS (illustrated here using bash shell syntax; for tcsh shell, use *setenv*):

```
export OMP_NUM_THREADS=16
```

The checkpoint interval can be changed using *dmtcp_command*, which sends the command to the *dmtcp_coordinator* already launched in Fig. 20.1:

```
dmtcp_command --interval <checkpoint interval in seconds>
```

Because Code 20.1 executes very quickly, a checkpoint request will be manually input into the *dmtcp_coordinator* command interface. The executable is launched with checkpoint capability using the *dmtcp_launch* tool:

```
dmtcp_launch ./checkpoint_openmp
```

The executable begins to run as normal, and if a checkpoint interval has been supplied, at every specified interval of wallclock time a checkpoint is written to the file system. Additionally, if the command "c" is supplied to the *dmtcp_coordinator* command interface, a checkpoint is written to the file system at that point. DMTCP checkpoint files have the naming convention of "ckpt_<executable name>_<client identity>.dmtcp" and are written in the directory where the executable was launched. A manually issued checkpoint request is illustrated in Fig. 20.2, which creates, in this example, a checkpoint file named *ckpt_checkpoint_openmp_16707112e4c8f-42000-8687a700c18a5.dmtcp*.

The checkpoint file is restarted using the *dmtcp_restart* command:

```
dmtcp_restart <checkpoint file>
```

A snippet of the standard output for Code 20.1 with and without checkpoint restart is shown in Fig. 20.3. The same OpenMP threads operate on the same array indices and all operations are identical in the restarted case and the nonrestarted case. No changes were made to the code to enable

```
c
[40367] NOTE at dmtcp_coordinator.cpp:1071 in startCheckpoint; REASON='starting checkpoint, suspending all nodes'
     s.numPeers = 1
[40367] NOTE at dmtcp_coordinator.cpp:1073 in startCheckpoint; REASON='Incremented computationGeneration'
     compId.computationGeneration() = 1
[40367] NOTE at dmtcp_coordinator.cpp:413 in updateMinimumState; REASON='locking all nodes'
[40367] NOTE at dmtcp_coordinator.cpp:419 in updateMinimumState; REASON='draining all nodes'
[40367] NOTE at dmtcp_coordinator.cpp:425 in updateMinimumState; REASON='checkpointing all nodes'
[40367] NOTE at dmtcp_coordinator.cpp:449 in updateMinimumState; REASON='building name service database'
[40367] NOTE at dmtcp_coordinator.cpp:465 in updateMinimumState; REASON='entertaining queries now'
[40367] NOTE at dmtcp_coordinator.cpp:470 in updateMinimumState; REASON='refilling all nodes'
[40367] NOTE at dmtcp_coordinator.cpp:510 in updateMinimumState; REASON='restarting all nodes'
```

FIGURE 20.2

A manually issued checkpoint request followed by the associated status messages from DMTCP for checkpointing Code 20.1.

```
andersmw@cutter:~/textbook$ dmtcp_restart ckpt_checkpoint_openmp_16707112e4c8f-42000-8687a700c18a5.dmtcp
 Thread id: 15 working on index 141
 Thread id: 14 working on index 138
 Thread id: 7 working on index 117
 Thread id: 12 working on index 132
 Thread id: 1 working on index 99
 Thread id: 2 working on index 102
 Thread id: 8 working on index 120
 Thread id: 5 working on index 111
 Thread id: 11 working on index 129
 Thread id: 13 working on index 135
 Thread id: 3 working on index 105
 Thread id: 10 working on index 126
 Thread id: 9 working on index 123
 Thread id: 6 working on index 114
 Thread id: 4 working on index 108
 Thread id: 0 working on index 96
```

```
Thread id: 15 working on index 141
Thread id: 14 working on index 138
Thread id: 8 working on index 120
Thread id: 1 working on index 99
Thread id: 2 working on index 102
Thread id: 4 working on index 108
Thread id: 12 working on index 132
Thread id: 7 working on index 117
Thread id: 0 working on index 96
Thread id: 13 working on index 135
Thread id: 11 working on index 129
Thread id: 5 working on index 111
Thread id: 3 working on index 105
Thread id: 9 working on index 123
Thread id: 6 working on index 114
Thread id: 10 working on index 126
```

FIGURE 20.3

The standard output from Code 20.1 after checkpoint restart (left) and without restart (right). The same OpenMP threads operate on the same indices and all operations are identical in the restarted case and the nonrestarted case. As is standard in system-level checkpointing, no changes to Code 20.1 were made to enable checkpoint capability.

checkpoint/restart capability, and the checkpoint files written could also be used for debugging, execution snapshots, or as part of a strategy for fault tolerance.

Interactive system-level checkpoint/restart using DMTCP for an MPI application is similar to that for an OpenMP application, but with small differences. An example MPI "pingpong" code, referred to as pingpong.c, using *MPI_Send* and *MPI_Recv* is shown in Code 20.2, which passes back and forth an integer and increments that integer for each iteration.

```
#include <stdio.h>
#include <stdlib.h>
#include <unistd.h>
#include "mpi.h"

int main(int argc,char **argv)
{
  int rank,size;
  MPI_Init(&argc,&argv);
  MPI_Comm_rank(MPI_COMM_WORLD,&rank);
  MPI_Comm_size(MPI_COMM_WORLD,&size);

```

```
13   if ( size != 2 ) {
14     printf(" Only runs on 2 processes \n");
15     MPI_Finalize();    // this example only works on two processes
16     exit(0);
17   }
18
19   int count;
20   if ( rank == 0 ) {
21     // initialize count on process 0
22     count = 0;
23   }
24   for (int i=0;i<10;i++) {
25     if ( rank == 0 ) {
26       MPI_Send(&count,1,MPI_INT,1,0,MPI_COMM_WORLD); // send "count" to rank 1
27       MPI_Recv(&count,1,MPI_INT,1,0,MPI_COMM_WORLD,MPI_STATUS_IGNORE); // receive it back
28       sleep(1);
29       count++;
30       printf(" Count %d\n",count);
31     } else {
32       MPI_Recv(&count,1,MPI_INT,0,0,MPI_COMM_WORLD,MPI_STATUS_IGNORE);
33       MPI_Send(&count,1,MPI_INT,0,0,MPI_COMM_WORLD);
34     }
35   }
36
37   if ( rank == 0 ) printf("\t\t\t Round trip count = %d\n",count);
38
39   MPI_Finalize();
40 }
```

Code 20.2. Example MPI "pingpong" code for demonstrating system-level checkpoint/restart using DMTCP. A "sleep" command has been added to line 28 to slow down the execution for checkpoint demonstration purposes. This code is designed to work on only two processes and will print out the "count" integer at each message epoch.

Just as in the OpenMP checkpoint/restart example, the code is not modified and is compiled as usual without including any extra libraries specific to checkpoint/restart:

```
mpicc -O3 -o pingpong pingpong.c
```

In this example MPICH-2 is the MPI implementation used; DMTCP supports several different implementations of MPI. After the *dmtcp_coordinator* is started in a separate window to issue manual checkpoint commands and monitor status messages, the pingpong executable is then launched on two processes using a combination of *dmtcp_launch* and *mpirun* as follows:

```
dmctp_launch --rm mpirun -np 2 ./pingpong
```

```
c
[22984] NOTE at dmtcp_coordinator.cpp:1071 in startCheckpoint; REASON='starting checkpoint, suspending all nodes'
     s.numPeers = 4
[22984] NOTE at dmtcp_coordinator.cpp:1073 in startCheckpoint; REASON='Incremented computationGeneration'
     compId.computationGeneration() = 1
[22984] NOTE at dmtcp_coordinator.cpp:413 in updateMinimumState; REASON='locking all nodes'
[22984] NOTE at dmtcp_coordinator.cpp:419 in updateMinimumState; REASON='draining all nodes'
[22984] NOTE at dmtcp_coordinator.cpp:425 in updateMinimumState; REASON='checkpointing all nodes'
[22984] NOTE at dmtcp_coordinator.cpp:449 in updateMinimumState; REASON='building name service database'
[22984] NOTE at dmtcp_coordinator.cpp:465 in updateMinimumState; REASON='entertaining queries now'
[22984] NOTE at dmtcp_coordinator.cpp:470 in updateMinimumState; REASON='refilling all nodes'
[22984] NOTE at dmtcp_coordinator.cpp:510 in updateMinimumState; REASON='restarting all nodes'
```

FIGURE 20.4

Status messages generated after issuing the checkpoint command ("c") to the *dmtcp_coordinator*. Each process generates a checkpoint file, which is stored in the directory where the executable was launched.

After five message epochs the command for generating the checkpoint ("c") is issued to the *dmtcp_coordinator*, as illustrated in Fig. 20.4.

Four checkpoint files result from the checkpoint command, one from each process and two associated with the MPI launcher. A restart script specific to the checkpoint files generated is also created to simplify the restart process. This script is created in the directory where the *dmtcp_coordinator* was launched and is called *dmtcp_restart_script_<client identity>.sh*. The script requires no arguments and already knows where to find the checkpoint files in the file system. Launching this shell script will restart the job, as illustrated in Fig. 20.5.

Both the OpenMP and MPI examples explored here using the DMTCP system-level checkpointing tool were performed interactively for ease of demonstration. However, on most supercomputing systems a user does not attempt to perform a checkpoint/restart interactively but launches applications through a resource management system like PBS or SLURM. DMTCP, like the other system-level checkpointing tools mentioned here, is integrated with PBS and SLURM and provides example scripts for launching and restarting applications through a resource management system. In the case of DMTCP, using a resource management system to checkpoint an MPI or OpenMP application requires the *dmtcp_coordinator* to be launched as a daemon in the PBS or SLURM script while the other commands (*dmtcp_launch, dmtcp_restart_script)* remain the same, as was demonstrated in interactive mode. On HPC resources with an Infiniband network, the *dmtcp_launch* command also requires the flag *–infiniband* for checkpoint/restart support of MPI-based applications using Infiniband.

```
[andersmw@cutter textbook]$ ./dmtcp_restart_script_129b065bca8bba11-56000-87bae5e9cb04.sh
 Count 6
 Count 7
 Count 8
 Count 9
 Count 10
                               Round trip count = 10
```

```
Count 1
Count 2
Count 3
Count 4
Count 5
Count 6
Count 7
Count 8
Count 9
Count 10
                  Round trip count = 10
```

FIGURE 20.5

The standard output from the MPI "pingpong" from Code 20.2 after checkpoint restart (left) and without using any checkpoint/restart (right). The checkpoint restart case (left) began from checkpoint data generated after the fifth epoch, and consequently the first output seen after restart is the sixth epoch.

20.3 APPLICATION-LEVEL CHECKPOINTING

In application-level checkpointing the application developer has the responsibility to perform all checkpoint/restart operations. As opposed to system-level checkpointing, application-level checkpointing requires changes to the application code. While inconvenient, application-level checkpoint/restart tends to produce checkpoint files that are smaller than system-level checkpoint/restart, where a full memory dump is performed. Checkpoint files originating from application-level checkpointing are generally smaller than those originating from system-level checkpointing approaches simply because the application developer will only output the most pertinent information necessary for application restart. The system, in contrast, has to dump the entire application memory because it cannot single out what data is relevant for restart.

For distributed-memory applications based on MPI, application-level checkpoint/restart approaches often share some basic characteristics:

- Only one checkpoint file is written per MPI process.
- Only one MPI rank accesses a single checkpoint file.
- Checkpoint files do not contain data from multiple checkpoint epochs.
- Checkpoint files are generally written to the parallel file system by the compute nodes.
- Checkpoint/restart overheads can be large.

Application-level checkpoint/restart implementations generally pick designated points in the computational phase in the simulation algorithm for checkpointing, to ensure computational phase consistency in the checkpoint epoch. For example, in a timestepping algorithm a natural place to incorporate checkpoint/restart would be at the end of one timestep, thereby ensuring that all checkpoint files are at the same computational phase even if they each reached this phase at different wallclock times. This is in contrast to system-level checkpointing, where, regardless at what phase of computation the process may be, a checkpoint is dumped as designated by a wallclock time interval or an event such as a manual request for checkpoint given in the command line. Consequently, application-level checkpoint/restart implementations may not specify a checkpoint interval in terms of wallclock time, as in system-level approaches, but rather require the interval of computational phases for checkpoint/restart.

Some of the I/O libraries explored in Chapter 10 are especially well suited for use in application-level checkpointing. For instance, the HDF5 library is widely used in this checkpointing because it is well suited for parallel I/O and creates data structured for different execution configurations as well as providing portability. As with any parallel I/O operation, however, the developer will still have to ensure that all application data is actually written to the checkpoint files and not just the pointer addresses to data. Because C codes frequently access data indirectly between different functions, it is a common novice C programmer mistake to output a pointer address rather than the data itself.

Application-level checkpoint/restart is very popular in large-scale MPI applications and toolkits because it can be tailored for the application to be as efficient and minimal as possible. However, the checkpoint/restart overhead is still very high and there are checkpoint/restart libraries written to assist in reducing this overhead for application-level checkpoint approaches. One such library is Scalable Checkpoint/Restart (SCR) for MPI [4].

The SCR library assists application-level checkpoint strategies by reducing the load on a parallel file system and partially utilizing nonparallel fast storage local to a compute node for checkpoint file storage, with some redundancy in the event of a failure on the local storage. SCR provides several different checkpoint file redundancy schemes with varying levels of resilience and performance. It requires the parallel remote shell command [5] and the Perl module for date/time interpretation [6], and works natively with the SLURM resource manager.

The SCR library is built around an application-level checkpoint strategy like that illustrated in Code 20.3 where only one checkpoint file is written by an MPI process. When using the SCR library, the library needs to know when to start a checkpoint and when to finish a checkpoint through API calls that are collective across all MPI processes. The SCR library can also determine if a checkpoint file is needed rather than having some user-defined checkpoint frequency, as was seen in Code 20.3. This is done by configuring SCR with system information to estimate checkpoint costs and frequency of failure, and then using the application programming interface (API) call *SCR_Need_checkpoint* to let SCR decide the frequency of checkpointing.

```
#include <stdio.h>
#include <stdlib.h>

#include “mpi.h”


int write_checkpoint()
{
  // get our rank
  int rank;
  MPI_Comm_rank(MPI_COMM_WORLD, &rank);

  char file[128];
  sprintf(file,“checkpoint/%d_checkpoint.dat”,rank);

  FILE *fp = fopen(file,“w”);

  // write sample checkpoint to file
  fprintf(fp,“ Hello Checkpoint World\n”);
  fclose(fp);

  return 0;
}

int main(int argc,char **argv)
{
  MPI_Init(&argc,&argv);

  int max_steps = 100;
  int step;
  int checkpoint_every = 10;

  for (step=0;step<max_steps;step++) {
    /* perform simulation work */
```

```
35
36     if ( step%checkpoint_every == 0 ) {
37       write_checkpoint();
38     }
39   }
40
41   MPI_Finalize();
42   return 0;
43 }
```

Code 20.3. Simple example of a common application-level checkpoint strategy. Each process writes its own checkpoint data to a single checkpoint file. The frequency of writing the checkpoint is determined by the user, set here to be 10 (line 31).

The modifications to Code 20.3 needed to incorporate the SCR library are limited to adding the calls *SCR_Init*, *SCR_Finalize*, *SCR_Start_checkpoint*, *SCR_Complete_checkpoint*, and *SCR_Route_file*. Optionally, the checkpoint frequency can be determined by SCR using the call *SCR_Need_checkpoint*, as already noted. *SCR_Init* and *SCR_Finalize* initialize and shut down the SCR library, analogous to *MPI_Init* and *MPI_Finalize*. *SCR_Start_checkpoint* and *SCR_Complete_checkpoint* indicate, respectively, that a checkpoint is about to begin to write and a checkpoint has successfully been written. *SCR_Route_file* is used for getting the full path and file name for SCR access. Each SCR API call is collective across all MPI processes. The SCR version of Code 20.3 is provided in Code 20.4.

```
#include <stdio.h>
#include <stdlib.h>
#include "scr.h"
#include "mpi.h"

int write_checkpoint()
{
  SCR_Start_checkpoint();

  // get our rank
  int rank;
  MPI_Comm_rank(MPI_COMM_WORLD, &rank);

  char file[128];
  sprintf(file,"checkpoint/%d_checkpoint.dat",rank);

  FILE *fp = fopen(file,"w");

  char scrfile[SCR_MAX_FILENAME];
  SCR_Route_file(file,scrfile);

  // write sample checkpoint to file
  fprintf(fp," Hello Checkpoint World\n");
  fclose(fp);

```

```
26     int valid = 1;
27
28     SCR_Complete_checkpoint(valid);
29
30     return 0;
31   }
32
33   int main(int argc,char **argv)
34   {
35     MPI_Init(&argc,&argv);
36
37    if ( SCR_Init() != SCR_SUCCESS ) {
38       printf(" SCR didn't initialize\n");
39       return -1;
40    }
41
42    int max_steps = 100;
43    int step;
44    for (step=0;step<max_steps;step++) {
45      /* perform simulation work */
46
47      int checkpoint_flag;
48      SCR_Need_checkpoint(&checkpoint_flag);
49      if ( checkpoint_flag ) {
50         write_checkpoint();
51      }
52    }
53    SCR_Finalize();
54    MPI_Finalize();
55    return 0;
56 }
```

Code 20.4. SCR version of Code 20.3 application-level checkpointing. Calls to the SCR API include SCR_Init (line 37), SCR_Finalize (line 53), SCR_Start_checkpoint (line 8), SCR_Complete_checkpoint (line 28), SCR_Need_checkpoint (line 48), and SCR_Route_file (line 20). The SCR_Need_checkpoint call is optional and allows SCR to control the checkpoint frequency. Relatively few changes are needed to an existing application-level checkpoint strategy to take advantage of the benefits of SCR.

To use SCR and execute Code 20.4, SCR must be integrated with the supercomputer's resource management system. In the case of SLURM, an SCR-enabled code would launch using *scr_srun* instead of *srun*.

20.4 SUMMARY AND OUTCOMES OF CHAPTER 20

- Applications with long execution times run a significant risk of encountering a hardware or software failure before completion.
- Long execution times also frequently violate supercomputer usage policies where a maximum wallclock limit for a simulation is established.
- The consequences of a hardware or software failure can be very significant and costly in terms of time lost and computing resources wasted for long-running jobs.
- At designated points during the execution of an application on a supercomputer, the data necessary to allow later resumption of the application at that point in the execution can be output and saved. This data is called a checkpoint.
- Checkpoint files help mitigate the risk of a hardware or software failure in a long-running job.
- Checkpoint files also provide snapshots of the application at different simulation epochs, help in debugging, aid in performance monitoring and analysis, and can help improve load-balancing decisions for better distributed-memory usage.
- In HPC applications, two common strategies for checkpoint/restart are employed: system-level checkpoint and application-level checkpointing.
- System-level checkpointing requires no modifications to the user code but may require loading a specific system-level library.
- System-level checkpointing strategies center on full memory dumps and may result in very large checkpoint files.
- Application-level checkpointing requires modifications to the user code. Libraries exist to assist this process.
- Application-level checkpoint files tend to be more efficient, since they only output the most relevant data needed for restart.

20.5 EXERCISES

1. List the trade-offs between system-level checkpointing and application-level checkpointing. Survey the some of the many scientific computing toolkits available for download that have checkpoint/restart capability. What form of checkpointing is the most popular in these toolkits?
2. How might checkpoint files be used for debugging? Illustrate this by introducing a race condition into Code 20.1, such as a reduction operation without the appropriate reduction clause, and expose the bug by using a checkpoint file. Use system-level checkpointing.
3. For an application that runs on 100,000 cores for 9 days of wallclock time, estimate the likelihood that the application will encounter a hardware failure during the simulation. Use the reported annualized failure rate for a hypothetical collection of hard drives, processors, and power supplies.
4. What could happen if a system failure occurs while a checkpoint is being written? What are the ways to mitigate this type of failure?
5. What is the trade-offs between checkpointing frequently and infrequently? Suppose the example in Code 20.2 is checkpoint every 1 s versus every 30 s. What are the performance consequences and benefits of these?

REFERENCES

[1] Berkely Laboratory, Berkeley Lab Checkpoint/Restart (BLCR) for LINUX. [Online] http://crd.lbl.gov/departments/computer-science/CLaSS/research/BLCR/.
[2] CRIU, Checkpoint/Restore In Userspace. [Online] https://criu.org/.
[3] DMTCP: Distributed MultiThreaded CheckPointing. [Online] http://dmtcp.sourceforge.net/.
[4] Lawrence Livermore National Laboratory, Scalable Checkpoint/Restart Library. [Online] http://computation.llnl.gov/projects/scalable-checkpoint-restart-for-mpi/software.
[5] Parallel Remote Shell Command (PDSH). [Online] http://sourceforge.net/projects/pdsh.
[6] Perl Date Maniputation. [Online] http://search.cpan.org/~sbeck/Date-Manip-6.56.

CHAPTER

NEXT STEPS AND BEYOND

21

CHAPTER OUTLINE

High Performance Computing. https://doi.org/10.1016/B978-0-12-420158-3.00021-6

21.1 INTRODUCTION

This textbook gives a comprehensive top-level coverage of high performance computing (HPC), both to present the complex interdisciplinary components of the field and to provide the basic skill-sets that an entry-level student practitioner requires and can use to employ such systems for end-user applications. It presents major classes of architecture, programming models, basic algorithmic techniques, and widely used tools and environments. More deeply, it shares the fundamental concepts that govern the challenges of efficiency, scalability, parallel semantics, and metrics. But while an excellent first coverage of the broad field, it is far from complete; it is more of a starting point than exhaustive. In this chapter the authors complete this treatise by noting what has not been covered that may be of interest and serve as a roadmap for further study in specific areas, incrementally building on what has already been presented. This is done in two domains. Sections 21.2 and 21.3 describe in brief the more sophisticated techniques currently employed in both programming models and hardware architectures. Section 21.4 discusses current directions toward exascale computing, which is occupying much energy in near-term research across the northern hemisphere, with likely impact in the early 2020s. Section 21.5 considers a shift in computing methods being explored, sometimes referred to as "asynchronous multitasking", that will enable dynamic adaptive techniques for improved efficiency and scalability. Section 21.6 on the "neodigital age" may be viewed for your curiosity. It projects ideas about what may happen with the end of Moore's law and nanoscale semiconductor technology, and where revolutionary approaches to computer architecture going beyond the von Neumann architecture and its decades of derivatives may take us. This includes "quantum computing", which is in a most inchoate phase, but if it proves possible will be able to perform some computations that could not be done even in the lifetime of the universe if performed on even the biggest conventional computer.

21.2 EXPANDED PARALLEL PROGRAMMING MODELS

21.2.1 ADVANCE IN MESSAGE-PASSING INTERFACE

The message-passing interface (MPI) is one of the most widely used means of describing programs to run on scalable distributed-memory systems comprising multiple computing nodes integrated via one or more interconnection networks. This textbook describes the programming principles of MPI consistent with the MPI-1 standard, including the basics of establishing virtual topologies among processes, send/receive message communication constructs, scalar data types and some complex data structures, collective operations for synchronization, data distribution, and collective reduction operations. But in total only a couple of dozen MPI functions are described. These are sufficient to represent a wide range of useful parallel algorithms and run these applications on a wide range of large-scale current-generation systems, yet only scratch the surface of the rich set of commands actually available even by MPI-1 for optimization and to facilitate sophisticated communication and shared computation patterns. Since the final specification of MPI-1 in 2008, including more than 120 functions, MPI has evolved as a model and a parallel programming interface, expanding to the advanced versions of MPI-2 and MPI-3. MPI-2 made important extensions to the original standard, including a strong set of input/output (I/O) calls to manage access to mass storage, dynamic process management, and single-sided functions on remote memory. MPI-3 added significant extensions to the previous versions, expanding the full set of collective operations specifically in the domain of non-blocking as well as other improvements.

21.2.2 ADVANCES IN OPENMP

OpenMP has been demonstrated as a popular programming interface for shared-memory computing systems. First introduced in 1997 with Fortran bindings and in 2002 with C/C++ bindings for OpenMP-2, OpenMP language extensions have provided environment variables, directives, and library functions for transforming sequential application codes into programs that include multiple-thread computing for a degree of parallelism and reduction in time to solution. This textbook presents the foundation concepts of OpenMP, and many of the key constructs and their syntax. The full OpenMP specification is far larger, with many valuable optimizations that are not covered. But even the chosen subset shows that substantive and diverse applications can be constructed and run on a wide array of systems. Further advances beyond the basic functions were devised in later versions of OpenMP. For example, the powerful capability of multitasking and the task construct were a centerpiece of OpenMP-3 in 2008. In 2013 OpenMP-4 was released with a number of significant improvements, such as support for heterogeneous systems incorporating accelerators, the inclusion of thread affinity to assist in managing some aspects of locality, and methods for exploiting single-instruction multiple data (SIMD) parallelism. OpenMP has been very successful, but has some shortcomings that bound its effectiveness in terms of efficiency and scalability. Because it assumes a shared-memory ecosystem, it is limited in scaling on single symmetric multiprocessor (SMP) systems. This is in part mitigated by increasing the number of cores integrated on chip and per socket. Its efficiency is constrained by its heavy use of fork–join semantics in which global barriers play a significant part. This is sensitive to Amdahl's law with the purely sequential parts of any OpenMP code. The tasking mechanisms can help offset this property.

21.2.3 MPI+X

In brief, MPI provides a form of scalability with coarse-grain parallelism across distributed-memory systems while OpenMP provides a form of medium-grain parallelism within the boundaries of shared-memory nodes. Neither is sufficient for the future challenges of exascale computing and beyond. But the combination of the two, each complementing the other, is viewed as a significant opportunity for the next stages in the field. MPI processes across distributed-memory system architectures will continue to provide the scalability required, while OpenMP delineates medium-grain threads that can be performed by the many cores within a single node. This permits a coarse-grained MPI process to span the entire node (as it did in the early days of massively parallel processors—MPPs), but allows the efficiencies of shared memory hardware to be exploited and greater parallelism to be exposed with the assistance of OpenMP constructs. The general concept has been referred to as "MPI+X", where "X" refers to another or additional programming interface working in cooperation with MPI. X could also mean OpenCL, or perhaps even configuring field programmable gate arrays (FPGAs) within a node. As Bill Gropp said, "The important part of MPI+X is the '+'." [1]

21.3 EXTENDED HIGH PERFORMANCE COMPUTING ARCHITECTURE

The end of Moore's law marks a milestone in HPC. Over multiple decades technology could be anticipated to deliver exponential growth in device density and clock rate. But this is rapidly changing, with parallel architecture being the only remaining strategy to continue performance growth, at least until some significant advance in enabling technology emerges to replace CMOS (such as superconducting Josephson junction logic) or an entirely new paradigm (such as quantum computing) is developed and made practical. This section touches on some advances in HPC system architecture that are being pursued.

21.3.1 THE WORLD'S FASTEST MACHINE

The world's fastest machine as of June 2017 is the third Chinese machine to make the number 1 slot of the Top 500 list in recent years: the Sunway TaihuLight (神威·太湖之光) based on Sunway microprocessors. It is an example of pursuing alternative approaches outside conventional architectures. This system, which has a peak performance greater than 100 Petaflops and a Linpack rating of almost that much, is based on a new architecture fully developed and manufactured in China. The architecture features an extremely lightweight core that dispenses with many of the conventional internal subcomponents such as data caches. While some efficiency, as measured by arithmetic logic unit utilization, is degraded, a much larger number of cores can be integrated on to a die, each using much less energy. This machine, although more than two times faster than its predecessor (also Chinese), uses less than half as much electrical power. This is a remarkable achievement. The Sunway architecture is also controversial, as its memory capacity is relatively small given its peak floating-point performance. But in a very short time it has demonstrated significant achievement in real-world applications. In all it has more than 10 million cores—an unprecedented record.

21.3.2 LIGHTWEIGHT ARCHITECTURES

The vast majority of the fastest supercomputers (see the Top 500 list) employ either Intel ×86 architecture microprocessors (including AMD variants) or IBM Power-based microprocessors with or without accelerators, including Nvidia and Intel Phi. However, there is a trend toward lightweight architectures to increase peak performance per socket and reduce power consumption and space costs.

As noted, a dramatic example is the TaihuLight, the world's fastest supercomputer measured by the high performance Linpack (HPL) benchmark in 2017. It comprises 10 million cores, each of which is very lightweight with only some scratchpad high-speed memory (with an instruction cache). Sixty-four of these are organized in a "group", and there are four groups in a processor socket for 256 cores plus four management processing elements to manage the computation. At a peak performance of 125 petaflops it is the first system to enter the 100 Pflops performance regime.

A second important trend is the evolution of the Intel Xeon Phi processor, derived from the failed Larrabee Project [2]. Intel chose to address the challenge of ultrahigh performance through pervasive integration of a semiconductor die with many lightweight cores rather than the fewer heavyweight

Xeon cores that have dominated MPPs and commodity clusters for 2 decades. These were originally treated like graphics processing units (GPUs), as attached processors with printed circuit boards (PCBs) incorporating Phi chips integrated via industry interface standards, principally PCI express (PCIe). While a convenient way to introduce a new technology rapidly, this approach suffered from the treatment of these devices as attached array processors controlled by master processors and separated by relatively slow Peripheral Component Interconnect (PCI) buses in terms of latency, bandwidth, and control overheads. The latest generation of Xeon Phi corrects these shortcomings by allowing the Phi processor sockets to operate in "self-hosting" mode; that is, to be their own masters, eliminating the PCI bottlenecks and equally important the control overheads. This is a big deal, and will be first demonstrated in the 2018 as currently planned.

An alternative path that is trending is the evolution of the long-serving ARM processor architecture. The heritage of ARM is in the vast operational space of mobile, embedded, and control processing. ARM can be custom configured by the end implementer to provide a wide variation in the ecosphere of the support logic and interfaces on die. Although primarily a 32-bit architecture, ARM has now been extended to several variants of 64-bit architecture, making it truly suitable in the context of supercomputing for conventional numeric applications such as simulation and data analysis. At least one major-scale experimental supercomputer, Mont Blanc, is under development in Europe using ARM as the principal processor core. Unconfirmed reports suggest that the National University of Defense Technology in China is pursuing a similar approach. While ARM is not currently regarded as part of the HPC field, this may change radically toward the end of this decade.

21.3.3 FIELD PROGRAMMABLE GATE ARRAYS

An FPGA is, as the name implies, a component comprising a large number of logic gates and other functional parts connected by a network, the connectivity of which can be determined by "programming" the device. That is, there is a protocol by which the end user can determine the logic circuitry of the component. While less dense and somewhat slower than application-specific integrated circuits (ASICs), FPGAs enable custom designs to be produced to optimize them for special-purpose functionality. This permits the rapid development of prototype designs and gives a means to distribute a small number of parts to end users. One area of use that may prove promising is application-specific FPGA logic circuits optimized for specific algorithms. Such structures as systolic arrays can be implemented readily with FPGAs to accelerate important applications by one to two orders of magnitude with respect to conventional microprocessors. Other uses may include logic designs to support future system software to reduce overheads.

The major challenge is to provide efficient functionality that best suits application algorithms and the means of rapidly programming FPGAs. Much work has been done in both domains, but use still demands expertise. Another problem is the integration of FPGAs with otherwise conventional systems. This is in part addressed through industry-standard interfaces to which custom boards are designed with FPGA components. But this still has its limitations. Now hybrid subsystems with both processors and FPGAs integrated together are being made available, again improving their mutual connectivity.

21.4 EXASCALE COMPUTING

IBM Blue Gene/Q. *Courtesy Argonne National Laboratory via Wikimedia Commons*

Alan Gara is the chief architect of the highly successful series of IBM Blue Gene supercomputers, named after its intended applications: study of gene development and protein folding. Blue Gene architecture was a significant departure from the then leading Earth Simulator computer emphasizing vector processing. Blue Gene instead incorporated a large number of simple cores derived from embedded processors, resulting in improved energy efficiency. Its first model, Blue Gene/L, employed dual processor nodes with compute logic and NIC integrated on a single ASIC. The central processing units (CPUs) were based on PowerPC 440 with added double-precision floating-point pipelines delivering a peak of 5.6 Gflops per node. Thanks to high-density packaging, a single rack contained 1024 such nodes. Blue Gene/L (shown in the right picture) included 32,768 cores and debuted as number 1 on the Top 500 list in November 2004, achieving over 70 Tflops or twice the performance of the previous incumbent. In an updated configuration Blue Gene maintained this position for the next 3.5 years, achieving a peak throughput of nearly 600 Tflops while consuming only 2.3 MW of electricity. The architecture is also notable for incorporation of three network types: three-dimensional torus for point-to-point communication, a dedicated collective communication interconnect, and a global interrupt network. The later versions of Blue Gene architecture included P revision with quad-core nodes and a performance-to-power metric of 0.35 Gflops/W and Q, utilizing 18-core four-way simultaneously multithreaded processors and scaling to 20 Pflops.

For his work on three generations of Blue Gene architecture, Alan Gara was recognized with the Seymour Cray Award in 2010. He also codeveloped high performance implementations of quantum chromodynamics applications; one on the QCDSP custom architecture and the other on Blue Gene/L, each of which won the Gordon Bell Prize.

Historically within the field of supercomputing there has been a natural tendency of the community as a whole to speculate, consider, and ultimately to achieve the next three orders of magnitude performance-gain milestone over the previous major one. The first megaflops computer was the CDC-6600 in 1968, followed by the first gigaflops computer, the Cray-YMP in 1988, the first teraflops machine, the Intel Red Storm in 1997, deployed at Sandia National Laboratories, and finally the first petaflops machine in 2008, the IBM Roadrunner deployed at Los Alamos National Laboratory. Roughly speaking these accomplishments occur approximately every 11 years. But this would suggest that the next milestone, exaflops, should be anticipated for 2019. While conceivable, this is not likely for a number of reasons. In recent years the fastest supercomputers measured by the HPL benchmark have been developed and deployed in China, with the most recent approaching 100 petaflops Rmax.

21.4.1 CHALLENGES TO EXASCALE COMPUTING

While most HPC systems within the mainstream are capable of one petaflops or less, the goal of exascale computing suggests 1000 times this norm, or more than 10 times the fastest computer in the world today. The challenges to achieving this are many and are application dependent. While technology is approaching the asymptote with respect to Moore's law and nanoscale semiconductors, exascale computing is still within the scope of Moore's law, even if approaching the end. The principal challenges as viewed by the industry and its users include the following:

- Energy and power—this is a limiting factor that goes beyond just the cost of the energy, which is about $1M/MWyear. It is also constrained by the maximum power that can feed a semiconductor die before it reaches a threshold of failure. A target goal is 20 MW or 50 Gflops/W.
- Hardware parallelism—expected to be in the order of a billion, which may be manifest by hundreds of millions of cores, each operating with 10-way parallelism like SIMD or vector.
- Software parallelism—application programs and algorithms using and exploiting more than a billionfold parallelism to take advantage of the hardware, including communication and secondary storage access.
- Overhead—the work required to manage the system and control each task. While a source of loss of efficiency, it also bounds the granularity of the tasks and therefore the available useful concurrency.
- Latency—with larger systems including more racks the physical distances for global access of data or services increase, requiring even more parallelism to hide the latency.
- Reliability—with the increase in the number of devices both on and off the die the chance of a single point failure increases and the potential reduction of the mean time to failure could make exascale computing impractical. Methods are required to provide resilience of both hardware and software with sufficient confidence that large and time-consuming computations can be performed.

21.4.2 DOING THE MATH, HOW BIG IS EXASCALE?

By any measure, exascale computing is enormous and its achievement, anticipated sometime in the next decade, will be a *tour de force*. In this textbook we have identified and considered a number of different dimensions by which a class of system can be measured. As a benchmark, the TaihuLight

Chinese system achieves about 100 petaflops with 10 million cores (a little less for Rmax, a little more for peak). This suggests that an exascale machine will require at least a 100 million cores for an exaflops. Of course these are lightweight cores with limited capability. Fewer cores would be required but at much more die space if heavyweight cores like the IBM Power 9 are employed, such as in the future (2018) Summit machine expected to operate at about 200 petaflops. But for real-world codes rather than for a friendly Linpack benchmark, much more will be required. With typical efficiencies around 10% (often less but sometimes more), this would project that there is significant room for dramatic improvements in delivered performance and reduced energy consumption.

21.4.3 THE ACCELERATED APPROACH

GPU accelerators are extremely effective for performing specific classes of streaming processing, and doing so with high-throughput performance. They incorporate many specialized processor cores interconnected to form useful dataflow paths to minimize the need for write-back of intermediate data and avoid control overheads. System nodes are heterogeneous, combining multicore CPU chips and GPU modules to permit computing workflows as appropriate running on the GPUs and the remaining computations being performed on the CPUs. An important path to exascale is a heterogeneous system architecture combining CPUs with GPUs which will provide high-density peak floating-point operations. A major challenge, programming such heterogeneous systems, is receiving significant attention, as is discussed in this book. The Summit supercomputer is planned to employ this kind of heterogeneous system architecture using GPUs; it will be deployed in 2018 at Oak Ridge National Laboratory with a delivered performance of approximately 200 petaflops.

21.4.4 LIGHTWEIGHT CORES

The alternative approach to achieving exascale performance is the use of a very large number of very lightweight cores. A typical core such as an Intel Xeon processor or IBM Power 8 architecture engages many mechanisms to keep the execution pipeline full and the time to execution of a thread to its minimum possible with the enabling technology. One school of thought is that to build the fastest system, one needs the fastest node; and to build the fastest node, the fastest core possible is required. But for a given socket package size and energy budget, a different strategy is to provide the highest number of cores possible, which means implementing the smallest-size core possible with full functionality. This was first tried with some success by IBM's Blue Gene systems using the lightweight PowerPC processor. Today Intel provides the Xeon Phi lightweight processor core with 76 cores per socket for Knights Landing. The next generation of Phi will be Knights Hill, which will provide the basis for the future systems to be deployed possibly in 2018. TaihuLight has 256 very lightweight cores per socket; a total of 10 million cores providing roughly 100 petaflops and using low energy. The ARM processor is emerging as yet another choice for large systems based on lightweight cores. Japan, China, and the European Union are all planning ARM-based systems of between 100 Petaflops and 1 Exaflops.

21.5 ASYNCHRONOUS MULTITASKING

Asynchrony is the property of uncertainty of timing and ordering of known events and operations. Greater scaling, such as remote data access or services performed, aggravates the variability of timing. Thus handling the effects of asynchrony becomes increasingly important as system scale and heterogeneity increase. A class of computing methodology referred to as "asynchronous multitasking" (AMT) is a topic of extensive research that shifts computing from static scheduling and conventional resource management methods to dynamic adaptive control of program execution and the application of available memory and processing resources. The following subsections describe aspects being considered as means for addressing the challenges imposed by asynchrony and exploiting the opportunities that asynchrony offers.

21.5.1 MULTITHREADED

Threads are generally considered as sequences of instructions sharing intermediate result data that can be scheduled on individual cores. Multithreaded computing is when there is more than one thread operating concurrently and possibly in parallel, in which case time to solution improves, perhaps proportionally with the number of threads. This is not a new concept, of course, but how it is implemented in terms of control, synchronization, scheduling, and resource allocation has evolved and differs substantially among different methodologies. Typically there is a one-to-one mapping of application threads to hardware threads, but having more application threads than physical threads opens opportunities to address asynchrony. This is commonly known as "overdecomposition", and if used opportunistically can avoid blocking of hardware resources. It is done by switching out an application thread that has been blocked while waiting for a long-duration access or service and putting a pending thread on the hardware to continue using these resource, improving efficiency and scaling. This requires the ability to do on-the-fly context switching. As the granularity of threads can be made finer and still be efficient, this permits an increase in scalability for strong scaling and more threads with weak scaling. Hardware for multithreaded execution has been developed, including the Tera MTA with 128 threads with single-cycle context switching times.

21.5.2 MESSAGE-DRIVEN COMPUTATION

The historical load/store architecture combined with message passing for scalability has proved effective over more than 25 years. But with increasing scale and resulting asynchrony, the effects of latency have proven increasingly costly in dimensions of both time and energy. Where both temporal and spatial locality could be exploited by caches, the deleterious effects of latency could be bounded, especially with cache-aware programming techniques. However, more general computation, extended scale, and broader access patterns expose system latencies and uncertainties. An alternative stratagem is message-driven computations that move work to the data rather than always demanding that data is moved to the nexus of the static work control state. Combined with multithreading, this technique can hide some latencies, especially long-distance latencies, and avoid blocking hardware as a result. By keeping the work and the data close together, it can reduce absolute latencies of action.

Within computing research there is a long heritage of exploration of message-driven computation. Dataflow architectures of the 1970s and 1980s considered lightweight messages called "tokens" to move intermediate result data between succeeding actors, referred to as "templates". The actors' model added semantic richness to this in the form of "futures". In 1992 Dally's J-machine provided hardware support for messages to instantiate methods for remote procedure calls. The University of California at Berkeley, as part of the threaded abstract machine model, devised a version of message-driven computing called "active messages", a term that has had some traction. More recently the ParalleX execution model and the HPX runtime systems it inspired incorporate "parcels" that convey actions to be performed on remote data, as well as the means to support the migration of continuations to provide for dynamic placement of the parallel control state.

In essentially every case, a lightweight message is structured to incorporate several fields of information. These include a destination, an action specification, a payload field, and in some cases a continuation. The destination can be a physical node, software process, core thread, or virtual data object. The action can be as simple as an operation, a sequence of instructions, a pointer to a method or procedure, or an effect on some element of control state or synchronization object. The payload varies from nothing or void to a set of independent scalars, vector, list, or a more general structure. These values (or pointers) are used along with the destination object data to perform the projected calculations. The final field is referred to as the "continuation", which in simplest terms tells the destination what to do after the specified action is completed. This can be as simple as return the result to the originating source of the action—typical of more conventional computing. It also can indicate what recovery response to an error should occur. But more interesting in some models is the effect on the global control state either by modifying the state of an existing control object or adding such a control object to the existing global parallel control state.

21.5.3 GLOBAL ADDRESS SPACE

A division in thinking about scalable computing has existed for more than two decades concerning support for global address spaces. This single issue has incited severe argument on occasion, as substantial investment has been made in both classes of system. In truth, it is much harder to design a very large computer of many, perhaps thousands, of nodes that retains uniformity of address spaces across the entire system. While delivering a means to access known physical addresses correctly is achievable, the more challenging problems are dealing with virtual addresses and cache coherency. One approach employed for virtual address is the partitioned global address space (PGAS). Here the virtual address space is partitioned as contiguous blocks among the physical nodes. The upper bits of the virtual address identify the node on which it will be found. This is efficient, but it has the unfortunate property that a word associated with a given virtual address cannot be moved between nodes and retain the same virtual address. Cache coherence is even more challenging, as any processor becoming the owner of a virtual location, i.e., it can write to it, must be able to invalidate all copies of that location throughout the distributed system. In some cases cache coherency is not assumed and remote accesses are differentiated from local accesses, only the latter of which within a given node is treated as cache coherent. Yet another problem is implicit: locality and latency. A strong argument for message passing in a distributed-memory address space such as that used with MPI is that it forces the programmer to deal explicitly with locality, optimizing local operations and minimizing global accesses through message passing. This has proven quite effective for many applications. Nonetheless, the inefficiencies of using message passing for lightweight remote data accesses and the increased difficulties in having to control data movement explicitly by this means has led to many experimental AMT software systems incorporating global address space frameworks, at least of the PGAS type.

21.5.4 ACTOR SYNCHRONIZATION

Conventional programming methods, particularly of the message-passing forms but also for multiple-thread operation, use global barriers, blocking message send/receives, or nonblocking send/receives with waiting. These are semantically weak, in that they accomplish relatively little in flow control while incurring significant overheads. They tend to be coarse grained, especially in the case of global barriers where all processes or threads must come to a stop until all tasks have completed their respective work prior to the barrier synchronization point. Some AMT systems incorporate advanced dynamic synchronization constructs such as dataflow and futures, both of which have a heritage extending back more than 3 decades. Dataflow addresses out-of-order completion of input operands and asynchrony of arrival prior to scheduling a specified operation to be performed. The futures synchronization extends this to different uses of the same prior result value requested by other streams of execution delivering the equivalent of an IOU that can be treated as a manipulatable pointer to an eventual value and employed in building data structures giving additional parallelism.

21.5.5 RUNTIME SYSTEM SOFTWARE

The concepts described in the subsection on AMT are found most readily in a small number of runtime software libraries developed for scalable and efficient HPC. Work on such runtimes as Charm++ from the University of Illinois Urbana–Champaign, OCR from Rice University, and HPX from Louisiana State University and Indiana University is representative, but these are by no means the only packages. They vary in detail, sometimes in important ways, but have many similarities in their main functionality and semantics. Runtime software is the easiest way to achieve dynamic adaptive computing, and for some classes of applications such as adaptive mesh refinement, molecular dynamics, particle in cell, fast multipole methods, and dynamic graph problems including data analytics it can serve well for improved efficiency, scalability, and user productivity. But for some applications there is little or no performance improvement, in part because runtime software actually adds to the total overhead imposed on the system. Some cases have been documented where performance actually degrades with scale for this reason. Runtime software can manage over-decomposition and this often makes better utilization of computing resources, at least up to a point. But runtime software behavior is also sensitive to scheduling policies, which may need to adapt to application algorithm requirements. In the future it is hoped that hardware architectures will evolve to incorporate mechanisms for accelerating certain aspects of runtime system operation to lower overhead and improve useful parallelism.

21.6 THE NEODIGITAL AGE

After decades of exponential growth of semiconductor technology, Moore's law is coming to an end, if it has not already done so (depending on how its defined). This explosion of on-chip components can no longer be relied upon to deliver continued performance gain. Even over the last decade clock rates have flattened due to power limitations, and instruction-level parallelism has also flatlined despite optimistic expectations. This period has seen performance delivery gains achieved principally through multicore and many-core processors using up the last vestiges of Moore's law as enabling technology reaches nanoscale. If Moore's law can no longer yield greater performance given the other limitations, what can?

Here we hypothesize a new generation of HPC systems that differ significantly from conventional practices and their incremental extensions. Design strategies include the following:

- *Execution models.* The history of high-end computing has experienced about half-a-dozen paradigm shifts over the last 7 decades to adopt new enabling technologies and exploit different forms of hardware parallelism. Such phase changes include the original von Neumann architecture, vector and SIMD processing, and communicating sequential processes and shared-memory multithreaded. But new execution models are required that dramatically increase both scalability and efficiency to drive future computing across the exascale performance region, even possibly to zetaflops.
- *Architecture fundamentals.* Originally, floating-point operations were the performance-limiting property of HPC systems and the early architectures were designed to achieve highest arithmetic unit utilization. Efficiency is often described as the ratio of sustained floating-point performance to peak floating-point performance. But today memory bandwidth is the critical resource and memory capacity the biggest single cost factor. Overall data movement system-wide is also time limiting. Future architectures need to be redesigned around these performance and energy boundaries rather than historical biases.
- *Parallel algorithms.* How we organize a computation is highly sensitive to the nature of the machine structure upon which a problem is to be executed. Changes in algorithms are required to adjust to new structures and expose and exploit parallelism intrinsic to the target problem domain, as well as effective memory usage. There have been many instances when algorithmic changes have dramatically improved overall computational time to solution.
- *Programming interfaces.* The semantics of control and data are reflected by the programming interfaces, including languages and libraries that determine the means of applying applications to HPC systems. As system architectures have evolved over the decades, changing the forms of parallelism they exploit, programming methods have to evolve as well to let programmers take advantage of the hardware. We have watched this as MPI has evolved from MPI-1 to MPI-4. Programming interfaces are often extended, and sometimes new ones are created. The creation and use of CUDA allow programmers to take advantage of the peculiarities and opportunities made possible by the architecture improvements.

In the following sections examples of approaches to computing beyond conventional practices are presented to hint at possible elements of future HPC systems and methods. Some of these ideas have a long legacy in the research community. Others have yet to be investigated in any depth but are considered (by the authors at least) to have future promise.

21.6.1 DATAFLOW

Dataflow is a parallel execution model originally developed in the 1970s but explored and enhanced as the basis for non-von Neumann computing architecture and techniques. While there were many contributors over a period of more than two decades, two investigators stand out: Jack Dennis and Arvind, both at Massachusetts Institute of Technology. These two leaders in the field, although at the same institution, led separate research groups and pursued distinct conceptual strategies. Jack Dennis, who may be considered the father of dataflow, founded what has now come to be called "static dataflow", while Arvind is credited with the introduction of the school of "dynamic dataflow". Strong research programs, especially in the 1980s, were conducted worldwide, with full implementations of hardware systems in the United States, Japan, and Europe. Some fundamental flaws in architecture reflecting the abstract model naively ultimately doomed this particular approach, largely due to overheads. But the underlying concepts are important and contribute to many hardware and software techniques, although not in the original forms anticipated by its founders. It is quite likely that innovative approaches exploiting the valuable aspects of dataflow will drive future system architectures and programming methods at the end of Moore's law in nanoscale fabrication technology.

Dataflow in its purest form represents a computation in terms of the data precedence constraints of the operations to be performed. A visual presentation of a dataflow program looks like a directed graph, with its vertices determining the operations to be performed and the links between vertices determining the flow of operand values, from the source vertices that produce the intermediate values of the computation to the destination vertices that consume the values as input operands to their own operation. "Tokens" were initially expected to serve as messages that carry these values from the output of the source where the values are calculated to the input of the destinations where the values are used for follow-on calculations. The operations themselves are designated by a small data structure or record referred to as a "template", which specifies the operation to be performed, buffers the input values, designates the destination templates for the result values, records and updates synchronization control state, and includes other information as required by the specific design.

Dataflow is a functional or value-oriented model of computation. There is no shared data; no global side-effects. Only actual values can be exchanged between operator templates. This has many advantages, at least in the abstract. In its original version dataflow was fine grained, revealing most of the intrinsic parallelism. It is very robust, avoiding many of the pitfalls associated with shared-memory models. As intrinsics, tokens provide event-driven computing through self-synchronization and templates maintain control state, permitting operations to be performed only when all operand values have been received, although order of arrival does not matter. Problems with aliasing and race conditions are thus avoided. Backus (inventor of Fortran) in his famous Turing Award lecture strongly advocated functional programming as the only means of writing robust code. A number of functional programming languages have been developed over the decades, with Haskell the most recently and widely used example.

Dataflow, at least as manifest, suffered from a number of inefficiencies which ultimately made it nonviable as a basis for hardware architecture. Perhaps most egregious was that it was inefficient due to overheads of operation control and scheduling. Many microoperations were required for each template operation performed, yet those operations were very lightweight and did not amount to a lot of work. This meant that more work was performed in managing a template than the resulting full operation performed. Compared to a typical program counter, this was far more effort. It was sensitive to bubbles or gaps in the operational pipeline because of the need for all these update events for each single useful operation. It was memory intensive due to requirements of template storage. Perhaps worse was that it was also memory bandwidth intensive, again due to all the data transfer and synchronization events. This was compounded by the dissemination of result values to possibly many destination templates. The failure to take advantage of usual accelerating mechanisms such as registers, caches, and reservation stations made it difficult for it to compete effectively with RISC uniprocessor architecture, although these were sequential and used execution pipelines with out-of-order completion, effective compiler methods, higher clock rates, and lower energy. Finally, in a period when parallel computers were limited to at most a few hundred processors, and this rare, coarse-grained parallelism was sufficient to keep the resources fully utilized. Full use of the fine-grained operation implied by dataflow was unnecessary and in fact wasteful.

In spite of these deficiencies of the original dataflow architecture designs, the underlying execution model is very powerful. It addresses the key challenge of asynchrony and the resulting uncertainty of order of operational events. It makes for cleaner composability of separately developed software. It provides a clean means of overdecomposition which can be used for dynamic adaptive resource management and task scheduling to avoid resource blocking and circumventing contention over shared resources. It provides a natural way to minimize starvation by using much of the available parallelism. There are many possible variations, compromises, and hybrid structures that may be able to benefit from the dataflow concept. Already there is increased use of directed acyclic graph representation of computations at the medium- or coarse-grained level to exploit more adaptive flow control for enhanced efficiency and scalability. For these reasons it is projected that where new architectures will be required to increase performance at the end of Moore's law, concepts embodied by the dataflow execution model will be employed, although in innovative ways.

21.6.2 CELLULAR AUTOMATA

Among the many contributions by the mathematician John von Neumann was the invention of a distinct model of computation, cellular automata, in 1949. The irony cannot be avoided: the cellular automaton is considered a "non-von Neumann architecture".

In its simple form, a cellular automaton consists of a two-dimensional array (it can be one- or three-dimensional as well) of cells, each of which is connected to its nearest neighbors (typically four: up, down, right, left). Each cell contains a small amount of state: sometimes a few bits or a few words, although it can be more. Finally, a cell incorporates a set of rules that determines how its own state will change depending on its current state and that of its immediate neighbors.

The classic example of cellular automata is Conway's Game of Life, in which each cell has one of two states (e.g., alive or dead), and a small set of simple rules as follows.

- A cell dies if it is alive and only one or none of its neighbors is alive.
- If two or three of the neighbors are live, then an alive cell remains in that state.
- But if an alive cell has four, five, or six live neighbors, then it dies.
- Finally, a dead cell with three live neighbors becomes live.

The evolution of this cellular automaton is determined entirely by its initial state, that is the state of all its cells. Von Neumann was able to demonstrate that there is a set of rules and state that is Turing equivalent and therefore, in principle, can serve as a general-purpose computer, although his solution was theoretical and did not reflect a practical framework for real-world computing. Conway's model is much simpler, and it too is a universal Turing machine.

A cellular automaton has a number of properties that makes it interesting as a future class of HPC architecture. It exposes an enormous amount of hardware parallelism, as each cell can be very small and thus for a given fabrication feature size and die area there can be a maximum number of execution units, although of modest capabilities. It has very large storage bandwidth, although the memory density may not be as good as other means. Latency for local storage access will be very low, as well as to the nearest neighbor state. If the communication is flat as described, remote access could take many hops and impose long latencies. However, hierarchical topologies can strongly mitigate this. Asynchrony across the very wide system can also be ameliorated by local synchronization built into the hardware functionality. A number of data and operation sequence layout patterns can be devised to take advantage of vector, systolic, SIMD, wave, dataflow, and graph algorithms derived from prior art.

There are many open questions, many tradeoffs in balancing storage capacity, operation functions, and communication, and the major challenge of achieving the global emergent behavior of general-purpose parallel computing from massive local basic operations across the array of cells. Essentially, what is the new execution model? It is not clear that this is ultimately possible. However, it does open a new class of HPC architecture at a time when architecture may be the only hope of a significant performance advance.

21.6.3 NEUROMORPHIC

The human brain is an extraordinary system, perhaps the most complex known. It incorporates more interconnections within a single cranium than all the stars in the Milky Way galaxy. With 89 billion neurons it consumes only 20 W of power, with each neuron on average communicating through 10,000 synaptic junctions. While each neuron operates at less than 1 kHz, a brain activates more than 10 trillion spikes per second. And it is constantly changing in topology to fix long-term memories. Certain forms of operation, such as associative processing of images, sounds, and patterns, are accomplished with a throughput unachievable by even the highest-performance supercomputer. Then, speculate researchers, cannot a future class of computers be developed around the same principles as the human brain to make artificial computing systems with similar remarkable capabilities? In the most general sense these are known as "neuromorphic" computers; there are many diverse approaches being explored at this time, but all are inspired by the brain.

21.6.4 QUANTUM COMPUTING

Trying to explain quantum computing is like teaching computer science at Hogwarts. But quantum computing is not magic, even if it seems like it. And in no practical sense is it real yet. But it is both theoretically possible and becoming ever more likely technically, although there is still some way to go. Why there is so much interest and investment in what is still a research domain is the capability and impact that it would have if actually achieved. Again theoretically, it would be possible to do certain calculations that would be impossible with conventional supercomputers even if running for the entire age of the planet. And this is not limited to some esoteric or obscure problem, but rather for areas of extreme criticality such as cryptanalytics or multidimensional nonlinear optimization.

The fundamental concepts behind quantum computing have been understood since the 1980s, including the foundational work by the Nobel Laureate Richard Feynman of Caltech, among other pioneers. The core idea for quantum computing is embodied in the idea of the "qubit" that stores quantum information as the Shannon bit stores binary information. But there the similarity ends. A qubit state is not a 0 or a 1 but rather the superposition of the probabilities of the data being either a 0 or a 1. A set of n qubits can store the probabilistic distribution of all possible values, that is 2^n possible values, and process all of these simultaneously, at least in principle. The sum of the probabilities must be equal to 1. When the values of the hypothetical qubit are measured (observed), the output value collapses to a single n-bit answer. The likelihood of any particular answer is the probability of the superimposed field associated with that value. That means that rerunning the computation a number of times is likely to deliver different values.

Important breakthroughs came with the development of particular algorithms that showed how theoretical quantum computers could be employed to accelerate certain problems. Shor's algorithm for factorization was an example that spawned significant interest and research in this field. A variant of such machines, called "quantum annealing" computers, perform a narrower range of optimization algorithms. In spite of its limitations, practical systems of this type have been built and operated, in particular by the Canadian company D-wave.

The technology required to achieve this functionality, at least as understood through actual experimentation, involves extremes in cryogenic superconductivity. Specifically, Josephson Junctions cooled to 10 s of millikelvins (degrees Celsius above absolute zero) are employed to maintain stability of the quantum state long enough to perform the required computation. It is not easy, and alternative methods are under research. Whether or not a viable technology solution is ultimately developed, the advantages of full quantum computing are still limited. There are certainly many classes of problems performed by conventional computers today that cannot be accelerated by a quantum computer as currently conceived. Also, it is not possible that a future quantum computer can in principle solve a problem not solvable by conventional computers, in that they are Turing equivalent. Nonetheless, for those problems with a conceivable performance advantage, the prospects for futuristic quantum computers are very exciting.

21.7 EXERCISES

1. Look up the most energy-efficient supercomputer on the Green 500 list [3]. Extrapolate the top system to exascale and estimate the power cost to operate. How close is it to the goal of 20 MW/year for an exascale machine?
2. Review the most recent Gordon Bell Prize winners [4]. How many applications used "MPI+X"? How many utilized GPUs? What architectures are represented?
3. What kinds of applications will benefit from exascale computing resources? What kinds of applications will not benefit from such resources?
4. What types of applications are currently being deployed on commercial quantum computers?
5. Explain why Moore's law has given a free ride to application developers in improving application performance. What are the consequences of Moore's law ending?

REFERENCES

[1] T. Sterling, Personal Communication.
[2] Wikipedia, Larrabee (Microarchitecture), [Online]. https://en.wikipedia.org/wiki/Larrabee_(microarchitecture).
[3] Green500, Green500 List, [Online]. https://www.top500.org/green500/.
[4] Association for Computing Machinery, ACM Gordon Bell Prize, [Online]. http://awards.acm.org/bell/.

Essential C

This appendix is intended to assist those who already know one or more programming languages and may need a brief introduction to C syntax and semantics. The approach provided here is driven by four examples which address a wide range of C usage: numerical integration, lower/upper (LU) decomposition, the fast Fourier transform (FFT), and the game of tic-tac-toe. In these examples the core C syntax is illustrated. Some of the key C syntax elements are highlighted in Table A.1.

A.1 NUMERICAL INTEGRATION

Integrating an ordinary differential equation using a method from the Runge–Kutta family of integrators is a common task in scientific computing. The classic fourth-order algorithm, frequently referred to as rk4, illustrates many important features of the C programming language. In the example presented in Code 1, which solves the ordinary differential equation

$$\frac{dx}{dt} = -\lambda x$$

for the function $x(t)$, there are only two routines required: *main* and *rhs*. While the *main* routine is present in all C codes, the *rhs* function provides the right-hand side evaluation of the ordinary differential equation evaluated at different function values and times. The header for the *rhs* function is declared in line 13, while the function itself is declared in lines 71–73. The header provides *main* with information on the expected input and output of the function and aids in type checking. Output from each step of the Runge–Kutta integration is written to a file. The file handler is declared in line 35, while the output file itself, *rk4.dat*, is opened in line 38 with "write" access, as indicated by the *w* in the last argument to the routine *fopen*. Output from each step of the integration is written to the file using the *fprintf* function in line 54, and the file is closed in line 65 using *fclose*. The rk4 integrator itself is listed in lines 56–63. The exact solution to this ordinary differential equation is

$$x(t) = Ce^{-\lambda t}$$

where the constant $C = 1$ based on the initial condition for $x(t)$ given in line 41. The exact solution is evaluated in line 49 and used to evaluate the error in the numerical solution throughout the integration.

High Performance Computing. https://doi.org/10.1016/B978-0-12-420158-3.15001-4

Table A.1 Some Key C Syntax Elements Used in the Four Example Codes Here

Operational or Functional Element	Location	Example
For loop	Code 1, line 44	`for (i=0;i<N;i++) {`
While loop	Code 3, line 11, 85	`while (nmoves++ < 9) {`
If statement	Code 4, line 90	`if (!p->level) return;`
Bitwise right shift	Code 3, line 12	`k >>= 1;`
Bitwise left shift	Code 3, lines 27,28	`if(n & (1 << (log2_int(N) - j)))`
Bitwise AND	Code 3, lines 20, 27,58	`if(!(i & n)) {`
Bitwise OR	Code 3, line 28	`p |= 1 << (j - 1);`
Modulo	Code 3, line 60	`double complex Temp = W[(i * a) % (n * a)] * f[i + n];`
Increment operator	Code 1 line 44 Code 4 line 148	`for (i=0;i<N;i++) {`
Subtract and assignment operator	Code 2, lines 71,74	`for (int j = 0; j < i; j++)` `x[i] -= ap[i][j]*x[j];`
Conditional Expression	Code 4 line 55	`char who = (upper->who == comp_mark)? user_mark: comp_mark;`
Structures	Code 4 line 10	`typedef struct move {`
Allocate and zero initialize	Code 4 line 60	`if (!m) m = calloc(1, sizeof(move_t));`
Complex allocation	Code 3, line 46	`W = (double complex *)malloc(N / 2 * sizeof(double complex));`
Powers of complex numbers	Code 3, line 52	`W[i] = cpow(W[1], i);`
File handling	Code 1, lines 38,54,65 Code 2, lines 19, 33,34	`FILE *f = fopen(path, "r");`
Getline	Code 2, line 23	`getline(&line, &n, f);`

```
/*
* Solving the Ordinary Differential Equation
*  dx/dt = -lambda x
*  using Runge-Kutta 4th order
*/

#include <stdio.h>
#include <stdlib.h>
#include <math.h>

#define lambda 5.0

double rhs(double x,double t);

int main(int argc, char *argv[]) {
  // Starting and Stopping integration time
  double A = 0.0;
  double B = 1.0;

  // Size of timestep
  double dt = 0.1;

  // Number of timesteps
  int N = (B-A)/dt+1;

  int i;

  // predictor-corrector rk4 steps
  double F1,F2,F3,F4;
  double x,t;
  double exact;
  double small_number = 1.e-15;

  // file for output
  FILE *rk4data;

  /* open a file for output */
  rk4data = fopen(“rk4.dat”,“w”);

  /* initial condition: x(A) = 1.0 */
  x = 1.0;

  fprintf(rk4data,“# t x(t) exact diff\n”);
  for (i=0;i<N;i++) {
  /* RK4 */
  t = A + dt*i;

  /* Exact solution */
  exact = exp(-lambda*t);
```

```
    /* Write to file the log of the difference
    * between the exact solution and integrated solution */
    //fprintf(rk4data,"%g %g\n",t,log(x-exact+small_number));
    fprintf(rk4data,"%g %g %g %g\n",t,x,exact,x-exact);

    // Runge-Kutta
    F1 = rhs(x,t);
    F2 = rhs(x+0.5*dt*F1,t+0.5*dt);
    F3 = rhs(x+0.5*dt*F2,t+0.5*dt);
    F4 = rhs(x+dt*F3,t+dt);

    // update x(t)
    x = x + 1.0/6.0*dt*( F1 + 2.0*F2 + 2.0*F3 + F4 );
  }
  fclose(rk4data);

  return 0;
}

// The right hand side of the first order differential equation
double rhs(double x,double t) {
  return -lambda*x;
}
```

Code 1. Integrating an ordinary differential equation using a Runge–Kutta method in C.

A.2 LOWER/UPPER DECOMPOSITION

The LU decomposition program is an example of dense algebra processing. Such problems deal with matrix and vector representation of systems of equations, potentially including thousands of interrelated equations and variables. Among many other applications, matrix-based equation solvers are used to generate numerical solutions of ordinary and partial differential equations, and thus are widely employed in simulations of real-world phenomena in nearly every branch of physics.

The program, listed in Code 2, solves the equation $Ax = b$ for x. Matrix A and vector b are given to and retrieved from files passed to the program as the required command-line arguments. To be able to solve the system, A must be square and contain linearly independent columns and rows. To calculate the solution taking into account a broad range of possible instances of A, the code employs a specific approach in which the matrix is expressed as a product of a lower triangular matrix L (all its elements above the main diagonal are zero) and an upper triangular matrix U (all elements below the main diagonal are zero). Since converting the original matrix to triangular form requires that the so-called pivot elements located on the main diagonal of A are nonzero (the algorithm divides by pivot value to compute values of other elements of the matrix), on occasion rows of the matrix must be swapped to avoid this issue. Note that this simply corresponds to changing the order in which original equations are listed, and therefore does not change the solution. The reordering is expressed by a permutation matrix P, which has a single 1 in every column and row and 0s elsewhere. The matrix is expressed thus as:

$$PA = LU$$

Leading to the problem definition as

$$LUx = Pb$$

This may be further decomposed into two related systems by introducing an intermediate vector y:

$$Ly = Pb$$

$$Ux = y$$

Thanks to the fact that L is triangular, obtaining the solution of the first equation may be done trivially via forward substitution. Note that the first element of y may be calculated by dividing the first element of permuted vector b by the element in row 1 and column 1 of L. Since the second row of L contains only two nonzero elements, the second element of y may be computed based on the value of the first element. This process continues row by row until all elements of y are known. The calculated y can be plugged into the second matrix equation involving U, and used to compute the values of vector x using an analogous approach (back substitution).

The contents of matrix A and vector b are fetched from storage using various file I/O operations seen in the *read_from_file* function (*fopen*, *getline*, *fread*, and *fclose*). The first of them (invoked in line 19) opens a file described by *path* for reading. The file contains a header with one or two decimal numbers separated by a space and terminated with a new-line character; they describe the dimensions of the matrix or vector. This part is extracted using the *getline* function (line 23) that stops after reading the full line, followed by the sscanf function (line 24) that converts the text representation of the numbers into integer variables. Since *sscanf* returns the number of items converted, the following switch statement explicitly zeroes out each dimension that could not be read. The routine allocates the storage for the array or vector and treats the remaining contents of the file as serialized binary data (a sequence of double-precision floating-point numbers without gaps). The data is stored in row-major form, starting with the lowest row index and the lowest column index in each row. While this approach results in efficient use of storage space, the files are not portable to architectures with incompatible memory layout, i.e., different endianness and different number size. Also, due to difficulties associated with inspecting the contents of such files, the use of portable and self-describing file formats such as HDF5 or NetCDF is recommended. The transfer of the file contents to data memory is performed by the *fread* function in line 33. After the number of retrieved elements (not bytes!) is verified, the file is closed by the *fclose* function (line 34).

The LU decomposition is performed by the *decompose* function. To conserve memory, a commonly used trick stores both L and U matrices in the space occupied originally by A. This is possible because matrix L has only ones on its diagonal, thus eliminating the need for their explicit storage, so the diagonal elements of A can be used to keep the corresponding elements of matrix U. To accelerate the computations and enable more familiar double-index notation when accessing the matrix elements, an array of pointers to rows *ap* is allocated and initialized. This allows for much faster row permutations. To swap two rows, only their pointers are exchanged; the contents of rows are kept in their original memory locations. The decomposition scans the values of elements underneath each diagonal component to select the largest (in absolute value sense) pivot in each row. This is both to avoid zero- or near zero-valued pivots and to obtain good numerical accuracy. Since the permutation matrix P is very sparse (recall that it has only one nonzero element per row), a permutation vector is used instead. It stores the updated index for each row that will be later used to fetch the elements of vector b correctly. Originally each index in P points to the initial position of the row; whenever the rows are swapped, the corresponding entries in P are swapped as well.

The *solve* function computes the solution vector x in two steps. The first calculates the intermediate vector from L and vector b accessed via the redirection vector p. The seconds step converts the elements of the intermediate vector into final solution values. No extra storage is needed, since the elements of the intermediate vector are consumed at the same rate as the elements of x are produced.

If the user specifies the third argument on the command line, it will be interpreted as a path name to the file storing the solution vector. Function *write_to_file* handles the data output using similar I/O functions as those used for reading, but with the exception of *fprintf* (line 84) and *fwrite* (line 85). The first behaves much like the regular *printf*, except it redirects its output to the stream specified as its first parameter. The *fwrite*, on the other hand, accepts the same arguments as *fread* and writes the raw data to the opened file. If the third argument is not given, the program prints out all elements of vector x (lines 106–108).

The program uses the *variadic* function (that is, a function accepting a variable number of arguments) *error* to handle critical execution problems. This is indicated by the ellipsis ("...") as the last formal parameter. Thanks to variadic support, the programmer may pass additional information to be included in the error messages. The definitions required to access this functionality are provided by the include file "stdarg.h".

```
0001 #include <stdio.h>
0002 #include <stdlib.h>
0003 #include <stdarg.h>
0004 #include <math.h>
0005
0006 #define EPS 1e-20
0007
0008 // handle error occurrence
0009 void error(char *fmt, ...) {
0010   va_list ap;
0011   va_start(ap, fmt);
0012   fprintf(stderr, "Error: ");
0013   vfprintf(stderr, fmt, ap);
0014   exit(1);
0015 }
0016
0017 // read in contents of matrix or vector from file
0018 double *read_from_file(char *path, unsigned dim[2]) {
0019   FILE *f = fopen(path, "r");
0020   if (!f) error("cannot open \"%s\" for reading\n", path);
0021   size_t n = 0;
0022   char *line = NULL;
0023   getline(&line, &n, f);
```

```
  switch (sscanf(line, “%u %u”, &dim[0], &dim[1])) {
    case 0: dim[0] = 0;
    case 1: dim[1] = 0;
      break;
  }
  if (!dim[0]) error(“invalid data file format in file \“%s\””, path);

  n = dim[0]*(dim[1]? dim[1]: 1);
  double *data = malloc(sizeof(double)*n);
  size_t cnt = fread(data, sizeof(double), n, f);
  fclose(f);
  if (cnt < n) error(“file \“%s\” seems to be truncated\n”, path);
  return data;
}

// perform LU decomposition
double **decompose(int n, double *a, double *b, int *p) {
  double **ap = malloc(sizeof(double)*n); // array of row pointers
  for (int i = 0; i < n; i++) {
    ap[i] = &a[i*n]; p[i] = i;
  }

  for (int i = 0; i < n; i++) {
    for (int j = i+1; j < n; j++) {
      int maxind = i;
      if (fabs(ap[j][i]) > fabs(ap[maxind][i])) maxind = i;
      if (maxind != i) {
        double *atmp = ap[i];
        ap[i] = ap[j]; ap[j] = atmp; // pivot row swap
        int ptmp = p[i];
        p[i] = p[j]; p[j] = ptmp; // permutation tracking
      }
      if (fabs(ap[i][i]) < EPS) error(“matrix A ill-defined, aborting\n”);
  }
  for (int j = i+1; j < n; j++) {
    ap[j][i] /= ap[i][i];
    for (int k = i+1; k < n; k++) ap[j][k] -= ap[j][i]*ap[i][k];
    }
  }
  return ap;
}

// solve system of equations
double *solve(int n, double **ap, double *b, int *p) {
  double *x = malloc(sizeof(double)*n);
  for (int i = 0; i < n; i++){ // forward substitution with L
    x[i] = b[p[i]];
    for (int j = 0; j < i; j++) x[i] -= ap[i][j]*x[j];
  }
```

```
  for (int i = n-1; i >= 0; i--) { // backward substitution with U
    for (int j = i+1; j < n; j++) x[i] -= ap[i][j]*x[j];
    x[i] = x[i]/ap[i][i];
  }
  return x;
}

// save result vector to file
void save_to_file(char *path, int n, double *x) {
  FILE *f = fopen(path, “w”);
  if (!f) error(“cannot open \"%s\“ for writing\n”, path);
  fprintf(f, “%d\n”, n);
  if (fwrite(x, sizeof(double), n, f) != n)
    error(“short write to \“%s\” file\n”, path);
  fclose(f);
}

int main(int argc, char **argv) {
  // initialization and sanity checks
  if (argc != 3 && argc != 4)
    error(“usage: %s matrix_file vector_file [result_file]\n”, argv[0]);
  int Asize[2], bsize[2];
  double *A = read_from_file(argv[1], Asize);
  if (Asize[0] != Asize[1]) error(“matrix A is not square\n”);
  double *b = read_from_file(argv[2], bsize);
  if (bsize[1] > 0) error(“b is not vector\n”);
  if (bsize[0] != Asize[0]) error(“size of b incongruent with A\n”);
  int *P = malloc(sizeof(int)*(*bsize)); // row permutation vector
  // decompose and solve
  double **Ap = decompose(*bsize, A, b, P);
  double *x = solve(*bsize, Ap, b, P);
  // output handling
  if (argc > 3) save_to_file(argv[3], *bsize, x);
  else { // if no output file specified, print out the solution
    for (int i = 0; i < *bsize; i++) printf(“%f ”, x[i]);
    printf(“\n”);
  }

  return 0;
}
```

Code 2. Source code for matrix LU decomposition and solver.

A.3 FAST FOURIER TRANSFORM

The FFT is a core computational science algorithm that usually involves complex numbers. Code 3 illustrates computing the FFT in C using the Cooley–Tukey algorithm. This implementation illustrates the use of the computing powers of complex numbers (line 52), bit right-shift assignment (line 12), the bitwise AND operator (lines 20, 27, and 58), bitwise OR assignment (line 28), bitwise left shift (lines 27 and 28), modulo (line 60), while-loops (lines 11 and 85), for-loops, and if conditionals. It is an example of a divide-and-conquer algorithm.

```
0001 #include <stdio.h>
0002 #include <stdlib.h>
0003 #include <math.h>
0004 #include <complex.h>
0005
0006 #define MAX 200
0007
0008 int log2_int(int N)    /*function to calculate the log2(.) of int numbers*/
0009 {
0010    int k = N, i = 0;
0011    while(k) {
0012       k >>= 1;
0013       i++;
0014    }
0015    return i - 1;
0016 }
0017
0018 int check(int n)    //checking if the number of element is a power of 2
0019 {
0020    return n > 0 && (n & (n - 1)) == 0;
0021 }
0022
0023 int reverse(int N, int n)    //calculating revers number
0024 {
0025   int j, p = 0;
0026   for(j = 1; j <= log2_int(N); j++) {
0027      if(n & (1 << (log2_int(N) - j)))
0028         p |= 1 << (j - 1);
0029   }
0030   return p;
0031 }
0032
0033 void ordina(double complex* f1, int N) //using the reverse order in the array
0034 {
0035   double complex f2[MAX];
0036   for(int i = 0; i < N, i++)
0037      f2[i] = f1[reverse(N, i)];
0038   for(int j = 0; j < N; j++)
0039   f1[j] = f2[j];
0040 }
0041
0042 void transform(double complex* f, int N) //
```

```
{
  ordina(f, N); //first: reverse order
  double complex *W;
  W = (double complex *)malloc(N / 2 * sizeof(double complex));
  double rho = 1.0;
  double theta = -2. * M_PI / N;
  W[1] = rho*cos(theta) + rho*sin(theta)*I;
  W[0] = 1;
  for(int i = 2; i < N / 2; i++) {
    W[i] = cpow(W[1], i);
  }
  int n = 1;
  int a = N / 2;
  for(int j = 0; j < log2_int(N); j++) {
    for(int i = 0; i < N; i++) {
      if(!(i & n)) {
        double complex temp = f[i];
        double complex Temp = W[(i * a) % (n * a)] * f[i + n];
        f[i] = temp + Temp;
        f[i + n] = temp - Temp;
      }
    }
    n *= 2;
    a = a / 2;
  }
}

void FFT(double complex * f, int N, double d)
{
  transform(f, N);
  for(int i = 0; i < N; i++)
    f[i] *= d; //multiplying by step
}

int main()
{
  int n;
  do {
    printf(" Give array dimension (needs to be a power of 2)\n");
    char str1[20];
    scanf("%s",str1);
    n = atoi(str1);
  } while(!check(n));
  double sampling_step = 1.0;
  double complex vec[MAX];
  double freq = 100;
  double x;
  printf(" Input vector\n");
```

```
    for(int i = 0; i < n; i++) {
      x = -M_PI + i*2*M_PI/(n-1);
      vec[i] = cos(-2*M_PI*freq*x);
      printf("%g + %g I\n",creal(vec[i]),cimag(vec[i]));
    }
    printf("-------------------\n");
    FFT(vec, n, sampling_step);
    printf(" FFT of the array\n");
    for(int j = 0; j < n; j++)
      printf("%g + %g I\n",creal(vec[j]),cimag(vec[j]));

    return 0;
}
```

Code 3. FFT in C. This code was adapted from a C++ version in Wikipedia [1].

A.4 GAME OF TIC-TAC-TOE

To illustrate a problem with dynamically generated and deleted data structures, Code 4 provides a simplified implementation of the popular tic-tac-toe game. The game begins with the user making the first move by placing an "X" anywhere in a 3°×°3 grid. At this point the computer generates the graph of all possible moves and selects the one giving it the best chance of winning. Since some of the reviewed moves are no longer necessary, the other graph branches will be removed to release the allocated memory. While this is not absolutely necessary for game play, it serves as an example of recursive function invocation coupled with dynamic memory operations and pointer manipulation.

The fundamental data structure used in the program is *move_t* (lines 10–15), storing the details of a single move (placement of "X" or "O") in the game. It is a C structure containing the *next* and *level* pointers to other like structures, and permits building graphs extending in two dimensions. The *next* pointer points to a structure containing the immediate follow-on move from the current state. Since there may be more than one move possible, they are stored in the list linked by *level* pointers. The *wins* and *losses* fields contain the sum of all wins and losses computed for the entire subtree below the current move. A leaf node in the graph is one that ends with one of the parties winning (and hence one of the *wins* and *losses* fields is 0 and the other is 1) or a draw when the board is completely filled with no winner identified. For the latter both *wins* and *losses* are 0. The structure also contains the column and row coordinates of the current move (*x* and *y*), as well as information about *who* was moving (a character field storing either "X" or "O").

The move space is generated by the *build_tree* function starting at line 54. This function allocates a new *move_t* structure for every empty field found on the board, adding it to the *level* list. The list is pointed to by the *next* pointer stored in the upper-level node. If any of the board layouts in the list is identified as a winning move, the *wins* and *losses* fields are filled out appropriately. Otherwise, *build_tree* is invoked recursively, with the current move set as the ancestor node. In either case the values of wins and losses for the current move are added to the corresponding fields of the upper node, ensuring the propagation of these values up to the starting node.

Selecting the next computer move (*make_next_move*, line 120) involves traversing the level list immediately below the node representing the most recently made move. The strategy is rather simplistic, but it works quite well in many cases. If a move with a nonzero number of wins and no losses can be found, it is selected immediately. Otherwise, the difference of *wins-losses* is calculated and a move with the best result is picked.

The user input is handled by the *get_user_input* function (starting in line 99). It uses the *scanf* call to convert the text supplied by the user to two short integer numbers corresponding to the row and column of the next move. This is invoked in an infinite loop, since the user may enter coordinates of an already occupied field by mistake. The loop is broken when the input is successfully validated.

Once the next move (by either user or computer) is known, the move space is cleaned to remove the move nodes that are no longer necessary. The graph is rearranged so that the path to the current move can be reached by traversing only the next links from the top node. All remaining entries on the level lists are deleted by the function *prune_untaken* at line 88. The recursive cleanup of memory is performed by the function *prune* starting in line 79.

The board state is stored in a 3×3 character array. Only one instance of the board is required both to generate the move tree and to play the game. The board is visualized on standard output by the *show_board* routine (lines 18–39), which also illustrates usage of a switch statement with multiple case label assignments to the same pieces of code.

```
0001 #include <stdio.h>
0002 #include <stdlib.h>
0003 #include <string.h>
0004
0005 // markers for computer, user and empty space
0006 const char comp_mark = 'O', user_mark = 'X', empty = ' ';
0007 // array type to hold the board state
0008 typedef char board_t[3][3];
0009 // structure describing single move
0010 typedef struct move {
0011    struct move *level, *next;
0012    int wins, losses;
0013    short x, y;
0014    char who;
0015 } move_t;
0016
0017 // display the board
0018 void show_board(board_t b) {
0019    for (int i = 0; i < 7; i++) {
0020    switch (i) {
0021      case 0:
0022      case 6:
0023        printf(“ -----------\n”);
0024        break;
0025      case 2:
0026      case 4:
0027           printf(“ |---+---+---|\n”);
0028         break;
```

```
      case 1:
      case 3:
      case 5: {
        short r = (i-1)/2;
        printf(“ %d | %c | %c | %c |\n”, r+1, b[r][0], b[r][1], b[r][2]);
        break;
      }
    }
  }
  printf(“  1 2 3\n\n”);
}

// test if the move described by m is a winning move
int winning_move(board_t b, move_t *m) {
  short x = m->x, y = m->y;
  if (b[y][x] == b[y][(x+1)%3] && b[y][x] == b[y][(x+2)%3]) return 1;
  if (b[y][x] == b[(y+1)%3][x] && b[y][x] == b[(y+2)%3][x]) return 1;
  if (x == y &&
      b[y][x] == b[(y+1)%3][(x+1)%3] && b[y][x] == b[(y+2)%3][(x+2)%3]) return 1;
  if (x+y == 2 &&
      b[y][x] == b[(y+1)%3][(x-1)%3] && b[y][x] == b[(y+2)%3][(x-2)%3]) return 1;
  return 0;
}

// build move search graph
void build_tree(move_t *upper, board_t b, int depth) {
  char who = (upper->who == comp_mark)? user_mark: comp_mark;
  move_t *m = NULL;
  for (int j = 0; j < 3; j++)
    for (int i = 0; i < 3; i++)
      if (b[j][i] == empty) {
        if (!m) m = calloc(1, sizeof(move_t));
        else {
          m->level = calloc(1, sizeof(move_t));
          m = m->level;
        }
        if (!upper->next) upper->next = m;
        m->x = i; m->y = j; m->who = b[j][i] = who;
        if (winning_move(b, m)) {
          m->wins = (who == comp_mark); m->losses = (who == user_mark);
        }
        else if (depth < 9) {
          build_tree(m, b, depth+1);
        }
        upper->wins += m->wins; upper->losses += m->losses;
        b[j][i] = empty;
      }
}
```

```

// delete no longer needed move branches
void prune(move_t *m) {
  if (m) {
    if (m->next != NULL) prune(m->next);
    if (m->level != NULL) prune(m->level);
    free(m);
  }
}

// delete all non-taken moves below curr with the exception of keep
void prune_untaken(move_t *curr, move_t *keep) {
  move_t *p = curr->next;
  if (!p->level) return;
  if (p != keep) {
    while (p->level != keep) p = p->level;
    p->level = keep->level; keep->level = curr->next->level; curr->next = keep;
  }
  prune(keep->level); keep->level = NULL;
}

// ask for and validate user input
void get_user_input(board_t b, short *x, short *y) {
  while (1) {
    printf("%c's move; enter row and column number separated by space: ", user_mark);
    scanf("%hd %hd", y, x);
    (*x)--; (*y)--;
    if (*x >= 0 && *x < 3 && *y >= 0 && *y < 3 && b[*y][*x] == ' ') return;
    printf("Invalid move, please try again!\n\n");
  }
}

// process user move
int get_user_move(board_t b, move_t *curr) {
  short x, y;
  get_user_input(b, &x, &y);
  b[y][x] = user_mark;
  for (move_t *p = curr->next->level; p; p = p->level)
    if (p->x == x && p->y == y) prune_untaken(curr, p);
  return winning_move(b, curr->next);
}

// calculate computer's move
int make_next_move(board_t b, move_t *curr) {
  move_t *best = NULL;
  for (move_t *p = curr->next; p; p = p->level) {
  if (p->losses == 0 && p->wins > 0) {
    best = p; break;
  }
```

```
    if (best) {
      if (best->wins-best->losses < p->wins-p->losses) best = p;
    }
    else best = p;
  }
  b[best->y][best->x] = comp_mark;
  prune_untaken(curr, best);
  printf(“%c plays at %hd %hd:\n”, comp_mark, best->y+1, best->x+1);
  return 2*winning_move(b, best);
}

int main() {
  // initialization and first move
  board_t board;
  move_t *game = calloc(1, sizeof(move_t)), *current = game;
  memset(board, empty, 9);
  show_board(board);
  get_user_input(board, &game->x, &game->y);
  game->who = user_mark; board[game->y][game->x] = user_mark;
  build_tree(game, board, 1);

  int status = 0, nmoves = 1;
  while (nmoves++ < 9) { // main game loop
    show_board(board);
    if ((status = make_next_move(board, current)) > 0) break;
    current = current->next; nmoves++;
    show_board(board);
    if ((status = get_user_move(board, current)) > 0) break;
    current = current->next;
  }

  show_board(board);
  switch (status) { // print the final status
    case 1:
      printf(“\n*** Congratulations, you won! ***\n”);
      break;
    case 2:
      printf(“\n*** I won! ***\n”);
      break;
    default:
      printf(“\n It’s a draw. Thanks for playing! \n”);
      break;
  }

  return 0;
}
```

Code 4. Source code of the tic-tac-toe game.

REFERENCE

[1] https://it.wikipedia.org/wiki/Trasformata_di_Fourier_veloce. Wikipedia, FFT, [Online].

ESSENTIAL LINUX

B.1 LOGGING IN

Most computers, including large installations, have various means to protect the stored information from unauthorized access. This is particularly important in systems that are shared by many users. The first line of defense consists of validating the access rights of a particular user, completely disabling access to storage contents and preventing the usage of system utilities when a user's identity cannot be properly confirmed. This is accomplished through the so-called login screen depicted in Fig. B.1. While the actual appearance may differ from system to system, the screen contains two fields that must be filled out. The first is the user identifier as assigned by the system administrator, which is a combination of letters, digits, and underscore ("_") and may be in some cases derived from the actual user's name. It has to be a unique, contiguous string of characters. The second entry accepts the user's password, or a secret combination of arbitrary printable characters, preferably including upper- and lower-case letters, digits, and punctuation marks. Note that the typed characters are replaced on screen by asterisks or dots to avoid showing the actual password text. For improved security, use of plain English words as listed in a dictionary should be avoided as much as possible. Many systems have rules governing password selection with which all users must comply, including the minimum password length. Of course, the user is obliged to remember his or her ID and password, and avoid disclosing the latter to anyone (including system administrators, since they have other means at their disposal to manage the user's account).

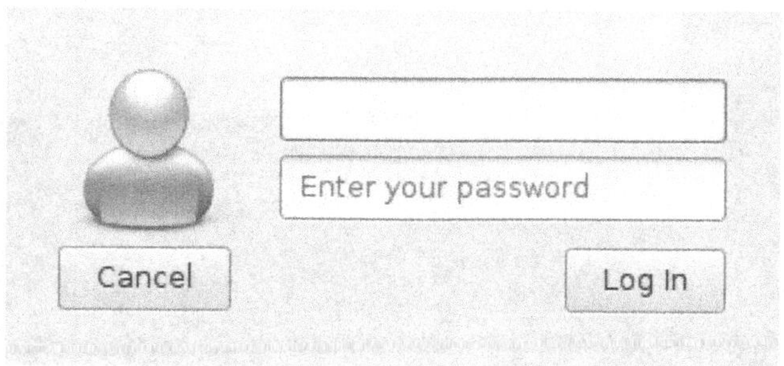

FIGURE B.1

Login dialog window used by a variant of Debian Linux distribution.

High Performance Computing. https://doi.org/10.1016/B978-0-12-420158-3.15002-6

After entering the correct user name and password and clicking on the "log in" button (or its equivalent), the user is presented with a graphical desktop. To take advantage of material described in this book, a terminal application must be invoked. Linux distributions typically offer several such applications that differ in their look and feel, configuration options, and capabilities. The most common include *xterm* (a basic terminal emulator for the X Window system), *urxvt* (a Unicode-capable version of the older *rxvt* terminal), *gnome-terminal* (available in the Gnome desktop environment), and *konsole* (a terminal emulator bundled with the KDE desktop environment). They may be found in the "system" entry of the "application" menu on most desktops. Clicking on the relevant entry opens a terminal window with a prompt (usually a ">" or "$" character, on occasion following some additional information such as current time or host name), at which point one enters commands to be executed. A snapshot of a graphical desktop with an opened terminal emulator is shown in Fig. B.2.

In some cases a graphical desktop may not be available when using a simple text-based console or when more advanced display modes have not been configured or were disabled on the machine. This does not make it unusable, but the operation may be limited to text mode on a single terminal (see Fig. B.3). The login proceeds as described previously, with the user entering the credentials at the appropriate prompts. The main difference is that during the password entry no characters are echoed to the screen.

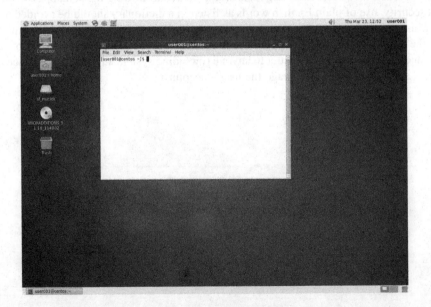

FIGURE B.2

Graphical desktop with a terminal emulator window (CentOS distribution).

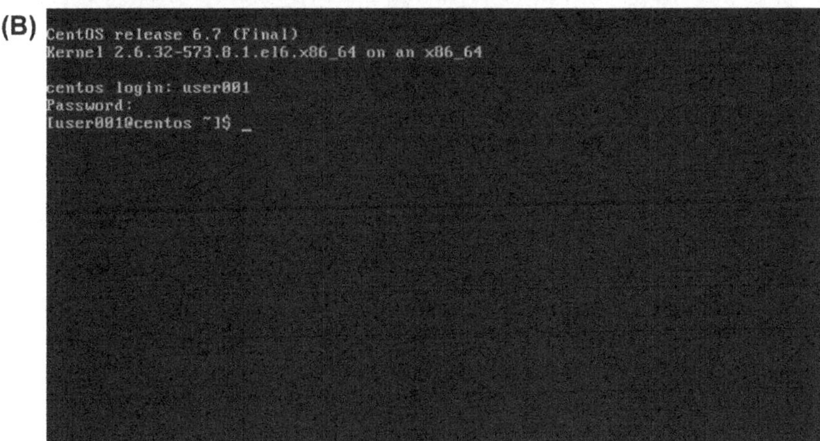

FIGURE B.3

Terminal login: (A) authentication prompt; (B) shell prompt after successful user authentication.

B.2 REMOTE ACCESS

The login procedure delineated above may be used to gain access to a local Unix (or Linux in particular) machine. However, permitting only local login to a supercomputer would be overly restrictive. The preferred approach is to enable remote login over the network to accommodate even the broadest base of users without forcing them to be in physical proximity to the machine.

The commonly used program for that purpose is Secure Shell, or *ssh*. It transmits all information, including login credentials, in encrypted format, thus preventing the potential eavesdroppers on the network from intercepting any useful data. A sample first-time *ssh* login sequence which may be executed on any terminal mentioned in Section B.1 is shown below:

```
> ssh user001@bigiron.some.university.edu
The authenticity of host 'bigiron.some.university.edu (10.0.0.1)' can't be
 established.
ECDSA key fingerprint is SHA256:pyYRR3L9EZXA1alJ/EyteIkfL2RJhwiAS2j174UbM1c.
Are you sure you want to continue connecting (yes/no)? yes
Warning: Permanently added "bigiron.some.university.edu" (ECDSA) to the list of
 known hosts.
user001@bigiron.some.university.edu's password:
[user001@bigiron ~]$
```

In this example the user name is "user001" and the login host is "bigiron.some.university.edu". Since this is the first time this user attempts to connect to "bigiron.some.university.edu", *ssh* warns that it does not have any previously collected information about the target machine. Unless there are good reasons to assume that host spoofing is indeed taking place, the user should answer "y" to the question about whether to continue connecting to the server. This produces the password prompt. Entering the password (which will not be shown on the screen) completes the login process by presenting the user with a shell prompt on the *remote* machine. The subsequent login sequence is much shorter, since the client machine is already in possession of the encrypted keys identifying the remote host. The warnings may reappear when the target machine changes its keys, which should happen relatively infrequently. As demonstrated in the example below, *ssh* also reports the time and origin of the last session to alert the user if a third party managed to gain illicit access to his or her account.

The connection to the remote host established in this way permits the use of arbitrary command-line applications that do not require a graphical environment to run. Occasionally, however, it is desirable to start a graphical user interface (GUI) application on the remote host to take advantage of improved user interface or to access graphical tools that are licensed only for local use. Adding a `-Y` option to the *ssh* command activates the X Windows protocol forwarding over the network connection:

```
> ssh -Y user001@bigiron.some.university.edu
Last login: Fri Mar 24 10:47:22 2017 from mybox.some.university.edu
[user001@bigiron ~]$ vtk
```

This results in the *vtk* window appearing on the client machine's display. Beware that slow network links may result in substantial delays between the command being issued and the resultant window being displayed (or even redrawn) on the client screen. Of course, the forwarding works only if the client machine supports and is actively running a graphical desktop environment.

B.3 NAVIGATING THE FILE SYSTEM

Persistent information in computer systems is stored in *files*, named entities organized in a hierarchy referred to as a *file system*. Unlike memory contents, once committed to physical storage the files survive machine reboots and shutdowns. All information that needs to be preserved, such as important datasets or programs to be executed, has to be stored in files. Files are explicitly created, read, and written by programs.

The file system provides its own naming scheme to facilitate access to specific files. Individual files have their own names, such as "*main.c*" or "*task_plan.txt*". While not strictly required, these names have typically two components separated by a period ("."): *base name* and *extension*. The base name may be anything the user has selected to hint at the file's purpose or suggest its contents. The extension describes the file's type. Thus for the two examples given above, "*main.c*" most likely contains source code of a program in C language, while "*task_plan.txt*" is probably a plain-text file containing the description of some planning activity. File names tend to be relatively short, as most file systems impose a fixed limit on their length. Since Unix file names may contain multiple periods, only the group of characters following the last of them is considered an extension.

Using plain file names as the only access method would quickly become unmanageable in systems that must handle thousands of them. It also does nothing to prevent collisions on the same file name. For example, to store two code versions of the same program source, one would have to be renamed; that change would in turn have to be propagated through scripts that build the final executable code, preventing reuse and creating unnecessarily replicas. To organize the file system contents better, the notion of *directory* was introduced. Directories are named groups of files and other directories. They may have (almost) any name, but unlike files they do not use extensions, although periods are permitted in their names. Directories may be arbitrarily nested. The top-level directory indicates the *root* (topmost entry) of the file system and is referred to as "*/*" (single forward slash). Forward slashes are used as separators of hierarchy levels leading to the specific file or directory. Thus "*/home/user001/src/heat.c*" uniquely identifies file named "*heat.c*", presumably a C source code, that is contained by the "*src*" directory stored in the "*user001*" directory, and that in turn resides in the "*home*" directory directly below the root of the file system. Note that this scheme allows for two or more different files called "*heat.c*" to exist within the file system as long as they are stored in different directories. The sequence of hierarchy elements necessary to reach the specific file starting from the root is called a *path*.

Using full paths to identify files being accessed may become tedious and verbose in the long run. Since commands are executed by the shell (see Section B.5), a more convenient solution is possible thanks to the notion of a *working directory*. The shell retains the path name of the working directory between command invocations, and updates it only when dedicated commands changing its value are called by the user. The working directory acts as a prefix that is prepended to the so-called *relative* paths, which are distinguished from full or *absolute* paths by the fact that they do not begin with a slash. Thus if the current working directory is set to user001's home, or "*/home/user001*", the C source file from the example may be referred to by typing only "*src/heat.c*". Other conveniences include syntax shortcuts that simplify the formation of various paths.

- The user's home directory is abbreviated to "~" (tilde character). The home directory is the current working directory set immediately following user login. Thus the file above could also be reached by using "*~/src/heat.c*".

- The current directory is represented by "." (single period). Thus the paths "*/home/user001/src*" and "*/home/./user001/src/.*" are equivalent. While it may look like this shortcut is not terribly useful, its benefits become more obvious when discussing commands that take directories as arguments.
- The parent directory may be expressed as ".." (double period). Hence "*/home*" and "*~/..*" refer to the same directory.

File systems typically conform to default layout rules to make computer users more effective and help them to find various utilities, documentation, and appropriate storage for data. See , Chapter 3 for a more detailed description of the standard directory structure utilized by Linux distributions.

A number of Linux system utilities have been developed, with a goal of simplifying the management of the file and directory hierarchy and accessing file contents. They are briefly described below, with simple usage examples. The shell prompts were shortened to a single ">" character for brevity. Due to context sensitivity, the examples were created with the assumption that they are executed in order on the same host.

- ***ls*** (list directory contents)

  Without arguments, this lists the contents of the current working directory. The arguments may include an arbitrary number of file and directory paths. Additional options may provide more information about the stored entries, such as access permissions, ownership, modification date, size, etc. The commonly used ones include "`-l`" to select the "long" format and "`-a`" to enable display of hidden entries (i.e., all files and directories whose names start with a period).

  Note: many distributions by default alias the *ls* command with frequently used options to "*ll*".

```
> ls -l /home/user001/src
total 8
-rw-r--r-- 1 user001 user001 361 Mar 24 17:55 Makefile
-rw-r--r-- 1 user001 user001 491 Mar 24 17:55  heat.c
```

- ***cd*** (change working directory)

  This changes the working directory to the specified path or, when invoked without arguments, to the user's home directory. The example below changes the working directory to the user's home, descends into the "*src*" subdirectory, and lists all files there:

```
> cd
> cd src
> ls -la
total 16
drwxr-xr-x 2 user001 user001 4096 Mar 24 20:03 .
drwxr-xr-x 3 user001 user001 4096 Mar 24 20:07 ..
-rw-r--r-- 1 user001 user001  361 Mar 24 17:55 Makefile
-rw-r--r-- 1 user001 user001  491 Mar 24 17:55 heat.c
```

- ***pwd*** (print working directory)

  This prints the current working directory.

```
> pwd
/home/user001/src
```

- ***mkdir*** (make directory)

  This creates new directories whose paths are specified as arguments to the command. Nominally, the new directory must be an immediate child of an existing path. To permit creation of arbitrarily nested paths, a "-p" option (for "parents") should be used. The example below has to use the parents option, since the "*src2*" directory currently does not exist:

```
> mkdir -p ~/src2/tmp
> ls -l ../src2
total 4
drwxrwxr-x 2 user001 user001 4096 Mar 24 20:44 tmp
```

- ***cp*** (copy files and directories)

  This takes at least two path arguments: the last argument is the destination for the copy operation, while all preceding arguments are considered to be the source arguments. Source arguments must exist. Multiple sources are permitted only if the destination is an existing directory. To copy source directories properly, a recursive option "-r" should be specified.

```
> cp heat.c ~/src2/heat2.c
> cp -r ~/src2 .
> ls -l src2
total 8
-rw-r--r-- 1 user001 user001  491 Mar 24 21:24 heat2.c
drwxrwxr-x 2 user001 user001 4096 Mar 24 21:24 tmp
```

  The example above copies the content of the *heat.c* file to the *src2* directory created before and stores it in a file named *heat2.c*. The second call copies the whole directory "/home/user001/src2" to the current working directory (note the use of "."). Since the whole subdirectory tree is replicated, a recursive option is used.

- ***mv*** (move files and directories)

  The move command is used to relocate files and directories within the file system. Its syntax resembles that of *cp*, but the recursive option is no longer necessary, since changing the location of a directory implies changing it for all its children. The *mv* command may also be used to rename either files or directories.

```
> mv src2/heat2.c src2/tmp
> mv src2/tmp ./other
> ls -l other src2
other:
total 4
-rw-r--r-- 1 user001 user001 491 Mar 24 21:24 heat2.c
src2:
total 0
```

The first command moves file *heat2.c* from the *src2* directory to its child subdirectory *tmp*. The second moves that subdirectory along with its contents to the current working directory and renames it to "*other*". The directory listing confirms that the operations have been carried out correctly: the *src2* directory is now empty and "*other*" directory is now a direct child of the current working directory and contains file *heat2.c* that was originally stored in *src2*.

- ***rm*** (remove files of directories)

  The *rm* command irreversibly deletes files or directories. For the latter, a recursive option ("`-r`") must be added. The example shows how to remove the now empty *src2* subdirectory:

```
> rm -r src2
> ls -l
total 12
-rw-r--r-- 1 user001 user001  361 Mar 24 17:55 Makefile
-rw-r--r-- 1 user001 user001  491 Mar 24 21:38 heat.c
drwxrwxr-x 2 user001 user001 4096 Mar 24 21:51 other
```

- ***find*** (look for specific files)

  The *find* command searches for files of predefined characteristics. While its option list is quite extensive, it is frequently used to find files or directories with specific names. This is controlled by the predicate "`-name` *filename*" for exact matches and "`-iname` *filename*" for case-insensitive matching. The search may be further restricted to report only directories by specifying "`-type d`" and regular files by using "`-type f`". The only argument of *find*, immediately following the command, is a path name identifying the top directory on whose contents the lookup will be performed recursively. The example below attempts to find all file system entries named *heat2.c* that exist at any hierarchy level under the user's home directory, and later all files starting with "heat" to demonstrate wildcard use (explained in detail in Section B.5). Note that the latter requires protecting the name argument from shell expansion by enclosing it in single quotes:

```
> find ~ -name heat2.c
/home/user001/src/other/heat2.c
/home/user001/src2/heat2.c
> find ~ -name 'heat*'
/home/user001/src/heat.c
/home/user001/src/other/heat2.c
/home/user001/src2/heat2.c
```

B.4 EDITING THE FILES

Having learned the basics of file system access, the next step is to create files with the desired contents. This capability is provided by text editors. Linux distributions offer many options of different complexity, resource footprint, supported environments, and integration features targeting code development. One of the main distinguishing factors for editor selection is GUI availability: some editors may only work invoked inside a text terminal, some support graphical desktops, and a subset provides both. For editors that are incapable of accessing remote files, terminal-based operation consumes much less network bandwidth, resulting in smoother editing when invoked on a remote machine (such as a supercomputer's login node). A short description of commonly used text editors is given below.

B.4.1 VI

Vi is a nonGUI editor with a broad user base and a long history in Unix environments originating in the 1970s. Its code has been updated many times and has inspired a number of clones. Perhaps the most characteristic feature of vi is modality. Text input using keystrokes (insert mode) and execution of editor commands (normal or command mode) are performed in dedicated modes of operation that the user explicitly switches between. Most current Linux versions bundle vim ("Vi IMproved"), which offers new features compared to the original, such as syntax highlighting (coloring of various syntactic constructs in programming languages to make the code makeup more apparent), mouse support, completion, file comparison and merging, regular expressions, scripting, spell checking, tab support, and many others. Vim is also available in a GUI variant, complete with menus and toolbars, as gVim.

B.4.2 EMACS

Another editor with an established presence in the Unix world is Emacs. Its name was derived as a contraction of "editor macros". Of a number of clones spawned over the years, the most popular remains GNU Emacs, a free software implementation based on a small core written in C with most functionality provided by the Elisp (a dialect of LISP) extension language. GNU Emacs layout consists of a main text window and a much smaller minibuffer that displays status information and acts a command interface. This layout works in both text-only mode and with a GUI, although the latter also provides a set of menus for common operations. The editor is highly extensible and configurable, implementing over 2000 commands. Another important feature is support of major and minor modes, in which a specific major mode is activated per file buffer and usually triggered by the file type (such as C code or HTML source), while further customizations, including on-the-fly spell checking, automatic line breaking, or highlighting of specific portions of text, may be enabled or disabled at any time. Any number of minor modes may be active at any time.

B.4.3 NANO

The GNU nano editor embraces interface simplicity as its main design goal, making it an obvious choice for beginners. The commonly used command key combinations are displayed on the same screen as edited text, thus not requiring their memorization for effective editing. Despite its small size, nano features colored text, multiple edit buffers, search-and-replace operations based on regular expressions, recent operation undo and redo, and modification of key bindings. Nano operates in text-only mode.

B.4.4 GEDIT

Gedit is a GUI-centered editor developed for the Gnome desktop environment, deployed by default on many Linux distributions including Ubuntu, Fedora, Debian, CentOS, and others. The editor's long list of features supports syntax highlighting, multilanguage spell checking, tabbed mode, session preservation, line numbering, parenthesis matching, automatic indentation, autosave, font configuration, etc. Gedit is also capable of editing files on remote hosts. Its core functionality may be further extended through plugins.

B.4.5 KATE

The other popular desktop environment, KDE, provides a default GUI-based editor called Kate. The basic feature set is similar to that of Gedit. Kate's indentation and tool functionality accessed through the command line may be additionally customized through javascript code. Kate is the source code editor used by the Kdevelop integrated development environment in KDE.

File editing using any of these editors is quite straightforward. The editor programs are started by typing their name (in lower case) on the command line, optionally followed by the path name of the file one wants to modify or create. The editor marks the place being edited with a *cursor*, or a single character-sized block or bar that may be blinking for faster visual location on the screen. The arrow keys on the keyboard move the cursor in any of the four principal directions (up, down, left, and right). Typing printable characters enters them at the cursor's current position and displaces the existing text to the right. Advancing the text by larger strides is possible using the page-up and page-down keys in most editors. With the exception of vi, the editors allow free mixing of text editing and command execution. In vi the insert mode (for typing the text directly) is activated by typing letter "i" in command mode, while switching back to command mode

Table B.1 Key Bindings for Frequently Used Commands in Popular Text Editors

Function	Vi	Emacs	Nano	Gedit	Kate
Display help	:h	Ctrl-h	Ctrl-g	F1	F1
Undo	:u	Ctrl-x u	Alt-u	Ctrl-z	Ctrl-z
Open a file	:r *filename*	Ctrl-x Ctrl-f	Ctrl-r	Ctrl-o	Ctrl-o
Save file	:w	Ctrl-x Ctrl-s	Ctrl-o	Ctrl-s	Ctrl-s
Save as another file	:w *filename*	Ctrl-x Ctrl-w	Ctrl-o	Ctrl-Shift-s	Ctrl-Shift-s
Find a string	/	Ctrl-s	Ctrl-w	Ctrl-f	Ctrl-f
Search and replace	:s/*pattern*/*replacement*/	Esc %	Alt-r	Ctrl-h	Ctrl-r
Cut text	dd	Ctrl-k	Ctrl-k	Ctrl-x	Ctrl-x
Paste text	P	Ctrl-y	Ctrl-u	Ctrl-v	Ctrl-v
Exit	:q	Ctrl-x Ctrl-z	Ctrl-X	Ctrl-q	Ctrl-q

All vi commands must be entered in the "normal" (command) mode. For other editors, Ctrl, Alt, Shift, and F1 denote specific keys on the keyboard. A dash following one of these keys and a letter signifies concurrent activation of several keys. For example, the Ctrl-h sequence is performed by first pushing the control key and then depressing the "h" key while the control key is held down.

is performed by pressing the escape key. Table B.1 summarizes the keyboard shortcuts for common editing operations.

B.5 ESSENTIAL BASH

Command invocation, job management, and many aspects of file handling may be vastly simplified by using various features provided by the shell. The shell is used to issue commands, display their output, and manage concurrent tasks. It also acts as an interpreter for a language that may express sequences of operations and implement elements of flow control that permit building custom execution scripts. Since *bash* is set up as the default login shell when creating new user accounts and is configured by default by many (if not all) Linux installations, this section focuses exclusively on its syntax and features.

B.5.1 PATH EXPANSION

The first important feature that permits easier manipulation of file groups is called path expansion. The characters "*" (asterisk), "?" (question mark), "[', ']" (square brackets), and "{', '}" (curly braces) have special meanings when used inside directory and file paths. The first matches any string of characters, including an empty string. Assuming the current working directory contains files as listed by the command below:

```
> ls
Makefile  example.txt  f1.txt  f2.txt  f22.txt  heat.c
```

matching all files with the extension ".txt" may be accomplished as:

```
> ls *.txt
example.txt  f1.txt  f2.txt  f22.txt
```

The question mark matches precisely one character. Thus to select only files from the above set with a single character between the "f" character and the extension ".txt", one could type:

```
> ls f?.txt
f1.txt  f2.txt
```

Square brackets match one of the specified characters. For example, to find files with the second letter in their names of either "a" or "e", the following pattern may be used:

```
> ls ?[ae]*
Makefile heat.c
```

Braces are used to list arbitrary substrings or patterns to be matched. Multiple substrings must be comma separated. Thus the following selects all files for which the ".txt" extension is immediately preceded either by a digit "2" or a string "ple":

```
> ls *{2,ple}.txt
example.txt f2.txt f22.txt
```

To verify that patterns work when specified within braces, try to match all text files whose base names are exactly two characters long or end in "ample":

```
> ls {??,*ample}.txt
example.txt f1.txt f2.txt
```

The path substitution forms discussed above may be applied to any portion of a path name, including directory components. However, the matching is always limited to the single level of the hierarchy. Thus "/*" will not select all entries present in the file system, but only files and directories contained by the root directory.

B.5.2 SPECIAL CHARACTER HANDLING

On occasion it may be necessary to refer to a path name that contains one or more special characters. In such situations these characters will have to be escaped using a backslash (“\”) or placed between single quotes. To refer to a file named “ready?”, the actual string argument appearing on the command line would have to be typed as “ready\?” (without the double quotes which serve here only as name delimiters) or “‘ready?’”. As the shell breaks down the command-line contents at blank spaces (which actually may be regular spaces or tabs) to identify command options and arguments, the same method may be used to refer to files whose names contain spaces. Shell language syntax assigns special meaning to several other characters, making escaping them necessary if used within path names. They include the pipe symbol (“|”), ampersand (“&”), semicolon (“;”), parentheses (“(‘ and ’)”), angle brackets (“<” and “>”), and the end-of-line character. To minimize the occurrence of related problems, avoiding use of these characters in file names is a good general rule, especially for users who are just beginning to learn the shell concepts.

B.5.3 INPUT/OUTPUT REDIRECTION AND PIPELINES

Some commands executed by the shell generate output and some expect input data. The shell provides dedicated operators to manage the standard input, standard output, and standard error streams mentioned in Appendix A. In Unix systems these streams are by convention associated with file descriptors numbered 0–2, respectively. So-called “redirection” may be used to channel the input to the application from a specific file (instead of requiring the user to type in the input data every time that application is run) or permit the capture of application output in a file (instead of making just an ephemeral appearance on the screen). The operators governing the I/O redirection include the following.

- “>” redirects the application’s standard output to the specified file. To illustrate this, a *cat* utility (described in Section B.7.1) is used to display the contents of the file:

```
> ls *.c > c_files
> cat c_files
heat.c
```

- “&>” redirects both standard output and standard error to the specified file. The example below tricks *ls* into generating error output by specifying an argument that refers to a nonexistent file:

```
> ls *.h > h_files
ls: cannot access *.h: No such file or directory
> cat h_files
> ls *.h &> h_files
> cat h_files
ls: cannot access *.h: No such file or directory
```

Since ">" only redirects the standard output, the error was not captured as the content of "*h_files*" but displayed in the terminal instead. The capture file is still created, but nothing is stored in it. The second invocation applies the "&>" operator that redirects both types of output. This is particularly useful when saving the output of installation or compilation scripts; using only the first kind of redirection might omit the actual error information, making the subsequent troubleshooting more difficult.

- ">>" redirects the standard output while appending it to the specified file. This variant may be used to merge the output of several commands into a single file, since the application of ">" to the same file would simply overwrite its contents. To illustrate this in action, a shell built-in *echo* command that outputs (echoes) strings to the standard output will be used. Since path expansion is applied to all unescaped arguments in commands executed by the shell, there is no need to invoke the *ls* command explicitly:

```
> echo "These are my C files:" *.c >> my_files
> echo "These are my text files:" *.txt >> my_files
> cat my_files
These are my C files: heat.c
These are my text files: example.txt f1.txt f2.txt f22.txt
```

- "&>>" redirects both standard output and error streams to be appended to the given file.
- "<" redirects the application's standard input to be read from the specified file. The somewhat contrived example below (since the *cat* utility can accept a file argument directly) demonstrates its use:

```
> cat < my_files
These are my C files: heat.c
These are my text files: example.txt f1.txt f2.txt f22.txt
```

As many applications both accept input and generate output, it stands to reason there is a way to daisy-chain them to implement more complex processing flows. This concept is called pipelining, and is realized using the pipe operator "|". It enables forwarding the standard output created by command *k* to be standard input of command *k+1* in the pipeline, as shown below:

```
command_1 | command_2 | ... | command_n
```

Of course, the output(s) of *command_n* may be captured in a file by applying the redirection mechanism described above. A variant of the pipe operator, "|&", supports redirection of merged standard output and error streams to the standard input of the next pipeline stage.

B.5.4 VARIABLES

Bash supports variables that may be used to store arbitrary strings produced by commands and applications or to retain control state in scripts. The fundamental variable assignment statement is

name=value

where *name* is a variable identifier consisting of an arbitrary combination of letters, digits, and underscores as long as the first character is not a digit. *Value* may be a string or an array. It may also be omitted, in which case an empty variable is created. Once assigned, the variable value can be retrieved by placing a dollar sign ("$") before its identifier:

```
> x=99
> echo $x
99
```

Array variables may be created by the explicit assignment of an element at a specific index, such as

name[*index*]=*value*

where *index* has to evaluate a number. Another way to create arrays is by assignment of list of values:

name=(*value_1 value_2 … value_n*)

To dereference a specific element of an array, ${*name*[*index*]} format should be used. Special subscripts of "@" or "*" retrieve all values of the array, but with one difference: the first produces a list of values very much mirroring the way they were originally assigned to the array, while the latter yields a single string containing concatenated values. The first element of an array is located at index 0, hence:

```
> numbers=(one 2 three 4 five)
> echo $numbers
one
> echo ${numbers[@]}
one 2 three 4 five
> echo ${numbers[2]}
three
```

The content of an array may be expanded using the "+=" operator. For instance:

```
> fruits=(apple peach)
> fruits+=(banana)
> echo ${fruits[@]}
apple peach banana
```

Defined variables are normally accessible within the scope of the current shell. Since shell scripts are executed in a subshell, they typically do not have access to the parent shell variables set up in the way described above. To enable such access, each variable must be explicitly exported.

This is accomplished by preceding the variable assignment (or just the variable name if already defined) by the keyword "export":

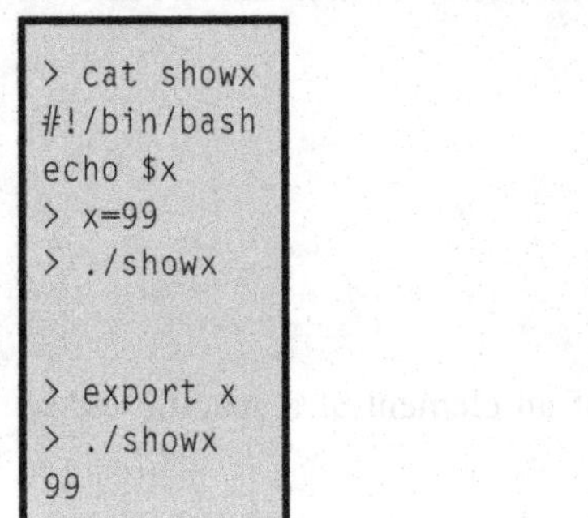

```
> cat showx
#!/bin/bash
echo $x
> x=99
> ./showx

> export x
> ./showx
99
```

In the example above, the first line of the script "*showx*" is a hint to the execution environment that the remainder of the file should be interpreted by a program residing at the specified path ("/bin/bash" in this case). The variable "x" is unknown to the script until it is exported. The same could have been accomplished at the variable definition time using "`export x=99`".

Variables may be deleted using a statement in the form:

unset *name*

```
> echo $x
99
> unset x
> echo $x
```

Bash provides a number of predefined variables that may provide useful information to scripts. The necessarily limited list below describes those most often used.

- **BASH** provides the full path name leading to the shell program currently executing.
- **BASHOPTS** lists enabled shell options in a colon-separated format.
- **BASH_VERSION** gives the version number of the currently executing shell.
- **HOSTNAME** contains the name of execution host.
- **MACHTYPE** describes the system (machine) type the shell is running on.
- **OSTYPE** identifies kind of operating system executing on the host.
- **PATH** contains a colon-separated list of directory locations (search paths) that the shell scans for commands. For any command invoked by name only (i.e., without specifying the path to its executable), Bash will try to determine its location by checking each specified search path in the order listed.
- **PWD** is the path name of the current working directory.

- **OLDPWD** is the path name value identifying the previous working directory.
- **GLOBIGNORE** contains a colon-separated list of patterns to be ignored when performing path name expansion.
- **HOME** stores the path name of the user's home directory.
- **GROUPS** is an array of identifiers of groups of which the user is a member.
- **PIPESTATUS** is an array storing exit status values of all processes comprising the most recently executed pipeline statement.
- **RANDOM** is a variable generating a random integer value between 0 and 32767 whenever read.
- **SECONDS** stores the number of seconds elapsed since the shell was started.

Bash supports many syntactic enhancements that provide additional information about existing variables or transform them into other forms of data. The commonly encountered constructs include the following.

- "**${#*name*}**" returns the length of the variable (the number of characters used by its string representation).
- "**${#*name*[@]}**" provides the count of elements stored in the array.
- "**${*name*:*offset*}**" or "**${*name*:*offset*:*length*}**" performs substring expansion, i.e., it extracts the section of string of *length* characters starting at an *offset.* If *length* is not specified, the substring starts at an *offset* and continues until the last character of *name*.
- "**#{*name*/*pattern*/*string*}**" substitutes the first longest occurrence of *pattern* with *string.* If *pattern* begins with "/", every occurrence of *pattern* is replaced. The *string* may be empty, in which case the second "/" may be omitted.
- "**${*name*#*pattern*}**" or "**${*name*##*pattern*}**" removes the matching prefix. The first deletes the shortest matching prefix, while the second form removes the longest. The pattern is transformed using path name expansion rules.
- "**${*name*%*pattern*}**" or "**${*name*%%*pattern*}**" is analogous to the previous construct except it removes the suffix portion of the string.

Examples:

```
> s=/home/user001/error.c
> echo ${#s}
21
> echo ${s/er/ing}
/home/using001/error.c
> echo ${s//er/ing}
/home/using001/ingror.c
> echo ${s##*/}
error.c
> echo ${s%/*}
/home/user001
```

B.5.5 ARITHMETIC ON VARIABLES

Variables representing numbers may be used in simple arithmetic expressions. The construct to accomplish this is "$((*expression*))" and may be nested.

```
> x=99
> echo $(((x+1)*10))
1000
```

The supported operators include "+" (addition), "-" (subtraction), "*" (multiplication), "/" (division), "%" (remainder), "**" (exponentiation), "~" (bitwise negation), "&" (bitwise and), "|" (bitwise or), "^" (bitwise exclusive or), "<<" (left bitwise shift), ">>" (right bitwise shift), "==" (compare for equality), "!=" (compare for inequality), "<" (less than), "<=" (less or equal), ">" (greater than), ">=" (greater or equal), "&&" (logical and), "||" (logical or), "*expr1?expr2:expr3*" (conditional operator), "*name++*" (postincrement), "*++name*" (preincrement), "*name–*" (postdecrement), and "*–name*" (predecrement). The last four operators change the value of variable *name*. While the post- variants return the variable value before the operation is performed, the pre-variants return the value of variable after the update. For example:

```
> echo $x
99
> echo $((x++))
99
> echo $x
100
```

B.5.6 COMMAND SUBSTITUTION

A particularly useful feature of the shell is the ability to capture directly the output of a command in a variable. There are two forms of syntax to do this: by encasing the command in a pair of backquotes ("`"), or by invoking it as "$(*command*)". The command may be compound, including a pipeline. Bash provides a faster option to read file contents into a variable with "$(< *file*)" rather than "$(cat *file*)". The following example stores paths of all files matched by the *find* command into the variable "text_files":

```
> text_files=`find . -name "*.txt"`
> echo $text_files
./f22.txt ./f2.txt ./example.txt ./f1.txt
```

B.5.7 CONTROL FLOW

Creation of sophisticated shell scripts takes advantage of more complex constructs that permit definition of loops and conditional execution. To introduce them, the concept of exit status needs to be explained. Every command and application run by a shell returns a numeric status value when it finishes the execution; this value is not displayed on the screen but kept internally by the shell. For C programs, this is the value of the expression following the "return" keyword in the main function or argument to the "exit" library function. For shell scripts, the status is that of the last command executed by the script, or zero if no commands were executed. By convention in Unix systems, zero exit status indicates success, while any nonzero value is a failure.

A brief overview of the commonly used constructs is presented below.

- "*command_1* ; *command_2* ; … ; *command_n*" executes each of the specified commands in order, waiting for command x to finish before starting the command x+1. The exit status is that of the last command.

```
> ls M*; ls *.h; ls *.c
Makefile
ls: cannot access *.h: No such file or directory
heat.c
```

- "*command_1* **&&** *command_2* **&&** … **&&** *command_n*" executes commands in sequence, stopping after the first failing command. The example below attempts to list different kinds of files and displays "Success!" if all of them exist:

```
> ls *.c && ls M* && echo "Success!"
heat.c
Makefile
Success!
```

- "*command_1* || *command_2* || … || *command_n*" attempts to execute command *k+1* only if all *k* preceding commands failed. None of the commands following the successful one is executed. For example:

```
> ls *.h || echo "Could not find any files!"
ls: cannot access *.h: No such file or directory
Could not find any files!
```

- "**for** *name* **in** *word1 word2* … **; do** *list* **; done**" implements a loop that iterates over values represented by *word1*, *word2*, etc. while storing them in a variable *name*. That variable may be referenced by any of the commands inside the loop body represented in the syntax above by *list*. For example:

```
> for f in 'ls *.txt'; do echo "Text file:" $f; done
Text file: example.txt
Text file: f1.txt
Text file: f2.txt
Text file: f22.txt
```

- "**for** ((*expr1* ; *expr2* ; *expr3*)) ; *list* ; **done**" implements an arithmetic loop which resembles the "for-loop" syntax in C language discussed in Appendix A. For instance:

```
> for ((x=2; x<5; x++)); do echo "square of $x is $((x*x))"; done
square of 2 is 4
square of 3 is 9
square of 4 is 16
```

- "**while** *list1* ; **do** *list2* ; **done**" behaves similarly to the while-loop in C language. As long as the status of the last command in *list1* is zero, commands in *list2* are executed. The exit status is that of the last executed command in *list2*, or zero if none was run. The following sequence of commands appends paths in reverse order from the "files" array to the "names" array until the latter includes four elements or there is nothing left to copy:

```
> files=(*.txt *.c Makefile)
> echo ${#files[@]}
example.txt f1.txt f2.txt f22.txt heat.c Makefile
> names=() > i=${#files[@]} > while ((${#names[@]}<4 && $i>0)); do names+=(${files
[$((--i))]}); done
> echo ${names[*]}
Makefile heat.c f22.txt f2.txt
```

- "**if** *list1* ; **then** *list2* ; [**else** *list3* ;] **fi**" executes statements in *list2* if the exit status of *list1* is zero. Otherwise, if the **else** branch is specified, statements of *list3* are executed. For example:

```
> for ((x=3; x<6; x++)); do echo -n "cube of $x is "; if ((x**3%2==0)); then echo even;
else echo odd; fi; done
cube of 3 is odd
cube of 4 is even
cube of 5 is odd
```

Note that the "-n" option to *echo* suppresses the output of the end-of-line character.

B.6 COMPILATION

Compilation is a process of converting the program description stored in one or more source files to executable code. Creation of executable files typically proceeds in two stages: generation of so-called object files for each C language source file, and linking the resultant files into a single final executable binary. Many compilers support invocation formats that permit combination of these two phases into a single command for convenience.

Object files normally have an ".o" extension. They contain machine instructions to be later executed by the CPU, but which cannot run by themselves. The "gcc" C compiler commonly found in Linux distributions uses the -c option to create them. Let us assume we have three source files (as shown in the example below) that together contain the full functionality of the program. The "main" function is defined within the "main.c" file; the other sources may not contain their own "main" functions, since it would make it ambiguous as to which one of them is the entry point to the program. Compilation of the "main.c" file to object code is invoked as follows:

```
> ls
main.c src1.c src2.c
> gcc -c main.c
> ls
main.c main.o src1.c src2.c
```

Note that the object file created in that way retains the base name of the input source file, only replacing the extension. If the source code does not contain any problematic constructs or undefined identifiers, the compiler typically will not produce any text output. The code generation is controlled by a plethora of options, of which the most common are listed below.

- **-O***number* performs code optimizations at a level determined by *number.* Generally, the higher the level and the more involved the optimizations, the better the resultant performance of the code, but also the longer compilation. In practice, "-O2" and "-O3" offer the best tradeoff between compilation time and code quality. The "-O0" turns off the optimizations—this is the default behavior when no optimization option is specified.
- **-g** embeds the debugging information, such as variable and function names, in the resultant object file. While gcc permits combining debugging and optimization options in the same command, one has to remember that higher optimization levels may severely modify flow control in the program, on occasion completely eliminating some variables or functions. A variant of this option, **-ggdb**, produces debug information specifically for use with the GNU debugger, potentially including gdb-specific extensions.
- **-o** *file* places the compiler output in an explicitly named *file.* When generating an object file, it should have an ".o" extension.
- **-I***directory* adds *directory* to the set of header (files with an ".h" extension) search paths. Multiple -I options are permitted in the same command. Header files installed under "/usr/include" (such as prototypes and macros used by the C library) are searched by default.

To make the object files into a self-contained program, a linker must combine them together, make sure there are no missing functions and variables, and add extra code that correctly sets up the execution environment. Conveniently, the gcc compiler may be also used to perform this operation. Remembering that there two more source files to compile, and the remaining sequence of commands is as follows:

```
> gcc -c src1.c
> gcc -c src2.c
> gcc main.o src1.o src2.o -o my_program
> ls
main.c main.o my_program src1.c src1.o src2.c src2.o
```

The newly created executable "my_program" may be now invoked at the shell prompt just like any other program. If the "-o" option is not used, a default executable name is assumed, typically "a.out" on Unix systems.

In simple cases similar to the example above, creation of the executables may be performed in a single command. The intermediate object files are not retained in this case, so from the user's perspective it appears as though the compiler produced the final binary directly from sources. The following example illustrates this, while at the same time performing code optimization:

```
> rm -f *.o my_program
> gcc -O2 main.o src1.o src2.o -o opt_program
> ls
main.c opt_program src1.c src2.c
```

The examples so far have not created or taken explicit advantage of external libraries. Actually, the latter is not quite correct: the linker silently links the object code with the system's C library, so if any of the listed sources invoked C library functions or used its internal variables, they would be automatically resolved. To learn how to create custom libraries, let us assume that "src1.c" and "src2.c" contain functionality that could be reused by several programs and is thoroughly debugged and fine-tuned for performance. It would thus make sense to avoid their recompilation every time a new version of the program needs to be built. This is accomplished by converting them into a library, with the familiar first step involving compilation to object files with the desired debugging and optimization flags:

```
> gcc -c -g -O2 src1.c
> gcc -c -g -O2 src2.c
> ar rcs libmy_library.a src1.o src2.o
```

The last command invokes the Unix archive tool "ar" that packages all specified object code files into a library file named "libmy_library.a". Customarily, code libraries have the ".a" extension and carry names starting with "lib". The remaining, not yet compiled, functionality of the program is now limited to the contents of the file "main.c". To create a correctly formed executable, just two more commands are needed:

```
> gcc -c -g -O2 main.c
> gcc main.o -o opt_deb_program -L. -lmy_library
> ls
libmy_library.a  main.o           opt_program   src1.o    src2.o
main.c           opt_deb_program  src1.c        src2.c
```

As a result, an "opt_deb_program" optimized executable with debug symbols has been created. Note that the linking command this time contained only one object file "main.o", since the other required program functions are already provided by the library. To tell the linker which libraries should be used when looking for missing symbols, **-l***name* option is used, where *name* is the library file name stripped of the "lib" prefix and extension. Since custom libraries may reside anywhere in the file system, the linker is informed about their location through the −L*directory* option. Of course, the linking command may specify multiple library search paths and multiple libraries.

B.7 OTHER COMMAND-LINE UTILITIES

B.7.1 TEXT TOOLS

less (file viewing utility)

The *less* program is a simple file visualization tool, also called a pager, that permits scrolling of file contents by an arbitrary number of lines (using arrow keys), pages (page-up and page-down keys), and jumping directly to a specific location (line number followed by a "G"). The supported navigation and text search operations are a subset of the vi editor commands.

cat (concatenate files and print them on standard output)

This command takes any number of file arguments and merges their contents in a specified order. The concatenated text is printed to the standard output. When used without arguments, it passes standard input to standard output.

```
> cat f1.txt
file 1
> cat f2.txt
file 2
> cat f*.txt
file 1
file 2
```

head (print the beginning part of files)

The *head* command outputs the first number of lines ("`-n` *number*" option) or characters ("`-c` *number*" option) of specified files to the standard output. If the *number* is preceded by a minus, the output includes all but the last *number* of lines or characters. Without options, it prints the first 10 lines of indicated files. If multiple files are given, the printout for each is preceded by a header indicating the file name. The example below shows that no extra end-of-line character is added at the end of output (hence the shell prompt is adjacent to the printed text), and that end-of-line characters are included in the count.

```
> cat example.txt
line 1
line 2
line 3
> head -c 10 example.txt
line 1
lin>
```

tail (print the last part of files)

Analogous to *head*, this outputs the last *number* of characters or lines (the same options are used) of files. The *number* may be prefixed with a "+" (plus sign) to force starting the output with the *number*th character or line of the file. The *tail* command is also often used to monitor growing files (with contents appended by other running applications). This behavior is activated by option "-f".

```
> tail -n +3 example.txt
line 3
```

cut (cut a section of each line)

The command selects a specific range of characters (option "-c *list*") or fields (option "-f *list*") from each line of the input files (or standard input if "-" is specified instead a file name) and prints it to the standard output. The fields are determined by splitting each line at every occurrence of a predefined delimiter character (controlled by the option "-d *character*"), or by default the tabulation mark. The list may be a single integer to identify a specific field or character, a range in the form *start-end* (inclusive), or with the first or last number of the range missing, indicating starting from the first or ending on the last field or character of the line, respectively. The example below illustrates how to set the space character as the field delimiter:

```
> cut -f 2- -d ' ' example.txt
1
2
3
```

grep (find lines matching a pattern)

The *grep* utility matches lines that contain a specific character pattern. Its arguments include text pattern to look for, and optionally names of the files to search (standard input is assumed if no files are given). With multiple files, for each line containing the pattern *grep* outputs the name of the relevant file followed by the contents of the line. Printing of line numbers may be requested with option "-n". The matching is normally case sensitive, but specifying "-i" suppresses this behavior. *Grep* behavior may be reversed to output all the lines which do not contain the specified pattern by adding the "-v" option. Finally, recursive searches on directories may be triggered with option "-r". The latter permits specification of directory paths as command arguments.

```
> grep —n 'e 2' f*.txt example.txt
f2.txt:1:file 2
example.txt:2:line 2
```

B.7.2 PROCESS MANAGEMENT

ps (output current process status)

Applications and system utilities that are not built-in shell commands have to be started as processes. To view a snapshot of their status, a *ps* command is used. Without options, it reports only processes that belong to the current user:

```
> ps
 PID TTY          TIME CMD
18441 pts/25 00:00:00 bash
18444 pts/25 00:00:00 ps
```

The processes are characterized by their process identifier (PID), a numeric handle that uniquely identifies the running process. To display all processes running in the system along with full information about them, "*ps auxw*" may be invoked (note there is no minus preceding the options). An interesting variant presented below reorganizes the output to display *process tree*, in which one can determine which processes are children of others:

```
> ps ax -H
  PID TTY    STAT   TIME COMMAND
...
    1 ?      Ss     0:04 /sbin/init
  370 ?      S      0:00    upstart-udev-bridge --daemon
  374 ?      Ss     0:00    /lib/systemd/systemd-udevd --daemon
  514 ?      S      0:01    upstart-socket-bridge --daemon
...
```

kill (deliver a signal to a process)

As its rather gruesome name suggests, the *kill* command may be used to terminate processes via Unix's signal mechanism. Not all signals result in a process termination; some may interrupt its execution, pause it, etc. Their full listing may be obtained with the "*kill —l*" command.

Without any options, a TERM (terminate) signal delivered to a process is in many cases sufficient to cause its more or less graceful termination. Some stubborn processes may ignore it, in which case a

KILL signal must be sent. The arguments of the *kill* command are PIDs of target processes. The example shows how to kill the user's *bash* process (which is usually a bad idea and is mentioned here only for illustrative purposes) with a PID obtained from the *ps* listing above:

```
> kill -KILL 18441
```

B.7.3 DATA COMPRESSION AND ARCHIVING

gzip (compress or expand a file)

The *gzip* utility is one of the most common compression programs, characterized by achieving substantial data compaction ratios (especially for text files) and fast operation. It takes as its argument path the name of the file or multiple files to be compressed:

```
> ls -l Makefile
-rw-r--r-- 1 user001 user001 361 Mar 24 17:55 Makefile
> gzip Makefile
> ls -l Makefile*
-rw-r--r-- 1 user001 user001 233 Mar 24 17:55 Makefile.gz
```

Gzip removes the original file if the compression is successful and adds the "*.gz*" extension to the compressed file name. If the compaction process fails, for example due to running out of disk space, the original file is left untouched. To restore the original file, one can use:

```
> gzip -d Makefile.gz
> ls -l Makefile*
-rw-r--r-- 1 user001 user001 361 Mar 24 17:55 Makefile
```

For convenience, the same effect may be achieved using the "*gunzip*" program (without the "-d" option).

Linux provides other file compression utilities that function in a similar fashion to *gzip*, such as *bzip2*, *lzma*, *7z*, and others. While they may achieve better data compression ratios, the compute time required to process the input files may be substantially longer.

tar (archive files)

The *tar* program has a long tradition as the primary file archiving tool for Unix. Its three primary invocation formats are:

tar −c −f archive options path…

tar −x −f archive options

tar −t −f *archive*

The first creates an archive containing all file system objects pointed to by paths (which may be files and directories). For any *path* identifying a directory, its content will be archived recursively. The options may specify the compression algorithm to be used: "-z" for *gzip*, "-j" for *bzip2*, "-J" for *xz*, and "--lzma" for *lzma*. Other useful options include verbose output "-v" and preservation of original permissions "-p".

The second form extracts the contents of the archive to the current working directory or location specified in the "-C *directory*" option. The decompression algorithm does not need to be specified, as it is automatically determined through examination of archive content. Finally, the third instance lists the contents of the specified archive.

Example:

```
> ls -l src
total 12
-rw-r--r-- 1 user001 user001  361 Mar 27 14:06 Makefile
-rw-r--r-- 1 user001 user001  491 Mar 27 14:06 heat.c
drwxrwxr-x 2 user001 user001 4096 Mar 24 21:51 other
> tar -c -f sources.tar.gz -z src
> ls -l sources.tar.gz
-rw-rw-r-- 1 user001 user001 540 Mar 27 14:08 sources.tar.gz
> tar -t -f sources.tar.gz
src/
src/other/
src/other/heat2.c
src/heat.c
src/Makefile
```

Glossary

Absolute Time in Pregroove (ATIP) An additional metadata segment that guides the process of data storage on recordable and rewritable optical media.

Abstract Device Interface for I/O (ADIO) A device-independent layer providing I/O functionality in MPI.

Accelerated Processing Unit (APU), formerly Fusion A processor architecture developed by AMD that combines conventional CPU cores and GPU logic on a single die, sharing external memory.

Accelerator A special-purpose hardware device used to speed up the execution of specific tasks.

Access Control List (ACL) Implementation of a fine-grain access control to file system entities.

Accumulator A dedicated processor register used for operand and result storage in ALU operations.

Adaptive Mesh Refinement (AMR) A numerical method employing multiple-resolution meshes adaptively in a simulation to improve efficiency and reduce the memory requirements for a simulation.

Advanced RISC Machine (ARM) A family of computer processors with fewer transistors but also lower power consumption and lower cooling requirements. RISC stands for "reduced instruction set computing."

American Standard Code for Information Interchange (ASCII) One of the most widespread character encoding standards, comprising 128 characters including all letters of the English alphabet.

AND Binary logic function that evaluates to one only when all its inputs are ones.

Andrew File System (AFS) A distributed file system developed at Carnegie Mellon University.

Antialiasing A signal processing technique that minimizes distortions due to artifacts outside the sampling band.

Apple Filing Protocol (AFP) A proprietary remote file access protocol developed by Apple; formerly AppleTalk Filing Protocol.

Application-Specific Integrated Circuits (ASICs) An integrated circuit designed for a specific application using predefined gates.

Arithmetic Logic Unit (ALU) The circuit that performs digital operations on integer numbers and logic values. Its counterpart for floating-point operations is the FPU.

ATA over Ethernet (AoE) A simple protocol for accessing block storage devices over Ethernet networks.

Automatically Tuned Linear Algebra Software Project (ATLAS) A project providing a BLAS implementation that is automatically tuned for performance.

Backfill Scheduling A job scheduling strategy that avoids starving the lower-priority jobs by scheduling them ahead of higher-priority jobs provided this will not delay the execution of the latter, effectively "filling back" the voids in the time–resource scheduling graph.

Ball Grid Array (BGA) A common high-density chip package type consisting of a grid of solder balls attached to a flat case.

Basic Linear Algebra Subprograms (BLAS) A standard interface to vector, matrix–vector, and matrix–matrix routines that have been optimized for various computer architectures.

Batch Processing A processing mode in which multiple, possibly parallel, compute jobs are executed without the involvement of a user; the opposite of interactive processing.

Binary-Coded Decimal (BCD) (a) Number encoding in which each decimal digit occupies a four-bit field; (b) several nonstandard encodings of upper-case letters, digits, and special codes using six-bit characters.

Bit Block Transfers (BitBLT) A set of memory copy and bit-wise compositing operations used in computer graphics and video processing.

Bit, "Binary Digit" The smallest unit of information used by most digital computers assuming one of two values, typically "0" or "1."

Block Smallest granularity of data used in transfers to and from some device types, particularly mass storage.

Blu-ray Disc (BD) Optical storage technology developed to support data volumes and transfer rates required by high-definition video.

Blu-ray Disc XL (BDXL) Blu-ray disc specification update introducing high-capacity (up to 128 GB per disc) media.

Bottleneck An execution hotspot that negatively impacts an application's performance.

Branch Prediction A hardware mechanism (frequently in combination with software support) used to determine with a high level of probability whether a conditional branch is taken or not.

Buffered File I/O An intermediate file access layer supported by the C library, often resulting in performance advantages.

Burst Buffer A high-bandwidth storage device capable of quickly storing moderate amounts of data and acting as an I/O buffer between compute nodes and (slower) secondary storage.

Byte The smallest unit of addressable memory in computers, commonly comprising eight bits.

Cache A component of CPU architecture that stores a subset of main memory contents providing lower access latency and higher data bandwidth.

Cell Broadband Engine (CBE) or Cell Processor A heterogeneous multicore processor based on Power architecture and developed by Sony, Toshiba, and IBM for embedded applications.

Central Processing Unit (CPU) A primary hardware device performing code execution and data processing in a computer system; a processor.

Checkpointing The process of saving the necessary data from a running application to allow later resumption of the application in the event of system failure or to work around wallclock time execution limitations on a supercomputer.

Collaboration of Oak Ridge, Argonne, and Livermore (CORAL) A joint procurement of supercomputing resources between two key US Department of Energy National Laboratories.

Common Internet File System (CIFS) A variant of SMB protocol for remote file access.

Compact Disc (CD) An optical storage technology on 120 mm discs developed by Sony and Philips and originally used to store digital audio.

Compact Disc Read-Only Memory (CD-ROM) A variant of a CD dedicated to data storage.

Compact Disc Recordable (CD-R) An optical storage technology based on the CD format that permits one-time writing of user-defined data to the medium.

Compact Disc Rewritable (CD-RW) A variant of CD technology permitting multiple updates of medium contents.

Complementary Metal-Oxide Semiconductor (CMOS) The currently dominant technology used to fabricate integrated logic circuits.

Complex Instruction Set Computer (CISC) A type of processor architecture supporting instructions that consist of multiple low-level operations or support complex addressing modes; the opposite of RISC.

Compute Unified Device Architecture (CUDA) Nvidia's application programming interface for parallel computing on graphics processing units.

Conjugate Gradient (CG) A Krylov subspace iterative solver used for solving positive definite systems of equations.

Coprocessor A dedicated circuit accelerating a specific kind of computation.

Cross-Interleaved Reed-Solomon Code (CIRC Code) An error-detecting and error-correcting code with good spatial efficiency and well suited to correcting random and burst errors. It is used to protect the information stored on some optical media.

Cycles per Instruction (CPI) A performance metric specifying average number of processor cycles for each instruction performed.

Cylinder One of the physical address components used to locate data blocks on a hard disk drive and identifying set of tracks equidistant from the spindle.

Daemon A process executing in the background and performing specific services.

Data Writes per Day (DWPD) Metric used to assess the endurance of SSDs due to a finite number of flash rewrites and equal to the number of full device capacity rewrites performed per day over the warranty period.

Debugger A tool to assist the programmer in stepping through a code in execution and examining program state.

Degrees of Freedom per Second (DOFS) The output metric for the HPGMG benchmark.

Department of Energy (DOE) The United States agency tasked with nuclear stockpile stewardship and research in science.

Die A semiconductor substrate for integrated circuit implementation.

Digital Audio Tape (DAT) A digital storage technology using magnetic tapes originally developed for digital audio recording by Sony.

Digital Data Storage (DDS) Magnetic-tape-based digital storage technology, now obsolete.

Digital Linear Tape (DLT) Digital storage technology using a magnetic tape format developed by Digital Equipment Corporation, no longer manufactured.

Digital Signal Processing (DSP) A computing technique used to extract features of, modify, or generate sampled signal values, frequently through the use of specialized hardware.

Digital Versatile Disc or Digital Video Disc (DVD) Digital storage technology involving 120 mm optical discs with increased capacity and data transfer rates compared to a CD.

Digital Versatile Disc Random Access Memory (DVD-RAM) A storage technology permitting a large number of rewrites of compatible DVD media; incompatible with either DVD-R and DVD+R.

Digital Versatile Disc Recordable (DVD-R and DVD+R) A one-time recordable version of DVD; DVD-R and DVD+R denote incompatible formats of similar technology.

Digital Versatile Disc Rewritable (DVD-RW and DVD+RW) A version of DVD storage whose contents may be updated multiple times; DVD-RW and DVD+RW are incompatible formats of similar technology.

Direct Memory Access (DMA) A hardware mechanism in computers allowing memory access by system devices without interaction with the CPU.

Directory A unit of content organization within a file system which functions as a container for other directories, files, and file system entities.

Disc at Once (DAO) A recording mode in optical storage in which all data is written to a medium in a single operation.

Diskless Node A type of compute node that does not include secondary storage devices.

Distributed Lock Manager (DLM) Implementation of an algorithm for coordinating accesses to shared resources in a distributed computer system.

Dual In-Line Package (DIP) A type of case used to package integrated circuits with a low pin count.

Dynamic Random Access Memory (DRAM) A high-density variant of random access memory that requires periodic refreshing of its contents.

Eigenvalue Solvers for Petaflop Applications (ELPA) An HPC library for computing the eigenvalues and eigenvectors of Hermitian matrices.

Eight-to-Fourteen Modulation (EFM) A run-length-limited encoding technique frequently used to store data on optical media such as CDs.

Elastic Computing A type of processing in which the footprint of utilized resources may significantly vary over time.

Electrically Erasable Programmable Read-Only Memory (EEPROM) A variant of semiconductor read-only memory whose contents may be electrically erased and reprogrammed.

Environment Variable A uniquely named string defined in a context (environment) of the underlying command shell and providing additional information or configuration to specific tools or applications.

Error-Correcting Code (ECC) An additional code accompanying a data segment that permits both detection and correction of data corruption; the extent of detection and correction relies on the data size and algorithm used.

Escape Opcode A predefined prefix used in assembly code causing the CPU to transfer control to a coprocessor for the duration of the next instruction.

Event-Triggered Scheduling A simple variant of scheduling in which only jobs at the front of system queues are considered for scheduling.

Exclusive Or (XOR, EXOR or EOR) A binary function evaluating to one only if the number of one-valued arguments is odd.

External Data Representation (XDR) Data serialization layer enabling interoperability between hosts using different internal data representations.

Extreme Science and Engineering Discovery Environment (XSEDE) An NSF-funded project aiming to provide coordinated and unified access to supercomputing resources, expertise, and related tools to researchers, scientists, and engineers around the world. Formerly known as Teragrid.

Failover The process of replacing failed services in a high-availability system.

Fast Fourier Transform (FFT) A transform frequently used in signal processing and solving partial differential equations.

Fibre Channel (FC) A custom high-speed network technology used to attach storage devices to servers.

Fibre Channel over Ethernet (FCoE) A protocol encapsulating Fibre Channel communication over an Ethernet network.

Fibre Channel Protocol (FCP) A protocol encapsulating SCSI communication over a Fibre Channel connection.

Fibre Connection (FICON) Mapping IBM's specific storage access protocols onto Fibre Channel, used primarily by mainframes.

Field-Effect Transistor (FET) A semiconductor device applying a field effect controlled by the potential of the gate electrode to modulate the conductance of a channel between the source and drain electrodes.

Field Programmable Gate Array (FPGA) A device whose logical functionality may be specified and reconfigured by the user at the hardware level.

File A named entity representing a collection of data in a file system.

File Access Delegation Optimization of file data operations implemented by some versions of NFS.

File Descriptor A handle, usually an integer, identifying an open file.

File Extent A contiguous storage space reserved for file data; a file fragment.

File Identifier (FID) A unique file name in the Lustre file system.

File Placement Optimizer (FPO) A feature of GPFS utilized to process "big data" workloads.

File System A high-level system for organizing and accessing data written to persistent storage devices exposing a relevant user interface and supported by the operating system.

First Come, First Serve (FIFO) A processing or data ordering structure in which individual entries are stored and processed in order of arrival; a queue.

Floating-Point Operations per Second (Flops) The output metric for the HPL and HPCG benchmarks.

Floating Gate MOS (FGMOS) Transistor A variant of MOSFET with an additional gate buried within the oxide layer which permits trapping of charge; a storage element in some nonvolatile memories.

Floating-Point Unit (FPU) A dedicated circuit performing floating-point arithmetic; a common part of CPUs and GPUs.

Gang Scheduling A scheduling strategy that groups a number of jobs, processes, or threads with similar resource requirements for the purpose of concurrent execution, allowing low latency communication between them or coordinated access to shared resources. In the Slurm Workload Manager, gang scheduling grants only one job in a gang the exclusive access to shared resources and cyclically preempts it at a timeslice boundary to enable execution of other gang members.

Gang-Partitioned (GP) Mode The initial mode of workload parallelization in OpenACC.

General Parallel File System (GPFS) A proprietary parallel file system developed by IBM, recently rebranded as IBM Spectrum Scale.

Generalized Minimum Residual Method (GMRES) A Krylov subspace iterative solver for solving general sparse systems of equations.

Generic Security Service Application Program Interface (GSS-API) A programming interface to security services standardized by the Internet Engineering Task Force (IETF).

Giant Magnetoresistance (GMR) A quantum-mechanical phenomenon in layered ferromagnetic and weakly magnetic materials providing the basis for construction of read–write heads in modern hard-disk drives.

Gigabit Ethernet (GigE) An implementation of an Ethernet network capable of a peak data rate of 1 billion bits per second.

GNU Debugger (GDB) An open source tool to assist the programmer in stepping through a code in execution.

GNU General Public License (GNU GPL) A free software license with distribution terms defined by the Free Software Foundation.

GNU Scientific Library (GSL) A library which provides a wide array of linear algebra routines, including an interface to BLAS for C and C++.

Gperftools A popular open-source code profiling and memory allocator package originally developed by Google.

Graphical User Interface (GUI) A type of interface permitting specification of input parameters and interaction with application execution through graphics-based (instead of text-only) dialogs.

Graphics Core Next (GCN) A GPU microarchitecture developed by AMD and used in its current line of products.

Graphics Processing Unit (GPU) A specialized device accelerating computations related to image or video generation.

Hadoop Distributed File System (HDFS) A file system in Hadoop which enables distributed file access across many linked storage devices.

Hamming Codes A family of error-correcting codes capable of correcting single bit errors and detecting single or double (extended hamming code) bit errors with optimal spatial overhead.

Hard Disk Drive (HDD) A storage device technology utilizing rigid, spinning, magnetic platters as media to store information.

Heap A segment of an application's memory space that hosts dynamically allocated storage.

Heterogeneous System Architecture (HSA) A set of specifications maintained by the HSA Foundation that simplifies the management and programming of heterogeneous devices sharing memory resources by providing unified architecture, API, and language support.

Hierarchical Data Format (HDF5) A library for self-describing portable data output frequently used in HPC applications.

High-Bandwidth Memory (HBM) A memory technology providing high data bandwidths utilizing a large number of interface pins and three-dimensional die stacking.

High-Density Complementary Metal-Oxide-Semiconductor (HCMOS) An older description of a CMOS process variant used to manufacture circuits with high transistor counts.

High Performance Computing (HPC) A parallel computing mode involving the use of supercomputers.

High Performance Conjugate Gradients (HPCG) A benchmark complementing the HPL benchmark which explores memory and data access patterns that are not well represented by HPL.

High Performance Linpack (HPL) The third iteration of the Linpack benchmark, used for the Top 500 supercomputer ranking list.

Highly Scalable Preconditioner (HYPRE) A library developed at Lawrence Livermore National Laboratory which provides a set of highly scalable preconditioners for sparse linear system solves.

High-Throughput Computing A parallel computing strategy in which a large number of loosely coupled tasks is executing on distributed execution resources.

Hotspot In performance analysis, a part of code dominating the program execution time.

HyperSCSI A protocol implementing SCSI communication over an Ethernet network.

Hyperthread Intel's variant of multithreading in which two threads may coexecute on a single CPU core.

IBM Spectrum Scale The current name of the IBM General Parallel File System.

IEEE754 An IEEE standard defining the format of floating-point numbers.

InfiniBand Architecture (IBA) A high-speed interconnect technology found in many current HPC cluster installations.

Inode An internal data structure in a Unix-compatible OS kernel containing low-level metadata of file system objects.

Input/Output Operations per Second (IOPS) A performance metric of storage devices specifying the number of small independent I/O requests processed by the device within a second; may be further qualified as read or write accesses, random or sequential, etc.

Instruction-Level Parallelism (ILP) A type of fine-grain parallelism due to multiple operations issued as result of instruction processing.

Instruction Mix Decomposition of a computational workload or benchmark by types of instructions it executes (such as ALU, branches, memory access, etc.).

Instruction Set Architecture (ISA) A description of computer architecture based on a command set it can execute.

Instrumentation A program modification that permits extraction of specific performance data or other execution-related details.

Interactive Processing A processing mode that grants the user control over job execution, frequently used to facilitate debugging of applications.

Internet Fibre Channel Protocol (iFCP) A communication protocol enabling Fibre Channel connectivity over an IP network.

Internet Protocol over InfiniBand (IPoIB) The encapsulation of Internet Protocol traffic over physical InfiniBand fabric.

Internet Small Computer Systems Interface (iSCSI) A protocol forwarding SCSI commands over an IP network.

Internet2 A nonprofit technology community of US academic, government, research, and industrial partners founded in 1996, primarily known for advancing global research by offering access to high-bandwidth networks on a national scale.

iSCSI Extensions for RDMA (iSER) An extension of the Internet Small Computer System Interface enabling the use of remote direct memory access over the underlying network.

Isosurfaces Surfaces that connect data points which have the same value.

Job Array A collection of a specific number of jobs with similar properties and characteristics, managed as a single group.

Job Queue A named entity in a resource management system allowing grouping of jobs with similar characteristics and associated with a specific set of execution resources.

Job Step A meaningful part of a larger computational job; a task.

Joint Test Action Group (JTAG) A formative body and a resulting standard that defines the signaling interface and protocol for in-circuit access to the internal state of hardware devices.

Journaling File System A file system implementation in which uncommitted transactions are stored in a dedicated log, resulting in improved reliability.

Kerberos A network-enabled authentication software layer.

Knights Landing (KNL) The code name for a revision of Intel Xeon Phi architecture.

Linear Algebra Package (LAPACK) A linear algebra library that provides driver routines designed to solve complete problems such as a system of linear equations, eigenvalue problems, or singular value problems.

Linear Tape-Open (LTO) A digital storage technology using magnetic tapes and developed as an open standard by the LTO Consortium.

Link A construct supported by some file systems and used to provide alternative names (aliases) for stored objects.

Linpack A linear algebra library for solving systems of linear equations. It has been superseded by LAPACK.

Linux A popular open-source operating system kernel based on Unix.

Low Infrastructure Public Key Mechanism (LIPKEY) A credential exchange protocol implemented as a layer above SPKM.

Low Level Virtual Machine (LLVM) An open-source compiler project that has become a key component of development tools for Apple's MacOS and iOS.

Lustre Distributed Lock Manager (LDLM) The component of a Lustre file system responsible for efficient synchronization of concurrent accesses to shared files.

Lustre File System Check (LFSCK) A distributed file system check utility customized for Lustre.

Lustre Networking (LNET) The communication infrastructure in a Lustre file system.

M.2 The form factor and interface specification of internal expansion cards (primarily storage) attached through a miniaturized edge connector.

Management-Processing Element (MPE) A conventional core that provides directive functions, as opposed to a compute-processing element intended for computation.

Management Server (MGS) The component of a Lustre file system responsible for maintaining and providing configuration information.

Management Target (MGT) Storage space for MGS in a Lustre file system.

Many-Integrated Core (MIC) Architectural concept and hardware product introduced by Intel in which multiple tens of interconnected identical computing cores are embedded in a single device; currently known under the brand name Xeon Phi.

Mass Storage A class of storage capable of accommodating large amounts of data.

Massively Parallel Processor (MPP) A class of parallel computing architecture consisting of very large number of nodes connected by a network.

Matrix Template Library (MTL) A library for linear algebra operations that retains the look and feel of the original mathematical notation of linear algebra.

Mean Time Between Failures (MTBF) An estimated measure of system or device reliability equal to the average period of time between consecutive failures.

Memory Wall A mismatch between the computational throughput of a processor and the data rate a connected storage device (memory) is capable of supporting.

Message-Passing Interface (MPI) A programming interface and software stack used in supercomputing environments for communication between participating processes.

Metadata Additional attributes or information about stored data, typically used to indicate the owner, access rights, creation time, size, etc.

Metadata Server (MDS) The Lustre file system component managing namespace and metadata.

Metadata Target (MDT) The metadata storage in a Lustre file system.

Metal-Oxide Semiconductor Field-Effect Transistor (MOSFET) A variant of field-effect transistor (FET) with an insulated gate; a building block of electronic CMOS circuits.

Microcode A translation layer in processing hardware permitting implementation of higher-complexity instructions.

Microprocessor without Interlocked Pipeline Stages (MIPS) An influential RISC processor architecture originally developed at Stanford University.

Mini-Compact Disc (Mini-CD) A smaller version of a CD with a diameter of 80 mm.

Mini-SATA (mSATA) A miniaturized variant of a SATA connector utilized by small form factor storage devices.

MoM A job execution daemon in PBS.

Moore's Law An observation made by Gordon Moore of Fairchild Semiconductor stating that the number of transistors in large integrated circuits doubles approximately every 2 years.

Motion Picture Experts Group (MPEG) A standards group founded by ISO and IEC tasked with creating specifications for compressed digital video and audio encoding; the standards names include "MPEG-" followed by a numerical or alphabetic suffix (such as MPEG-2).

Mount Point Directory under which the contents of another file system is exposed in a process called "mounting."

MPI+X The concept of using coarse-grained MPI processes to span an entire node but allowing the efficiencies of shared-memory hardware to be exploited with the assistance of an additional programming interface like OpenMP working in cooperation with MPI.

Multi-Chip Module (MCM) A type of electronic device assembly and packaging combining several dies on a common carrier.

Multilevel Cell (MLC) Nonvolatile storage organization in which each storage cell of a device contains two bits of information.

Multiple-Mount Protection The aspect of failover management in a Lustre file system preventing simultaneous mounts on different nodes.

Multithreading A parallel execution paradigm employing multiple control flow contexts (threads) sharing an address space.

Myrinet High performance network developed by Myricom and deployed as cluster interconnect.

National Aeronautics and Space Administration (NASA) A US government agency that manages and directs the civilian space program and is a frequent driver of high performance computing applications.

National Television System Committee (NTSC) A standard defining video stream properties, color encoding, and the transmission modulation scheme for the analog television signal used in most of the Americas and some Pacific territories.

National University of Defense Technology (NUDT) The top military academy and defense research university in Changsha, Hunan, China. NUDT supports both supercomputing research and the Chinese space program.

Network Attached Storage (NAS) A shared network-connected storage pool accessible remotely through specialized protocols and software.

Network File System (NFS) A remote, shared file access service with a protocol defined by several open RFC standards and commonly used in Unix environments.

Network Interface Controller (NIC), also Network Interface Card A specialized electronic device or adapter board that allows connecting the computer to a specific network type.

Network Shared Disk (NSD) Storage abstraction in IBM Spectrum Scale (GPFS).

Noise-Predictive Maximum Likelihood (NPML) A set of digital signal processing methods used to improve the reliability of retrieved information from noisy channels or media (such as magnetic disks).

Nonuniform Memory Access (NUMA) A memory architecture in which memory access latency varies depending on the relative location of the issuing processor and targeted memory module.

Nonvolatile Memory Express (NVMe) The interface specification for attaching nonvolatile storage devices over a PCI express bus.

Nonvolatile Random Access Memory (NVRAM) A class of memory whose contents are retained after device power is turned off.

NAND Binary logic function that evaluates to zero only when all its inputs are ones.

NOR Binary logic function that evaluates to one only when all its inputs are zeroes.

NVLink A short-range communications protocol between a GPU and a CPU or multiple GPUs, developed by Nvidia.

Object Storage Server (OSS) Processes file data requests in a Lustre file system.

Object Storage Target (OST) The underlying physical storage for OSS in a Lustre file system.

Offline Storage A variant of archival storage in which access to storage media is explicitly managed by a human operator.

Open Accelerators (OpenACC) A programming model for accelerators using an approach similar to OpenMP.

Open Computing Language (OpenCL) An application programming framework providing a unified interface to execution resources, including conventional CPUs and various accelerator types.

Open Multiprocessing (OpenMP) A compiler-supported programming environment enabling application parallelization on shared-memory multiprocessors.

OpenFabrics Enterprise Distribution (OFED) A set of software stack components and protocols developed and distributed by OpenFabrics Alliance in support of InfiniBand technology.

Operating System (OS) A system software layer that allocates and manages hardware resources, enforces resource protection, provides standardized services, and schedules execution of applications.

OR Binary logic function that evaluates to zero only when all its inputs are zeroes.

Overhead An additional amount of work required to manage a computation.

Packet Writing A method of contents modification on recordable or rewritable optical media that permits addition and deletion of files and directories at any time.

Page A unit of memory organization and address translation, ranging from a few KB to a few GB.

Parallel Boost Graph Library (PBGL) A library for high performance graph algorithms.

Parallel File System A file system optimized for concurrent access to data objects.

Parallel NFS (pNFS) An extension to NFS supporting parallel access to shared files.

Partial Response Maximum Likelihood (PRML) A set of algorithms in signal theory used to increase the reliability of information retrieved from weak or interfering signals.

Path The name identifying a specific entity or object in a file system.

Perf (on occasion perf_events, perf tools or Performance Counters for Linux, PCL) A performance-monitoring and event-tracing tool available for Linux systems.

Performance Application Programming Interface (PAPI) A library which provides tools for performance measurement and portable access to hardware performance counters.

Peripheral Component Interconnect (PCI) A parallel expansion bus standard.

Peripheral Component Interconnect Express (PCIe or PCI Express) A serial expansion bus standard with a control protocol derived from and extending that of PCI.

Perpendicular Recording A method of storing information on a magnetic medium that results in increased bit density compared to more traditional horizontal recording.

Picture Element (Pixel) The smallest, indivisible element of a digital image.

Pin Grid Array (PGA) An integrated circuit enclosure placing I/O leads on the bottom of ceramic or plastic case.

Plastic Leaded Chip Carrier (PLCC) A type of enclosure used to house integrated circuits with leads arranged along the four sides of a rectangular case.

Portable Batch System (PBS) A common cluster-oriented resource management system developed and maintained by Altair Engineering; recently open sourced.

Portable, Extensible Toolkit for Scientific Computation (PETSc) A suite of data structures and routines for solving partial differential equations on distributed-memory architectures.

Portable Operating System Interface (POSIX) A collection of IEEE standards specifying operating environment, programming interfaces, and interaction and management of executing entities for compatibility and interoperability across variants of the Unix operating system.

Preemption A scheduler feature allowing it to interrupt and suspend an already running lower-priority task to start the execution of a higher-priority task.

Prefetch A mechanism reducing data access latency by initiating data transfer ahead of actual data use.

Primary Storage The top level of storage hierarchy, including CPU registers, caches, and main memory.

Printed Circuit Boards (PCB) An insulated board providing mechanical support for interconnected electrical components.

Process Identifier (PID) A number used by the operating system to identify an active process.

Processing Element A primitive hardware computing unit; one of many replicated components of a processing array or a vector unit.

Profiling A performance analysis technique that measures the dynamic properties of program execution.

Programmed Input/Output (PIO) A method of data transfer between computer memory and a system device explicitly performed by the CPU.

Pseudo File System A data structure or service exposing an access interface compatible with a file system API.

Raster Operation (ROP) An operation executed during one of the final steps in computer image rendering, generating the actual displayed pixel value.

Reduced Instruction Set Computer (RISC) A processor architecture paradigm emphasizing ISAs with fewer, simpler, and more generic instructions rather than complex ones.

Redundant Array of Independent Disks, formerly Redundant Array of Inexpensive Disks (RAID) A form of aggregated storage incorporating multiple HDDs or SSDs capable of tolerating a limited number of device failures.

Remote Direct Memory Access A low-overhead data transfer technique between the memories of two machines that avoids direct involvement of their processors.

Remote Procedure Call (RPC) A distributed computing paradigm in which the client node supplies input arguments and requests the invocation of a function using these arguments on a remote server in a specific application's address space.

Request for Comments (RFC) A publication body maintained by the IETF and Internet Society, and used as a forum for internet standard development.

Request Replay Cache A data structure in some NFS implementations used to avoid duplicate request execution.

Resource Management A collection of methodologies, algorithms, and tools supporting efficient allocation of computing resources to executable tasks.

Restart At designated points during the execution of an application on a supercomputer the data necessary to allow later resumption of the application at that point in the execution can be output and saved. This data is called a checkpoint, and the resumption of application execution is called restart.

Round-Robin A task scheduling or data distribution method in which tasks or data units are repetitively assigned to resources in the same predefined order.

Scalable Library for Eigenvalue Problem Computations (SLEPc) An extension of PETSc for solving very large sparse eigenvalue problems.

SCSI RDMA Protocol or SCSI Remote Protocol (SRP) A protocol leveraging the use of remote direct memory access for SCSI commands over supporting networks such as InfiniBand or 10 Gbps Ethernet.

Secondary Storage The second level of storage hierarchy, incorporating high-bandwidth mass-storage devices for persistent preservation of data.

Sector A unit of data access on storage devices; a block.

Self-Monitoring, Analysis, and Reporting Technology (SMART) A self-contained, built-in monitoring system analyzing the health status of storage devices such as HDDs and SSDs.

Serial Advanced Technology Attachment (SATA) A high-speed serial interface bus used to connect storage devices to motherboards and I/O expansion cards.

Server Message Block (SMB) A proprietary protocol with currently open specifications for remote file, printer, and hardware port access originated in the Microsoft Windows environment.

Service Unit (SU) A metric for charging supercomputer time against a user account. While defined locally for each supercomputer, it is generally considered the wall time in hours multiplied by the number of cores used for a simulation.

Setgid Analogous to "setuid," but applied to user groups.

Setuid A flag associated with an executable file changing the effective program's ownership even when executed by ordinary users; typically used to elevate the privilege level.

Shader A replicated processing component in a GPU that supports a number of bit-wise and arithmetic operations.

Shell An interface facilitating the execution of operating system commands and user programs as well as visualization of their output.

Simple Public Key GSS-API Mechanism (SPKM) An authentication protocol defined by RFC2025.

Single Instruction, Multiple Data (SIMD) An element of Flynn's taxonomy for achieving parallelism where several processing units perform the exact same operation simultaneously on multiple data inputs.

Single Program, Multiple Data (SPMD) An element of Flynn's taxonomy for achieving parallelism, and the most common style of parallel programming for distributed-memory architectures.

Single-Level Cell (SLC) Nonvolatile storage organization in which each storage cell of a device contains exactly one bit of information.

Slurm Partition Slurm's equivalent of a job queue.

Slurm Workload Manager, "Slurm" A popular open-source resource management suite for cluster computers, originally an acronym of "Simple Linux Utility for Resource Management."

Small Computer System Interface (SCSI) A standard family describing electrical and mechanical interfaces, communication protocols, and supported device functions for various peripherals such as HDDs, tape drives, scanners, and others.

Small-Scale Integration (SSI) A scale of integrated circuit minimization placing tens of transistors on a single die.

Socket A physical connector on the motherboard accommodating a CPU or a representation of physical resources provided by a single CPU package.

Solid-State Drive or Solid-State Disk (SSD) A storage device technology leveraging solid-state devices (such as flash memory) for persistent data storage and thus containing no moving components.

Starvation, Latency, Overhead, Contention, Energy, Resilience (SLOWER) Sources of performance degradation.

Stateless Protocol A communication protocol in which neither client nor server is required to retain session-related information.

Static Random Access Memory (SRAM) A variant of memory technology with the fastest access time but a higher unit cost and lower storage density than DRAM.

Sticky Bit A flag associated with files or directories that restricts when they may be deleted.

Storage Area Network (SAN) A storage virtualization layer using a network to provide block-level accessibility to remote storage devices.

Stream Multiprocessor (SM) A component of Nvidia GPU architecture consisting of multiple shader units with related infrastructure that execute concurrent compute threads.

Streamlines Streamlines take a vector field as input and show curves that are tangent to the vector field

Stripe In distributed storage, the smallest sequence (or its size) of data blocks spanning all devices in the array.

Supercomputer A computing system exhibiting high-end performance capabilities and resource capacities within practical constraints of technology, cost, power, and reliability.

Superconducting Josephson Junction Logic (Superconducting JJ) Two superconductors coupled together across a thin insulating barrier or nonsuperconducting metal.

Symmetric Multiprocessor (SMP) The most common type of shared-memory compute node.

System on Chip (SoC) An integrated circuit containing multiple components of a computing system (CPU, memory, signal converters, graphics processors, analog functions, etc.) on a single die.

TaihuLight Currently the fastest supercomputer in the world, located in China.

Tarball A file that contains a group of archived files with the extension .tar. It is often compressed using gzip, resulting in the filename extension .tar.gz.

TeraBytes Written (TBW) A metric estimating the maximum aggregate volume of data that may be written to a storage device without causing its failure or data loss.

Tertiary Storage A storage hierarchy level maintaining large amounts of data, frequently supporting automated media changes.

Texture Element (Texel) In computer graphics, a basic unit of texture.

Time-Limited Error Recovery (TLER) A property of a storage device that bounds the time required to process an internal error, making is suitable for use with RAID controllers.

TOP500 List A ranked listing of the world's fastest 500 supercomputers, updated twice a year.

Track at Once (TAO) A recording mode used in optical storage in which data may be added to a disc in several sessions.

Translation Lookaside Buffer (TLB) A critical component of modern CPUs, accelerating virtual to physical address translation.

Transmission Control Protocol (TCP) One of the commonly used internet protocols providing reliable, connection-oriented data transfer.

Traverse Edges per Second (TEPS) The output metric for the Graph500 benchmark.

Triple-Level Cell (TLC) Nonvolatile storage organization in which each storage cell of a device contains three bits of information.

Tuning and Analysis Toolkit (TAU) An open-source performance measurement, analysis, and visualization suite developed by the University of Oregon.

Uniform Memory Access (UMA) UMA shared memory is a memory architecture in which memory access latency does not vary depending on the relative location of the issuing processor and targeted memory module.

Universal Standard Bus (USB) A short-range peripheral interconnect standard.

Unix A family of multiuser operating systems descended from the original Unix developed at AT&T Bell Laboratories.

User Datagram Protocol (UDP) A simple connectionless communication protocol supporting messaging over the internet.

VampirTrace A fine-grain trace collection tool commonly used to profile MPI and OpenMP applications.

Vector-Partitioned (VP) Mode The finest grain of workload parallelization in OpenACC that uses the SIMD capabilities of the accelerator.

Very Large-Scale Integration (VLSI) The currently highest level of integrated circuit miniaturization, placing several thousands to billions of transistors on a single die.

Vienna Ab Initio Simulation Package (VASP) A widely used density functional theory toolkit for HPC systems.

Virtual Address Extension (VAX) An ISA, and a family of microcomputers based on it, developed by Digital Equipment Corporation in the 1970s.

Virtual File System (VFS) A system-independent abstraction of a file system.

Virtual Memory A memory abstraction and management technique allowing mapping of regions of an address space to different types of underlying physical storage devices.

Virtual Node or Vnode A system-independent representation of an inode in a virtual file system.

Visualization Toolkit (VTK) A visualization library that provides hundreds of visualization algorithms.

Von Neumann Bottleneck See "memory wall."

Wide Area Network (WAN) A communication network that spans large distance.

Worker-Partitioned (WP) Mode A method of workload parallelization supported by OpenACC that uses multiple workers per gang.

Xeon Phi See "many integrated core."

Yet Another Resource Negotiator (YARN) A central resource manager used in Hadoop.

Z-Buffer A data structure used in computer graphics to provide the accurate depth coordinate for each rendered pixel.

ZFS (initially Zettabyte File System) An advanced-featured file system developed by Sun Microsystems and currently owned by Oracle.

Index

'*Note:* Page numbers followed by "f" indicate figures, "t" indicate tables, and "b" indicate boxes.'

D

E

F

M

Q

R

S

T

Printed in the United States
By Bookmasters